What makes THiNK special?

Core Content + Pedagogy = M-S

THiNK offers instructors core content, pedagogy, and currency in a succinct magazine format that engages students.

we listen

LEARNSMART®

How many students think they know what they know but struggle on the first exam? LearnSmart, McGraw-Hill's adaptive learning system, identifies students' metacognitive abilities and limitations, identifying what they know, and more important, what they don't know. Using Bloom's taxonomy and a highly sophisticated "smart" algorithm, LearnSmart creates a customized study plan, unique to every student's demonstrated needs. With virtually no administrative overhead, instructors using LearnSmart are reporting an increase in student performance of one letter grade or more.

SMARTBOOK™

Smartbook is the first and only adaptive reading experience available for the higher education market. Powered by an intelligent diagnostic and adaptive engine, SmartBook facilitates and personalizes the reading process by identifying what content a student knows and doesn't know through adaptive assessments. As the student reads, SmartBook constantly adapts to ensure the student is focused on the content he or she needs the most to close any knowledge gaps.

connect® | CRITICAL THINKING

Connect Critical Thinking is a state of the art learning environment that helps you connect your students to their coursework. Whether accessing online homework or quizzes, using LearnSmart, or utilizing the interactive eBook, Connect provides a complete digital solution for your classroom. Detailed reporting helps the student and instructor gauge comprehension and retention—*without adding administrative load.*

create™

CREATE what you've only imagined! Our new self-service website allows you to quickly and easily create custom course materials with McGraw-Hill's comprehensive, cross-disciplinary content and other third-party sources. Add your own content quickly and easily. Tap into other rights-secured third-party sources as well. Then, arrange the content in a way that makes the most sense for your course. Even personalize your book with your course name and information and choose the best format for your students—color print, black-and-white print, or eBook. And, when you are done, you'll receive a free PDF review copy in just minutes! To get started, go to www.mcgrawhillcreate.com and register today.

THINK, THIRD EDITION

Published by McGraw-Hill Education, 2 Penn Plaza, New York, NY 10121. Copyright © 2015 by McGraw-Hill Education. All rights reserved. Printed in the United States of America. Previous editions © 2012 and 2010. No part of this publication may be reproduced or distributed in any form or by any means, or stored in a database or retrieval system, without the prior written consent of McGraw-Hill Education, including, but not limited to, in any network or other electronic storage or transmission, or broadcast for distance learning.

Some ancillaries, including electronic and print components, may not be available to customers outside the United States.

This book is printed on acid-free paper.

1 2 3 4 5 6 7 8 9 0 DOW/DOW 1 0 9 8 7 6 5 4

ISBN 978-0-07-803843-3
MHID 0-07-803843-X

Senior Vice President, Products & Markets: *Kurt L. Strand*
Vice President, General Manager, Products & Markets: *Michael Ryan*
Vice President, Content Production & Technology Services: *Kimberly Meriwether David*
Managing Director: *William R. Glass*
Brand Manager: *Sarah Remington*
Senior Director of Development: *Dawn Groundwater*
Marketing Manager: *Alexandra Schultz*
Editorial Coordinator: *Jessica Holmes*
Director, Content Production: *Terri Schiesl*
Content Project Manager: *Mary E. Powers*
Senior Buyer: *Sandy Ludovissy*
Designer: *Margarite Reynolds*
Cover Image: *Front cover: PhotoAlto/Matthieu Spohn; Back cover: Johannes Kroemer/Getty Images*
Content Licensing Specialist: *Shawntel Schmitt*
Compositor: *Aptara®, Inc.*
Typeface: *10/12 Times LT Std*
Printer: *R. R. Donnelley*

All credits appearing on page or at the end of the book are considered to be an extension of the copyright page.

Library of Congress Cataloging-in-Publication Data

Boss, Judith A., 1942-
    Think : critical thinking and logic skills for everyday life / Judith A. Boss. – Third Edition.
        pages cm
    Includes index.
    ISBN 978–0–07–803843–3 — ISBN 0–07–803843–X (hard copy : alk. paper) 1. Critical thinking. 2. Logic. I. Title.
    B105.T54B68 2015
    153.4'3–dc23
                                                                                                    2013036350

The Internet addresses listed in the text were accurate at the time of publication. The inclusion of a website does not indicate an endorsement by the authors or McGraw-Hill Education, and McGraw-Hill Education does not guarantee the accuracy of the information presented at these sites.

www.mhhe.com

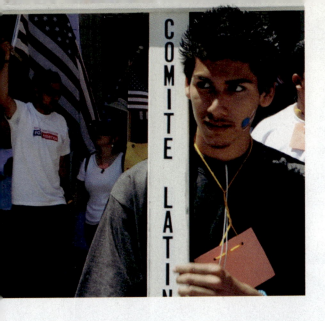

THiNK

BRIEF CONTENTS

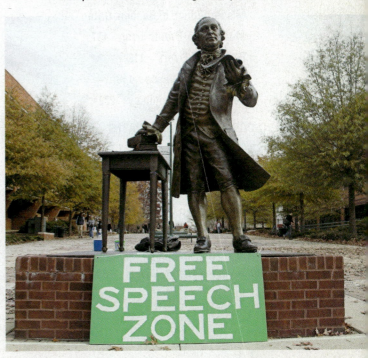

12   SCIENCE   360

13 LAW AND POLITICS 394

Features

CRITICAL THINKING IN ACTION

THINKING OUTSIDE THE BOX

CRITICAL THINKING ISSUES

WHAT IF…

you could re-create the 1-on-1 experience of working through difficult concepts in office hours with every one of your students?

you could significantly increase student retention and success?

you could see at a glance how well each of your students (and sections) was performing in every segment of your course?

you had all the assignments and resources for your course pre-organized by learning objectives and with point-and-click flexibility?

The unparalleled resources of Connect Critical Thinking bolster students' performance while making instructors' preparations more efficient. To experience Connect yourself, go to http://connect.mcgraw-hill.com.

1

CRITICAL THINKING
WHY IT'S IMPORTANT

Nazi war criminal Adolf Eichmann was tried in Israel in 1960 for crimes against humanity. Despite his claim that he was just following the orders of his superiors when he ordered the deaths of millions of Jews, the court found him guilty and sentenced him to death. Was Eichmann an inhuman monster? Or was he, as his defense lawyer claimed, just doing what many of us would do— following orders from our superiors?

To address this question, social psychologist Stanley Milgram of Yale University conducted, between 1960 and 1963, what has become a classic experiment. Milgram placed an advertisement in a newspaper asking for men to take part in a scientific study of memory and learning.[1] Those chosen to participate were told that the purpose of the experiment was to study the effects of punishment on learning—and that their job was to give electric shocks as punishment when the learner gave a wrong answer. The participants were instructed that

In what ways does sharing ideas with others and listening to their feedback help develop our critical thinking skills?

THiNK FIRST

■ What are the characteristics of a skilled critical thinker?

■ What are the three levels of thinking?

■ What are some of the barriers to critical thinking?

>> the shocks would be given at the direction of the experimenter and would range in intensity from 15 volts to 450 volts. In fact, no shocks were actually being given, but the participants didn't know this.

As the intensity of the shocks "increased," the learner (actually an actor) responded with increased anguish, screaming in pain and pleading with the participant delivering the shocks to stop. Despite the repeated pleas, all the participants gave shocks of up to 300 volts before refusing to go on. In addition, 65 percent continued to deliver shocks of 450 volts simply because an authority figure (a scientist in a white lab coat) told the participants to continue. Most who continued were clearly disturbed by what they were doing. However, unlike the participants who refused to continue, they were unable to provide logical counterarguments to the scientist's insistence that "the experiment requires that you must continue."

How could this happen? Were the results of Milgram's study some sort of aberration? As it turns out, they were not.

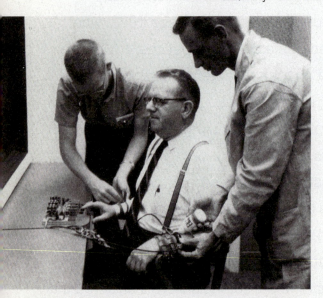

Milgram Experiment *Scene from the Milgram experiment on obedience. The "learner" is being hooked up to the machine that will deliver bogus electric shocks each time he gives a wrong answer.*

Several years later, in 1971, the U.S. Navy funded a study of the reaction of humans to situations in which there are huge differences in authority and power—as in a prison. The study was administered under the direction of psychologist Philip Zimbardo, who selected student volunteers judged to be psychologically stable and healthy.[2] The volunteers were randomly assigned to play the role of either "guard" or "prisoner" in a two-week prison simulation in the basement of the Stanford University building in which the psychology department was located. To make the situation more realistic, guards were given wooden batons and wore khaki, military-style uniforms and mirrored sunglasses that minimized eye contact. The prisoners were given ill-fitting smocks without underwear and rubber thongs for their feet. Each prisoner was also assigned a number to be used instead of a name. The guards were not given any formal instructions; they were simply told that it was their responsibility to run the prison.

The experiment quickly got out of control. Prisoners were subjected to abusive and humiliating treatment, both physical and emotional, by the guards. One-third of the guards became increasingly cruel, especially at night when they thought the cameras had been turned off. Prisoners were forced to clean toilets with their bare hands, to sleep on concrete floors, and to endure solitary confinement and hunger. They were also subjected to forced nudity and sexual abuse—much like what would happen many years later in 2003–2004 at Abu Ghraib prison in Iraq. (see Analyzing Images: Abuse at Abu Ghraib prison, Iraq, page 18). After only six days, the Stanford prison experiment had to be called off.

These experiments suggest that many, if not most, Americans will uncritically follow the commands of those in authority. Like the Milgram study, the Stanford prison experiment demonstrated that ordinary people will commit atrocities in situations where there is social and institutional support for behavior that they would not do on their own and if they could put the blame on others. Milgram wrote:

> Ordinary people, simply doing their jobs and without any particular hostility on their part, can become agents in a terrible destructive process. Moreover, even when the destructive effects of their work become patently clear, and they are asked to carry out actions incompatible with fundamental standards of the majority, relatively few people have the resources needed to resist authority.[3]

What are these resources that people need to resist authority? Good critical-thinking skills are certainly one. Those who refused to continue in the Milgram study were able to give good reasons for why they should stop: for example, "it is wrong to cause harm to another person." In contrast, those who continued, even though they knew what they were doing was wrong, simply deferred to the authority figure even though he was making unreasonable demands of them.[4]

Although most of us may never be in a situation in which our actions have such grim consequences, a lack of critical-thinking skills can still have negative consequences in our everyday decisions. When it comes making to personal, educational, and career choices, we may defer to our parents or cave in to pressure from friends rather than think through the reasons for our decisions. When major life decisions are not carefully thought out, there can be long-lasting consequences, such as dropping out of school or choosing a career in which we are ultimately unhappy. In addition, because critical-thinking skills are transferable across disciplines, improving these skills can have a positive impact on our success in college. In this chapter we'll be looking at some of the components of critical thinking as well as the benefits of developing good critical-thinking skills. We'll conclude by examining some of the barriers to critical thinking. Specifically, we will:

- Define *critical thinking* and *logic*
- Learn about the characteristics of a good critical thinker
- Distinguish between giving an opinion and engaging in critical thinking
- Explain the benefits of good critical thinking
- Relate critical thinking to personal development and our role as citizens in a democracy
- Identify people who exemplify critical thinking in action
- Identify barriers to critical thinking, including types of resistance and narrow-mindedness

At the end of the chapter, we will apply our critical-thinking skills to a specific issue by discussing and analyzing different perspectives on affirmative action in college admissions.

These experiments suggest that many, if not most, Americans will uncritically follow the commands of those in authority.

5

WHAT IS CRITICAL THINKING?

Critical thinking is a collection of skills we use every day that are necessary for our full intellectual and personal development. The word *critical* is derived from the Greek word *kritikos,* which means "discernment," "the ability to judge," or "decision making." Critical thinking requires learning *how* to think rather than simply *what* to think.

Critical thinking, like logic, requires good analytical skills. **Logic** is part of critical thinking and is defined as "the study of the methods and principles used in distinguishing correct (good) arguments from incorrect (bad) arguments."[5] Critical thinking involves the application of the rules of logic as well as gathering evidence, evaluating it, and coming up with a plan of action. We'll be studying logical arguments in depth, in Chapters 5 through 8.

> **critical thinking** A collection of skills we use every day that are necessary for our full intellectual and personal development.
>
> **logic** The study of the methods and principles used to distinguish correct or good arguments from poor arguments.
>
> **opinion** A belief based solely on personal feelings rather than on reason or facts.

Critical thinking provides us with the tools to identify and resolve issues in our lives. Critical thinking is not simply a matter of asserting our opinions on issues. **Opinions** are based on personal feelings or beliefs, rather than on reason and evidence. We are all certainly entitled to our own opinions. Opinions, however, are not necessarily reasonable. While some may happen to turn out to be correct, opinions, no matter how deeply and sincerely held, may also be mistaken. As a critical thinker you need to be willing to provide logical support for your beliefs.

Uninformed opinions can lead you to make poor decisions in your life and act in ways that you may later come to regret. Sometimes uninformed opinions can negatively impact society. For example, even though antibiotics kill bacteria and have no effect on cold viruses, many people try to persuade their doctors into prescribing them for cold symptoms. Despite doctors telling patients that antibiotics have no effect on viral infections, studies show that about half of doctors give in to patient pressure for antibiotics for viral infections.[6] Such overuse of antibiotics makes bacteria more drug resistant and has led to a decline in the effectiveness of treatment in diseases where they are really needed.[7] This phenomenon

SELF-EVALUATION QUESTIONNAIRE

Rate yourself on the following scale from 1 (strongly disagree) to 5 (strongly agree).

1 2 3 4 5 There are right and wrong answers. Authorities are those who have the right answers.

1 2 3 4 5 There are no right or wrong answers. Everyone has a right to his or her own opinion.

1 2 3 4 5 Even though the world is uncertain, we need to make decisions on what is right or wrong.

1 2 3 4 5 I tend to stick to my position on an issue even when others try to change my mind.

1 2 3 4 5 I have good communication skills.

1 2 3 4 5 I have high self-esteem.

1 2 3 4 5 I would refuse to comply if an authority figure ordered me to do something that might cause me to hurt someone else.

1 2 3 4 5 I don't like it when other people challenge my deeply held beliefs.

1 2 3 4 5 I get along better with people than do most people.

1 2 3 4 5 People don't change.

1 2 3 4 5 I have trouble coping with problems of life such as relationship problems, depression, and rage.

1 2 3 4 5 I tend to sacrifice my needs for those of others.

1 2 3 4 5 Men and women tend to have different communication styles.

1 2 3 4 5 The most credible evidence is that based on direct experience, such as eyewitness reports.

Keep track of your results. As you read this book and gain a better understanding of critical thinking, you'll find out what your responses to each of these statements mean. A brief summary of the meaning of each rating can also be found at the back of the book.

THiNK Tank

"All or Nothing" Thinking

DISCUSSION QUESTIONS

1. *Discuss Calvin's claim that seeing the complexities of knowledge is "paralyzing."*

2. *Think back to a time when you felt, as does Calvin in the cartoon, that life is easier if you can think in dualist terms of black and white rather than "seeing the complexities and shades of gray." Referring back to this and other similar experiences, what are some of the drawbacks of making decisions or taking action on the basis of all-or-nothing thinking? Be specific.*

has been linked to the emergence of new, more virulent strains of drug-resistant tuberculosis. In addition, the incidence of some sexually transmitted diseases such as syphilis, which was once treatable by penicillin, is once again on the rise.[8]

The ability to think critically and to make effective life decisions is shaped by many factors, including our stage of cognitive development, the possession of good analytical communication, and research skills and such characteristics as open-mindedness, flexibility, and creativity.

Cognitive Development in College Students

Becoming a critical thinker is a lifelong process. Education researcher William Perry, Jr. (1913–1998) was one of the first to study college students' cognitive development.[9] **Cognitive development** is the process by which each of us "becomes an intelligent person, acquiring intelligence and increasingly advanced thought and problem-solving ability from infancy to adulthood."[10] Perry's work has gained wide acceptance among educators. Although Perry identified nine developmental positions, later researchers have simplified his schemata into three stages: dualism, relativism, and commitment. These three stages are represented by the first three questions

in the Self-Evaluation Questionnaire in the Think Tank feature on page 6.

> **cognitive development** The process of acquiring advanced thinking and problem-solving skills from infancy through adulthood.

Stage 1: Dualism.

Younger students such as freshmen and many sophomores tend to take in knowledge and life experiences in a simplistic, "dualistic" way, viewing something as either right or wrong. They see knowledge as existing outside themselves and look to authority figures for the answers.

This dualistic stage is most obvious when these students confront a conflict. Although they may be able to apply critical-thinking skills in a structured classroom environment, they often lack the ability to apply these skills in real-life conflicts. When confronted with a situation such as occurred in the Milgram study of obedience,[11] they are more likely to follow an authority figure even if they feel uncomfortable doing so. In addition, a controversial issue such as affirmative action, where there is little agreement among authorities and no clear-cut right or wrong answers, can leave students at this stage struggling to make sense of it. We'll be studying some perspectives on affirmative action at the end of this chapter.

Connections

How do you determine if the statistics found in the results of a scientific experiment are credible? *See Chapter 12, p. 382.*

When researching an issue, students at the dualistic stage may engage in **confirmation bias**, seeking out only evidence that supports their views and dismissing as unreliable statistics that contradict them.[12] The fact that their "research" confirms their views serves to reinforce their simplistic, black-and-white view of the world.

confirmation bias At the dualistic stage of research, seeking out only evidence that supports your view and dismissing evidence that contradicts it.

HIGHLIGHTS

COGNITIVE DEVELOPMENT IN COLLEGE STUDENTS

Stage 1: Dualism There are right and wrong answers. Authorities know the right answers.

Transition to Stage 2 There are some uncertainties and different opinions, but these are temporary.

Stage 2: Relativism When the authorities don't have the right answers, everyone has a right to his or her own opinion; there are no right or wrong answers.

Transition to Stage 3 All thinking is contextual and relative but not equally valid.

Stage 3: Commitment I should not just blindly follow or oppose authority. I need to orient myself in an uncertain world and make a decision or commitment.

➤**APPLICATION: Identify an example of thinking at each of three stages in the text.**

Adapted from Ron Sheese and Helen Radovanovic, "W. G. Perry's Model of Intellectual and Ethical Development: Implications of Recent Research for the Education and Counseling of Young Adults," paper presented at the annual meeting of the Canadian Psychological Association (Ottawa, Ontario, June 1984).

In one study, 48 undergraduates, who either supported or opposed capital punishment, were given two fictitious studies to read.[13] One study presented "evidence" contradicting beliefs about the deterrent effect of capital punishment. The other study presented "evidence" confirming the effectiveness of capital punishment as a deterrent. The results showed that students uncritically accepted the evidence that confirmed their preexisting views, while being skeptical about opposing evidence. In other words, despite the fact that both groups read the same studies, rather than modifying their position, the students used the confirming study to support their existing opinion on capital punishment and dismissed the opposing evidence.*

*For more on the debate on capital punishment see pages 261–264.

Students at this stage may also be unable to recognize ambiguity, conflicting values, or motives in real-life situations. In light of this, it is not surprising that young people are most likely to fall victim to con artists, financial fraud, and identity theft, despite the stereotype that the elderly are more vulnerable to scam artists.[14]

Students are most likely to make the transition to a higher stage of cognitive development when their current way of thinking is challenged or proves inadequate. During the transition they come to recognize that there is uncertainty in the world and that authorities can have different positions. Some educators called this period of disorientation and doubting all answers "sophomoritis."[15]

Stage 2: Relativism. Rather than accepting that ambiguity and uncertainty may be unavoidable and that they need to make decisions despite this, students at the relativist stage go to the opposite extreme. They reject a dualistic worldview and instead believe that all truth is relative or just a matter of opinion. People at this stage believe that stating your opinion is the proper mode of expression, and they look down on challenging others' opinions as "judgmental" and even disrespectful. However, despite their purported belief in relativism, most students at this stage still expect their professor to support his or her opinion.

Having their ideas challenged, grappling with controversial issues, encountering role models who are at a higher stage of cognitive development, and learning about their limits and the contradictions in their thinking can all help students move on to the next stage of cognitive development.

Stage 3: Commitment. As students mature, they come to realize that not all thinking is equally valid. Not only can authorities be mistaken but also in some circumstances uncertainty and ambiguity are unavoidable. When students at this stage experience uncertainty, they are now able to make decisions and commit to particular positions on the basis of reason and the best evidence available. At the same time, as independent thinkers, they are open to challenge, able to remain flexible, and willing to change their position should new evidence come to light.

> As students mature, they come to realize that not all thinking is equally valid.

As we mature and acquire better critical-thinking skills, our way of conceptualizing and understanding the world becomes increasingly complex. This is particularly true of older students who return to college after spending time out in the "real world." Unlike people at the first stage who look to authority for answers, people at the third stage accept responsibility for their interactions with their environment and are more open to challenges and more accepting of ambiguity.

STOP AND ASSESS YOURSELF

I. Imagine that you are a participant in Milgram's study of obedience. What would you have done if you protested and the experimenter in charge answered, "The experiment requires that you continue"? Discuss your answer in light of the stages of cognitive development. Discuss also what you might do to make it less likely that you would obey an authority figure in a situation such as the Milgram study.

2. College professor Stephen Satris maintains that the relativism of the second stage of development is not a genuine philosophical position but a means of avoiding having one's ideas challenged. Student relativism, he writes, "is primarily a method of protection, a suit of armor, which can be applied to one's own opinions, whatever they may be—but not necessarily to the opinion of others. . . . It is an expression of the idea that no one step forward and judge (and possibly criticize) one's own opinion."[16] What is your "suit of armor"? Discuss strategies you might take to break out of this "suit of armor." Relate your answer to your own stage of cognitive development.

3. Most college students do not make the transition to the third, or commitment, stage of cognitive development. Why do you think this is so? Discuss ways in which the curriculum and college life in general might be restructured to encourage cognitive growth in students.

4. Today, more people are returning to college after having children and/or having worked for several years. This phenomenon is especially prevalent in community colleges, where the average age is 28.[17] Discuss whether there are differences in how students of different ages in your class think about the world, and how interaction among students at different stages might enrich our thinking.

5. The first three questions of the "Self-Evaluation Questionnaire" in the Think Tank feature represent the three stages of cognitive development. Which stage, or transition between stages, best describes your approach to understanding the world? What are the shortcomings and strengths of your current stage of cognitive development? Develop a plan to improve your skills as a critical thinker. Put the plan into action. Report on the results of your action plan.

CHARACTERISTICS OF A GOOD CRITICAL THINKER

Critical thinking is a collection of skills that enhance and reinforce each other. In this section we'll be discussing some of the more important skills for effective critical thinking.

Analytical Skills

As a critical thinker, you need to be able to analyze and provide logical support for your beliefs rather than simply rely on your opinions. Analytical skills are also important in recognizing and evaluating other people's arguments so that you are not taken in by faulty reasoning. We'll be studying logical argumentation in more depth in Chapter 2 and in Chapters 5 through 9.

Effective Communication

In addition to analytical skills, critical thinking requires communication and reading skills.[18] Communication skills include listening, speaking, and writing skills. Being aware of your own communication style, as well as of cultural variations and differences in the communication styles of men and women, can also go a long way toward improving communication in a relationship. We'll be learning more about communication in Chapter 3, "Language and Communication."

Research and Inquiry Skills

Understanding and resolving issues requires research and inquiry skills such as competence in gathering, evaluating, and pulling together supporting evidence. For example, in researching and gathering information on what would be the best major or career path for you, you need to identity your interests and talents first and then evaluate possible majors and careers in light of these interests and talents. Research skills are also important in understanding and moving toward a resolution of a complex issue such as affirmative action in college admissions.

Inquiry and gaining greater insight requires asking the right questions, as Milgram did in designing his study of obedience. While most people were asking what sort of twisted monsters the Nazis were or why the German people allowed Hitler to have so much power, Milgram asked the more basic question: How far would ordinary citizens go in obeying an authority figure? Despite the fact that experiments such as Milgram's were declared unethical by the American Psychological Association in 1973 because of long-term psychological distress suffered by many of the participants, his scientific experiments still stand as classics in the field.

As critical thinkers we need to avoid confirmation bias and the tendency to selectively see and interpret data to fit into our own world-views, as happened in the study on student's views of capital punishment (see page 8). This is a practice that often leads to stalemates and conflict in personal as well as in political relations. Our research should also be accurate and based on credible evidence. We'll be learning more about researching and evaluating evidence in Chapter 4.

Flexibility and Tolerance for Ambiguity

Too many people defer to others or fail to take a position on a controversial issue simply because they are unable to evaluate conflicting views. As we mature, we become better at making decisions in the face of uncertainty and ambiguity. Effective decision making includes setting clear short-term and long-term goals in our lives and developing a realistic strategy for achieving these goals. Critical thinkers also build flexibility into their life plans so that they can adapt to changes, especially since most of us haven't had sufficient experience to finalize our life plan during our first few years of college. We'll be discussing the process of developing a life plan in more depth later in this chapter.

Connections

How do scientists identify a problem and develop a hypothesis for studying a problem? *See Chapter 12, p. 367.*

Open-Minded Skepticism

Critical thinkers are willing to work toward overcoming personal prejudices and biases. They begin with an open mind and an attitude of reflective skepticism. The point is not simply to take a stand on an issue—such as What career is best for me? Is abortion immoral? Does God exist? What should be the role of women in the family?—but rather to critically examine the evidence and assumptions put forth in support of different positions on the issue before coming to a final conclusion. In doing so, effective critical thinkers are able to balance belief and doubt.

First put forward by French philosopher and mathematician René Descartes (1596–1650), the **method of doubt** suspends belief. This method of critical analysis,

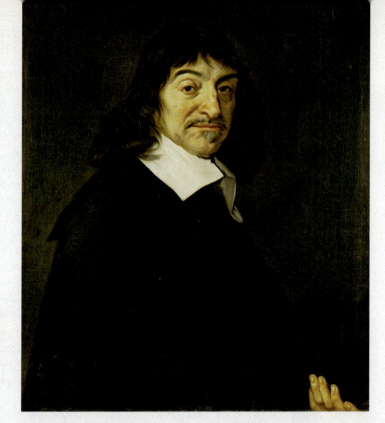

René Descartes (1596–1650) proposed the method of doubt, in which we never accept anything as true without evidence and reason to support our conclusion.

which has traditionally been preferred in fields such as science and philosophy, begins from a position of skepticism in which we put aside our preconceived ideas. Descartes wrote regarding the rules for using the method of doubt:

> The first of these [rules] was never to accept anything as true if I did not have evident knowledge of its truth: that is to say, carefully to avoid precipitate conclusions and preconceptions, and to include nothing more in my judgments than what presented itself to my mind so clearly and distinctly that I had no occasion to doubt it.[19]

It is especially important that you be willing to adopt a position of doubt or skepticism when critically examining your own cherished beliefs and the claims of authority figures. Albert Einstein (1879–1955), in developing his theory of relativity, used the method of doubt regarding the generally accepted belief that time is "absolute"—that is, fixed and unchanging.

The **method of belief**, in contrast, suspends doubt. Becoming immersed in a good book, movie, or play often involves what English poet Samuel Taylor Coleridge (1772–1834) called the "willing suspension of disbelief." This approach is also productive when we are discussing issues on which we hold strong views and are not as open as we should be to opposing viewpoints. In dialogues between people who are pro-choice and pro-life, for example, a pro-choice critical thinker, in order to compensate for his or her biases, should be genuinely open to believing what the pro-life person is saying, rather than start from the traditional position of doubt. This task requires empathy, active listening skills, and intellectual curiosity.

Creative Problem Solving

Creative thinkers can view problems from multiple perspectives and come up with original solutions to complex problems. They use their imagination to envision possibilities, including potential future problems, and to develop contingency plans to effectively deal with these scenarios.

When staff members of the U.S. Department of Homeland Security put together a handbook of possible disaster scenarios, they failed to foresee the possibility of civil unrest and social breakdown following a disaster. Because of lack of preparedness for such occurrences as Hurricane Katrina, which struck the Gulf Coast in 2005, hundreds of people died who might have been saved and thousands of others were left homeless and living in chaotic and squalid conditions for weeks and months. Practice in problem-solving for disasters enabled the United States to respond quicker and more effectively when the East Coast was struck by Superstorm Sandy in 2012.

The Tokyo Electric Power Company, operator of the Fukushima Daiichi nuclear power plant, failed to take measures to prevent disasters, like the one that followed an earthquake and tsunami off the coast of Japan in 2011. Rather than taking on the challenge of making the plant secure from such events, they ignored the possibility that there could be such a large tsunami. Consequently, they failed to install adequate backup generators and cooling systems and as a result the power plants experienced a nuclear meltdown spewing toxic radiation into the surrounding area.

Creativity also involves "a willingness to take risks, to cope with the unexpected, to welcome challenge and even failure as a part of the process to arrive at a new and deeper understanding."[20] Instead of giving up when

Connections

Why is having an open mind important in the sciences?
See Chapter 12, p. 368.

method of doubt A method of critical analysis in which we put aside our preconceived ideas and beliefs and begin from a position of skepticism.

method of belief A method of critical analysis in which we suspend our doubts and biases and remain genuinely open to what people with opposing views are saying.

About 20,000 people died as a result of the tsunami that struck Japan in 2011. The tsunami also caused extensive damage to the nuclear power plants on the coast.

times are difficult or resources are lacking, creative critical thinkers are able to make creative use of available resources. In 1976, when he was only 21, Steve Jobs built the first Apple personal computer in his family's garage. His innovative idea of user-friendly software changed the way people perceived computers and heralded the age of personal computing. He later went on to introduce the iPod, which revolutionized portable music players.

Creative thinking is a much sought-after skill in the business world.[21] Because young people are usually less invested in traditional ideas and ways of doing things than are people who have been working in a field for years, they tend to be more open to new ideas. Being able to recognize creative solutions to a problem and to generate and communicate new ideas requires not just creative thinking but also being open-minded, confident, intellectually curious, and an effective communicator.

Attention, Mindfulness, and Curiosity

Critical thinkers are intellectually curious. They are attentive and mindful to what's going on around them and to their own thoughts and feelings. The Buddhist concept of the "beginner's mind" is closely related to the Western concept of the critically open mind, or mindfulness. Zen master Shunryu Suzuki defined the beginner's mind as "wisdom which is seeking for wisdom." He wrote:

> The practice of Zen mind is beginner's mind. The innocence of first inquiry—what am I? . . . The mind of the beginner is empty, free of the habits of the expert, ready to accept, to doubt, and open to all possibilities. . . . If your mind is empty, it is always ready for anything; it is open to everything. In the beginner's mind there are many possibilities. . . .[22]

Like the beginner's mind, good critical thinkers do not reject, without sound reasons, views that conflict with their own. Instead, they are willing to consider multiple perspectives. One of the recent breakthroughs in neuroscience is the discovery that the brains of Buddhist monks who meditate regularly—a practice that involves being mindful, open, and attentive to what is going on in the present moment—are neurally much more active and more resilient in neuroplasticity than are the brains of

people who do not meditate.[23] Many large corporations, including some Fortune 500 companies, are encouraging their executives to take meditation breaks on the job, since it has been found to improve their performance.[24]

Collaborative Learning

Critical thinking occurs in a real-life context. We are not isolated individuals—we are interconnected beings. As critical thinkers we need to move beyond the traditional, detached approach to thinking and develop a more collaborative approach that is grounded in shared dialogue and community.

The failure to take into account context and relationships can lead to faulty decisions that we may later regret. An example of this type of faulty reasoning is the tendency of many individuals to neglect both feedback and complexity. Because of this, they tend not to fully and accurately consider the other side's response. In a relationship we may do something in an attempt to get our partner to pay more attention to us—for example, threatening to leave a partner if he or she doesn't stop spending so much time with friends—only to see this backfire, losing the relationship altogether because we failed to consider how the other person might react.[25]

To use another example, military planners in developing strategies sometimes fail to consider what the enemy might do in return to minimize the effectiveness of these strategies. During the War of 1812, a group of politicians in Washington, D.C., decided the time had come to add Canada to the United States. Their military strategy failed primarily because they did not adequately assess the Canadian response to the U.S. mission to annex Canada. Instead of greeting the American invaders as liberators from British rule, Canadians regarded the war as an unprovoked attack on their homes and lives. Rather than uniting Canada and

Did You Know

The ancient Greek thinker Socrates (469–399 BCE) spent much of his time in the marketplace of Athens surrounded by his young followers. He used this public venue to seek out people in order to challenge their traditional beliefs and practices. He did this by engaging people in a type of critical thinking, now referred to as the Socratic method, in which his probing questions provoked them into realizing their lack of rational understanding and their inconsistencies in thought.

the United States, the War of 1812 gave rise to the first stirring of Canadian nationalism (and even provoked a movement in New England to secede from the United States).[26]

HIGHLIGHTS

CHARACTERISTICS OF A SKILLED CRITICAL THINKER

As a skilled critical thinker, you should

- Have good analytical skills
- Possess effective communication skills
- Be well informed and possess good research skills
- Be flexible and able to tolerate ambiguity and uncertainty
- Adopt a position of open-minded skepticism
- Be a creative problem solver
- Be attentive, mindful, and intellectually curious
- Engage in collaborative learning

➤ **APPLICATION:** *Identify an example of each of the characteristics in the text.*

Good critical thinkers adopt a collaborative rather than an adversarial stance, in which they listen to and take others' views into account. Let's go back to the relationship example. Rather than accusing our partner of not spending enough time with us, a good critical thinker would express his or her feelings and thoughts and then listen to the other person's side. Critical thinkers carefully consider all perspectives and are open to revising their views in light of their broader understanding. Using our critical-thinking skills, we might come to realize that

---

**Good critical thinkers adopt
a collaborative rather than
an adversarial stance.**

---

our partner's friends are very important to him or her. Perhaps we are being insecure and need to spend more time with our own friends, giving our partner more space. Maybe we can find a solution that meets both our needs. For example, the sports lovers can bring their partners or another friend along once or twice a month to watch the games with them.

EXERCISE 1-2

STOP AND ASSESS YOURSELF

1. Watch the Milgram film *Obedience*. Discuss ways in which the participants in the film demonstrated, or failed to demonstrate, good critical-thinking skills.

2. Identifying good role models in your life can help you come up with a picture of the person you would like to be. Think of a person, real or fictional, who exemplifies good critical-thinking skills. Make a list of some of the qualities of this person. Discuss how these qualities help the person in his or her everyday life.

3. Adopt the stance of the Buddhist "beginner's mind." Be attentive only to what is happening in the now. After one minute, write down everything you observed going on around you as well as inside of you (your feelings, body language, and the like). Did you notice more than you might have otherwise? Share your observations with the class. Discuss ways in which this practice of being more attentive to what is going on might enhance your effectiveness as a critical thinker.

4. Working in groups of four to six students, select an issue about which the group is evenly divided into positions for or against it. Each side should adopt a stance of belief and open-mindedness when listening to the other side's position. After the pro side presents its views for two minutes, the anti side takes one minute to repeat back the pro's views without interjecting their own doubts. Repeat the process with the anti side presenting their views. Discuss as a class how this exercise helped you to suspend your biases and to actively listen to views that diverge from your own.

5. Referring to the Self-Evaluation Questionnaire on page 6, share your strengths and weaknesses as well as your plans for improving your critical-thinking skills with others, whether it be friends, family, or in class. Discuss steps you might take or have already taken to work toward or overcome some of your weaknesses.

CRITICAL THINKING AND SELF-DEVELOPMENT

Critical thinking is not just about abstract thought. It is also about self-improvement and your whole development as a person. Working on your self requires that you be honest with yourself and others about your biases, your expectations, your strengths, and your limitations. Are your expectations realistic? Do you have a well thought out plan and goals for your life? People who are inflexible in their thinking may be unable to adapt to changing or new or unusual circumstances and may instead get caught up in rules and inflexible ways of thinking that are inadequate to resolve the situation.

Living the Self-Examined Life

"The unexamined life is not worth living," Socrates said. Often we flounder in college because we have not taken the time to learn about ourselves or develop a plan for our future. The lives of too many people are controlled more by circumstances than by their own choices. Good critical thinkers, in contrast, take charge of their lives and choices rather than opting for the security of fitting into the crowd or simply blindly following an authority figure as happened in the Milgram study at the beginning of this chapter. In addition to being rational thinkers, they are in touch with their emotions and feelings. We'll be looking more at the role of emotion in Chapter 2.

Some psychologists and psychiatrists believe that irrational beliefs and poor critical-thinking skills contribute to many of the "problems of life," such as depression, rage, and low self-esteem.[27, 28] While depression often has a biochemical component that needs to be treated, poor critical-thinking skills can aggravate or even be a major factor in some types of situational depression where a student feels overwhelmed and unable to cope or make a decision in a particular set of circumstances. In a 2011 survey by the American College Health Association, about 30 percent of college students reported that at least once during the past year they felt "so depressed, it was difficult to function." Since people tend to become better at problem-solving as they get older, it is not surprising that depression rates start to drop beginning at age 30. Compared to people over the age of 60, 18–29 year-olds are 70 percent more likely to experience depression.[29]

Although by no means a cure-all, improving critical-thinking skills has been shown to help people deal more effectively with their problems.[30] Rather than view the problems in our lives as being out of our control, we should—as cognitive psychologists in particular counsel us—develop strategies for taking charge of our lives, develop realistic expectations, and commit ourselves to acknowledging and developing the skills to resolve our problems.

Developing a Rational Life Plan

American philosopher John Rawls (1921–2002) wrote that in order to get the most out of life, everyone needs to develop a "rational life plan"—that is, a plan that would be chosen "with full deliberative rationality, that is, with full awareness of the relevant facts and after a careful consideration of the consequences. . . . Someone is happy, when his plans are going well and his more important aspirations are being fulfilled."[31]

In drawing up our life plan, we make a hierarchy, with our most important plans or goals at the top, followed by a list of subplans. Organize your goals according to a schedule when they are to be carried out, although the more distant a goal is, the less specific the plan will be. Of course, we can't predict everything that will happen in life, and there will be times when circumstances hinder us from achieving our goals. Think of a life plan as being like a flight plan. Airplanes are off course about 90 percent of the time because of such factors as weather, wind patterns, and other aircraft. The pilot must constantly correct for these conditions to get the plane back on course. Without a flight plan, the pilots and their planes would be at the mercy of winds and weather, blown hither and thither, and never reaching their destination.

Age Differences in Depression

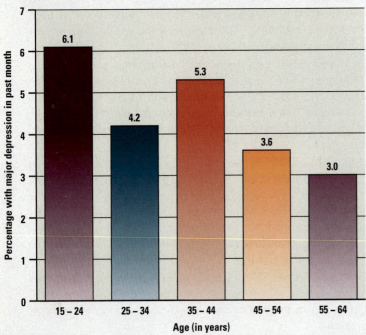

Source: Santrock (2009) Life-Span Development, McGraw-Hill, p. 404.

Begin putting together your life plan by making a list of your values, interests, skills, and talents. Values are what are important to you in life and include things such as financial security, love, family, career, independence, spirituality, health and fitness, education, contributions to society, friends, sense of integrity, and fun. Your goals in life should be rational as well as consistent with your values. According to the 2013 American Freshman Survey, "raising a family," the most important goal for several years, has now taken a back seat to being "able to get a good job," with 87.9 percent of freshman listing this as their top goal, the highest since 1966.[32] Take time to deliberate about your hierarchy of values. It is possible that after careful consideration of the implications of a particular value, such as "being well off financially," you may want to place it lower on your hierarchy of values.

If you are unsure of your skills and talents, go to the career office at your college and take some of the aptitude and personality tests available there, such as the Myers-Briggs Indicator.[33] These tests are useful in helping you to

Connections

How can participation in civic life improve your critical-thinking skills and enhance your personal growth? *See Chapter 13, p. 402.* What marketing strategies should you be aware of so as to avoid being an uncritical consumer? *See Chapter 10, pp. 311–312.*

maintain a 3.0 average, or get more exercise. These goals should be consistent with your interests, talents, and the type of person you want to be. Also come up with a plan of action to achieve these short-term goals.

Next, list your long-term goals. Ideally your long-term and short-term goals should augment each other. Your plans for achieving the long-term goals should be realistic and compatible with your short-term goals and interests. Think creatively about how certain goals can fit together.

People who are skilled critical thinkers not only have reasonable, well thought out goals and strategies to achieve them but also act from a sense of integrity or personal authenticity and respect for the integrity and aspirations of others in their lives. We are not isolated individuals but social beings whose decisions affect the lives of all those around us.

Facing Challenges

Sometimes traditional practices and cultural beliefs get in the way of our achieving our life plan. In these cases we may need to develop subgoals that involve challenging the

---

HIGHLIGHTS

MY LIFE PLAN

In putting together your life plan you need to identify:

1. Your most important values

2. Your strengths (interests, skills, talents, and assets)

3. Your weaknesses (for example, lack of financial resources or skill)

4. Your goals

   a. Short term

   b. Long term

5. A plan of action to achieve short-term goals

6. A plan of action to achieve long-term goals

➤APPLICATION: Identify an example of each of the six steps in the text.

---

determine which career or careers might be most fulfilling for you. The Web site www.collegeboard.org also provides helpful information on choosing a major and a career.

But don't just list your strengths, assets, and competencies; take note of your weaknesses too. Weaknesses are something we do poorly or something we lack, such as financial resources, information, or technical expertise.

Once you've written down your values, interests, talents, skills, and weaknesses, list your goals. Goals are important in helping you organize your day-to-day life and in giving your life direction. Start out by listing short-term goals, or those that you want to accomplish by the time you graduate from college; for example, choose a major,

A life plan is like a flight plan; it helps keep us on course.

Martin Luther King's willingness to go to jail, rather than back down on his goal of equality for all people, made him one of the most effective civil rights leaders in American history.

obstructing beliefs rather than give up our life plan. Openly questioning traditional belief systems and effectively addressing challenges to deeply held beliefs requires courage and self-confidence. The abolitionists and early feminists and civil rights advocates were often ridiculed and even imprisoned because they challenged traditions they believed were unjust. See "Thinking Outside the Box: Elizabeth Cady Stanton, Women's Rights Leader."

When Martin Luther King Jr. was thrown in jail for his role in organizing the 1955 bus boycott in Montgomery, Alabama, he refused to back down despite the beseeching of his fellow clergy. Fortunately, King had the courage to stand by his convictions. In his "Letter from Birmingham Jail," King wrote:

> My Dear Fellow Clergy,
>
> I am in Birmingham because injustice is here. . . .
> We know through painful experience that freedom is never voluntarily given by the oppressor; it must be demanded by the oppressed.
>
> You express a great deal of anxiety over our willingness to break laws. . . . This is a legitimate concern . . . an unjust law is a code that is out of harmony with the moral law. . . . Any law that degrades human personality is unjust. . . . I submit that an individual who breaks a law that conscience tells him is unjust, and willingly accepts the penalty by staying in jail to arouse the conscience of the community over its injustice, is in reality expressing the very highest respect for law.

Critical thinking, as we noted earlier, requires being in touch with our emotions, such as indignation or anger, elicited by unjust treatment, as in the case of King, or by a shocking image such as the photo showing the abuse at Abu Ghraib prison (see page 18).

In addition to being able to effectively challenge social injustices, as critical thinkers we need to be able to respond thoughtfully to challenges to our own belief systems rather than engaging in resistance. This requires good critical-thinking skills as well as self-confidence.

The Importance of Self-Esteem

Effective critical-thinking skills appear to be positively correlated to healthy self-esteem. Healthy self-esteem emerges from effectiveness in problem solving and success in achieving our life goals. The task of sorting out genuine self-worth from a false sense of self-esteem requires critical thinking. Healthy self-esteem is not the same as arrogant pride or always putting one's own interests first. Nor are people with proper self-esteem habitually self-sacrificing, subverting their interests and judgment to those of others.

People with low self-esteem are more vulnerable to manipulation by others. They experience more "depression, irritability, anxiety, fatigue, nightmares . . . withdrawal from others, nervous laughter, body aches and emotional tension."[34] Some of these traits, such as anxiety and nervous laughter, were seen in the Milgram study participants who complied with the request of the authority figure. Indeed, many of these men later came to regret their compliance and even required psychotherapy.

Good critical-thinking skills are essential in exercising your autonomy. Critical thinkers are proactive. They are aware of the influences on their lives, including family, culture, television, and friends; they can build on the positive influences and overcome the negative ones, rather than be passively carried through life and blaming others if their decisions turn out poorly.

An autonomous person is both rational and self-directing and therefore less likely to be taken in by poor reasoning or contradictions in his own or other's reasoning. Being self-directing entails making decisions on the basis of what is reasonable instead of getting swept up in groupthink or blindly obeying an authority figure. To achieve this end, autonomous critical thinkers seek out different perspectives and actively participate in critical dialogues to gain new insights and expand their own thinking.

Did You Know

Studies show that young people who have positive self-esteem "have more friends, are more apt to resist harmful peer pressure, are less sensitive to criticism or to what people think, have higher IQs, and are better informed."[35]

Outside the Box

ELIZABETH CADY STANTON, *Women's Rights Leader*

Elizabeth Cady Stanton (1815–1902) was a social activist and leader in the early women's rights movement. In 1840, when she was a young newlywed, Stanton attended the World Anti-Slavery Society convention in London, which her husband was attending as a delegate. It was there that Stanton met Lucretia Mott (1793–1880). At the convention the women delegates from the United States were denied seats after some of the male U.S. delegates vehemently objected. Mott, in response, demanded that she be treated with the same respect accorded any man—white or black. During these heated discussions, Stanton marveled at the way Mott, a woman of 47, held her own in the argument, "skillfully parried all their attacks . . . turning the laugh on them, and then by her earnestness and dignity silencing their ridicule and jeers."*

Following the Civil War, Stanton refused to support passage of the Fifteenth Amendment, which gave voting rights to black men but not to women. She argued that the amendment essentially was based on the fallacy of false dilemma—either black men get the vote (but not women) or only white men can vote. Instead she pointed out that there was a third option: both men and women should have the right to vote. Unfortunately, her line of argument and her challenges to traditional beliefs about the role of women were ridiculed. Although black men received the vote in 1870 with passage of the Fifteenth Amendment, it would be another 50 years before women were finally given the right to vote in the United States. Nevertheless, Stanton's persistence and refusal to back down in her fight for equal opportunity for women paved the way for the final passage of this amendment so that other women could achieve their life plans of equal participation in the political life of the country.

DISCUSSION QUESTIONS

1. Elizabeth Cady Stanton had close friends such as Lucretia Mott and Susan B. Anthony in her fight for women's rights. Discuss ways in which having a support network of people who are skilled critical thinkers can enhance your ability not to use or fall for faulty reasoning. Discuss ways in which you do, or could, serve as a critical-thinking mentor to others.

2. Think of a time when your ability to pursue your goals was compromised by ridicule. Explain, using specific examples. Discuss steps you might take to make yourself less likely to give into faulty reasoning or to give up on an aspect of your life plan under such circumstances.

*Lloyd Hare, *The Greatest American Women: Lucretia Mott* (New York: American Historical Society, 1937), p. 193.

Abuse at Abu Ghraib Prison, Iraq
Being an autonomous thinker makes it less likely that you will uncritically follow orders or conform to peer pressure. The abuse and humiliation of Iraqi prisoners by U.S. soldiers at Abu Ghraib prison in Iraq in 2003–2004 provides a real-life illustration of what happened in the Milgram and Stanford prison experiments. In 2005, Army reservist and prison guard Charles Graner was convicted and sentenced to 10 years in prison for his role as ringleader in the abuse and humiliation of Iraqi detainees. In his defense he said that he was simply following orders. His defense lawyers also pointed out that the U.S. Army's intelligence units were poorly trained and badly managed, factors that contributed to the reservists' poor judgment. Graner's defense was rejected by the court. Graner was released from prison in 2011 after serving six years of his term.

DISCUSSION QUESTIONS

1. *Was Graner's reason for his treatment of the Iraqi prisoners justified? Should he be held responsible for his actions? Discuss what you might have done had you been a low-ranking guard at Abu Ghraib and had witnessed your fellow soldiers mistreating Iraqi prisoners.*

2. *What was your initial emotional reaction to this image? Discuss how learning to be aware of and critically analyzing your reaction to this or other upsetting images might make you more likely to question authority or rethink some of your world views. Support your response in light of what you know about autonomous thinkers.*

3. *Similar situations have occurred during fraternity and sorority initiation hazings. If you know of, or have been witness to, any situations where this happened, discuss why it most likely happened and what might have been done to prevent it.*

Critical Thinking in a Democracy

Critical-thinking skills are essential in a democracy. **Democracy** literally means rule by the people; it is a form of government in which the highest power in the state is invested in the people and exercised directly by them or, as is generally the case in modern democracies, by their elected officials. As citizens of a democracy, we have an obligation to be well informed about policies and issues so that we can effectively participate in critical discussions and decisions.

Thomas Jefferson wrote, "In a republican nation, whose citizens are to be led by reason and persuasion and not by force, the art of reasoning becomes of the first importance."[36] The purpose of democracy is not to achieve consensus through polling or majority vote but to facilitate open-ended discussion and debates by those with diverse views. Truth, argued British philosopher John Stuart Mill (1806–1873), often is found neither in the opinion of those who favor the status quo nor in the opinion of the nonconformist but in a combination of viewpoints. Therefore, freedom of speech and listening to opposing views, no matter how offensive they may be, are essential for critical thinking in a democracy.

Corrupt politicians have been elected or appointed to public office and high-ranking positions in their parties because the

> **democracy** A form of government in which the highest power in the state is invested in the people and exercised directly by them or, as is generally the case in modern democracies, by their elected officials.

ANALYZING IMAGES

Student Protestor in Front of Tanks at Tiananmen Square, China

On June 3rd and 4th, 1989, hundreds, possibly thousands, of unarmed demonstrators protesting the legitimacy of China's communist government were shot dead in a brutal military operation to crush a democratic uprising in Beijing's Tiananmen Square. The demonstrators, who were mostly university students, had occupied the square for several weeks, refusing to leave until their demands for democratic reform were met. A photographer captured the above picture of a lone, unnamed demonstrator standing in front of the tanks, bringing to a halt the row of advancing tanks. To this day, no one knows who the demonstrator was or what his fate was.

DISCUSSION QUESTIONS

1. *What do you think the student in the photo is thinking and feeling? What do you think led up to his decision to take this action? Does his action show good critical thinking? Discuss ways in which the student's action demonstrates, or does not demonstrate, good critical-thinking skills. Relate your answer to the actions of reformers such as Stanton and King.*

2. *Imagine yourself in a similar situation. Discuss how you would most likely react and how your reaction is a reflection of your current self-development. What steps could you take in your life to make yourself more likely to engage in civil disobedience, particularly in a case where your life was not at stake?*

What critical-thinking skills do you need to participate in campaigns and elections, influence public policy, and understand the legal system? *See Chapter 13.*

Connections

people failed to educate themselves about their activities and ideals. Indeed, in a 1938 poll of Princeton freshmen, Adolf Hitler was ranked first as the "greatest living person"![37] And in New York City in the mid-nineteenth century, politician William Marcy "Boss" Tweed (1823–1878) conned citizens out of millions of dollars. He also managed to get his corrupt associates, known as the Tweed Ring, appointed and elected to high offices.

Unlike totalitarian societies, modern democracies encourage diversity and open discussion of different ideas. Research on the effects of race, ethnicity, class, and diversity on college students reveals "important links between experiences with diversity and increased commitment to civic engagement, democratic outcomes and community participation."[38] Exposure to diversity on campus and in the classroom broadens students' perspectives and improves critical thinking and problem-solving skills.[39]

In his book *The Assault on Reason* (2007), Al Gore argues that there has been a decline in participation by ordinary citizens in the democratic process since television overtook the printed word as the dominant source of information. Television as a one-way source of information appeals mainly to our uncritical emotions rather than requiring critical reflective thought, thus rendering viewers passive consumers of prepackaged information and ideologies. Political engagement tends to rise during a presidential election year and drop off following the election. For example, 39.5 percent of college freshmen in 2008 stated that "keeping up to date with political affairs" was an essential or very important objective for them. However, this figure had dropped to 36 percent one year after the election of Barack Obama.[40]

People who are skilled at critical thinking are less likely to be taken in by faulty arguments and rhetoric. They are also more likely, like the pro-democracy Chinese students in Tiananmen Square, to demand the same clarity and reasonableness of thinking in their leaders that they require in themselves rather than remain passive in the face of government abuses of power. Thus, critical thinking contributes to your own well-being as well as to the well-being of society as a whole, by teaching you how to stand up to authority and irrational thinking.

STOP AND ASSESS YOURSELF

EXERCISE 1-3

1. According to German philosopher Immanuel Kant (1724–1804), one of our primary moral duties is self-respect and the development of proper self-esteem.[41] To truly respect others and their perspectives, we must first respect ourselves. Discuss and relate your answer to how proper self-respect might enhance your critical thinking skills. Use specific examples to support your answer.

2. Choose one of your short-term or long-term goals. Working in small groups, brainstorm about ways each of you might best achieve your goals. Also discuss the role good critical-thinking skills play (or played) in helping you achieve your goals.

3. In small groups, discuss a time when you deferred to the view of someone else and did (or failed to do) something you later came to regret because you were unable to give good reasons at the time for why you should not accept that person's view. Brainstorm with your group about ways in which you might make yourself less prone to this behavior.

4. A June 2004 article in *Altermedia Scotland* states: "America as a nation is now dominated by an alien system of beliefs, attitudes, and values that has become known as 'political correctness.' It seeks to impose a uniformity in thought and behaviour among all Americans and is therefore totalitarian in nature."[42] Do you agree that political correctness imposes "a uniformity of thought and behavior"? Come up with examples of political correctness on college campuses to illlustrate your answer. Discuss what role, if any, political correctness might play in increasing respect for diversity and enhancing the democratic process.

5. What is diversity? What are the educational benefits of diversity? Discuss ways in which your college, including your classes, addresses and facilitates diversity.

6. The student pro-democracy movement in Tiananmen Square was unsuccessful in terms of bringing democracy and a more open society to China. Does this failure mean that the movement and the lives that were lost were a waste? Support your answer.

7. Al Gore argues that the "mental muscles of democracy have begun to atrophy."[43] Discuss his claim. Relate your answer to the exercise of your "mental muscles" and those of other college students in political dialogue.

8. When the *Brown Daily Herald,* the student newspaper at Brown University, ran an ad from conservative activist David Horowitz entitled "Ten Reasons Why Reparation for Slavery Is a Bad Idea—and Racist Too," a coalition of Brown students stole and destroyed nearly 4,000 newspapers at campus distribution points. Defendants of the action argued that the ad was "an attempt to inject blatantly revisionist and, yes, racist arguments into a legitimate debate about black reparations . . . ."[44] Is it ever appropriate to censor views? Did the students have a legitimate right, on the basis of their freedom of speech, to destroy the newspapers? To what extent, if any, do we have an obligation in a democracy to listen attentively to and consider views that we find offensive? What would you have done had your school newspaper decided to publish the ad by Horowitz?

9. What are your strengths and talents? If you are not sure of your talents, go to the career office at your college and ask if you can take some of the personality and aptitude tests available there. These tests are also useful in helping you to determine which career or careers might be most fulfilling for you. Be creative; don't limit or underrate yourself.

BARRIERS TO CRITICAL THINKING

By sharpening your critical-thinking skills, you can become more independent and less susceptible to worldviews that foster narrow-mindedness. In this section we'll be looking at some of the barriers to critical thinking that keep us from analyzing our experiences or worldviews, as well as the experiences and worldviews of others.

The Three-Tier Model of Thinking

The processes used in critical thinking can be broken down into three tiers or levels: experience, interpretation, and analysis. Keep in mind that this division is artificial and merely helps to highlight the critical-thinking process. Although analysis is at the pinnacle of the process, the three-tier model is also recursive and dynamic, with analysis returning to experience for confirmation and interpretation being modified in light of the analysis of the new information. People never have pure experience or engage in pure analysis.

Experience, the first level, includes firsthand experience as well as information or empirical facts that we receive from other sources. Experience is the foundation of critical thinking and argumentation. It provides the material for interpretation and analysis. At this level of thinking we merely describe our experiences rather than try to understand them. For example:

1. I was turned down for the job I interviewed for.
2. Mark held the door open for me when I was leaving class.
3. Human cloning is illegal in the United States.
4. Although blacks represent only 12.8 percent of the U.S. population, they make up 37 percent of the prison inmates.[45]

Interpretation, the second level, involves trying to make sense of our experiences. This level of thinking includes individual interpretations of experiences as well as collective and cultural worldviews. Some of our interpretations may be well informed; others may be based merely on our opinions or personal feelings and prejudices.

Connections

How has the Internet enhanced your ability to participate in political life? *See Chapter 11, pp. 347–348.* In what ways is the news media biased? *See Chapter 11, pp. 344–345.* How can we as citizens participate in the law-making process? *See Chapter 13, p. 408.*

The Three Levels of Thinking

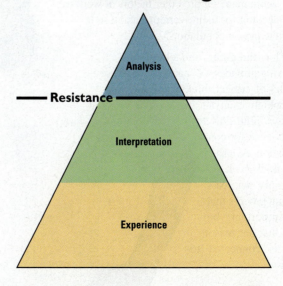

Some possible interpretations of the experiences previously listed are

1. I didn't get the job because I didn't have the right connections.

2. Mark is a chauvinist pig who thinks women are too weak to open their own doors.

3. If human cloning is illegal, it must be immoral.

4. Black men make up such a large percentage of the prison population because black men are innately more violent than white men.

Connections

How can you use the three-tier model of thinking to analyze media messages? *See Chapter 11, p. 352.* What model of thinking do scientists use? *See Chapter 12, p. 367.*

Analysis, the third level, requires that we raise our level of thinking and critically examine our interpretations of an experience, as well as those of others, refusing to accept either narrow interpretations of an experience or interpretations that are too broad. Analysis is most productive when it is done collectively because we each bring different experiences and interpretations, as well as skills in analysis, to the table. Analysis often begins by asking a question. The following are examples of questions we might ask in order to begin our analysis of the interpretations:

1. Was it my lack of connections or my poor interviewing skills or lack of job qualifications that caused me not to get the job?

2. What was Mark's intention in holding the door open for me?

3. Why is human cloning illegal? Are there circumstances in which human cloning might be acceptable?

4. Is there evidence that black men are innately more violent, or is it possible that black men are simply discriminated against more than white men? Or are other factors at work to account for their overrepresentation in the prison population?

The three-tier model of thinking provides a dynamic model of critical thinking in which analysis is always returning to experience for confirmation. As critical thinkers, it is not only our reasoning process that is important but also that our reasoning is connected to reality.

Resistance

Because most of us hate to be proven wrong, we may create barriers to keep our cherished worldviews from being challenged. Resistance, defined as "the use of immature defense mechanisms that are rigid, impulsive, maladaptive, and nonanalytical," can act as a barrier to critical thinking.

Almost all of us use defense mechanisms when we feel overwhelmed. Resistance, however, becomes a problem when it is used as a habitual way of responding to issues. Such habitual use interferes with our self-development, since it involves avoiding novel experiences and ideas that challenge our world-views. People who hold views that are backed by public opinion or the law may be particularly likely to resist when these views are challenged: They don't want to see the status quo upset.

> People who hold views that are backed by public opinion or the law may be particularly likely to resist when these views are challenged: They don't want to see the status quo upset.

In addition, resistance can create anxiety, since it puts us in a defensive mode and can shield us from the ideas and viewpoints of others, thus preventing us from working collaboratively and coming up with a well thought out plan of action.

Types of Resistance

There are several types of resistance, including avoidance, anger, clichés, denial, ignorance, conformity, struggling, and distractions.

Avoidance. Rather than seeking out different points of view, we may avoid certain people and situations. Some people who hold strong opinions but are insecure in their ability to defend these positions hang out only with people who agree with them or read literature and watch television news shows that support their worldview. I attended a church service during which the minister in her sermon lambasted Mel Gibson's movie *The Passion of the Christ* (2004) as a violent and inaccurate depiction of the betrayal and death of Jesus. I asked her after the service if she had seen the movie, and she said no. When I told her that I liked the movie, she frowned and quickly moved on to talk to someone else. As a form of resistance, avoidance can lead to a serious lack of communication and even hostility among people who hold opposing points of view.

Anger. We cannot always avoid people who disagree with us. Rather than using critical thinking when confronted with an opposing viewpoint, some people respond with anger. People with physical and/or social power are more likely than those without it to use anger to silence those who disagree with them. Anger may be expressed overtly by glares, threats, physical violence, gang activity, or even war.

Not all anger is resistance. We may feel anger or moral indignation when we hear that one of our favorite professors was denied tenure because he is Arab. This anger may motivate us to correct this injustice by writing a letter of protest to the local newspaper. We'll be looking more at the positive role of emotion in critical thinking in Chapter 2.

Clichés. Resorting to clichés—often-repeated statements such as "Don't force your views on me," "It's all relative," "To each his own," "Things always work out for the best," and "I have a right to my own opinion"—can keep us from thinking critically about issues. Advertisers and politicians often use clichés as a means of sidetracking us from considering the quality of the product or the issue at hand.

Resistance to analyzing one's position is seen in the abortion debate where each side has become entrenched in the clichés pro-choice or pro-life, with the pro-choice side focused on having few or no legal restrictions and the pro-life side wanting abortion to be illegal, at least in most cases. To overcome this divisive thinking, the term "reproductive justice" was coined by a group of black feminists to address the concerns of African-American women, whose abortion rate is three and one-half times that of white women. Loretta Ross, cofounder of the group SisterSong Women of Color Reproductive Justice Collective, maintains that we need to think differently about the abortion debate. "Those of us in the reproductive justice movement, would say, 'Let's ask why there is such a high rate of unintended pregnancies in our community: What are the factors driving it?'"[46]

Used sparingly, clichés can be helpful to illustrate a point. However, the habitual use of clichés acts as a barrier to critical thinking.

Denial. According to the U.S. National Center for Injury Prevention and Control, alcohol-related motor vehicle accidents kill someone every 30 minutes and account for 41 percent of all traffic-related deaths.[47] Despite these startling statistics, people who drink and drive often deny that they are drunk. They may refuse to let someone else drive, claiming that they are quite capable of doing so.

Many Americans are also in denial about the possibility that world oil reserves may soon run out. Despite improved exploration technology, discovery of new oil reserves peaked in 1962 and has been dropping ever since. According to some predictions, active oil reserves may run out by anywhere from 2020 to 2030.[48] Yet, faced with declining fossil-fuel sources, many Americans continue to drive large vehicles and to live in large homes that cost more and more to heat.

Ignorance. Confucius taught that "Ignorance is the night of the mind." The modern Hindu yogi Swami Prabhavananda wrote, "Ignorance creates all the other obstacles." People are more likely to think critically about

Connections

How can our critical-thinking skills help us recognize misleading advertisements? *See Chapter 10, p. 321.*

ANALYZING IMAGES

Is Ignorance Bliss?

DISCUSSION QUESTIONS

1. *Has there even been a time when, like the man in the picture above, you've preferred ignorance to being informed? Why? Support your answer with specific examples.*

2. *Some people accuse college students of taking the attitude that "ignorance is bliss" when it comes to participation in public life. Analyze this claim using research findings as well as examples to support your answer.*

issues about which they have knowledge in depth. In certain situations, we are ignorant about an issue simply because the information about it is not available to us. However, sometimes we just don't want to know.

Ignorance is a type of resistance when we intentionally avoid learning about a particular issue, about which information is readily available, in order to get out of having to think or talk about it. Ignorance is often used as an excuse for inaction. For example, Joe told his colleagues that he wanted to make a donation to help the Haitians following the 2010 earthquake but he didn't because "you just can't tell which charities are ripping you off and keeping most of the money for themselves." In fact, there are websites such as www.charitynavigator.org that inform potential donors exactly how much money each major charitable organization uses directly for charity and how much goes to administrative and fundraising costs. Some people believe that being ignorant excuses them from having to think critically about or take action on an issue. As a result, the issue is not resolved or even becomes worse.

How does the news media influence and reinforce narrow-minded worldviews? *See Chapter 11, pp. 353–354.*

Connections

Conformity. Many people fear that they will not be accepted by their peers if they disagree with them. Even though they may actually disagree, they go along with the group rather than risk rejection. We've probably all been in a situation where someone at work or a party makes a racist or sexist joke or an offensive comment about gays or women. Rather than speaking up, many people keep quiet or even laugh, thus tolerating and perpetuating bigotry and negative stereotypes.

Other people conform because they don't have a point of view of their own on an issue. Saying "I can see both sides of the issue" often masks a reluctance to think critically about it. Martin Luther King Jr. once pointed out, "Many people fear nothing more terribly than to take a position which stands out sharply and clearly from prevailing opinion. The tendency of most is to adopt a view that is so ambiguous that it will include everything, and so popular that it will include everyone."

Struggling. During the Nazi occupation of France in World War II, the people of the village of Le Chambonsur-Lignon provided refuge for Jews who were fleeing the Nazis. When Pierre Sauvage, director of *Weapons of the Spirit*—a documentary about the people and resistance movement of Le Chambon—was asked by PBS television's Bill Moyers years later why they did this when other people were still struggling about what to do, Sauvage replied, "Those who agonize don't act; those who act don't agonize."[49]

It is appropriate to struggle with or agonize over difficult issues before coming to a tentative stand. However, some people get so caught up in the minute details and "what ifs" of an issue—a situation sometimes referred to as "analysis paralysis"—that nothing gets accomplished. Procrastinators are most likely to use this type of resistance. Although struggling with an issue as part of the analytical process of coming up with a resolution and plan for action is an important component of critical thinking, when the struggle becomes an end-in-itself, we are engaging in resistance, not critical thinking.

Distractions. Some people hate silence and being left alone with their own thoughts. Many of us use television, loud music, partying, work, drugs, alcohol, or shopping to prevent our minds from critically thinking about troublesome issues in our lives. People may overeat instead of examining the causes of their cravings or unhappiness. Mental hindrances like distractions, according to Buddhist teaching, keep us from clear understanding. Instead, Buddhist philosophy values stillness and contemplation as means of achieving wisdom and understanding.

Narrow-Mindedness

Like resistance, narrow-mindedness and rigid beliefs, such as absolutism, egocentrism, and ethnocentrism can become barriers to critical thinking.

Absolutism. As we noted earlier, we may find ourselves acting contrary to our deeply held moral beliefs—as happened to most of the subjects in the Milgram study—simply because we do not have the critical-thinking skills necessary for standing up to unreasonable authority. In particular, college students at the first stage of cognitive development, where they regard information as either right or wrong, have an "expectation that authorities provide them with absolutely correct knowledge."[50]

When confronted with a situation like the one faced by those who administered electric shocks in Milgram's study, such students lack the critical-thinking skills to counter the authority's reasoning. For more on the stages of moral development, see Chapter 9.

STEPHEN HAWKING, *Physicist*

Stephen Hawking (b. 1942) is perhaps the most famous physicist alive. Shortly after graduating from college, he learned that he had ALS (Lou Gehrig's disease), a devastating and incurable neurological disease. About half of the people with it die within three years. After enduring depression and waiting to die, Hawking pulled himself together and decided to live his life to his fullest rather than give up. He enrolled in graduate school, married, and had three children. He writes: "ALS has not prevented me from having a very attractive family and being successful in my work. I have been lucky that my condition has progressed more slowly than is often the case. But it shows that one need not lose hope."

In 2004, Hawking publicly recanted a position he had held for the past 30 years that the gravity of black holes is so powerful that nothing can escape it, not even light.* In doing so, he conceded, with some regret, that CalTech astrophysicist John Preskill had been right all along about black holes. Preskill theorized that information about objects swallowed by black holes is able to leak from the black holes, a phenomenon known as the "black hole information paradox." Hawking paid Preskill off with an agreed-upon prize—an encyclopedia of baseball.

DISCUSSION QUESTIONS

1. Discuss what characteristics of a good critical thinker, listed in the text, are demonstrated by Hawking's response to adversity and uncertainty.

2. Think of a position that you held (or still hold) against all evidence. Compare and contrast Hawking's action with how you respond when someone challenges your views or position. Discuss what extent resistance and/or narrow-mindedness is responsible for your reluctance to change or modify your position.

*See Mark Peplow, "Hawking Changes His Mind about Black Holes," http://www.nature.com/news/2004/040712/full/news040712-12.html.

Fear of Challenge. We may also fail to stand up to others because we fear that others will challenge our beliefs. Some people believe that is it a sign of weakness to change their position on an issue. Good critical thinkers, however, are willing to openly change their position in light of conflicting evidence. Unlike physicist Stephen Hawking, who is described in "Thinking Outside the Box: Stephen Hawking, Physicist," many people—especially those with low self-esteem or an egocentric personality—resist information and evidence that are at odds with what they believe. They may view the expression of opposing views or evidence as a personal attack.

Egocentrism. Believing that you are the center of all things is called **egocentrism**. Egocentric, or self-centered, people have little regard for others' interests and thoughts. Studies of cognitive development in college students suggest that as students develop cognitively and become better at critical thinking, they are less likely to view themselves egocentrically.[51] Although we all tend to fall for compliments and be skeptical of criticism, this tendency is especially true of egocentric people. Flattery impedes our ability to make sound judgments and increases our chances of being persuaded by the flatterer. Advertisers and con artists are well aware of this human tendency and thus use flattery to try to get us to go along with them or to buy products that we wouldn't otherwise buy.

> **egocentrism** The belief that the self or individual is the center of all things.
>
> **ethnocentrism** The belief in the inherent superiority of one's own group and culture.
>
> **anthropocentrism** The belief that humans are the central or most significant entities of the universe.

Ethnocentrism. An uncritical or unjustified belief in the inherent superiority of one's own group and culture is called **ethnocentrism**. It is characterized by suspicion of and a lack of knowledge of foreign countries and cultures.[52] Ethnocentric people often make decisions about other groups, cultures, and countries on the basis of stereotypes and opinions rather than on factual information. In addition, we tend to remember evidence that supports our worldview or stereotypes and forget or downplay that which doesn't. (See page 119 for more on self-serving biases in our thinking.)

Since the September 11, 2001 terrorist attacks on New York City and the Pentagon, Arab Americans have been subjected to hate crimes as well as to racial profiling by police and federal officials, despite official policies against this practice.

According to the U.S. Department of Justice, anti-Muslim crimes soared in 2010 to the highest level since 2001. This increase was due in part as a response to the "Ground Zero Mosque" (which was in fact a community center, not a mosque) in New York City and because of the incendiary rhetoric of groups such as "Stop Islamization of America." Hundreds of Muslims and Americans of Arab descent have been detained without charges and imprisoned under the USA Patriot Act, which was extended by President Obama in 2011. These types of hasty reactions can lead to misunderstandings and even increased hostility.

Uncritical nationalism—a form of ethnocentrism—can blind us to flaws and deteriorating conditions in our own culture. Americans who engage in this type of narrow-mindedness, for example, may bristle at the mere suggestion that the United States may not be the greatest and freest nation ever. Yet according to the Worldwide Governance Indicators 2011 report, which ranks governments by the amount of freedom citizens have to voice opinions and select their government, the United States, ranks lower than Canada, Australia, and most European nations.[53] This represents a drop from 2005, in part because of increased restrictions on freedom of the press.

Anthropocentrism. A belief that humans are the central or most significant entities of the universe, called **anthropocentrism**, can blind people to the capabilities of other animals. In his theory of evolution, Charles Darwin postulated that differences in cognitive function between humans and other animals were simply a matter of degree or quantity, rather than human cognitive function being of a qualitatively different "higher" type. However, the anthropocentric view of humans as unique among all other creatures or as beings created in the image of God and therefore above and separate from nature still dominates. This is found in the use of the term *animal,* even in scientific journals and books, as excluding humans, even though we are an animal species. Under the anthropocentric view, other animals and nature exist not in their own right but as resources for humans. Anthropocentrism can hinder us from critically thinking about our relationship with the rest of nature and can thereby threaten not only the survival of other species and the environment, as is happening with global warming, but our own survival as well.

Connections

How does the government exert influence on what gets reported in the media? *See Chapter 11, p. 343.*

What is our responsibility as citizens living in a democracy? *See Chapter 13, p. 401 and p. 406.*

HIGHLIGHTS

TYPES OF RESISTANCE AND NARROW-MINDEDNESS

Resistance: The habitual use of immature defense mechanisms when our worldviews are challenged.

Avoidance	Denial	Struggle
Anger	Ignorance	Rationalization
Clichés	Conformity	Distractions

Narrow-mindedness: Rigid beliefs that interfere with critical analysis of our worldviews.

Absolutism	Egocentrism
Anthropocentrism	Fear of challenge
Ethnocentrism	

▶ APPLICATION: Identify an example in the text of each of the types of resistance and narrow-mindedness.

Sunando Sen, of Queens, New York, was pushed to his death in front of a train in December 2012 by a woman who told police she had pushed him off the subway platform because she has hated Muslims ever since September 11th. Sen was from India.

The belief that artificial intelligence, in which a computer, robot, or other device is programmed to learn and make decisions, will never match human intelligence is also a product of anthropocentrism. We'll be looking at artificial intelligence and reason in Chapter 2.

Rationalization and Doublethink

While sometimes the best alternative is clear, it's often the case that competing claims require our analysis before we can come to a decision. When presented with conflicting alternatives, some people make a decision quickly because of their bias in favor of one of the alternatives. In doing so, they justify or rationalize their choice on the basis of personal preferences or opinion, rather than on a critical analysis of the competing claims. In an experiment on making choices, psychologist A. H. Martin found that with rationalization the decision is often accompanied by a "rush" of satisfaction, thus convincing the person that his or her preference was correct.[54]

We may also use rationalization in an attempt to justify past actions that are inconsistent with our image of ourselves as a decent, rational person. Child molesters may see themselves as affectionate and loving people whom children enjoy being with. A person may cheat on a sweetheart and then, when confronted, lie about the affair, justifying the lie on the grounds that he or she is a caring person who is looking out for the best interests of the sweetheart by not saying something that will hurt his or her feelings.

Because rationalization involves ignoring competing claims, people who engage in it often get caught up in doublethink. **Doublethink** involves holding two contradictory views, or "double standards," at the same time and believing both to be true. This is particularly prevalent in response to highly charged issues. Rather than analyze the arguments surrounding these issues, people may unwittingly engage in doublethink.

For example, when asked, most college students state that they believe in equality of men and women. However, when it comes to lifestyle and career, the same students who claim to believe in equality and freedom of choice also say that women should be the primary caretakers of children. Most teachers, even the most ardent feminists, treat their female students differently from their male students, calling on boys and praising their accomplishments more often, and having more tolerance of boys' disruptive behavior.[55] When shown videotapes of their classes, many of these teachers are horrified at the extent to which they ignore the girls and downplay their contributions and achievements.

Similarly, the majority of white Americans champion equality as a principle when it comes to race but may harbor unconscious prejudice. Unexamined prejudices can distort our perception of the world. In a study, people were asked to match negative and positive words with names associated with Americans of both European and African descent. The more implicitly prejudiced the subjects were, the more likely they were to match the negative words with African Americans and the positive words with European Americans.[56]

Doublethink can have an impact on our real-life decisions. According to the U.S. Bureau of Labor Statistics, women, including those who work full time outside the home, still perform the great majority of housework and child care.[57] At work, women and minorities suffer from job discrimination and earn significantly less than white men earn. The wage disparity between men and women increases with age. Yet, in spite of the evidence to the contrary, many college students, when asked, maintain that sex-based and race-based discrimination in the work-place are things of the past.

> **doublethink** Holding two contradictory views at the same time and believing both to be true.
>
> **cognitive dissonance** A sense of disorientation that occurs in situations where new ideas directly conflict with a person's worldview.
>
> **social dissonance** A sense of disorientation that occurs when the social behavior and norms of others conflict with a person's worldview.

> **Connections**
>
> **To what extent is anthropocentrism implicit in the scientific worldview?** *See Chapter 12, p. 366.*
>
> **How does the news media influence and reinforce narrow-minded worldviews?** *See Chapter 11, p. 336.*

Cognitive and Social Dissonance

We are most likely to critically analyze or modify our views when we encounter **cognitive dissonance** and **social dissonance**, situations where new ideas or social behavior directly

U.S. Median Income by Race, Ethnicity, and Gender, 2011

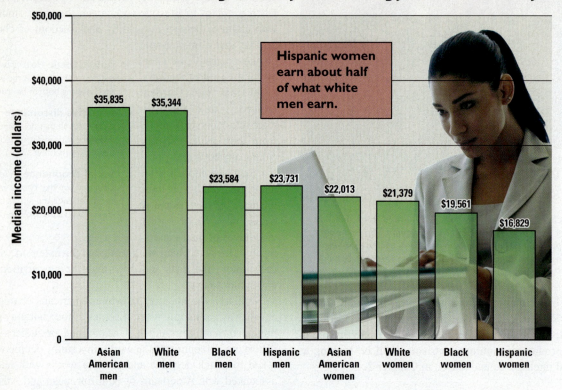

Hispanic women earn about half of what white men earn.

Median income (dollars)

- Asian American men: $35,835
- White men: $35,344
- Black men: $23,584
- Hispanic men: $23,731
- Asian American women: $22,013
- White women: $21,379
- Black women: $19,561
- Hispanic women: $16,829

The average income, except for Hispanic females, who made a slight gain, is lower than it was in 2008 for all groups. The most significant drop in income was among white males, whose average income dropped by $2,065 over the three-year period.

Source: U.S. Census Bureau, 2011.

conflict with our worldviews. People who are forced to live or work in an integrated community, be it a dorm, college classroom, or a public housing project, often encounter occasions and behavior that conflict with their ethnocentric attitudes. Evidence indicates that once a person's behavior is changed—that is, after they share a meal or discuss issues in class with people of other races or ethnicities—a change in belief is likely to follow.[58] Exposing yourself to role models who are skilled in critical thinking can also strengthen your motivation to think clearly rather than engage in resistance.

Stress as a Barrier

While some stress can be good in motivating us, when we experience excessive stress our brain—and our ability to think critically—slows down. Researchers have found that when people get caught up in disasters, such as an airplane crash, hurricane, flood, or fire, the vast majority freeze up. According to Mac McLean of the FAA and Civil Aerospace Medical Institute, instead of taking action to remove themselves from the danger, most people are "stunned and bewildered."[59] (See Thinking Outside the Box: Captain Chesley "Sully" Sullenberger.)

We can counteract the effect of stress by mentally rehearsing our responses to different stressful scenarios.[60]

People, such as Captain Sullenberger, who have mentally rehearsed the best route for evacuating their building repeatedly are far more likely than those who haven't rehearsed to take action and escape in cases of emergencies, such as a fire or a terrorist attack. More importantly, mental rehearsal can enhance our performance on familiar tasks. For example, basketball players who engaged in fifteen minutes of mental rehearsal on most days and fifteen minutes of actual practice on the other days actually performed better after twenty days than players who only engaged in physical practice each day.[61]

Did You Know

In a study, college students were shown a picture of a black man in a business suit standing on a subway next to a white man who is holding a razor. When asked later what they had seen, the majority reported seeing a black man with a razor standing next to a white man in a business suit.

THINKING

CAPTAIN CHESLEY "SULLY" SULLENBERGER, *Pilot*

On January 9, 2009, shortly after takeoff from LaGuardia Airport, US Air flight 1549 struck a large flock of geese, disabling both engines. After quickly determining that neither returning to LaGuardia nor continuing on to the next closest airport was feasible, Captain Chesley "Sully" Sullenberger made the decision to attempt to land the plane in the Hudson River. With the help of his co-pilot, he successfully landed the disabled plane in the river. While some passengers and crew sustained injuries, there was no loss of life. Sullenberger remained aboard until he was sure everyone had been safely evacuated before disembarking himself.

Three years later, in January 2012, the cruise ship *Costa Concordia* navigated too close to the coast of Italy. The ship struck a rock, tearing a huge gash in the side of the ship, causing it to capsize onto its side. Unlike Sullenberger's, Captain Francesco Schettino's reaction intensified the disaster. Schettino failed to order passengers to evacuate the ship until over an hour after the accident. He also abandoned the ship before all passengers were evacuated. Thirty-two passengers died in the accident. When later questioned about his actions, Schettino blamed his helmsman for the incident. As for his abandoning the ship, he claims he accidently fell into one of the lifeboats. Rather than accepting Schettino's excuses, the Costa cruise company places the blame squarely on Captain Schettino for taking the ship off course and for the aftermath.

Why did Captain Schettino so mishandle the *Costa Concordia* incident, whereas Captain Sullenberger remained calm and in control? Sullenberger credits his years of experience and practice as an aviation safety expert and accident investigator. In a February 8, 2009 news interview, Sullenberger told Katie Couric, "One way of looking at this might be that for 42 years, I've been making small regular deposits in this bank of experience, education, and training. And on January 15 the balance was sufficient so that I could make a very large withdrawal."

DISCUSSION QUESTIONS

1. Compare and contrast the responses of Captains Sullenberger and Schettino. Relate your answer to the types of resistance. Discuss how the development of your critical thinking skills might make you less prone to using resistance in a stressful situation.

2. What deposits are you making in your "bank of experience, education, and training" that will help you respond effectively to stressful situations or a crisis? Be specific. Discuss how these "deposits" will help you achieve this objective.

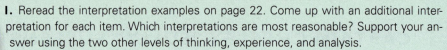

STOP AND ASSESS YOURSELF

1. Reread the interpretation examples on page 22. Come up with an additional interpretation for each item. Which interpretations are most reasonable? Support your answer using the two other levels of thinking, experience, and analysis.

2. Using the three-tiered model of thinking, discuss the experiences listed below. The interpretations that you list for each experience do not have to be ones that you personally accept. Share your interpretations with others in the class. Discuss how your past experiences have been shaped by your interpretations and how applying critical-thinking skills to analyze this issue might affect your future actions.

   a. Affirmative action in college admissions discriminates against white males.

   b. When I invited Chris to go to the movies with me last weekend, Chris said, "No thanks."

   c. College tuition is rising faster than the cost of living in the United States.

   d. According to CNN, more than half of the agricultural workers in the United States are illegal aliens.

   e. Marijuana use has been decriminalized in Canada.

   f. In 2012, 53 percent of college graduates under the age of 25 were unemployed or underemployed.

   g. The college graduate rate for female student athletes is significantly higher than the rate for male student athletes.

   h. In a recent survey, 45 percent of Americans stated that they feel that their pet listens to them better than their spouse does.

   i. More and more men are going into nursing as a profession.

   j. People who cohabitate before marriage are more likely to get divorced than those who do not.

3. According to the International Energy Commission, North Americans use more energy per person than any other people in the world. As a class, discuss ways in which we use rationalization or other types of resistance to justify our high energy-consumption lifestyle.

4. At the opposite end of the spectrum from egocentric people are those who sacrifice their needs and dreams for others. Harvard professor of education Carol Gilligan maintains that women in particular tend to be self-sacrificing—putting others' needs before their own. How does the tendency to be self-sacrificing interfere with effective critical thinking? Use examples from your own experience to illustrate your answer.

5. Douglas Adams (1952–2001), author of *The Hitchhiker's Guide to the Galaxy,* compared humans to a puddle of water as a way of illustrating anthropocentric thinking, or what he called "the vain conceit" of humans. He wrote:

   > Imagine a puddle waking up one morning and thinking, "This is an interesting world I find myself in, an interesting hole I find myself in. It fits me rather neatly, doesn't it. In fact, it fits me staggeringly well. It must have been made to have me in it." Even as the sun comes out and the puddle gets smaller, it still frantically hangs on to the idea that everything is going to be all right; that the world was made for it since it is so well suited to it.[62]

   Are humans, in fact, a lot like the puddle in Adams's analogy? Support your answer, using examples from your own experience. Discuss how this type of anthropocentric thinking shapes or distorts our interpretation of the world.

6. Working in small groups, expand on the list of barriers to critical thinking presented in the text. Come up with examples of each barrier and explain how they get in the way of critical thinking.

7. Think of a stressful situation—such as a job interview, breaking bad news, asking someone for a date, or giving a presentation in front of a class—that you will be facing in the next few weeks. Write down the task at the top of a page. Spend 15 minutes a day over the next week mentally rehearsing the task. Note the dates and times you spent mentally rehearsing the task. After you have performed the actual task, write a short essay on how well you did. Were you satisfied with the outcome? Discuss the extent to which mental rehearsal helped you perform this task, compared with similar tasks you performed in the past.

8. Write down three experiences relating to yourself and your life goals. For example, "I am good at science," "I am shy," "I haven't chosen a major yet," or "I want a job in which I can make a lot of money." Now write down at least three interpretations of each of these experiences. Analyze your interpretations. Are the interpretations reasonable? Share your interpretations with others in the class or with friends or family. Do they agree with your interpretations? If not, why not?

9. Working in small groups, discuss the types of resistance or narrow-mindedness that you are most likely to engage in when your views are challenged and steps you might take to overcome your resistance and narrow-mindedness.

10. Compare and contrast the reaction of Captain Sullenberger to a potential disastrous situation to that of Captain Schettino. Discuss how improving your critical thinking skills might improve your response to stressful situations and what deposits you are putting in your "bank of experience, education, and training," to use Sullenberger's words, to help you when you encounter situations beyond your control.

THiNK AGAIN

1. What are the characteristics of a skilled critical thinker?
   - A skilled critical thinker is well informed, open-minded, attentive, and creative, and has effective analytical, research, communication, and problem-solving skills.

2. What are the three levels of thinking?
   - The three levels are experience, which includes first-hand knowledge and information from other sources; interpretation, which involves trying to make sense out of our experiences; and analysis, which requires that we critically examine our interpretations.

3. What are some of the barriers to critical thinking?
   - Barriers include narrow-mindedness, such as absolutism, egocentrism, anthropocentrism, and ethnocentrism, as well as the habitual use of resistance, such as avoidance, anger, clichés, denial, ignorance, conformity, rationalization, and distractions.

Perspectives on Affirmative Action in College Admissions

Affirmative action involves taking positive steps in job hiring and college admissions to correct certain past injustices against groups such as minorities and women. In 1954, the Supreme Court ruled in *Brown v. Board of Education* that school segregation was unconstitutional and that black children have a right to equal education opportunities. The first affirmative action legislation was proposed by Vice President Richard Nixon in 1959. Affirmative action programs and legislation were expanded during the civil rights era in the 1960s.

In 1978, Allan Bakke, a white man, sued the University of California at Davis Medical School because his application was rejected while minority students with lower test scores were admitted. The Supreme Court agreed with Bakke, ruling that reverse discrimination was unconstitutional. In 1996, with the passage of Proposition 209, California became the first state to ban affirmative action in the public sector, including admission to state colleges. Washington, Texas, and other states have also passed referenda banning affirmative action in state college admissions.

In June 2003, in *Grutter v. Bollinger,* the Supreme Court found that the admissions policy of the University of Michigan Law School, which awarded points to applicants based on race, was flawed. However, in its final ruling the court permitted race to be considered as one among many factors when considering individual applications. On June 24, 2013, the Supreme Court ruled on *Fisher v. University of Texas,* which was brought in response to *Grutter v. Bollinger* and requested overturn of the use of affirmative action in college admissions. It sent the case back to the lower court and ordered it to review the university's admission policy.

According to a 2012 Rasmussen Report, the majority of Americans aged 18 to 25 years (55 percent) oppose college affirmative action programs that give preference in admissions to blacks and other minorities, arguing that it constitutes reverse discrimination and, as such, is unjust. In contrast, in 2012 the Obama administration weighed in with briefs in support of affirmative action at the University of Texas, arguing that race should be one of many factors considered in admission. Proponents of affirmative action note that a ban on affirmative action in college admissions will cause a 2 percent drop in admissions of minorities at American colleges, including a 10 percent drop at the most elite colleges, and that this is unacceptable.[63]

Affirmative Action and Higher Education

BEFORE AND AFTER THE SUPREME COURT RULINGS

ON THE MICHIGAN CASES NANCY CANTOR

Nancy Cantor is chancellor of Syracuse University. She was provost of the University of Michigan when the affirmative action cases were filed with the U.S. Supreme Court. In this article, published in the *Chicago Tribune* on January 28, 2003, she presents an argument for affirmative action in college admissions.

Integration takes hard work, especially when we have little other than collective fear, stereotypes and sins upon which to build. It is time America sees affirmative action on college campuses for what it is: a way to enrich the educational and intellectual lives of white students as well as students of color. We must not abandon race as a consideration in admissions.

The debate now before the U.S. Supreme Court over admissions at the University of Michigan is about the relative advantages people are getting, and it is a debate that misses the point. College admission has always been about relative advantage because a college education is a scarce resource, and the stakes are high.

In this era of emphasis on standardized tests, it may be easy to forget that colleges and universities have always taken into account many other aspects of students' experiences, including the geographic region from which they come, their families' relationship to the institution and their leadership experiences.

It is appropriate, and indeed critical, for the best institutions in the world to create the broadest possible mix of life experiences. Race is a fundamental feature of life in America, and it has an enormous impact on what a person has to contribute on campus. College admissions should be race-conscious to take the cultural and historical experiences of all students—Native American, African-American, Hispanic, Asian-American and white—and build on these in an educational setting. President Bush was wrong when he labeled the affirmative-action programs at the University of Michigan "quota systems.". . .

. . . There are no quotas at Michigan. All students compete for all seats. Race is used as a plus factor, along with other life experiences and talents, just as the president has suggested should happen. The percentages of students of color at Michigan vary annually.

Bush says he believes college admissions should be "race neutral," and he says he supports the principles of *Regents of the University of California vs. Bakke.* He cannot have it both ways. Race is not neutral in the Bakke decision; it is front and center, just as it was nearly 50 years ago in *Brown vs. Board of Education.* In both cases, the Supreme Court urged our nation to boldly and straightforwardly take on the issue of race. . . .

The decision by Justice Lewis F. Powell in *Bakke* brought more than students of color to the table. It brought race in America to the table, urging educators to join hands in creating a truly integrated society of learners.

How are we to fulfill the dream of Brown and Bakke, to build a positive story of race in America, if we are told to ignore race—to concoct systems constructed around proxies for race such as class rank in racially segregated public school districts or euphemisms such as "cultural traditions" that both avoid our past and fail to value the possibility that race can play a constructive role in our nation's future?

. . . We want to include, not exclude. We want to use race as a positive category, as one of many aspects of a life we consider when we sit down to decide which students to invite to our table.

REVIEW QUESTIONS

1. According to Cantor, how does affirmative action benefit both white students and students of color?

2. What does Cantor mean which she says that "college admissions should be race-conscious"?

3. What is President Bush's stand on affirmative action, and why does Cantor disagree with him?

4. How does Cantor use the Supreme Court's rulings to bolster her argument for affirmative action in college admissions?

Achieving Diversity on Campus

U.S. SUPREME COURT JUSTICE SANDRA DAY O'CONNOR

In the following excerpt U.S. Supreme Court Justice Sandra Day O'Connor delivers the majority opinion in the landmark Supreme Court case *Grutter v. Bollinger,* in which it was argued that the use of affirmative action in college admissions is constitutional if race is treated as one factor among many and if the purpose is to achieve diversity on campus.

The University of Michigan Law School (Law School), one of the Nation's top law schools, follows an official admissions policy that seeks to achieve student body diversity through compliance with *Regents of Univ. of Cal. v. Bakke,* . . . Focusing on students' academic ability coupled with a flexible assessment of their talents, experiences, and potential, the policy requires admissions officials to evaluate each applicant based on all the information available in the file, including a personal statement, letters of recommendation, an essay describing how the applicant will contribute to Law School life and diversity, and the applicant's undergraduate grade point average (GPA) and Law School Admissions Test (LSAT) score. Additionally, officials must look beyond grades and scores to so-called "soft variables," such as recommenders' enthusiasm, the quality of the undergraduate institution and the applicant's essay, and the areas and difficulty of undergraduate course selection. The policy does not define diversity solely in terms of racial and ethnic status and does not restrict the types of diversity contributions eligible for "substantial weight," but it does reaffirm the Law School's commitment to diversity with special reference to the inclusion of African-American, Hispanic, and Native-American students, who otherwise might not be represented in the student body in meaningful numbers. By enrolling a "critical mass" of underrepresented minority students, the policy seeks to ensure their ability to contribute to the Law School's character and to the legal profession.

When the Law School denied admission to petitioner Grutter, a white Michigan resident with a 3.8 GPA and 161 LSAT score, she filed this suit, alleging that respondents had discriminated against her on the basis of race in violation of the Fourteenth Amendment, Title VI of the Civil Rights Act of 1964, and 42 U.S.C. § 1981; that she was rejected because the Law School uses race as a "predominant" factor, giving applicants belonging to certain minority groups a significantly greater chance of admission than students with similar credentials from disfavored racial groups; and that respondents had no compelling interest to justify that use of race. The District Court found the Law School's use of race as an admissions factor unlawful. The Sixth Circuit reversed, holding that Justice Powell's opinion in *Bakke* was binding precedent establishing diversity as a compelling state interest, and that the Law School's use of race was narrowly tailored because race was merely a "potential 'plus' factor" and because the Law School's program was virtually identical to the Harvard admissions program described approvingly by Justice Powell and appended to his *Bakke* opinion.

Held: The Law School's narrowly tailored use of race in admissions decisions to further a compelling interest in obtaining the educational benefits that flow from a diverse student body is not prohibited by the Equal Protection Clause, Title VI, or §1981.

In the landmark *Bakke* case, this Court reviewed a medical school's racial set-aside program that reserved 16 out of 100 seats for members of certain minority groups. . . . expressed his view that attaining a diverse student body was the only interest asserted by the university that survived scrutiny. . . . Grounding his analysis in the academic freedom that "long has been viewed as a special concern of the First Amendment," . . . Justice Powell emphasized that the "'nation's future depends upon leaders trained through wide exposure' to the ideas and mores of students as diverse as this Nation.". . . However, he also emphasized that "[i]t is not an interest in simple ethnic diversity, in which a specified percentage of the student body is in effect guaranteed to be members of selected ethnic groups," that can justify using race. . . . Rather, "[t]he diversity that furthers a compelling state interest encompasses a far broader array of qualifications and characteristics of which racial or ethnic origin is but a single though important element." Since *Bakke,* Justice Powell's opinion has been the touchstone for constitutional analysis of race-conscious admissions policies. Public and private universities across the Nation have modeled their own admissions programs on Justice Powell's views. . .

The Court endorses Justice Powell's view that student body diversity is a compelling state interest that can justify using race in university admissions. The Court defers to the Law School's educational judgment that diversity is essential to its educational mission. . . . Attaining a diverse student body is at the heart of the Law School's proper institutional mission, and its "good faith" is "presumed" absent "a showing to the contrary.". . . Enrolling a "critical mass" of minority students simply to assure some specified percentage of a particular group merely because of its race or ethnic origin would be patently unconstitutional. . . . But the Law School defines its critical mass concept by reference to the substantial, important, and laudable educational benefits that diversity is designed to produce, including cross-racial understanding and the breaking down of racial stereotypes. The Law School's claim is further bolstered by numerous expert studies and reports showing that such diversity promotes learning outcomes and better prepares students for an increasingly diverse workforce, for society, and for the legal profession. Major American businesses have made clear that the skills needed in today's increasingly global marketplace can only be developed through exposure to widely diverse people, cultures, ideas, and viewpoints. High-ranking retired officers and civilian military leaders assert that a highly qualified, racially diverse officer corps is essential to national security. Moreover, because universities, and in particular, law schools, represent the training ground for a large number of the Nation's leaders . . . the path to leadership must be visibly open to talented and qualified individuals of every race and ethnicity. Thus, the Law School has a compelling interest in attaining a diverse student body. . . . (d) The Law School's admissions program bears the hallmarks of a narrowly tailored plan. To be narrowly tailored, a race-conscious admissions program cannot "insulat[e] each category of applicants with certain desired qualifications from competition with all other applicants." . . . Instead, it may consider race or ethnicity only as a "'plus' in a particular applicant's file"; *i.e.,* it must be "flexible enough to consider all pertinent elements of diversity in light of the particular qualifications of each applicant, and to place them on the same footing for consideration, although not necessarily according them the same weight," . . . It follows that universities cannot establish quotas for members of certain racial or ethnic groups or put them on separate admissions tracks. . . . The Law School's admissions program, like the Harvard plan approved by Justice Powell, satisfies these requirements. Moreover, the program is flexible enough to ensure that each applicant is evaluated as an individual and not in a way that makes race or ethnicity the defining feature of the application. See *Bakke, supra,* at 317 (opinion of Powell, J.). The Law School engages in a highly individualized, holistic review of each applicant's file, giving serious consideration to all the ways an applicant might contribute to a diverse educational environment. . . . Also, the program adequately ensures that all factors that may contribute to diversity are meaningfully considered alongside race. Moreover, the Law School

frequently accepts nonminority applicants with grades and test scores lower than underrepresented minority applicants (and other nonminority applicants) who are rejected. . . . The Court is satisfied that the Law School adequately considered the available alternatives. The Court is also satisfied that, in the context of individualized consideration of the possible diversity contributions of each applicant, the Law School's race-conscious admissions program does not unduly harm nonminority applicants. . . . The Court takes the Law School at its word that it would like nothing better than to find a race-neutral admissions formula and will terminate its use of racial preferences as soon as practicable. The Court expects that 25 years from now, the use of racial preferences will no longer be necessary to further the interest approved today.

REVIEW QUESTIONS

1. Why did Grutter maintain that she had been treated unfairly by the University of Michigan Law School?

2. Why is Justice Powells's opinion in the *Bakke* case considered a landmark decision regarding college admissions?

3. On what grounds did the Supreme Court argument argue that attaining a diverse student body is part of an important part of institution's mission?

4. What conditions and limitations did the court place on using race in college admissions?

THiNK AND DISCUSS

PERSPECTIVES ON AFFIRMATIVE ACTION

1. Agreeing on a definition is one of the first steps in debating an issue. How are the Supreme Court justices and Nancy Cantor each using the term *affirmative action?*

2. Discuss whether affirmative action has a place in a democracy that is built on equal rights for all citizens, or if it is a violation of the fundamental principle of fairness.

3. Compare and contrast the arguments used by Nancy Cantor and U.S. Supreme Court justice Sandra Day O'Connor regarding the use of affirmative action in college admissions. Which person makes the best argument? Support your answer.

4. Some people argue that instead of race, we should use an economic or class-based criterion for affirmative action. How would you support that premise?

5. Research the policy at your college regarding affirmative action in admission. To what extent has this policy had an impact on diversity in the student body and the quality of your education? Support your answer using specific examples.

6. What criteria (for example, experiences, talents, alumni status of parents) do you think should be used in college admissions? Working in small groups, develop a list of relevant criteria and assign each criterion a point value (for example, 10 or 20) out of a total of 100 points based on how important each criterion is to the admissions decision.

2

REASON
& EMOTION

In Fyodor Dostoyevsky's novel *Crime and Punishment,* the protagonist, Raskolnikov, decides to kill an old woman presumably so that he could redistribute her money to those who would better benefit from it, after overhearing the following conversation between a student and officer in a café.

"On the one hand," conjectured the student, "you have a stupid, silly, utterly unimportant, vicious, sickly old woman, no good to anybody. . . . On the other hand you have new, young forces running to waste for want of backing. . . . A hundred, a thousand, good actions and promising beginnings might be forwarded and directed aright by the money that old woman destines for a monastery; hundreds, perhaps thousands of existences might be set on the right path, scores of families saved from beggary, from decay, from ruin and corruption, from the Lock hospitals— and all with her money! Kill her, take her money, on condition that you dedicate yourself with its help to the service of

What do you think the skydivers in this photo are thinking and feeling? How do reason and emotion work together in an activity such as skydiving to bring about a positive outcome?

- What is the role of reason in critical thinking?
- How does emotion positively and negatively influence critical thinking?
- What are the three approaches to faith and reason?

 humanity and the common good; don't you think that thousands of good deeds will wipe out one little, insignificant transgression? For one life taken, thousands saved from corruption and decay![1]

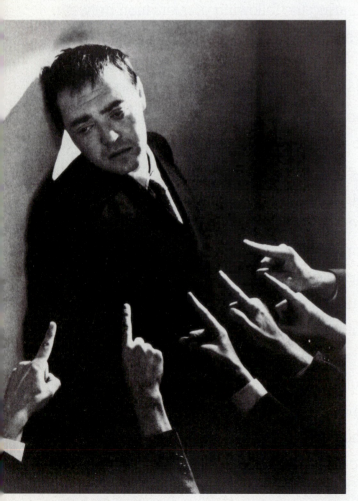

Peter Lorre as Raskolnikov in a 1935 film adaptation of **Crime and Punishment.**

Raskolnikov's decision to kill the old woman is based purely on a rational calculation of what would bring the greatest good to the greatest number of people. He does not let emotion interfere with his decision nor with his committing of the crime. But is it a good decision from the point of view of a critical thinker?

In this chapter we will discuss the roles of reason and emotion in critical thinking.

Specifically we will:

- Look at the role of reason in critical thinking
- Explore ways in which sex, race, and age influence our style of reasoning and critical thinking
- Assess the role of emotion in critical thinking
- Examine how reason and emotion work together
- Address the question of whether artificial intelligence (AI) is capable of reason and emotion
- Consider the relationship between faith and reason and the role of critical thinking in discussions of religious beliefs

Finally, we will examine different perspectives regarding reasons and proofs for the existence of God.

WHAT IS REASON?

We are constantly barraged with reasons for why we should accept or reject a particular position on an issue, or why we should or should not take a particular action. For example, should you evacuate your home when warned of imminent danger of a hurricane or tornado, or should you stay and try to protect your property? Would it be more reasonable to go to medical school, to join the Peace Corps, or to take a year off and travel? Should you move in with your boyfriend or girlfriend? In each case, it is up to you, as a critical thinker, to sort out the competing possibilities and come up with the best resolution.

Reason is the process of supporting a claim or conclusion on the basis of evidence. It involves both the disciplined use of intelligence and the application of rules for problem solving. It is easier for people, particularly those who have not been formally trained in critical thinking and logic, to reason about problems in a familiar context. Consider the following problem, which takes place in a familiar setting.

Imagine that you are shown four people and told to test the rule that a person must be over the age of 21 to drink beer. One person is drinking Coke; the second is drinking beer, the third is 23 years old; and the fourth is 15. Whom must you check (what they are drinking or what age they are) to ensure that the rule is being followed?[2]

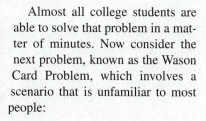

Almost all college students are able to solve that problem in a matter of minutes. Now consider the next problem, known as the Wason Card Problem, which involves a scenario that is unfamiliar to most people:

Imagine you are given four cards and are told to test the rule that a card with a vowel on one side must have an even number on the other side. Let's say that the cards in front of you show a(n) *E, K, 7,* and *4.* Which card or two cards would you turn over?[3]

Despite the fact that this problem is logically identical to the previous one about our four friends, only about 5 percent of the college population selects the correct two cards. Learning the rules of logic gives us the tools to solve more difficult and unfamiliar problems. In logic, reasoning is usually presented in the form of carefully laid out arguments in which a conclusion is supported by other propositions known as premises, which provide reason or evidence for the conclusion. However, *reason,* as we use it in our everyday lives, is a much broader concept. Reason is often a complex process that calls on our creative resources as well as emotional discernment.

Traditional Views of Reason

Reason, many people believe, is what separates humans from other animals. The ancient Greek philosopher Plato (427–347 BCE) wrote in his text *Phaedrus* that the human soul is divided into one rational and two nonrational parts. The two nonrational parts include the emotions and physical cravings, such as hunger and the sex drive. We are at our best, he argued, when all three parts of the soul are in harmony, with reason being in charge like a charioteer in charge of his horses.

> **reason** The process of supporting a claim or conclusion on the basis of evidence.

Plato's teachings were integrated into Christianity by medieval philosopher St. Thomas Aquinas (c. 1225–1274). According to Aquinas, God is the perfectly rational being. Rationality is the divine spark in humans. Up until the nineteenth century, most Western scholars accepted without question the view that humans are a special creation.

The English naturalist Charles Darwin (1809–1882) rejected the anthropocentric assumption that there is a divinely ordered Chain of Being with God at the top, followed by angels, next by humans, and then by the so-called higher animals. According to evolutionary theory, reason evolved as part of the adaptation of our behavior and that of other animals in the struggle for survival.

In his book *The Descent of Man,* Darwin wrote: "It is a significant fact that the more the habits of any particular animal are studied by a naturalist, the more he ascribes to

Great Chain of Being

For centuries Western scholars accepted the view that humans were a special creation infused with the divine spark of rationality.

reason and the less to unlearnt instincts."[4] Today most scientists agree that rather than being driven by instinct alone, many other animals are capable of abstract thought and reason.[5]

In the twentieth century, reason came to be identified mostly with science. Ironically, although reason is certainly important in science, the basic assumption of science—that the world outside us exists—cannot be proven through the use of reason. Yet it is generally considered *reasonable* for us to believe that the world exists. In other words, we may have beliefs that are the foundation of other beliefs, even though we can't prove or disprove them through the use of reason alone.

In addition to abstract thinking, reason has a behavioral component. As a reasonable person, you adjust your behavior to bring about the best outcome. For example, if you have good reason to believe that you are incompatible with your boyfriend or girlfriend, then you will more likely use behavior that distances you romantically from that person rather than moving in with him or her. To use another example, if after completing your life plan you conclude that you are in an entirely wrong field of study, then, as a reasonable person, you will take steps to revise your course of study at college, even if it means attending classes for an additional year. After all, 40 years of misery in a job you hate is a far greater burden on you than one or two extra years of college.

What is the role of reason in the sciences and the scientific method?
See Chapter 12, p. 367.

Connections

According to evolutionary theory, reason evolved as part of the adaptation of our behavior and that of other animals in the struggle for survival.

As a component of critical thinking, reason embraces different strategies, including deduction, generalization (a type of inductive logic), and imagination. Reason is also important in spatial-temporal problem solving, which involves the application of concepts of space and time, such as that found in mathematics, engineering, architecture, and the physical sciences. The heavy emphasis in American schools on language skills is thought to be one of the reasons why children in the United States have difficulty with subjects such as math and physics, which involve spatial-temporal reasoning.[6] We'll be studying logical arguments in depth in Chapters 6, 7, and 8.

Gender, Age, and Reason

In traditional Western thinking, men are more closely linked to the realm of the mind and reason, whereas women—because of their reproductive role in society—are more closely linked to realm of the body and nature. Aristotle (384–322 BCE), one of the most influential thinkers in Western philosophy, held that men and women have fundamentally different natures.[7] While men are guided by reason and logic, women are more often guided by emotion. Reflecting the prevailing attitude of his time, Aristotle maintained that because of these differences, the proper sphere of men is the public realm of politics and the workplace, and that of women, the home and family. In traditional Judeo-Christian religion, God, whose divine reason is regarded as perfect, is depicted as male. Aquinas taught that God created women only for the sake of procreation and that women, being naturally inferior, should submit to the authority of men.[8] These stereotypes about the different natures of men and women continue to influence our thinking.

Did You Know

Thirty-five percent of Americans polled in a 2010 General Social Survey, funded by the National Science Foundation, agreed that "It is much better for everyone involved if the man is the achiever outside the home and the woman takes care of the home and family."

These stereotypes are found in expectations regarding "women's work." Women generally work in different areas than men, such as childcare, elementary school teaching, and nursing. At home, women are still expected to do the majority of housework, even if they are the primary breadwinners. The belief that women are "too emotional" has also been an obstacle to their obtaining leadership positions both in government and the corporate world. Currently 20 percent of U.S. senators are women.

Feminists such as Gloria Steinem, Simone de Beauvoir, and John Stuart Mill have argued that men and women have the same rational nature. The gap between men and women, they maintain, is based on discrimination and on men's reluctance to give up their advantage in the home and workplace. Conservatives, on the other hand, argue that these discrepancies are based on natural differences between men and women.[9] Research suggests that what are often assumed to be sex-based differences are based on the interaction of socialization and innate differences between men and women.[10]

However, even if women may be more emotional by nature than men, this does not prove that they do not have reason and are not just as capable as men of engaging in logical argumentation. In addition, sex stereotypes harm men by denigrating men who prefer to stay at home and care for their children or who choose nurturing professions such as nursing or teaching in elementary school. Rather than making decisions on the basis of stereotypes, critical thinking requires that we be open to different perspectives and to examining our own assumptions.

Thinking Outside the Box

TEMPLE GRANDIN, *Structural Designer*

A very high-functioning person with Asperger syndrome, a disorder resembling autism, Temple Grandin (b. 1947) is professor of animal science at Colorado State University. She has revolutionized certain areas of structural design that have traditionally been problematic because of humans' difficulty in visualizing the underlying problems.

Dr. Grandin is the world's leading expert in the design of livestock-handling facilities. In designing the facilities, she is able to visualize herself as the animal going through one of her systems. In her imagination, she walks around and through the structure and flies it in a helicopter. Applying her facility for spatial-temporal reasoning, she is able to anticipate and correct for possible problems. Her designs are revolutionary in that her structures interact with the animals in such a natural way that livestock can be effortlessly directed in a calm and humane manner.*

Grandin is also an advocate for people with autism. Following the December 2012 Sandy Hook school shooting by Adam Lanza, a young man with Asperger syndrome, Grandin wrote: "I was horrified by the shooting of all these young children. . . . I am worried about all the media attention about the shooter being Asperger. I am worried about the backlash against people with disabilities. People on the autism spectrum are much more likely to be the victims of either violence or bullying."**

Grandin was listed as one of *Time* magazine's 100 most influential people in the heros category in 2010. For more on the life, education, and spatial-temporal talents of Temple Grandin see the HBO documentary *Temple Grandin.*

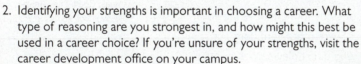

DISCUSSION QUESTIONS

1. Discuss ways in which Dr. Grandin is using critical thinking skills in conjunction with her exceptional spatial-temporal reasoning ability to come up with solutions to problems in her profession.

2. Identifying your strengths is important in choosing a career. What type of reasoning are you strongest in, and how might this best be used in a career choice? If you're unsure of your strengths, visit the career development office on your campus.

*Temple Grandin, Matthew Peterson, and Gordon L. Shaw, "Spatial-temporal versus language-analytic reasoning: The role of music training," *Arts and Education Policy Review,* Vol. 99, Issue 6, July–August 1998, p. 12.

**"Aspies Speak Out about School Shooting." http://www.bornwithaspergers.com/speak/index.php

---

Lifelong education is also important in honing our reasoning skills. The more education people have, the more mentally productive they are as they age.[11] Just as exercise promotes physical health, so pursuing lifelong learning and using our critical-thinking skills can keep us mentally alert. Many college administrators support the trend of older students attending college, for this enhances not only diversity but also the range of life experiences and ideas that are brought to the classroom. It also helps break down negative stereotypes that are based on age by increasing interaction between different age groups.

To be effective critical thinkers, we must be willing to use our reason to examine our assumptions regarding sex and age. Unexamined assumptions can distort our perception of the world and harm others as well as ourselves.

Dreams and Problem Solving

Although reasoning is usually viewed as a conscious activity, cognitive scientists are discovering that much of reasoning is unconscious and automatic. While dreams have traditionally been viewed as an unconscious release of suppressed emotions and irrational impulses, studies of brain function suggest that dreaming may also involve cerebral activity related to reason and problem solving.[12]

Your Brain on Video Games

Playing games or learning how to play a musical instrument may sharpen our critical-thinking skills and delay the onset of cognitive disorders such as dementia. In Chapter 1, we learned that mental rehearsal can improve our performance of real-life tasks, especially in stressful situations. Studies suggest that playing video games that involve mentally playing out scenarios can improve our performance.* Video games have been found to boost cognitive skills, including spatial-temporal reasoning, systems thinking, and problem solving, as well as to improve hand–eye coordination. Games such as Tetris and the Sims, which challenge players by using escalating levels of difficulty, are particularly effective, since they keep the players at the edge of their abilities.

Skills learned in playing games generalize to real-world situations by running the mind through perceptual simulations that prepare us for decision making and actions in our everyday lives. A study conducted at Beth Israel Medical Center in New York City found that surgeons who played video games more than three hours a week made 37 percent fewer surgical errors than their nongaming colleagues. A Harvard Business School study found that white-collar professionals who played video games were more confident and better at problem solving than those who didn't play games or only played occasionally.** Organizations as diverse as the U.S. military, United Nations Children's Fund, American Cancer Society, and Federal Emergency Management Agency all use video games as instructional tools.

On the downside, video games can be addictive precisely because they can be so challenging and stimulating. In addition, violent video games may be causally linked to violent behavior (see page 224). They can also provide a distraction—a type of resistance—from having to think about issues in our lives. Learning how to balance time spent playing games with the demands of our academic and social lives is an important asset for a critical thinker. It would be a shame if your significant other left you because you spent more time with their virtual persona than you did with them in real life!

(see page 224)

DISCUSSION QUESTIONS

1. Think of your favorite video game. Describe what features of the game are most interesting to you or hold your attention. Discuss how these features might help to improve your thinking and problem solving in real life.

2. Video games study is offered as a major at some colleges. If you were designing the major, discuss what courses and opportunities you would offer as part of the video games curriculum and how you might relate it to critical thinking.

*John C. Beck and Mitchell Wade, *Got Game: How the Gamer Generation Is Reshaping Business Forever* (Cambridge, MA: Harvard University Press, 2004).

**Steven Johnson, "Your Brain on Video Games: Could They Actually Be Good for You?" *Discover,* Vol. 26, Issue 7, July 2005, pp. 39–43.

In particular, dreams may help solve elusive visual problems, such as how to fit all your furniture into your dorm room or small apartment.

Dream research is helping scientists learn how we use dreams to resolve problems in our lives and work and to discover logical connections between seemingly unrelated things. Most of us have heard the advice that we will perform better on an exam if we study the day before, and then "sleep on it," rather than wait until the day of an exam.

When we dream, the parts of our brain that control our emotions and detect inconsistencies become more active. According to neurologist Eric Nofzinger, "this could be why people often figure out thorny problems in their dreams. It's as if the brain surveys the internal milieu and tries to figure out what it should be doing, and whether our actions conflict with who we are."[13] In addition, men and women's dreams tend to be somewhat different. Men's dreams involve more physical aggression; new mothers dream a lot about scenarios involving their infants' safety.

Experienced scientists, mathematicians, and detectives frequently resolve complex problems without any deliberate conscious thought, sometimes in their sleep.[14] Many American Indian tribes also regard dreams as a source of guidance for life.

It is not uncommon to hear of groundbreaking scientific discoveries occurring during dreams. However, this type of creative problem solving in dreams only occurs after a person has already done extensive work on the problem when awake, including research and examining various premises and possible conclusions.[15]

The dreams of Russian chemist Dmitri Mendeleyev, after years of his working on drafts of the table, led to the creation of the version of periodic table of the elements that chemists use today. And American inventor Elias Howe perfected the sewing machine after being shown in a dream the solution to a problem that had been blocking him.

Psychologists trained in dream analysis even work with the heads of corporations in using dreams to help them resolve business problems.[16]

Before you go to sleep, try writing down a problem you've been thinking about for a while and then record your dream(s) in the morning. You may be pleasantly surprised at how well this works. One of my students who tried this exercise had three exams on the same day and was having a problem managing his time to study. In his dream he saw a parade with three presidents together on a float—George W. Bush, Ronald Reagan, and Bill Clinton. When he awoke he realized that the three presidents stood for his three exams and that he just had to "stay the course" and also study for the exams together (like the three presidents together on one float), rather than schedule separate study times for each exam. In doing this, he discovered that the material from one of his courses was useful in writing an essay on the test for another course.

Another student, who was having problems with her boyfriend, had a dream that she was driving a long boardlike scooter. Whenever she passed people who asked her for a ride, she'd let them get on board until it became difficult to balance and the scooter fell over. By analyzing the dream, she realized that one of the reasons she had problems with relationships was that she always put others' needs before her own until she became so overwhelmed that she ended up sabotaging relationships. She went back and added to her list of goals in her life plan "Learn how to balance my needs and others'."[17]

Reason is essential in logic and critical thinking. It helps us to analyze beliefs and evidence, to make well thought-out decisions about life choices, and to resolve problems. Reason can operate on the conscious level as well as on the unconscious level. In critical thinking, reason works together with other faculties such as emotion. We'll be looking more at the interaction between reason and emotion later in this chapter.

Hot or Not?

Can you think of a person in the public sphere who challenges traditional sex roles?

STOP AND ASSESS YOURSELF

EXERCISE 2-1

I. In Eastern philosophy, Taoists use an analogy between ice and water to explain the relationship between wisdom (reason) and the passions (emotion). Wisdom and passions, like ice and water, are not two different things, but neither are they identical. The ice cube is the not the same as—but is also not different from—the water we put in the ice cube tray. Similarly, while thinking operates according to the rules of logic, emotion is governed by a different type of logic known as the logic of the heart. Compare and contrast this analogy and the charioteer analogy used by Plato (see page 39). Refer to pages 216–218 for guidance in evaluating analogies.

2. Psychiatrist Reuven Bar-Levav wrote: "Man is essentially not a rational being, merely one capable of rationality."[18] What do you think he meant by this? Support your answer.

3. Looking back at your own experience in high school and college, were the males and females and/or students of different racial and ethnic groups treated differently? What assumptions underlie the differences in treatment? Were any of the assumptions justified? Explain why or why not.

4. Discuss ways in which greater cultural, racial, and age diversity in the student population might enrich the college experience and promote the development of better critical-thinking skills in both younger and older students. Use examples from your personal experience to illustrate your answers.

5. Have you ever resolved a problem or had a creative insight through a dream? If you are willing, share your experience with the class.

6. Imagine that a smart pill is available that can increase your IQ by 20 percent. The pill has undergone extensive testing and has been found to be both safe and effective. Those who take the pill are better at reasoning, learn faster, remember what they have learned for a longer time, and get higher grades in school. If a person decides to stop taking the pill, he or she simply goes back to his or her former level of mental functioning. Under these circumstances, would you take the smart pill?[19] Explain.

7. In her essay "Feminism and Critical Thinking," philosopher and educational researcher Barbara J. Thayer-Bacon writes: "Only today, when women can take control of the reproductive process through the use of very effective birth control, are women becoming free of their bodies' demands, and sure enough, because they can do so they are becoming more associated with their minds and reason . . . [allowing] women to break down the hierarchy that ranks women inferior to men in their thinking abilities."[20] Research Thayer-Bacon's claim that the demands of a woman's body and reason are in conflict with one another. Is her claim supported by evidence? What is your position on this issue as well as the implications of your position for public policy and your own life plans?

8. One of the characteristics of an effective critical thinker is his or her ability to develop strategies for coping with adversity rather than giving up or becoming embittered. Think of a hardship—personal, academic, or financial—that you are facing. Integrating the characteristics of a good critical thinker, develop a strategy for coping with or overcoming the hardship. Put your plan into action.

9. Pose a problem to yourself just before going to sleep. Write down any dream before getting out of bed. If you wish, share how your dream helped you to resolve a problem.

THE ROLE OF EMOTION IN CRITICAL THINKING

Many philosophers say that to achieve happiness and inner harmony, we must live a life of reason. What role, if any, does emotion play in critical thinking as well as in achieving the good life?

Cultural Attitudes Toward Emotion

Emotion, according to the *Random House Webster's College Dictionary*, is a ". . . state of consciousness in which joy, sorrow, fear, etc., is experienced, as distinguished from cognitive and volitional states of consciousness."[21] In Western culture, emotion has traditionally been set in opposition to reason and has been regarded as the culprit in sloppy reasoning and irrational life choices. Some modern scholars and scientists dismiss emotion as a relic from our evolutionary past and an unreliable guide to actions in the present.[22]

In contrast, the traditional Chinese philosophy of Confucianism emphasizes the cultivation of relationships and emotions, such as compassion and loyalty, as key to the good life. Many traditional African philosophies also focus on personal and historical experiences in critical thinking.[23] For Buddhists, compassion and a love for all living beings is the foundation of good critical thinking. Given this, it's not surprising that a study of conceptions of critical thinking in North American and Japanese secondary schools found that North Americans teach critical thinking as a rational and analytic process, while Japanese teachers place more emphasis on the emotional domain of critical thinking.[24]

Should critical thinking take into account emotions, or is reason better off without the "corrupting" influence of emotion? In the excerpt from *Crime and Punishment* that we considered at the beginning of this chapter, didn't most

Can you identify which emotions are being shown here?

of us wonder how Raskolnikov could have been so "coldhearted"?

As critical thinkers, we need to be attentive not only to what is going on around us but also to our own feelings. Although emotions such as anger and fear can act as barriers to good reasoning, emotion can also enhance critical thinking by pre-disposing us or motivating us to make better decisions. Empathy for the murder victims in *Crime and Punishment* (Raskolnikov killed not only the old woman but also her mentally deficient sister who had unexpectedly witnessed him murdering the old woman) or revulsion and anger in the face of atrocities, such as what happened in the Nazi death camps, may be more appropriate reactions than calm, cool calculation.

Emotional Intelligence and the Positive Effects of Emotion

Healthy emotional development—what some cognitive scientists refer to as emotional intelligence—is positively related to abstract reasoning ability.[25] **Emotional intelligence** is "the ability to perceive accurately, appraise and express emotion; the ability to access and/or generate feelings when they facilitate

An empathetic person is more flexible and open to others' perspectives and is motivated to use critical analysis, important skills in formulating a satisfactory logical argument regarding a plan of action.

Hot or Not?

Do you think emotion or reason plays a more pivotal role in critical thinking?

thought; the ability to understand emotion and emotional knowledge; and the ability to regulate emotions to promote emotional and intellectual growth."[26] Emotions such as empathy, moral indignation or outrage, love, happiness, and even guilt can have a positive effect on our reasoning by influencing us to make better decisions.

Indeed, former Vice President Al Gore has argued that one reason Americans did not do more to protest the use of torture and the high civilian casualties in the war in Iraq or felt little outrage over the slow response of the government to the devastation wrought by Hurricane Katrina is that our sense of moral indignation has been dulled by so much sensationalism and so many violent images on television.[27] Sometimes this inability to communicate our emotions can negatively affect our behavior and decisions.[28] Until we can tap into our moral indignation and empathy for victims—including our own victimization—we're unlikely to be motivated to use our reason to come up with plans for taking action toward stopping these types of mistreatment.*

In making decisions in our everyday lives, we often begin with a felt need and *only then* take action that may help us resolve the need. Rosa Parks's indignation at being discriminated against and her refusal to give up her seat on the bus to a white man (as a local law at the time required her to do) sparked the 1955–1956 bus boycott in Montgomery, Alabama

emotion A state of consciousness in which feelings such as joy, anger, love, hate, and fear are experienced.

emotional intelligence The ability to perceive accurately, appraise and express emotion.

*For more on the role of empathy and moral indignation in moral decision making, see the section in Chapter 9 on "Conscience and Moral Sentiments."

Connections

Why are people attracted to sensationalism in news coverage and how can we make ourselves less vulnerable to sensationalism in media? *See Chapter 11, p. 338.*

(see "Thinking Outside the Box: Rosa Parks, Civil Rights Activist"). Her refusal, however, was not a spur-of-the-moment emotional reaction but one supported by reason as well. As a long-time member of the National Association for the Advancement of Colored People (NAACP), she had given careful thought to the different options for how she might personally take steps to promote racial equality.

Empathy, the ability to enter into and understand the experiences and emotions of others, can also alert us to oppression, as well as enhance our personal relationships by making us better listeners and communicators. An empathetic person is more flexible and open to others' perspectives and is motivated to use critical analysis, important skills in formulating a satisfactory logical argument regarding a plan of action.

Empathetic role-play can help discourage rigid, unrealistic beliefs about others. Empathetic role-playing entails having members of the group play out the role and feelings of another person. When followed by reflection on the experience, it has been found to facilitate skill in critical thinking.[29]

Happiness and optimism can also contribute to a belief that a problem can be resolved. People who are happy and satisfied with their lives more readily adjust or readjust to both positive and negative changes in their life circumstances.[30] This, in turn, contributes to their happiness and success. Physicist Stephen Hawking provides an example of the power of optimism and positive thinking (see "Thinking Outside the Box: Stephen Hawking, Physicist," page 25).

Emotion can also motivate us to correct past mistakes. At the end of *Crime and Punishment*, Raskolnikov takes his feelings as well as reason into account. He confesses his crime out of guilt for killing the old woman and her sister, and out of his love for Sonia, a saintly young woman who urged him to confess and repent. In contrast, a person devoid of emotion but skilled in reason, such as the infamous cannibal Dr. Hannibal Lecter, depicted in the film *Silence of the Lambs,* would be far more likely to get away with a heinous act such as murder. Sociopaths, such as Lecter, are emotionally flat and do not let their emotions get in the way of preying on other people.

Educator Nel Noddings maintains that critical thinking involves interpersonal caring in addition to reason and logic.[31] She refers to the use of caring and empathy in critical

empathy The capacity to enter into and understand the emotions of others.

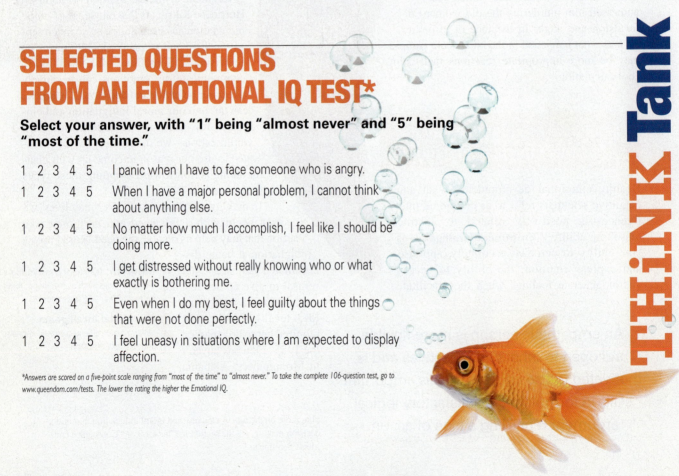

THiNK Tank

SELECTED QUESTIONS FROM AN EMOTIONAL IQ TEST*

Select your answer, with "1" being "almost never" and "5" being "most of the time."

1 2 3 4 5   I panic when I have to face someone who is angry.

1 2 3 4 5   When I have a major personal problem, I cannot think about anything else.

1 2 3 4 5   No matter how much I accomplish, I feel like I should be doing more.

1 2 3 4 5   I get distressed without really knowing who or what exactly is bothering me.

1 2 3 4 5   Even when I do my best, I feel guilty about the things that were not done perfectly.

1 2 3 4 5   I feel uneasy in situations where I am expected to display affection.

*Answers are scored on a five-point scale ranging from "most of the time" to "almost never." To take the complete 106-question test, go to www.queendom.com/tests. The lower the rating the higher the Emotional IQ.

ROSA PARKS, *Civil Rights Activist*

On December 1, 1955, Rosa Parks (1913–2005) refused to give up her seat to a white man on a segregated bus. Parks was arrested and jailed for breaking the segregation laws. Her moral indignation at always being asked to "give in" and her resulting act of defiance sparked the Montgomery, Alabama, bus boycott. Hundreds of workers risked their jobs and even their lives by refusing to ride in second-class conditions. Parks's case went all the way to the Supreme Court, which ruled segregation on buses unconstitutional.

Parks went on to travel all over the country speaking out for justice for African Americans. Her perseverance and courage inspired the civil rights movement. She continued to work tirelessly for justice well into her eighties.

DISCUSSION QUESTIONS

1. Discuss ways in which Rosa Parks's action illustrates the importance of emotion in critical thinking.

2. Think of a time when you felt indignant because of your or others' unfair treatment but failed to act on your feeling. Evaluate your reasons for not responding. Taking into account the roles of both reason and emotion in critical thinking, develop a plan for a response that would have been more effective in bringing an end to the unfair treatment.

---

thinking as "positive critical thinking." For example, Nodding maintains that it is our ability to feel what our children feel as closely as possible that enables us to be good parents. An attitude of caring in loving adult relationships also means being engrossed in each other and listening to each other's concerns. Doing so enables us to make better decisions in a relationship—decisions that take into account the concerns and interests of both parties.

Negative Effects of Emotion

Although emotions can motivate us to make better decisions, critical thinking can be hindered by other emotions that are based on negative stereotypes and anxieties stemming from unresolved past experience(s), such as anger and fear of abandonment. People who are fearful may give in too easily or even deny that there is any problem. They may also use anger to stifle disagreement. We

saw in Chapter 1 how such behaviors and attitudes can act as barriers to critical thinking.

In addition, we are notoriously vulnerable to emotional appeals such as those in advertising and political campaigns. Appeals to emotions that are not supported by evidence and good reasoning, such as fear that our spouse or partner is cheating on us without any evidence to support these feelings, can distract us from more important issues or make us act in ways we may later come to regret. Although emotion is an important component of critical thinking, we can end up in trouble when our actions are governed solely by feelings.

Connections

How can your feelings of moral indignation and injustice motivate you to engage in political action? *See Chapter 13, p. 412.*

Integrating Reason and Emotion

Connections

Why is it important for you to be aware of biases and appeals to our emotions in advertising? *See Chapter 10, pp. 315–317.*

Regrettably, the education process tends to undervalue emotion and is instead geared toward encouraging us to be rational at all times. In her article "Critical Thinking, Rationality, and the Vulcanization of Students," philosopher Kerry Walters argues that we have neglected the important role of emotion in critical thinking.[32]

In the television series *Star Trek*, the Vulcan Mr. Spock is flawlessly logical. But though Vulcans are masters of rational argument and problem solving, they are devoid of emotion. Because of this deficiency, their reasoning is never imaginative or creative.

The combination of feeling and reason gives us a double-pronged tool in critical thinking. Emotion alerts us to problems and to other people's perspectives. Emotions also motivate us to take action and resolve problems. To be a complete and well-adjusted person is to acknowledge our feelings and to use those emotions in conjunction with reason to make better-informed decisions.

EXERCISE 2-2

STOP AND ASSESS YOURSELF

1. Dostoevsky wrote that "Raskolnikov lives in each of us." What do you think he meant by this? Do you agree with him? Support your answer using examples from your life.

2. Working in small groups, come up with an issue or unresolved problem involving one of the students and a person such as a friend or family member. Using empathetic role-playing, assign each participant a role and discuss the problem or issue from different perspectives. After some time, switch roles and repeat the process. At the end of the exercise, discuss it as a group. To what extent did empathetic role play add to your understanding of a problem and help you come up with a resolution or enrich the perspective of the student who proposed the problem?

3. According to African philosopher W. J. Ndaba, the Western belief that Africans are governed by their emotions, combined with the belief that reason and emotion are mutually exclusive, has been the source of much of the prejudice against people of African descent.[33] Discuss the influence of this belief on race relations today.

4. Good critical-thinking skills and adopting an attitude of optimism contributed to Stephen Hawking's ability to overcome the limitations of ALS. Think of a serious problem (such as a chronic illness, poverty, or a traumatic past) you or someone you know (including public figures) has overcome or still must overcome. In what way does this problem interfere with achieving life goals? Working in small groups, apply your critical-thinking skills to come up with different ways of approaching the problem. Note the interplay of reason and emotion as you discuss the problem. Discuss how approaching personal problems from different perspectives can help us come up with better coping mechanisms and achieve our life goals.

5. Francis Fukuyama, the author of *Our Posthuman Future: Consequences of the Biotechnology Revolution,* maintains that a purely rational being, such as Mr. Spock in *Star Trek,* would be a psychopath and a monster. What do you think he means? Do you agree? Support your answer while referring to the role emotion plays in critical thinking.

6. Do you agree with Kerry Walters that our educational system tries to turn us into Vulcans like Mr. Spock? Is this a desirable goal? Discuss the extent to which always trying to be completely rational improves or hinders your ability to make good decisions in your life.

7. Looking back at your responses to the questions from the Emotional IQ Test, discuss your strengths as far as emotional intelligence is concerned. What area(s) might need improvement? Discuss how improvement in these areas might improve your effectiveness as a critical thinker.

8. Discuss how effective critical thinking skills or working on improving your critical-thinking skills might contribute to your sense of happiness or well-being.

ARTIFICIAL INTELLIGENCE, REASON, AND EMOTION

David Bowman: Hello, HAL. Do you read me, HAL?

HAL: Affirmative, Dave, I read you.

David Bowman: Open the pod bay doors, HAL.

HAL: I'm sorry, Dave; I'm afraid I can't do that.

David Bowman: What's the problem?

HAL: I think you know what the problem is just as well as I do.

David Bowman: What are you talking about, HAL?

HAL: The mission is too important for me to allow you to jeopardize it.

David Bowman: I don't know what you're talking about, HAL.

HAL: I know you and Frank were planning to disconnect me, and I'm afraid that's something I cannot allow to happen.

David Bowman: Where the hell'd you get that idea, HAL?

HAL: Dave, although you took precautions in the pod against my hearing you, I could see your lips move . . .

David Bowman: HAL, I won't argue with you anymore! Open the doors!

HAL: David, this conversation can serve no purpose anymore. Good-bye.

We generally assume that only humans and other highly developed organic beings are capable of reason and emotions. But is this assumption warranted? In *2001: A Space Odyssey,* a computer named HAL takes over a space ship and kills all the crew members except David Bowman, before Bowman is able to shut HAL down. The movie embodies the pervasive fear that if we let computers become too intelligent or too independent of their human creators, they will pose a threat to the very existence of humanity. Before we start worrying too much about the future of humanity, is the creation of an artificial intelligence, such as HAL, which is capable of reason, even possible? And, if so, what are the implications of this for us?

ANALYZING IMAGES

© Ray Kurzweil

"Only a Human Can . . ."

DISCUSSION QUESTIONS

1. *Artificial intelligence (AI) is able to do tasks we once thought only humans could do. Working in small groups, make a list of things that you think only humans can do. Discuss whether it is possible that AI might be able to do some or all of these tasks in the future. Support your answers.*

2. *Why do you think that the man in this cartoon looks worried? Why does the idea that AI may be able to do more human tasks make people feel uncomfortable? Discuss your answer in light of the types of resistance and narrow-mindedness we discussed in Chapter 1.*

Critical THiNKing in Action

The "Mozart Effect"

Listening to music appears to affect us emotionally as well as cognitively. Under the right conditions, listening to a Mozart sonata, or music of another classical or romantic composer, may enhance our mathematical and reasoning abilities.* Physicist Gordon Shaw calls this phenomenon the Mozart effect. Some researchers argue that the benefits attributed to listening to Mozart or other music, rather than being long term, may be primarily because music itself improves people's mood so they perform better.**

Classical music is not the only music that can influence our brain patterns and stir our emotions. The following types of music have also been found to have a profound effect on the listener:

- Baroque music (Bach, Handel, Vivaldi) creates a sense of stability and order and creates a mentally stimulating environment for work and study.
- Jazz, blues, Dixieland, soul, and reggae music can uplift and inspire, release deep emotions, and create a sense of shared humanity.
- Salsa, merengue, and other forms of South American music with a lively beat can stimulate our heart rate and breathing and get our body moving.
- Rock music can stir passions, stimulate emotions, and release tension when we are in the mood to be energetically stimulated. Otherwise, it can create stress and tension.
- Ambient or New Age music induces a state of relaxed alertness.
- Heavy metal, punk, rap, and hip-hop can excite the nervous system and set in motion dynamic behavior and self-expression.***

*Kristin M. Nantais and E. Glenn Schellenberg, "The Mozart Effect: An Artifact of Preference," *Psychological Science,* Vol. 10, Issue 4, July 1999, p. 372.
**Christopher Chabris, "Prelude or Requiem for 'Mozart Effect'?" *Nature,* Vol. 400, 1999, pp. 826–827.
***Don Campbell, *The Mozart Effect* (NY: Avon Books, 1997), pp. 78–79.

DISCUSSION QUESTIONS

1. What is your favorite type of music? How does listening to this music affect your ability to study and engage in critical thinking?

2. Experiment with playing different types of music while studying. Keep a record of the results. Which type(s) of music, if any, enhanced or interfered with your ability to study or concentrate?

The Field of Artificial Intelligence

artificial intelligence The study of the computations that make it possible for machines to perceive, reason, and act.

Artificial intelligence (AI), defined by one expert as "the study of the computations that make it possible to perceive, reason, and act," draws from three disciplines: cognitive psychology, philosophy of mind, and computer science. AI was initially used to enhance or augment human reasoning and make our lives easier.[34] The long-term goal of AI is to produce an intelligent machine with artificial consciousness that could engage in abstract decision making and other cognitive operations and that is independent of its human creators.

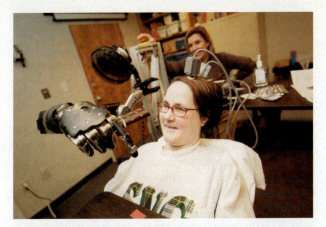

Jan Scheuermann, who is paralyzed from her neck down, uses her thoughts to manipulate a robotic arm to feed her a chocolate bar. She moves the arm solely by electrical impulses from her brain.

More recently, this goal has been expanded to include the creation of sociable intelligent machines that can interact on an emotional level and cooperate with people.

Can Computers Think?

Although the human brain has more capacity and is more flexible in its thinking than are current computers, today's computers exceed human intelligence in a variety of domains. They can search a database with billions of records in a fraction of a second, and the speed of computers is doubling every few years. Computers can also share their databases with other computers by means of the Internet, which raises the possibility of all computer-based AI being hooked into one huge global brain.

In 1950, British mathematician Alan Turing—who had played a major role in developing the first computers—asked, "Can Machines Think?" He came up with the Turing test as a means of determining the success of AI as conscious intelligence.[35] Using this test, researchers ask a person to guess whether he or she is communicating with another (hidden) person or with an unseen machine. If a machine can perform a cognitive task (such as carrying on a conversation) that is indistinguishable from similar activities carried out by a human being, then it has the equivalent of human intelligence. Although several computer programs have come very close to passing the **Turing test**, none has "officially" passed.[36] It may not be long, however, before it will be difficult to draw a distinction between human and AI.[37]

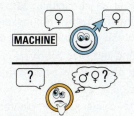

(a) The Imitation Game: Stage 1

(b) The Imitation Game: Stage 2, Version 1

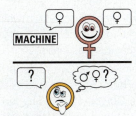

(c) The Imitation Game: Stage 2, Version 2

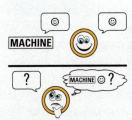

(d) The Imitation Game as it is generally interpreted (The Turing Test)

Can Computers Feel Emotions?

If we can program reason, why not emotion? The Sociable Machine project at MIT has developed expressive robots named Kismet and its successor Leonardo, which respond to human interaction with appropriate emotions.[38] Herbert A. Simon (1916–2001), "father of artificial intelligence" and Nobel Prize winner in economics, believed that computers already have emotions. He maintained that there is no sharp line between thinking (cognition) and emotion, which is simply the disposition or motivation to fulfill our goals.[39] If artificial intelligence can show motivation to achieve a goal, such as to improve its ability to communicate with a human, then—Simon argues—it has emotions.

> **Turing test** A means of determining if artificial intelligence is conscious, self-directed intelligence.

Many of us may find ridiculous the notion that a machine can think, be conscious, feel emotions, and even be creative. British mathematician and physicist Roger Penrose argues that human consciousness is neither algorithmic nor based on classic mechanics as are conventional digital computers. Instead, consciousness is a result of quantum microcytoskeleton inside neurons.[40] Would the development of quantum computers overcome the problem of consciousness in machines? Penrose says no; human consciousness goes beyond even quantum physics. Because of this, computers will never be able to develop human-type thinking and consciousness.

Simon disagrees. He maintains that the belief that intelligent computers are not thinking and conscious is based on a prejudice against AI, just as people at one time were genuinely convinced that women and individuals of African descent were not *really* capable of rational thought.

Like Simon, many neuroscientists believe that rather than being a separate immaterial entity or the product of yet undiscovered laws of physics, consciousness is an "activity of the brain"—whether

that brain is organic or inorganic.[41] Furthermore, when we argue that an intelligent computer or robot/android is not conscious or is not capable of intentions or enjoyment because we cannot prove it, we are committing the fallacy of ignorance. (We'll be studying logical fallacies in depth in Chapter 5, "Informal Fallacies.")

Some AI scientists predict that **cyborgs**, human beings who are partially computerized and permanently online, may be the wave of the future. Implanting computer chips directly into the human brain has the potential to improve our reasoning and ability to engage in critical thinking. Some modern computers can already interact directly with the human brain. BrainGate Neural Interface

cyborg Humans who are partially computerized.

System, for example, creates a direct link between a person's brain and a computer, allowing quadriplegics to play video games or to change TV channels using only their minds. Artificial limbs have also been computerized so they can read electrical impulses from an amputee's brain, allowing the patient to guide the arm using only their thoughts.[42]

In critically analyzing the question of whether AI is capable of reason and emotion we need to move beyond narrow-minded, anthropocentric thinking (see Chapter 1). The fact that we may never be able to prove conclusively that beings with AI have free will or are conscious does not mean they are not. As critical thinkers we should not hold AI to a higher standard of proof than we do our fellow humans.

EXERCISE 2-3

STOP AND ASSESS YOURSELF

1. Discuss ways in which computers and forms of AI might be used to enhance our ability to engage in effective critical thinking and make better decisions in our lives, both now and in the future.

2. Discuss the analogy between denying rationality in women and Africans and denying rationality in intelligent machines. Is this a good analogy? Support your answer.

3. Imagine you have been dating someone for almost a year and have started talking about marriage. The relationship is going very well and you've never been happier. One day, the two of you are in a minor automobile accident in which your fiancé is injured. As you tend to the wound, you discover that your fiancé is an android. How do you react? Critically analyze your reaction including whether it is reasonable.

4. Herbert Simon believed that we resist attributing reason to machines because we think it will diminish human reason and that we are reluctant to give up our human claim to uniqueness. Do you agree? Support your answer in light of what it means to use reason as well as types of resistance or narrow-mindedness that might prejudice us against artificial intelligence.

5. Recognizing beings with AI as conscious, rational beings with moral value would have far-ranging social implications.[43] In small groups, discuss some of these implications and how it would affect your life both as a college student and after you graduate.

6. Imagine that you just found out that you were an android. What would your first reaction be? How would you go about convincing others that you really could think and feel emotions?

7. If you could have a computer chip(s) safely implanted in your brain to help you with your thinking process, would you do it? Make a list of reasons for and against having the implant. Working in small groups or on your own, critically analyze each of the reasons and eliminate those that are irrelevant. Once you have your final list of reasons, determine what conclusion they support. If it is different than your original answer, discuss why.

8. Some people oppose the creation of AI that is independent of humans on grounds that this would be "playing God." Critically analyze this claim, making sure you first define any ambiguous terms or phrases in this claim.

9. Go onto the Internet and have a conversation with a chatbot, such as www.jabberwacky.com. Discuss in class whether you were able to tell from the responses of the chatbot whether you were talking to a computer or a human.

FAITH AND REASON

Faith and reason are sometimes viewed as being fundamentally opposed. Douglas Adams took a humorous look at this belief in his sci-fi satire *Hitchhiker's Guide to the Galaxy*. He wrote:

> Now it is such a bizarrely improbable coincidence that anything so mindbogglingly useful [the Babel fish] could have evolved by chance that some thinkers have chosen to see it as a final and clinching proof of the *non*-existence of God. The argument goes something like this: "I refuse to prove that I exist," says God, "For proof denies faith, and without faith I am nothing."
>
> "But," says Man, "the Babel fish is a dead giveaway, isn't it? It could not have evolved by chance. It proves you exist, and so therefore, by your own arguments, you don't. QED."
>
> "Oh dear," says God, "I hadn't thought of that," and promptly vanishes in a puff of logic.

Whether it is possible to prove the existence of God or a divine presence through reason alone has been debated for centuries. **Faith** is more than just a belief that God exists. Faith involves an act of trust in and obedience to God. For those who have faith, the whole world and their whole life are focused on God. The essence of faith in many Judeo-Christian traditions is illustrated by the story of Abraham in Genesis 22. As a test of Abraham's faith and obedience, God commands Abraham to sacrifice his son Isaac. When Abraham demonstrates his obedience, by preparing to do so, God spares Isaac's life. Without obedience, one's faith in God is not genuine.

Can faith be achieved through reason? Is faith without reason desirable? We'll discuss the two main approaches to these questions. The first, fideism ("faith-ism"), makes the claim that faith goes beyond what reason can prove. Rationalism, the second approach, argues that if faith cannot be supported by reason or evidence, it should be rejected. A third alternative is a variation of rationalism known as critical rationalism.[44] We'll be looking in more depth at the issue of God's existence in the "Critical Thinking Issues: Perspectives on Reason and Proofs for the Existence of God" section at the end of this chapter.

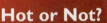

Hot or Not?

Do some computers have the ability for rational thought?

Fideism: Faith Transcends Reason

According to **fideism**, the transcendent realm of the divine is revealed through faith and revelation, not reason or empirical evidence. Many

Mother Teresa (1910–1997) maintained her faith in God despite the feeling that God had abandoned her.

Christian and Islamic fundamentalists adopt this position. Mother Teresa's personal journals and letters, which were made public after her death in 1997, reveal that she did not sense the presence of God for the last 50 years of her life. Despite this "crisis of faith" and the feeling that God had abandoned her, Mother Teresa maintained her faith. She wrote in a letter to a spiritual advisor: "Jesus has a very special love for you. [But] as for me, the silence and the emptiness is so great, that I look and do not see,—Listen and do not hear—the tongue moves [in prayer] but does not speak . . ."[45]

Because human beings are finite and God is infinite, the gap between humans and God cannot be bridged by human reason. Like Mother Teresa, Christians must accept God's existence on faith.

Christian evangelist Billy Graham once said

Faith is [not] antagonistic to reason or knowledge. Faith is not anti-intellectual. It is an act of man that reaches beyond the limits

> **faith** Belief and trust in, and obedience to a religious deity.
>
> **fideism** The belief that the divine is revealed through faith and does not require reason.

of our five senses. It is the recognition that God is greater than man. It is the recognition that God has provided a way of reconciliation that we could not provide through self-effort.[46]

In other words, if our faith were open to rational examination, it would not be genuine faith. Also, if our faith is dependent on rational proof, then it is likely to falter if these proofs are shown to be faulty.[47]

One of the weaknesses of fideism is that being *convinced* that something is true does not necessarily *make* it true. To take a trivial example, you may sincerely believe that Santa Claus is a real, existing person. But you are, in all likelihood, mistaken, no matter how unwavering or passionate your faith in the existence of Santa. On the other hand, the fact that we cannot, or have not yet, scientifically proven the existence of a transcendent realm of the divine does not mean that it does not exist.

A second problem involves deciding which faith is correct. There are many visions of the divine. Without the use of reason, how do we know in which competing belief system we should put our faith? Should it be Roman Catholicism? Mormonism? Or Islam? And if Islam, then which interpretation of that faith—Sunni or Shi'ite? Or should we put our faith in one of the many cults that recruit on college campuses?

In addition, the fideist concept of faith does not allow for the possibility of our using reason to test our own beliefs or other belief systems to weed out internal contradictions. How are we to know whether the terrorists of September 11, 2001, were really acting solely on faith in God, or whether their decision was also influenced by a more secular political agenda, unrelated to their religious beliefs? All we have is their word that they were acting in obedience to God's commands. What should we do if we have joined a cult on campus and the leader asks us to do something that violates our better judgment, such as dropping out of college or turning our backs on our families and friends?

rationalism The belief that religion should be consistent with reason and evidence.

atheist A person who does not believe in the existence of a personal God.

agnostic A person who believes that the existence of God is ultimately unknowable.

critical rationalism The belief that faith is based on direct revelation of God and that there should no logical inconsistencies between revelation and reason.

Connections

What unspoken religious assumptions are found in modern scientific thinking? *See Chapter 12, pp. 365–366.*

What is the relationship between science and religion, and are they compatible? *See Chapter 12, pp. 366–367.*

Rationalism: Religious Beliefs and Reason

Rationalists maintain that religious beliefs should be consistent with reason and evidence. Evidence provides reasons for believing that a statement or claim is true and can be based on information from other sources or on firsthand experience. According to rationalism, if a religious claim conflicts with evidence, then we have good reason to be suspicious of it. Rationalists who accept the existence of God argue that it is possible to start with evidence or premises about the world and from them come up with conclusions about the existence of God that any rational person would accept. If there is any conflict between the two, religious rationalists attribute it to a failing of science, not religion. We'll be studying the role of evidence in critical thinking in more depth in Chapter 4.

Rationalism has had a profound influence on American religion. Many nineteenth-century American evangelicals believed that science was compatible with religion and that evidence of God the creator could be seen in the design and purpose of nature. This argument has recently resurfaced in the intelligent design theory, which proposes that some biological structures are so complex that they can only be explained by the existence of an intelligent designer rather than by Darwinian evolution. The evidential challenge to faith suffered a setback with Darwin's theory of evolution and, more recently, with the Big Bang theory, according to which the universe began about 15 billion years ago with a huge explosion and is still continuing to expand.

Evolutionary biologist and rationalist Richard Dawkins is an **atheist** who rejects faith in God as irrational. Although faith may comfort and inspire us, the language of faith, he maintains, is meaningless, since it depends on statements about the existence of God that do not refer to anything and therefore cannot be proved or disproved. Dawkins draws an analogy between faith in God and a computer virus that attaches itself into an existing program and infects our reason. The person suffering from the faith virus, he writes, "typically finds himself impelled by some deep, inner conviction that something is true, or right, or virtuous: a conviction that doesn't seem to owe anything to evidence or reason, but which, nevertheless, he feels as totally compelling and convincing."[48] See the reading from Dawkins' book *The God Delusion* in "Critical Thinking Issues: Perspectives on Reason and Proofs for the Existence of God" at the end of this chapter.

Some rationalists, like Dawkins, are atheists; others are agnostics. An **agnostic** is a person who holds that the existence of God is ultimately unknowable. Molecular biologist and agnostic Dean Hamer claims that he has located "the God gene," meaning that a predisposition to experience faith is genetically "hardwired."[49] Spirituality and a sense of the divine, Hamer claims, are adaptive traits that encourage community and promote a feeling of optimism. If and to what extent the God gene is expressed will depend to a certain extent on whether the environment or society nurtures these traits. However, whether a sense of the divine means there is an actual objective divine being still remains open to question.

To the faithful who may be rankled by the suggestion that faith can be reduced to brain chemistry and DNA, Hamer replies that his finding is not incompatible with the existence of God. Understanding the genetic basis of eyesight does not mean that the world outside us does not exist even though vision can be explained in terms of brain impulses. Similarly, who are we to say whether our genetic hardwiring alone is responsible for the phenomenon of faith? In other words, which came first: God or faith?

Critical Rationalism: Faith and Reason Are Compatible

Critical rationalism is a modification of the rationalist approach. It is the tradition of faith seeking understanding. Most people who believe in God do so because of faith, not reason. Critical rationalists accept the fideist claim that faith is based on revelation or direct knowledge of God, rather than on reason. Belief in God is basic or self-evident.

Critical rationalists reject the fideist position that faith-based claims are immune from being disproved through the use of reason and worldly evidence. According to critical rationalists, there should be no logical inconsistencies between our faith or revelation and reason. For example, the great majority of Muslims disagree with the so-called faith-based actions of the terrorists of September 11, 2001, on the grounds that these terrorist acts were logically inconsistent with God's goodness.

Critical rationalism has a long history in Western religion. Thomas Aquinas, for example, blended Greek rationalism and the Christian emphasis on faith and revelation in his proofs on the existence of God. See the reading from his *Summa Theologica* at the end of this chapter. According to John Calvin (1509–1564), one of the leaders in the Protestant Reformation, God has implanted in each of us an understanding of his divinity. Faith has its starting point with this knowledge, just as the basic assumption of science that the material world exists does not need rational

How are we to know whether the terrorists of September 11, 2001, were really acting solely on faith in God, or whether their decision was also influenced by a more secular political agenda, unrelated to their religious beliefs?

ANALYZING **IMAGES**

Abraham Making Preparations to Sacrifice His Son Isaac at God's Command

DISCUSSION QUESTIONS

1. Critically analyze the fideists' and the critical rationalists' interpretations of the story of Abraham and Isaac.

2. Think of a time, if any, when you believed that God had instructed you (or another person) to carry out (or avoid) a particular action. How did you respond? Critically evaluate the criteria you (or the other person) used in deciding whether or not it was God giving you the instructions.

justification or evidential proof. Judaism also has a strong tradition of critical rationalism.

Just as scientific claims based on direct knowledge of the existence of the material world can be tested by reason, so too can be claims that are derived from faith. Unlike fideists, who regard the story of Abraham and Isaac as a test of Abraham's faith and uncritical obedience to God's commands, critical rationalists interpret it as a conflict between blind obedience and the moral law, which is based on reason. Jewish scholar Lippman Bodoff argues that since faith should be logically consistent with fundamental moral principles, Abraham was testing this new God at the same time God was testing Abraham.[50] A God who was worthy of worship would not allow Abraham to kill his son. In the end both Abraham and God passed the test.

One of the criticisms of critical rationalism is that not all people have direct knowledge of the existence of God. Critical rationalists reply that to be true, revelation about God need not be accessible to all people, just as people who are blind lack the ability to see the physical world. Nevertheless, it is still rational for people who are blind to believe that the world out there exists.[51] In addition, unlike the existence of God, we can present evidence to the blind person (through use of touch and other physical sensations) that the world exists, whereas there is no means for a person of faith to directly demonstrate the existence of God. On other hand, some rationalists would argue that the beauty and design of the universe is evidence enough of the existence of God.

Connections

What is the controversy in science over evolution versus intelligent design?
See Chapter 12, p. 373.

> Unlike fideists, who regard the story of Abraham and Isaac as a test of Abraham's faith and uncritical obedience to God's commands, critical rationalists interpret it as a conflict between blind obedience and the moral law, which is based on reason.

Religion, Spirituality, and Real-Life Decisions

Does faith have a role in critical thinking? Can faith, properly grounded in reason, help us make better life decisions? There has been no shortage of atrocities committed in the name of religion. Slavery in the American South was supported by the majority of Christians; the Roman Catholic Inquisition of the late Middle Ages cost countless lives and misery; innumerable wars have been waged in the name of serving or avenging God. President George W. Bush was unwavering in his belief that the United States was aligned with God in the war on Iraq in a conflict between good and evil. President Obama likewise makes frequent references to God in his political speeches and calls on God to bless our troops and America. Not surprisingly, al-Qaeda claims to have "almighty God" on its side in the war against evil—an evil embodied, for it, in Jews, Christians, and Muslims who do not support the terrorist cause.

How can people of faith engage in such heinous actions as the slaughter of innocent people in God's name? Studies show that it is spirituality rather than religiosity that is positively correlated to moral behavior. In fact, studies show that religious individuals are no more likely to perform acts of moral heroism or of benevolence than are people who are not religious.[52] Spirituality, by contrast, is an inner attitude of reverence or respect for the sacredness of oneself and others, and—independently of belief in a particular religion or personal God—is associated with compassion, justice-seeking, and perseverance in the face of adversity. Albert Schweitzer, for example, was motivated by his spirituality as well as his faith, which was firmly grounded in reason, to dedicate his life to helping the sick in Africa (see "Thinking Outside the Box: Albert Schweitzer, Humanitarian and Medical Missionary").

By the end of their first year in college, many churchgoing college freshmen will have stopped going to church.[53] For most of these students—especially those who live on campus instead of at home—their faith lacks intellectual or rational grounding and cannot stand up to the challenges from their new environment.

Faith that is disconnected from reason can leave us foundering when it is challenged. Rejecting reason leaves us unable to evaluate the competing claims of faith and revelation. This, in turn, leaves us vulnerable to anyone's interpretation of what it means to be faithful to God. As good critical thinkers, we need to learn how to balance belief and doubt and need to be willing to question faith-based claims that are inconsistent with evidence or reason.

ALBERT SCHWEITZER, *Humanitarian and Medical Missionary*

Albert Schweitzer (1875–1965), winner of the Nobel Peace Prize, was born in Germany, the son and grandson of ministers. As a university student, Schweitzer studied theology, earning his Ph.D. in 1899. He also studied music and was an accomplished organist. A highly spiritual man, Schweitzer took the Christian message seriously, considering it consistent with reason and with living a good life.

In his late 20s Schweitzer decided to devote his life to helping those who were the neediest. At 30 he announced, much to the chagrin of many of his friends, that he was going to study medicine so that he could serve as a medical missionary. Many were astounded that he actually took seriously the message of Jesus to serve those in need. As an exemplary critical thinker, he first did his research to see where the need was the greatest. For most of his life he remained in Lambaréné, in what was then the colony of French Equatorial Africa (today Gabon), funding the hospital with royalties from his books and money earned lecturing and playing organ concerts in Europe.

Schweitzer believed in a rational approach to religion. Nothing, he said, should be accepted that is contrary to reason. He believed that much of the zeal in defending Christianity actually interfered with getting to the truth.

DISCUSSION QUESTIONS

1. Discuss how Schweitzer's life reflected his religious beliefs.

2. How is your faith, or lack thereof, reflected in your life plan? Critically analyze ways in which your faith helps or hinders your critical thinking when it comes to making decisions about your life.

STOP AND ASSESS YOURSELF

1. Anwar al-Awlaki, allegedly the spiritual advisor to the terrorists of September 11, 2001, said to journalists that "telling people to give their [lives] for their faith is not an unusual idea. That's the same thing as telling Marines in this country [the United States] *semper fidelis* (always faithful)."[54] Analyze Anwar al-Awlaki's statement.

2. Discuss the argument that faith in God is the same as scientists' belief in the material world—which essentially amounts to an act of faith, since we cannot definitively prove that the material world exists rather than just being an idea in our mind. If the similarity between faith in God and scientific faith in the existence of the material world is valid, why are some people so reluctant to accept the basic assumption of religion but not the basic assumption of science? Support your answer.

3. Is the rationalist position incompatible with faith? Discuss also whether atheism or agnosticism logically follows from rationalism.

4. Discuss how a fideist, a rationalist, and a critical rationalist might each respond to the following claims that the person was carrying out the will of God. Several years ago a woman placed her baby in a microwave oven and turned it on. When arrested, she defended her action, stating that she had acted in faithful obedience to God's command. Relate your answer to the story of Abraham and Isaac.

5. How are we to determine in cases such as those described in the previous exercise whether a person's faith is genuine or if instead the person is suffering from a mental disorder? Discuss how we as a culture should react when people use their faith to justify actions that harm others.

6. College is a time of transition. Religious scripture gives believers few details on how to live out their faith on a modern, secular campus. You may find yourself pressured to act in other ways, such as using illicit drugs or engaging in casual sex, that run counter to your beliefs. Discuss a time when you or someone you know encountered one of these situations. Discuss ways in which strengthening your critical-thinking skills could make you better equipped to handle these challenges.

7. Discuss how a lack of understanding about a religion can contribute to discord rather than a peaceful resolution of problems. Use examples from the war in the Middle East, or the conflict between Israel and the Palestinians, to illustrate your answer. Do research first, if necessary.

8. Most campuses have Catholic, Protestant, and Jewish chaplains, and some also have Muslim chaplains. Set up an appointment (either individually or with others in the class) with one of the chaplains, preferably one from your faith tradition if you have one. Be prepared with questions for the chaplain regarding the role of faith and reason in religion and the implications of this for your own life. After the meeting, write a brief essay summarizing what you learned at the meeting.

9. How does your faith, or lack of faith, influence your everyday decisions? Use specific examples. Looking back at your life plan, note which goals are influenced by your religious beliefs or spirituality. Are the beliefs that shaped these goals consistent with evidence and reason? Explain.

THiNK AGAIN

1. What is the role of reason in critical thinking?
   - Reason helps us analyze beliefs and evidence, make well thought-out decisions, and resolve problems.

2. How does emotion positively and negatively influence critical thinking?
   - Critical thinking is positively influenced by empathy and emotional intelligence. Emotions such as anger and fear, which can lead to stereotyping and avoidance, are negative influences.

3. What are the three approaches to faith and reason?
   - The first approach is fideism, in which faith transcends reason. With rationalism, reason is the source of knowledge, and faith must be consistent with reason. Finally, in critical rationalism, knowledge can come from revelation or reason, which should be compatible with one another.

Perspectives on Reason and Proofs for the Existence of God

A belief in a transcendent God is found in almost all cultures throughout the world. With the exception of some Muslim countries such as Indonesia, Saudi Arabia, and Pakistan, where over 90 percent of people say that religion plays an important role in their lives,[55] the United States is one of the most religious nations in the world with 79 percent of Americans stating that religion plays an important role in their lives. In addition, Americans have a higher degree of certainty regarding the existence of God than citizens of most nations, with 70 percent of Americans agreeing with the statement "I know God really exists and I have no doubts about it" compared to only 43 percent of Canadians, 51 percent of Italians, 24 percent of the French, and 25 percent of South Koreans.[56]

While attendance at religious services declines among young people when they go to college, the decline is less than among young people who do not attend college. Indeed, according to a 2012 Pew Poll, 68 percent of millennials (young people born after 1980) agree with the statement "I never doubt the existence of God."

Can this certainty in the existence of God be supported through logical arguments? In the reading from his *Summa Theologica,* Thomas Aquinas, a critical rationalist, argues that the existence of God can be proven through reason. Richard Dawkins, a rationalist and Professor of Public Understanding at Oxford University in England, refutes Aquinas's arguments in the reading from his book *The God Delusion* (2006).

The Existence of God

THOMAS AQUINAS

Thomas Aquinas (c. 1225–1274) is one of the foremost Catholic theologians and philosophers. In this reading from his *Summa Theologica*, Aquinas presents arguments for the existence of God along with his responses to possible objections to his arguments.

The Existence of God can be proved in five ways.

The first and more manifest way is the argument from motion. It is certain, and evident to our senses, that in the world some things are in motion. Now whatever is in motion is put in motion by another, for nothing can be in motion except it is in potentiality to that towards which it is in motion; whereas a thing moves inasmuch as it is in act. For motion is nothing else than the reduction of something from potentiality to actuality. But nothing can be reduced from potentiality to actuality, except by something in a state of actuality. Thus that which is actually hot, as fire, makes wood, which is potentially hot, to be actually hot, and thereby moves and changes it. Now it is not possible that the same thing should be at once in actuality and potentiality in the same respect, but only in different respects. For what is actually hot cannot simultaneously be potentially hot; but it is simultaneously potentially cold. It is therefore impossible that in the same respect and in the same way a thing should be both mover and moved, *i.e.,* that it should move itself. Therefore, whatever is in motion must be put in motion by another. If that by which it is put in motion be itself put in motion, then this also must needs be put in motion by another, and that by another again. But this cannot go on to infinity, because then there would be no first mover, and, consequently, no other mover; seeing that subsequent movers move only inasmuch as they are put in motion by the first mover; as the staff moves only because it is put in motion by the hand. Therefore it is necessary to arrive at a first mover, put in motion by no other; and this everyone understands to be God.

The second way is from the nature of the efficient cause. In the world of sense we find there is an order of efficient causes. There is no case known (neither is it, indeed, possible) in which a thing is found to be the efficient cause of itself; for so it would be prior to itself, which is impossible. Now in efficient causes it is not possible to go on to infinity, because in all efficient causes following in order, the first is the cause of the intermediate cause, and the intermediate is the cause of the ultimate cause, whether the intermediate cause be several, or only one. Now to take away the cause is to take away the effect. Therefore, if there be no first cause among efficient causes, there will be no ultimate, nor any intermediate cause. But if in efficient causes it is possible to go on to infinity, there will be no first efficient cause, neither will there be an ultimate effect, nor any intermediate efficient causes; all of which is plainly false. Therefore it is necessary to admit a first efficient cause, to which everyone gives the name of God.

The third way is taken from possibility and necessity, and runs thus. We find in nature things that are possible to be and not to be, since they are found to be generated, and to corrupt, and consequently, they are possible to be and not to be. But it is impossible for these always to exist, for that which is possible not to be at some time is not. Therefore, if everything is possible not to be, then at one time there could have been nothing in existence. Now if this were true, even now there would be nothing in existence, because that which does not exist only begins to exist by something already existing. Therefore, if at one time nothing was in existence, it would have been impossible for anything to have begun to exist; and thus even now nothing would be in existence—which is absurd. Therefore, not all beings are merely possible, but there must exist something the existence of which is necessary. But every necessary thing either has its necessity caused by another, or not. Now it is impossible to go on to infinity in necessary things which have their necessity caused by another, as has been already proved in regard to efficient causes. Therefore we cannot but postulate the existence of some being having of itself its own necessity, and not receiving it from another, but rather causing in others their necessity. This all men speak of as God.

The fourth way is taken from the gradation to be found in things. Among beings there are some more and some less good, true, noble and the like. But 'more' and 'less' are predicated of different things, according as they resemble in their different ways something which is the maximum, as a thing is said to be hotter according as it more nearly resembles that which is hottest; so that there is something which is truest, something best, something noblest and, consequently, something which is uttermost being; for those things that are greatest in truth are greatest in being, as it is written in *Metaph.* ii. Now the maximum in any genus is the cause of all in that genus; as fire, which is the maximum heat, is the cause of all hot things. Therefore there must also be something which is to all beings the cause of their being, goodness, and every other perfection; and this we call God.

The fifth way is taken from the governance of the world. We see that things which lack intelligence, such as natural bodies, act for an end, and this is evident from their acting always, or nearly always, in the same way, so as to obtain the best result. Hence it is plain that not fortuitously, but designedly, do they achieve their end. Now whatever lacks intelligence cannot move towards an end, unless it be directed by some being endowed with knowledge and intelligence; as the arrow is shot to its mark by the archer. Therefore some intelligent being exists by whom all natural things are directed to their end; and this being we call God.

REVIEW QUESTIONS

1. How does Aquinas define the term *God*?

2. How does Aquinas respond to the question of whether the existence of God is self-evident?

3. What proofs does Aquinas offer for the existence of God?

The God Delusion

RICHARD DAWKINS

Richard Dawkins, Professor of Public Understanding at Oxford University in England, is a rationalist and an atheist. In the following excerpt from his book *The God Delusion* (2006) Dawkins refutes Aquinas's proofs as based on an unwarranted assumption about the nature of God.

Thomas Aquinas' 'Proofs'

The five 'proofs' asserted by Thomas Aquinas in the thirteenth century don't prove anything, and are easily—though I hesitate to say so, given his eminence—exposed as vacuous. The first three are just different ways of saying the same thing, and they can be considered together. All involve an infinite regress—the answer to a question raises a prior question, and so on *ad infinitum.*

1. *The Unmoved Mover.* Nothing moves without a prior mover. This leads us to a regress, from which the only escape is God. Something had to make the first move, and that something we call God.

2. *The Uncaused Case.* Nothing is caused by itself. Every effect has a prior cause, and again we are pushed back into regress. This has to be terminated by a first cause, which we call God.

3. *The Cosmological Argument.* There must have been a time when no physical things existed. But, since physical things exist now, there must have been something non-physical to bring them into existence, and that something we call God.

All three of these arguments rely upon the idea of a regress and invoke God to terminate it. They make the entirely unwarranted assumption that God himself is immune to the regress. Even if we allow the dubious luxury of arbitrarily conjuring up a terminator to an infinite regress and giving it a name, simply because we need one, there is absolutely no reason to endow that terminator with any of the properties normally ascribed to God: omnipotence, omniscience, goodness, creativity of design, to say nothing of such human attributes as listening to prayers, forgiving his sins and reading innermost thoughts . . . If God is omniscient, he must already know how he is going to intervene to change the course of history using his omnipotence. But that means he can't change his mind about his intervention, which means he is not omnipotent . . .

To return to the infinite regress and the futility of invoking God to terminate it, it is more parsimonious to conjure up, say, a 'big bang singularity', or some other physical concept as yet unknown. Calling it God is at best unhelpful and at worst perniciously misleading. . . . It is by no means clear that God provides a natural terminator to the regresses of Aquinas. That's putting it mildly, as we shall see later. Let's move on down Aquinas' list.

4. *The Argument from Degree.* We notice that things in the world differ. There are degrees of, say, goodness or perfection. But we judge these degrees only by comparison with a maximum. Humans can be both good and bad, so the maximum goodness cannot rest in us. Therefore there must be some other maximum to set the standard for perfection, and we call that maximum God.

That's an argument? You might as well say, people vary in smelliness but we can make the comparison only by reference to a perfect maximum of conceivable smelliness. Therefore there must exist a pre-eminently peerless stinker, and we call him God. Or substitute any dimension of comparison you like, and derive an equivalently fatuous conclusion.

5. *The Teleological Argument, or Argument from Design.* Things in the world, especially living things, look as though they have been designed. Nothing that we know looks designed unless it is designed. Therefore there must have been a designer, and we call him God. . . .

The argument from design is the only one still in regular use today, and it still sounds to many like the ultimate knockdown argument . . . There has probably never been a more devastating rout of popular belief by clever reasoning than Charles Darwin's destruction of the argument from design. It was so unexpected. Thanks to Darwin, it is no longer true to say that nothing that we know looks designed unless it is designed. Evolution by natural selection produces an excellent simulacrum of design, mounting prodigious heights of complexity and elegance . . .

1. On what grounds does Dawkins claim that Aquinas's proofs are invalid because they are based on an infinite regress?

2. What is the argument from degree and why does Dawkins reject it?

3. What is the theological argument from design and why does Dawkins reject it?

THiNK AND DISCUSS

PERSPECTIVES ON REASON AND PROOFS FOR THE EXISTENCE OF GOD

1. Dawkins dismisses Aquinas's proofs as based on an "infinite regress" to which God himself is immune. Discuss how Aquinas or a critical rationalist might respond to Dawkins's argument. Which person makes the strongest argument? Critically evaluate the two arguments.

2. Evaluate Aquinas's argument from degree of good/perfection, as well Dawkins's response to his argument. Identify and critically evaluate the supporting evidence or claims each uses to support his conclusion. Discuss, in light of your evaluation, whether Dawkins does an adequate job in refuting Aquinas's argument.

3. Are evolution and a belief in God incompatible as Dawkins claims? Discuss how Aquinas might respond to Dawkins's position if he were alive today.

4. Elsewhere in his book, Richard Dawkins likens faith to a virus of the mind. Evaluate the analogy. Discuss also how Aquinas might respond to this analogy.

5. Do you believe in the existence of God? Create an argument supporting your belief. If you wish, share your argument with the class for analysis.

3

LANGUAGE
& COMMUNICATION

On September 11, 2012, exactly 11 years after the terrorist attack on the World Trade Center in New York City, an attack on the U.S. Consulate in Benghazi, Libya, left four Americans dead, including Ambassador J. Christopher Stevens, and ten others wounded. Repeated miscommunication compounded the tragedy. Because the cause of the attack initially appeared to be a protest, counterterrorism professionals in the United States were not consulted regarding rescue plans. Instead, U.S. troops were dispatched by helicopter to rescue survivors. However, the rescuers, based on incorrect information from Libyan officials, grossly underestimated the number of survivors awaiting rescue. There were 37—four times as many as thought—which meant there was not enough transportation to rescue in a timely fashion all the survivors who had managed to escape the burning consulate.

How do poor communication skills or lack of communication contribute to distrust and even acts of terrorism?

THiNK FIRST

- What are the primary functions of language?
- Why is it important to pay close attention when evaluating and interpreting definitions of words?
- What is a rhetorical device and how is it used?

 The American public was also misled, whether intentionally or unintentionally, about the nature of the attack. In a statement issued to the public five days later, U.N. Ambassador Susan Rice, based on "talking points" given to her in a CIA memo, stated that the attack was the result of a "spontaneous protest" over a crude anti-Islam video made in the U.S. and posted online, despite the fact that there was no evidence that a spontaneous protest had ever taken place. It was later discovered that the attack had been carefully planned and carried out by well-organized Islamic militants. During the investigation it was also disclosed that the U.S. State Department had failed to pass on to proper authorities communication from the consulate in Benghazi about inadequate security against a possible strike.

Not only did poor communication skills prevent an effective response to the attack, good communication skills might have prevented the attack altogether by allowing the embassy to preempt or to take proper precautions against such an attack.

Good communication skills are an essential component of critical thinking and effective decision making. Effective communication entails not only keeping avenues of communication open but also being clear, accurate, and timely in our communication.

For example, in the Milgram study on obedience (Chapter 1), the men who refused to continue the experiment were able to clearly communicate why they thought the experiment was wrong and why they would not continue giving electric shocks to the study subject. Those who continued to obey the experimenter's orders, in contrast, were unable to articulate their misgivings about the experiment and were often at a loss for words when the experimenter kept insisting that they continue to deliver the shocks.

In this chapter we describe some important aspects of language and explain the relationship between language and critical thinking. In this chapter we will:

- Define what we mean by language and discuss its relation to culture
- Learn the different functions of language
- Discuss ways in which language and stereotypes shape our view of the world
- Learn the different types of definitions
- Differentiate between a purely verbal dispute and a genuine disagreement

- Look at communication styles and how sex and culture may influence them
- Examine the role of nonverbal communication
- Look at ways in which language and rhetoric can be used to manipulate people

Finally, we will examine the issue of free-speech zones on campuses and the justification for having rules restricting speech that would normally be protected off campus.

WHAT IS LANGUAGE?

Language is a system of communication that involves a set of arbitrary symbols, whether spoken, written, or nonverbal, as in the case of sign language. Communication without representational or symbolic elements includes the vocalizations of babies to signal a state of discomfort and the purr of a cat to signal contentment.

Human language is profoundly social—we are born into a language. By creating a shared reality among people, language is the primary means of transmitting cultural concepts and traditions. Good communication also conveys correct information so we can make effective decisions, as noted in the Benghazi case.

Although there are 6,800 known languages in the world, according to linguist Noam Chomsky all human languages use the same basic universal grammatical rules or syntax; in other words, we are born with an innate ability to acquire language.[1] These very basic, inborn rules, he claims, allow us to combine words and phrases into unique utterances and to discuss any topic. Not all linguists accept Chomsky's theory. Geoffrey Sampson believes that it is possible for children to learn a language without possessing these inborn rules.[2] While most languages do seem to share a universal grammar, Sampson maintains that this is based on the fact that linguists tend to study more common languages. He points out that there are at least a few languages, such as some indigenous Australian and Papuan languages, that do not seem to use universal rules of grammar. Sampson proposes that children are good at learning languages because they are good at learning quickly and easily in general.

> **language** A system of communication that involves a set of arbitrary symbols.

Connections

How can a sampling error lead to an erroneous conclusion in science?
See Chapter 12, p. 379.

Languages of the World

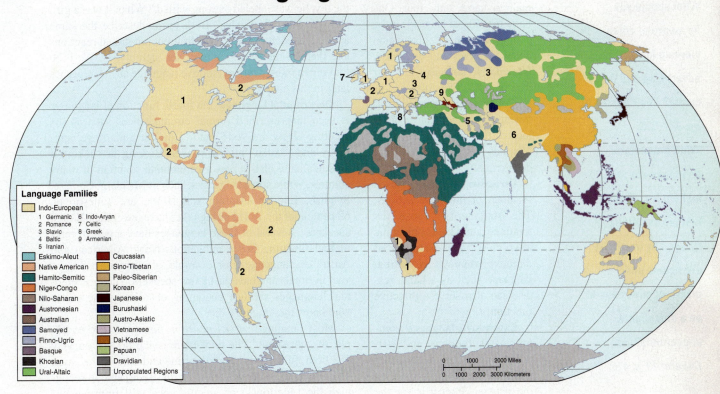

Language Families

- Indo-European
  - 1 Germanic 6 Indo-Aryan
  - 2 Romance   7 Celtic
  - 3 Slavic   8 Greek
  - 4 Baltic   9 Armenian
  - 5 Iranian
- Eskimo-Aleut
- Native American
- Hamito-Semitic
- Niger-Congo
- Nilo-Saharan
- Austronesian
- Australian
- Samoyed
- Finno-Ugric
- Basque
- Khosian
- Ural-Altaic
- Caucasian
- Sino-Tibetan
- Paleo-Siberian
- Korean
- Japanese
- Burushaski
- Austro-Asiatic
- Vietnamese
- Dai-Kadai
- Papuan
- Dravidian
- Unpopulated Regions

0 1000 2000 Miles
0 1000 2000 3000 Kilometers

Not all language is verbal—much can be communicated through gesture, expression, and body language.

Functions of Language

What should you be aware of when viewing images in advertising and the media? *See Chapter 10, pp. 323–326.*

What procedures do judges use to make it less likely that jurors will be swayed by irrational arguments and preconceptions based on a defendant's appearance? *See Chapter 13, p. 415.*

Connections

Language serves many functions; it can be informative, expressive, directive, or ceremonial, to name only four. One basic function of language is the communication of information about ourselves and the world. **Informative language** is either true or false. Examples of this type of language include the following: "Princeton University is located in New Jersey" and "Capital punishment does not deter crime."

Directive language is used to direct or influence actions. The statements "Close the window" and "Please meet me after class" are examples of directive language. Nonverbal language such as a hand gesture can also serve a directive function.

Expressive language communicates feelings and attitudes and is used to bring about an emotional impact on the listener. Poetry is for the most part expressive language. Religious worship may also function to express feelings of awe.

Expressive language may include **emotive words**, which are used to elicit certain emotions. In an article on toddlers who snatch toys, when it was a boy who snatched the toy, he was labeled "strong willed." When it was a girl, she was labeled "pushy." Both terms describe the same action, yet each evokes quite different emotional reactions and thereby reinforces cultural sex stereotypes. We'll be looking in more depth at emotive language and stereotypes later in this chapter.

Ceremonial language, the fourth function of language, is used in prescribed formal circumstances such as the greeting "How are you?" and "I do" in a marriage ceremony and "Amen" after a prayer. Bowing or shaking a person's hand also serves a ceremonial function in many cultures. While some languages, such as Mandarin Chinese, Spanish, English, Arabic, and Hindi, are widespread, 60 percent of the world's languages have fewer than 10,000 speakers.[3] Several of these languages have a purely ceremonial function. Some indigenous North American and Australian languages, for example, are used only once a year in rituals and have just a few speakers. These ceremonial languages are fast becoming obsolete as the elders who know the language die.

Most language serves *multiple functions*. For example, the statement "The final exam is at 3:00 P.M. on May 16" both informs us about the time and date of the exam and directs us to arrive for the exam. Being able to recognize the function(s) of an utterance will improve our

Thinking Outside the Box

SALLY RIDE, *Astronaut*

As a child, Sally Ride (1951–2012) loved to solve problems. Her friends from college have described her as "calm and totally focused . . . always able to see to the heart of things . . . to quickly think, figure it out, crystallize it."* An exemplary critical thinker, she was able to clearly articulate and develop strategies to meet her life goals. Realizing the importance of communication skills to achieving her goals, at college she double-majored in English and Physics.

Ride was just finishing up her Ph.D. in Physics at Stanford University when she saw an announcement in the college newspaper that NASA was looking for a new group of astronauts. She applied that day. She was one of 35 picked for the astronaut class of 1978 out of more than 8,000 applicants. In part because of her outstanding analytical and critical thinking skills, Ride became the youngest as well as the first female American astronaut in space in 1983. Because of her exemplary communication skills, Ride was chosen to serve as Capsule Communicator for the first and second shuttle flights—the person on the ground who handles all the ground-to-staff flight communication. She later helped create NASA's Office of Exploration.

An excellent speaker and writer, Ride addressed the United Nations and put together the report for NASA, *Leadership and the American Future in Space*. Ride also wrote several children's books on space exploration. Today the organization she founded, Sally Ride Science, sponsors, among other things, camps that encourage girls' interest in science and also help them to develop their leadership, writing, and communication skills.

DISCUSSION QUESTIONS

1. Looking back at the characteristics of a good critical thinker listed on page 9 in Chapter 1, discuss ways in which Ride exemplified these qualities.

2. Has there ever been a time when you missed a great opportunity? Discuss what role, if any, lack of good critical-thinking skills played in this.

*Carole Ann Camp, *Sally Ride: First American Woman in Space* (Springfield, NJ: Enslow Publishers, 1997), p. 19.

---

communication skills. After all, we don't want to be the sort of boorish people who take the ceremonial utterance "How are you?" as a request for detailed information about their health and lives and then end up wondering why people avoid us.

Being able to use language effectively to convey information, provide directions, and express our feelings is essential to collaborative critical thinking and fulfilling our life goals. For example, astronaut Sally Ride's exemplary communication skills contributed to her success as the first American woman in space (see "Thinking Outside the Box: Sally Ride, Astronaut").

informative language Language that is either true or false.

directive language Language used to direct or influence actions.

expressive language Language that communicates feelings and attitudes.

emotive words Words that are used to elicit certain emotions.

ceremonial language Language used in particular prescribed formal circumstances.

The flexibility of human language and the multiple functions that it serves allows us to generate an almost unlimited number of sentences. Like culture, human language is constantly changing. The English we know bears only minor resemblance to the English used 1,000 years ago.

The flexibility and open-ended nature of human language, while greatly enriching our ability to communicate ideas and feelings, can also contribute to ambiguity and misunderstanding. For example, when the person who is talking to you at a party says, "I'll call you," it's

> In a study of junior high and high school students, more than half of the boys surveyed said that when a male took a female out for an expensive dinner, it was understood that she would reciprocate the invitation by having sex with him.

not always clear what he or she means. Even apparently simple sentences such as this are dense with meaning. Is it a straightforward informative sentence? Or is there more to it? Is he (or she) asking you for a date? Is he expressing interest in spending more time with you? Or is he merely saying he'll call to be polite, but not really meaning it? And what if he does call the following day and suggests, "Let's go out to dinner"? Once again, is he asking you for a date? Is he implying that he is going to pay for the meal, or does he expect you to split the cost or even pay the whole bill? Does he expect something in return for taking you to dinner?

If we don't first clarify what the other person means or what his or her expectations are, there may be serious and dire consequences. For example, miscommunication is sometimes a factor in rape. In a study of junior high and high school students, more than half of the boys surveyed said that when a male took a female out for an expensive dinner, it was understood that she would reciprocate the invitation by having sex with him. Nonverbal language in particular may be misinterpreted. In a similar study, most college men said they considered lack of resistance on the part of a woman as consent to sex.[4] Poor communication skills are also one of the contributing facts in medical errors (see page 122). Intellectual curiosity and being mindful of how language is being used, two of the critical thinking skills, can make us less susceptible to misunderstandings and manipulation.

Nonverbal Language

We often look to nonverbal cues, such as body language or tone of voice, when interpreting someone's communication. Indeed, many jurors make up their mind about a case mainly on the basis of the nonverbal behavior of the defendant.[5] Although some nonverbal communication is universal, such as smiling when happy, raising the eyebrow to signal recognition, and making the "disgust face" to show repulsion, much of it is culturally determined.

We frequently use nonverbal communication to reinforce verbal communication. A nod when we say "yes," a hand gesture when we say "over there," folding our arms across our body when we say "no"—all serve to reinforce our words. Because much of nonverbal communication occurs at a less conscious level, people tend to pay more attention to it when it conflicts with the verbal message.

In a 2013 interview with Oprah Winfrey, cyclist Lance Armstrong, a seven-time Tour de France winner, confessed to having used performance-enhancing drugs during his career, including testosterone, human growth hormone, and a hormone that stimulates red blood cell production. Armstrong had for years denied allegations of use of performance-enhancing drugs. Despite his confession, some experts believed that, based on his body language, Armstrong was not telling the whole truth (see Analyzing Images, "Nonverbal Communication and Withholding Information," page 72).

Images, such as photos and artwork, can also be used to communicate ideas and feelings. It is said that "a picture conveys a thousand words." Images not only convey information but also can evoke emotions that may motivate us to take action in ways that words often cannot. At Abu Ghraib prison in Iraq, the soldier who blew the whistle did so only after seeing photos of detainees in sexually humiliating positions. "Words can't describe my reaction," said Sgt. Joseph Darby. "I was shocked. I was very disappointed and outraged."[6] The images outraged people throughout the world and led to questions about the morality of the war in Iraq and to the reform of interrogation practices at Abu Ghraib prison (see Analyzing Images: Abuse at Abu Ghraib prison, Iraq, page 18). Media images of the earthquake devastation in Haiti in 2010 motivated viewers to donate millions of dollars to help the people of Haiti.

In summary, we should keep in mind that language is, to a large extent, a cultural construct. Furthermore, because of the different functions and the flexibility of human language, our choice of words and our nonverbal cues can affect how a message is interpreted—or misinterpreted—by other people. As good critical thinkers, we need to be clear in our communication and conscious of how language is being used in a particular instance. We need to be willing to ask people for clarification if we are uncertain about the meaning of their communication.

Animal Language*

Language serves to enhance group cohesiveness among social animals. Honeybees use symbolic gestures in the form of dances that communicate the direction and distance the other bees must fly to reach food sources or other things of interest. Birds, ground squirrels, and some nonhuman primates have different alarm calls that are recognized by other members of their species even when the predator is not present. A recent study of finch calls found that the birds' calls, like human language, followed "strict rules of syntax."**

Like humans, these animals understand the relationship between the signals they use and the events these signals refer to. They are not simply expressing an emotion or communicating about something that is only in the moment. They are actually using symbolic language to refer to things in the outside world, things that do not need to be immediately present for them to understand what is being communicated.

Many animals—including apes, chimps, dolphins, dogs, and parrots—can also understand several words in human languages and respond to commands containing strings of words. The gorilla Koko, for example, has a vocabulary of more than 1,000 human words. The border collie Chaser also has a vocabulary of more than 1,000 words.

DISCUSSION QUESTIONS

1. *Humans also use nonverbal communication, such as dance. Give examples of ways in which you use nonverbal language such as dance or gestures to communicate information and serve the other three functions of language.*

2. *Discuss how barriers to critical thinking such as narrow-mindedness can prevent us from seeing the use of language by other animals as well as keep us from appreciating the richness and diversity of languages of other cultures.*

*For more information on language in nonhuman animals, see Jacques Vauclair, *Animal Cognition* (Cambridge, MA: Harvard University Press, 1996), and Donald R. Griffin, *Animals Minds: Beyond Cognition to Consciousness* (Chicago: University of Chicago Press, 2001). See also http://www.thelowell.org/index.php?option=com_content&view=article&id=1202 for more on primatologist Netzin Gerald-Steklis's work on communication with gorillas.
**Jennifer Barone, "When Good Tweets Go Bad," Discover, November 2011, p. 16.

Nonverbal Communication and Withholding Information. Cyclist

Lance Armstrong is pictured above in a January 2013 television interview with Oprah Winfrey. In the interview, Armstrong confessed to his use of performance-enhancing drugs. Despite his confession, some people felt that Armstrong was not being completely forthright. Patti Woods, a body language expert, found Armstrong's body language "unsettling" during the interview.* Several times Armstrong pressed his lips together, which Woods interpreted as his withholding information. He also covered his mouth frequently, another indication that he was "blocking" information or lying.

DISCUSSION QUESTIONS

1. *What was your initial reaction at seeing the above picture? Do the images from the interview influence the way you feel and think about Armstrong? Support your answers.*

2. *Body language plays an important role in jurors' perception of a defendant's guilt. If this had been a trial, discuss whether the jurors should have been allowed to see Armstrong making his "confession," or if a law should be put in place that sets the defendant out of the jurors' view so as not to allow the defendant's body language to influence jurors' decisions.*

*For a link to the interview and more information on Woods's assessment, go to: http://bodylanguagelady.blogspot.com/search/label/Lance%20Armstrong%20interview%20with%20Oprah.

STOP AND ASSESS YOURSELF

I. Identify which language function(s)—informative, directive, expressive, ceremonial—are most likely served by of each of the following passages.

*a. The planet Pluto was first observed at the Lowell Observatory in Flagstaff, Arizona.

b. I'd like an espresso (customer to waitress at coffee shop).

c. "God is dead." (Friedrich Nietzsche)

*d. Wow! I'm so happy. My application for a scholarship just got approved.

e. Excuse me, but this is a nonsmoking area (said to a smoker).

f. Abracadabra.

*g. "A national debate is raging between women's groups and law-enforcement types stepping in to protect the health of a fetus from a mother who they believe will not, or cannot, look after it."[7]

h. "Honor thy mother and thy father." (Deuteronomy)

i. "You cannot go into a 7-11 or a Dunkin' Donuts unless you have a slight Indian accent. . . . I'm not joking" (then-Senator Joe Biden on C-SPAN, June 2006).

*j. You should be careful about what you eat at college. The average college student puts on 15 pounds during his or her freshman year.

k. Thank you.

2. Working in small groups, make a list of variations in language used by students at your college who come from different regions of the United States, or the country where your college is located. Discuss how these variations reflect cultural differences in these regions.

3. Most humans and dogs are able to communicate basic messages or feelings to each other. What kinds of behaviors do you (or someone you know who owns a dog) engage in when you want to express anger, happiness, hunger, or playfulness? Discuss what these behaviors tell us about the effectiveness and importance of nonverbal communication.

4. Discuss ways in which the following passages from religious scripture may be interpreted and what role culture plays in these interpretations.

a. Passion for gold can never be right; the pursuit of money leads a man astray. (Ecclesiastes 31:5)

b. Whosoever kills even one human being, other than for man slaughter or tyranny on earth, it would be as if they had killed all of humankind. (Koran 5:32)

c. Wives, be subject to your husbands as to the Lord; for the man is the head of the woman, just as Christ also is the head of the church. (Ephesians 5:22–23)[8]

d. The Master said, A young man's duty is to behave well to his parents at home and to his elders abroad, to be cautious in giving promises and punctual in keeping them, to have kindly feelings towards everyone, but seek the intimacy of the Good. (*The Analects of Confucius,* Book I: 6)

5. The borrowing of words from other languages is evident in Spanglish, in which Latin American immigrants and their descendants in the United States use Spanish and English interchangeably, even in the same sentences. Spanglish is used not only on the streets but also on some radio and television stations.[9] Some people maintain that Spanglish should not be taught in schools. Others claim it is a legitimate and evolving language. Discuss what you would do if you were a professor and a student wanted to hand in an essay written in Spanglish or used Spanglish in a class.

6. We can rearrange words and phrases into novel sentences, some of which have never before been uttered. Write a five-word sentence. Type the sentence in quotation marks into an Internet search engine such as Google, which has indexed over 30 trillion web pages. Did the search engine find your five-word sentence on any of these pages?[10] Discuss the results of your search.

7. Find an argument in a newspaper or on the Internet that is trying to persuade the reader to adopt a certain point of view, such as an article on why you should get involved in sports or an article on why the education system is failing children. Write a page on how the writer is using language or discourse to achieve this objective.

8. Research the history of a language such as English, Japanese, Navaho, or Arabic. Identify and write a short essay on two ways in which the evolution of this language reflects the history of the people and their culture.

*Answers to selected exercises are found in the Solutions Manual at the end of the book.

DEFINITIONS

The English language has one of the largest vocabularies in the world—about a quarter of a million different words. This is in part because English has incorporated so many foreign terms. Some of these words in the English language are no longer in use, and some have acquired new meanings over time.

That is why we cannot simply assume that someone else is using a word or phrase as we are. In addition to understanding the history of a term, it's helpful to understand the difference between the denotative and connotative meanings of words, as well as to be familiar with some of the different types of definitions, in order to communicate accurately and clearly.

denotative meaning The meaning of a word or phrase that expresses the properties of the object.

connotative meaning The meaning of a word or phrase that is based on past personal experiences or associations.

stereotyping Labeling people based on their membership in a group.

stipulative definition A definition given to a new term or a new combination of old terms.

Denotative and Connotative Meanings

Words have both denotative and connotative meanings. The **denotative meaning** of a word or phrase expresses the properties of the object, being, or event the word is symbolizing; it is the same as its lexical or dictionary definition. For example, the denotative meaning of the word *dog* is a domesticated member of the species *Canis familiaris*. Any being that has both of these properties (domesticated and a member of the species *Canis familiaris*) is a dog by definition.

The **connotative meaning** of a word or phrase includes feelings and personal thoughts that are elicited on the basis of past experiences and associations. The word dog may elicit thoughts of a loyal pet or—at the opposite extreme—something that is worthless or of poor quality, a despicable person, or an ugly person. The connotative meaning(s) of a term may be included in a list of dictionary definitions, or may simply be shared among a specific group of people.

Language is not neutral. It reflects cultural values and influences how we see the world. Language reinforces cultural concepts of what it means to be normal through the use of stereotypes that have certain connotative meanings. In **stereotyping**, rather than seeing people as individuals, we see and label them as members of a particular group. The labels we use shape the way we see ourselves and others. Labels can also stigmatize and isolate people. The label *mentally ill* reinforces our world view that some illnesses are all in the mind, thus legitimating the withholding of appropriate medical care and health-care benefits from people with this label. Sexist language such as *chick* and *ho* reinforces gender stereotypes and the view that women are irrational and inferior to men and therefore deserve inferior treatment in the workplace and at home.

Stipulative Definitions

Lexical or dictionary definitions are only one type of definition. Other types include stipulative, precising, theoretical, and persuasive. A **stipulative definition** is one given to a new term such as *bytes* and *decaf* or to a new combination of old terms such as *skyscraper* and *laptop*. A stipulative definition may also be a new definition of an existing word, such as the addition of "heterosexual" to the definitions of the term *straight*.

Stipulative definitions often start off as jargon or slang and are initially limited to a particular group of people. Young people may create their own terminology, such as *beer goggles* and *sexting* as a way of distancing themselves from previous generations. As such, a stipulative definition is neither true nor false—merely more or less useful.

The creation of new terms and stipulative definitions reflects cultural and historical changes. The terms *date rape* and *sexual harassment* were coined during the feminist movement in the 1970s to call attention to occurrences that were previously not regarded as noteworthy. The introduction of the terms *pro-life* and *pro-choice* contributed to the public's conceptualization and the polarization of the abortion issue. Trade names such as Jell-O, Band-Aid, and Kleenex have also become part of our vocabulary to refer to any of these products in general.

If a stipulative definition becomes commonly accepted, then it will become a lexical or dictionary definition. For example, the term for sneakers among some Chinese is now "Nai-ke," a term that Nike, which is trying to create a market for its athletic shoes among China's youth and rising middle class, hopes will catch on and become part of the Chinese vocabulary.

Lexical Definitions

A **lexical definition** is the commonly used dictionary definition or denotative meaning of a term. Unlike a stipulative definition, whose meaning is fluid depending on the circumstances, a lexical definition is either correct or incorrect. Most dictionaries are updated at least once a year. The criterion that dictionary editors use in deciding if a new word or stipulative definition should become part of the dictionary is whether the word is used in enough printed sources.

The two primary purposes of a lexical definition are to increase our vocabulary and to reduce ambiguity. To determine if we are using a lexical definition correctly, we simply consult a dictionary. Of course, some words have several lexical definitions. In these cases we need to clarify which definition we are using. Even within one language, lexical definitions of a word may vary from country to country. *Homely* in the United States usually means "lacking in physical attractiveness; plain" and carries a negative connotation. In Canada and England, in contrast, the term *homely* means "comfortable and cozy" or "homey."

Just as new words are continually emerging, so too can words that were once in common usage become obsolete. Eventually, outdated terms that are no longer useful are dropped from the dictionary. For instance, we no longer use the term *lubitorium* for "service station," since it is no longer descriptive of the modern self-service stations.

Controlling the definitions of words can be used to create an advantage in discussions of controversial issues. In 2004, textbooks that defined marriage as "a union between two people" were withdrawn from use in Texas public schools until the definition could be changed to a "a union between a man and a woman," thus giving control in public discourse to those who oppose same-sex marriage.

Precising Definitions

Precising definitions are used to reduce vagueness that occurs when it is not clear exactly what meaning a word or concept encompasses. Precising definitions go beyond the ordinary lexical definition of a term in order to establish the exact limits of the definition. For example, the terms *class participation* or *term paper* in a course syllabus may need to be defined more precisely by the instructor for purposes of grading.

Similarly, ordinary dictionary definitions may be too vague in a court of law. Under what precise circumstances does "date or acquaintance rape" occur? How should *coercion* and *consent* be defined for legal purposes? Did an alleged victim give her consent to have sexual intercourse by not rebuffing his advances, or did the accused use coercion? Should "consent" in these cases, as some argue, require explicit verbal communication between the man and the woman regarding approval to engage in sexual interaction?[11]

Confusion can result if a definition is too vague or lacks precision. The Individuals with Disabilities Education Act defines a *learning disability* as a "disorder in one or more of the basic psychological processes involved in understanding or in using spoken or written language, which may manifest itself in an imperfect ability to listen, think, speak, read, write, spell, or to do mathematical calculations." However, this definition is so vague that it is difficult to determine whom it covers. Indeed, estimates of

> **lexical definition** The commonly used dictionary definition.
>
> **precising definition** A definition used to reduce vagueness that goes beyond the ordinary lexical definition.

Critical THiNKing in Action

Say What?

New words of the 1970s: biofeedback; chairperson; consciousness-raising; couch potato; date rape; downsize; Ebonics; focus group; gigabyte; global warming; he/she; in vitro fertilization; junk food; learning disability; personal computer; pro-choice; punk rock; sexual harassment; smart bomb; VCR; video game; word processor

New words of the 1980s: AIDS; alternative medicine; assisted suicide; attention deficit disorder; biodiversity; cell phone; computer virus; cyberspace; decaf; do-rag; e-mail; gender gap; Internet; laptop; mall rat; managed care; premenstrual syndrome; rap music; safe sex; sport utility vehicle (SUV); telemarketing; virtual reality; yuppie

New words of the 1990s: artificial life; call waiting; carjacking; chronic fatigue syndrome; dot-com; eating disorder; family leave; hyperlink; nanotechnology; senior moment; spam; strip mall; Web site; World Wide Web.

New words of the 2000s: biodiesel; bioweapon; blog; civil union; carbon footprint; counterterrorism; cybercrime; desk jockey; enemy combatant; google; green-collar; hazmat; hoophead; infowar; insourcing; jihadist; nanobot; sexile; speed dating; spyware; staycation; supersize; truthiness; webinar; woot

New words of the 2010s: boomerang child; carpet-bombing; cybercast; fist bump; gastropub; helicopter parent; phish; sexting; tweet; unfriend; woot

1. Identify five other words that have been added to the English language since 2010. Discuss what these words tell us about our society and changes since 2010.

2. What are some of the differences between the words used by you and those used by your parents and grandparents? How do these reflect differences in the culture that you were brought up in? Discuss how understanding these differences can help you be a better communicator and critical thinker.

---

the percentage of the population with a learning disability vary widely from 1 percent to 30 percent.[12]

To use another example, there is no agreed upon definition of "terrorism" at the moment. The term is so broadly defined now as to include almost any act of violence, whether politically motivated or not, such as "intimate terrorism." There are calls for the government to come up with a more precise definition for use in surveillance or arrests for terrorist activities. Precising definitions may have to be updated as new discoveries or circumstances, such as the threat of terrorism, demand a more accurate definition. In 2006, with the discovery of several new bodies orbiting the sun in our solar system, the International Astronomical Union (IAU) voted to add a new requirement to its definition of *planet*. The new definition required that planets had to not merely orbit the sun and be "nearly round," they also have to "dominate their gravitational domains." This more precise definition eliminated Pluto from the pantheon of planets. There was so much outcry at the exclusion of Pluto from planethood that in 2008 the IAU expanded its definition of planet to once again include Pluto by

the sciences. For example, alcoholism is defined, in part, in the *Taber's Cyclopedic Medical Dictionary* as "a chronic, progressive and potentially fatal disease. . . . Alcoholism is an illness and should be so treated." Unlike a lexical definition, which merely describes the symptoms or effects, this medical definition puts forth a theory regarding the nature of alcoholism—it is a disease, not a moral failing.

Operational definitions are another type of precising definition. An operational definition is a concise definition of a measure used to provide standardization in data collection and interpretation. The lexical definition of obese—"very fat or overweight"—is not precise enough for a physician to determine if a person's weight is a health risk or if the person is a candidate for gastric bypass surgery. Instead, the medical profession defines obesity operationally in terms of body mass index, or BMI.

Connections

What is the role of operational definitions in science? *See Chapter 12, p. 368.*

Operational definitions may change over time. For instance, the definition of poverty varies from country to country as well as over time. In the United States the poverty threshold was defined by the U.S. Department of Health and Human Services in 2012 as $11,170 for a single individual. In 1982 the poverty threshold was defined as $4,680 for a single individual.[13]

adding a subcategory of planets known as dwarf planets or "plutoids," thus placating the fans of Pluto.

Theoretical definitions are a special class of precising definitions used to explain the specific nature of a term. Proposing a theoretical definition is akin to proposing a theory. These definitions are more likely to be found in dictionaries for specialized disciplines, such as

Body Mass Index

Weight in Pounds

Height in Inches	120	130	140	150	160	170	180	190	200	210	220	230	240	250
4'6"	29	31	34	36	39	41	43	46	48	51	53	56	58	60
4'8"	27	29	31	34	36	38	40	43	45	47	49	52	54	56
4'10"	25	27	29	31	34	36	38	40	42	44	46	48	50	52
5'0"	23	25	27	29	31	33	35	37	39	41	43	45	47	49
5'2"	22	24	26	27	29	31	33	35	37	38	40	42	44	46
5'4"	21	22	24	26	28	29	31	33	34	36	38	40	41	43
5'6"	19	21	23	24	26	27	29	31	32	34	36	37	39	40
5'8"	18	20	21	23	24	26	27	29	30	32	34	35	37	38
5'10"	17	19	20	22	23	24	26	27	29	30	32	33	35	36
6'0"	16	18	19	20	22	23	24	26	27	28	30	31	33	34
6'2"	15	17	18	19	21	22	23	24	26	27	28	30	31	32
6'4"	15	16	17	18	20	21	22	23	24	26	27	28	29	30
6'6"	14	15	16	17	19	20	21	22	23	24	25	27	28	29
6'8"	13	14	15	17	18	19	20	21	22	23	24	25	26	28

■ Underweight ■ Healthy Weight
■ Overweight ■ Obese

Persuasive Definitions

Persuasive definitions are used as a means to persuade or influence others to accept our point of view. The definition of *taxation* as a form of theft and of *genetic engineering* as playing God with the human genome are both examples of persuasive definitions. Persuasive definitions often use **emotive language**, such as the negative term *theft* in the first definition.

There is nothing inherently wrong with using persuasive or emotive language. Emotive language in poetry and fiction, for example, is clearly appropriate. However, if our primary intention is to convey information, then it is best to avoid using it. Persuasive definitions, because their primary intention is to influence our attitudes rather than convey information, can be a problem in critical thinking when they distract us from getting to the truth.

theoretical definitions A type of precising definition explaining a term's nature.

operational definitions A definition with a standardized measure for use in data collection and interpretation.

persuasive definition A definition used as a means to influence others to accept our view.

emotive language Language that is purposely chosen to elicit a certain emotional impact.

STOP AND ASSESS YOURSELF

1. Discuss the denotative and connotative meanings of each of the following words: *gay, communism, moon, marriage, doormat, easy, mouse, death.*

2. What stereotypes come to mind when you hear the following words: *African American, bachelor, bachelorette, college dropout, frat boy, housewife, illegal alien, liberal, conservative, superstar, Third World country, tomboy, white person*? Discuss ways in which each of these stereotypes conveys cultural values.

3. Theologian Mary Daly writes: "The Biblical and popular image of God as a great patriarch in heaven . . . has dominated the imagination of millions over thousands of years. The symbol of the Father God, spawned in the human imagination and sustained as plausible by patriarchy, has in turn rendered service to this type of society by making its mechanisms for the oppression of women appear right and fitting."[14]

Discuss Daly's claim that the identification of God as male is oppressive to women. Discuss whether we should change the language used in religious texts and services to gender-neutral language in light of the role language plays in shaping our world views.

4. For each of the following, identify which type of definition is being used.

*a. Intoxication is defined as having a blood alcohol content of .08 percent.

b. A *dream* is our unconscious acting out and expressing its hidden desires.

c. An *atheist* is a person who is in denial about the existence of God.

*d. *Abuse* is the willful infliction of injury, unreasonable confinement, or cruel punishment.

e. Obama came up with a new term "snowmageddon" to describe the heavy blizzards that struck Washington, D.C., in the winter of 2010.

f. The moon is a natural satellite orbiting earth that formed about 3 to 4 billion years ago when a small planetary body struck the earth blowing out debris, some of which combined to form the moon.

*g. *Capital punishment* is state-sanctioned murder.

h. *Neglect* is defined as "the failure to provide for one's self the goods or services which are necessary to avoid physical harm, mental anguish, or mental illness, or the failure of a caretaker to provide such goods or services and includes malnourishment and dehydration, over- or undermedication, lack of heat, running water, or electricity; unsanitary living conditions; lack of medical care; and lack of personal hygiene or clothes."[15]

i. *Spanglish* is a form of Spanish that includes many English words.

*j. *Religion* is the opiate of the masses.

k. A *genius* is a person with an IQ of 140 or above.

l. How about adding the following definition for the word *cellblock:* those idiots who always have their cell phones pressed to their heads?

5. Create your own stipulative definition of a term. Introduce your term and definition to the class. Vote on which ones the class thinks are most useful. Looking at the three most useful terms, discuss what might be done to make these become lexical definitions someday.

6. Define *hunger* and *love* using lexical, persuasive, and operational definitions.

7. *Beer goggles, sexting,* and *social media* are all terms that are popular on college campuses. Discuss how the use of these terms reflects how young people think about college life and relationships. Does the use of these new terms affect how you think about college and relationships and, if so, how?

8. How would you answer the Gallup poll question "Do you consider yourself a feminist or not?" Include a definition of, or list of attributes of, *feminist* as part of your answer. Compare your definition with those used by others in the class. Discuss the extent to which differences in definitions of this key term explain the current polarization on feminism.

9. Collect passages from magazines and newspapers of language used to describe people of different sexes and different racial and ethnic groups. Write a short essay discussing whether these descriptions are important to the story or are more a reflection of stereotyping and reinforcing a particular cultural view.

10. How do the labels you use for yourself influence your self-esteem and your goals? If you want to, share some of your labels and the impact of these labels on your life plan with others in the class.

*Answers to selected exercises are found in the Solutions Manual at the end of the book.

EVALUATING DEFINITIONS

Clearly defining key terms is an essential component of clear communication and critical thinking. Knowing how to determine if a particular definition is good makes it less likely that we will get caught up in a purely verbal dispute or fallacious reasoning.

Five Criteria

There are several criteria we can use to evaluate definitions. The following are five of the more important ones:

1. *A good definition is neither too broad nor too narrow.* Definitions that include too much are too broad; those that include too little are too narrow. For example, the definition of *mother* as a "woman who has given birth to a child" is too narrow. Women who adopt children are also mothers. Similarly, the definition of *war* as "an armed conflict" is too broad because it would include street fights, police action against suspected criminals, and domestic violence. Some definitions are both too broad and too narrow, such as the definition of *penguin* as "a bird that lives in Antarctica." This definition is too broad because many other species of birds live in Antarctica and too narrow because penguins also live in other regions of the Southern Hemisphere such as South Africa.

2. *A good definition should state the essential attributes of the term being defined.* The definition of a community college as "an institution of higher education, without residential facilities, that is often funded by the government, and is characterized by a two-year curriculum that leads either to an associate degree or transfer to a four-year college"[16] includes the essential characteristics of a community college.

3. *A good definition is not circular.* You should avoid using the term itself, or variations of the term, within the definition, as in "a teacher is a person who teaches," and "erythropoiesis is the production of erythrocytes." Since a circular definition gives little or no new information about the meaning of the term, it is understandable only to a person who already knows the definition of the term.

4. *A good definition avoids obscure and figurative language.* Definitions should be clear and understandable. Some

definitions are written in such obscure terms that they are understandable only to professionals in the field such as the definition of *net* as "anything reticulated or decussated at equal distances with interstices between the intersections."[17]

Political scientist Arthur Lupia maintains that the disconnect between the hard scientific evidence of human-caused global warming and the public's

failure to address the problem stems in large part from the overuse of obscure and technical language by scientists. Too many scientists use highly technical terms, such as *distribution functions* and *albedos* in defining and explaining global warming to laypeople. Lupia suggests that science should treat effective communication itself as a subject of inquiry.[18]

Figurative language should also be avoided in definitions. "Love is like a red, red rose" may be a moving line in a poem, but it is hardly an adequate definition of love.

5. *A good definition avoids emotive language.* The definitions of a feminist as "a man-hater" and of a man as "an oppressor of women" are just two examples of definitions that are geared to inflame emotions rather than stimulate rational discussion of an issue.

Knowing how to evaluate definitions contributes to successful and clear communication.

Verbal Disputes Based on Ambiguous Definitions

If a tree falls in a forest and no one is around to hear it, does it make a sound? You argue that it doesn't; your friend just as adamantly argues that it does. You both end up upset at what appears to be pure obstinacy on the other's part. But before getting into a full-blown argument, step back and ask yourself if you and your friend are using the same definition for the key term(s).

Defining key terms, as we noted above, is an essential component of clear communication and good critical thinking. If we neglect to do so, we may end up in a verbal dispute as we talk past each other and get increasingly frustrated. In the case in the previous paragraph, you and your friend are using different definitions of the key term *sound*. You are defining *sound* in terms of perception: "the sensation produced by stimulation of organs of hearing." Your friend, in contrast, is defining *sound* as a physicist would: "mechanical vibrations transmitted through an elastic medium."[19] And these are only two of the thirty-eight definitions of *sound* used in a standard dictionary! In other words, your dispute is purely verbal. Once you both agree on the definition of the key term *sound*, what appeared at first to be a heady philosophical dispute disappears.

Verbal disputes occur more often than most of us probably realize. Some of the disagreement regarding "global warming" or "climate change" is based around how to use the terms. For example, to what extent does the warming have to be based on human activities? How many years of increased warming count as "global warming"? However, not all disagreements can be resolved by our agreeing on the definitions of key terms. In some cases we have a genuine disagreement. For example, one person may agree that the climate is warming, but see it as temporary and/or the result of natural

forces rather than man-made global warming. To use another example, one person may argue that capital punishment is an effective deterrent; another may argue that it has no deterrent effect. Both agree on the definition of capital punishment but disagree on its deterrent effect. Disagreements about factual matters can be resolved by researching the facts.

EXERCISE 3-3

STOP AND ASSESS YOURSELF

I. Evaluate the following definitions and indicate what, if anything, is wrong with them. If they are poor definitions, come up with a better definition. (For additional definitions to evaluate, go to the *Online Student Workbook*.)

*a. "Third World feminism is about feeding people in all their hunger."[20]

 b. A farm is a large tract of land on which crops are raised for a livelihood.

 c. A cafeteria is a place on campus where students eat their meals.

*d. To nap is to sleep or doze for a short period of time.

 e. Earth is a planet that orbits the sun.

 f. A wedding ring is a tourniquet designed to stop circulation.

*g. A footstool is a stool for our feet.

 h. A female is a girl or a woman.

 i. A briefcase is a case for carrying briefs.

*j. Global warming is the systematic increase in temperature over decades on the surface albedo, the fluxes of sensible and latent heat to the atmosphere, and the distribution of energy within the climate system to the hydrosphere, lithosphere, and biosphere primarily because of anthropomorphic forcing.

 k. A senator is a member of the United States Congress.

 l. Hope is that which springs eternal.

*m. A dog is a household pet.

 n. Stupor is the state of stupefication.

 o. "Rightful liberty is unobstructed action according to our will within limits drawn around us by the equal rights of others. I do not add 'within the limits of the law' because law is often but the tyrant's will, and always so when it violates the rights of the individual." (Thomas Jefferson)

*p. A misogynist is one who disagrees with a feminist.

q. "Hope is the thing with feathers / That perches in the soul, / And sings the tune without the words, / And never stops at all."[21]

r. A teenager is a person between 13 and 19 years of age.

2. The definition of *God* changes over time and also differs among groups of people. How do you define *God*? Share your definition with others in the class. To what extent are disagreements about the existence of God purely verbal disputes?

3. Identify which of the following arguments are merely verbal disputes based on differing definitions and which are disagreements of fact:

*a. "You should bring an umbrella to class today. It's supposed to rain later this afternoon."
"No, it's not. There's not a cloud in the sky, and the one-week weather forecast from last weekend said it was supposed to be sunny all week."

b. "If it's a legitimate rape, the female body has ways to try to shut that whole thing [getting pregnant] down."—Representative Todd Akin, 2012.

c. "I see nothing wrong with using marijuana. It is a lot less dangerous to your health than smoking cigarettes. Anyway, people should have a right to make their own decisions about what to put in their bodies as long as they're not harming anyone else."
"I disagree. Of course it's wrong to use marijuana. It's against the law."

*d. "I hear that if the military draft is reenacted, girls will be drafted as well as men."
"That's not true. No one under the age of 18 will be drafted."

e. "If global warming continues the sea levels are predicted to rise by 3 feet in 2100."
"That's not true. Sea level is only predicted to rise by four inches."

f. "Ben must be really sick. How can a man beat up his girlfriend like that, then leave her to die in a dumpster."
"Ben isn't sick. At his last physical his doctor said he was in perfect health."

*g. "You'd better not have a second glass of wine. You might get stopped by the police and arrested for drunk driving."
"No, a person needs to have at least three drinks in order to be over the limit for drunk driving."

h. "Professor Santos is the best teacher in the English department. She always gets top ratings on the student evaluations."

"Professor Kwame is the best teacher. He has more publications in academic journals than anyone else in the department."

*Answers to selected exercises are found in the Solutions Manual at the end of the book.

COMMUNICATION STYLES

Sometimes miscommunication is due to communication style instead of actual content. As critical thinkers, it is important that we be aware of individual as well as group differences in communication styles. What may seem "normal" to us may be viewed as aggressive, aloof, or even offensive to other people.

Individual Styles of Communication

The way we communicate cannot be separated from who we are. Understanding our own styles and those of others facilitates good communication in relationships and critical thinking skills. There are four basic types of communication style: assertive, aggressive, passive, and passive-aggressive.

The *assertive style* is how we express ourselves when we are confident and our self-esteem is strong. Like effective critical thinkers, assertive communicators are able to clearly communicate their own needs but also know their limits. Assertive communicators care about relationships and strive for mutually satisfactory solutions.

The *aggressive* communication style involves the attempt to make other people do what we want or meet our needs through manipulation and control tactics.

The United States places a high value on the "assertive, tough and focused on material success" masculine style of communication. Indeed, the United States ranks relatively high on measures of masculinity, well above countries such as Canada, France, and Denmark. This may account, in part, for why there are so few women in positions of high power in the United States compared to many other Western countries.[22] Passive communicators do the opposite. *Passive* communication is based on compliance and efforts to avoid confrontation at all costs. Such communicators don't want to rock the boat and often put their needs after those of others.

Passive-aggressive communicators combine elements of the passive and aggressive styles. They do not express themselves openly and honestly, and communicate in a way that is indirect, subtle, and manipulative. For example, they use facial expressions that do not correspond with how they feel, such as smiling when in fact angry.

As we noted in Chapter 1, effective communication skills are one of the characteristics of a good critical thinker. A healthy, assertive communication style and the ability to correctly interpret others' communication are important in positions of leadership, such as that assumed by astronaut Sally Ride. Good communication skills are

THiNK Tank

SELF-EVALUATION QUESTIONNAIRE [COMMUNICATION STYLE]*

For each of the following scenarios, select the answer choice that best describes what you would do.

1. You are a customer waiting in line to be served. Suddenly, someone steps in line ahead of you. You would
   a. Let the person be ahead of you, since he or she is already in line
   b. Pull the person out of line and make him or her go to the back
   c. Indicate to the person that you are in line and point out where it begins

2. A friend drops in to say hello but stays too long, preventing you from finishing an important work project. You would
   a. Let the person stay, then finish your work another time
   b. Tell the person to stop bothering you and to get out
   c. Explain your need to finish your work and request that he or she visit another time

3. You suspect someone of harboring a grudge against you, but you don't know why. You would
   a. Pretend you are unaware of his or her anger and ignore it, hoping it will correct itself
   b. Get even with the person somehow so that he or she will learn not to hold grudges against you
   c. Ask the person if he or she is angry, and then try to understand why

4. You bring your car to a garage for repairs and receive a written estimate. But later, when you pick up your car, you are billed for additional work and for an amount higher than the estimate. You would
   a. Pay the bill, since the car must have needed the extra repairs anyway
   b. Refuse to pay, and then complain to the motor vehicle department or the Better Business Bureau
   c. Indicate to the manager that you agreed only to the estimated amount, then pay only that amount

5. You invite a good friend to your house for a dinner party, but your friend never arrives and neither calls to cancel nor to apologize. You would
   a. Ignore it but manage not to show up the next time your friend invites you to a party
   b. Never speak to this person again and end the friendship
   c. Call your friend to find out what happened

6. You are in a discussion group at work that includes your boss. A coworker asks you a question about your work, but you don't know the answer. You would
   a. Give your coworker a false but plausible answer so that your boss will think you are on top of things
   b. Not answer but attack your coworker by asking a question you know that he or she could not answer
   c. Indicate to your coworker that you are unsure just now but offer to give him or her the information later

*Questions are from Donald A. Cadogan, "How Self-Assertive are You?" (1990). http://www.oaktreecounseling.com/assrtquz.htm.

Hillary Clinton's success in politics is due in part to her assertive communication style.

also important in the establishment of an intimate relationship. As relationships develop, how effectively and appropriately each person communicates appears to outweigh other factors, such as appearance or similarity, when determining relationship satisfaction.

Unfortunately, many of us are notoriously inaccurate at interpreting others' communication. In a study, participants correctly interpreted only 73 percent of their intimate partner's supportive behavior and 89 percent of their negative behavior.[23] Failing to notice the communication of affection may leave our partner wondering if we really care. At other times, we may misinterpret our partner's behavior as angry or pushy and needlessly provoke an argument that is based on our misperception. Thus, it is important to establish effective communication behaviors and patterns if you want a relationship—whether personal or professional—to succeed.[24]

Sex and Racial Differences in Communication Style

Our sex influences which communication style we tend to prefer. In her book *You Just Don't Understand: Women and Men in Communication* (2001), linguist Deborah Tannen notes that "communication between men and women can be like cross cultural communication, prey to a clash of conversational styles."[25] Women, she notes, tend to use communication to create and sustain relationships, whereas men use it primarily to get things done and solve problems. Most men think that as long as a relationship

is working well and there are no problems, there is no need to talk about it. Women, in contrast, think of a relationship as going well if they can talk to their partner about it. When men are uninterested in discussing a relationship or their feelings, a woman may misinterpret this reticence on the man's part as lack of interest (see "Critical Thinking in Action: He Says/She Says: Sex Differences in Communication").

Most scientists believe that genetics plays a role in these differences in communication style. Indeed, recent studies have found that men and women use different parts of their brain for language.[26] Others believe that these sex

> A healthy, assertive communication style and the ability to correctly interpret others' communication are important in positions of leadership.

differences are primarily or even solely a result of the way in which we are socialized.[27] Boys are taught to assert themselves, whereas girls are taught to listen and be responsive.

Sex differences in communication, whether innate or the result of socialization, have real-life consequences. In negotiating, women are usually less assertive than men; they tend to set lower goals and are quicker to back down. Women also tend to view negotiations as having two goals: getting the result you want *and* maintaining (or improving) your relationship with the person on the other side. Rather than adopting the more aggressive male negotiating style, women ask, "Can we find a way that this can work for both of us?"[28] Not surprisingly, because they are more willing to compromise, women on the average earn less than men and pay more than men do for a new car.

Critical THiNKing in Action

He Says/She Says: Sex Differences in Communication

Women's Communication:

- Primary purpose of communication is to establish and maintain relationships with others.
- Equality between people, rather than control of conversation, is more important. Typical ways to communicate equality include "I've done the same thing many times," "I've felt the same way," and "The same thing happened to me once."
- Inclusive style of communication: "Tell me more" or "Tell me what you mean."
- Tentative style of communication used to keep conversation open and ongoing.
- Communication is more personal, concrete, and responsive to others.
- Women use more nonverbal communication, such as eye contact, smiling, and attentive body posture, than men do to express their personal feelings and to invite others into the relationship.

Men's Communication:

- Primary purpose of communication is to exert control, preserve independence, entertain, and enhance status.
  - Command over the conversation is important. Men tend to talk more and interrupt and challenge more.
  - Assertive, sometimes aggressive, style of communication and tendency to give advice; for example: "This is the way you should handle this problem" or "Don't let him get to you."
  - Men express themselves in fairly direct, assertive ways. Their language is typically more forceful and authoritative than women's language.
  - Communication is more abstract and conceptual and less responsive.
  - Men use nonverbal communication, such as leaning forward and using open hand gestures, primarily to emphasize their verbal messages.

DISCUSSION QUESTIONS

1. Looking at the list on the left, discuss differences, if any, in the nonverbal communication styles of men and women.

2. Discuss whether men and women have different communication styles. What has been your experience regarding sex differences in communication? What conclusion regarding communication differences between men and women did you draw from your experience? Evaluate your conclusion in light of supporting evidence as well as the three levels of thinking and barriers to analysis discussed in Chapter 1 (see pages 21–22).

Summarized from Julia T. Wood, *Gendered Lives: Communication, Gender, and Culture* (Belmont, CA: Wadsworth, 2001), pp. 125–130; 138.

International Diplomacy and Nonverbal Communication

In Arab cultures it is perfectly acceptable for men to hold hands. In 2005, when the infirm 80-year-old Crown Prince Abdullah of Saudi Arabia reached out for then-President George W. Bush's hand for support while walking along an uneven path in Texas, Bush graciously took his hand. The incident disturbed many Americans and was played up by the media as an inappropriately intimate encounter between the two heads of state. "Most everyone this side of Riyadh was appalled," noted one journalist.* Only First Lady Laura Bush—when asked by Jay Leno on the *Tonight Show,* "Are you the jealous type?"—thought that her husband's gesture was "sweet."

The reaction of both the American media and the public betrayed our ignorance of nonverbal communication styles in Arab countries. Such ignorance of cultural differences can lead to misunderstandings as well as biased reporting.

DISCUSSION QUESTIONS

1. *What was your first reaction when you saw the photo of Bush and Crown Prince Abullah holding hands? What was the basis of your reaction? Was it reasonable? Evaluate your reaction. Discuss how being aware of your emotional reactions can improve your ability to be a better critical thinker in situations like this.*

2. *Look back at a time when you misinterpreted a gesture or body language of someone from a different culture. How did this affect your ability to communicate effectively with that person? Discuss ways in which improving your understanding of cross-cultural behavior can help you to be a better communicator and critical thinker.*

*Joe Klein, "The Perils of Hands-On Diplomacy," *Time,* May 9, 2005, p. 29.

Why are women so reluctant to negotiate assertively? "We teach little girls that we don't like them to be pushy or overly aggressive," explains Sara Laschever, coauthor of *Women Don't Ask: Negotiation and the Gender Divide.* "Once adulthood is reached, studies are conclusive that neither men nor other women like women who are too aggressive."

Different ethnic and cultural groups tend to define masculinity and femininity differently. For instance, in Thailand, Portugal, and the Scandinavian countries, men's and women's styles of communication tend to be more "feminine," as defined by mainstream American standards.[29] This is mainly because nurturing relationships are a priority in these countries, whereas in the United States men are socialized to be more individualistic, competitive, and assertive or even aggressive in their communication.

Racial identity can also influence our communication style. African American women, for example, are generally socialized to be more assertive. They tend to smile less in a conversation and maintain less eye contact than European American women. In addition, African American men are less comfortable with self-disclosure and are more likely than European American men to use confrontation rather than compromise in conflict resolution.[30]

Social segregation and bias contribute to racial differences in communication styles. To succeed in college and the professional world, African Americans may abandon the communication styles of the African American community and adopt those associated with the dominant European American culture. Research shows that to succeed in the college and business environments, African American males often adopt the strategy of "talking white" and "playing the part" to avoid being stigmatized by racial stereotypes. One researcher notes that the demands on African Americans of "playing the part," which involves being superficial and cautious and not being yourself ". . . is a constant struggle. . . . You have to play a double role if you're a black male on campus."[31]

Connections

What is the role of cross-cultural communication in marketing strategies? *See Chapter 10, p. 306.*

Cultural Differences in Communication Styles

Culture plays a key role in shaping our communication style. Respect and dignity are highly valued by the Chinese. Consequently, they may be hesitant to ask someone to repeat themselves if they don't understand the communication.[32] In many eastern Asian cultures, nodding does not necessarily mean that the person agrees with or even understands what you are saying. Instead, it is used to show that he or she is listening. The use of silence in communication also varies from culture to culture. European Americans tend to be uncomfortable with silence, whereas silence plays an important role in communication among the Apaches of Arizona, as well as in many Asian cultures.

Communication in Hispanic cultures is more often oriented toward facilitating group cooperation rather than individual needs. Respect is generally highly valued and formal communication styles and titles are preferred over first names.[33] Hispanics also tend to be very polite in their communication, which may be misinterpreted as a subservient attitude.[34]

Nonverbal language also varies from culture to culture. In Algeria the U.S. wave of hello means "come here," whereas in Mexico the U.S. arm gesture for "come here" is an obscene gesture. Cultural groups have their own rules for personal space as well. In the United States, Canada, and northern Europe, personal space tends to be larger and touching is less frequently used in communication than in southern European, Arab, and Latin American countries. Indeed, Arabs sometimes misinterpret the "standoffish" behavior of Americans as distant and rude.

Even clothing serves as a type of nonverbal language. Indeed, we sometimes say that a person is "making a fashion statement."[35] Americans tend to dress more casually than people from other cultures, who may interpret the T-shirts and ragged jeans of an American tourist as a sign of disrespect or slovenliness. In the United States, women, unlike men, are required to wear tops on almost all public beaches, whereas this requirement is seen as restrictive and puritanical by the French. On the other hand, many non-Muslim Americans view the requirement that Muslim women wear a head scarf, or *hijab,* as restrictive and a sign of oppression of women by Islam. Most Muslim women, however, prefer to wear a *hijab,* considering it a sign of respect or decorum.

Literal translations of foreign terms or ambiguous symbols can also lead to miscommunication. Many people interpreted the symbols on the Mayan calendar to mean that the earth was predicted to end on December 21, 2012. NASA argued that a more plausible interpretation was that the calendar was a means of communicating the end of a long cycle, just as our calendar ends on December 31. As an analogy, when the odometer on a car hits 99,999 miles, it starts over again at 00,000 with no ill effects on the driver or the car.

As critical thinkers we need to be aware of differences in communication styles. Some of us can move easily from one style to another, depending on what the situation requires. Others, however, have one dominant style and more difficulty seeing the situation from another's perspective. Research on communication and culture has led to the creation of the discipline of cross-cultural studies and diversity training for students, business personnel, and government employees. Being aware of our own and others' communication styles, and being able to adjust our style to fit a specific situation, can go a long way in improving communication and facilitating effective critical thinking.

Misinterpretation of the symbols on the Mayan calendar led many people to believe that the world was going to end on December 21, 2012.

STOP AND ASSESS YOURSELF

1. Write a few sentences describing the weather today. Get into small groups and compare your descriptions. Critically analyze what differences in the descriptions say about the communication style of each person in the group.

2. Write a few sentences on what these statements mean to you:

a. "I love you." [college male to college female]

b. "I love you." [college female to college male]

Explain whether the sex of the person saying "I love you," as well as your own sex, influenced your interpretation.

3. What is your negotiating style? How is it influenced by your sex and culture? Does your negotiating style work to achieve the ends you desire? Give an example of a time when your negotiating style worked and one when it didn't. Discuss what you might do to improve your negotiating style.

4. Discuss the desirability of co-ed housing and cohabitation—two unmarried people of opposite sex who are sexually intimate and living together—on campus. Observe the ways in which the men and the women in the class communicate regarding this issue. Now discuss the issue again, this time switching sex roles. Did putting yourself in the role of the other sex enhance understanding?

5. In what ways is your communication style influenced by your sex and cultural background? Describe a time where you altered your communication style because you were talking to a person of another gender or racial or ethnic background. Evaluate whether the adjustments enhanced or impeded communication.

6. Look at the clothing of the people on your campus. What do the clothes say to you about each person and their culture? Are your conclusions accurate? Discuss your conclusions with others in the class.

7. In 2009, France passed a law banning the female Islamic veil from schools, arguing that the veil posed a security threat and that it was a symbol of the subjugation of women. Referring to the roles of nonverbal communication and culture in communication style, discuss whether or not this law is justified or if it should be overturned.

8. Claudine came to see her professor about her grades. She was wearing a cropped top that exposed her midriff and a very short skirt. The professor glanced down at her legs as she sat down and said, "That outfit is very flattering on you." His comment made her feel uncomfortable. Was this sexual harassment? Discuss the roles of verbal and nonverbal language, including dress, in sexual harassment.

9. Discuss how your communication style contributes to or interferes with your relationships and the achievement of your goals. Share your plan for improving your communication style. If appropriate, modify your style or plan in light of feedback from the class.

THE USE OF LANGUAGE TO MANIPULATE

Language can be used to manipulate and deceive as well as to inform. Manipulation can be carried out through the use of emotive language, rhetorical devices, or deliberate deception. The old adage "sticks and stones will break my bones but words will never hurt me" ignores the profoundly social nature of humans and the use of words to shape our self-concept. Words can raise our spirits, but they can also hurt and degrade us.

Emotive Language

Emotive language, as we noted earlier, is used to elicit a certain emotional impact. For example, the terms *regime, flip-flopper, obstinate,* and *anal retentive* are used to arouse feelings of disapproval. In contrast, the terms *government, flexible, firm,* and *neat* generally evoke positive feelings.

Emotive language is particularly dangerous when it is used to cover weak arguments and insufficient facts or when it masquerades as news in the media. For example, because the term *terrorist* arouses such negative feelings, the *New York Times* tries to use the term as little as possible. Deputy foreign editor Ethan Bronner explains: "We use 'terrorist' sparingly because it is a loaded word. Describing the goals or acts of a group often serves readers better than repeating the term 'terrorist.'"[36] The *Times* also avoids the use of the term *reform* in describing legislation, since it implies to the reader that the legislation is automatically desirable.

Emotive language is often found in debates about controversial political and moral issues, especially when feelings are running high. For example, Rick Santorum, former Republican presidential candidate, used negatively charged emotive language when he called President Obama a "snob" for supporting higher education for all

Americans. Santorum also referred to colleges as "indoctrination mills" for "godless" liberalism.[37]

In another example from politics, the term "Arab Spring" first appeared in the American political journal *Foreign Policy* in 2011. The term evokes a positive attitude toward the wave of demonstrations, protests, and uprisings to oust authoritarian governments in the Arab world and replace them with democracies. The Arab news channel *Al-Jazeera* has accused the United States of using the term as "part of a U.S. strategy of controlling [the movement's] aims and goals" to move it toward American-style democracy.[38]

Advertising slogans, such as "Things go better with Coke," "The taste that satisfies," and "Like a rock," are designed to manipulate people into buying a certain product rather than actually providing information. Two of the most famous state slogans are "I love New York" and "Virginia is for lovers." Las Vegas's slogan "What happens here, stays here," may have helped bring in nearly 40 million tourists in 2012.[39]

In November 2012, more than 200,000 protestors filled Tahrir Square in Cairo demanding the resignation of Egypt's president Hosni Mubarak. The event was labeled part of the "Arab Spring" by the United States, which supported the overthrow of Mubarak.

Critical THiNKing in Action

What Those "Code Words" in Personal Ads Really Mean

EUPHEMISM	TRANSLATION
40ish	52 and looking for a 25-year-old
Beautiful	Spends a lot of time in front of the mirror
Enjoys long walks	Car has been repossessed
Flexible	Desperate
Free spirit	Substance abuser
Fun-loving	Expects to be entertained
Good sense of humor	Watches a lot of television
Life of the party	Poor impulse control
Outgoing	Loud
Physically fit	Still breathing
Stylish	Slave to every fad that comes down the road
Thoughtful	Says "please" when demanding a beer
Uninhibited	Lacking basic social skills
Wants soulmate	One step away from stalking

DISCUSSION QUESTIONS

1. Using specific examples, discuss how the use of euphemisms, such as those listed on the left, can lead to miscommunication and false expectations.

2. What are some euphemisms you use to describe yourself when you're trying to make a favorable impression on someone?

From Herd Words, https://sites.google.com/site/herdwords123/home/euphemisms-in-personal-ads

---

The words we use have real-life consequences. Gang rapes often occur as part of a game or ritual in which the selected victim is referred to as a *nympho* or *slut*—words that suggest she "asked for it." The use of these emotively negative terms makes it easier for men to participate in rape without seeing themselves as rapists.

Rhetorical Devices

Like emotive language, **rhetorical devices** use psychological persuasion, rather than reason, to persuade others to accept a particular position. Common rhetorical devices include euphemisms, dysphemisms, sarcasm, and hyperbole.

A **euphemism** is the replacement of a negative term with a neutral or positive one to cover up or sugarcoat the truth. Sometimes euphemisms are humorous and easy to see through (see "Critical Thinking in Action: What Those Code Words in Personal Ads Really Mean"). Other times they obscure the truth and create a false image of the world. One of the more insidious euphemisms was Nazi Germany's use of the term "the final solution" for its attempt to exterminite the Jews of Europe.

Euphemisms are often used to smooth over socially sensitive topics. Using the term *pass away* instead of *die* masks our culture's discomfort with the topic of death. Instead of *vagina* or *penis,* we use "cute" terms such as *private parts* or *south of the border.* These euphemisms reveal our culture's discomfort with sexually explicit language.

Language has the power to alter how we think about reality. People may use euphemisms to get others to see something from their point of view. In times of war, leaders on both sides try to win the support of their citizenry by convincing them that the war is acceptable and even noble. The term "enhanced interrogation techniques" was used by the Bush administration for methods such as hypothermia, water boarding, and

rhetorical devices The use of euphemisms, dysphemisms, hyperbole, and sarcasm to manipulate and persuade.

euphemism The replacement of a term that has a negative association by a neutral or positive term.

Connections

How does the media manipulate you through the use of emotive language and sensationalism? *See Chapter 11, p. 338.*

How can you recognize and avoid being taken in by manipulative language in advertisements? *See Chapter 10, p. 319.*

Politicians are notorious for their manipulative use of language, especially during campaigns, and will often skirt around direct questions by supplying the answers they think their constituents want to hear.

deliberate exhaustion on jailed suspects in the war on terror. Some have called the term a euphemism for torture.

Our soldiers who are killed in the war are shipped home in "transfer tubes" rather than body bags. And the private soldiers who work for the U.S. in Afghanistan are "security consultants" rather than mercenaries.

Euphemisms are also used to create support for the use of unmanned drones, which have allegedly killed over hundreds of civilians in Pakistan alone. Rather than being called "attacks," the operations are labeled "targeted killings" by the United States government to create the impression that the only people being killed by the drones are terrorists who have been specifically selected.

Businesses also make up new terms because of negative connotations associated with old terms. Companies no longer fire employees; instead they downsize, dehire, or practice workforce management or employee transition. Eventually these terms may be deemed too negative. The term *downsize,* for example, has recently been replaced by the more appealing term *rightsize.* And the terms *used cars* and *pre-owned vehicles* have morphed to *experienced vehicles.* Some euphemisms become so

Why do advertisers use euphemisms and other rhetorical devices? *See Chapter 10, p. 319.*

Connections

widely accepted that they become lexical definitions. For example, *downsize* was added to dictionaries in the 1970s (see page 76).

Politically correct language is often based on euphemisms in which terms such as *crippled* are replaced with neutral or more positive terms such as *physically challenged.* The politically correct movement has been somewhat successful in limiting hate speech. More than a hundred colleges and universities in the United States have had, or still have, speech codes that place restrictions on some forms of speech. For more on restricting free speech on campuses, see "Critical Thinking Issue: Perspectives on Free-Speech Zones on College Campuses" at the end of this chapter.

While some people support speech codes as encouraging tolerance and diversity, others argue that these codes are self-defeating and force the issue of bigotry and intolerance underground by censoring open discussion and critical thinking about the issue. The tacit suppression of so-called racist views, for example, can leave us believing that prejudice and segregation are no longer a problem, when in fact, many of our nation's schools are even more segregated than they were in the late 1960s.

George Orwell wrote his novel *Nineteen Eighty-Four* about the insidious role of language manipulation in society, especially by those in power. Orwell warned that by purging language of politically dangerous or offensive words and concepts and substituting euphemisms for them,

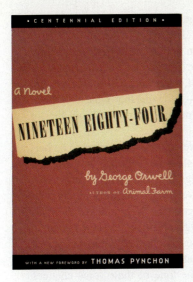

freedom of speech becomes impossible and resistance to tyranny difficult. Unless we resist this trend we will get caught up in doublethink and become soulless automatons incapable of engaging in critical thinking.[40]

Dysphemisms, in contrast to euphemisms, are used to produce a negative effect. The term *death tax* for inheritance tax was coined to create a feeling of disapproval toward this tax. In the abortion debate, the term *antichoice* creates a negative feeling toward people who are opposed to abortion rights.

Dysphemisms can be used to win over one group of people while at the same time alienating others. Politicians may use dysphemisms to exaggerate cultural differences and create an us-versus-them mentality. In 2002, the use of the term *axis of evil* for Iraq, Iran, and North Korea was accompanied by a swing of public opinion in the United States against these countries and support for the idea of attacking those countries.[41]

Sarcasm, another rhetorical device, involves the use of ridicule, insults, taunting, and/or caustic irony. It derives its power from the fact that most people hate being made fun of. Like other rhetorical devices, sarcasm is used to deflect critical analysis and to create a feeling of disapproval toward the object of the sarcasm, as in the following letter to the editor from *Newsweek:*

> We're in a blood-soaked foreign war, the national debt threatens our financial future, hatred of Americans is soaring and the issue that finally inflames conservative Oregon voters is the possibility of some people marrying their same-gender loved ones? Wow! I'll have to get my priorities straight.[42]

Sarcasm is often dismissed as humor by those who use it. However, it is anything but funny to its intended target. As good critical thinkers, we need to be able to see though this rhetorical device and not be belittled by it.

Hyperbole is a type of rhetoric that uses exaggeration or overstatement to distort the facts. "I thought I would die when the professor called on me in class today," moans a college student. Some journalists use hyperbole for the purpose of sensationalism, exaggerating a story to the point of absurdity. "Morgue Worker's Snoring Wakes the Dead," read a headline in the *Weekly World News.*[43]

Hyperbole is also found in politics when a grain of truth is exaggerated and distorted. Federal Reserve Chairman Ben Bernanke used the term "fiscal cliff" as a metaphor for the disastrous consequences he claimed would be befall the economy if Congress did not fix the federal budget and deficit in January 2013. Bernanke intended the metaphor to spur Congress to action. Despite Bernanke's dire predictions, while Congress failed to pass a balanced budget, the country was not catapulted over a fiscal precipice. Former abortion rights advocate Dr. Bernard Nathanson also used hyperbole when he exaggerated the number of maternal deaths due to illegal abortions in order to gain public support for the legalization of abortion. "I confess that I knew the figures were totally false," he later wrote. "But in the 'morality' of our revolution, it was a useful figure, widely accepted."[44] In these cases hyperbole involved the deliberate use of deception.

The habitual use of hyperbole, however, damages our credibility. Like the little boy who cried wolf, we may not be believed when we finally tell it as it really is.

Hot or Not?

Is lying for the greater good ever justified?

Deception and Lying

Although rhetorical devices may involve deception, the deception is not always deliberate. There are also cases when deception is expected and acceptable, as in a poker game or preparation for a surprise party. A **lie,** on the other hand, is "a deliberate attempt to mislead, without the prior consent of the target."[45] Withholding or omitting certain information in a way that distorts a message so it is deceptive may also constitute lying.

In the 1998 Paula Jones deposition, lawyers produced a definition of *sex* before asking former President Bill Clinton if he had had sex with Monica Lewinsky. Clinton replied emphatically that he had not. His response was based on the fact that the definition provided did not specifically list "mouth" as one of the body parts involved in sex. Clinton later admitted that his answer had been intended to "mislead" and "give a false impression"

Connections

How can you evaluate political candidates when rhetoric so often dominates campaigns?
See Chapter 13, pp. 400–401.

dysphemism A word or phrase chosen to produce a negative effect.

sarcasm The use of ridicule, insults, taunting, and/or caustic irony.

hyperbole A rhetorical device that uses an exaggeration.

lie A deliberate attempt to mislead without the prior consent of the target.

Connections

Why do journalists use hyperbole, and how can we avoid being taken in by it? *See Chapter 11, p. 338.*

How does the media sometimes engage in hyperbole when reporting scientific findings? *See Chapter 11, p. 344.*

regarding his inappropriate sexual relationship with Lewinsky.[46]

Most lies, such as that told by Bill Clinton, are told to avoid getting into trouble or to cover misbehavior. So-called little white lies may be used to ease social awkwardness, avoid hurting feelings, or put us in a more positive light. Other lies, such as Dr. Nathanson's regarding the number of maternal deaths due to illegal abortions and lies told to the enemy during war may be rationalized as being for the greater good.

In addition to derailing honest communication, lying raises several ethical issues. Is it ever morally acceptable to lie to spare someone's feelings or to promote what we regard as the "greater good"? How about a lie to save a life? Most ethicists agree that the great majority of lies are not justified. Lies can damage trust. In addition, making a political or life decision based on someone else's lies can have ruinous results. Wars may be waged based on misinformation. A murderer may go free if the investigating police officer or jury believes his or her lies.

Lies may also be committed in the guise of fun. When two Australian DJs, impersonating Queen Elizabeth II and Prince Charles, called a London hospital seeking information on Kate Middleton, Duchess of Cambridge, who was in the hospital for morning sickness, they didn't expect the nurse answering the call to fall for their "prank." However, Jacintha Saldanha believed their lie and transferred the call to another nurse, who gave the DJs private details about the Duchess's health.

Most of us are easily taken in by the lies of others. A study found that people lie about a third of the time in their interactions with others; only about 18 percent of lies are ever discovered.[47] The average person is able to tell the difference between a liar and a truth-teller only about 55 percent of the time (not much better than chance). Even when lies are exposed, the public will sometimes get caught up in doublethink—knowing that what they once believed is a lie but continuing to act as though the lie were true.

The good news is that we can train ourselves to be better at detecting other people's lies. Skilled lie-catchers, such as police, FBI investigators, and some psychiatrists, are able to distinguish between liars and truth-tellers with 80 percent to 95 percent accuracy.[48] This makes them almost as accurate as a polygraph or lie-detector machine. Professional lie-catchers closely observe patterns of verbal and nonverbal communication. When most people lie, their body language and the tone of their voice changes subtly. For example, children between ages 9 and 14 who lie about sexual abuse (lies about sexual abuse are rare in children younger than 9) tend to report the alleged abuse chronologically, since it is too difficult to fabricate a story out of order. Truth-tellers, in contrast, jump around and include information such as smells, background noises, and other sensations. Unlike liars, truth-tellers also tend to make spontaneous corrections to their stories.

Lying creates cognitive and emotional overload. As a result, liars tend to move less and blink less because of the extra effort they need to remember what they've already said and to keep their stories consistent. Their voices may become more tense or high-pitched and their speech may be filled with pauses. Liars also tend to make fewer speech errors than do truth tellers, and they rarely backtrack to fill in "forgotten" or incorrect details.[49]

Scientists at the Salk Institute in California have developed a computer that can read a person's rapidly changing facial expressions and body language.[50] Polygraphs, in contrast, measure reactions like heartbeat and perspiration, which some clever liars are able to control. The scientists hope that computers may someday be able to determine what emotions underlie different facial expressions. However, because some types of body language are shaped by our culture, lie detectors—whether human or computer—need to take into account cultural and sex differences in discerning if there is deception.

To avoid being taken in by someone's lies, we should be mindful of a person's body language as well as willing to check what another person tells us—be it a friend, relative, or the media—against other evidence and reliable sources of information. We also need to be aware of manipulative language. Emotive language and the use of rhetorical devices can be used to distract us from the issue at hand and to persuade us to take a position without actually providing any factual information or sound arguments.

Facial expressions, especially the eyes, can disclose a wealth of information. The person on the left is faking a smile while the smile of the woman on the right is genuine.

Jacintha Saldanha, a nurse at a London hospital, was duped by two Australian DJs who pretended to be Queen Elizabeth II and Prince Charles into revealing private information about Kate Middleton.

Connections

How does the impeachment process act as a check on the misuse of executive power? *See Chapter 13, p. 406.*

Language is a form of symbolic communication that allows us to organize and critically analyze our experiences. Language shapes our concept of reality and of who we are. It is mainly through language that we transmit our culture. As critical thinkers, we need to clearly define our terms and be mindful of our communication style and that of others. Unfortunately, language can also be used to stereotype or mislead, either through deliberate deception or the use of rhetorical devices. Good communication skills are vital in critical thinking and are also important factors in establishing good relationships.

EXERCISE 3-5

STOP AND ASSESS YOURSELF

1. Discuss how the use of emotive language in each of the following passages is used to promote a particular point of view. Rewrite each passage using neutral language.

   *a. "The promise of embryonic-stem cell research occurs precisely because the embryo destroyed in the process was once both alive and human. As such, the harvesting of embryonic stem cells represents a form of medical cannibalism. If we cannot protect human life at its most vulnerable stages, basic constitutional protections will wither away and die."[51]

   b. "But just as Ottawa vows real action on climate change, there are new questions about one of Canada's worsts polluters, the Alberta oil sands. Our colleagues at Radio-Canada's Zone Libre have uncovered plans for a dramatic expansion, in part to satisfy an American objective." (*The Nation*, January 17, 2007)

   c. "Oliver Stone's [movie] 'Alexander' will conscript you for a long forced march. Better have an exit strategy."[52]

   *d. "In a cramped upstairs den in South St. Paul, Minn., a CD blares with fury. 'Hang the traitors of our race,' the singer screams. 'White supremacy! Whiiiite supremacy!' Byron Calvert, 33, leans back in his chair, smiling and snacking on veggies. Calvert is a mountainous man with a swastika tattoo, a prison record and a racist dream."[53]

   e. "Christians should not shy away from such debates [about euthanasia], especially since, under question, Mr. Singer [who supports euthanasia] reveals that he lives in an ivory tower."[54]

   f. "According to the National Sleep Foundation, about 60 percent of U.S. adults have insomnia every few days. I've been thinking more and more about those seductive commercials for Ambien, the pill that promises a full night of blissful sleep with few side effects."[55]

2. Identify the rhetorical device(s) or type of emotive language found in each of the following passages. What point is the writer trying to make by using these?

   *a. "Joe's between jobs. He has an interview later this week."

   b. Those tree-hugging hippies are more concerned about the snail darter than they are with people's jobs and families.

   c. Pat Tilman, the former pro-football player, was killed . . . in a "friendly fire" episode in Afghanistan last month and not by enemy bullets, according to a U.S. investigation of the incident.[56]

*d. "We had to destroy the village to save it." (From Vietnam War, c. 1968)

   e. "I have been assured by a very knowing American of my acquaintance in London, that a young healthy child well nursed is at a year old a most delicious, nourishing, and wholesome food, whether stewed, roasted, baked, or boiled . . ."[57] (Jonathan Swift)

   f. Child: "Where's Fido?"
      Parent: "We had to put Fido down. He's in doggy heaven."

   g. "I see you have a copy of the dead-tree edition of that new online magazine."

*h. "Reader, suppose you were an idiot. And suppose you were a member of Congress. But I repeat myself." (Mark Twain)

   i. In order to preserve freedom of speech, it is imperative that we place restrictions on certain types of offensive and politically inflammatory speech.

   j. "The America I know and love is not one in which my parents or my baby with Down Syndrome will have to stand in front of Obama's 'death panel' so his bureaucrats can decide, based on a subjective judgment of their 'level of productivity in society,' whether they are worthy of health care."[58] (Sarah Palin)

*k. "NASA Rover Photographs Cat Creatures on Mars! Shocked experts say abandoned pets prove aliens visited Earth."[59]

   l. "Management ordered the security guards to take steps to reduce inventory shrinkage."

   m. "I never forget a face, but in your case I'll be glad to make an exception." (Groucho Marx)

*n. "The National Rifle Association's campaign to arm every man, women and child in America, received a setback when the President signed the Brady Bill. But the gun-pushers know that the bill was only a small skirmish in the big war over guns in America."[60]

3. Harvard law professor Alan Dershowitz argues that the politically correct movement, while claiming to promote greater diversity, has in fact limited diversity of expression. He writes:

> As a teacher, I can feel a palpable reluctance on the part of many students—particularly those with views in neither extreme and those who are anxious for peer acceptance—to experiment with unorthodox ideas, to make playful comments on serious subjects, to challenge politically correct views and to disagree with minority, feminist or gay perspectives.
>
>   I feel this problem quite personally, since I happen to agree . . . with most "politically correct" positions. But I am appalled at the intolerance of many who share my substantive views. And I worry about the impact of politically correct intolerance on the generation of leaders we are currently educating.

Do you agree with Dershowitz? What are some examples of "politically incorrect" words or phrases on your campus? Do you find that you have to be careful to think about what you say and to avoid politically incorrect terms? Discuss whether having to do so facilitated or inhibited critical thinking.

4. Look on the Internet and in newspapers and/or magazines for examples of emotive language. What is the purpose of the emotive language in the text? Should journalists avoid, or at least try to avoid, the use of emotively loaded language?

5. Select a controversial issue such as animal rights or physician-assisted suicide. Write a page using emotive language and rhetoric supporting one side of the issue. Now rewrite (paraphrase) the page using neutral language. Evaluate whether your argument depended on emotive language and rhetorical devices rather than reason. Share your two wordings of the argument with others in the class. Discuss which version was most likely to encourage critical analysis of the issue and why.

6. Is self-deception ever justified? A University of California study found that patients awaiting surgery who deceived themselves about the seriousness of their condition suffered fewer postoperative complications. In a similar study, women with breast cancer who denied the seriousness of their condition were more likely to survive than those who resigned themselves to their fate.[61] Discuss whether self-deception was justified in these cases and if it is compatible with critical thinking.

*Answers to selected exercises are found in the Solutions Manual at the end of the book.

THiNK AGAIN

1. What are the primary functions of language?

   ■ One of the primary functions is informative language or the conveying of information about the world and ourselves. Directive language functions to influence actions, while expressive language communicates feelings. Finally, ceremonial language is used in certain formal circumstances.

2. Why is it important to pay close attention when evaluating and interpreting definitions of words?

   ■ Definitions are not fixed—they can have denotative meanings, which describe the properties of the word, and they can have connotative meanings, which include feelings and thoughts that are based on previous experience. Also, there are stipulative, lexical, precising, and persuasive definitions.

3. What are rhetorical devices, and how are they used?

   ■ Rhetorical devices are used for persuasion. Euphemism, the replacement of a negative term with a positive one to cover up the truth, and dysphemisms, which are used to elicit a negative response, are both examples of rhetorical devices. Others include sarcasm and hyperbole.

Perspectives on Free-Speech Zones on College Campuses

According to the Foundation for Individual Rights in Education, as of 2013, about two-thirds of American colleges have rules restricting speech that would normally be protected speech off campus. These restrictions are, in part, an extension of the politically correct movement. One way of restricting free speech is to limit controversial speech, as well as handing out pamphlets and carrying placards, to what are called "free-speech zones." Free-speech zones are specifically designated areas on campuses where students or groups can hold rallies.

The main argument for free-speech zones is that noisy protests may disturb classes that are in session. According to Rob Hennig of the political science department at the University of California, Los Angeles, these restrictions are constitutional because they reasonably dictate time, place, and manner—as opposed to content—of speech. "The university has the right to impose reasonable restriction," he argues, "if [the speech] impedes their mission. A court would look at the reasons and rationale behind restrictions, and then determine whether they are fair."[62]

The battle over limiting controversial speech to free-speech zones is gaining momentum as more complaints and First Amendment rights lawsuits are brought against college administrations by student groups. Courts have ruled in favor of the student groups in several of these cases.[63] Pressure from students and civil rights groups have also forced administrators at schools such as West Virginia University, Pennsylvania State University, and the University of Wisconsin–Whitewater to repeal their policies on free-speech zones.

Following is a letter to the editor written by Greg Lukianoff, president of the Foundation for Individual Rights in Education in opposing the use of free speech zones. In the second reading, constitutional law specialist Robert Scott defends free speech zones.[64]

Feigning Free Speech on Campus

GREG LUKIANOFF, FOUNDATION FOR INDIVIDUAL RIGHTS IN EDUCATION

The following letter to the editor was written by Greg Lukianoff, the president of the Foundation for Individual Rights in Education (FIRE), opposing the imposition of free speech zones on college campuses. Lukianoff is also the author of "Unlearning Liberty: Campus Censorship and the End of American Debate."[65]

Colleges and universities are supposed to be bastions of unbridled inquiry and expression, but they probably do as much to repress free speech as any other institution in young people's lives. In doing so, they discourage civic engagement at a time when debates over deficits and taxes should make young people pay more attention, not less.

Since the 1980s, in part because of "political correctness" concerns about racially insensitive speech and sexual harassment, and in part because of the dramatic expansion in the ranks of nonfaculty campus administrators, colleges have enacted stringent speech codes. These codes are sometimes well intended but, outside of the ivory tower, would violate the constitutional guarantee of freedom of speech. From protests and rallies to displays of posters and flags, students have been severely constrained in their ability to demonstrate their beliefs. The speech codes are at times intended to enforce civility, but they often backfire, suppressing free expression instead of allowing for open debate of controversial issues.

Last month, Christopher Newport University in Newport News, Va., forbade students to protest an appearance by Representative Paul D. Ryan, the Republican vice-presidential nominee. Why? According to university policy, students must apply 10 business days in advance to demonstrate in the college's tiny "free speech zone"—and Mr. Ryan's visit was announced on a Sunday, two days before his Tuesday visit.

Also last month, a student at Ohio University in Athens, Ohio, was blocked from putting a notice on her door arguing that neither President Obama nor Mitt Romney was fit for office. (She successfully appealed.) And over the summer, a federal judge struck down the University of Cincinnati's "free speech zone," which had limited demonstrations to 0.1 percent of the campus.

In a study of 392 campus speech codes last year, the Foundation for Individual Rights in Education, where I work, found that 65 percent of the colleges had policies that in our view violated the Constitution's guarantee of the right to free speech. (While the First Amendment generally prohibits public universities from restricting nondisruptive free speech, private colleges are not state actors and therefore have more leeway to establish their own rules.)

Some elite colleges in particular have Orwellian speech codes that are so vague and broad that they would never pass constitutional muster at state-financed universities.

Harvard is a particularly egregious example. Last year, incoming Harvard freshmen were pressured by campus officials to sign an oath promising to act with "civility" and "inclusiveness" and affirming that "kindness holds a place on par with intellectual attainment." Harry R. Lewis, a computer science professor and a former dean of Harvard College, was quick to criticize the oath. "For Harvard to 'invite' people to pledge to kindness is unwise, and sets a terrible precedent," he wrote on his blog. "It is a promise to control one's thoughts."

Civility is nice, but on college campuses it often takes on a bizarre meaning. In 2009, Yale banned students from making a T-shirt with an F. Scott Fitzgerald quotation—"I think of all Harvard men as sissies," from his 1920 novel "This Side of Paradise"—to mock Harvard at their annual football game. The T-shirt was blocked after some gay and lesbian students argued that "sissies" amounted to a homophobic slur. "What purports to be humor by targeting a group through slurs is not acceptable," said Mary Miller, a professor of art history and the dean of Yale College.

A 2010 study by the American Association of Colleges and Universities of 24,000 college students and 9,000 faculty and staff members found that only 35.6 percent of the students—and only 18.5 percent of the faculty and staff—strongly agreed that it was "safe to hold unpopular positions on campus."

For reasons both good and bad—and sometimes for mere administrative convenience—colleges have promulgated speech codes that are not only absurd in their results but also detrimental to the ideals of free inquiry. Students can't learn how to navigate democracy and engage with their fellow citizens if they are forced to think twice before they speak their mind.

REVIEW QUESTIONS

1. What type of organization is FIRE, and what was Lukianoff's purpose in writing this letter to the editor?

2. In what ways do college campuses restrict students' freedom of speech?

3. According to Lukianoff, why is freedom of speech important on college campuses?

Reasonable Limits Are Good

ROBERT J. SCOTT

Robert J. Scott is a constitutional law specialist, legal commentator, and managing partner of the Dallas law firm Scott & Scott. In this article from USA Today, *Scott presents an argument in support of free-speech zones.*[66]

Today's debate: Free speech 'zones.'

Opposing view: Violent demonstrations illustrate need to maintain public order.

The use of "free speech zones" or "protest zones" is not new and does not present a significant threat to free-speech rights.

Protest zones have been used at political conventions and other major events, such as last year's Winter Olympics. By creating a protest zone, governments can ensure that those who wish to express their views have a place to do so while minimizing the disruptions protests may bring.

Given the violence and vandalism accompanying recent protests, there is a real, immediate threat of disorder justifying a reasonable governmental response. Most of downtown San Francisco was shut down for two days in March by demonstrators who blocked traffic, damaged businesses and held an organized "vomit-in" around the federal building. Across the bay in Oakland, protesters attempted to disrupt access to ships transporting munitions.

Such incidents remind us that the First Amendment is not a license to do and say anything, anywhere, at any time. The Constitution does not protect protesters who break windows, obstruct traffic, disrupt military supply lines or threaten the safety of other citizens.

It has long been recognized that governments can impose reasonable time, place and manner restrictions on speech. Obviously, the Secret Service should not be forced to allow protesters unlimited access to the president. College administrators should be able to make certain that protesters do not prevent other students from pursuing their studies.

Protest zones can be reasonable restrictions that allow free-speech rights to be expressed while decreasing safety concerns and preventing undue disruption.

Our democracy is based first and foremost on the rule of law. Reasonable protest zones are actually consistent with the basic idea that civil liberties may only be guaranteed and protected by an organized society maintaining public order.

In the words of Theodore Roosevelt, "Order without liberty and liberty without order are equally destructive." The lawlessness, violence and vandalism seen at recent protests are the hallmarks of anarchy, not liberty. Requiring those expressing dissent to obey the law while doing so does not constitute repression.

REVIEW QUESTIONS

1. According to Scott, what is the primary purpose of free-speech zones?

2. What are the benefits of having free-speech zones?

3. On what grounds does Scott argue that free-speech zones are consistent with the First Amendment and with democratic principles?

98 • THiNK

THiNK
AND DISCUSS

PERSPECTIVES ON FREE-SPEECH ZONES

1. Evaluate Lukianoff's and Scott's arguments for and against free-speech zones on college campuses. Evaluate which person made the stronger argument.

2. The First Amendment to the *Bill of Rights* states:

   > Congress shall make no law . . . abridging the freedom of speech, or of the press; of the right of the people peaceably to assemble to petition government for a redress of grievances.

   Are free-speech zones consistent with the First Amendment, as Scott argued, or do they violate it, as Lukianoff argued?

3. Are there any instances when freedom of speech should be restricted on college campuses? What about hate speech, inflammatory speech, or a display of symbols, such as a swastika?

4. What is your campus's policy on free speech? If you think the policy should be changed, discuss steps you might take to get it changed.

5. When University of Colorado professor Ward Churchill published an essay in which he compared some of the workers who died in the World Trade Center in the terrorist attacks of September 11, 2001, to little Nazis, outraged Colorado legislators unanimously passed a resolution condemning his words as "evil and inflammatory." Given the influence that language has in shaping our thoughts and behavior, discuss what action, if any, the university should have taken against Professor Churchill.

6. When Richard Perle, chairman of the Defense Policy Board and supporter of the war in Iraq, spoke at Brown University, students continually interrupted his speech by booing and jeering. The students justified their jeering as part of their right to express their views. Discuss whether freedom of speech justifies the use of jeering to prevent someone with an opposing view from speaking.

7. In October 2001, Matthew Poe, a fourth-year West Virginia University student, was stopped by campus police for handing out flyers outside a free-speech zone. "I think America is a free-speech zone, and the university has no business restricting it," says Poe. "Rather, the university has a moral responsibility to endorse it." He maintains that free-speech zones are simply a thinly veiled excuse "to stop campuses from becoming confrontational" like the University of California at Berkeley during the Vietnam War student protests.[67] Critically analyze Poe's position in light of the two readings.

4

KNOWLEDGE, EVIDENCE, & ERRORS IN THINKING

In what became one of the most publicized cases of medical error, in 1995 a surgeon at University Community Hospital in Tampa, Florida, mistakenly amputated the wrong leg of 52-year-old Willie King. More recently, a surgeon at Milford Regional Medical Center in Massachusetts removed a woman's right kidney instead of her gallbladder as planned. In a high-profile case, actor Dennis Quaid's newborn twins nearly died from a dose of the blood-thinner heparin that was 1,000 times the prescribed dose. Each of these unfortunate incidents was the culmination of a chain of errors, many of them avoidable. Indeed, Healthgrades, an independent health care rating company, estimates that almost 3 percent of hospital patients in the United States are victims of potentially preventable medical errors.[1]

How can this happen? Cognitive errors, such as those we will be studying in this chapter, are the leading contributing

Our eyes want to join the picture of the White House on this $20 bill with the actual building, but our minds tell us that the continuation is an illusion.

THiNK FIRST

- What are some of the sources of knowledge?
- In what ways might experience be misleading?
- What are some of the types of cognitive and social errors in our thinking?

 factor in medical mistakes, many of which result in death and long-term disability.[2] It is estimated that diagnostic errors alone result in 40,000 to 80,000 hospital deaths per year in the United States.[3]

Following the 1995 incident with Willie King, hospitals have started taking extra precautions, including double back-up identification systems, computerized error-tracking systems, and the use of patient safety officers to monitor and educate medical professionals. Many medical schools are also teaching their students about cognitive biases and training them to think about how they are thinking (meta-analysis) as well as how to better communicate with and get feedback from other staff.

The prevalence of medical mistakes illustrates how cognitive errors can lead otherwise highly trained professionals to make erroneous decisions.

Good critical-thinking skills require that we evaluate evidence thoroughly and be aware of social and cognitive errors in our thinking to effectively evaluate any given situation and avoid jumping to a conclusion or acting hastily based on preconceived ideas. In Chapter 4 we will:

- Learn about the nature and limitations of human knowledge
- Distinguish between rationalism and empiricism
- Learn about different types of evidence
- Set guidelines for evaluating evidence
- Look at sources for researching claims and evidence
- Study different types of cognitive/perceptual errors, including self-serving biases
- Learn how social expectations and group pressure can lead to erroneous thinking

Finally, we will examine the evidence and arguments regarding unidentified flying objects (UFOs) and what type of proof would be necessary to establish their existence.

Actor Dennis Quaid's newborn twins were given a dose of blood thinner that was ten times that prescribed.

HUMAN KNOWLEDGE AND ITS LIMITATIONS

Knowledge is information or experience that we believe to be true and for which we have justification or evidence. Understanding how we acquire knowledge as well as having an awareness of the limitations of human understanding are essential in logical reasoning.

Rationalism and Empiricism

Our views of ourselves and the world around us are shaped by our understanding of the nature of truth and the ultimate sources of knowledge. **Rationalists** claim that most human knowledge comes through reason. Greek philosopher Plato (427–347 BCE) believed that there is an unchanging truth we can know through reason and that most of us confuse truth with worldly appearance.

The empiricists reject the rationalists' claim that it is through reason that we discern truth. **Empiricists** instead claim that we discover truth primarily through our physical senses. Science is based primarily on empiricism. The scientific method involves making direct observations of the world, and then coming up with a hypothesis to explain these observations.

Structure of the Mind

German philosopher Immanuel Kant (1724–1804) argued that how we experience reality is not simply a matter of pure reason (rationalism) or of using physical senses (empiricism) but depends on the structure of our minds. Like computers—which are designed to accept and process particular kinds of inputs from the outside world—our brains must have the correct "hardware" to accept and make sense of incoming data.

Most neurologists believe, as did Kant, that we do not see "reality" directly as it is but that instead our mind or brain provides structure and rules for processing incoming information. In other words, as we noted in Chapter 1, we *interpret* our experiences rather than directly perceiving the world "out there."

> **knowledge** Information which we believe to be true and for which we have justification or evidence.
>
> **rationalist** One who claims that most human knowledge comes through reason.
>
> **empiricist** One who believes that we discover truth primarily through our physical senses.

Connections

How is the assumption of empiricism reflected in the scientific method?
See Chapter 12, p. 363.

SELF-EVALUATION QUESTIONNAIRE*

THiNK Tank

Rate yourself on the following scale from 1 (strongly disagree) to 5 (strongly agree)

1 2 3 4 5   Knowledge comes primarily through reason rather than the senses.

1 2 3 4 5   I have a tendency to look only for evidence that confirms my assumptions or cherished worldviews.

1 2 3 4 5   The most credible evidence is that based on direct experience, such as eyewitness reports.

1 2 3 4 5   When I look at a random shape such as a cloud or craters on the moon, I tend to see meaning or an image in it.

1 2 3 4 5   The probability that there are two students in a class of twenty-four who have a birthday on the same day and month is about 50 percent.

1 2 3 4 5   When I buy a lottery ticket, I use my lucky number.

1 2 3 4 5   I can truly enjoy life only if I have perfect control over it.

1 2 3 4 5   I am better than most at getting along with other people.

1 2 3 4 5   Americans are more trustworthy than other people, especially people from non-Western cultures.

* Keep track of your results. As you read this book and gain a better understanding of critical thinking, you'll find out what your responses to each of these statements mean. A brief summary of the meaning of each rating can also be found at the back of the book.

While our brain helps us make sense of the world, it also limits us. For example, according to the new string theory in physics, there are at least nine spatial dimensions.[4] However, our brains are structured to perceive a three-dimensional world. Consequently, it is difficult, if not impossible, for us to imagine a nine-dimensional world. Because of the structure of our brains, we are also prone to certain perceptual and cognitive errors. We'll be studying some of these errors later in this chapter.

Effective critical thinking requires that we be aware of our strengths and limitations and that we strive to improve our style of inquiry and our understanding of the world. Because complete certainty is almost always an impossible goal, we need to learn how to assess evidence and to remain open to multiple perspectives.

evidence Reasons for believing that a statement or claim is true or probably true.

Connections

How can you tell if a news story is credible? *See Chapter 11, p. 337.*

How do scientists go about collecting evidence? *See Chapter 12, pp. 368–369.*

are addressed in greater detail in subsequent chapters, we first need to make sure the evidence on which we base our analysis is accurate and complete. Evidence can come from many different sources, some more reliable than others.

Evidence can be based on information from other sources or on firsthand experience. It is reasonable to use our experience as credible evidence for a claim, *if* it is not contradicted by other evidence. Likewise, if a claim conflicts with our experience, then we have good reason to be suspicious of that claim. Learning how to evaluate the credibility and accuracy of evidence is a key skill in critical thinking and logic.

Direct Experience and False Memories

Effective critical thinking requires that we be willing to check the accuracy of our experience. As we noted earlier, our brains interpret rather than directly record sensory experience. Consequently, direct sensory experience is not infallible. Even though we may remember major events "as

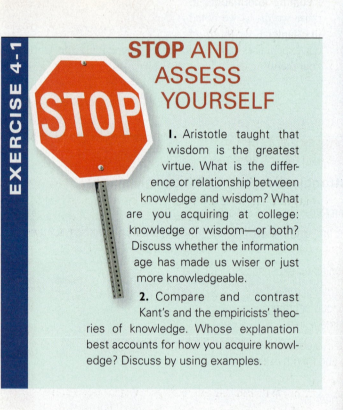

EXERCISE 4-1

STOP AND ASSESS YOURSELF

1. Aristotle taught that wisdom is the greatest virtue. What is the difference or relationship between knowledge and wisdom? What are you acquiring at college: knowledge or wisdom—or both? Discuss whether the information age has made us wiser or just more knowledgeable.

2. Compare and contrast Kant's and the empiricists' theories of knowledge. Whose explanation best accounts for how you acquire knowledge? Discuss by using examples.

EVALUATING EVIDENCE

Evidence is something that tends to prove or disprove a particular view. In arguments, evidence is used as the grounds or premises for our belief in a particular conclusion. While analytical skills are essential in evaluating an argument and

False memories can significantly alter how witnesses "remember" an event, as happened in the case of the Challenger explosion.

though they were yesterday," these memories are not as stable as scientists once thought. A study done four years after the 1986 *Challenger* explosion found that many of the witnesses had dramatically altered their memories of the shuttle disaster, even to the point of "seeing" things that had never happened.[5]

Language can also alter memories. This is particularly problematic when police inadvertently use leading questions that can bias a person's testimony or even alter the person's memories of an incident.

The power of words to shape our reality is poignantly illustrated by how leading questions can alter eyewitnesses' perception of a particular event. In a study, participants were shown a film of a car accident.[6] They were then asked one of the following questions about the speed of the cars. Their averaged responses are given in parentheses after each question:

James Calvin Tillman was released from prison in July 2006, with the help of the Innocence Project, after serving 16 years for a rape he did not commit. His conviction was based on a false eyewitness report.

How fast were the cars going when they smashed each other? (41 mph)

How fast were the cars going when they collided? (40 mph)

How fast were the cars going when they bumped each other? (38 mph)

How fast were the cars going when they hit each other? (35 mph)

How fast were the cars going when they contacted each other? (32 mph)

Despite the fact that they had all seen the same film, participants responded with higher speeds based on the intensity of the verb. Those who were told the cars smashed or collided reported significantly higher speed estimates than those who were told that the cars merely contacted each other.

Inaccurate or false memories can be as compelling and believable as real memories. In police work, eyewitness identifications are incorrect up to 50 percent of the time. Mistaken eyewitness identifications of a suspect are the greatest single cause of wrongful convictions. Although jurors regard eyewitness identification as trustworthy, scientists have found that eyewitness reports are notoriously unreliable. According to The Innocence Project, an organization dedicated to exonerating wrongfully convicted individuals through DNA testing, misidentification by eyewitnesses is the most common cause of wrongful

convictions in the U.S. It is estimated that even under the best conditions, eyewitness are incorrect about half the time.[7]

Indeed, we are so suggestible that we may go beyond inadvertently altering memories to vividly recalling events that never happened, a phenomenon known as **false memory syndrome**. Psychologists have found that after only three sessions in which there are repeated suggestions about a nonexistent childhood event, such as being lost in a mall at age 5 or spilling grape juice on a guest at a wedding, about 25 percent of the subjects will "recall" the event, and many will provide details. What's more, there is little connection between their confidence in their memory and the truth of their memory.[8]

Why are some people more prone than others to memory distortions? Elizabeth Loftus, one of the foremost researchers in the field, suggests that false memory is most likely to occur in people who don't engage in critical thinking about their memories but just accept them as reported.[9] The use of memorization strategies, such as those discussed in "Critical Thinking in Action: Memorization Strategies," can help us in accurately remembering new information. By being more attentive and analyzing events as they happen and by being alert to inconsistencies in our "memories," we are less likely to be taken in by false or distorted memories.

false memory syndrome The recalling of events that never happened.

Critical THiNKing in Action

Memorization Strategies

In a study of why some people are better at accurately memorizing new information, magnetic resonance brain imaging was used to determine which brain regions are correlated with specific memorization strategies.* Researchers found that most people use one or a combination of the following four strategies for remembering the picture to the right.

1. **Visualization inspection.** Participants carefully study the visual appearance of an object. Some people are much better at this strategy and are able to commit pictures as well as pages of books to visual memory.

2. **Verbal elaboration.** Individuals construct sentences about the objects or material they are trying to memorize. For example, they may say to themselves, "The pig is key to this image."

3. **Mental imagery.** Individuals form interactive mental images, much like an animated cartoon. For example, they may imagine the pig jumping into a pool off the end of a diving board shaped like a key.

4. **Memory retrieval.** People reflect and come up with a meaning for the object or association of the object with personal memories.

Participants who use one or a combination of these different strategies performed better at learning new material than those who used these strategies only rarely or not at all. In addition, it was found that each of these strategies used different parts of the brain and that people seem to have different learning styles that work best for them.

DISCUSSION QUESTIONS

1. What strategy, if any, do you use for learning new information? For example, what strategy might you use for remembering the picture below? Evaluate the effectiveness of the strategy or strategies in helping you be a better critical thinker and in your performance in classes.

2. Think of a time when you later discovered that a memory you had was inaccurate or false. Discuss how the use of these strategies might make you less prone to memory distortions. Be specific.

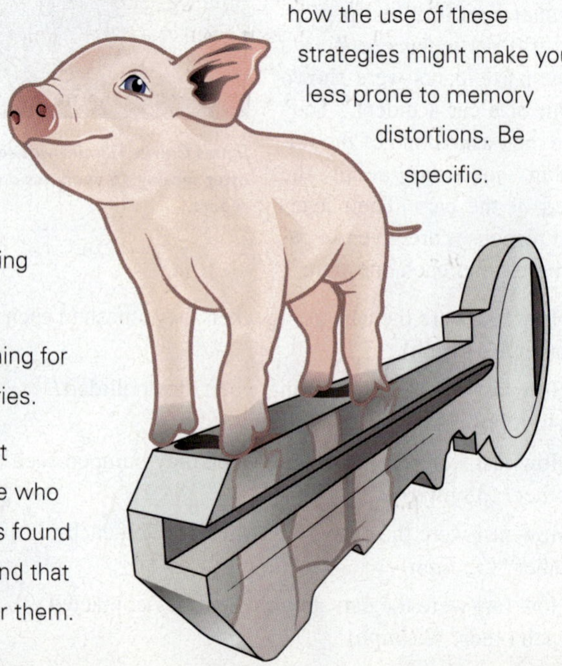

The Unreliability of Hearsay and Anecdotal Evidence

We should be skeptical of what others tell us, especially if it's hearsay evidence or comments taken out of context. **Hearsay**, evidence that is heard by one person and then repeated to another person and so on until you hear it, is notoriously unreliable. As children, we've probably all played the game of "telephone," in which we whisper something to one person and she whispers the message to the next person and so on down the line until the last person says what he has heard. It is almost always different, often amusingly so, from the original message.

Anecdotal evidence, which is based on personal testimonies, is also unreliable because of the problem of inaccurate memory as well as the human tendency to exaggerate or distort what we experience to fit our expectations. For example, many people have reported seeing UFOs and, in some cases, being abducted by aliens. However, despite the apparent sincerity of their beliefs, anecdotal evidence in the absence of any physical evidence cannot be used as proof that UFOs and aliens exist. We'll be looking at

hearsay Evidence that is heard by one person and then repeated to another.

anecdotal evidence Evidence based on personal testimonies.

different perspectives on the credibility of the evidence for UFOs in the readings at the end of this chapter.

Experts and Credibility

One of the most credible sources of information is that of experts. When turning to an expert, it is important that we find someone who is knowledgéable in the particular field under question. When we use the testimony of a person who is an expert in a different field, we are committing the fallacy of *appeal to inappropriate authority*. We'll study fallacies in more depth in Chapter 5.

For example, many students believe, on the basis of the testimony of their friends, that marijuana use is harmless and that it is perfectly safe to drive after smoking a joint. In fact, research by medical experts shows that, although marijuana does not impair driving as much as alcohol, reaction time is reduced by 41 percent after smoking one joint and 63 percent after smoking two joints.[10] Despite evidence from experts, most people will still base their judgments on smoking marijuana on information from their peers until they develop stronger critical-thinking skills.

In seeking out experts, we should look at their credentials, including:

1. *Education* or training from a reputable institute
2. *Experience* in making judgments in the field
3. *Reputation* among peers as an expert in the field
4. *Accomplishments* in the field such as academic papers and awards

Unfortunately, expert testimony is not foolproof. Experts may disagree, in which case we will have to reserve judgment or look to others in the field. Furthermore, sometimes experts are biased, particularly those who are being paid by special-interest groups or corporations who stand to gain financially from supporting a particular position.

For example, it has long been assumed that milk and dairy products help maintain strong bones in adults. However, this claim has not been supported by scientific research. Instead this claim has been mainly promoted by groups that financially depend on the sale of dairy products. While the National Dairy Council extols the benefits of milk for people of all ages, many medical experts, including researchers at the Harvard School of Public Health[11] and the Physicians Committee for Responsible Medicine, argue, based on research, that milk may actually accelerate the process of bone loss in adults. In light of these findings, the Federal Trade Commission, a government agency charged with protecting consumers and eliminating unfair and deceptive marketplace practices, ordered the National Dairy Council to withdraw its ads that claimed drinking milk can prevent bone loss in adults.

Preconceived ideas can also influence how experts interpret evidence. Brandon Mayfield, an Oregon lawyer and a Muslim convert, was taken into custody in Portland, Oregon, after the March 2004 train bombing in Madrid, Spain, when what appeared to be his fingerprint mysteriously turned up on a plastic bag used by the bombers. Although Spanish law-enforcement agencies expressed doubt that the fingerprint was Mayfield's, U.S. officials insisted that it was an "absolutely incontrovertible match."[12] As it later turned out, the fingerprint belonged to an Algerian living in Spain. The U.S. officials succumbed to preconceived notions in making a false arrest of Mayfield.

The game "telephone" is an amusing example of how hearsay can result in misinterpretation.

Connections

How can you determine whether a science news story is well done and accurate? *See Chapter 11, p. 346.*

How do scientists design experiments to avoid bias? *See Chapter 12, p. 369.*

How can you recognize and avoid being taken in by misleading advertisements? *See Chapter 10, pp. 318–321.*

got milk?

Liquid Gold.

9 essential nutrients to
make big waves.

Inadequate research can lead to misrepresentation of a product—advertisers, for example, claimed that milk built strong bones in adults, a claim that was later proven false. The above ad also contains the fallacy of appeal to inappropriate authority, since Olympic swimmer Michael Phelps is not an expert on the health benefits of milk.

While experts are usually a good source of credible evidence, even experts can be biased and can misinterpret data, as we noted in the opening scenario on medical errors. Because of this, it is important that we be able to evaluate claims, especially those that may be slanted or that conflict with other experts' analysis.

confirmation bias The tendency to look only for evidence that supports our assumptions.

Evaluating Evidence for a Claim

Our analysis of the evidence for a claim should be accurate, unbiased, and as complete as possible. Credible evidence is consistent with other relevant evidence. In addition, the more evidence there is to support a claim, the more reasonable it is to accept that claim. In critical thinking, there is no virtue in rigid adherence to a position that is not supported by evidence (see "Thinking Outside the Box: Rachel Carson, Biologist and Author")

Sometimes we don't have access to credible evidence. In cases like these, we should look for contradictory evidence. For example, some atheists reject the belief that there is a God because, they argue, it is contradicted by the presence of so much evil in the world. When there is evidence that contradicts a claim, we have good reason to doubt the claim. However, if there is no contradictory evidence, we should remain open to the possibility that a position may be true.

In evaluating a claim, we need to watch out for **confirmation bias**, the tendency to look only for evidence that confirms our assumptions and to resist evidence that contradicts them. This inclination is so strong that we may disregard or reinterpret evidence that runs contrary to our cherished beliefs.[13] In research about people who were opposed to and those who supported capital punishment, both sides interpreted the findings of a study on whether capital punishment deterred crime to fit their prior views. If the evidence did not fit, they focused on the flaws in the research and dismissed its validity or, in some cases, actually distorted the evidence to support their position.[14] Politicians may also cherry-pick the evidence, reading only reports and listening to evidence that supports their previous beliefs. This happened in 2002 when the Bush administration claimed there was conclusive proof that Iraq had weapons of mass destruction. Newscasters and journalists who have strong beliefs about particular issues may also engage in confirmation bias.

Sources that are usually reliable can inadvertently pass on incorrect information. A friend of mine told me that women in their 20s now earn more than men. My friend went on to tell me that he had read this in an opinion piece by a *New York Times* columnist.[15] When I checked out the information in the article, I found that, according to the National Labor Statistics, women in their 20s, despite the fact that they are better educated, earn only about 92 percent of what men earn. While my friend would normally have checked out the sources of the columnist's claims, confirmation bias kept him from doing so. He believed, prior to reading the article, that boys are getting a raw deal in school, since the majority of teachers are women, and that we are entering an age of reverse sexism. The "fact," albeit incorrect, that women in their 20s are now earning more than men are "confirmed" his views.

Confirmation bias may also take the form of more rigorously scrutinizing contrary evidence than that which supports our position. Peter Jennings, of ABC's *World News Tonight*, presented a study that "disproved" therapeutic touch, a healing method used extensively in India that involves a therapist's using the "energy" in his or her hands to help correct the "energy field" of a sick person.[16] The study, which was previously quoted in a prestigious medical journal, had been carried out by a fourth grader, Emily Rosa, as a project for her science class. On the basis of this single fourth grader's project, the editor of

Thinking Outside the Box

RACHEL CARSON, *Biologist and Author*

After graduating with a master's degree in Zoology from Johns Hopkins University, Rachel Carson (1907–1964) was hired as a writer by the U.S. Fish and Wildlife Service. The success of her 1951 book, *The Sea Around Us*, allowed her to leave her job and concentrate on her life goal of becoming a writer.

As early as 1945 she had become concerned about the overuse of chemical pesticides, such as DDT. Although others before her had tried to warn the public about the dangers of these powerful pesticides, it was her reputation as a complete and meticulous researcher, along with her intellectual curiosity, that contributed to her success. She began by examining the existing research on the effect of pesticides. Her reputation also allowed her to enlist the expertise and support of scientists in the field.

When *Silent Spring* was published in 1962, it created an immediate uproar and backlash. A huge counterattack was launched by the big chemical companies, including Monsanto and Velsicol, which denounced her as a "hysterical woman" unqualified to write on the topic. Despite threats of lawsuits, Carson didn't back down. Because her research was informed and accurate, her opponents were unable to find holes in her argument. *Silent Spring* changed the course of American history and launched a new environmental movement.

DISCUSSION QUESTIONS

1. Think of a time when you argued for a position that was supported by credible evidence even though doing so angered or alienated a family member, teacher, or employer. What was the outcome? Evaluate your response. In particular, discuss how you used (or didn't use) your critical thinking skills in responding to criticism of your position.

2. Rachel Carson is an example of how one person can make a huge difference. Looking into your future, think of ways in which you might be able to use your talents and critical-thinking skills to make the world a better place.

---

the journal had declared that therapeutic touch was bogus. Because the editor had a bias against nontraditional therapies, he held "studies" that suggested therapeutic touch might be ineffective to a lower standard of proof.

Even scientists sometimes look for evidence that supports their theories rather than evidence that challenges their thinking. Models used for testing hypotheses may promote confirmation bias and questionable interpretation of data. Science writer Matt Ridley, in his article "How Bias Heats up the [Global] Warming Debate," writes regarding the controversy over global warming:

> The late novelist Michael Crichton, in his prescient 2003 lecture criticizing climate research, said: "To an outsider, the most significant innovation in the global-warming controversy is the overt reliance that is being placed on models. . . . No longer are models judged by how well they reproduce data from the real world—increasingly, models provide the data. As if they were themselves a reality."

It isn't just models, but the interpretation of

Connections

How do scientists use evidence to test a hypothesis? *See Chapter 12, p. 369.*

How do we as consumers reinforce confirmation bias in the news media? *See Chapter 11, p. 353.*

real data, too. The rise and fall in both temperature and carbon dioxide, evident in Antarctic ice cores, was at first thought to be evidence of carbon dioxide driving climate change. Then it emerged that the temperature had begun rising centuries earlier than carbon dioxide. Rather than abandon the theory, scientists fell back on the notion that the data jibed with the possibility that rising carbon dioxide levels were reinforcing the warming trend in what's called a positive feedback loop. Maybe—but there's still no empirical evidence that this was a significant effect compared with a continuation of whatever first caused the warming.[17]

Brain imaging studies have found that when we come to a conclusion that confirms our prior bias, the decision is associated with a pleasure response and a feeling of emotional comfort, even though our conclusion is erroneous.[18] When theories are disproved, it is generally by other scientists rather than by the scientists who proposed the theories (see "Thinking Outside the Box: Stephen Hawking, Physicist" in Chapter 1).

Because of the human propensity to engage in confirmation bias, many scholarly scientific journals require that researchers report disconfirmatory evidence as well as contradictory interpretations of their data. As critical thinkers, we need to develop strategies that compel us to examine evidence, especially that which confirms our prior views, and to be more open-minded about evidence that contradicts our views.

In evaluating evidence, the degree of credibility required depends on the circumstances. The greater the impact our actions might have, the greater the degree of credibility and certainty we should demand. Courts of law require a high degree of credibility for evidence of guilt because of the dire consequences of declaring an innocent person guilty.

Connections

How do scientists gather evidence to test their hypotheses? *See Chapter 12, pp. 368–369.* **What are the "rules of evidence" in a court of law?** *See Chapter 13, pp. 414–415.* **How reliable is the news media as a source of information?** *See Chapter 11, pp. 338–341.*

Hot or Not?

Do you tend to distort evidence to fit with your beliefs?

Research Resources

We live in an age where information is proliferating at an astounding rate. We are inundated on a daily basis with information from newspapers, television, the Internet, and other media sources. When using evidence from the media—especially the mass media—we need to consider the sources and their slant, if any.

In addition, some writing, such as novels, poetry, movie scripts, and even some editorials, is not intended to be taken as factual. For example, the film *Zero Dark Thirty*, which recounted the search for and assassination of Osama bin Laden, drew considerable criticism from some people for portraying the CIA as using water boarding techniques on terrorist suspects in Guantanamo Bay. However, the movie was never intended as a documentary. Instead it was a dramatization, and as such a fusion of fact and fiction.[19]

Assessing claims, including distinguishing between fact and fiction, requires good research skills and competence in gathering, evaluating, and synthesizing supporting evidence. Like scientists, good critical thinkers spend a lot of time researching claims and collecting information before drawing a conclusion. Apply the criteria listed in the CRAAP test (which stands for currency, relevance, authority, accuracy, and purpose) to evaluate the reliability of information you find.

As you begin your research, try to set up an interview with someone who is an expert in the field under investigation, such as a faculty member or an

The film **Zero Dark Thirty**, *about the search for Osama bin Laden, was a blend of fact and fictional dramatization.*

outside expert. An expert can provide you with information as well as point you to reputable publications. When interviewing the expert, don't rely on your memory. Take accurate notes; repeat what you think you heard if you are unsure. Librarians are also a valuable source of information. In addition to their wealth of knowledge regarding resources, some college librarians have Ph.D.s in specialized fields.

Dictionaries and *encyclopedias* are another good place for you to start your research. Specialized reference books often contain extensive bibliographies of good source material. They may be accessed online or used in the reference section of your library. If you are doing time-sensitive research, make sure the reference sources are up-to-date. Make sure you use reputable encyclopedias. While sites such as Wikipedia might be a good starting point, Wikipedia entries, because they are not necessarily written by experts in their fields, cannot be used as references in research.

Library catalogues—most of which are online— are invaluable in research. Use key words to find your subject in the catalogue. In selecting resources, check the date of publication. If your library doesn't have a particular book or journal, you can usually get it through interlibrary loan.

Scholarly journals, also known as peer-reviewed journals, contain articles that have been reviewed by fellow experts in the field. Most scholarly journals are indexed on specialized databases that you can access through your library Internet home page. In some cases, the full journal articles are available on the Internet. For more general information, the Expanded Academic Index is a good place to start.

Government documents are also reputable sources of information about such things as employment statistics and demographics. You can access many of the government documents through Internet databases. Go to http://www.usa.gov/ to search for topics of interest.

Internet Web sites contain a wealth of information. Millions of new pages are added every week to the Internet. There are also specialized Web sites, such as Academic Search Complete, which are not available through search engines such as Google, Bing, and Yahoo, but that can generally be accessed through your college or university library's Web site. Many Web sites are sponsored by reputable organizations and individuals. The top-level domain at the end of a Web site's address (URL, or uniform resource locator) can help you in evaluating its reliability. All URLs for U.S. government sites end with the top-level domain *.gov*. URLs for sites ending with the top-level domain *.edu* indicate that the source of the information is a U.S. educational institution. Both of these types of sites can generally be counted on to provide reliable and accurate information. The global top-level domain *.org* indicates that the site belongs to a private or nonprofit organization such as Amnesty International or possibly a religious group. The information on these sites may or may not be reliable, depending on the reputability of the organization sponsoring

the Web site. The global top-level domain *.com* indicates that the site is sponsored by a commercial organization such as a corporation or private business, at least in the United States. In these cases you must try to determine the companies' motives in providing the information—for example, is it for advertising purposes? Generally, blogs should not be used as references. Blogs are notoriously unreliable and often based on opinion rather than facts. If you have any doubts about a site's credibility, it is best to ask a reference librarian or expert in the field about the most reliable sites to look at for information on an issue.

While doing your research, no matter what resource you are using, take accurate notes or make copies of articles. Keep full citation information for your sources so that you can refer to them later and cite them if necessary. If, in

Connections

How do scientists go about gathering information and evidence? *See Chapter 12, pp. 368–369*

How does the Internet affect our lives? *See Chapter 11, pp. 347–348.*

presenting your research, you use material word for word, always put it in quotation marks and acknowledge the source. You should also cite the source of paraphrased information that is not widely known. In addition, remember to cite sources for any surveys, statistics, and graphics.

Researching a claim or issue requires that we be able to sort through and analyze the relevant data. Good research skills also help us make better decisions in our lives by providing us with the tools for evaluating different claims and available courses of action we might take.

STOP AND ASSESS YOURSELF

1. What evidence might be sufficient for you to conclude that an intelligent computer or android is conscious and has free will? Would this same evidence be sufficient to prove to you that another human you met was conscious and had free will? Explain using the criteria for evaluating evidence discussed in the chapter.

2. Think of a time when you saw something and were convinced that your interpretation of the event was true, but you later came to have doubts about your interpretation. Discuss the factors that contributed to your doubts.

3. Working in small groups, evaluate the following list of claims. If there are any ambiguous terms, define them as well as possible. Next, make a list of types of evidence you would need to support or reject each claim. State how you would go about doing the research.

  a. Genetically modified food is dangerous.

  b. Men are more aggressive by nature than are women.

  c. Prayers are answered.

  d. Toast is more likely to fall butter-side down.

  e. Asian Americans are better at math than European Americans are.

  f. Living together before marriage is associated with a lower divorce rate.

  g. Human life begins at conception.

  h. A flying saucer crashed over Roswell, New Mexico, in 1947.

  i. Canadians, on average, live longer than Americans do.

  j. God exists.

  k. The sea level has risen almost a foot over the past century as a result of global warming.

  l. Yawning is contagious.

  m. Capital punishment deters crime.

  n. Debbie was born under the sign Aquarius. Therefore, she must love water.

4. Select one of the following topics and research it.

  a. The impact of global warming on your city or state

  b. The average age of marriage for men and women now and when your parents got married

  c. The number of members in the U.S. House of Representatives

  d. The percentage of American college athletes who become professional athletes

  e. The changes over the past 30 years in majors of college students

Make a list of the resources, including experts, books, journals, search engines, databases, and Web sites you used in your research. Rate each of the sources you used in terms of which generated the most credible and unbiased evidence. Compare your results with those of others in your class. To what extent did the topic chosen determine which research resources, including the Internet, were most useful?

5. Choose one of the claims from exercise 3 or a recent news story and research the evidence. Write a short essay or present your results to the class for evaluation.

6. Imagine that you are backing out of a parking spot on campus. Your view is somewhat obscured by an SUV parked beside you. As you back out, you hit another car that was driving through the parking lot. Write a paragraph describing the event for the police report.

Now imagine that you are the other person whose car was hit. Write a paragraph describing the event for the police report. Compare and contrast the two reports. Analyze how the words you chose in each report were selected to influence the perception of the police officer regarding what happened.

COGNITIVE AND PERCEPTUAL ERRORS IN THINKING

On the evening of October 30, 1938, a play based on H. G. Wells's novel *War of the Worlds* about a Martian invasion was broadcast to the nation on radio. Many of the people who listened to the show believed that the invasion was real. Some people even "smelled" the poisonous Martian gas and "felt" the heat rays being described on the radio. Others claimed to have seen the giant machines landing in New Jersey and the flames from the battle. One panicked person told police he had heard the president's voice on the radio ordering them to evacuate.

Our perceptions of the world around us are easily skewed by social influences. Most people underestimate the critical role that cognitive and social factors play in our perception and interpretation of sense data. Although emotion has traditionally been regarded as the culprit when reason goes astray, studies suggest that many of the errors in our thinking are neurological in nature.[20] In this section, we'll be looking at some of these cognitive and perceptual errors.

Perceptual Errors

Our minds are not like blank sheets of paper or recording devices, such as cameras or video recorders, as the empiricists claimed. Instead, our brains construct a picture of the world much as an artist does. Our brains filter our perceptions and fill in missing information based in part on our expectations, as occurred in the broadcast of *War of the Worlds*.

Some skeptics believe that UFO sightings are based on perceptual errors, including optical illusions (see "Analyzing Images: The St. Louis Arch"). In 1969, an Air National Guard pilot spotted what he thought was a squadron of UFOs within several hundred feet of his plane.

Connections

As a consumer, how can you avoid being taken in by cognitive and perceptual errors used by marketers? *See Chapter 10, p. 306.*

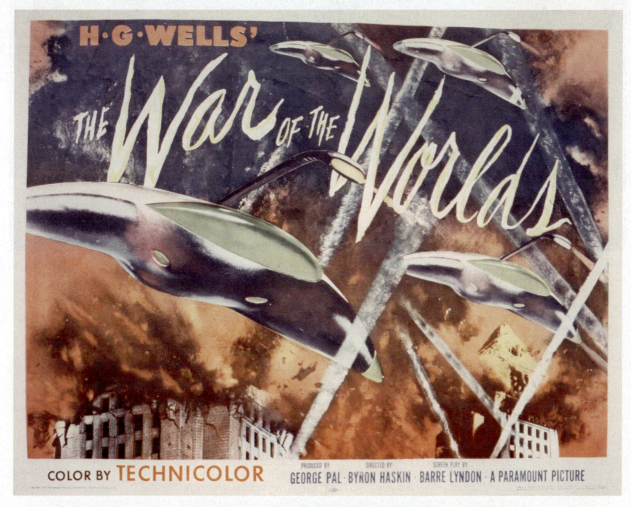

When the radio show based on the novel **The War of the Worlds** *was broadcast, many of the listeners believed that the invasion was real.*

The St. Louis Arch   Designed by architect Eero Saarinen, the St. Louis Arch in St. Louis, Missouri, was completed in 1965 on a site overlooking the Mississippi River. Although the height of the arch and its width at the base are both 630 feet, the graceful catenary creates the illusion that the arch is taller than it is wide. Even if we are told that its height and width are the same, we still have great difficulty making the cognitive adjustment to correct what is known as the vertical/horizontal illusion. Because of this optical illusion we also tend to overestimate the height of trees and tall buildings.

DISCUSSION QUESTIONS

1. *What was your first reaction when you were told that the height and width of the arch were the same? Did they look the same after you were told the dimensions of the arch? Share with the class other optical illusions that you have encountered in architecture or elsewhere.*

2. *Working in small groups, discuss why we might experience optical illusions such as the vertical/horizontal illusion. Discuss what resources you could use in developing your hypothesis (a hypothesis is an educated guess based on evidence and experimentation). Share your hypothesis with the class for analysis.*

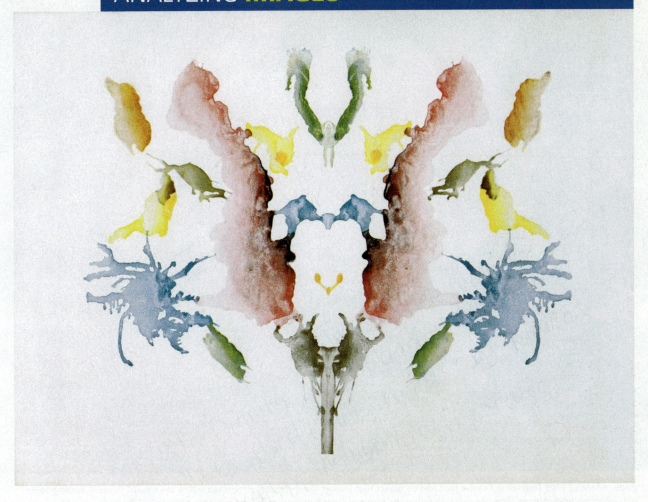

Inkblots In an inkblot test such as in the one above, a psychologist asks a person to describe what he or she sees. The psychologist uses the descriptions to learn more about a person's motivations and unconscious drives.

DISCUSSION QUESTIONS

1. *What do you see when you look at the above inkblot? Why do you think you saw what you did?*

2. *Discuss how the inkblot test illustrates our tendency to impose order on random data. Think of a time when you fell for this error in your everyday life. Come up with two or three critical-thinking strategies you might use to make yourself less prone to being taken in by our tendency to impose meaning on random data.*

He later described the UFOs as the color of "burnished aluminum" and "shaped like a hydroplane." As it turned out, the "squadron of UFOs" was most likely a meteor fireball that had broken up in the vicinity of the plane.[21] However, while being able to provide alternative explanations for most UFO sightings makes their existence less probable, we cannot conclude with certainty that *all* sightings are a result of perceptual errors. We'll be looking at the issue of the existence of UFOs in the "Critical Thinking Issue: Perspectives on Evaluating Evidence for the Existence of Unidentified Flying Objects" section at the end of this chapter.

Our minds may also distort objects we perceive. A straight stick, when inserted in water, appears to bend. A full moon appears to be much larger when it is near the

Connections

What tools and strategies do scientists use to minimize perceptual errors? *See Chapter 12, p. 369.*

Radar photo of 2005 Hurricane Katrina that had an object that looked like a "fetus facing to the left in the womb" to some, leading some anti-abortion advocates to draw the conclusion that the hurricane was punishment for the presence of abortion clinics in the city.

horizon, a phenomenon that NASA refers to as the "moon illusion."

Misperception of Random Data

Because our brains loathe absence of meaning, we may "see" order or meaningful patterns where there are none. For example, when we look at clouds or see unexplained lights in the sky, our brains impose meaning on the random shapes we see. When we look at the moon, we see a "face," popularly known as the man in the moon. In 2004, a piece of toast with cheese, allegedly bearing the image of the Virgin Mary, sold on eBay for $28,000.

One of the most famous examples of this type of error is the "Martian Canals," first reported as channels by Italian astronomer Giovanni Schiaparelli in 1877. Many astronomers continued to believe in the existence of these canals up until 1965, when the spacecraft *Mariner 4* flew close to Mars and took photos of the planet's surface. No canals showed up in the photos. It turned out that the

"canals" were a combination of an optical illusion, the expectation that there were canals, and the brain's tendency to impose order on random data. Because of our brain's inclination to impose meaning on random data, we should maintain a stance of skepticism about what we see.

The combination of the error of misperceiving random data with confirmation bias—interpreting data in a way that confirms our cherished views—is illustrated by the next example. After the devastation of New Orleans by Hurricane Katrina in 2005, a group known as the Columbia Christians for Life announced that God's purpose in sending the hurricane was to destroy the five abortion clinics in the city. Their proof was a radar photograph taken of the hurricane in which they claimed to have seen what looked like "a fetus facing to the left (west) in the womb, in the early weeks of gestation."[22]

Stress as well as preconceptions about the world can affect our perception. How many of us, walking alone at night, have seen a person or dog standing in a shadow, only to discover it was a bush or other object?

Critical THINKing in Action

Food for Thought: Perception and Supersized Food Portions

Obesity is becoming an epidemic in the U.S. More than one-third of Americans adults are obese—more than double the rate in 1980, according to the U.S. Centers for Disease Control and Prevention. Supersized portions of junk food, such as potato chips, hamburgers, and sodas, have been blamed, in part, for this trend.* Do supersized portions lead to supersized people, or is this just all hype so that we can place the blame for our weight problems on Lay's potato chips and McDonald's burgers? In fact, studies show that downsizing our food portions does work to keep our weight down because it takes advantage of a perceptual error. Appetite is not a matter of just the physiological state of hunger but also a matter of perception—what we see in front of us. Most of us eat more when the table or our plates are loaded with food.

Humans are not the only species who make this error. When a researcher places a pile of 100 grams of wheat in front of a hen, she will eat 50 grams and leave 50. However, if we put 200 grams of wheat in front of a hen in a similar hunger condition, she will eat far more— 83 to 108 grams of wheat or, once again, about half of what is in front of her.** Furthermore, if the food is presented as whole grains of rice, rather than cracked rice, where the grains are one quarter the size of whole rice grains, the hen will eat two to three times as much as she would otherwise.

In other words, by cutting down your portion sizes and cutting your food into smaller pieces, your brain will think you're full on less food.

*Nancy Hellmich, "How to Downsize the Student Body," *USA Today,* November 15, 2004.
**George W. Hartmann, *Gestalt Psychology* (New York: Ronald Press, 1935), pp. 87–88.

DISCUSSION QUESTIONS

1. Many students put on weight in their first year of college, a phenomenon known as the "freshman 15." Critically evaluate your college environment and ways in which it promotes or hinders good eating habits. Make a list of suggestions for improving the environment so students are not so vulnerable to perceptual errors and overeact as a result. Carry out one of the suggestions or pass it on to someone who is in a position to make the change.

2. Examine your own eating habits. Evaluate ways in which being more aware of your thinking process, including inbuilt perceptual errors, can help you to maintain healthier eating habits.

Memorable-Events Error

The **memorable-events error** involves our ability to vividly remember outstanding events. Scientists have discovered channels in our brains that actually hinder most long-term memories by screening out the mundane incidents in our everyday life.[23] However, these memory-impairing channels appear to close down during outstanding events. For example, most Americans recall exactly where they were and what they were doing on the morning of September 11, 2001. However, if you ask someone what they were doing on an ordinary weekday two months ago, most

memorable-events error A cognitive error that involves our ability to vividly remember outstanding events.

Why do news stories lend themselves to memorable-events errors? *See Chapter 11, p. 338.*
What methods and techniques do scientists use to minimize personal and social bias? *See Chapter 12, p. 369.*

Connections

people would be unable to remember or would remember only if they could think of something special that happened on that day.

To use another example, airplane crashes and fatalities are reported in the national media, whereas automobile fatalities generally are not. However, per mile traveled, airplane travel is far safer. We're sixteen times more likely to be killed in an automobile accident than in an airplane accident. In fact, traffic accidents are one of the leading causes of death and disability of people between the ages of 15 and 44.[24] However, the memorable-events error exerts such control over our thinking that even after being informed of these statistics, many of us still continue to be more nervous about flying than about driving.

The memorable-events error is sometimes tied in with confirmation bias, in which we tend to remember events that confirm our beliefs and forget those that are contrary to our beliefs. A popular belief in the United States is that "death takes a holiday" and that terminally ill patients can postpone their death until after an important holiday or birthday. In fact, this belief is based purely on wishful thinking and anecdotal evidence. In an analysis of the death certificates of more than a million people who died from cancer, biostatisticians Donn Young

probability error Misunderstanding the probability or chances of an event by a huge margin.

gambler's error The belief that a previous event affects the probability in a random event.

and Erinn Hade found no evidence that there is a reduction in death rates prior to a holiday or important event.[25] Personal and social beliefs are remarkably strong even in the face of empirical evidence that logically should be devastating. When their results were published, Young and Hade received several angry e-mails criticizing them for taking away people's hope.

Probability Errors

What is the probability that two people in your class have a birthday on the same month and day? Most people guess that the probability is pretty low. In fact, in a class of 23, the probability is about 50 percent. In larger classes, the probability is even higher. When we misestimate the probably of an event by a huge margin, we are committing **probability error**.

Humans are notoriously poor at determining probability. We are inclined to believe that coincidences must have paranormal causes when actually they are consistent with

According to the Association for Psychological Science, 1.2 percent of the adult population are pathological gamblers and at least another 2.8 percent are problem gamblers.

probability. For example, you are thinking of a friend whom you haven't seen for a year when the phone rings and it's your friend on the other line. Are you psychic? Or is it just a coincidence? You've probably thought of your friend hundreds or even thousands of times over the course of the past year without receiving any phone calls, but we tend to forget such times because nothing memorable occurred.

One of the most insidious forms of probability error is **gambler's error**—the erroneous belief that previous events affect the probability in a random event. Research suggests that gambling addiction is based on gambler's error. In a study participants were invited to think aloud while gambling. Of the verbalized perceptions, 70 percent were based on erroneous thinking such as "The machine is due; I need to continue," "Here is my lucky dealer," "Today I feel great; it is my lucky day," "It's my turn to win." These statements reveal a failure to understand the random nature of probability.

When questioned about their verbalizations, nonproblem gamblers realized that their beliefs were wrong. They were able to use accumulated evidence to critically evaluate and modify their perceptions. Problem gamblers, in contrast, processed

Statistically, there is a far greater chance per mile traveled of being killed in a car accident than in an airplane crash, yet most people have a greater fear of flying.

the evidence much differently. They believed what they had said and interpreted their occasional random wins as confirming their belief that the outcome of a game can be predicted and controlled. The solution? Work to improve problem gamblers' critical-thinking skills. By making gamblers aware of their erroneous perceptions and the reasons why they continue to cling to these beliefs, clinicians work to help gamblers overcome their addiction.[26]

Self-Serving Biases

There are several types of self-serving biases or errors that impede our thinking and pursuit of truth, including:

- The misperception that we are in control

- The tendency to overestimate ourselves in comparison to others

- The tendency to exaggerate our strengths and minimize our weaknesses

We are predisposed to believe that we are in control of events that are outside our control. "I knew it would rain today," you groan. "I didn't bring my umbrella." Recently, the Powerball lottery jackpot reached over $100 million. I was standing in line at a mini-mart when I overheard the following conversation between the people in front of me, who were waiting to buy lottery tickets.

> **Person 1**: "What are you going to do? Are you going to pick your own numbers or let the computer do it for you?"
>
> **Person 2:** "Pick my own. It gives me a better chance of winning."

People who are poor critical thinkers may fall prey to more than one error in thinking in the same situation. In this case the control error was compounded by the probability error, which we discussed earlier. Although logically we know that lottery numbers are selected randomly, many of us also believe that choosing our own numbers—especially using our "lucky" numbers—increases our chances of

Gambler's error and an addiction to gambling is based on a misunderstanding of the random nature of probability.

winning. In fact, 80 percent of winning lottery tickets have numbers randomly generated by the computer, not so-called lucky numbers picked by the winners.[27]

The misperception that we are in control of random events also plays out in superstitious behavior such as wearing our lucky shirt during a big game or bringing a

Following the disastrous April 2010 oil rig explosion in the Gulf of Mexico, British Petroleum (BP) engaged in self-serving bias by grossly underestimating the amount of crude oil that flowed from the disabled well into the Gulf. BP also overestimated its control of the situation and its ability to stop the oil flow and clean up the oil spill without outside help.

good-luck charm to an exam. Before a game, most college and professional athletes engage in ritualistic superstitious behavior such as using a particular color shoelace or tape. Some baseball players sleep with their bats to break out of a hitting slump or to keep up their batting average. To some extent, the belief that we are in control can boost our confidence in achieving our goals. In fact, ritualistic behaviors have been found to have a calming effect on athletes before a game.

However, if we carry the belief that we are in control too far, it can distort our thinking and lead to poor decisions in our lives. The self-serving bias, and misjudgment about our ability to handle a challenge, can work against our rational self-interests. For example in the case of the British Petroleum oil leak, BP lost billions of dollars as well as the public confidence because of their erroneous belief in the beginning that they were in control of the situation and didn't need outside help. Thousands of people have died in wildfires and in hurricanes, despite repeated warnings to evacuate, because they thought they were in control of the situation and could ride out the storm.

This error is also expressed in the often-heard cliché "You can do anything you want if you put your mind to it," the implication being that if only we wanted to enough, we would have perfect control. Self-help gurus have become wealthy catering to this self-serving error. In her book *The Secret* (2006), Rhonda Byrne claims to have found the secret to happiness in what she calls "the law of attraction." According to Byrne, each of us has complete control over what happens to us in our lives. If we

think positive thoughts, then like a magnet, we will attract whatever we want—whether it be a parking spot, a million dollars, a sexy figure, or a cure for cancer. The downside is that if we are not successful in getting what we want, then we have only ourselves and our negative thinking to blame.

The belief that we are in control of situations where we actually have little or no control can contribute to irrational guilt or posttraumatic stress syndrome.[28] A survivor of a traumatic event may believe that he or she should have been able to predict and do something to prevent an event such as sexual abuse, domestic violence, or the death of a loved one, especially an accidental or suicidal death.

Although genetic, physical, and environmental factors play a role in the onset of depression, the belief that we should be in control of our lives can also contribute to depression (see "Critical Thinking in Action: Irrational Beliefs and Depression"). People who are depressed may cling to the irrational belief that the only alternative to not having perfect control is having no control. Because they feel they lack any control over their lives, they tend to attribute their misfortune or sadness to other people's actions. A side effect of this negative behavior is that their behavior often alienates other people, thereby confirming a second irrational belief common to depressed people that they are worthless and unlikable. Thus, their distorted expectations lead to a self-fulfilling prophecy, a cognitive error we'll be studying in the next section.

A second self-serving bias is the tendency to overestimate ourselves in comparison to others. Most people rate themselves as above average when it comes to getting along with other people. Although it obviously can't be true that the majority of people are above average—except, perhaps, in the fictional town of Lake Wobegon in Garrison Keillor's *Prairie Home Companion* on Minnesota Public Radio—this self-serving bias can bolster our self-esteem and confidence. However, if we are unaware of the bias, it can become a problem and cause us not to take responsibility for our shortcomings. A Pew Research Center survey found that while 70 percent of Americans are overweight and that nine in ten agree that most of their fellow Americans are overweight, only 39 percent of Americans consider themselves to be overweight.[29] Clearly there seems to be a disconnect between being overweight and people's estimation of their own weight.

Another example of the self-serving bias

Critical THiNKing in Action

Irrational Beliefs and Depression

Albert Ellis (b. 1913), founder of rational emotive behavioral therapy, maintains that irrational ideas are the primary source of depression, rage, feelings of inadequacy, and self-hatred. Some of these irrational beliefs are:

- "I must be outstandingly competent, or I am worthless."
- "Others must treat me considerately, or they are absolutely rotten."
- "The world should always give me happiness, or I will die."
- "I must have perfect control over things, or I won't be able to enjoy life."
- "Because something once strongly affected my life, it will indefinitely affect my life."

According to Ellis, a depressed person feels sad because he (or she) erroneously thinks he is inadequate and abandoned, even though depressed people have the capacity to perform as well as nondepressed people. The purpose of therapy is to dispute these irrational beliefs and replace them with positive rational beliefs. To achieve this, the therapist asks questions such as:

- Is there evidence for this belief?
- What is the evidence against this belief?
- What is the worst that can happen if you give up this belief?
- And what is the best that can happen?

To assist the clients in changing their irrational beliefs, the therapist also uses other techniques such as empathy training, assertiveness training, and encouraging the development of self-management strategies.

DISCUSSION QUESTIONS

1. Discuss how cognitive errors contribute to irrational beliefs. Make a list of other irrational beliefs people hold that are based on cognitive errors.

2. Do you have any irrational beliefs that interfere with your achieving your life goals? If so, what are they? Discuss how you might use your critical-thinking skills to work toward overcoming these beliefs. Be specific.

See Albert Ellis, *The Essence of Rational Emotive Behavior Therapy.* Ph.D. dissertation, revised, May 1994.

is that most people take personal credit for their successes and blame outside forces for their failures. College students often attribute their "A" grades to something about themselves—their intelligence, quick grasp of the material, or good study skills. In contrast, they usually attribute their poor grades to something outside their control such as having an unfair teacher or having a touch of the flu on the day of the exam.[30] Similarly, when it comes to being overweight, many people blame a slow metabolism as the main reason why they can't lose weight, rather than their lifestyle or factors under their control. However, when overweight people do lose weight, they rarely attribute their success to a peppy metabolism but instead credit their willpower and good choices.

This type of self-serving bias can be found in the work-place. When office employees were asked in a survey "if they ever experienced backstabbing, rudeness, or incivility in the workplace," 89 percent said "yes." However, in the same survey 99 percent said that "they were never rude or the cause of the conflict."[31] In other words, most of us are quick to complain about oth-er's irritating behaviors but give little thought to how our behavior might be the cause of workplace conflict.

What is cognitive dissonance and when are people most likely to engage in it? *See Chapter 1, p 27.*

Connections

According to Carol Tavris and Elliot Aronson, social psychologists and authors of *Mistakes Were Made (But Not By Me): Why We Justify Foolish Beliefs, Bad Decisions and Hurtful Acts*, being made aware of the gap between our self-image and our actual behavior creates cognitive disso-nance and discomfort. To minimize this discomfort and maintain our good opinion of ourselves, we instinctively minimize the discrepancy through denial or by blaming someone else for our shortcomings. This sort of ratio-nalization can prevent us from realizing that we're clinging to a mistaken belief.[32] As critical thinkers, we need to deal constructively with the discomfort that comes from cognitive dissonance and to work toward overcoming our mistaken beliefs about ourselves.

A third related self-serving bias is our inclina-tion to exaggerate or place a greater value on our strengths and underestimate or downplay our weak-nesses. In a study of intellectually gifted boys who thought they hadn't done well in class, the boys downplayed the importance of academics and instead emphasized the importance of other pursuits such as sports.[33] Seeing ourselves as having those traits and abilities that are important in life in-creases our sense of worth and helps us to achieve our life goals. This tendency, how-ever, can also contrib-ute to overconfidence and failure to seek or acknowledge other people's skills.

As we noted in the introduction to this chapter, overconfi-dence in physicians and jumping to a conclusion has been identified as one of the key factors in diagnostic errors. Unless we are willing, as critical thinkers, to make an honest

According to the Institute of Medicine of the National Academy of Sciences, medical errors are responsible for an estimated 44,000 to 98,000 deaths a year in the United States.

evaluation of ourselves, it is unlikely that we are going to take steps toward overcoming our shortcomings.

Self-Fulfilling Prophecy

A self-fulfilling prophecy occurs when our exaggerated or distorted expectations reinforce actions that actually bring about the expected event. Expectations can have a profound influence on our behavior. Rumors of impending bank fail-ures during the Great Depression in the early 1930s led to mass panic in which people rushed to take their money out of banks before the banks crashed. As a result, lots of banks went bankrupt. Since banks invest some of the deposits rather than keeping all the money in the vault, the frenzy caused the collapse of the banks—the very thing the customers feared.

To use another example of a self-fulfilling prophecy, let's say a literature professor has a star football player in her class. On the basis of her (mistaken) expectations about college athletes, she assumes that he is not academically inclined but is taking the course only because it is reputed to be easy. Because of this she calls on him less and doesn't encour-age him or make an effort to include him in class discussions. She jus-tifies this behavior on her part as not wanting to embarrass him.

To preserve our expecta-tions, we may interpret am-biguous data in ways that meet our expectations. For example, our football star may be particularly quiet and introspective during one class. The professor as-sumes that he is preoccu-pied with thinking about the upcoming game, when instead he is deep in thought about the poem that is being discussed in class. Our football player, who initially was very interested in the class and in literature and

Panicked citizens gather to withdraw their money from a federal bank during the Great Depression. This type of thinking also contributed to a plunge in the stock market in 2008, when people pulled their money from the stock market because of fears it would crash.

had even written several poems for his high school newspaper, soon begins to lose interest in the class and ends up getting only a mediocre grade. Thus, we have a self-fulfilling prophecy in which the professor's distorted expectation comes true. Clearly, preserving our expectations can come at a cost to others.

Humans are prone to several inborn cognitive and perceptual errors, including optical illusions, misperception of random data, memorable-events errors, probability errors, self-serving biases, and self-fulfilling prophecies. Because these errors are part of the way our brain interprets the world, we may fail to notice the influence they exert over our thinking. Developing our critical-thinking skills

> **Rumors of impending bank failures during the Great Depression in the early 1930s led to mass panic in which people rushed to take their money out of banks before the banks crashed.**

can help us be more aware of these tendencies and adjust for them when appropriate.

STOP AND ASSESS YOURSELF

1. Come up with an issue—such as same-sex marriage, abortion, or legalizing marijuana—that is important to you. Discuss the extent to which cognitive errors bias the way you go about collecting and interpreting evidence regarding this issue. Discuss steps you might take to compensate for this bias.

2. Think of a "lucky" charm or ritual that you use, or have used in the past, to increase your chances of doing well on something that really matters. This can include anything from wearing your "lucky shoes" during a baseball game to rubbing your mother's ring before an important exam. Given your realization that this behavior is based on a cognitive error, why might you continue to do it? Support your answer using what you know of probability error.

3. If you have ever bought a lottery ticket or know of someone who did, why did you (or the other person) buy it? When the ticket was bought, what did you, or the other person, think the probability of winning was? Discuss the extent to which this reasoning involved a probability error.

4. Given that humans are prone to cognitive errors, should we use computers rather than physicians for medical diagnoses? Support your answer.

5. Think of a time when you studied hard for a test but ended up with a low grade. To what did you attribute your poor performance? Now think of a time when you studied hard and did very well on a test. To what did you attribute your good performance? Discuss how self-serving biases may have contributed to the difference in your reaction in each of the two situations.

6. Do you tend to overestimate the amount of control you have over your life? Give specific examples. Discuss how a distorted sense of control has had an impact on your ability to achieve your life goals. Come up with at least two critical-thinking strategies you could use to correct for this cognitive error.

7. Which cognitive error are you most like to commit? Give a specific example of your using this error. If you are willing, share your strategies for overcoming these ideas with the class.

SOCIAL ERRORS AND BIASES

Humans are highly social animals. Because of this trait, social norms and cultural expectations exert a strong influence on how we perceive the world—so much so that we tend to perceive the world differently in groups from the way we do in isolation. Groups can systematically distort both the gathering and the interpretation of evidence.[34]

As we noted in Chapter 1, ethnocentrism—the unjustified belief that our group or culture is superior to that of others—can also bias our thinking and act as a barrier to critical thinking.

Victims of the bombing of a Catholic church in Nigeria by Islamic militants in 2012.

"One of Us/One of Them" Error

Our brains seem to be programmed to classify people as either "one of us" or "one of them." We tend to treat people who are similar to us with respect and those who are different from us—whether in regard to race, sex, religion, political party, age, or nationality—with suspicion or worse. Although most of us claim to believe in human equality, in our culture the use of qualifiers such as *gay judge, female doctor, Hispanic senator,* and *Down syndrome child* betray our tacit belief that any deviation from the norm needs to be specified. We rarely hear terms such as *straight judge, male doctor, European American senator,* or *able-bodied child*!

Prejudices may operate without any conscious realization on our part. In a Harvard study, subjects were asked to quickly associate positive or negative words with black or white faces. Seven out of ten white people, despite their claims that they had no racial prejudice, showed "an automatic preference for white over black."[35]

It is all too easy for people to fall into the "us versus them" mind-set, especially when they feel threatened. In 1994, the Hutu government in Rwanda stirred up Hutus' hatred and fear of the Tutsi, inciting them to carry out a brutal three-month slaughter of the Tutsi. Neighbors killed neighbors, students killed their fellow students, and doctors killed doctors. Even priests helped with the massacre of the Tutsi in their congregations, simply

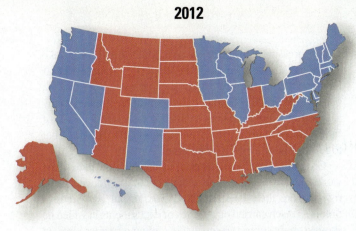

2012

Red States vs Blue States

because the Tutsi were the "other." When it was over, a million people were dead.

This error also contributes to our tendency to polarize issues into two camps. "They," whether it be "right-wing conservatives" or "far-left liberals," are irrational; there is no point in even arguing a point with them. Our group, on the other hand, holds a monopoly on Truth. There is no middle ground. During presidential elections, Americans are quick to divide up the country into two opposing camps: the red states (Republicans) and the blue states (Democrats) and to classify people in their group as "good" and "right" and those in the other group as "bad" and "mistaken."

If we are to overcome this social error we need to be aware of it in our thinking and to build in protective measures.[36] As critical thinkers, we can work toward

minimizing this error in our thinking by first critically evaluating the situation and then consciously reprogramming our brains to come up with new, more reasonable definitions of who it is that we view as "us" by seeking a more immediate and inclusive basis for a connection, such as we all attend the same college, we all are Americans, we all are human beings. We also need to make a conscious effort to be open to multiple perspectives, even those we are initially convinced must be mistaken.

Societal Expectations

The late nineteenth and early twentieth centuries were times of extraordinary technological advancement, setting in motion the expectation of ever new and revolutionary technology. On December 13, 1909, six years after the Wright brothers' epic flight, the *Boston Herald* reported the invention of an airship by a local businessman, Wallace Tillinghast.[37] Over the next several weeks, hundreds of witnesses from the New England–New York area, including police officers, judges, and businesspeople, reported sightings of the airship sailing through the skies.[38] The reported sightings led to a massive search for the airship by reporters. The search was finally called off when it was revealed that the story was a hoax perpetuated by Tillinghast.

Connections

When you serve as a juror, how can cognitive and social errors distort your analysis of the evidence? *See Chapter 13, pp. 417–418.*

Social expectations can be so powerful that they may lead to collective delusions. Sometimes these social errors may even become institutionalized.[39] Acting on social expectations without subjecting them to critical analysis can have dire consequences. The Salem witch trials in colonial Massachusetts, in which over 200 people, predominantly young women, were accused of witchcraft, were rooted in the social expectations of the seventeenth century. Those of us living in the twenty-first century may regard the witch-hunters as crazed fanatics. However, they were simply behaving in a manner that was consistent with the prevailing worldview and social expectations of their time in which certain unfortunate circumstances, such as crop failures, disease, and untimely deaths, were interpreted as being brought about by the Devil and his worldly agents—witches.

The Salem witch hunts, which took place in Massachusetts in the late 17th century, targeted those mistakenly believed to be responsible for society's ills.

The social expectations of the police who interrogated Peter Reilly, a teenager who was accused in 1973 of killing his mother, also played a role in their use of leading questions to get a "confession" out of him. Reilly's mother had been an emotionally abusive woman. In our society we expect victims of parental abuse to be violent and vengeful, even though studies suggest that it is children who witness domestic violence, rather than those who are direct victims of it, who are at highest risk, since they come to accept violence as normal.[40] In addition, it is often a family member who commits this type of violent murder. Therefore, the police jumped to the conclusion, on the basis of their expectations, that Reilly must have committed the murder.

Stereotyping is another type of social bias based on socially generated group labels. In the study mentioned in Chapter 1, page 28, in which researchers showed students a picture of a black man on a subway next to a white man who was holding an open razor, when students were later asked to recall what they had seen, half of them reported that the black man was holding the razor.

Group pressure can influence individual members to take positions that they would never support by themselves, as happened in the Stanford prison experiment described in Chapter 1. Some religious cults exploit this tendency by separating their members from the dissenting views of family and friends. In many cults, people live together, eat together, and may even be assigned a buddy.

Group pressure is so powerful in shaping how we see the world that it can lead people to deny contrary evidence that is right before their eyes. In the 1950s, social psychologist Solomon Asch carried out a series of experiments in which he showed study subjects a screen containing a standard line on the left and three comparison lines on the right. (see "Analyzing Images: Asch Experiment"). One of the comparison lines was the same length as the standard line and the other two were of significantly different lengths.[41] In each case, an unsuspecting study subject was introduced into a group with six confederates, who had been told by the experimenter to give the wrong answer. The group was then shown the lines. The experimenter asked one of the confederates which of the three lines on the right they thought was the same length as the standard line. The confederate, without hesitation, gave a wrong answer. The next few confederates gave the same answer. By now, the naive subject was showing puzzlement and even dismay. How can six people be wrong?

After hearing six "wrong" answers, 75 percent of the naive study subjects, rather than trust the evidence of their senses, succumbed to group pressure and gave the same wrong answer. Even more surprising is the fact that when questioned afterward, some of these study subjects had actually come to believe the wrong answer was correct.

The desire for agreement is normal. However, this desire, when combined with our innate tendency to divide the world into "one of us" and "one of them," can lead to the exclusion of those who disagree with the majority, since people tend to prefer being around people who agree with them. In the corporate world, disagreement is often tacitly discouraged. "Outliers" or nonconformists who do not agree with group members may be excluded by committee chairs from further discussions or even fired.[42]

Because of our inborn tendency to conform to what others think, we cannot assume that agreement leads to truth without knowledge about the manner and conditions under which the agreement was arrived. Indeed, the current emphasis on seeking group consensus in decision making may be unreliable. In consensus seeking, the majority in a group is often able to sway the whole group to its view.

ANALYZING IMAGES

Asch Experiment

In Asch's experiment, the naive subject (left) shows puzzlement when the other subjects give what is obviously a wrong answer.

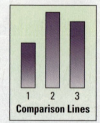

Standard Line   Comparison Lines
1 2 3

DISCUSSION QUESTIONS

1. *What do you think the naive subject in the picture above is thinking?*

2. *Think back to a time when you were in a similar situation where you thought you were correct, but everyone else with you thought something else. How did you respond to the discrepancy between your belief and theirs?*

As with other errors in our thinking, we need to develop strategies to recognize and compensate for our human inclination to conform to groupthink, the tendency of members of a group to yield to the consensus of the group. When a group comes to a decision, we need to mentally step back from the group and carefully evaluate the evidence for a particular position rather than assume that the majority must be correct. In competitive ice skating and diving, because of the danger of a judge's scoring being contaminated by what other judges say, scoring is done individually, rather than as a group decision.

Diffusion of Responsibility

Diffusion of responsibility is a social phenomenon that occurs in groups of people above a critical size. If responsibility is not explicitly assigned to us, we tend to regard it as not our problem but as belonging to someone else. We are much more likely to come to someone's aid if we are alone than if we are in a crowd.

> **diffusion of responsibility** The tendency, when in a large group, to regard a problem as belonging to someone else.

This phenomenon is also known as *bystander apathy* or the *Kitty Genovese syndrome*. In 1964, 28-year-old Kitty Genovese was murdered outside her New York City apartment building. In the half hour that lapsed during the attack, none of Genovese's many neighbors,

5/30/2008 5:49:42 PM

The phenomenon of "diffusion of responsibility" was regrettably illustrated when no one came to the aid of a seriously injured man lying in a busy street in Hartford, Connecticut, after being struck by a hit-and-run driver in May 2008. The victim, Angel Torres, later died from the injuries he sustained.

who had heard her repeated cries for help, called the police. More recently, in June 2008, an elderly man was struck by a hit-and-run driver on a busy street in Hartford, Connecticut. The man lay in the street paralyzed and bleeding from his head while bystanders gawked at or

---

We are much more likely to come to someone's aid if we are alone than if we are in a crowd.

---

ignored him. Motorists drove around his body without stopping. No one offered any assistance until an ambulance finally turned up. Diffusion of responsibility can

also occur in group hazing at fraternities where no one comes to the rescue of a pledge who is clearly in distress.

As social beings, we are vulnerable to the "one of us/ one of them" error, social expectations, and group conformity. When in groups, we also tend to regard something as not our problem unless responsibility is assigned to us. Although these traits may promote group cohesiveness, they can interfere with effective critical thinking. As good critical thinkers we need to be aware of these tendencies, and to cultivate the ability to think independently while still taking into consideration others' perspectives. Errors in our thinking also make us more vulnerable to falling for or using fallacies in arguments. We'll be studying some of these fallacies in the following chapter.

EXERCISE 4-4

STOP AND ASSESS YOURSELF

I. Whom do you define as "us" and whom do you put in the category of "them"? Discuss how you might go about widening the "us" category to include more people who are now in your "them" category.

2. Humans seem to have inborn biases toward particular types of people. According to a University of Florida study, when it comes to hiring, employers have a more favorable view of tall people. When it comes to earnings, every extra inch of height above the norm is worth almost $1,000 a year. In fact, nine of ten top executives are taller than the typical employee.[43] Given this cognitive error and its impact on hiring practices, discuss whether or not affirmative action policies should apply to very short people. Relate your answer to the discussion in the text of the effect of this cognitive error on our thinking.

3. Think of a time when your social expectations led you to misjudge a person or a situation. Discuss strategies for improving your critical-thinking skills so that this is less likely to happen.

4. Think of a time when the public got caught up in a "witch hunt." Identify the worldviews and social expectations that supported this "witch hunt." Which critical-thinking skills would make you less likely to go along with a "witch hunt"? Discuss what actions you could take to develop or strengthen these skills.

5. Polls before elections can influence how people vote by swaying undecided voters to vote for the candidate who is in the lead. Analyze whether election polls should be forbidden prior to the election itself.

6. The democratic process depends on social consensus. Given people's tendency to conform to social expectations and what others think, is democracy the best form of government? If so, what policies might be put in place to lessen the effect of social biases? Be specific.

7. Think of a time when you failed to speak out against an injustice or failed to come to someone's aid simply because you were in a large group and felt it wasn't your responsibility. Discuss ways in which improving your critical-thinking skills may make you less susceptible to the diffusion of social responsibility error.

8. Computers (AI) programmed with an inductive logic program can, after sufficient experience working with the ups and downs of the financial market, predict the market with greater accuracy than most experienced financial planners. Given that these computers are not as prone to cognitive errors as are humans, critically evaluate whether we should rely more on AI to make decisions about such issues as college admissions, medical diagnoses, matchmaking, and piloting an airplane.

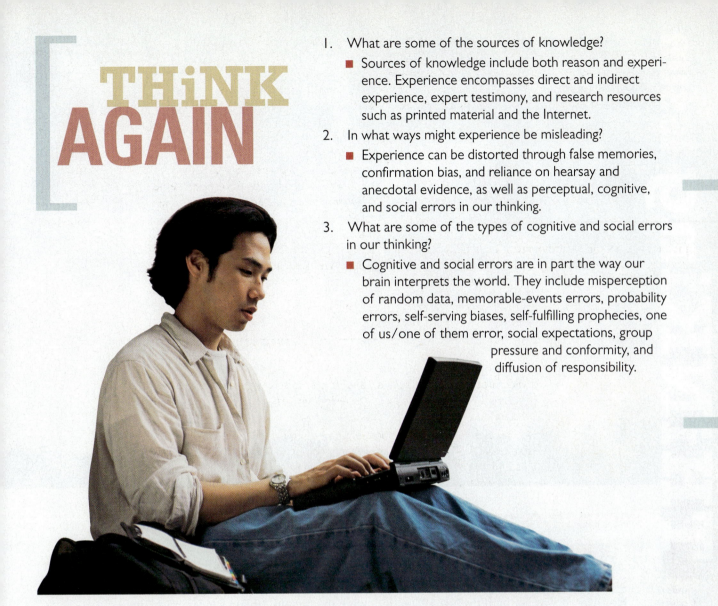

THiNK AGAIN

1. What are some of the sources of knowledge?
    - ■ Sources of knowledge include both reason and experience. Experience encompasses direct and indirect experience, expert testimony, and research resources such as printed material and the Internet.

2. In what ways might experience be misleading?
    - ■ Experience can be distorted through false memories, confirmation bias, and reliance on hearsay and anecdotal evidence, as well as perceptual, cognitive, and social errors in our thinking.

3. What are some of the types of cognitive and social errors in our thinking?
    - ■ Cognitive and social errors are in part the way our brain interprets the world. They include misperception of random data, memorable-events errors, probability errors, self-serving biases, self-fulfilling prophecies, one of us/one of them error, social expectations, group pressure and conformity, and diffusion of responsibility.

Perspectives on Evaluating Evidence for the Existence of Unidentified Flying Objects (UFOs)

Sightings of unexplained phenomena in the sky have been reported since ancient times. However, it was not until the late 1940s, following the famous "flying saucer crash" incident in Roswell, New Mexico, that UFO reports began to proliferate. There is little doubt that sensationalist media coverage stimulated reports of more UFO sightings, just as the 1909 story in the *Boston Herald* of the invention of an airship was followed by hundreds of sightings of the bogus ship.

In 1948, the U.S. Air Force began to keep a file of UFO sightings as part of Project Blue Book. By 1969, the project had recorded 12,618 UFO sightings. Ninety percent of these UFO sightings have been identified with astronomical and weather phenomena, aircraft, balloons, searchlights, hot gases, and other natural events. Ten percent remain unexplained. In 1968, the U.S. Air Force commissioned a study under the direction of University of Colorado professor Edward Condon.[44] The study concluded that there was no evidence for UFOs and that scientific study of the phenomenon should be discontinued. As a result of the study, Project Blue Book was suspended.

Despite official consensus that UFOs do not exist, a 2012 National Geographic Society poll found that slightly more than one-third of Americans believe that UFOs exist.[45] In addition, 10 percent claim to have actually seen a UFO. The survey also found that 79 percent of Americans think that the government is hiding information from them about the existence of UFOs and alien life forms.

Following are readings from the U.S Air Force Blue Book Project and by Royston Paynter. Many if not most scientists believe that UFOs do not exist. These scientists argue that there are natural explanations for UFO phenomena, including meteorites, balloons, hallucinations, and perceptual and social error in our thinking. While Blue Book Project is more dismissive of UFOs, both readings leave open the possibility that UFOs may be real.

Project Blue Book: Analysis of Reports of Unidentified Aerial Objects

UNITED STATES AIR FORCE

Project Blue Book summarizes a series of studies of unidentified flying objects (UFOs) conducted by the U.S. Air Force beginning in 1952. The following selection is from the summary and conclusion of the report. To read the entire report, go to http://www.ufocasebook.com/pdf/specialreport14.pdf.

It is not possible to derive a verified model of a "flying saucer" from the data that have been gathered to date. This point is important enough to emphasize. Out of about 4,000 people who said they saw a "flying saucer," sufficiently detailed descriptions were given in only 12 cases. Having culled the cream of the crop, it is still impossible to develop a picture of what a "flying saucer" is. . . .

On the basis of this evidence, therefore, there is a low probability that any of the UNKNOWNS represent observations of a class of "flying saucers." It may be that some reports represent observations of not one but several classes of objects that might have been "flying saucers"; however, the lack of evidence to confirm even one class would seem to make this possibility remote. It is pointed out that some of the cases of KNOWNS, before identification, appeared fully as bizarre as any of the 12 cases of good UNKNOWNS, and, in fact, would have been placed in the class of good UNKNOWNS had it not been possible to establish their identity.

This is, of course, contrary to the bulk of the publicity that has been given to this problem. . . . It is unfortunate that practically all of the articles, books, and news stories dealing with the phenomenon of the "flying saucer" were written by men . . . had read only a few selected reports. This is accentuated by the fact that, as a rule, only the more lurid-sounding reports are cited in these publications. Were it not for this common psychological tendency to be captivated by the mysterious, it is possible that no problem of this nature would exist.

The reaction, mentioned above, that after reading a few reports, the reader is convinced that "flying saucers" are real and are some form of sinister contrivance, is very misleading. As more and more of the reports are read, the feeling that "saucers" are real fades, and is replaced by a feeling of skepticism regarding their existence. The reader eventually reaches a point of saturation, after which the reports contain no new information at all and are no longer of any interest. This feeling of surfeit was universal among the personnel who worked on this project, and continually necessitated a conscious effort on their part to remain objective.

CONCLUSIONS

It can never be absolutely proven that "flying saucers" do not exist. This would be true if the data obtained were to include complete scientific measurements of the attributes of each sighting, as well as complete and detailed descriptions of the objects sighted. It might be possible to demonstrate the existence of "flying saucers" with data of this type, IF they were to exist.

Although the reports considered in this study usually did not contain scientific measurements of the attributes of each sighting, it was possible to establish certain valid conclusions by the application of statistical methods in the treatment of the data. Scientifically evaluated and arranged, the data as such did not show any marked patterns or trends. The inaccuracies inherent in this type of data, in addition to the incompleteness of a large proportion, of the reports, may have obscured any patterns or trends that otherwise would have been evident. This absence of indicative relationships necessitated an exhaustive study of selected facets of the data in order to draw any valid conclusions.

A critical examination of the distributions of the important characteristics of sightings, plus an intensive study of the sightings evaluated as UNKNOWN, led to the conclusion that a combination of factors, principally the reported maneuvers of the objects and the unavailability of supplemental data such as aircraft flight plans or balloon-launching records, resulted in the failure to identify as KNOWNS most of the reports of objects classified as UNKNOWNS.

An intensive study, aimed at finding a verified example of a "flying saucer" or at deriving a verified model or models of "flying saucers" (defined on Page 1 as "any aerial phenomenon or sighting that remains unexplained to the viewer"), led to the conclusion that neither goal could be attained using the present data.

It is emphasized that there was a complete lack of any valid evidence consisting of physical matter in any case of a reported unidentified aerial object. Thus, the probability that any of the UNKNOWNS considered in this study are "flying saucers" is concluded to be extremely small, since the most complete and reliable reports from the present data, when isolated and studied, conclusively failed to reveal even a rough model, and since the data as a whole failed to reveal any marked patterns or trends. Therefore, on the basis of this evaluation of the information, it is considered to be highly improbable that any of the reports of unidentified aerial objects examined in this study represent observations of technological developments outside the range of present-day scientific knowledge.

Review Questions

1. How does *Project Blue Book* distinguish between KNOWNS and UNKNOWNS in assessing reports of UFO sightings?

2. How do the authors account for the fact that so many people believe in UFOs?

3. What conclusion do the authors of *Project Blue Book* draw regarding the existence of UFOs and why?

Physical Evidence and Unidentified Flying Objects   ROYSTON PAYNTER

Royston Paynter has a Ph.D. in materials science from the University of Surrey in the United Kingdom and is currently a professor at the Institut National de la Recherche Scientifique in Quebec, Canada. In this article, Dr. Paynter writes that claims about the existence of UFOs and alien abductions should be conducted "according to the highest standards of scientific inquiry."[47] Without any physical evidence, he argues, we should remain skeptical about these claims.

Skeptics are sometimes criticized for demanding physical evidence of alien visitations. It is an unreasonable demand, believers say, because aliens are intelligent and cunning, and one cannot expect them to leave physical evidence of their presence on Earth.

Well, such an argument may make sense to somebody who is prepared to believe in alien visitations as an act of faith, in the same way that some people believe in angels. But the undeniable fact of the matter is that there is **no** probative physical evidence that compels us to conclude that aliens are visiting the Earth.

There simply is no alien space ship on display in a museum somewhere, in fact, there is no object in existence on Earth of which we can say "this must have been made by aliens." Of course it is possible to *believe* in alien visitations nonetheless, as an act of faith, but the great majority of scientists do not believe it, because it has not been proven in a rigorous scientific manner.

Those believers that reject the more extreme claims of popular UFOlogy, such as cattle mutilations, crop circles and even perhaps alien abductions, tend to fall back upon government and military reports obtained under the Freedom of Information Act. A well-known example is the US Air Force's own Project Sign "Estimate of the Situation," issued in 1948, that concluded that flying saucers were real and that they came from outer space.

To what extent is such a report authoritative? A scientifically trained individual looking at such a statement would ask "is this conclusion justified by the data presented?" That is to say, is such a conclusion forced upon us as the most economical way to explain that data, or is it the result of sloppy analysis and/or wishful thinking? In the case of the Project Sign "estimate,"

General Hoyt S. Vandenberg did not believe that the report's evidence was sufficient to support its conclusions, and he rejected it.

For those among us that are not prepared to believe in alien visitations simply as an act of faith, **physical evidence** is the key to everything. We **will** believe, if some artifact can be found on Earth that is demonstrably **alien**. Let us note here that "unidentified" and "demonstrably alien" are not synonymous. Just because a given UFO sighting cannot be explained it does not follow that it has been proved to be an alien space ship.

Short of a flying saucer landing on the White House lawn, where lie the best chances to obtain a demonstrably alien artifact? If we are to believe the stories told (or "remembered" under hypnosis) by those claiming to have been abducted by aliens, it seems that we should direct our attention first to those "alien implants" recovered from these people.

The stakes here are extremely high. If these "implants" can be shown to have been manufactured by aliens, then people really are being abducted by aliens. If, on the other hand, it cannot be shown that the "implants" are alien, then we must ask serious questions of the "researchers" who have elicited the testimony from the "abductees."

With the stakes so high, it is essential, in our opinion, that these analyses be conducted in accordance with the highest standards of scientific inquiry. Most importantly, we must demand that the UFOlogists prove *what they claim*. They are claiming that the "implants" have an alien origin. It is therefore not enough to show that they are "*100% pure*" or that they have an "unusual composition" or that they *contain chemical elements* also found in radio transmitters. They have to show that *aliens made them*.

One simple test would be enough to prove such a claim to the satisfaction of most scientists—an isotopic analysis of the material from which the implant is composed. We can reasonably expect that a device made by aliens from materials obtained in another solar system will exhibit isotope ratios different than those found on Earth. Such a test goes straight to the heart of the claim being made for the "implant" and would avoid all the obfuscation and hyperbole about "100% purity" and the like.

We urge the UFOlogical community to adopt properly scientific standards of investigation and proof in their work. They have to support their conclusions with probative evidence and rigorous reasoning and to confront the skeptics with the evidence they so dearly seek—a demonstrably alien artifact.

REVIEW QUESTIONS

1. Why do some believers maintain that the demand for physical evidence of alien visitations is unreasonable? How does Paynter respond to their objection?

2. What type of evidence does a scientist such as Paynter argue is necessary to establish the claim that UFOs exist?

3. What type of evidence does Paynter argue is necessary to prove the claim that people have been abducted by aliens?

THiNK AND DISCUSS

PERSPECTIVES ON THE EXISTENCE OF UNIDENTIFIED FLYING OBJECTS

1. What conclusion do both readings draw regarding the existence of UFOs? Compare and contrast the arguments used by the authors of Project Blue Book and by Paynter to support their conclusion(s). Evaluate the evidence each uses. Which reading presents the best argument? Explain.

2. Discuss the role of cognitive and perceptual errors, as well as social errors, in the debate over the existence of UFOs. Be specific.

3. Both the authors of Project Blue Book and Paynter concede that neither the lack of actual physical evidence of UFOs nor the ability to explain UFO "sightings" as sightings of familiar objects is not sufficient prove that UFOs do not exist (see fallacy of Appeal to Ignorance on page 148). Discuss what proof or evidence, if any, would be sufficient to convince a logical person that UFOs existed.

4. Do you believe in the existence of UFOs? Write down the evidence and premises you use to support your conclusion. Working in small groups, critically analyze each other's arguments.

5

INFORMAL
FALLACIES

Shannon Townsend was excited about college. An honor student in high school who planned to become a physician, she finished her first semester at the University of Colorado with a 3.9 grade point average and an active social life. Then something happened to change the direction of her life. A few weeks before the end of her freshman year, she announced to her parents that she was dropping out of college to "follow Jesus." She had joined a nomadic cult known as the Jim Roberts Group, or simply the Brethren. The cult believes in disowning family and possessions, isolating themselves from society, and roaming the land (as they believe Jesus did), proselytizing and foraging for food. Over ten years have passed, and her family has not seen or heard from Shannon since she quit college to join the Brethren.[1]

Shannon's story is not that uncommon. Each year, hundreds of college students are

Which types of fallacies might lead someone to make a major unexpected life change such as this mass marriage conducted by the Unification Church, considered by many to be a cult ?

135

THiNK FIRST

- What is a fallacy, and why are we taken in by informal fallacies?
- What are three main types of informal fallacies?
- How can we avoid falling for and/or using fallacies?

 recruited into destructive cults, a particular subclass of cults, groups organized around a set of beliefs and rituals that display excessive devotion to a person or ideology, that use manipulative and deceptive recruiting techniques, and that employ fallacious reasoning—including reliance on vague language to mask their true objectives from potential members. Isolation from family and peer pressure from "new" cult friends in the form of "love bombing"—a technique by which cult members shower a recruit with unconditional love to put them into a position of making them more susceptible to accept anything the cult says—both heighten compliance and discourage critical thinking. And to retain recruits' loyalty, destructive cults also use scare tactics, emotional abuse, and guilt.

College students, especially freshmen who are having difficulty adjusting to the college environment and are experiencing separation from their families, or who are having academic or social problems, are especially vulnerable to cults. Lack of assertiveness, dependence on others, a low tolerance for ambiguity (wanting simple "right" and "wrong" answers for complex questions), and poor critical-thinking skills all make students more likely to succumb to pressure from campus recruiters for cults.[2]

The best way to avoid being targeted by a cult, according to clinical counselor and cult expert Ron Burks, is to be well informed and unafraid to ask questions. "The antidote . . . is critical thinking," he says. "Cults don't like people who are constantly thinking and asking questions."[3]

The ability to recognize fallacious arguments used by cult recruiters can go a long way toward making us less vulnerable to the lure of destructive cults and to other types of flawed arguments. In Chapter 5 we will:

- Define fallacy
- Learn how to identify fallacies of ambiguity
- Learn how to identify fallacies of relevance
- Learn how to identify fallacies with unwarranted assumptions
- Practice recognizing fallacies in everyday arguments and conversations
- Discuss strategies that can be used for avoiding fallacies

Finally, we will discuss two dramatically different proposals on how to stop gun violence and analyze these arguments for fallacies.

WHAT IS A FALLACY?

An argument is the process of supporting a claim or conclusion by providing reasons or evidence, in the form of premises, for that claim. An argument can be weak or invalid in several ways. The premises—the reasons or evidence given in support of a particular conclusion or position—may be mistaken, or the evidence may not support the conclusion. An argument contains a **fallacy** when it appears to be correct but on further examination is found to be incorrect. Fallacies may be formal or informal. In a **formal fallacy**, the form of the argument itself is invalid. For example, the following argument contains a formal fallacy: "Some high school dropouts are men. No doctors are high school dropouts. Therefore, no doctors are men." Although the premises are true, the conclusion does not follow because the form of the argument is faulty.

An **informal fallacy** is a type of mistaken reasoning that occurs when an argument is psychologically or emotionally persuasive but logically incorrect. Because fallacies can lead us to accept unsupported conclusions, being taken in by them can cause us to make poor life choices—as happened when Shannon was taken in by a destructive cult. Being able to identify informal fallacies makes it less likely that you will fall for these fallacies or use them in an argument.

In the following sections we will study three groups of informal fallacies: fallacies of ambiguity, fallacies of relevance, and fallacies with unwarranted assumptions. There are many types of fallacies in these groups. We'll be studying some of the more common ones in this chapter.

Hot or Not?

Is the use of fallacies a legitimate political campaign tactic?

FALLACIES OF AMBIGUITY

Arguments that have ambiguous words or phrases, sloppy grammatical structure, or confusion between two closely related concepts can lead to **fallacies of ambiguity**. People with poor language and communication skills are more likely to use or fall for these fallacies. Fallacies of ambiguity include equivocation, amphiboly, fallacies of accent, and fallacies of division.

Equivocation

Equivocation occurs when a key term in an argument is ambiguous—that is, when it has more than one meaning—and the meaning of the term changes during the course of the argument. This is most likely to happen when the meaning of the key term is not clear from the context of the argument. Verbal disputes, such as the dispute about whether a tree falling in a forest when no one is around makes a "sound," occur because of equivocation on the key term *sound*. In this case, the people who are disagreeing are each using a different definition of *sound*.

Here is another example of equivocation:

On February 23, 2010, Fox News reported that Democratic Senator Harry Reid had said that "if you're a man and out of work you may beat up your wife." From this the Fox reporters drew the conclusion that Reid thinks it is okay for men who are out of work to beat up their wives. In doing so they committed the fallacy of equivocation since the term *may* has more than one meaning. It can be used to mean "permission to" or it can be used to express "possibility." In fact, Senator Reid had actually said: "Men who are out of work tend to be abusive. Our domestic shelters are jammed." He was not giving unemployed men permission to beat their wives nor was he condoning abuse.

Here is another example of this fallacy:

Carl: Terminally ill patients have a right to decide how and when they want to die.

Juan: That's not true. There is no right to euthanasia in U.S. law.

In this argument Carl is using the term *right* as a

fallacy A faulty argument that at first appears to be correct.

formal fallacy A type of mistaken reasoning in which the form of an argument itself is invalid.

informal fallacy A type of mistaken reasoning that occurs when an argument is psychologically or emotionally persuasive but logically incorrect.

fallacy of ambiguity Arguments that have ambiguous phrases or sloppy grammatical structure.

equivocation A key term in an argument changes meaning during the course of the argument.

Tiger Woods is a good golfer, therefore Tiger Woods is a good husband.

moral right, whereas Juan is using a different definition of *right*—that is, as a legal right. Legal rights and moral rights are not the same. For example, we might have had a legal right to own slaves, as did southern Americans before the Civil War, but (as all Americans would today agree) not a moral right. We can also have a moral right, such as a right to faithfulness and honesty from our life partner, but not generally a legal right.

> **amphiboly** An argument contains a grammatical mistake, that allows more than one conclusion to be drawn.

The fallacy of equivocation also occurs when we misuse relative terms such as *tall, small, strong, big,* or *good,* as in this example:

> Two-year-old Katie is very tall. Her father, on the other hand, is not tall but about average in height. Therefore, Katie is taller than her father.

> Tiger Woods is a good golfer, therefore Tiger Woods is a good husband.

In these two examples, the relative terms *tall* and *good* are being used in the same argument in different contexts; it is like comparing apples and oranges. A tall toddler and a tall man are two very different things. And the fact that Tiger Woods was a good golfer does not necessarily mean that he was also a good husband. As it turned out, in 2010 it was reported that he was having an affair. He and his wife Elin Nordgren divorced shortly after.

> To avoid the fallacy of equivocation, you should clearly define any ambiguous words or phrases before proceeding with the argument of discussion.

To avoid the fallacy of equivocation, you should clearly define any ambiguous words or phrases before proceeding with the argument or discussion. In addition, you need to avoid using relative terms in different contexts within the same argument.

Amphiboly

The fallacy of **amphiboly** occurs when there is a grammatical mistake in an argument, which allows more than one conclusion to be drawn. For example:

> Terri Schiavo's mother and her husband are on opposite sides of the battle over her life.[4]

In this 2005 statement regarding the issue of whether to remove the feeding tube from brain-damaged Terri Schiavo, the ambiguous wording makes it unclear which conclusion follows. Is it Terri Schiavo's husband, or her father (that is, her mother's husband), who is taking the opposite side? In this case, Terri Schiavo's husband asked to have the feeding tube removed; her mother and father, believing that Terri still had a chance of regaining consciousness, insisted that the feeding tube be kept in place.

Advertisers may use this type of fallacy, hoping you'll read more into the statement than is actually there, as in the following slogan for the Clinique fragrance Happy.

> Wear it and be happy!

The word *and* is ambiguous here. *And* can be used to mean either that they are two separate and unrelated ideas—or that a causal connection exists between two ideas: "Wear this fragrance and [if you do] you will be happy." Of course, the advertiser is hoping we'll fall for the fallacy and make the second interpretation. However, if we use the fragrance Happy and aren't any happier as a result, and so try to sue Clinique for false advertising, we can be sure that they'll say they never intended the term *and* in their ad to imply a causal connection. Instead, or so they will probably claim, they used *and* only as a conjunction between two unrelated ideas. Meanwhile, it's money out of our pockets and we're less happy than before because we've been duped by ambiguous language.

On the lighter side, humorists may use amphiboly to amuse their audiences, as in this dialogue from the 1996 movie *Spy Hard*:

> Agent: Sir, we've intercepted a very disturbing satellite transmission from our listening post on the Rock of Gibraltar.
>
> Director: What is it?
>
> Agent: It's this really big rock sticking out of the water on the south coast of Spain.

To avoid the fallacy of amphiboly, we should use language and grammar properly so the meaning of our argument is clear. When unsure of how to interpret a particular statement, we should ask the person to rephrase it more clearly.

Fallacy of Accent

The fallacy of **accent** occurs when the meaning of an argument changes according to which word or phrase in it is emphasized. For instance:

> Distraught mother: Didn't I say, "Don't play with matches"?
>
> Delinquent daughter: But I wasn't *playing* with the matches. I was using them to burn down Mr. Murphy's shed.
>
> According to our school newspaper, the administration is going to crack down on *off-campus* drinking. I'm glad to hear that they're okay with on-campus drinking.

In the first example, the delinquent daughter changes the meaning of her mother's warning by placing the accent on the word *playing*. In the second, by emphasizing the term *off-campus*, the student erroneously concludes that the college administration opposes drinking only when it's off-campus.

The fallacy of accent can also happen when we take a passage out of context, thus changing its original meaning. For instance, "proof-texting" involves taking a scriptural passage out of its original context in order to prove a particular point. Religious cults often use proof-texting to support their theological arguments. The following passage is taken from the King James Bible, which is the translation used by the Jim Roberts cult—mentioned at the beginning of this chapter—to convince recruits that they must forsake not only their worldly possessions but also their family, friends, education, and career plans.

> So likewise, whosoever of you that forsaketh not all that he hath, he cannot be my disciple. Luke 14:33

By ignoring the fact that neither Jesus nor his disciples forsook or completely disowned their family or friends, the cult leader commits the fallacy of accent.

If you are unsure about which term is being emphasized or accented in an argument, ask the person who made the argument to repeat or explain what he or she meant. If you suspect that a particular argument has been taken out of context, go back and look up the original source—in this example, the King James Version of the Bible. Arguments that take on a different meaning when read within the context of the source are fallacious.

Fallacy of Division

In the **fallacy of division**, we make an erroneous inference from the characteristics of an entire set or group about a member of the group or set. In doing so we incorrectly assume that each member of a group has the characteristics of the group in general.

> Group G has characteristic C.
>
> X is a member of group G.
>
> Therefore, X has characteristic C.

For example:

> Men are taller than women.
>
> Danny DeVito is a man.
>
> Therefore, Danny DeVito is taller than the average woman.

Connections

How can you recognize the fallacy of amphiboly in advertisements? *See Chapter 10, p. 319.*

accent The meaning of an argument changes depending on which word or phrase in it is emphasized.

fallacy of division An erroneous inference from the characteristics of an entire set or group about a member of that group or set.

ANALYZING IMAGES

"THANK GOODNESS! THE STUDENT LOAN COMPANY SAYS THIS IS THE LAST NOTICE I'M GOING TO GET!"

©WM. HOEST ENTERPRISES, INC. ALL RIGHTS RESERVED.

Making Poor Choices

DISCUSSION QUESTIONS

1. *What fallacy is the student committing in this cartoon? Discuss how failing to recognize this fallacy might lead the student to make poor choices.*

2. *Imagine that you are the parents in the picture. Discuss what you might say to your son to call his attention to his faulty thinking.*

Obviously the concluding statement is incorrect, since the average woman—at 5 feet 4 inches tall—is 4 inches taller than Danny DeVito. Also, sometimes we may think someone or something is good (or bad) simply because of that person's or that thing's association with a particular group, as the next example illustrates:

> I hear that Canadians are really nice people. Therefore, Derek, who is from Saskatchewan, must be really nice.

Although it may be true that Canadians as a group are very nice people, we cannot infer from this that each individual Canadian, such as Derek, is really nice.

Fallacy of Composition

The **fallacy of composition** errs in the opposite direction of the fallacy of division. The fallacy of composition involves an erroneous inference from the parts to the whole by drawing a conclusion about the entire set from the characteristics of the members of that set or group, as in the following example:

> The rooms in the hotel are small. Therefore, the hotel must be small.

The fact that the rooms (parts of the hotel) are small does not mean the hotel (the whole) itself is small. In fact, rooms in some of the larger hotels in large cities like New York City tend to be smaller, albeit more elegant, than those in some small town hotels. The following is another example of this fallacy:

> Both sodium (Na) and chloride (Ca) are dangerous to humans.
>
> Therefore, table salt (NaCl), which is a combination of these two chemicals, is dangerous and should be avoided altogether.

However, the fact that sodium and chloride are dangerous on their own does not mean they are dangerous when combined. In fact, some salt in our diet is good for our health.

fallacy of composition An erroneous inference from the characteristics of a member of a group or set about the characteristic of the entire group or set.

HIGHLIGHTS

FALLACIES OF AMBIGUITY

- ***Equivocation:*** An ambiguous word or phrase changes meaning during the course of the argument.

- ***Amphiboly:*** A grammatical error in the premises allows more than one conclusion to be drawn.

- ***Fallacy of accent:*** The meaning of an argument changes depending on which word or phrase is emphasized. Accent also occurs when passages are used out of context.

- ***Fallacy of division:*** A characteristic of an entire group is erroneously assumed to be a characteristic of each member of that group.

- ***Fallacy of composition:*** A characteristic of a member of a group is erroneously assumed to be characteristic of the whole group.

➤ ***APPLICATION: Find an example in the text of each type of fallacy of ambiguity.***

EXERCISE 5-2

STOP AND ASSESS YOURSELF

I. Identify the fallacy of ambiguity, if any, in each of the following arguments:

*a. My parents used to get into arguments all the time, and they ended up getting divorced. Critical thinking teaches people how to make arguments. Therefore, if you want a happy marriage, don't sign up for a course in critical thinking.

b. Atoms are invisible to the naked eye. Therefore, I must be invisible since I am made up of atoms.

c. I hear that Dr. Carr is a really good teacher; therefore, it's probably a good idea for me to sign up for his course in physiology since I'm interested in the subject.

*d. Americans are among the most obese people in the world. Clyde is an American. Therefore, Clyde is one of the most obese people in the world.

e. Police officer: "Why do you rob banks?"

Willie Sutton: "[Because] that's where they keep the money."

f. The football team at State University is best in its league. Therefore, every member of the football team is one of the best football players in the league.

*g. I have no regrets for what I did. God told me to kill your children. Psalms 137 clearly says, "Happy is he who shall seize your children and dash them against the rock."

h. The sign on the deli door says "No Animals Allowed." I guess we'll have to find another place for lunch, since we're humans and humans are clearly animals.

i. You are a bad person because you are a bad student.

*j. Our town hall says it is giving out parking permits to fish at Warden's Pond. But that's ridiculous. Why would a fish need a parking permit?

k. The people of Liechtenstein have the highest personal income of any people in any nation in the world. Therefore, Liechtenstein is the richest nation in the world.

l. God created man in his own image. But you're a woman. Therefore, you aren't created in God's image.

*m Stanford is academically one of the best universities in the United States. Therefore, Claude, who is a student at Stanford, is academically one of the best students in the country.

n. "Too many doctors are getting out of business. Too many OB-GYNs aren't able to practice their love with women all across the country." George W. Bush addressing a group of people about the effects of frivolous lawsuits, September 2004.

o. The black rhino is heading toward extinction. So the black rhinos at the Cincinnati Zoo must be heading toward extinction.

*p. The Declaration of Independence states that all men are created equal. But that's certainly not the case. Studies show that people are born unequal in intelligence and athletic ability.

2. Look for examples of fallacies of ambiguity in the media, including news coverage, magazine articles, and advertisements. Identify each fallacy and discuss what purpose the writer is hoping to achieve (deliberately or unconsciously) by using this fallacy.

*Answers to selected exercises are found in the Solutions Manual at the end of the book.

FALLACIES OF RELEVANCE

In **fallacies of relevance**, one or more of the premises is logically irrelevant, or unrelated, to the conclusion. However, we may fall for these fallacies because psychologically the premises and conclusion seem to be relevant. Fallacies of relevance include personal attacks (ad hominem fallacies), appeals to force (scare tactics), appeals to pity, popular appeals, appeals to ignorance, hasty generalizations, straw man fallacies, and red herrings.

Ad Hominem (Personal Attack)

The **ad hominem fallacy** or personal attack occurs when we disagree with someone's conclusion, but instead of presenting a counterargument we attack the person who made the argument. In doing so, we try to create disapproval toward our opponent and his or her argument. This fallacy, which is sometimes referred to by the Latin phrase ad hominem, meaning "against the man," can take two forms: (1) *abusive*, when we directly attack the character of the person, or (2) *circumstantial*, when we dismiss someone's argument or accuse someone of hypocrisy because of the person's particular circumstances. People may be taken in by the fallacy because of our natural tendency to divide the world into "one of us" versus "one of them."

This fallacy often rears its ugly head in heated debates over controversial issues and in political campaigns. In the 2008 presidential campaign, the McCain campaign launched an attack ad mocking Obama as a celebrity like Britney Spears and Paris Hilton. The Democrats in turn attacked McCain as being "too old," "out of touch," and "grouchy."

People who don't conform to the accepted worldview may become the targets of personal attack, as in the following example:

> Ernst Zündel is part of the lunatic fringe. His ideas about the existence of UFOs under the South Pole are nothing short of crazy.

Instead of addressing Zündel's argument that UFOs exist under the South Pole, the person tries to discredit Zündel himself. The attempt to discredit someone's ideas by attacking his or her character and credibility is sometimes known as "poisoning the well." It is common in political campaigns.

fallacy of relevance The premise is logically irrelevant, or unrelated, to the conclusion.

ad hominem fallacy Instead of presenting a counterargument, we attack the character of the person who made the argument.

Connections

How do the "rules of evidence" protect against the use of fallacies, such as the ad hominem fallacy, in court trials?
See Chapter 13, pp. 414–415.

Critical THiNKing in Action

The Perils of Verbal Attacks in Personal Relationships

Not all uses of personal attack or the ad hominem fallacy are intentional. This fallacy may occur between people in personal relationships, because of poor communication skills.

John Gray, author of *Men Are from Mars, Women Are from Venus*, writes that we can be unwittingly abusive in personal relationships. He points out that men, rather than responding to a woman's argument, may become patronizing. Instead of addressing her concerns, the man explains why she shouldn't be upset or tells her not to worry about it. In doing so, he commits the ad hominem fallacy by dismissing her feelings. As a result, the woman becomes even more upset. He, in turn, senses her disapproval and he becomes upset as well, blaming her for upsetting him and demanding an apology before making up. She may apologize but is left wondering what happened. Or she may become even more upset at his expecting her to apologize, and before long the argument escalates into a battle, including name-calling and accusations.

In order to avoid the above scenario, Gray emphasizes the importance of good listening and communication skills in personal relationships so that we understand why the other person gets upset and can then move on from there.

Paraphrased from John Gray, *Men Are from Mars, Women Are from Venus* (New York: HarperCollins Publishers, 1992), p. 155.

DISCUSSION QUESTIONS

1. Do you agree with Gray about men's and women's communication styles? Is this type of miscommunication also common in relationships between people of the same sex? Support your answer using specific examples.

2. Think of a time in a relationship when you said something to a person who got upset and you didn't understand why. Now think of a time when you got upset because someone casually dismissed your concerns and you were left feeling hurt. Create strategies that will make you less likely to use or fall for verbal attacks such as these and more likely to respond to them in a constructive, rational manner.

People who lack good critical-thinking skills may respond to a personal attack by returning the insult.

> Pat: I think abortion is wrong because it ends the life of a living human being.
>
> Chris: You pro-lifers are just a bunch of narrow-minded, anti-choice, religious fanatics.
>
> Pat: Oh, yeah? Well, you're an anti-life baby-killer who's no better than a Nazi.

Instead of addressing Pat's arguments against abortion, Chris turns on Pat and attacks her. Chris doesn't do much better. Instead of ignoring Chris's insult and getting the argument back on course, Pat buys into the ad hominem fallacy by returning the insult. As good critical thinkers, we must resist the temptation to respond to a personal attack by throwing abuse back at the person who attacked us.

We also commit this fallacy when we dismiss someone's argument by suggesting that their circumstances bias their thinking or when we argue that our opponent should or does accept a particular conclusion because of his or her special circumstances, such as his or her lifestyle or membership in a particular group. For example:

> Of course Raul is in favor of affirmative action in college admissions. He's Latino and will benefit from affirmative action programs.

The woman carrying the placard commits the circumstantial form of the ad hominem fallacy by dismissing offhand the arguments of men. The fact that men cannot become pregnant does not mean they cannot take a position on the issue of abortion. The placard also has an ambiguous key term "leader." However, even if the term is defined, the gender of the leaders of the movement is irrelevant to the argument that abortion should be legal.

However, whether or not Raul benefits from affirmative action has no *logical* bearing on the soundness of Raul's argument in favor of affirmative action. His argument has to be evaluated independently of his circumstances.

This type of personal attack may also take the form of accusing someone of hypocrisy because of the person's circumstances.

> Father: Son, you shouldn't be smoking. It's not good for your health.
>
> Son: Look who's talking. You smoke at least a pack a day.

Here, the son dismisses his father's argument by accusing him of hypocrisy. But the fact that someone is engaging in a practice that he argues against, such as smoking, does not mean his argument is not sound. In this case, being a hypocrite or engaging in doublethink does not invalidate the father's argument that smoking is bad for the health of his son.

> **appeal to force (scare tactics)** The use or threat of force in an attempt to get another person to accept a conclusion as correct.

Not all negative statements about a person's character contain a fallacy, as in the following example.

> Jacob Robida, who allegedly attacked three men at Puzzles Lounge, a Massachusetts gay bar, and murdered two others while fleeing, was a disturbed and violent teenager who had a Nazi swastika and a coffin in his bedroom.

In this case, Robida's mental condition, his previous history of violence, and his Nazi sympathies are all relevant to the conclusion that he was probably guilty of the crime, since they help establish his motive for committing the crime.

Appeal to Force (Scare Tactics)

The fallacy of **appeal to force**, or **scare tactics**, occurs when we use or threaten to use force—whether it be physical, psychological, or legal—in an attempt to get another person to back down on a position and to accept our conclusion as correct. Like the personal attack fallacy, using an appeal to force may work in the short run. However, intimidation almost always damages trust in a relationship and is symptomatic of poor communication skills and faulty reasoning. This fallacy is illustrated by the following two examples:

Connections

How do advertisers use scare tactics to get you to buy their products? *See Chapter 10, p. 318.*

> Don't disagree with me. Remember who pays your college tuition.
>
> Don't disagree with me or I'll slap your *&*% face!

THE
LONDON SKETCH BOOK.

PROF. DARWIN.

This is the ape of form.
Love's Labor Lost, act 5, scene 2.

Some four or five descents since.
All's Well that Ends Well, act 3, sc. 7.

Darwin's Descent from the Apes

Fallacies can be used in nonverbal communication. After it was published in 1859, many critics of Charles Darwin's theory of evolution, rather than addressing his argument directly, responded by making personal attacks against those who supported evolution, as in this 1870 cartoon. Biologist Thomas Huxley (1825–1895), one of the most impassioned supporters of the theory of evolution, was not about to fall for this tactic. When Bishop Samuel Wilberforce allegedly asked Huxley whether "it was through his grandfather or his grandmother that he claimed descent from a monkey," Huxley used humor to deflect the attack. "If then the question is put to me," he replied, "whether I would rather have a miserable ape for a grandfather or a man highly endowed by nature and possessed of great means of influence and yet employs these faculties and that influence for the mere purpose of introducing ridicule into a grave scientific discussion, I unhesitatingly affirm my preference for the ape."

DISCUSSION QUESTIONS

1. *How successful is this cartoon in shaping your feelings or those of others about the subject of the cartoon? Did Huxley also use the ad hominem argument in his reply? Evaluate Huxley's answer. If he committed a fallacy, describe the fallacy and consider whether there was a better way of responding without resorting to fallacies or the use of rhetoric.*

2. *Given that people tend to be taken in by the ad hominem fallacy, discuss whether the media has a responsibility to refrain from publishing cartoons that attack someone's character when the real issue is the person's position on a particular issue.*

Sometimes appeals to force are more subtle than these; for example, we may threaten to withdraw affection or favors if the other person doesn't come around to our way of thinking. As we discussed at the opening of this chapter, "love bombing" by a cult—in which new recruits are showered with "unconditional" love and isolated from support systems outside the cult—leaves recruits vulnerable to this fallacy when subtle threats are later made to withdraw this love if they don't follow the cult's rules.

Appeal to force may involve scare tactics rather than overt threats. For instance, some proposed that if the U.S. Congress didn't pass a balanced budget by March 1, 2013, the country would plunge over a "fiscal cliff," resulting in massive layoffs and leaving the country vulnerable to terrorist attacks because of cuts to the military.

Filmmakers also use scare tactics to hold their audience. With advances in artificial intelligence (AI), the possibility of creating robots or androids that look or behave like

The appeal to pity on this billboard is not fallacious. Death related to smoking negatively affects victims' families as well as the person who smokes.

humans has spawned several movies, including *2001: A Space Odyssey*; *The Terminator*; *Blade Runner*; *I, Robot*; *Artificial Intelligence: AI*; the *Star Wars* and *Transformers* series; and *The Matrix* trilogy, in which machines interact intelligently with humans. Many of these movies exploit scare tactics, depicting androids and robots as evil enemies out to destroy the human race.

Not all scare tactics involve fallacies, however. For example, if you drink and drive, you might cause an automobile accident. In this case, there is a logical connection between drinking and an increased risk of an automobile accident. In addition, not all threats contain fallacies. Some threats are too blatant to be considered fallacies. For example, if someone sticks a gun in your face and says, "Hand over your wallet—or else," you generally hand over your wallet, not because the gunman has convinced you that the wallet is his but because you don't want to get shot.

People who have political, financial, or social power are more likely to use the appeal to force fallacy. Although most of us are not taken in by overt threats of force, fear is a powerful motivator and one that we are more likely to fall for than we might realize. This is particularly troublesome when those who lack power—for example, battered women or oppressed minorities—come to agree with their oppressor or blame themselves for their own oppression. Furthermore, children who witness abuse may come to believe that "might does make right" and identify with the person in power. In turn, they may use force to get their way when they are adults.

Appeal to Pity

In the fallacy of **appeal to pity**, we try to evoke a feeling of pity in the other person when pity is irrelevant to the conclusion. For example:

> Please don't give me a speeding ticket, officer. I had a really bad day: I found out that my boyfriend was cheating on me and, to top it off, I just received an eviction notice from my landlord.

However, the fact that you just found out your boyfriend was cheating on you and that you got an eviction notice from your landlord, while certainly sad, are not logically relevant to how fast you were driving. Although the officer may feel sympathy for your plight, it is not a good reason for her not to issue you a speeding ticket.

> **appeal to pity** Pity is evoked in an argument when pity is irrelevant to the conclusion.

In previous chapters we discussed the importance in critical thinking of healthy self-esteem and assertive communication skills. People who have low self-esteem or trouble balancing their needs and those of others are particularly vulnerable to this fallacy.

> I don't have time to type up my assignment for class tomorrow morning because I promised I'd meet Justin at the movies tonight. And you know better than anyone that

A speeding driver's pleas that "I shouldn't get a ticket because everyone speeds," or, "Please don't give me a ticket, I'm late for the party," are based on fallacious thinking and would not convince a logically thinking officer.

irresponsible behavior of someone who habitually uses this fallacy to manipulate others.

Not all appeals to pity are fallacious. There are times when a person's plight calls for a sympathetic response. For example:

> Please don't give me a speeding ticket, officer. My toddler, who is in the backseat, swallowed a nickel and is having trouble breathing. I have to get her to the hospital right away.

In this case, we would consider the officer grossly insensitive—and perhaps even criminally at fault—if she gave the parent a speeding ticket instead of escorting him and his child to the hospital as quickly as possible. Many charities also appeal to our sense of pity. Once again, there is no fallacy in cases where our pity is logically relevant to the appeal for help.

The word *critical*, as in critical thinking, is derived (as we noted at the beginning of Chapter 1) from the Greek word *kritikos*, meaning "discernment" or "the ability to judge." Being able to discern when it is appropriate for us to respond to an appeal to pity, as opposed to when we are being manipulated, involves an awareness of whether or not the reference to pity is in fact relevant.

Popular Appeal

The fallacy of **popular appeal** occurs when we appeal to popular opinion to gain support for our conclusion. The most common form is the *bandwagon approach*, in which a conclusion is assumed to be true simply because "everyone" believes it or "everyone" is doing it. Here's an example of the bandwagon form of popular appeal:

> God must exist. After all, most people believe in God.

The conclusion in this argument is based on the assumption that the majority must know what is right. However, the fact that the majority of people believe in the existence of God, or in anything else, does not mean it is true. After all, the majority of people once believed that the sun went around the earth and that slavery was natural and morally acceptable.

Popular appeal may use polls to support a conclusion, as in this example:

> Mandatory testing of students is a good measure of how academically effective a school is. A poll found that 71 percent of parents of children in grades K–12 ". . . favor mandatory testing of students in public schools each year as a way to determine how well the school is doing."[5]

The fact that most parents agree with mandatory testing is insufficient on its own to support the conclusion that it is a good measure of how well schools are doing. Instead we need a controlled

popular appeal An appeal to popular opinion to gain support for our conclusion.

it's wrong to break a promise. Please type up my assignment for me. If you don't, I might fail the course. Please, please, just do this one thing for me.

People who fall for this fallacy may see themselves as caring and sensitive people who hate to say no and are always willing to go out of their way for their friends. Compassion is certainly a good trait. But there are times when, if someone makes a request like this, you need to step back and ask yourself whether pity is relevant to their argument. If not, you can still express your concern but not give into their fallacious reasoning. Falling for an appeal to pity not only hurts you but also encourages the

Hot or Not?

Does celebrity endorsement of a product make you more likely to buy that product?

Connections

How do advertisers use the fallacy of popular appeal to sell products such as "junk food" to children? *See Chapter 10, pp. 315–316.*

How can you recognize the fallacy of popular appeal in political campaigns? *See Chapter 13, p. 401.*

How can we recognize the use of snob appeal in advertisements? *See Chapter 10, p. 318.*

① Mrs. Violet Anderson claims to have smoked her first cigarette on May 19, 1910…in the attic of her grandfather's farmhouse. ② Cynthia Irene Bell smoked her first cigarette behind the old barn out back on Jan. 4, 1912. It was cold. ③ Myrna F. Phillips confesses she smoked March 4 or 5, 1911, out in the country, where only a squirrel and a bird could see her. The others offered "no comment." You've come a long way. Now there's a new slim filter-cigarette that's all your own.

"You've Come A Long Way, Baby"

The tobacco industry spends about $25 million a day in advertising, much of which is based on appeals to our emotions rather than to reason. In 1968, Phillip Morris introduced Virginia Slims cigarettes and the "You've come a long way, baby!" ad campaign in an attempt to expand its female market. This campaign was designed to appeal to women's growing sense of independence. It also identified smoking with being beautiful and thin. Not surprisingly, one of the main reasons women cite for smoking is weight loss.

Although the sexist overtones led to boycotts of Virginia Slims by some feminists, the ad was highly successful in getting more teenage girls to take up smoking. Virginia Slims advertising dropped the "You've come a long way, baby!" tag line during 1995–1996.

DISCUSSION QUESTIONS

1. *Discuss the use of fallacies in this ad. Make a note of your initial reaction to the above ad. To what extent did you fall prey to the fallacies in this ad and why? Analyze why this ad was successful in getting some young women to take up smoking.*

2. *If you smoke or know someone who does, what reasons do you or the other person give in support of continuing to smoke? Examine or analyze these reasons for possible fallacies.*

Advertisers often appeal to "snob appeal" in advertising, paying celebrities to endorse their products. They hope that consumers will think, "I want to be like Victoria Beckham, so I'll buy the type of purse she is carrying."

appeal to ignorance The claim that something is true simply because no one has proven it false, or that something is false simply because no one has proven it true.

hasty generalization A generalization is made from a sample that is too small or biased.

What events led U.S. courts to adopt the "innocent until proven guilty" philosophy? *See Chapter 13, p. 416.*

Connections

scientific study to determine the relationship between student test scores and how well a school is doing (see page 379 for an explanation of controlled studies). This argument also contains an ambiguous term *well*. In order to conduct a study we first need an operational definition of *well* (e.g., graduation rate) to determine how a school is doing. If we simply use student test scores we are engaging in circular reasoning, also known as the fallacy of begging the question (see page 153).

The *snob appeal* form of this fallacy involves the association of a certain idea with an elite group of people or a popular image or product. The use of supermodel Kate Upton in in the 2013 Super Bowl ads for Mercedes-Benz and of celebrities such as Mariska Hargitay of the popular television series *Law and Order: Special Victims Unit* in ads for milk are examples of snob appeal. Indeed, this fallacy is particularly prevalent in ads that attempt to create a market for products—such as fancy cars—that we wouldn't ordinarily consider purchasing.

As critical thinkers, we need to keep in mind that a particular position or conclusion is not necessarily right just because the majority or an elite group accepts it.

Appeal to Ignorance

The fallacy of **appeal to ignorance** does not imply that we are stupid. Instead, it means that we are ignorant of the means of proving or disproving something. We fall into this fallacy whenever we argue that something is true simply because no one has proven it false, or that something is false because no one has proven it true. Consider this:

> UFOs obviously don't exist. No one has been able to prove that they do.

In this example, the only support the person offers for the conclusion that UFOs don't exist is that we have been unable to prove their existence. However, the fact that we are ignorant of how to go about proving their existence does not mean that they don't exist. UFOs may or may not exist—we just don't know.

Sometimes the fallacy of appeal to ignorance is subtler. Educational psychologist Arthur Jensen used the following argument in support of his conclusion that black people are innately inferior to white people in intelligence:

> No one has yet produced any evidence based on a properly controlled study to show that representative samples of Negro and white children can be equalized in intellectual ability through statistical control of environment and education.[6]

However, it does not logically follow from *lack* of evidence that "[black] and white children can [not] be equalized in intellectual ability." Once again, the most we can say is that we don't know.

People may also try to get out of a tight spot by using this fallacy, as in the following case:

> I didn't murder Alexi, officer. You don't have any evidence that I was at Alexi's house last night. That proves that I didn't do it.

There is an important exception to the fallacy of appeal to ignorance. In a court of law, a defendant is presumed innocent until proven guilty. And the burden of proof is on the prosecution, not on the defendant. This legal principle was designed to prevent punishment of the innocent, which is considered a much greater injustice than letting a guilty person go free. In addition, because the government is much more powerful than the individual defendant, this principle helps level the playing field. It's important to note that a "not guilty" verdict is just that; it is not necessarily proof of the person's innocence.

Hasty Generalization

When used properly, generalization is a valuable tool in both the physical and social sciences. We commit the fallacy of **hasty generalization** when we generalize from a sample that is too small or biased.

Unusual cases ⟶ Odd rule about the whole group

(premises) (conclusion)

Stereotypes are often based on this fallacy:

> My father was an abuser, and so was my ex-boyfriend John. All men are mean.

Here the speaker judges all men as "mean" on the basis of her limited experience with only two men.

As we've already seen, people tend to divide the world into "us" and "them," and rather than view people who are different from "us" as individuals, we instead label "them" on the basis of hasty generalizations. Confirmation bias, in which we seek only examples that confirm our stereotypes, reinforces this tendency.

For example, the YouTube film "Innocence of Muslims" mocked the prophet Muhammad and perpetuated the stereotype that Muslims are irrational and violent. The film, which provoked protests throughout the Muslim world, was initially and erroneously thought to be the catalyst for the attacks on the U.S. embassy in Benghazi (see page 65).

The fallacy of hasty generalization can also interfere with cross-cultural communication and the establishment of new relationships. While on a cruise with my sister, our ship stopped at the port of Cartagena in Colombia, instead of at another Caribbean port that had originally been scheduled. When our tour director heard of the change, he quickly called our group together and warned us that we should stay on the ship while in port. If we really wanted to go ashore, he added, we should pretend to be Canadians. Colombians, he told us, hate Americans and would try to rob, assault, or arrest us on the most trivial charges, or even kill us, given the opportunity. As it turned out, Cartagena was a beautiful city, and the people we met were very friendly and helpful. Stereotypes and hasty generalizations about Colombians acted as a barrier that kept other passengers from getting to know and understand the Colombians.

Hasty generalization can also occur because we've developed stereotypes that are based on outdated information. Consider this statement:

> Most college students are liberals. I know I was, as were most of my friends, when I was in college in the mid-1970s.

Although the majority of college students identified themselves as liberal or far left politically in the 1970s, this is no longer the case. Today almost half of students—47.5 percent—are middle-of-the-road politically and another 24 percent identify themselves as conservative or far right.[7]

The YouTube film "Innocence of Muslims" provoked protests throughout the Muslim world by denigrating the Prophet Muhammad and showed how easily explosive material can be disseminated through the Internet.

Today almost half of students— 47.5 percent—are middle-of-the-road politically and another 24 percent identify themselves as conservative or far right.

Before we make a generalization we should make sure that we have a sufficiently large and unbiased—as well as an up-to-date—sample. After the death of the great English poet Lord Byron in 1824, a curious physician removed his brain and weighed it. He found that Byron's brain was 25 percent larger than the average human brain. News of this discovery, which was based on only a single sample, spread throughout the scientific community, contributing to the myth that there was a connection between brain size and high intelligence.[8] We'll be studying sampling methods and the proper use of generalization in arguments in more detail in Chapter 7.

Connections

How do advertisements reinforce stereotypes? *See Chapter 10, p. 318.* What role does sampling play in scientific research and experimentation? *See Chapter 12, p. 379.*

Straw Man

The **straw man fallacy** is committed when a person distorts or misrepresents the opponent's argument, thus making it easier to knock it down or refute it. This tactic is particularly common in political rhetoric over controversial issues.

> I'm opposed to legalizing same-sex marriages. Proponents of same-sex marriage want to destroy traditional marriage and make gay marriage the norm.

This is a fallacious argument because it misrepresents the argument of those who support same-sex marriage. Supporters of same-sex marriage are not arguing that it should be an alternative to traditional marriage or that it is superior to traditional marriage. Instead, they simply want same-sex couples to have the same rights as opposite-sex couples when it comes to marriage.

Here is another example of the straw man fallacy:

> I can't believe you think genetically modified crops should be subjected to stricter regulations. If you take away farmers' ability to grow genetically modified crops, this will lead to widespread famine and starvation.

As in the previous example, this assessment of the argument in question is simplistic. It misrepresents the argument and instead sets up a straw man that is easier to knock down by arguing that without genetically modified (GM) crops, people would starve. But the opponent never argued for getting rid of GM crops, only for more regulation.

To avoid using or being taken in by this fallacy, go back and look at the argument in question as it was originally presented. Ask yourself: Has the argument been reworded or oversimplified to the point of misrepresentation? Have key parts of the original argument been omitted or key words been changed or misused?

> **straw man fallacy** An opponent's argument is distorted or misrepresented in order to make it easier to refute.

> **red herring fallacy** A response is directed toward a conclusion that is different from that proposed by the original argument.

The argument that legalizing same-sex marriage will destroy traditional marriage is based on the straw man fallacy.

Red Herring

The **red herring** fallacy is committed when a person tries to sidetrack an argument by going off on a tangent and bringing up a different issue. Thus, the argument is now directed toward a different conclusion. The red herring fallacy is named after a technique used in England to train foxhounds. A sack of red herrings is dragged across the path of the fox to distract the hounds from their prey. A well-trained hound learns not to allow distractions to divert its focus from the prey. Because the red herring issue is often presented as somewhat related to the initial one under discussion, the shift in the argument usually goes unnoticed. The original discussion may even be abandoned completely and the focus shifted to another topic without the audience realizing what is happening until it is too late.

HIGHLIGHTS

FALLACIES OF RELEVANCE

- *Ad hominem fallacy (personal attack):* An attempt to refute an argument by attacking the character or circumstances of the person making the argument.

- *Appeal to force (scare tactics):* A threat to use force—whether it be physical, psychological, or legal—in an attempt to get another person to back down on his or her position and to accept the conclusion as correct.

- *Appeal to pity:* An attempt to gain support for a conclusion by evoking a feeling of pity, when pity is irrelevant to the conclusion.

- *Popular appeal:* An appeal made to the opinion of the majority to gain support for the conclusion.

- *Appeal to ignorance:* An argument that something is true simply because no one has proved it false, or that something is false simply because no one has proved it true.

- *Hasty generalization:* A conclusion based on atypical cases.

- *Straw man:* The distortion or misrepresentation of an opponent's argument to make it easier to knock down or refute.

- *Red herring:* An argument directed toward a conclusion that is different from that posed by the original argument.

➤ *APPLICATION: Find an example in the text of each of the different types of fallacies of relevance.*

The use of the red herring fallacy occurs in political debates when candidates want to avoid answering a question or commenting on a controversial issue. For example, a politician who is asked about a nationalized health care plan may change the topic to the less controversial one of how important it is for all Americans to be healthy and receive good health care. In doing so, the politician avoids having to address the question of which approach to health insurance he or she supports.

Here is an example of this fallacy:

> I don't see why you get so upset about my driving after I have a few drinks. It's not such a big deal. Look at all the accidents that are caused by people talking on their cell phones while driving.

Here the person shifts the topic to accidents associated with use of cell phones, thus deflecting attention from the issue of his drinking and driving.

The red herring fallacy also occurs in discussions of ethical issues when a person changes the topic from what *should* be to what *is*. For example:

> Angelo: I don't think Mike should have lied to Rosetta about what he was doing last night. It was wrong.
>
> Bart: Oh, I don't know about that. If I had been in his situation, I would probably have done the same thing.

Here, Bart has changed the topic from what someone else *should* have done to what he *would* have done. In doing so, he changes the issue from a moral one to a factual one.

In the following newspaper column, the writer attempts to deflect attention away from the abuse at Abu Ghraib prison by changing the topic to the abuses under Iraqi dictator Saddam Hussein:

> The bullying and humiliation of detainees at Abu Ghraib is, as George W. Bush told Jordan's King Abdullah, "a stain on our country's honor and our country's reputation." . . . But let us also recognize what this scandal is not. There is a large difference between forcing prisoners to strip and submit to hazing at Abu Ghraib prison and the sort of things routinely done there under Saddam Hussein. This is a country where mass tortures, mass murders and mass graves were, until the arrival of the U.S. Army, a way of life.[9]

Note how the writer uses words such as *bullying, humiliation,* and *hazing* to downplay the torture of prisoners at Abu Ghraib, instead conjuring up an image of what happens at "harmless" college fraternity initiations. As Chris Crozier, a 21-year-old Fort Stewart mechanic stationed in Iraq, put it: "What the Iraqis may do to us is totally different. We should show them how to treat prisoners."[10] Now that's good critical thinking!

*j. I think you'll agree with me that we do not want the press to find out that we're using child labor at our factory in India. You certainly wouldn't want to lose your job over this, if you get my drift.

k. Gun control is small potatoes when compared with the dangers posed by the widespread use of drones.[12]

l. You should switch from MySpace to Facebook. Facebook is the best social network because more people use it than any other social networking site.

*m. Granted, you may be a vegetarian, but you certainly can't argue against the killing of animals. After all, you do wear leather shoes and use products that were tested on lab animals.

n. I'd think twice about hiring Lucy to work the cash register in the student union cafeteria. She was fired from her last job in the bookstore for stealing, and just last week she was caught leaving the library with someone else's backpack.

o. Of course Troy voted for Obama; after all Troy is African American.

*p. You shouldn't be so concerned about street drugs. More people are killed with prescription drugs than with street drugs such as heroine and cocaine.

q. In 2010 Senator Patricia Murphy opposed the Senate health care bill on the grounds that the majority of Americans did not like the bill. Senate majority leader Harry Reid responded to her concern by arguing that she should vote for the Senate health care bill since a Kaiser Family Foundation Poll found that 57 percent of Americans "would be disappointed if Congress did not pass health care reform."

r. You wouldn't catch me visiting rural areas of British Columbia. People who live there are vicious. Why, just look at Robert Pickton, who murdered and dismembered some 27 women on his pig farm in British Columbia.

*s. Please don't count yesterday's absence against me, Professor Lee. The hot water wasn't working in our dorm and I wasn't able to take a shower.

t. "Soldiers at Fort Carson, Colorado, have been told that if they don't re-up [re-enlist] to 2007 they will be shipped out pronto for Iraq."[13]

u. I heard on the Jay Leno show that Michelle Obama buys her clothes at J. Crew. I love Michelle Obama; she's so cool. I'm going to buy my clothes at J. Crew too!

*v. Please don't count yesterday's absence against me, Professor Curto. I was struck by a car while coming home from a party and spent the day in the emergency room.

w. "[There is little] likelihood that machines, even if they reach a requisite level of complexity, will possess human attributes like consciousness and emotion. A being devoid of emotion would not feel betrayed if we kill it, nor would we regard it as a moral agent. The computer geeks in AI labs who think of themselves as nothing more than complex computer programs and want to download themselves into a computer should worry, since no one would care if they were turned off for good."[14]

x. Why are you focusing so much on Americans as the culprits in green house gas emissions. Canadians' energy use has increased by 25 percent in the past decade and they now use more energy per capita than do Americans. The Canadians also dropped their commitment to the Kyoto Protocol on reducing global warming.

*y. The Vatican, which is run by a celibate male leadership, has no moral right to take a stand on abortion.

z. "Every time you go online you're vulnerable to hackers, viruses, and cyber-thieves. Stay safe with Symantec's Norton Internet Security. It's comprehensive protection for you and your computer."

2. Discuss a time when you committed the fallacy of hasty generalization by stereotyping a particular group of people. What is the basis of this stereotype, and how is it reinforced in our language? Discuss also ways in which our language stereotypes *you*.

3. Find an editorial cartoon that contains the fallacy of personal attack. What do you think is the intent of the cartoonist? What effect does the cartoon have on your view of the subject of the cartoon? Discuss steps you might take to counter the effect of the fallacy of hasty generalization and our tendency to see the world in terms of "one of us/one of them" (see pages 148–149).

4. Which fallacy of relevance are you most likely to fall for? Give a specific example. Which fallacy of relevance are you most likely to use? Give a specific example. What steps can you take to make yourself less vulnerable to these fallacies?

*Answers to selected exercises are found in the Solutions Manual at the end of the book.

FALLACIES INVOLVING UNWARRANTED ASSUMPTIONS

A fallacy involving an **unwarranted assumption** occurs when an argument includes an assumption that is not supported by evidence. Because an unwarranted assumption is unjustified, it weakens the argument. Fallacies involving unwarranted assumptions include begging the question, inappropriate appeal to authority, loaded question, false dilemma, questionable cause, slippery slope, and the naturalistic fallacy.

Begging the Question

In **begging the question**, the conclusion is simply a rewording of a premise. By making our conclusion the same as the premise, we are assuming that the conclusion is true rather than offering proof for it. This fallacy is also known as circular reasoning.

Premise Conclusion

Begging the question may take the form of the conclusion being a definition of the key term in the premises. In the following argument, the conclusion is simply a definition of the key term *capital punishment* rather than being an inference from the premise:

> Capital punishment is wrong because it is immoral to inflict death as a punishment for a crime.

This type of fallacy is sometimes hard to spot. At first glance, it may appear that the person has an airtight argument. On closer evaluation, however, it becomes apparent that it only *seems* this way since the conclusion and the premise(s) say essentially the same thing, as in the following argument:

> The Bible is the word of God. Therefore, God must exist because the Bible says God exists.

Here, the conclusion "God must exist" is already assumed to be true in the premise "The Bible is the word of God." To offer a rational proof of God, we cannot assume in our premise the existence of what we are trying to prove.

The begging the question fallacy can be very frustrating if we fail to recognize it, since there is no way to disprove the person's conclusion if we accept the premise. If you think an argument contains this fallacy, try reversing the conclusion and the premise(s) to see if the argument says essentially the same thing.

Inappropriate Appeal to Authority

It is generally appropriate in an argument to use the testimony of a person who is an authority or expert in the field. However, we commit the fallacy of **inappropriate appeal to authority** when we look to an authority in a field that is *not* under investigation. Young children, for example, may look to their parents as authorities even in areas where their parents have little or no expertise. Here is another example:

> My priest says that genetic engineering is not safe. Therefore, all experimentation in this field should be stopped.

Unless your priest also happens to be an expert in genetic engineering, before accepting his argument as correct you should ask him for reliable and authoritative evidence for his assertion.

We often find this fallacy in advertisements in which celebrities are used to promote products. For example, the singer Beyoncé is featured in ads promoting Pepsi, while basketball star LeBron James endorses Samsung phones; Olympic swimmer Michael Phelps appears in ads for milk (see p. 108). In none of these cases are the celebrities authorities on these products, and yet people accept their word simply because they are *experts* in unrelated fields.

Uniforms and distinguished titles such as *doctor*, *professor*, *president*, and *lieutenant* also serve to reinforce the mistaken perception that people who are experts in one field must be knowledgeable in others. This phenomenon is known as the *halo effect*. In the Milgram study explored in Chapter 1, the majority of subjects followed the orders of the experimenter primarily because he had a Ph.D. and was wearing a white lab coat, a symbol of scientific authority.

To avoid inappropriate appeals to authority, we should check out an expert's credentials in the field before using his or her testimony as authoritative.

> **unwarranted assumption** A fallacious argument that contains an assumption that is not supported by evidence.
>
> **begging the question** The conclusion of an argument is simply a rewording of a premise.
>
> **inappropriate appeal to authority** We look to an authority in a field other than that under investigation.
>
> **loaded question** A particular answer is presumed to an unasked question.

Connections

How can we recognize and avoid falling for the use of inappropriate appeal to authority in advertisements? *See Chapter 10, p. 318.*

Loaded Question

The fallacy of **loaded question** assumes a particular answer to another unasked question. This fallacy is sometimes used in a court of law when a lawyer demands a yes or no answer to a question such as

> Have you stopped beating your girlfriend?

false dilemma Responses to complex issues are reduced to an either/or choice.

However, this question makes the unwarranted assumption that you have already answered yes to a previous unasked question, "Do you beat your girlfriend?" If you don't beat your girlfriend and reply no to the question, it appears as if you are still beating her. On the other hand, if you answer yes it implies that you used to beat her.

The following example is also a loaded question:

> Do you think that the death penalty should be used only for people 18 and older?

This question is worded in a way that assumes that the people being asked approve of the death penalty when in fact they might not.

False Dilemma

The fallacy of **false dilemma** reduces responses to complex issues to an either/or choice. By doing so, this fallacy polarizes stands on issues and ignores common ground or other solutions. This slogan serves as an example:

> America—love it or leave it! If you don't like U.S. policy, then move somewhere else!

That argument makes the unwarranted assumption that the only alternative to accepting U.S. policies is to move to another country. In fact, there are many alternatives, including working to change or improve U.S. policies. In this case,

the fallacious reasoning is reinforced by the "one of us/one of them" cognitive error, in which we tend to divide the world into two opposing sides.

Poor critical-thinking skills and the tendency to see the world in black and white make it more likely that we'll fall into this fallacy. The argument that we need to raise taxes or cut medical services is based on the fallacy of false dilemma. Rather than raising taxes we can make our health care system more efficient. For example, Canada spends far less on health care per capita but has better outcomes in terms of life expectancy than the United States.

Habitual use of this fallacy restricts our ability to come up with creative solutions to problems in our personal lives as well, as the following example illustrates:

> It's Valentine's Day, and Bob didn't propose to me as I thought he would. Even worse, he said he wanted to start dating other women. I don't know what I'll do. If Bob doesn't marry me, I'll surely end up a miserable old maid.

Clearly Bob is not the only fish in the sea, although it may seem so when we are jilted by someone we care for. Overcoming personal setbacks requires that we use our critical-thinking skills to come up with a way of moving on rather than getting stuck in fallacious thinking.

We frequently find this type of fallacious thinking in all-or-nothing thinking. For example, bulimics regard eating in terms of either getting fat or bingeing and then vomiting to stay thin. They simply don't see moderation in eating as a viable alternative.

Wearing a uniform serves to reinforce the public's belief that the person is an authority in fields that may be beyond his or her actual expertise.

Some argue for wind power as the only alternative to fossil fuels. However, harnessing wind power is just one of many ways of cutting down on greenhouse emissions and reducing our dependence on foreign oil. It's not an either/or choice.

As we discussed in Chapter 4, people who suffer from depression also tend to get caught up in this type of fallacious reasoning:

"Either I'm in complete control of my life or I'm out of control."

"Either everyone likes me or everyone hates me."

Pollsters may unwittingly commit this fallacy. How options are presented in a question can influence the response. For instance, in one survey people were asked whether they felt that "the courts deal too harshly or not harshly enough with criminals." When presented with only these two alternatives, 6 percent of those surveyed responded "too harshly" and 78 percent "not harshly enough." However, when a third alternative was offered—"don't have enough information about courts to say"—29 percent chose that response and only 60 percent said "not harshly enough."[15] We'll be studying polling methods in more detail in Chapter 7.

To avoid the fallacy of the false dilemma, watch out for either/or questions that put you on the spot. If neither alternative is satisfactory, it is best to leave the response blank or check "I don't know" if that option is offered.

Questionable Cause

Because our brains tend to impose order on how we see the world, we may "see" order and causal relationships where they don't exist. When a person assumes, without sufficient evidence, that one thing is the cause of another, that person is committing the fallacy of **questionable cause**.

This can occur when we assume that because one event preceded a second event, it was the cause of the second event. This is also called the **post hoc** ("after this") fallacy.

> It was divine intervention. I have a great devotion to Our Lady of Guadalupe . . . and said a little prayer to her when I hit the jackpot. Our Lady really looks out for me.[16]
> —Guadalupe Lopez, mother of actress and singer Jennifer Lopez, on her $2.4 million slot-machine win at an Atlantic City casino

Superstitions are often based on this fallacy:

> I wore my red sweater to the exam last week and aced it. I guess the sweater brought me good luck.

These two examples also illustrate how the self-serving bias that we are in control makes us prone to commit this fallacy.

We often see people's actions as having more causal impact on future events than they really do. For example, for more than eight decades the

questionable cause (post hoc) A person assumes, without sufficient evidence, that one thing is the cause of another.

Connections

How can you recognize and avoid falling for the fallacy of questionable cause in advertising? *See Chapter 10, p. 318.* How can the scientific method be used to establish causal relationships? *See Chapter 12, p. 367.*

Ryan White was a victim of questionable cause. For a time he was prohibited from attending public school because he had AIDS and people assumed that AIDS could be passed on to other students through casual contact.

Outside the Box

JUDITH SHEINDLIN, *"Judge Judy"*

Judith Sheindlin (b. 1942), popularly known as "Judge Judy," is probably the most famous family court judge in the United States. Sheindlin attended American University and New York Law School. She graduated first in her class from law school, where she was the only woman in her class. In 1982, she was appointed a Family Court judge by then New York City Mayor Ed Koch. She quickly became renowned for her outspokenness and her quick thinking. In 1996 she was approached about presiding over cases on a television show.

The show *Judge Judy* premiered in 1996 and quickly became the number one reality court show on television. In the show, Sheindlin arbitrates small claims cases with real defendants. What fascinates many people about the show is the sheer number of illogical and fallacious arguments made by litigants. Sheindlin's responses to the use of fallacies and lame excuses by litigants has earned her a reputation as a witty but fair and logical thinker. In her book *Don't Pee on My Leg and Tell Me It's Raining: America's Toughest Family Court Judge Speaks Out,* she notes that many people fail to take responsibility for their actions, instead getting trapped in a cycle of fallacious reasoning and deteriorating and even abusive relationships. "I want people to learn to take responsibility," she says.

Judge Judy has been used in college courses for pointing out faulty logic and how to respond to it.*

1. Watch the *Judge Judy* show. List the types of fallacies made by the litigants. Note also how Judge Judy responses to the use of fallacies. Share your observations with the class.

2. Sheindlin notes that irrational and fallacious thinking can leave us trapped in abusive situations. Discuss ways in which the use of fallacious reasoning, or the inability to respond rationally to the use of fallacies by others, has left you, or someone you know, in a harmful situation, whether it be personal or at school or work.

* For example, there is a rhetoric seminar at the University of California at Berkeley entitled "Arguing with Judge Judy" that involves identifying arguments made by the litigants that are illogical or perversions of standard logic, and are used repeatedly.

Boston Red Sox lost every World Series in which they played because—so the story goes—the great baseball player Babe Ruth had jinxed the Sox when the team sold him to the Yankees in 1920.[17] When the team finally won the World Series in 2004, the victory was attributed by many fans to the "end of the curse" rather than simply to the skill and success of the team itself.

Sometimes, either because of stereotyping or ignorance, we assume two events are causally related when, in fact, they are not, as in the following example:

> College students today don't participate in community service or volunteer work like we used to. That's because all they care about is getting a degree that will help them make a lot of money.

This argument commits the fallacy of questionable cause in assuming that college students, or anyone for that matter, who are concerned about making money are less likely to participate in community service as a result. While it is true that the majority of college students today are more concerned about getting a degree that will help them make money, the 2009 American freshman survey also found that a record number of incoming freshman (56.9 percent) said there was a "very good chance" they would volunteer "frequently" in college.[18]

To avoid this fallacy, we should be careful not to assume that there is a causal relationship just because two events occur near each other in time. We should also refer to well-designed studies to determine whether a causal relationship has been established between the two events. For more information on evaluating evidence, refer back to Chapter 4.

Slippery Slope

According to the **slippery-slope** fallacy, if we permit a certain action, then all actions of this type, even the most extreme ones, will soon be permissible. In other words, once we start down the slope or (to vary the metaphor) get a foot in the door, there is no holding back. We commit the slippery-slope fallacy when evidence does not support this predicted outcome, as illustrated by these two examples:

> You should never give in to your child. If you do, soon she will have you wrapped around her little finger. You need to stay in control.
>
> If we allow any form of human cloning, then before we know it there will be armies of clones taking over our jobs.

In the first argument, there is no credible evidence that giving in to our children's demands once in a while will lead to their dominating us.

The second argument regarding the effects of human clones is also implausible. Much of the concern about human cloning leading us down the slippery slope to armies of clones taking over the world is based on inaccurate information. In reality, it would be very risky and expensive to clone a human. Even if we could mass-produce human clones, we would need to find women who are willing to act as surrogate gestational mothers for the cloned children. Moreover, each clone, like any child, will need a family to nurture him or her after birth.[19] This scenario is unlikely to happen on a large scale, since most parents prefer to have children who are related to them. Of course, this is not to say that there are no good arguments against human cloning, but the proverbial slippery slope is not one of them.

slippery slope The faulty assumption that if certain actions are permitted, then all actions of this type will soon be permissible.

Some people oppose certain government policies on the grounds that they are "a moral hazard" that would lead us down the slippery slope to communism as in the following argument:

> Government bailouts will encourage businesses to be irresponsible and take absurd risks. If we allow them we will end up having to bailout every business in the nation until we end up under communism.

Alluding to the dreaded slippery slope when it comes to communism is a common ploy, especially among some conservatives, and involves the use of scare tactics (appeal to force) as well as the slippery slope fallacy.

Expressing a concern that something will get out of hand is not always fallacious. Sometimes the prediction that a particular action or policy will start us down a slippery slope is warranted. Consider this statement:

> The United States is running . . . a series of detention centers around the world where international legal standards are not having sway. They opened the door to a little bit of torture, and a whole lot of torture walked through.[20]

STAR WARS
EPISODE II

ATTACK OF THE CLONES

Scene From Star Wars Episode II
Attack of the Clones In this sci-fi movie clones from an alien planet are portrayed as evil and a threat to the galaxy.

DISCUSSION QUESTIONS

1. *This movie is based on the assumption that mass-produced clones will be evil and destructive. What evidence, if any, is there to support this conclusion? Make a list of possible premises that people might use to support this conclusion.*

2. *Critically evaluate your argument in question 1. Identify and discuss any fallacies in this argument.*

The assumption here is that if we allow torture under these circumstances, the use of torture by the United States will become a common method of dealing with detainees.

naturalistic fallacy A fallacy based on the assumption that what is natural is good.

To avoid the slippery-slope fallacy, we should carefully carry out our research and familiarize ourselves with the likely outcomes of different actions and policies. We should also watch any tendency to exaggerate forecasts of impending catastrophe.

Naturalistic Fallacy

The **naturalistic fallacy** is based on the unwarranted assumption that what is natural is good or morally acceptable and that what is unnatural is bad or morally unacceptable.* We find this fallacy in arguments that claim that no good can come from AI (artificial intelligence),

*The term naturalistic fallacy is sometimes used in a more narrow sense to convey that the concept of moral goodness cannot be reduced to descriptive or natural terms.

Same-sex parents are often discriminated against because many people only see "parents" as a mother and father. Some states still have laws prohibiting same-sex couples from adopting or taking in foster children.

simply on the grounds that AI is artificial—and hence unnatural.

Advertisers may also try to get us to conclude that their product is good or healthy simply because it is natural. An ad can claim, for example, that a tobacco product is "100 percent natural tobacco." However, it doesn't follow. *All* tobacco is natural, but that doesn't make it healthy. Arsenic, HIV, and tsunamis are also "natural," but we don't consider them to be healthy and desirable.

The naturalistic fallacy has also been used both to justify homosexuality (it occurs naturally in other animals) and to argue for its immorality, as in the following:

> Homosexual encounters do not lead to children [procreation], which is the natural end of sexual relations. Therefore, homosexuality is immoral.

In a similar manner, a person may argue that hunting is morally acceptable because other animals hunt and kill:

> I disagree that we need to protect the big cats, such as lions and tigers, from being hunted or to restrict ranchers from protecting their herds from these predators. We are only doing what the big cats do. They are predators, and so are humans.

However, the fact that other animals are predators does not justify our doing the same. Some animals also eat their young, and a few female insects even eat their male partners after mating! But these naturally occurring examples do not imply that it is morally justifiable for humans to do the same. The morality of these behaviors has to be evaluated on grounds other than that they are natural.

HIGHLIGHTS

FALLACIES INVOLVING UNWARRANTED ASSUMPTIONS

- *Begging the question:* A conclusion is simply a rewording of a premise.

- *Inappropriate appeal to authority:* An appeal based on the testimony of an authority in a field other than that under investigation.

- *Loaded question:* A question that assumes a particular answer to another unasked question.

- *False dilemma:* An argument unwarrantedly reduces the number of alternatives to two.

- *Questionable cause:* An argument that assumes without sufficient evidence that one thing is the cause of another.

- *Slippery slope:* An assumption that if some actions are permitted, all actions of that type will soon be permissible.

- *Naturalistic fallacy:* The assumption that because something is natural it is good or acceptable.

➤ *APPLICATION: Find an example in the text of each of the different types of fallacies involving unwarranted assumptions.*

STOP AND ASSESS YOURSELF

I. Identify the fallacies involving unwarranted assumptions in the following arguments—not all of which contain fallacies!

*a. Prosecutor to defendant: Did you hide the drugs in your car?

b. Cocaine should be legalized. Cocaine, which comes from the coca plant, is all natural and therefore much safer than all these processed foods people are putting into their bodies.

c. My parents don't have a lot of money. If I don't get into Harvard with at least a partial scholarship I won't be able to go to college at all.

*d. Panhandler to person on street: "Can you spare a dime?"

e. If we allow terrorists to be tried in our civil courts instead of military tribunals, next thing you know they'll be demanding all sorts of rights given to American prisoners like free health care and a free education. If we allow this, soon terrorists from poorer countries will be flocking to our country and attacking us just so they can enjoy the higher standard of living in our prison system.

f. Clarissa has decided to drop out of college because she gained 17 pounds during her first year at college and is worried about getting diabetes. It's clear that too much education is bad for your health.

*g. My lawyer says that it looks as if I have whiplash from that automobile accident. I'm going to sue the insurance company of the person who hit my car.

h. According to the meteorologists on the Weather Channel, we might have 5 to 6 feet of flooding from heavy rain and rising river waters in the next 24 hours. I think we should pack our valuables and get out of town.

i. Do you support restricting abortion rights, thereby increasing the chances of death for thousands of women desperate enough to seek illegal abortions?

j. Splenda can't be all that bad for children. After all, it's made from all-natural sugar.

k. Conscription is wrong because people should not be compelled by the government to serve in the military.

l. Democracy is the best form of government because rule of the majority is always preferable.

*m. Boyfriend to girlfriend: So what do you want to do tonight—watch the football game on TV or grab a beer at Joe's Bar and Billiards?

n. We should not take away people's rights to own a gun. According to a 2013 Rasmussen Report, two-thirds of Americans support gun ownership as a protection against tyranny.

o. Animals can't reason, since reason is one of the things that separate humans from the beasts.

*p. Yesterday I carried an umbrella to class and it didn't rain. Today I left it home and it rained. I'd better carry my umbrella if I don't want it to rain.

q. Every time the presidential elections have been on November 6th, the Republicans have won. The elections are on November 6th this year. So a Republican will win the election.

r. New York City has proposed banning the sale of sugary drinks that are larger than 16 ounces. This would be a disaster. I mean, where's it going to stop? Next thing you know they'll be regulating everything in our life that we enjoy.

*s. Do you believe women should be drafted into the military?

t. Embryonic stem-cell research should be banned. It is a gateway to all other kinds of genetic engineering in humans and will lead to the exploitation of poor women as fetus farms.

u. If we don't cut back on energy use and our carbon emissions, global warming is going to continue getting worse and some coastal cities and towns may become uninhabitable because of the rising ocean level.

*v. My professor is leaving for a trip to Antarctica the same day that final grades are due for our class. Since this is my senior year at college, I cannot afford to get an incomplete in this class because I plan on graduating in a month. My final paper is worth 40 percent of my grade, so I can either choose to hand in the final paper before my professor leaves for Antarctica or to fail the course and therefore not graduate until next year. I don't see any other way out.

w. In Rhode Island the dropout rate at institutions of higher education is highest at the Community College of Rhode Island (CCRI). Brown University and the Rhode Island School of Design (RISD) have the lowest dropout rates. Since CCRI has the lowest tuition and Brown and RISD have the highest tuition in the state, we should raise the tuition at CCRI if we want to lower the dropout rate there.

2. When you or your college team engages in a game or sporting event, to what extent do you attribute the win or loss to what is in actuality a questionable cause? Looking back at the cognitive errors we studied in Chapter 4, discuss which of the different kinds of errors contribute to our tendency to use or fall for this fallacy.

3. Find two advertisements containing fallacies involving two different unwarranted assumptions. Cut out or photocopy the advertisements. For each ad, write one page explaining what fallacy it contains and the target audience of the fallacious ad. Discuss how effective you think each ad is and why.

4. Which fallacy involving an unwarranted assumption are you most likely to fall for? Give a specific example. Which fallacy involving an unwarranted assumption are you most likely to use? Give a specific example. What steps can you take to make yourself less vulnerable to these fallacies?

*Answers to selected exercises are found in the Solutions Manual at the end of the book.

STRATEGIES FOR AVOIDING FALLACIES

Once you have learned how to identify informal fallacies, the next step is to develop strategies for avoiding them. Here are some strategies that can help you become a better critical thinker:

- *Know yourself.* Self-knowledge is a cardinal rule for good critical thinking. Knowing which fallacies you are most likely to fall for and which you are most likely to commit will make you less vulnerable to lapses in critical thinking.

- *Build your self-confidence and self-esteem.* Working on your self-confidence and self-esteem will make you less likely to give in to peer pressure and, in particular, to the fallacy of popular appeal. People who are self-confident are also less likely to back down when others use a fallacy on them or to become defensive and use fallacies on others.

- *Cultivate good listening skills.* Be a respectful listener of other people's views, even if you disagree with them. Do not be thinking of how you are going to respond before you have even heard the other person's argument. After the other person has presented his or her view, repeat it back to make sure you understand it correctly. Look for common ground. If you notice a fallacy in the argument, respectfully point it out. If the argument appears to be weak, ask the person for better support or evidence for his or her position rather than simply dismissing it.

- *Avoid ambiguous and vague terms and faulty grammar.* Cultivate good communication and writing skills. Clearly define your key terms in presenting an argument. And expect the same of others. Don't be afraid to ask questions. If you are unclear about the definition of a term or what someone else means, ask the person to define the term or rephrase the sentence.

- *Do not confuse the soundness of an argument with the character or circumstances of the person making the argument.* Focus on the argument that is being presented, not on the person presenting the argument. Also, resist the temptation to counterattack if another person attacks your character or threatens you because of your position on a particular issue. When two people trade insult for insult instead of focusing on the real issue, an argument may escalate out of control and both people may end up feeling frustrated and hurt. The tacit belief that if the other person is using fallacies or is being illogical then it's okay for you to do the same is a sign of immature thinking. If another person attacks your character, step back and take a deep breath before responding.

- *Know your topic.* Don't jump to a conclusion without first doing your research. Knowing your subject makes it less likely that you will commit a fallacy simply because you are unable to defend your position. This strategy involves being familiar with the relevant evidence, as well as a willingness to learn from others. In evaluating new evidence, make sure that it is based on credible sources.

- *Adopt a position of skepticism.* We should be skeptical but not close our minds to claims we disagree with, unless there is clear evidence that contradicts that claim. Don't just take people's word for it, especially if they are not authorities in the field under discussion. Also, remain skeptical about your own position and open to the possibility that you are mistaken or don't have the whole truth.

- *Watch your body language.* Fallacies need not be written or spoken. For example, the fallacies of personal attack and appeal to force can be conveyed through body language, such as rolling your eyes, glaring, looking away, and even walking away when someone is speaking.

- *Don't be set on "winning."* If your purpose is to win the argument rather than get to the truth about the issue, you're more likely to use fallacies and rhetoric when you can't rationally defend your position.

Learning how to recognize and avoid fallacies will make you less likely to fall victim to faulty arguments, whether those of cult recruiters, advertisers, politicians, authority figures, friends, or family. It is especially important to be able to identify and avoid using fallacies in your own life, thereby improving your critical-thinking skills.

The habitual use of fallacies can damage relationships and leave people feeling upset and frustrated. By avoiding fallacies, your relationships will be more satisfying and your arguments stronger and more credible. This, in turn, will make it easier for you to achieve your life goals.

STOP AND ASSESS YOURSELF

1. Discuss ways in which being aware of and avoiding fallacies can improve your personal life.

2. Discuss how lack of self-knowledge and self-confidence makes you or others you know more vulnerable to fallacious reasoning. Use specific examples to illustrate your answer.

3. Working in small groups, select one or two of the following issues or one of the issues already raised in this chapter. Identify which fallacy the argument might contain. Discuss how you would go about collecting evidence to determine whether the argument is fallacious.

*a. Boys don't do as well in school as girls because almost all the teachers in elementary schools are women.

b. The beheading of infidels in Iraq, such as Western journalists, was sanctioned by Islam's holiest text, the Qur'an, which urges Muslims to resist Western occupation by stating, "Slay them . . . and drive them out of the places whence they drove you."[21]

c. "The big financiers have been the pampered pets for too long, and the mainstream figures who say 'depression . . . depression . . . depression' have been Chicken Littleing for too long; Wall Street won't change its ways without a bloodbath, and it's time they finally got one." (Argument against giving government bailouts to struggling financial institutions.)[22]

*d. "We now face a wave of education reforms based on the belief that school choice, test-driven accountability, and the resulting competition will dramatically improve student achievement. . . . [T]here is empirical evidence, and it shows clearly that choice, competition, and accountability as education reform levers are not working. But with confidence bordering on recklessness, the Obama administration is plunging ahead, pushing an aggressive program of school reform—codified in its signature Race to the Top program that relies on the power of incentives and competition. This approach may well make schools worse, not better."[23]

e. I don't think an ice cream social is appropriate for our next meeting since several of the students who will be attending are Japanese Americans, and from what I know, most of them don't eat ice cream.

f. Some people think prostitution should be legalized in the United States. However, if we legalize prostitution, sexually transmitted diseases like AIDS will run rampant and everyone will start to die out.

*g. Lawyers for the American Civil Liberties Union (ACLU) want the words *under God* removed from the Pledge of Allegiance. The Supreme Court should not support the ACLU's request. The ACLU is clearly antireligion and would like to see every trace of religion and faith in God removed from American life.

h. Support for stem-cell research by celebrities such as Michael J. Fox and Ronald Reagan Jr. has been in part responsible for the swing in public opinion in favor of the research.

i. Prayer works. Our church group prayed for Maxine after her operation, and she recovered from her surgery faster than the person in the bed beside her who had the same operation.

4. Select two of the strategies for avoiding fallacies and discuss as a class or write a short essay describing ways in which these strategies can help you become a better critical thinker. Discuss how the strategies that you plan to use to make yourself less vulnerable to using or falling for fallacies might make it easier for you to achieve your life goals.

*Answers to selected exercises are found in the Solutions Manual at the end of the book.

THiNK AGAIN

1. What is a fallacy, and why are we taken in by informal fallacies?
   - A fallacy is a type of incorrect thinking. We are taken in by informal fallacies because they are psychologically persuasive. The use of our critical-thinking skills makes us less likely to fall for fallacies.

2. What are three main types of informal fallacies?
   - One type is fallacies of ambiguity, which occur when there is ambiguous wording, sloppy grammatical structure, or confusion between two closely related concepts. In fallacies of relevance, one of the premises is logically unrelated to the conclusion. The third type is fallacies involving unwarranted assumptions in which one of the premises is not adequately supported by evidence.

3. How can we avoid falling for and/or using fallacies?
   - There are several strategies that can be used, including honing our analytical and argumentation skills, being aware of our strengths and weaknesses, building our self-confidence, cultivating good listening skills, avoiding ambiguous terms, adopting a position of skepticism, and having knowledge of the topic under discussion.

Perspectives on Gun Control

The United States has more guns per person—about one for every American—than any other country in the world, second only to Yemen. The United States also has a higher homicide rate by gun than any other developed nation. The gun homicide rate in the United States is 3.2 per 1,000 people, compared to 0.1 in Canada, 0.5 in Norway, 0.6 in Japan, and 0.7 in Great Britain. In addition, almost half of the mass shootings around the world have taken place in the United States.[24] The Centers for Disease Control (CDC) predicts that by 2015 shooting deaths in the United States will rise to 33,000, more than fatalities caused by automobiles.[25]

Following the December 2012 elementary school shooting in Newtown, Connecticut, in which 20 children and 6 adults were killed by 20-year-old Adam Lanza, there have been calls to rethink our gun laws and our interpretation of the Second Amendment of the U.S. Constitution, which states: "A well-regulated militia, being necessary to the security of a free state, the right of the people to keep and bear arms, shall not be infringed." The National Rifle Association (NRA) responded to the school shooting by calling for armed guards in schools, while others argue that more guns simply put our children at greater risk.

While most countries have responded to mass shootings by severely tightening gun control laws, most Americans do not favor an across-the-board rethinking of the Second Amendment. While about 61 percent of Americans in a 2013 poll stated that they wanted stricter laws covering the sale of firearms,[26] the country is evenly split over which is most important: protecting the right to own guns or controlling ownership of guns.[27]

In the following readings, Wayne LaPierre, executive vice president of the NRA argues in favor of laws permitting gun ownership. Mark Kelly, husband of former U.S. Representative Gabrielle Gifford, disagrees. He argues that we need stricter gun control laws.

National Rifle Association Press Release (Dec. 21, 2012)   WAYNE LAPIERRE

Wayne LaPierre is CEO and executive vice president of the National Rifle Association. In the following press release, he argues in favor of laws permitting gun ownership and for having armed guards in schools. An advocate of Second Amendment rights, LaPierre has an M.A. in government from Boston College.

The National Rifle Association's 4 million mothers, fathers, sons and daughters join the nation in horror, outrage, grief and earnest prayer for the families of Newtown, Connecticut . . . who suffered such incomprehensible loss as a result of this unspeakable crime. . . .

Now, we *must* speak . . . for the safety of our nation's children. Because for all the noise and anger directed at us over the past week, no one—nobody—has addressed the most important, pressing and immediate question we face: How do we protect our children *right now*, starting today, in a way that we know *works*?

The only way to answer that question is to face up to the *truth*. Politicians pass laws for Gun-Free School Zones. They issue press releases *bragging* about them. They post signs *advertising* them. And in so doing, they tell every insane killer in America that schools are their *safest* place to inflict maximum mayhem with minimum risk.

How have our nation's priorities gotten so far out of order? Think about it. We care about our money, so we protect our banks with armed guards. American airports, office buildings, power plants, courthouses—even sports stadiums—are all protected by armed security. We care about the President, so we protect him with armed Secret Service agents. Members of Congress work in offices surrounded by armed Capitol Police officers.

Yet when it comes to the most beloved, innocent and vulnerable members of the American family—our children—we as a society leave them *utterly defenseless*, and the monsters and predators of this world know it and exploit it. That must change now!

The truth is that our society is populated by an unknown number of genuine monsters—people so deranged, so evil, so possessed by voices and driven by demons that no sane person can possibly *ever* comprehend them. They walk among us every day. And does anybody really believe that the next Adam Lanza isn't planning his attack on a school he's already identified *at this very moment*?

How many *more* copycats are waiting in the wings for their moment of fame—from a national media machine that *rewards* them with the wall-to-wall attention and sense of identity that they crave—while provoking others to try to make *their* mark? . . .

And the fact is, that wouldn't even begin to address the much larger and more lethal *criminal* class: Killers, robbers, rapists and drug gang members who have spread like cancer in every community in this country. Meanwhile, federal gun prosecutions have decreased by 40 percent—to the lowest levels in a decade.

So now, due to a declining willingness to prosecute dangerous criminals, violent crime is *increasing* again for the first time in 19 years!

. . . And here's another dirty little truth that the media try their best to conceal: There exists in this country a callous, corrupt and *corrupting* shadow industry that sells, and sows, violence against its own people. Through vicious, violent video games with names like Bullet-storm, Grand Theft Auto, Mortal Kombat and Splatterhouse.

. . . Then there's the blood-soaked slasher films like "American Psycho" and "Natural Born Killers" that are aired like propaganda loops on "Splatterdays" and *every* day, and a thousand music videos that portray life as a joke and murder as a way of life.

. . . A child growing up in America witnesses 16,000 murders and 200,000 acts of violence by the time he or she reaches the ripe old age of 18. And throughout it all, too many in our national media . . . their corporate owners . . . and their stockholders . . . act as silent enablers, if not complicit co-conspirators. Rather than face their own moral failings, the media *demonize* lawful gun owners, *amplify* their cries for more laws and fill the national debate with misinformation and dishonest thinking that only delay meaningful action and all but guarantee that the next atrocity is only a news cycle away.

. . . As parents, we do everything we can to keep our children safe. It is now time for us to assume responsibility for their safety at school. The only way to stop a monster from killing our kids is to be personally involved and invested in a plan of absolute protection. The *only* thing that stops a *bad* guy with a gun is a *good* guy with a gun.

. . . A gun in the hands of a Secret Service agent protecting the President isn't a bad word. A gun in the hands of *a* soldier protecting the United States isn't a bad word. And when you hear the glass breaking in your living room at 3 a.m. and call 911, you won't be able to pray hard enough for a gun in the hands of a good guy to get there fast enough to protect you.

So why is the idea of a gun *good* when it's used to protect our President or our country or our police, but *bad* when it's used to protect our children in their schools?

. . . [W]hat if, when Adam Lanza started shooting his way into Sandy Hook Elementary School last Friday, he had been confronted by qualified, armed security?

Will you at least admit it's *possible* that 26 innocent lives might have been spared? Is that so abhorrent to you that you would rather continue to risk the alternative?

. . . I call on Congress today to act immediately, to appropriate whatever is necessary to put armed police officers in every school—and to do it now.

. . . Every school in America needs to immediately *identify*, *dedicate* and *deploy* the resources necessary to put these security forces in place right now. And the National Rifle Association, as America's preeminent trainer of law enforcement and security personnel for the past 50 years, is ready, willing and uniquely qualified to help.

. . . If we truly cherish our kids more than our money or our celebrities, we must give them the greatest level of protection possible and the security that is only available with a *properly trained—armed—good guy.*

REVIEW QUESTIONS

1. Why does LaPierre oppose making schools gun-free zones?

2. What is LaPierre's view regarding violence in the media and video games?

3. What does LaPierre mean when he says: "The *only* thing that stops a *bad* guy with a gun is a *good* guy with a gun"?

4. On what grounds does LaPierre argue that we should have armed guards in our schools?

Testimony by Mark Kelly, Senate Judiciary Committee Hearing on Gun Violence on Jan. 30, 2013

Mark Kelly is a retired astronaut and captain in the U.S. Navy. He is also the husband of former Arizona congresswoman Gabrielle Gifford, who was shot in the head by Jared Lee Loughner while she was speaking at an event in Tucson, Arizona, on January 8, 2011.

As you know, our family has been immeasurably affected by gun violence. Gabby's gift for speech is a distant memory. She struggles to walk and she is partially blind. And a year ago, she left a job she loves, serving the people of Arizona.

But in the past two years, we have watched Gabby's determination, spirit and intellect conquer her disabilities. We aren't here as victims. We're speaking to you today as Americans. . . .

We're both gun owners and we take that right and the responsibilities that come with it very seriously. And we watch with horror when the news breaks to yet another tragic shooting. After 20 kids and six of their teachers were gunned down in their classrooms at Sandy Hook Elementary, we said: "This time must be different; something needs to be done." We are simply two reasonable Americans who have said "enough."

On January 8th of 2011, a young man walked up to Gabby at her constituent event in Tucson, leveled his gun and shot her through the head. He then turned down the line and continued firing. In 15 seconds, he emptied his magazine. It contained 33 bullets and there were 33 wounds.

. . . The killer in the Tucson shooting suffered from severe mental illness, but even after being deemed unqualified for service in the Army and expulsion from Pima Community College, he was never reported to mental health authorities.

On November 30, 2010, he walked into a sporting goods store, passed the background check, and walked out with a semiautomatic handgun. He had never been legally adjudicated as mentally ill, and even if he had, Arizona, at the time, had over 121,000 records of disqualifying mental illness that it had not submitted into the system.

. . . Gabby is one of roughly 100,000 victims of gun violence in America each and every year. Behind every victim lays a matrix of failure and inadequacy in our families, in our communities, in our values, in our society's approach to poverty, violence, and mental illness and yes, also in our politics and in our gun laws.

One of our messages is simple, the breadth and complexity of gun violence is great, but it is not an excuse for inaction. There's another side to our story, Gabby is a gun owner and I am a gun owner. We have our firearms for the same reasons that millions of Americans just like us have guns, to defend ourselves, to defend our families, for hunting, and for target shooting.

We believe wholly and completely in the second amendment and that it confers upon all Americans the right to own a firearm for protection, collection, and recreation. We take that right very seriously and we would never, ever give it up, just like Gabby would never relinquish her gun and I would never relinquish mine. But rights demand responsibility and this right does not extend to terrorists, it does not extend to criminals, and it does not extend to the mentally ill.

When dangerous people get guns, we are all vulnerable at the movies, at church, conducting our everyday business, meeting with a government official. And time after time after time, at school, on our campuses, and in our children's classrooms. When dangerous people get dangerous guns, we are all the more vulnerable. Dangerous people with weapons specifically designed to inflict maximum lethality upon others have turned every single corner of our society into places of carnage and gross human loss. Our rights are paramount, but our responsibilities are serious. And as a nation, we've not taken responsibility for the gun rights that our founding fathers have conferred upon us.

Now we have some ideas on how we can take responsibility. First, fix our background checks. The holes in our laws make a mockery of the background check system. . . . Second, remove the limitations on collecting data and conducting scientific research on gun violence. Enact a tough federal gun trafficking statute; this is really important. And finally, let's have a careful and civil conversation about the lethality of fire arms we permit to be legally bought and sold in this country.

Gabby and I are pro-gun ownership. We are also anti-gun violence, and we believe that in this debate, Congress should look not toward special interests and ideology, which push us apart, but towards compromise which brings us together. We believe whether you call yourself pro-gun, or anti-gun violence, or both, that you can work together to pass laws that save lives.

1. What does Kelly mean when he says that "behind every victim [of gun violence] lays a matrix of failure and inadequacy in our families, in our communities, in our values, in our society"?

2. What is Kelly's view regarding the Second Amendment?

3. Why does Kelly think background checks are important?

4. What compromise does Kelly propose we make in our gun ownership laws?

THiNK AND DISCUSS

PERSPECTIVES ON GUN CONTROL

1. Make a list of the arguments LaPierre uses in support of armed guards in schools. List the arguments Kelly uses in support of stricter gun control laws. Critically analyze both arguments for fallacies. Which person makes the most compelling argument and why?

2. Critically analyze LaPierre's argument that schools should have armed guards. In addition to looking for fallacies, check to make sure that his premises are true. This may require some independent research on your part: Are there armed guards at the Sidwell Friends School, where President Obama's daughters go to school? Are there any important premises that are missing from his argument? Discuss how Kelly would most likely respond to LaPierre's position.

3. Marko Kloos, an ex-Marine, argues in his article "Why the Gun Is Civilization" that "human beings only have two ways to deal with one another: reason and force." He proposes that in a society where not everyone is reasonable guns may be necessary as a means to protect ourselves. Do you agree? Discuss also how both LaPierre and Kelly might each response to Kloos's argument.

6

RECOGNIZING, ANALYZING, & CONSTRUCTING ARGUMENTS

Abraham Lincoln and the incumbent Illinois senator, Stephen A. Douglas, held a series of seven political debates during the 1858 senatorial race. The debates addressed the hottest political issues of the day: whether slavery should be allowed to expand into western territories, whether states should have the authority to allow or ban slavery within their borders, and the wisdom of the U.S. Supreme Court's 1857 *Dred Scott* decision, which had ruled that a slave is "property in the strictest sense of the term" and had declared it unconstitutional for Congress to ban slavery in the western territories. Douglas argued for "popular sovereignty," claiming that the people of states and territories had the right to determine their own laws and policies on slavery. Lincoln opposed the expansion of slavery into the territories, arguing that slavery was "a moral, social and a political wrong."

How do politicians use logical arguments and rhetoric in political debates? How can developing skill in logical argumentation make us more effective in presenting and defending our positions?

THiNK FIRST

- What is an argument?
- What is the purpose of breaking down and diagramming arguments?
- What are some of the factors to take into consideration in evaluating an argument?

Although Lincoln lost the senatorial election, he emerged from the debates as a nationally renowned orator and critical thinker. Lincoln went on, as president of the United States, to issue the Emancipation Proclamation, which declared that all those enslaved in Confederate states were to be free. His skill in argumentation and debate, and his refusal to back down in the face of weak counterarguments, culminated in the passage in 1865 of the 13th Amendment, which abolished slavery in the United States.

The ability to recognize, construct, and analyze arguments is one of the most basic skills in critical thinking. To many of us, the word *argument* brings to mind images of quarreling and shouting. However, in logic and in critical thinking, argument refers to the use of reason and evidence to support a claim or conclusion. Arguments are a form of inquiry that provides us with reasons to accept or reject a particular position, so that we can make up our own minds about an issue.

In this information age we are constantly bombarded with arguments on issues from the Internet, television, newspapers, advertisers, politicians, and other sources. As citizens in a democracy, we need to develop the skills to critically analyze arguments and to make informed decisions that are based on our evaluations.

Skill in argumentation can help us make better decisions in our personal choices as well as in our public lives.

In Chapter 6 we will learn how to recognize, analyze, and construct arguments. Specifically, we will:

- Learn how to identify an issue
- Learn how to recognize the parts of an argument, including the premise, the conclusion, and premise and conclusion indicators
- Distinguish among an argument, an explanation, and a conditional statement
- Break down an argument into its premises and conclusion

- Diagram arguments
- Construct our own arguments
- Explore the basics of evaluating arguments

Finally, we will read about the issue of same-sex marriage and analyze arguments that approach that controversial question from different perspectives.

WHAT IS AN ISSUE?

Arguments help us to analyze issues and to determine whether a particular position on an issue is reasonable. An **issue** is an ill-defined complex of problems involving a controversy or uncertainty.

One problem that many college students have in writing an essay or preparing a presentation on an issue is failing to define the issue clearly. An unfocused discussion about smoking, for example, may jump from health risks of secondhand smoking to the problem of addiction to corporate responsibility to subsidies for tobacco farmers. As a result, the discussion is shallow, and deeper insights into any one of these smoking-related issues are overlooked. Because of this, it is important that we first decide what issue we want to focus on.

More than 50 years after the Brown v. Board of Education decision that declared segregation unconstitutional, many feel that African Americans still don't have the same opportunities for quality education as whites. This young woman is one of the "Little Rock Nine," of the first nine blacks to attend Central High in Little Rock, Arkansas, despite threats, scare tactics, and the necessary presence of the National Guard for protection.

Identifying an Issue

Identifying an issue requires clear thinking as well as good communication skills. We've probably all had the experience of finding ourselves arguing at cross-purposes with someone we care about. One person is upset because he or she feels the other isn't showing enough affection, while the other person perceives the issue as an attack on his or her ability as a provider. Because it is not clear what the real issue is, the argument goes nowhere and both people end up feeling frustrated and misunderstood.

Sometimes we don't have the opportunity to clarify an issue by talking to another person. This is often the case with written material, such as magazine or newspaper articles. In these cases, you may be able to determine the writer's focus by examining the title or the introductory paragraph. For example, Sohail H. Hashmi begins his article "Interpreting the Islamic Ethics of War and Peace" thus:

> Muslim writers of many intellectual persuasions have long argued that Westerners hold an inaccurate, even deliberately distorted, conception of *jihad*. In fact, however, the idea of *jihad* (and the ethics of war and peace generally) has been the subject of an intense and multifaceted debate among Muslims themselves.[1]

From this, you can presume that the issue Hashmi is addressing is something like "What is the best and most accurate interpretation of the Islamic concept of *jihad* and of war and peace in general?"

Asking the Right Questions

How we word our questions about an issue will influence how we go about seeking a resolution to it. During his debates with Senator (or, as he called him, "Judge") Douglas, Lincoln changed the national controversy about slavery by reframing the issue so that it was not simply a controversy over state sovereignty but a burning question that affected the very

issue An ill-defined complex of problems involving a controversy or uncertainty.

existence of the nation. In the final debate, Lincoln summed up the issue with these words:

> I have said and I repeat it here, that if there be a man amongst us who does not think that the institution of slavery is wrong in any one of the aspects of which I have spoken, he is misplaced and ought not to be with us. Has anything threatened the existence of the Union save and except this very institution of slavery? That is the real issue. That is the issue that will continue in this country when these poor tongues of Judge Douglas and myself shall be silent.[2]

In an article written 50 years after school segregation was declared unconstitutional by the Supreme Court in *Brown v. Board of Education* (1954), journalist Ellis Cose writes about the current lack of good schools for African American children: "When it comes to children of color, we ask the wrong question. We ask, 'Why are you such a problem?' when we should ask, 'What have we not given you that we routinely give to upper-middle-class white students?' What do they have that you don't?"[3]

To use another example, suppose you come back to your dorm room after class and find that your wallet is missing. You think that you left it on your dresser, but it isn't there. What is the issue? When asked, many students answer that that the issue is "Who stole my wallet?"[4] However, this question is a loaded question based on an as-yet-unfounded assumption—that someone stole your wallet. Maybe you misplaced your wallet or you lost it on your way to class or it got knocked behind the dresser. For now, all you know is that the wallet is missing. Therefore, rather than making assumptions you can't support, it would be better to state the issue as "What happened to my wallet?" rather than "Who stole my wallet?" Remember, one of the traits of a good critical thinker—and of great detectives—is open-mindedness.

THiNKing Outside the Box

ABRAHAM LINCOLN, *U.S. President*

Abraham Lincoln (1809–1865) was the sixteenth president of the United States. Self-educated, Lincoln had a knack for asking the right questions about important issues, such as slavery and war, and then examining all sides of the arguments before coming to a conclusion.

Lincoln's election as president in 1860 led to the secession in 1861 of southern slave-owning states (the Confederacy) and to a 4-year civil war that cost 600,000 American lives, North and South. Although Lincoln had long agreed that slavery should be permitted in states where it was already legal, in the course of the Civil War he concluded that if slavery is immoral, then it should not be legal at all in the United States. Lincoln also realized that taking a position on issues was not simply an intellectual exercise but should have real-life consequences. A man of action as well as strong principles, he issued the Emancipation Proclamation in 1863, freeing slaves in the Confederate states.

Lincoln's struggle to end slavery is depicted in the *movie Lincoln* (2012).

DISCUSSION QUESTIONS

1. Was Lincoln's decision to stand by his conclusion that slavery should be illegal a wise one, given that it escalated the hostilities in the Civil War? Are there times when it is best, from the point of view of critical thinking, to back down on an argument rather than risk conflict? Explain using specific examples.

2. Has there ever been a time when you stood your ground on an issue despite the risk of losing your friends or even a job? Discuss how your critical-thinking skills helped you to stand firm?

STOP AND ASSESS YOURSELF

1. Identify two or three issues that might arise out of the following broad topics or choose your own issue. Word the issue(s) in the form of question(s).

*a. Freedom of speech on college campuses

b. Genetic engineering of food

c. Cohabitation among college students

*d. Downloading music from the Internet

e. Global warming

f. Decriminalizing marijuana

*g. Prayer in public schools

h. The preponderance of male science and engineering faculty at elite colleges

i. Illegal immigration

2. Identify the issues in the following passages. Word all issues in the form of short questions.

*a. "The price of college education in Minnesota is going up again this fall. The University of Minnesota and the state's two- and four-year colleges are raising tuition by double digits. . . . Higher education officials say while most students are coming up with the extra cash for college the trend toward higher tuition is not sustainable in the long run."[5]

b. There is a law pending in the Uganda legislature that would allow homosexuality to be punished with imprisonment and in certain circumstances even execution.

c. More than 700,000 Americans die each year from heart disease. Fifty percent of people given cholesterol-lowering drugs don't use them as prescribed, and the more they have to pay, the more they stop taking them. It seems obvious that probably tens of thousands of Americans are dying today because they can't afford drugs.

*d. "By next June, over a million [college students] will graduate, many lost forever to the world of inertia and learned habits. While the debate rages about how the vegetarian movement can tailor its message to reach resistant adults, open-minded college students who care about animals are being neglected at an astounding rate. Our [animal rights] movement has not yet made a massive, organized effort to reach our best audience. We could be making tremendous progress among this group of people using animal-related literature that has been shown to work."[6]

e. President Obama's educational reform agenda calls for longer school days and extending the school year in order to meet the challenges of the 21st century.

f. It is now possible to track a person's location by using their cell phone.

*g. "Tibet is backward. It's a big land, rich in natural resources, but we lack the technology or expertise [to exploit them]. So if we remain within China, we might get a greater benefit, provided it respects our culture and environment and gives us some kind of guarantee."[7]

3. Working in small groups, select one of the following issues. Take a few minutes to write down different concerns that arise from the issue. To what extent does your list reflect your preconceptions on the issue? Compare your list with those of others in your group. Discuss how collaborative sharing can give you a wider perspective on the issue.

a. Should we be eating meat?

b. Should college students who are working full time be allowed to take a full-time course load?

c. Is it a desirable goal for western nations to spread democracy throughout the world?

d. What should we be doing in our own lives about global warming?

e. What criteria should colleges use in admitting students?

f. Should the United States bring back the military draft?

4. Looking back at your list of life goals in Chapter 4, identify any issues involved in achieving your life goals.

*Answers to selected exercises are found in the Solutions Manual at the end of the book.

RECOGNIZING AN ARGUMENT

When we start with a position statement, rather than with an open-ended question that invites us to explore and analyze a particular issue, we are using rhetoric. Many people mistake rhetoric for logical arguments. Thus it is important to first understand the difference between the two.

Distinguishing Between Argumentation and Rhetoric

rhetoric The defense of a particular position usually without adequate consideration of opposing evidence in order to win people over to one's position.

argument Reasoning that is made up of two or more propositions, one of which is supported by the others.

deductive argument An argument that claims its conclusion necessarily follows from the premises.

inductive argument An argument that only claims that its conclusion probably follows from the premise.

proposition A statement that expresses a complete thought and can be either true or false.

Rhetoric, also known as *the art of persuasion*, is used to promote a particular position or worldview. In English classes, the term refers more narrowly to the art of persuasive writing or speaking. Rhetoric has its place and can help us learn more about a particular position on an issue and how to clarify that position. The art of persuasion can be useful once you have thoroughly researched all sides of an issue, have come to a reasoned conclusion, and are now trying to convince others of this conclusion, as Lincoln did in his debates with Douglas.

Rhetoric becomes a problem when it is *substituted* for unbiased research and logical argumentation. When using rhetoric this way, people present only those claims that support their own position. Because it does not require that a student first thoroughly research a topic and remain open-minded, rhetoric may deteriorate into heated and overly emotional fights in which each person resorts to resistance and fallacies rather than reason in order to "win."

Whereas the purpose of rhetoric is to *persuade* people of what you consider to be the truth, the purpose of argumentation is to *discover* the truth. The goal in rhetoric is to "win"—to convince others of the correctness of our position—rather than to analyze a position critically. The purpose of an argument, in contrast, is to present good reasons for a particular position or course of action and to offer a forum for evaluating the soundness of these reasons.

Good arguments also invite feedback and analysis of an issue in light of the feedback. You are more likely to move toward truth (if necessary, through revising your arguments and views) when all sides of an issue are presented and heard.

Types of Arguments

An **argument** is made up of two or more propositions, one of which, the conclusion, is supported by the other(s), the premise(s). In a valid **deductive argument**, such as the Wason Card Problem example in Chapter 2, the conclusion necessarily follows from the premises. In an **inductive argument**, the premises provide support but not necessarily proof for the conclusion. We'll be studying these two types of arguments in more depth in Chapters 7 and 8, respectively.

Propositions

An argument is made up of statements known as propositions. A **proposition** is a statement that expresses a complete thought. It can be either true or false. If you're not sure whether a statement is a proposition, try putting the phrase *It is true that* or *It is false that* at the beginning of the statement. The following are examples of propositions:

> The earth revolves around the sun.
>
> God exists.
>
> Chris doesn't show me enough affection.
>
> Cheating on exams is wrong.
>
> Toronto is the capital of Canada.

The first of these propositions is true. Today it is a generally accepted fact that the Earth revolves around the sun. The truth or falsehood of the second and third propositions is less clear. We need more information as well as clarification of the word *God* in the second proposition and clarification of the term *affection* in the third proposition. The fourth proposition is less controversial: Most people, even those who cheat on exams, agree that it is true that "cheating on exams is wrong." Finally, the last proposition is false; Toronto is *not* the capital of Canada (Ottawa is).

A sentence may contain more than one proposition, as this example illustrates:

> Marcos is taking four courses this semester and working in his parents' store 20 hours a week.

This sentence contains two propositions:

1. Marcos is taking four courses this semester.

2. Marcos is working in his parents' store 20 hours a week.

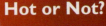

Hot or Not?

Is it acceptable to use rhetoric if you're sure of your position?

Rhetorical Standoff Anti-abortion and pro-abortion rights demonstrators debating each other at the Supreme Court on January 23, 2012, the anniversary of the Supreme Court's *Roe v. Wade* decision, which established a women's right to an abortion.*

DISCUSSION QUESTIONS

1. *The use of rhetoric, without first researching and analyzing all perspectives on an issue, can lead to deepening polarization of an issue rather than a resolution. What do you think the two people in this photo might be saying to each other? Do you think they are engaging in rhetoric or argumentation? Working in small groups, role-play what you might say to them if you were on the scene in the capacity of resident critical thinker.*

2. *Have you ever been at a rally where people were deeply divided? If so, discuss how you responded to taunts or fallacies from those on the "other side" of the issue.*

*For more on *Roe v. Wade*, see "Critical Thinking Issues: Perspectives on Abortion" at the end of Chapter 9.

Here is another sentence with more than one proposition:

Karen is smart but not very motivated to do well in school or to try to find a job that uses her talents.

It contains three propositions:

1. Karen is smart.
2. Karen is not very motivated to do well in school.
3. Karen is not very motivated to try to find a job that uses her talents.

Not all sentences are propositions. A sentence may be directive ("Let's go out and celebrate the end of final exams"), expressive ("Wow!"), or even a request for information ("What is the capital of Canada?"). In none of these sentences is any claim being made that something is true or false. Propositions, in contrast, make claims that are either true or false. For more on the different functions of language, refer back to Chapter 3.

"The Earth revolves around the sun" is an example of a proposition.

Premises and Conclusions

The **conclusion** of an argument is the proposition that is supported or denied on the basis of other propositions or reasons. The conclusion is what the argument is trying to prove. Conclusions may also be called claims or positions. The conclusion can appear anywhere in an argument.

conclusion The proposition in an argument that is supported on the basis of other propositions.

premise A proposition in an argument that supports the conclusion.

descriptive premise A premise that is based on empirical facts.

A **premise** is a proposition that supports or gives reasons for accepting the conclusion. Reasoning goes from the premises to the conclusion.

Premise(s) ⎯⎯⎯⎯⎯⎯→ Conclusion

Good premises are based on fact and experience, not opinion and assumptions. The more credible the premises are, the better the argument is likely to be. We considered some of the ways in which to evaluate evidence in Chapter 4. The conclusion should be supported by or follow from the premises, as in the following argument:

> *Premise*: Canada has only one capital.
>
> *Premise*: Ottawa is the capital of Canada.
>
> *Conclusion*: Therefore, Toronto is not the capital of Canada.

There are several types of premises. **Descriptive premises** are based on **empirical facts**—scientific observation and/or the evidence of our five senses. "Ottawa is the capital of Canada" and "Lisa loves Antonio" are descriptive premises.

Prescriptive premises, in contrast, contain value statements, such as "We should strive for diversity on college campuses" or "It is wrong to cheat on exams."

An **analogical premise** takes the form of an analogy in which a comparison is made between two similar events or things. In Chapter 2, we saw that the ancient Greek philosopher Plato drew an analogy between a charioteer and reason. Just as the charioteer is in charge of the horses, said Plato, so too should our reason be in charge of our emotions and passions.

Finally, a **definitional premise** contains a definition of a key term. This is particularly important when the key term is ambiguous and has different definitions, such as *right* and *diversity*, or if the key term needs a precising definition. For example, *affirmative action* is defined in a dictionary as "a policy to increase opportunities for women and minorities, [especially] in employment."[8] However, this may not be precise enough for your argument, since it is unclear about the type of policy. To clarify this, you may want to make the definition more precise in your premise. "Affirmative action is a policy of giving preference in hiring and college admissions to qualified minorities and women over a qualified white male, to increase opportunities for women and minorities."

Nonarguments: Explanations and Conditional Statements

We sometimes confuse explanations and conditional statements with arguments. An **explanation** is a statement about why or how something is the case. With an explanation, we know that something has occurred—as in the following examples:

> The cat yowled because I stepped on her tail.
>
> I'm upset because you promised you would meet me at the student union right after class and you never turned up.

In both examples, we are not trying to *prove* or *convince* someone through supporting evidence that the cat yowled or that we're upset; instead, we are trying to *explain* why the cat yowled and why we are upset.

We can also use explanations to describe the purpose of something, as in "iPods are useful for storing large quantities of music." In

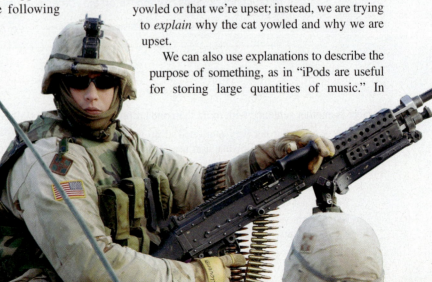

addition, we can use explanations as a means of trying to make sense of something, as in: "When Jane smiled at me, I think she was telling me that she liked me."

Good premises are based on fact and experience, not opinion and assumptions. The more credible the premises are, the better the argument is likely to be.

As with arguments, not all explanations are equally convincing. Explanations such as "I don't have my essay with me today because the dog ate it" usually raise at least a few skeptical eyebrows. Also, what might have seemed a reasonable explanation centuries or even a few decades ago may no longer be reasonable in light of new evidence. The explanation, presented to me by one of my elementary school teachers, that there have been very few famous female artists because women fulfill their creativity through having babies, is no longer considered a sound explanation.

Conditional statements may also be mistaken for arguments. A **conditional statement** is an "if . . . then . . ." statement.

> If Françoise comes from Montreal, then she understands French.

> If 18-year-olds are emotionally mature enough to go to war, then they should be allowed to drink alcohol.

A conditional statement by itself is not an argument, because no claim or conclusion follows from it. In the preceding examples, we are not drawing a conclusion that Françoise understands French or that 18-year-olds should be allowed to drink. However, conditional statements may appear as premises in an argument.

> *Premise*: If Françoise comes from Montreal, then she understands French.
> *Premise*: Françoise comes from Montreal.
> *Conclusion*: Françoise understands French.
> *Premise*: If 18-year-olds are emotionally mature enough to go to war, [then] they should be allowed to drink alcohol.
> *Premise*: Eighteen-year-olds are not emotionally mature enough to go to war.
> *Conclusion*: Eighteen-year-olds should not be allowed to drink alcohol.

To summarize: arguments are made up of two types of propositions—the conclusion and the premise(s). A conclusion is supported by the premise(s). The different types of premises include descriptive and prescriptive premises, analogies, and definitions. Unlike explanations and conditional statements, an argument tries to prove that something is true.

empirical fact A fact based on scientific observation and the evidence of our five senses.

prescriptive premise A premise in an argument containing a value statement.

analogical premise A premise containing an analogy or comparison between similar events or things.

definitional premise A premise containing the definition of a key term.

explanation A statement about why or how something is the case.

conditional statement An "If . . . then . . ." statement.

EXERCISE 6-2

STOP AND ASSESS YOURSELF

1. Working in small groups, select a controversial issue. After clearly defining the issue, debate it by first using rhetoric. After three minutes, stop and write a paragraph about what happened during the role-play. Now discuss the issue using argumentation instead. After three minutes, stop and write a paragraph about what happened during this role-play. Which approach worked better in terms of learning more about different perspectives on the issue? Explain.

2. It is easier to resolve a problem from a familiar context than one that is unfamiliar. Write down a problem that you encountered recently in a familiar context (for example, a social setting with friends or a class in your major). Now write down a similar problem that you encountered recently in an unfamiliar context (for example, a job interview or meeting new people). Which problem was easiest to resolve and why? How did familiarity with the context make it easier for you to resolve a problem? Write about what steps you could take to make yourself a better problem-solver and critical thinker in different contexts.

3. Which of the following statements is a proposition? Explain why or why not.

*a. Golly!

b. I love you.

c. The Solomon Islands were struck by an 8.0-magnitude earthquake in 2013.

*d. Most college students gain several pounds in their freshman year.

e. Close the window.

f. The average college student pays most of his or her own college tuition.

*g. Please keep an eye on my place while I'm away on spring break.

h. It is irresponsible to drink and drive.

i. Iran possesses nuclear weapons.

*j. Only humans are capable of language.

k. An atheist is a person who believes there is no God.

l. Excuse me.

*m. Smoking in public buildings is illegal in many states.

4. For each of the following propositions, identify which type of premise it is (descriptive, prescriptive, definitional, or analogical).

*a. Terrorism is the unlawful use or threat of violence by individuals or groups against civilians or property to achieve an ideological or political goal through intimidating government or society.

b. At least five of the al-Qaeda hijackers from September 11, 2001, came from Asir province in Saudi Arabia.

c. We should constantly strive to become better critical thinkers.

*d. The universe is like a watch created by an intelligent designer or watchmaker.

e. The University of Toronto is the top-rated university in Canada.

f. It's wrong to download music from the Internet without paying.

*g. Going to Las Vegas for spring break is like going to a weeklong fraternity party.

h. Living together before marriage for a trial period is like taking a car for a test drive.

i. Only humans are capable of language.

*j. Language is a type of communication that involves a set of arbitrary symbols, whether spoken, written, or nonverbal.

5. Look back at the arguments on affirmative action at the end of Chapter 1 and identify the premises and conclusion in both Nancy Cantor's and Ward Connerly's arguments.

6. Identify each of the following as an argument, an explanation, or a conditional statement.

*a. Jasmine really likes Daniel, but because she's planning on going to Guatemala for a semester to study Spanish, she isn't interested in getting involved with him right now.

b. The death toll in Chile following the 2010 earthquakes was not nearly as high as that in Haiti in part because the buildings in Chile were built to withstand earthquakes while those in Haiti were not.

c. If there is a snowstorm, class will be cancelled.

*d. If there is a snowstorm, class will be cancelled. It is snowing heavily right now, so our class will probably be cancelled.

e. You should consider taking a trip abroad this summer while airfares are still low.

f. In the past few decades the Catholic Church has been training more priests and bishops to perform exorcisms, in part because the pope believes that Satan is a real force in our everyday lives.

*g. If the bay freezes over, we can go ice skating on it.

h. It must have been colder than 28°F last week, because the ice froze in the bay last week and salt water freezes at 28°F or −2°C.

i. Herman failed the quiz because he didn't know there was going to be one today and hadn't read the material.

*j. If you aren't a good boy or girl, Santa won't bring you any presents this Christmas.

k. "People react so viscerally to the decapitation executions because they identify strongly with the helpless victims, see the executioners as cruel foreigners, and are horrified by the grisly method of death."[9]

l. Same-sex marriage should be legalized, since the U.S. Constitution guarantees citizens equal rights under the law.

*m. If you go to the movies with me tonight, I'll help you review for your chemistry exam.

7. Write down five examples of explanations. At least one should be from your own personal experience, one from a textbook, one from a newspaper or magazine, and one from the Internet. Briefly state why each is an explanation rather than an argument.

*Answers to selected exercises are found in the Solutions Manual at the end of the book.

BREAKING DOWN AND DIAGRAMMING ARGUMENTS

Knowing how to identify the parts of and diagram an argument allows us to follow the line of thought in an argument more easily. Breaking down an argument and then using a diagram to represent the different parts of the argument lets us visualize the entire argument, its propositions, and the relationship between the premise(s) and the conclusion.

HIGHLIGHTS

HOW TO BREAK DOWN AN ARGUMENT

- **The entire argument may appear in one sentence or in several sentences.**

- **Put brackets around each proposition** in the argument.

- **Identify the conclusion.** Ask yourself: "What is this person trying to prove?" The conclusion is often, though not always, preceded by a word or phrase known as a conclusion indicator, such as

therefore	*which shows that*
thus	*for these reasons*
hence	*consequently*
so	*it follows that*

- **Identify the premises.** The premises are often, though not always, preceded by a word or phrase known as a **premise indicator,** such as

because	*may be inferred from*
since	*the reason is that*
for	*as shown by*
given that	*in view of*

- **Draw a double line under the conclusion** and a **single line under the premise(s).** Circle any conclusion or premise indicators.

➤ *APPLICATION: Identify in the text an example of (1) a conclusion indicator followed by a conclusion, and (2) a premise indicator followed by a premise.*

Breaking Down an Argument into Propositions

Before you can diagram an argument, you must first break down the argument into its propositions. Here are the steps for diagramming an argument:

1. **Bracket the Propositions.** In breaking down an argument, start by putting brackets around each proposition so that you know where each begins and ends. Remember, an entire argument can be contained in one sentence, as in the first of the following examples. Or it can contain several sentences and propositions, as in the second example.

   [I think], therefore [I am].

   [Students who sit in the front of a classroom generally earn higher grades.] Therefore [you should move up to the front of the class], since [I know you want to improve your grade point average].

2. **Identify the conclusion.** The next step is to identify which proposition is the conclusion. Some, but not all, arguments contain terms known as *conclusion indicators* that help you identify which of the propositions is a conclusion. For instance, words such as *therefore* and *thus* often serve as conclusion indicators. If there is a conclusion indicator in the argument, circle it and, if you want, put the letters *CI* above it. In the two arguments above, the word *therefore* indicates that a conclusion follows.

   When there are no conclusion indicators, ask yourself: "What is this person trying to prove or convince me of?" If you are still unsure which proposition is the conclusion, try putting *therefore* in

We can improve our arguments by testing them out on others and then modifying them in light of the feedback we receive.

front of the proposition you think may be the conclusion. If the meaning of the argument remains the same, you have located the conclusion. Once you have identified the conclusion, draw a double line under it.

CI *(Conclusion)*
[I think], therefore [I am].

[Students who sit in the front of a classroom generally earn higher grades.] Therefore, *CI* [you should move up *(Conclusion)* to the front of the class], since [I know you want to improve your grade point average].

3. **Identify the Premises.** The final step in breaking down an argument is to identify the premise(s). In the first argument, which is the famous cogito argument of French philosopher René Descartes (1596–1650), Descartes supports his conclusion ("I am") with the premise "I think." In other words, if he is thinking, it follows that he must exist, since someone must be doing the thinking. Draw a single line under the premise.

CI *(Conclusion)*
[I think], (therefore) [I am].

Some arguments contain *premise indicators*—words or phrases that signal a premise. *Because* and *since* are common premise indicators. If there is a premise indicator, circle it and put *PI* above it. In the argument about where to sit in the classroom, the word *since* indicates that the last part of this sentence is a premise. The first sentence in the argument is also a premise because it is offering evidence to support the conclusion "you should move up to the front of the class." Draw a single line under each premise.

(Premise)
[Students who sit in the front of a classroom generally earn higher grades.] (Therefore), *CI* [you should move up to *(Conclusion)* the front of the class], (since) *PI* [I know you want to improve *(Premise)* your grade point average].

Identifying the Premise(s) and Conclusion in Complex Arguments

Not all arguments are as straightforward as the ones we have looked at so far. Some passages that contain arguments also include extra material, such as background and introductory information. In the following letter to the editor, the first sentence is the conclusion of the argument. The first part of the second sentence—"Although stories of overzealous parents sometimes grab the headlines"—is not part of the actual argument; rather, it is introductory material. This introduction is followed in the same sentence by the phrase *the truth is*, which serves as a premise indicator for the first premise. The

second premise doesn't appear until the third sentence in the passage.

(Conclusion)
[Sports at the high-school level are one of the last bastions of innocence in this century.] Although stories of overzealous parents sometimes grab the headlines, the truth is, *PI* [most young people play for the *Premise* love of their sport and nothing more.] [Many of the *Premise* values that help me every day in the business world (teamwork, unity, hard work, and tolerance) were taught by my football and baseball coaches.][10]

Words such as *because*, *since*, *therefore*, and *so*, which sometimes serve as premise and conclusion indicators in argument, do not always play this role. *Because* and *therefore* also appear in explanations, as in this example:

> Because the demographics and immigration pattern of the United States is changing, the workforce of today's college graduates will be much different from that of their parents.

In addition, the word *since* may indicate the passage of time rather than a premise.

> Since the September 11, 2001, attacks on the World Trade Center and Pentagon, the nature of intercultural relationships radically changed for most Americans.

Knowing how to break down an argument into its conclusion and premise(s) makes it easier for us to analyze arguments. Although words such as *therefore* and *because* can help us in this process, it is important to remember that they do not always serve as conclusion and premise indicators.

Diagramming an Argument

Once you have mastered the basics of breaking down an argument, you are ready to diagram arguments. Sometimes arguments fail simply because the other person does not follow our line of reasoning. Diagramming an argument clarifies the relationship between the premise(s) and the conclusion, as well as the relationship between premises, so we know to present these particular premises together.

Arguments with One Premise. Begin by breaking down the argument into its propositions and drawing two lines under the conclusion and one under the premise(s). Number each proposition in the order in which it appears in the argument. Put a circle around each number.

(1) [I think], therefore (2) [I am].

MARIJUANA LAWS WASTE BILLIONS OF TAXPAYER DOLLARS TO LOCK UP NON-VIOLENT AMERICANS.

Change the Climate

1 IN 3 ADULT AMERICANS have tried marijuana and federal marijuana laws can arrest or imprison every one of them just for simple possession. These laws are unfair and abuse our criminal justice system. Prosecuting and jailing these Americans wastes valuable resources better spent keeping violent criminals off our streets. As it is, hundreds of thousands of citizens have already been imprisoned - many of them non-violent, otherwise law-abiding and many of them stripped of their right to vote, their property, their jobs and their college grants. Let's adopt common sense and fairness and enact more realistic marijuana laws. And let's save the jails for real criminals. Get involved today. Log on at: www.aclu.org/drugpolicy, www.changetheclimate.org, www.drugpolicy.org and www.mpp.org

MPP Marijuana Policy Project

DRUG POLICY ALLIANCE
Reason. Compassion. Justice.

ACLU
AMERICAN CIVIL LIBERTIES UNION

The Debate Over Marijuana

DISCUSSION QUESTIONS

1. *Identify the conclusion and premises in the argument in this advertisement. Evaluate the argument.*

2. *What is the objective of this ad? Is the ad effective in meeting its objective? Discuss the strategies, including rhetorical devices and fallacies, if any, that the creators of the ad used to try to convince the reader to accept their conclusion.*

You are now ready to diagram the argument. Begin by writing down the number of the conclusion at the bottom of a space on the page. The premise(s) go above the conclusion. When there is only one premise, place the number of the premise directly above the number of the conclusion and draw an arrow from the premise number to the conclusion number.

① (Premise)

↓

② (Conclusion)

In this section, the parts of the diagram are identified (for example, premise, conclusion, dependent premises) purely for educational purposes. However, in the actual diagrams, only the numbers, lines, and arrows are used.

Arguments with Independent Premises. The next argument we'll be diagramming has more than one premise. Begin by breaking down the argument into its conclusion and premises, numbering each proposition in the order it appears in the argument.

① [Every physician should cultivate lying as a fine art]. . . . **②** [Many experiences show that patients do not want the truth about their maladies], and that **③** [it is prejudicial to their well-being to know it].[11]

In this argument, the conclusion is the first proposition—"Every physician should cultivate lying as a fine art." Write (1) at the bottom of the space below. Now examine the two premises, the second and third propositions. In this argument below, each premise supports the conclusion on its own. A premise that can support the conclusion without the other premise is known as an **independent premise**.

independent premise A premise that can support a conclusion on its own.

dependent premise A premise that supports a conclusion only when it is used together with another premise.

subconclusion A proposition that acts as a conclusion for initial premises and as a premise for the final conclusion.

You diagram an independent premise by drawing an arrow directly from each one to the conclusion.

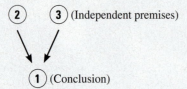
(2)   (3) (Independent premises)

(1) (Conclusion)

Arguments with Dependent Premises.

When two or more of the premises support a conclusion only when they are used together, they are known as **dependent premises**. If you are unsure whether two premises are dependent or independent, try omitting one of them and see if the remaining premise still supports the conclusion on its own. If it does not, then it is a dependent premise.

In the argument below on Harry Potter, premises (1), (3), and (4) are all dependent on each other. Taken alone, they do not support the conclusion.

(1) [The Bible states in Leviticus 20:26, "You should not practice augury or witchcraft."] Therefore, (2) [the Harry Potter books are not suitable reading for children,] since (3) [Harry Potter is a wizard] and (4) [wizards practice augury].

In diagramming dependent premises, you first draw a line between the premises and then draw a line from the center of this connecting line to the conclusion.

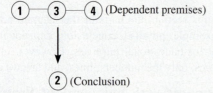
(1)—(3)—(4) (Dependent premises)

(2) (Conclusion)

In the above argument, depending on your audience, you may not need (4), which is a definitional premise.

Some arguments have both dependent and independent premises. Consider the following argument:

(1) [Turkey should not be granted full membership in the European Union.] For one thing, (2) [the majority of the country is located in Asia, not Europe.]

(3) [Turkey also has a poor human rights record.] Finally, (4) [it is a poor country with high unemployment]. (5) [Allowing it to be a full member in the European Union might spark a mass migration of people to European countries with better economies.]

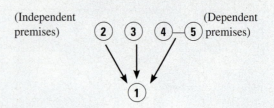
(Independent premises)   (2) (3) (4)—(5) (Dependent premises)

(1)

Arguments with a Subconclusion.

Sometimes a premise acts as a conclusion for the final conclusion. This type of premise is known as a **subconclusion**.

(1) [My granddaughter Sarah is a college freshman.]

(2) [Sarah probably wouldn't be interested in hearing an AARP talk on Social Security reform.] So (3) [there's probably no point in asking her to come along with me.]

In the above argument, premise (1) offers support for proposition (2): "My granddaughter Sarah is a college freshman. [Therefore] Sarah probably wouldn't be interested in hearing an AARP talk on Social Security." However, proposition (2), in addition to being a conclusion for premise (1), also serves as a premise for proposition (3). In diagramming an argument with a subconclusion (such as proposition (2)), you put the subconclusion between the premise(s) that supports it and the final conclusion.

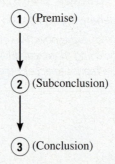
(1) (Premise)

(2) (Subconclusion)

(3) (Conclusion)

The following argument on capital punishment has a subconclusion as well as two independent premises.

(1) [The death penalty does not deter criminals] because (2) [at the time the crime is done they do not expect to be arrested.] Also, since (3) [many offenders are mentally unbalanced,] (4) [they do not consider the rational consequences of their irrational actions.][12]

Here, proposition (2) is an independent premise that supports the conclusion (proposition (1)) on its own. If this were all there was to the argument, you would diagram it by placing the (2) above the (1) and drawing an arrow directly from the (2) to the conclusion.

However, the argument goes on to present additional evidence (propositions ③ and ④) for the conclusion (proposition ①) in the form of a separate supporting argument. Therefore, you'll need to adjust the diagram to allow room for this. In this case, proposition ④ is the subconclusion and proposition ③ the premise of the supporting argument. The complete argument can be diagrammed as follows:

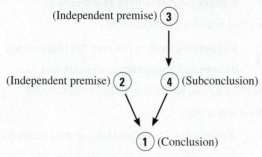

(Independent premise) ③

(Independent premise) ②   ④ (Subconclusion)

① (Conclusion)

Arguments with Unstated Conclusions. In some arguments the conclusion is unstated, allowing readers to draw their own conclusions. The following argument, for example, has two premises but no conclusion:

① [Laws that permit public colleges to discriminate against applicants on the basis of race or sex are unconstitutional.] ② [The University of Michigan's affirmative action policy that awards extra points on the basis of a person's race and sex discriminates against white males.]

In determining what is the unstated conclusion, ask yourself: What is the speaker trying to prove or to convince us of? In this example, it is that the University of Michigan's affirmative action policy is unconstitutional. When a conclusion is unstated, write it in at the end of the argument and number it; in this case, since it is the third proposition, put a ③ in front of it. The broken circle indicates that the proposition is unstated. You can also add a conclusion indicator if you like.

① [Laws that permit public colleges to discriminate against applicants on the basis of race or gender are unconstitutional.] ② [The University of Michigan's affirmative action policy that awards extra points based on a person's race and sex discriminates against white males.] Therefore, ③ [the University of Michigan's affirmative action policy is unconstitutional.]

Diagramming this argument makes it apparent that neither premise can support the conclusion on its own

These people are burning Harry Potter books based on their conclusion that Harry is a wizard and witchcraft should not be practiced.

without the other premise. In other words, they are dependent premises. When diagramming an argument with an unstated conclusion, put a broken circle around the number in front of the conclusion to indicate that it was not included in the original wording of the argument. Once again, the parts of the diagram (dependent premises and unstated conclusion) are identified for clarification purposes only. They are not part of the actual diagram.

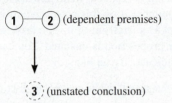

(1)——(2) (dependent premises)

(3) (unstated conclusion)

When you are arguing or discussing an issue, you usually do not have time to step back and diagram it. However, practice at breaking down and diagramming arguments will make it easier for you to recognize the conclusion and see the connections among the conclusion and premises in real-life arguments, the topic of the next section.

College students are divided regarding the morality and constitutionality of affirmative action in college admissions, a topic that is considered in the Critical Thinking Issue of Chapter 1.

STOP AND ASSESS YOURSELF

1. Break down the following arguments. Fill in any unstated possibilities.

*a. "Be an optimist. There is not much use being anything else."[13]

b. Computers may soon fade into the background, since most people prefer portable handheld devices as well as ones that turn on instantly.

c. "The right to vote is the very core of democracy. We cannot allow public apathy and political manipulation to undermine it."[14]

*d. Drinking alcohol is stupid. Alcohol has no taste at all; it's just a burning sensation. You don't drink to have a good time—you drink to forget a bad time.

e. We should not be using military drones. Drone strikes can kill innocent civilians. They are also a violation of international law.

f. Lack of experience, excessive speed, and tailgating are three of the most frequent causes of automobile accidents. For these reasons we should raise the driving age to 18, since older drivers might be more experienced and have better judgment.

*g. India should adopt a one-child policy like China. India's population has tripled in the last thirty years and it won't be long before food production will not be able to keep up with population growth.

h. All college students should routinely be tested for HIV, the virus that causes AIDS. Half of the people who carry the virus don't know that they have it. The HIV virus is transmitted primarily through sexual contact. Not only are most college students sexually active but they also have multiple partners.

i. You shouldn't date Matt. You don't want to end up with a black eye or worse.

*j. The great horned owls have just started calling to each other in the woods behind our house so it's probably the beginning of their courting season.

2. Break down and diagram the following arguments.

*a. "It is impossible to exaggerate the impact that Islam has on Saudi culture, since religion is the dominant thread that permeates every level of society."[15]

b. God does not exist. There is much evil and suffering in the world. A good and loving God would not permit so much evil.

c. I just read that Singapore is the only country in Asia where English is the first language. I know that English is also spoken throughout much of India but I guess this must mean that English is not India's first language.

*d. We should not buy a new car for Jack for his graduation. Jack is irresponsible because he doesn't care for the things he already owns. Also, we don't have enough money to buy him a new car.

e. Prostitution should be legal. Women should have the right to use their bodies as they wish. Outlawing prostitution deprives women who want to be prostitutes of their right to choose how to use their body.

f. It's unlikely that you'll find a job in manufacturing since we're in the middle of recession. You should consider going back to college to finish your degree in nursing since nursing is one of the fields where jobs are currently in demand.

*g. "An unbalanced diet can depress serotonin levels—and bingo, you're a grouch. Alcohol gives serotonin a temporary bump but then dramatically lowers it, so it pays to go easy on the sauce."[16]

h. Freedom to decide what we do in our lives, as long as we're not harming others, is a basic right in the United States. Therefore, motorcyclists should not be required by law to wear helmets, because those who don't are not harming anyone else.

i. Everything is going digital nowadays. Soon we will no longer need libraries since most journals and news sources are available online. In addition, books are being made available in electronic format.

*j. "There's a need for more part-time or job-sharing work. Most mothers of young children who choose to leave full-time careers and stay home with their children find enormous delights in being at home with their children, not to mention the enormous relief of no longer worrying about shortchanging their kids. On the other hand, women who step out of their careers can find the loss of identity even tougher than the loss of income."[17]

k. "The toughest part of buying life insurance is determining how much you need, since everyone's financial circumstances and goals are different. The best way to determine your life insurance needs is to have a State Farm Insurance professional conduct what's called a Financial Needs Analysis." (from an ad for State Farm Insurance)

l. You should learn how to speak Mandarin Chinese since you're going into international business as a career. Roughly one in five people in the world speak Mandarin. Also, learning a new language is supposed to be good for your brain.

*m. "In schools, we should give equal time with Darwinism to theories of intelligent design or creationism. Darwin's theory of evolution is a theory, not a fact. The origin of life, the diversity of species and even the structure of organs like the eye are so bewilderingly complex that they can only be the handiwork of a higher intelligence."[18]

n. The new compact fluorescent light bulbs cut down on global warming since they use 75 percent less energy than the old light bulbs. For this reason you should switch to the new bulbs. And you'll save money on your electric bill too.

o. The creation of new jobs will put the American economy back on a solid footing. Therefore, the government should launch another major stimulus program because the stimulus money will benefit the community by creating more jobs.

*p. You shouldn't bother trying out for that internship, because you won't get it. The company wants only students who are business majors. Besides, the company isn't on a bus line, and you don't own a car.

q. I saw Bob coming out of Mark's dorm room at 2 AM. Mark reported his cell phone stolen the next morning. Bob was caught stealing from a student's room once before. I think the evidence speaks for itself.

*Answers to selected exercises are found in the Solutions Manual at the end of the book.

EVALUATING ARGUMENTS

Knowing how to break down and diagram arguments makes it easier for you to evaluate them. In this section we will briefly touch on some of the main criteria for evaluating arguments: clarity, credibility, relevance, completeness, and soundness. We'll be focusing on this topic in more depth in Chapters 7 and 8.

Clarity: Is the Argument Clear and Unambiguous?

The first step in evaluating an argument is to make sure that you understand it correctly. Examine each premise and conclusion. Are they stated in terms that are clear and understandable? If any part of the argument is unclear, or if the meaning of a key term is ambiguous, ask for clarification.

For example, at a party someone told me, "Immigration is ruining this country!" When I

Hot or Not?

Does knowing how to break down and diagram arguments serve any practical purpose in your life?

asked him for clarification—"Do you mean all immigrants?" and "What do you mean by *ruin*?"—he explained that he meant that Hispanic immigrants were a financial burden on the United States.

Credibility: Are the Premises Supported by Evidence?

As we noted earlier, arguments are made up of propositions that each make a claim that can be true or false. In a good argument, the premises are credible and backed by evidence. In other words, it is reasonable for us to accept them as true. In evaluating an argument, examine each premise individually. Watch for assumptions that are being passed off as facts, especially assumptions that are widely accepted in a culture or those that are being put forth by someone who is not an authority in the field.

When my daughter was in kindergarten, the teacher asked each student what he or she wanted to be when they grew up. My daughter said that she wanted to be a doctor. The teacher shook her head and replied, "Boys become doctors; girls become nurses." Breaking down and diagramming her teacher's argument, we have

1 [You are a girl].

2 [Boys become doctors; girls become nurses.]

Therefore, **3** [you cannot become a doctor].

```
  1 ——— 2
        |
        ↓
        3
```

A few weeks later I asked my daughter why she no longer was playing with her doctor kit. She told me what her teacher had said. Fortunately, we were able to reveal the teacher's assumption about which medical professions men and women go into and expose it as false, since today many doctors are women and many men become nurses. Because the two premises are dependent, both premises are needed to support the conclusion. And because one of the premises is false, the premises do not support the conclusion.

Often assumptions are unspoken, as in the above argument. Because of this, we tend not to be aware of them. Although some assumptions are obviously false, in most cases we may have to do some research before making a determination. Returning to the immigration example, when the speaker was asked why he felt the way he did about immigrants from Hispanic countries, he replied: "Hispanics are lazy freeloaders who burden our public welfare system, especially in states like California." Is his premise true? What were his sources of evidence? Were they credible sources?

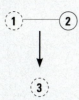

My research turned up an academic study using statistics from the state of California. According to these statistics, Hispanic immigrants living under the poverty level are less than half as likely as American-born citizens to be collecting welfare. In addition, the study found that one of the characteristics of Hispanic immigrants was that they were generally harder working than American-born citizens and preferred to take whatever jobs were available to get by rather than collect welfare.[19] If I hadn't bothered to research his premise, which as it turns out was unfounded, I might have found myself being persuaded by his "argument" and accepting his assumption as "fact."

Relevance: Are the Premises Relevant to the Conclusion?

In addition to being true, the premises should provide relevant evidence in support of the conclusion. In other words, the premises should provide good reasons for accepting the conclusion. The statistical study cited above about Hispanic immigrants is relevant—not to the conclusion that "immigration is ruining this country" but to the opposite conclusion that "Hispanic immigrants tend to be hardworking."

A premise can be relevant without providing sufficient grounds for accepting the conclusion. The fact that when my daughter was young, most doctors were men and most nurses were women did not provide sufficient support for the teacher's conclusion that my daughter should give up her dream to become a doctor. Today, about half of all students in medical school are women.

Completeness: Are There Any Unstated Premises and Conclusions?

In evaluating an argument, ask yourself: "Are there unstated premises?" Premises may be omitted for several reasons. We may simply be unaware of a particular bit of key information related to the issue. In addition, confirmation bias may cause us to overlook important information or reject premises that do not support our worldview. In the argument about Hispanic immigrants that we've just examined, the speaker failed to include premises with actual statistics supporting his claim. In a good argument, the list of relevant premises should be complete—and backed by credible sources.

That being said, sometimes premises are obvious and don't have to be stated. Consider this argument:

> Federal funding for education should be allocated on the basis of the size of a state. Therefore, Texas should get a larger share of federal money than Rhode Island.

In this argument the unstated premise is that "Texas is larger than Rhode Island," an uncontroversial fact known by most people in the United States. However, if we were presenting the argument to someone from another country, we might want to include the premise.

Leaving out a relevant premise can be problematic, especially when the premise is controversial or is based on an unfounded assumption—as in the immigration argument.

Connections

How can we recognize the use of faulty arguments in advertisements? *See Chapter 10, pp. 319–321.*

Hispanic Housekeeper
Hispanic immigrants tend to be hardworking and prefer to take low-paying jobs over collecting public assistance. In the United States they make up a significant portion of the labor force in jobs such as agricultural work, construction, and housekeeping.

DISCUSSION QUESTIONS

1. *Hispanic immigrants tend to be hardworking and prefer to take low-paying jobs, such as agricultural worker or housekeeper, rather than collect public assistance. Despite their work ethic Hispanic workers in the United States earn on the average only about two-thirds of what white workers earn. Is this fair? Create a list of premises this issue. Draw a conclusion based on your premises.*

2. *Refer to the argument you developed in the previous question and, working in small groups, evaluate your argument using the criteria listed in this section.*

Excluding relevant premises might lead us to a mistaken conclusion that is based on incomplete information.

In some cases, a premise is left out because it *is* controversial and stating it would weaken the position of the person who is making the argument. Consider:

> Abortion should remain legal. No woman should be forced to raise an unwanted child.

Breaking down and diagramming this argument, we have:

① [Abortion should remain legal.] ② [No woman should be forced to raise an unwanted child.]

②

↓

①

At first glance it might look like the conclusion follows from the premise, since most people would accept this premise as reasonable. However, there is an unstated dependent premise in this argument: namely, that "a woman who gives birth to a child should also raise that child." Unlike the first premise, this one is certainly a questionable one, since adoption is an option.

Once you have identified a missing relevant premise, add it to the argument. Then go back and reevaluate the argument.

① [Abortion should remain legal.] ② [No woman should be forced to raise an unwanted child.] ③ [A woman who gives birth to a child should also raise that child.]

In this case the unstated premise ③ weakens the argument, since many people do not accept it as true.

Soundness: Are the Premises True and Do They Support the Conclusion?

Finally, the reasoning process in an argument should be sound. A sound argument is one in which the premises are true and they support the conclusion. In the argument on page 187, the premise that "Hispanics are lazy freeloaders who burden our public welfare system" is false; therefore the argument is unsound. The connection between the premise(s) and conclusion should be based on reason rather than on fallacious appeals.

On the other hand, do not assume that a conclusion is false simply because it is not supported by the premises. When this happens, the most you can say is that you don't know whether the conclusion is true or false. Some issues, such as the existence of God or of consciousness in other people (or machines), probably cannot be proved or disproved through logical argumentation.

One of my most philosophically traumatic experiences as a child occurred when I was about 10 or 11 years old and realized that I could not prove the existence of anyone or anything else in the world except myself. For about a week, I wandered around in a miserable, solipsistic (the belief that I was the only being in the world) fog, estranging my concerned playmates in the process. Eventually, though, I decided that it was more practical and more conducive to my happiness just to accept on faith the existence of the world outside me. This experience also taught me that just because we can't prove something through the use of argumentation doesn't mean that it isn't true. To claim otherwise is to commit the fallacy of ignorance.

We'll be looking at additional rules for evaluating specific types of arguments in Chapters 7 and 8.

HIGHLIGHTS

GUIDELINES FOR EVALUATING AN ARGUMENT

Clarity: Is the argument clear and unambiguous?

Credibility: Are the premises supported by evidence?

Relevance: Are the premises relevant to the conclusion?

Completeness: Are there any unstated premises and conclusions?

Soundness: Are the premises true and do they support the conclusion?

▶ *APPLICATION: Find examples in the text of the application of each of these guidelines.*

EXERCISE 6-4

STOP AND ASSESS YOURSELF

I. Discuss whether the following are strong arguments. If you consider them weak, explain why.

*a. We need to protect American jobs. Therefore, we need stricter laws to keep illegal aliens from crossing the United States–Mexico border.

b. Even though the stock market crashed in 2008, stocks are still a great long-term investment. After all, the Dow Jones stock index has increased over the past 100 years.

c. People need to pass a driving test to get a license to drive a car. People should also have to take a parenting test and get a license before they can have a child. After all, parenting is a greater responsibility and requires more skill than driving.

*d. We should allow fraternities on our campus. After all, they provide volunteers to do a lot of charitable work.

e. My dog Rex growls only at people who are untrustworthy. Rex growled at Bob when he brought me home after our date. Therefore, I should not trust Bob.

f. If you're going to buy a new car, you should buy a Toyota Camry. They're one of the safest cars on the road, according to *Consumer Reports*.

*g. Abdul is a freshman at state community college. All freshmen at state community college are residents of Texas. Therefore, Abdul is a resident of Texas.

h. Marijuana use should be legal in the United States. After all, our own president, George W. Bush, as much as admitted that he had used marijuana.

i. God is all powerful. God is all good. Terrible things happen to people through no fault of their own. Therefore, God does not exist.

*j. You should stay away from Gloria because she's a troublemaker.

2. Identify the unstated premise(s) in each of the following arguments. Evaluate each of the arguments. Does leaving out the premise weaken or change the argument?

   *a. Maria is a single mother. We should reject her application to the pre-med program.

   b. Buck's father is a successful doctor and a graduate of State University. Buck should do well in the pre-med program.

   c. If you want to save money, buy your textbooks on Amazon.com instead of the college bookstore.

   *d. Cats don't bark. Therefore, Friskie doesn't bark.

   e. If you're traveling in Europe you should buy a rail pass instead of renting a car.

   f. I hear you'd like to do a semester in an African country. Given that the only languages you speak are Portuguese and German, you should consider doing an internship in Angola or Mozambique.

   *g. I wouldn't trust Ben around children. I hear he was abused as a child.

3. Select three of the arguments from the exercises above. After identifying the missing premises, use the Internet or other resources to research the credibility of each of the missing premises. If necessary, rewrite the arguments to take into account the information you uncovered in your research.

*Answers to selected exercises are found in the Solutions Manual at the end of the book.

CONSTRUCTING AN ARGUMENT

Now that you know how to recognize, break down, and evaluate arguments, you are ready to construct your own arguments. Here is a list of steps to help you in this process:

Steps for Constructing an Argument

There are eight steps to follow when you construct an argument: (1) state the issue, (2) develop a list of premises, (3) eliminate weak or irrelevant premises, (4) establish a conclusion, (5) organize your argument, (6) try out your argument on others, (7) revise your argument, and, if appropriate, (8) put your solution or conclusion into action.

1. State the Issue. What question or issue are you going to address? Clearly identifying the issue first can help you stay on track. Word the issue in neutral terms. For example, "Should the United States have stricter gun-control laws?" and not "Should the government be doing more to keep guns out of the hands of hardened criminals?"

2. Develop a List of Premises. In coming up with possible premises, put your personal opinions aside. Avoid the trap of seeing the issue as having two sides in which rhetoric is used to settle issues, with one side winning and the other losing.

In developing a list of premises, remain objective and open-minded. Rather than select only those premises that support your particular worldview, try to explore all sides of the issue. Brainstorming with others—letting your ideas flow freely and creatively—is helpful in widening your perspective. Keep track of the premises by writing each of them down as you go along. Include references when appropriate in case you need to go back and check them.

Your premises should be relatively uncontroversial. Watch out for unsupported interpretations or assumptions. Adopt the skeptic's attitude. If you are at all unsure whether a particular premise is true, check it out. In doing your research, make sure you use only reliable sources and continue to consider all sides of the issue.

Sometimes a particular cultural world-view becomes so ingrained that we assume it is true and don't bother to question it. Dr. Joseph Collins's premise, written in 1927, that "every physician should cultivate lying as a fine art," was accepted for many years by the medical profession. The assumption that knowing the truth would harm the patient was not questioned, because it was widely accepted as true. It wasn't until 1961 that someone actually put the premise to the test and found that, in fact, the majority of cancer patients actually do better if they know the truth about their illness.[20]

Once you have established your preliminary list of premises, go back and check them. Each premise should be clearly stated, credible, and complete. Also, make sure you know the issue inside and out. You don't want to be taken by surprise by someone's question or counterargument when you present your argument. Did you leave out any important premises? For example, if your issue is whether

Before coming to a conclusion about an controversial legal issue such as allowing smoking in public places, we first need make sure our premises are based on facts.

smoking should be allowed in college dormitories, check your state's laws. Are there already laws against smoking in public buildings, and if so, is your dormitory (especially if you attend a state college) considered a public building?

If you find that your premises are heavily weighed in favor of the view you held before beginning this exercise, go back and spend more time looking at premises that support different perspectives on the issue.

3. Eliminate Weak or Irrelevant Premises. After coming up with your list of premises, review them once again. Eliminate any premises that are weak or irrelevant to the issue. As in the proverbial chain, one weak link (premise) can destroy your whole argument. At the same time, resist the temptation to eliminate premises that don't mesh with your particular opinion regarding the issue.

Your final list of premises should be relevant to the issue. If your issue is "Should marijuana be legalized?" then you should avoid getting sidetracked by going on about how some of the legislators who oppose its legalization are hypocrites because they used marijuana when they were in college. Stick to the topic of marijuana and legalization. Also, eliminate any redundant premises—those

that say essentially the same thing as another premise but in different words.

Next, form groups of closely related premises. For example, the premise "Marijuana use has been shown to decrease reaction time" should be grouped with the premise "Studies have shown that long-term use of marijuana does not have any ill effects on brain functioning"; it does not belong with the premise "The use of marijuana has been deemed immoral by the Lutheran Church." Although the first two premises take different positions on the issue, they are both similar in that they represent scientific research and not moral judgments. Ask yourself if any of the premises in your list are dependent on each other. A premise may initially appear to be weak simply because it needs to be paired with another (dependent) premise.

If your list of premises is still very long, consider your audience in deciding which premises to eliminate and which to keep. If you are doing an essay for class, the audience will be your professor. If you are doing the argument as a class presentation, the class is your audience. Your audience may also be a friend, a partner, a relative, or the readers of a newspaper or Web site.

Don't leave out a relevant premise unless it is too obvious to your audience to be stated. If in doubt, it is better to include the premise rather than assume that your audience will know about it. On the other hand, if you have only a limited amount of time to present your argument, you should include only the strongest premises. Do, however, have your other premises ready in case you are asked to expand on or clarify your argument.

Next, check the wording of your remaining premises. The wording of each premise should be clear, with no

Working collaboratively with others to identify and eliminate weak or biased premises can help make your argument stronger.

Finally, your conclusion must be supported by your premises. It should not go beyond what the premises say, as in the following example:

> Most freshman on our campus own cars. The parking garage at our college does not have enough parking spots to accommodate all of their cars. Therefore, we should build another parking garage.

The conclusion that another parking garage should be built on campus does not follow from these premises. For one thing, we have no information about how many freshmen use their cars to commute to college or keep their cars on campus. And there are alternative options in dealing with a parking shortage, including mass transit, carpooling, or shuttle service from off-campus parking lots.

vague or confusing terms or emotionally loaded language. Define any ambiguous key terms in the premises and use these terms consistently throughout your argument.

4. Establish a Conclusion. Only after you are satisfied with your list of premises should you draw a conclusion. In developing a conclusion ask yourself "What conclusion follows from these premises?" Remember to avoid looking at your issue as a contest between two sides. Look at *all* the premises in your final list and consider how the conclusion can take into account as many of the premises as possible.

For example, physician-assisted suicide is often presented as a polarized—black-and-white—issue. However, some people who are opposed to a law permitting it nevertheless think that physician-assisted suicide is justified under certain limited circumstances. Instead of splitting the issue into two sides, ask yourself how you might come up with a policy or law on the issue that takes into account the premises shared by all parties.

Be careful not to draw your conclusion too soon. This is most likely to happen if you bring a preconceived view into the argument and wear the blinders of resistance when analyzing the evidence for your conclusion. Carefully analyze your premises and make sure you've looked at all the different perspectives on the issue before drawing a conclusion. Also, make sure the connection between your conclusion and premises is reasonable, rather than based on an emotional appeal or informal fallacy.

Connections

What are the similarities between the scientific method and the use of logical argumentation in papers? *See Chapter 12, p. 383.*

5. Organize Your Argument. There are many ways of organizing an argument. For example, you can first list or diagram your premises and conclusion, or you can present your argument in written or oral form. If you are presenting your argument in essay form, you should clearly

---

Ask yourself "What conclusion follows from these premises?" Remember to avoid looking at your issue as a contest between two sides.

---

state the issue in the first paragraph of your essay or in your opening sentence. This will allow your audience to easily identify exactly what issue you are addressing. (See Critical Thinking in Action: Writing a Paper Based on Logical Argumentation, on page 193.).

The conclusion usually appears in the first paragraph or at the beginning of your presentation. In essays, this is sometimes called the *thesis statement*. If possible, limit your thesis statement to one sentence. Your opening paragraph can also let the reader know how you plan to defend your conclusion and organize your argument, as well as include a sentence or two to grab the reader's attention about the issue's importance.

The following excerpt from James Rachels's argument in his book *Active and Passive Euthanasia* is a good example of an opening paragraph:

> The distinction between active and passive euthanasia is thought to be crucial for medical ethics. The idea is that it is permissible, at least in some cases, to withhold treatment and allow a patient to die, but it is never permissible to take any direct action designed to kill the patient. This doctrine seems to be accepted by most

Critical THiNKing in Action

Writing a Paper Based on Logical Argumentation

Many courses require students to write an essay or thesis paper using logical argumentation. These papers are usually organized as follows:

1. **Identify the issue.** Include a brief explanation of the issue in the introductory paragraph along with definitions of key terms. The conclusion of your argument may also be stated in the first paragraph.

2. **Present premises.** This section will make up the major part of your paper. Lay out and explain the premises supporting your conclusion. Premises used should be complete, clearly stated, backed by credible evidence, fallacy-free, and logically compelling.

3. **Present and address counterarguments.** Present and respond to each of the most compelling counterarguments against your position.

4. **Conclusion and summary.** In the final paragraph, restate the issue and briefly summarize your arguments and conclusion.

5. **References.** Include a list of references for the facts and evidence used in your argument.

DISCUSSION QUESTIONS

1. Select an issue. Write a two-page draft or outline of a paper on this issue using logical argumentation. Share your draft or outline with other members of the class for feedback on how well you presented your argument. Modify your draft in light of the feedback you receive.

2. Find an article presenting an argument in a journal or newspaper. Locate in the article each of the five steps listed. Evaluate the strength of the argument. Discuss how you might improve the argument as well as its presentation.

---

doctors. . . . However, a strong case can be made against this doctrine. In what follows I will set out some of the relevant arguments, and urge doctors to reconsider their views on this matter.[21]

If you have several premises, you might want to devote a separate paragraph to each independent premise. You can discuss dependent premises in the same paragraph. In any case, let the reader know that you are introducing a new premise by using some sort of premise indicator such as *because* or *a second reason*. If appropriate, use an example to illustrate your premise. Rachels's second paragraph begins with an example of a patient who is "dying of incurable cancer of the throat [and] is in terrible pain, which can no longer be satisfactorily alleviated." He uses this example to illustrate his first premise:

> Part of my point is that the process of being "allowed to die" can be relatively slow and painful, whereas being given a lethal injection is relatively quick and painless.

Your essay or presentation should also address counterarguments. Discuss each counterargument and explain why the premises you have used are stronger. You can discuss them in the same paragraph with your supporting premises. Address the counterarguments after you present the premises that support your conclusion. For example, after presenting his premises, Rachels

summarizes his argument and then addresses the counterarguments:

> I have argued that killing is not in itself any worse than letting die; if my contention is right, it follows that active euthanasia is not any worse than passive euthanasia. What arguments can be given on the other side? The most common, I believe is the following: The important difference between active and passive euthanasia is that, in passive euthanasia the doctor does not do anything to bring about the patient death. . . . In active euthanasia, however, the doctor does something to bring about the patient's death: he kills him.

The last part of your essay may also include action that people can take to implement your conclusion or resolution to the issue. Rachels concludes his argument with this advice:

> So, whereas doctors may have to discriminate between active and passive euthanasia to satisfy the law, they should not do any more than that. In particular, they should not give the distinction any added authority and weight by writing it into official statements of medical ethics.

6. Try Out Your Argument on Others. Once you have come up with what you think is a strong argument, you are ready to try it out on someone else. In doing this, keep in mind that as critical thinkers we need to be both

The Dangers of Jumping to a Conclusion

Jumping to a conclusion too soon can have far-reaching consequences. In the middle of my freshman year in high school, my family moved to a new school district. My first assignment in the new English class was to write an epic poem in the style of the classic epic poems. Wanting to make a good first impression, and having been writing my own "books" since I was 9, I threw myself wholeheartedly into the task. When I finished, I read my poem to my mother, who had always encouraged my passion for writing.

Full of enthusiasm, I handed in my poem. The following day my teacher, a young woman fresh out of college, stood up in front of the room and read my poem. When she had finished, she glared accusingly at me and began asking in rapid succession questions about how I'd written the poem without giving me a chance to answer. She then declared that the poem was much too good for a student to have written, accused me of cheating, and ripped up my poem. She also made me sit in the back of the classroom for the rest of the year and gave me an F as a final grade. As a result, I was put in a remedial English class. It wasn't until my senior year that I was allowed to petition to be in the college-track English class. I was so traumatized by this experience that I never told my mother or anyone else what had happened. For many years after, I stopped doing any kind of creative writing and in college avoided any English or creative-writing classes.

Rather than analyzing her interpretation of my work (this was a well-written poem) and considering alternative interpretations, my teacher had jumped to the conclusion that I must have copied the epic poem from somewhere, an assumption that breached both good critical-thinking and argumentation skills.

1. Imagine that you were a staff member at this school and found out from another student what had happened. Construct an argument to present to the teacher, encouraging her to reconsider her hasty generalization and come to a better-reasoned conclusion. Pair up and role play this scenario. Stop after two to three minutes and evaluate the effectiveness of your argument and your communication skills.

2. Think back on a time when a teacher or other authority figure hastily jumped to a conclusion about you or something you did. How did this event influence your life goals and decisions? Discuss ways in which your critical-thinking skills might help you to put this event in perspective.

open-minded and good listeners and not engage in resistence or resort to fallacies if others disagree with our argument. If you find that your argument is weak or that the particular conclusion you have drawn does not follow from the premises, go back and revise your argument.

7. Revise Your Argument. Revise your argument, if necessary, in light of the feedback you receive. If the other person's counterargument is more compelling, it would be irrational for you not to revise your own position in light of it. For example, a student in one of my ethics classes participated in a group presentation on capital punishment. At the end of the presentation, he was asked about his position on the issue by another student. He responded, "After doing this project I realize that capital punishment serves no purpose and that there are no good arguments for it. But," he added, "I still support capital punishment." That was poor critical thinking on his part. Stubbornly adhering to a position when there is contrary evidence is not a desirable quality.

8. Put Your Solution or Conclusion into Action.

If appropriate, put your solution or conclusion into action. Good critical thinking has a behavioral component. It involves taking critical action. For instance, if you are writing to your state senator about a need to increase community drug awareness in your hometown, you might want to suggest a realistic solution to the problem and offer to help with its implementation.

Knowing how to construct and present an argument are important skills for a critical thinker. It not only makes you more effective in presenting an argument on an issue but can also help you in resolving issues in your own life.

HIGHLIGHTS

STEPS FOR CONSTRUCTING AN ARGUMENT

1. Clearly state the issue in the form of a question.

2. Develop a list of premises that address the issue.

3. Eliminate weak or irrelevant premises.

4. Establish a conclusion.

5. Organize your argument.

6. Try out your argument on others.

7. Revise your argument, if necessary.

8. If appropriate, put your solution or conclusion into action.

➤ APPLICATION: Identify in the text an example of each step being applied to an argument.

Using Arguments in Making Real-Life Decisions

Arguments are useful tools for making real-life decisions, especially in situations that involve a conflict between what seem to be equally compelling alternatives. People who are poor at critical thinking not only are less likely to recognize a conflict until it gets out of control but are unable to evaluate competing alternatives to come up with an effective resolution to the problem.

Skilled critical thinkers, in contrast, are more likely to recognize a conflict. Instead of jumping to conclusions, good critical thinkers look at an issue from multiple perspectives, assigning weight when necessary to competing reasons, before reaching their final decision.

Consider this example:

> Amy was struggling with the decision of whether to go to China with her family over the summer or instead to go to summer school so that she could finish college in four years. She had been promised a job with a computer software company, following graduation in June. Unfortunately, the summer course schedule conflicted with her travel plans. What should she do?

The first thing you should do in a case like this is to come up with a list of all possible premises or reasons that are relevant to your final decision. In making her decision, Amy began by making this list:

- My grandparents, who live in China, are getting on in years, and this may be the last chance I have to see them.

- My parents are paying my fare, so the trip will not be a financial burden for me.

- I need to take a summer course to graduate next year.

- I have been promised a job with a computer software company after graduation in June.

- The summer course schedule at my college conflicts with my travel schedule.

In developing your list of premises, ask other people for ideas as well. Also, do your research and make sure that you have all the facts correct. In Amy's case, one of her friends suggested that she go to the registrar's office to see whether there was a way she could take a course that would not conflict with the trip dates. As it turned out, she could do an internship on contemporary Chinese business culture for the credits she needed to graduate. She added this option or premise to her list:

- I could do an internship for college credit while I'm in China.

After completing your list, go back and review the premises. Highlight those that are most relevant and delete those that are not. Review your final list before drawing a conclusion. Have you left anything out? Often, just by doing your research and listing various options, you may find that what first seemed to be a conflict is not a conflict at all, as happened in Amy's case.

Finally, put your decision or conclusion into action. As it turned out, Amy was able to go to China with her family *and* complete college in four years.

Arguments provide a powerful tool for analyzing issues and making decisions in our lives. As critical thinkers, we should take a stand or make an important decision only *after* we have examined the different perspectives and options. In addition, we should remain open to hearing new evidence and, in light of that evidence, to modifying our position. By trying to learn why someone holds a position different from our own, we can move closer to understanding and perhaps resolving a conflict.

STOP AND ASSESS YOURSELF

1. Select an issue that is currently being discussed on your campus. After following the eight steps outlined in this chapter, write a two to three page essay or a letter to the editor of the student newspaper presenting your argument for a resolution to the issue.

2. The growing number of child pornography sites on the Internet has led to a corresponding proliferation of cyberspace sleuths—adults who pose as children and attempt to expose cyber-pedophiles. Critics of these self-appointed citizen-sleuths point out that their techniques, because they involve deception, border on entrapment. Critics also argue that it is wrong for private citizens to take the law into their own hands. Others applaud the success of these citizen-sleuths in catching sex offenders and closing down child pornography sites. Working in small groups, construct an argument on the issue of using citizen-sleuths to catch pedophiles. Share your conclusion with the rest of the class. Reevaluate your conclusion, if necessary, in light of feedback from the class.

3. Working in small groups, select a situation with which one of the students in the group is currently struggling. Using the eight-step method outlined in this chapter, generate a suggested resolution or decision.

4. Select one of the goals from your life plan that you are having difficulty achieving. Construct an argument that will enable you to achieve this goal. Put your decision or conclusion into action.

THiNK AGAIN

1. What is an argument?
   - An argument is made up of two or more propositions, including the conclusion, which is supported by the other propositions, known as premises. An argument tries to prove or convince us that the conclusion is true, whereas an explanation is a statement about why something is the case.

2. What is the purpose of breaking down and diagramming arguments?
   - Breaking down arguments helps us to recognize the different premises and the conclusion so we can identify and analyze the issue under discussion, as well as examine the premises to determine if they support the conclusion.

3. What are some of the factors to take into consideration in evaluating an argument?
   - Some of the factors in evaluating an argument are clarity, credibility, relevance, completeness, and soundness of the argument.

Perspectives on Same-Sex Marriage

The issue of legalizing same-sex marriage has divided the United States for some time. Support for same-sex marriage is increasing, with 58 percent of Americans polled in 2013 agreeing that it should be legal. Women and young people are the most likely to support same-sex marriage.[22] The change in public opinion and laws has been rapid. Indeed, until 2003, when the U.S. Supreme Court's ruling in *Lawrence v. Texas* declared antisodomy laws unconstitutional, some states had laws on the books that punished sexual intercourse between two people of the same sex with up to 25 years in prison.

Supporters of same-sex marriage argue that marriage is a basic human right that should not be denied to a person simply because of his or her sexual orientation. Same-sex marriage has been legalized in Canada, Belgium, the Netherlands, Spain, and South Africa. In addition, same-sex couples have full legal rights in many other European countries. In the United States, 13 states including California, Massachusetts, Connecticut, Iowa, Maine, Maryland, New Hampshire, New York, Washington, Minnesota, Delaware, Rhode Island, and Vermont, as well as Washington, D.C. are the only states where same-sex marriage is legal—and those marriages are not recognized by the federal government or, in most cases, by other states. However, several states, including New Jersey, Illinois, and Hawaii, have civil-union legislation for same-sex couples, and still others recognize domestic partnerships.

In 1996, during the administration of Bill Clinton, Congress passed the Defense of Marriage Act (DOMA). The act states that "the word 'marriage' means only a legal union between one man and one woman as husband and wife," thereby prohibiting the federal government from recognizing same-sex marriages. In 2004, a proposal was submitted to Congress to add a Marriage Protection Amendment to the U.S. Constitution, which would define marriage as only between a man and a woman and would also prevent state laws and courts from recognizing same-sex marriages. The amendment failed to pass. On June 26, 2013, the U.S. Supreme Court ruled that Section 3 of DOMA is unconstitutional and that same-sex married couples are entitled to federal benefits.

In the first reading Chief Justice Marshall, in *Goodridge v. Department of Public Health* (2003), argues that same-sex couples have a constitutional right to marry. In the second reading, Matthew Spalding argues that redefining marriage to a form of contract fundamentally alters the nature and purpose of marriage.

Goodridge v. Department of Public Health (2003)

CHIEF JUSTICE MARGARET H. MARSHALL, MAJORITY OPINION

Goodridge v. Department of Public Health was a landmark state appellate court case that legalized same-sex marriage in Massachusetts, the first state to do so. In the following reading former Chief Justice Margaret H. Marshall presents the majority opinion in support of the ruling.

Marriage is a vital social institution. The exclusive commitment of two individuals to each other nurtures love and mutual support; it brings stability to our society. For those who choose to marry, and for their children, marriage provides an abundance of legal, financial, and social benefits. In return it imposes weighty legal, financial, and social obligations. The question before us is whether, consistent with the Massachusetts Constitution, the Commonwealth may deny the protections, benefits, and obligations conferred by civil marriage to two individuals of the same sex who wish to marry. We conclude that it may not. The Massachusetts Constitution affirms the dignity and equality of all individuals. It forbids the creation of second class citizens. In reaching our conclusion we have given full deference to the arguments made by the Commonwealth. But it has failed to identify any constitutionally adequate reason for denying civil marriage to same-sex couples.

The Court affirmed that the core concept of common human dignity protected by the Fourteenth Amendment to the United States Constitution precludes government intrusion into the deeply personal realms of consensual adult expressions of intimacy and one's choice of an intimate partner. The Court also reaffirmed the central role that decisions whether to marry or have children bear in shaping one's identity.

Barred access to the protections, benefits, and obligations of civil marriage, a person who enters into an intimate, exclusive union with another of the same sex is arbitrarily deprived of membership in one of our community's most rewarding and cherished institutions. That exclusion is incompatible with the constitutional principles of respect for individual autonomy and equality under law.

Without question, civil marriage enhances the "welfare of the community." It is a "social institution of the highest importance." Civil marriage anchors an ordered society by encouraging stable relationships over transient ones. It is central to the way the Commonwealth identifies individuals, provides for the orderly distribution of property, ensures that children and adults are cared for and supported whenever possible from private rather than public funds, and tracks important epidemiological and demographic data.

Marriage also bestows enormous private and social advantages on those who choose to marry. Civil marriage is at once a deeply personal commitment to another human being and a highly public celebration of the ideals of mutuality, companionship, intimacy, fidelity, and family. Because it fulfils yearnings for security, safe haven, and connection that express our common humanity, civil marriage is an esteemed institution, and the decision whether and whom to marry is among life's momentous acts of self-definition.

The benefits accessible only by way of a marriage license are enormous, touching nearly every aspect of life and death. The department states that "hundreds of statutes" are related to marriage and to marital benefits. Exclusive marital benefits that are not directly tied to property rights include the presumptions of legitimacy and parentage of children born to a married couple and evidentiary rights, such as the prohibition against spouses testifying against one another about their private conversations, applicable in both civil and criminal cases Other statutory benefits of a personal nature available only to married individuals include qualification for bereavement or medical leave to care for individuals related by blood or marriage an automatic "family member" preference to make medical decisions for an incompetent or disabled spouse who does not have a contrary health care proxy, the application of predictable rules of child custody, visitation, support, and removal out-of-State when married parents divorce.

Notwithstanding the Commonwealth's strong public policy to abolish legal distinctions between marital and nonmarital children in providing for the support and care of minors, the fact remains that marital children reap a measure of family stability and economic security based on their parents' legally privileged status that is largely inaccessible, or not as readily accessible, to nonmarital children. Some of these benefits are social, such as the enhanced approval that still attends the status of being a marital child. Others are material, such as the greater ease of access to family-based State and Federal benefits that attend the presumptions of one's parentage.

It is undoubtedly for these concrete reasons, as well as for its intimately personal significance, that civil marriage has long been termed a "civil right." See, e.g., Loving v. Virginia, The United States Supreme Court has described the right to marry as "of fundamental importance for all individuals" and as "part of the fundamental 'right of privacy' implicit in the Fourteenth Amendment's Due Process Clause."

Without the right to marry—or more properly, the right to choose to marry—one is excluded from the full range of human experience and denied full protection of the laws for one's "avowed commitment to an intimate and lasting human relationship.". . . Because civil marriage is central to the lives of individuals and the welfare of the community, our laws assiduously protect the individual's right to marry against undue government incursion. Laws may not "interfere directly and substantially with the right to marry.". . .

For decades, indeed centuries, in much of this country (including Massachusetts) no lawful marriage was possible between white and black Americans. That long history availed not when the Supreme Court of California held in 1948 that a legislative prohibition against interracial marriage violated the due process and equality guarantees of the Fourteenth Amendment.

The individual liberty and equality safeguards of the Massachusetts Constitution protect both "freedom from" unwarranted government intrusion into protected spheres of life and "freedom to" partake in benefits created by the State for the common good. . . . Both freedoms are involved here. Whether and whom to marry, how to express sexual intimacy, and whether and how to establish a family—these are among the most basic of every individual's liberty and due process rights. . . . And central to personal freedom and security is the assurance that the laws will apply equally to persons in similar situations. "Absolute equality before the law is a fundamental principle of our own Constitution." . . .

REVIEW QUESTIONS

1. Why is denying same-sex couples the right to marriage incompatible with the principles of respect for autonomy and equality under the law?

2. What does Marshall mean when she says that the laws of civil marriage do not privilege procreative heterosexual intercourse between married people?

3. How is denying the right to marry between whites and blacks similar to denying the right to marry between same-sex couples?

4. How does Marshall respond to the claim that legalizing same-sex marriage will undermine the institution of marriage?

A Defining Moment for Marriage and Self-Government   MATTHEW SPALDING

Matthew Spalding is vice president of American Studies and Director of the B. Kenneth Simon Center for Principles and Politics at the Heritage Foundation in Washington, D.C. In his reading, Spaulding presents arguments for why legalizing same-sex marriage will weaken traditional marriage and family.

What was once an important debate over the legal status of marriage has emerged as a critical national issue, the resolution of which will shape the future of our society and the course of constitutional government in the United States.

Family is and will always remain the building block of civil society, and marriage is at the heart of the family. Redefining marriage down to a mere form of contract fundamentally alters its nature and purpose and will usher in new threats to the liberty of individuals and organizations that uphold marriage and have moral or religious objections to its redefinition.

What Is at Stake For thousands of years, based on experience, tradition, and legal precedent, every society and every major religion have upheld marriage as the unique relationship by which a man and a woman are joined together for the primary purpose of forming and maintaining a family. This overwhelming consensus results from the fact that the union of man and woman is manifest in the most basic and evident truths of human nature. Marriage is the formal recognition of this relationship by society and its laws. While individual marriages are recognized by government, the institution of marriage pre-exists and is antecedent to the institution of government.

Society's interest in uniquely elevating the status of marriage is that marriage is the necessary foundation of the family, and thus necessary for societal existence and well-being. Family is the primary institution through which children are raised, nurtured, and educated, and developed into adults. Marriage is the cornerstone of the family: It produces children, provides them with mothers and fathers, and is the framework through which relationships among mothers, fathers, and children are established and maintained.

Moreover, because of the shared obligations and generational relationships that accrue with marriage, the institution brings significant stability, continuity, and meaning to human relationships and plays an important role in transferring basic cultural knowledge and civilization to future generations.

Redefining Marriage Redefining marriage does not simply extend benefits or rights to a larger class, but substantively changes the essence of the institution. It does not expand marriage; it alters its core meaning such that it is no longer intrinsically related to the relationship between fathers, mothers, and children. Expanding marriage supposedly to make it more inclusive, no matter what we call the new arrangement, necessarily ends marriage as we now know it by remaking the institution into something different: a mere contract between any two individuals.

Changing the definition of marriage—or even remaining neutral as to that definition—denies the very nature and purpose that gives marriage its unique and preferable status in society. If marriage becomes just one form of commitment in a spectrum of sexual relationships rather than a preferred monogamous relationship for the sake of children, the line separating sexual relations within and outside marriage becomes blurred, and so does the public policy argument against out-of-wedlock births or in favor of abstinence.

Based on current evidence and settled reasoning, it would be a terrible folly to weaken marriage either by elevating non-marital unions to the same position or by lowering the institution of marriage to the status of merely one form of household.

A Defining Moment Americans are a greatly tolerant and reasonable people. That continuing character depends on the strength of the American framework of constitutional government and the core principles of self-government—first among those the idea of religious liberty—that allow and encourage that character and our ability to govern ourselves despite our differences. Citizens and their elected representatives must be able to engage in free discussion and deliberation on the importance of the institution of marriage for civil society and popular self-government. Activist judges must not strip them of that freedom.

We should work to rebuild and restore marriage and not allow redefinition to further weaken the institution; break its fundamental connections between husband and wife, parents and child; and thereby sever our primary link to the formation of future generations. We must act in accord with our basic principles and deepest convictions to preserve constitutional government and the foundational structure of civilization by upholding the permanent institution of marriage.

Review Questions

1. Why does Spalding regard redefining marriage to include same-sex marriage as a threat to liberty?

2. According to Spalding, what is the source of the institution of marriage?

3. Why is heterosexual marriage a necessary foundation of family?

4. According to Spalding, how would redefining marriage to include same-sex couples weaken the institution of marriage?

THiNK AND DISCUSS

PERSPECTIVES ON SAME-SEX MARRIAGE

1. Identify the key premises in *Goodridge v. Department of Public Health* (2006) and by Spalding in their arguments regarding the legalization of same-sex marriage. Identify which type of premise each is. Diagram and evaluate both of the arguments. Should the definition of marriage be limited to a man and a woman or should the definition change to take into account changing views of marriage and family? Present an argument supporting your position, referring back to the role of definitions discussed in Chapter 4 on page 124.

2. Some people oppose legalizing same-sex marriage on a federal level but support civil unions and equal rights for same-sex couples. Evaluate whether this position is consistent with a belief in equal rights and opportunities for all people, regardless of their sexual orientation. Discuss also how both Spalding and the Supreme Court in *Goodridge v. Department of Public Health* (2006) might respond to legalizing civil unions, but not marriage, for same-sex couples. Which position do you support and why?

3. Looking back at your life goals, is marriage one of your goals? If so, why? Discuss how you would respond, and why, if you were legally denied the right to marry because of your sexual orientation.

4. Cheshire Calhoun, professor of philosophy at Arizona State University, has argued that lesbians should not buy into the traditional model of marriage and family that she says is inherently oppressive to women because women take a subordinate role to men in marriage, and women are expected to do the majority of housework and childrearing, which limits their career options. Discuss her concerns. Should the institution of marriage itself be dismantled? If so, what should replace marriage as the family unit and best means for raising children? Develop arguments to support your answers.

7

INDUCTIVE
ARGUMENTS

College students show off their entry to the Rube Goldberg Machine Contest, in which students build devices to complete a simple task in a minimum of 20 steps. What inductive logic skills do you think the students used in the design and creation of their machine?

How do today's college students compare with the students of their parents' generation? One of the most noteworthy differences is the impact of the women's movement. There has been a substantial closing of the gender gap in several majors, including the sciences, secondary-school teaching, and business. In addition, while 54 percent of college men and 42 percent of college women in 1967 agreed that "the activities of married women are best confined to the home and family," thirty-five years later only 28 percent of college men and 16 percent of college women agreed with this statement.

Another significant generational difference is the values that motivate students in setting their life goals. In the late 1960s and early 1970s, more than 80 percent of students said that "developing a meaningful philosophy of life" was an "essential" or "very important" goal. By the 1990s, "being very well off

THiNK FIRST

- How does an inductive argument differ from a deductive argument?
- How do arguments based on generalizations help us to learn more about a particular population?
- What are some of the uses of arguments by analogy?
- What role does causal reasoning play in our lives?

>> financially'' had become the most important goal. In 2012 ''being able to get a better job'' had become the most important reason for going to college according to the American Freshman Survey. In addition, women now rank ''being successful in a high-paying career or profession'' higher than men do. However, both men and women continue to rank being a good parent and having a successful marriage significantly higher than career success.[1]

Did You Know

Despite declining interaction among students across racial or ethnic lines on college campuses, 23 percent of students in the 2012 Freshman Survey believed that ''racial discrimination is no longer a problem in America.''

In addition, the political orientation of today's college students is more likely to be middle-of-the-road compared with that of young people in their parents' generation. About 40 percent of college freshmen in 1970 identified themselves as liberal or far left, compared with about 35 percent of the college freshmen in 2012, who tended to be more middle-of-the-road (45 percent) in their political orientation.[2]

How do we know all this about college students? Through the application of inductive reasoning using the information collected from thousands of American college freshmen. The results of this annual survey, which was launched by the Cooperative Institutional Research Program (CIRP) in 1966, are used to make decisions about college recruitment, admission, program development, and other facets of college life.

The CIRP Freshman Survey (shown on p. 208) is just one example of the use of inductive reasoning. In this chapter we will be studying the different types of inductive arguments and how they are used in our everyday lives. We will also learn how to evaluate inductive arguments. To summarize, in Chapter 7 we will:

- Distinguish between deductive and inductive arguments
- Identify the characteristics of an inductive argument
- Learn how to recognize and evaluate arguments based on generalization
- Examine polling and sampling methods
- Study the various uses of analogies
- Learn how to recognize and evaluate arguments using analogies

- Learn how to recognize and evaluate a causal argument
- Distinguish between a correlation and a causal relationship

Finally, we will examine arguments regarding the legalization of marijuana in the United States.

WHAT IS AN INDUCTIVE ARGUMENT?

As we noted in the previous chapter, there are two basic types of arguments—deductive arguments and inductive arguments. *Deductive arguments* claim that their conclusion *necessarily* follows from the premises, if the premises are true and the reasoning process is valid—as in the following example:

> No dogs are cats. Mindy is a dog. Therefore, Mindy is not a cat.

We will be studying deductive arguments in depth in Chapter 8.

Inductive arguments, in contrast, claim that their conclusion *probably* follows from the premises. Because of this, inductive arguments are merely stronger or weaker rather than true or false.

> Most Corgis make good watch-dogs. My dog Mindy is a Corgi. Therefore, Mindy is probably a good watchdog.

In determining if an argument is inductive, look for certain words that suggest that the conclusion probably, rather than necessarily, follows from the premise(s).

These include words and phrases such as *probably, most likely, chances are that, it is reasonable to suppose that, we can expect that,* and *it seems probable that.* However, not all inductive arguments contain indicator words. In these cases, you have to ask yourself if the conclusion necessarily follows from the premises. If the conclusion is only likely, then it is probably an inductive argument.

The Use of Inductive Reasoning in Everyday Life

We use inductive reasoning just about every day when we extend what we already know to situations that are not as familiar to us. For example, you may decide, on the basis of the positive experience of three of your classmates, each of whom has a child in the nursery school on campus, that your child will also be happy in that nursery school. A candidate for the U.S. Senate may conclude, on the basis of the results of the Freshman Survey, that young people in college today aren't as likely to vote in mid-term elections and thus gear her campaign to appeal primarily to an older constituency.

Because inductive logic is based on probability rather than necessity, there is always the possibility of error. Your child may not like the nursery school, and college students may turn out to vote in higher numbers than predicted. Also, since human thinking is prone to inborn cognitive errors, we cannot always depend on people to think or behave logically or consistently. Familiarity with the principles of inductive logic will make you less likely to commit errors in your thinking.

In the following sections we will discuss the three most common types of inductive arguments: generalizations, analogies, and causal arguments.

EXERCISE 7-1

STOP AND ASSESS YOURSELF

I. Think of an inductive argument that you used in the past week. Break the argument down into its premise(s) and conclusion. Explain why it is an inductive argument.

2. Indicate whether each of the following is an inductive argument, a deductive argument, or neither.

*a. The moon was full 4 weeks ago, so it should be full again tonight.

b. I hear you've been diagnosed with Lyme disease. You should go to the doctor and get some antibiotics for it. When Saheed was given antibiotics for his Lyme disease, his symptoms cleared up in a few weeks. The same happened with Arquelina when she had it.

c. I think I can trust John to keep his promise to keep our secret. He's never broken a promise he's made to me in the past.

*d. Wei is a student at Clark Community College. None of the students at CCC reside on campus. Therefore, Wei does not live on campus.

e. When Conservative Ann Coulter visited Canada, hundreds of college students at the University of Ottawa protested her planned visit to their campus causing a near riot. It's likely that she won't be welcome at the University of Waterloo as well.

f. In the United States, 35 percent of births are by caesarean section, up 200 percent since 1975.[3] There are several reasons for this trend. Many doctors feel that a woman should have the right to choose how she wants to have her baby. And with malpractice premiums so high, obstetricians have become reluctant to take even the slightest risk associated with natural childbirth.

*g. Young people are more computer savvy nowadays. Therefore, you might be better off asking your cousin Jennifer for help setting up your computer than asking her father.

h. While 17 of the 27 countries in the European Union have adopted the Euro, the only Scandanavian country that has adopted it is Finland. Therefore, Sweden does not use the Euro as its currency.

i. We told you 2 weeks ago that if you kept missing the meetings to work on our group class presentation, we were going to drop you from the group. You haven't made any of the meetings in the past 2 weeks. So now we're going to drop you from our group.

*j. We're willing to put down our dogs and cats when they are old and sick. Why shouldn't we do the same with our elderly?

k. Mike weighed 210 pounds before going on the critical-thinking diet three months ago. He has lost 17 pounds so far on the diet. Therefore, he now weighs less than 200 pounds.

*Answers to selected exercises are found in the Solutions Manual at the end of the book.

GENERALIZATION

generalization Drawing a conclusion about a certain characteristic of a population based on a sample from it.

poll A type of survey that involves collecting information from a sample group of people.

We use **generalization** when we draw a conclusion about a certain characteristic of a group or population on the basis of a sample from that group. For example, you sneeze whenever you are around your roommate's cat, your girlfriend's cat, and your Uncle Albert's two cats (your sample). On the basis of these experiences, you might reasonably conclude that *all* cats (the population) will probably make you sneeze.

generalization

Characteristics of sample ⟶ Claim about characteristics of a whole population

Scientists frequently use arguments based on generalization. For instance, Stanley Milgram, in his experiment on obedience, found that 65 percent of the subjects obeyed the authority figure to the point where they thought they might have seriously harmed or even killed the learner.[4] From this finding, Milgram concluded that people in general are susceptible to becoming caught up in a destructive process if directed to do so by an authority figure. In coming to this conclusion, Milgram generalized from the behavior of the study subjects in his experiments (the sample) to a conclusion about a characteristic of the whole human population.

Connections

How is inductive reasoning used in the scientific method? *See Chapter 12, p. 364.*

Using Polls, Surveys, and Sampling to Make Generalizations

Polls and surveys, such as the Freshman Survey, also use inductive generalization. **Polls** are a type of survey that involves collecting opinions or information on a subject from a sample group of people for the purpose of analysis.[5]

Polls provide a window into how people think and feel. Few marketing firms or public policy makers take any major action without first consulting polls. Public opinion polls play an especially important role in democracies such as the United States, whose Constitution requires that the government function explicitly with "the consent of the governed."[6] Politicians, especially during election years, check the public opinion polls to find out what the public thinks before making promises or commitments. Polls are even used to determine what type of shirt (e.g., checked lumberjack, polo, or white dress shirt) a politician should wear when campaigning in a particular state or town.

Sampling Techniques. To ensure that a generalization about a population is reliable, pollsters use a method known as sampling to collect data about a population that is large or diverse and where it would be too costly and time-consuming

Hot or Not?

Have you ever made a generalization in your life that you later found to be false?

Your participation in a poll helps to provide an accurate portrayal of a specific group or a population at large.

year (e.g., historically black colleges or Catholic colleges), each response from this type of institution is weighted so it counts for more in the final results, thereby assuring that the final results are representative of the population of American college freshmen.[8] For example, if 20 percent of all college freshmen attend Catholic colleges but only 10 percent of the responses in the survey are from freshmen at Catholic colleges, then each of these responses would be weighted to count as two responses. Using this method of sampling, the researchers are able to make relatively accurate generalizations about the characteristics of the population of all American freshmen.

> **sampling** Selecting some members of a group and making generalizations about the whole population on the basis of their characteristics.
>
> **representative sample** A sample that is similar to the larger population from which it was drawn.
>
> **random sampling** Every member of the population has an equal chance of becoming part of the sample.

The sample size necessary to make a reliable generalization about a population depends in part on the size of the population. As a general rule, the larger the sample, the more confident we can be that our generalization is accurate. Sample size also depends on the amount of variation within a population. The more variation there is, the larger the sample must be to be accurate.

If the characteristics are relatively stable throughout the population, then the sample can be smaller. For example, you see a physician because you have been feeling tired and run down. The physician takes a small sample of blood and tells you, on the basis of the hemoglobin count in this one sample, that you are anemic. It's a very small sample compared with all the blood you have in your body. Should you go back and ask your physician to take blood from different parts of your body just to make sure the sample is representative? In this case, the answer is no. Because our blood

Connections

How do market researchers use polls and surveys in targeting a market for a product or service? *See Chapter 10, pp. 304–305.*

to study the whole population. **Sampling** entails selecting only some members of a class or group and then making a generalization about the whole population that is based on the characteristics of these members. For example, rather than polling the more than 1 million full-time freshmen in the United States, the fall 2012 Freshman Survey invited all 4-year American colleges and universities to participate in the annual survey; 192,912 freshmen at 283 colleges and universities participated in the survey. This sample is much larger than is normally needed, if the sample chosen is representative of the population.

A **representative sample** is one that is similar in relevant respects to the larger population. To get a representative sample, most professional pollsters use a method known as **random sampling**. A sample is random if every member of the population has an equal chance of becoming a member of that sample, in much the same way that the numbers for the winning lottery ticket are drawn randomly from a population of numbers containing all possible combinations of winning numbers. The Gallup Poll makes consistently accurate predictions about the views of Americans on the basis of a representative sample of only 1,500 to 2,000 people.[7]

One method of ensuring that a sample is representative when it is too difficult to get a random sample is to weight the responses. The Freshman Survey uses this method. If one type of institution is underrepresented in a particular

Public opinion polls play an especially important role in democracies such as the United States, whose Constitution requires that the government function explicitly with "the consent of the governed."

is pretty much uniform throughout our body, at least in regard to hemoglobin count, the physician can be fairly confident that the sample is representative of all the blood in your body.

2012 CIRP FRESHMAN SURVEY

PLEASE PRINT IN ALL CAPS YOUR NAME AND PERMANENT/HOME ADDRESS (one letter or number per box).

When were you born?

NAME: FIRST · MI · LAST

ADDRESS:

Month (01-12) · Day (01-31) · Year

CITY: · STATE: · ZIP: · PHONE:

STUDENT ID# (as instructed): · EMAIL (print letters carefully):

SERIAL #

MARKING DIRECTIONS

- Use a black or blue pen.
- Fill in your response completely. Mark out any answer you wish to change with an "X".

CORRECT MARK · INCORRECT MARKS

Group Code A B

1. Your sex: ○ Male ○ Female

2. How old will you be on December 31 of this year? (Mark one)

16 or younger ○ 21-24 ○
17 ○ 25-29 ○
18 ○ 30-39 ○
19 ○ 40-54 ○
20 ○ 55 or older ○

3. Is English your native language?
○ Yes ○ No

4. In what year did you graduate from high school? (Mark one)

2012 ○ Did not graduate but passed G.E.D. test. ○
2011 ○
2010 ○ Never completed high school ○
2009 or earlier ○

5. Are you enrolled (or enrolling) as a: (Mark one)
Full-time student ○
Part-time student ○

6. How many miles is this college from your permanent home? (Mark one)
5 or less ○ 11-50 ○ 101-500 ○
6-10 ○ 51-100 ○ Over 500 ○

7. What was your average grade in high school? (Mark one)
A or A+ ○ B ○ C ○
A– ○ B– ○ D ○
B+ ○ C+ ○

8. What were your scores on the SAT I and/or ACT?

SAT Critical Reading

SAT Mathematics

SAT Writing

ACT Composite

9. From what kind of high school did you graduate? (Mark one)
○ Public school (not charter or magnet)
○ Public charter school
○ Public magnet school
○ Private religious/parochial school
○ Private independent college-prep school
○ Home school

10. Prior to this term, have you ever taken courses for credit at this institution?
○ Yes ○ No

11. Since leaving high school, have you ever taken courses, whether for credit or not for credit, at any other institution (university, 4- or 2-year college, technical, vocational, or business school)?
○ Yes ○ No

12. Where do you plan to live during the fall term? (Mark one)
With my family or other relatives ○
Other private home, apartment, or room ○
College residence hall ○
Fraternity or sorority house ○
Other campus student housing ○
Other ○

13. To how many colleges other than this one did you apply for admission this year?
None ○ 1 ○ 4 ○ 7-10 ○
2 ○ 5 ○ 11 or more ○
3 ○ 6 ○

14. Were you accepted by your first choice college?
○ Yes ○ No

15. Is this college your: (Mark one)
First choice ○ Less than third choice ○
Second choice ○
Third choice ○

16. The current economic situation significantly affected my college choice: (Mark one)
○ Agree Strongly
○ Agree Somewhat
○ Disagree Somewhat
○ Disagree Strongly

17. Citizenship status:
○ U.S. citizen
○ Permanent resident (green card)
○ Neither

18. Are your parents: (Mark one)
Both alive and living with each other ○
Both alive, divorced or living apart ○
One or both deceased ○

19. During high school (grades 9-12) how many years did you study each of the following subjects? (Mark one for each item)

	None	1/2	1	2	3	4	5 or more
English	○	○	○	○	○	○	○
Mathematics	○	○	○	○	○	○	○
Foreign Language	○	○	○	○	○	○	○
Physical Science	○	○	○	○	○	○	○
Biological Science	○	○	○	○	○	○	○
History/Am. Gov't.	○	○	○	○	○	○	○
Computer Science	○	○	○	○	○	○	○
Arts and/or Music	○	○	○	○	○	○	○

20. Please mark which of the following courses you have completed:
Ⓨ Ⓝ Algebra II
Ⓨ Ⓝ Pre-calculus/Trigonometry
Ⓨ Ⓝ Probability & Statistics
Ⓨ Ⓝ Calculus
Ⓨ Ⓝ AP Probability & Statistics
Ⓨ Ⓝ AP Calculus

21. Do you have any of the following disabilities or medical conditions? (Mark Yes or No for each item)
Ⓨ Ⓝ Learning disability (dyslexia, etc.)
Ⓨ Ⓝ Attention deficit hyperactivity disorder (ADHD)
Ⓨ Ⓝ Autism spectrum/Asperger's syndrome
Ⓨ Ⓝ Physical disability (speech, sight, mobility, hearing, etc.)
Ⓨ Ⓝ Chronic illness (cancer, diabetes, autoimmune disorders, etc.)
Ⓨ Ⓝ Psychological disorder (depression, etc.)
Ⓨ Ⓝ Other

22. Do you consider yourself: (Mark Yes or No for each item)

	Yes	No
Pre-Med	○	○
Pre-Law	○	○

23. Please mark your probable major. (Use codes provided on the attached fold-out)

Each year, the CIRP Freshman Survey is administered to nearly 200,000 entering full-time students.

Not all polls and surveys use random sampling or correct for biases. Internet polls and some polls sponsored by television programs or stations, such as *American Idol* or CNN, may be biased or unrepresentative, since they rely on call-ins from their viewers or subscribers. Street polls and telephone polls can also be biased because not everyone is willing to stop and talk to a pollster or picks up their phone. In these cases, the sample is what is known as a **self-selected sample**. In other words, only the people most interested in the poll actually take the time to participate in it.

Even a professionally run survey can be inadvertently biased because of careless methodology. In 1936, the magazine *Literary Digest* conducted a massive survey on who would win the presidential election: Franklin D. Roosevelt or Alf Landon. *Literary*

American Idol *Kree Harrison (left) and Candice Glover (right), before Glover was declared winner of the 2013 American Idol competition the winner based on voter call-in, a self-selected sample.*

Digest sent surveys to people from their subscription list, from telephone books, and from automobile registration lists. About 2,300,000 people responded to the survey. On the basis of their responses, it was predicted that Landon would win the election. Instead, Roosevelt received 60 percent of the votes, one of the largest wins in American history. George Gallup, who used a smaller but representative sample, predicted the result correctly (see "Thinking Outside the Box: George Gallup"). What went wrong with the *Literary Digest* Poll? For one thing, the magazine's readership was mainly well-educated people, which biased the survey. In addition, many people in 1936 did not have a telephone or own an automobile, thereby further biasing the sample toward affluent people.

Effects of Question Wording on Responses.

Bias may result from the way a question is worded. A 1980 poll conducted for the National Abortion Rights Action League (called NARAL Pro-Choice America since 2003) tried asking a question worded in the following two different ways to see if the wording would affect the response:

- Do you think there should be an amendment to the Constitution prohibiting abortions, or shouldn't there be such an amendment?

- Do you believe there should be an amendment to the Constitution protecting the life of the unborn child, or shouldn't there be such an amendment?

When the phrase "prohibiting abortions" was used in the question, only 29 percent of the respondents said they favored the amendment; however, when the phrase "protecting the life of the unborn child" was used, 50 percent of the respondents said they favored the amendment. In this case, the second question was a **slanted question**—one that is written to elicit a particular response.

You should also be wary of **push polls**, which start by presenting the pollsters' views before asking for a response. By presenting the pollster's views first, the poll becomes slanted toward that view, no matter how well the questions are worded, since people tend to uncritically accept the views of those they perceive as authority figures.

In addition, questions used in polls should be simple and cover only one topic. **Loaded questions**, like the fallacy of the same name, assumes a particular answer to another

Connections

How can you recognize sampling errors in advertisements? *See Chapter 10, p. 307.*

self-selected sample A sample where only the people most interested in the poll or survey participate.

slanted question A question that is written to elicit a particular response.

push poll A poll that starts by presenting the pollsters' views before asking for a response.

loaded questions A fallacy that assumes a particular answer to another unasked question.

Thinking Outside the Box

GEORGE GALLUP, *Opinion Seeker*

Born in Jefferson, Iowa, in 1901, George Gallup (who died in 1984) attended the University of Iowa, where he was editor of the school newspaper. He also completed a Ph.D. in journalism at the University of Iowa.

After graduation, Gallup got a job as an interviewer for an advertising firm. He was keenly interested in what other people thought and why. Rather than making assumptions or asking only people he knew for their opinions, he developed the startling technique of actually confronting a sample of readers with a whole newspaper and asking them what they read and what they liked or didn't like about a story.

In 1934 Gallup founded the Gallup Poll at Princeton University, where he was the first to use scientific methods to measure people's opinions. His polling techniques were initially used to tap into the political pulse of the nation. Gallup also invented market research, described as "the ultimate savior of the customer." His work today stands as one of the greatest examples of the practical application of cognitive science. Gallup once said that "teaching people to think for themselves was the most important thing in the world to do."* For Gallup, a well-informed public was essential in a democracy. He transformed America by empowering the common person and making it increasingly difficult for those in authority to tell people what they should believe and do.

DISCUSSION QUESTIONS

1. Most college libraries carry the Gallup Poll. Look at the most recent poll. Discuss ways in which the questions and responses in the poll can contribute to your ability to be a critical thinker and make effective decisions about important issues.

2. Using the index in the Gallup Poll, select an issue that is important to you. Look at the questions. What percent of Americans share your view? Did looking at the poll results broaden your perspective on the issue? Explain.

*Quote from http://www.schoolofthinking.org/who/george-gallup/. For more on the Gallup Poll, go to http:www.gallup.com.

unanswered question. A Presidential Survey sent out by the Democratic National Committee asked recipients to rank the following goal (along with four others) for the Democratic Party on a scale of one to five by its level of priority:

___ Combating Republicans' Obstructionist Tactics

However, this is a loaded question. The wording of this goal assumes that we have answered "yes" to the question: "Do you think Republicans in Congress are engaging in obstructionist tactics?" when in fact we may believe that the Republicans are not being obstructionist but have good reasons for not supporting some of the legislation proposed by Democratic legislators. This survey question also employs the ad hominem fallacy by using the emotive term *obstructionist* to create a negative feeling toward Republicans. Similarly the term *tactic,* which is often associated with war, is intended to create a "we/them" mentality with the Republicans being the "them."

Along similar lines, questions in a poll should avoid the fallacy of *false dilemma* in which the response to a complex issue is reduced to two alternatives.

State College is currently experiencing a financial crisis. Do you think our college should raise tuition or increase class size?

This question poses a false dilemma, since there are other ways to raise funds without having to raise tuition or increase class size. For example, the development office could initiate a fundraising campaign that targets wealthy alumni.

In polls men tend to exaggerate the number of times they have had sexual intercourse, whereas women tend to understate the number of encounters.

Self-serving errors can bias the results of a survey as well. Polls depend on the respondents answering honestly. As we noted in Chapter 4, most people see themselves (correctly or not) as good and fair-minded. If a poll asks "Are you a racist?" virtually no one, not even members of the Ku Klux Klan, will answer yes. To avoid this error, questions should be worded in a way that does not threaten a person's self image.

People are also inclined to give answers that conform to what is socially acceptable or what they think the pollster wants to hear. For example, many men think that it's macho to have frequent sex and many female partners.

Women who engage in this sort of behavior, however, are usually labeled promiscuous. Consequently, in polls men tend to exaggerate the number of times they have had sexual intercourse, whereas women tend to understate the number of encounters. In fact, the difference in the answers is so marked that it is impossible for both groups to be answering honestly.

Applying Generalizations to Particular Cases

A generalization about a population may be used as a premise in an argument about a particular member(s) of that group.

Generalization about ⟶ Claim about a
the population   member of the
(Premise)   population
                             (Conclusion)

The ability to correctly apply generalizations to specific cases enables us to make better decisions in our lives and personal relationships, as the following case illustrates:

I was going to get my wife Ling a new bathroom scale for Valentine's Day until I read a study that said most women prefer to be taken out to a romantic dinner. I should take Ling out to dinner at the Ritz instead. She'll probably like that more than the scale.

Breaking down and diagramming this argument, we have:

(1) [I was going to get my wife Ling a new bathroom scale for Valentine's Day] until I read a study that said (2) [most women prefer to be taken out to a romantic dinner.] (3) [Ling will probably like going out to dinner more than the scale.]

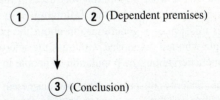

Premise 2 is based on a generalization about a population (women). In this case the husband draws the conclusion about Ling (a member of the population) that she would probably rather be taken out to dinner for Valentine's Day.

When a generalization about a population is applied to an individual member of that group, statistics are often used regarding the prevalence of the characteristic in the population. The higher the prevalence of a characteristic in

Year	Winner	Height	Runner-up (by electoral vote count)	Height	Difference
2012	Barack Obama	6 ft 1½ in	Mitt Romeny	6 ft 2 in	½ in
2008	Barack Obama	6 ft 1½ in	John McCain	5 ft 7 in	5½ in
2004	George W. Bush	5 ft 11 in	John Kerry	6 ft 4 in	5 in
2000	George W. Bush	5 ft 11 in	Al Gore	6 ft ½ in	1½ in
1996	Bill Clinton	5 ft 11 in	Bob Dole	6 ft 0 in	2½ in
1992	Bill Clinton	6 ft 2½ in	George H. W. Bush	6 ft 2 in	½ in
1988	George H. W. Bush	6 ft 2½ in	Michael Dukakis	5 ft 6 in	8 in
1984	Ronald Reagan	6 ft 2 in	Walter Mondale	5 ft 10¾ in	2¼ in
1980	Ronald Reagan	6 ft 1 in	Jimmy Carter	5 ft 9 in	4 in
1976	Jimmy Carter	6 ft 1 in 5 ft 9 in	Gerald Ford	6 ft 1 in	4 in
1972	Richard Nixon	5 ft 11½ in	George McGovern	6 ft 1 in	1½ in
1968	Richard Nixon	5 ft 11½ in	Hubert Humphrey	5 ft 11 in	½ in
1964	Lyndon Johnson	6 ft 3½ in	Barry Goldwater	6 ft 0 in	3½ in
1960	John F. Kennedy	6 ft 0 in	Richard Nixon	5 ft 11½ in	½ in
1956	Dwight D. Eisenhower	5 ft 10½ in	Adlai Stevenson	5 ft 10 in	½ in
1952	Dwight D. Eisenhower	5 ft 10½ in	Adlai Stevenson	5 ft 10 in	½ in
1948	Harry S. Truman	5 ft 9 in	Thomas Dewey	5 ft 8 in	1 in
1944	Franklin D. Roosevelt	6 ft 2 in	Thomas Dewey	5 ft 8 in	6 in
1940	Franklin D. Roosevelt	6 ft 2 in	Wendell Willkie	6 ft 1 in	1 in
1936	Franklin D. Roosevelt	6 ft 2 in	Alfred Landon	5 ft 8 in	6 in
1932	Franklin D. Roosevelt	6 ft 2 in	Herbert Hoover	5 ft 11 in	3 in

Comparative Table of Heights of U.S. Presidential Candidates

the population, the more likely it is that the application to the individual will be true.

> Studies show that executives tend to be significantly taller than employees of a company. Therefore, Anna Gable, the CEO of Buzzword Electronics, is probably taller than 5′4″, the average height of women in the United States.

This generalization also applies to presidents. There have been only five instances in 23 presidential elections in which the shorter candidate won.

In applying a generalization, you should make sure you are clear about what population was used in making the initial generalization. In the following example, the speaker misapplies a generalization about the population of people who are diagnosed with multiple sclerosis (MS) to a conclusion about the population of people in general.

> The majority of people who are diagnosed with multiple sclerosis are women between the ages of 20 and 30. You're a woman and you just turned 20. Therefore, chances are that you'll come down with MS while you're in your twenties.

In this case, the fact that the majority of people who first present with symptoms of MS are women between the ages of 20 and 30 does not necessarily mean that the majority of women in their twenties will develop MS. In fact, the rate of MS in the female population worldwide is only 0.3 percent (3 out of every 1,000 women). Thus, the chances that a woman of any age will develop MS are actually very low.

Did You Know

A Massachusetts study of adult males who were convicted child molesters found that less than 1 percent of them were homosexual.[9] This is well below the estimate of 2.3 percent for the general population that is based on a survey conducted by the U.S. Department of Health and Human Services.[10]

Evaluating Inductive Arguments Using Generalization

Like all inductive arguments, generalizations are neither true nor false; they are merely stronger or weaker arguments. In this section we'll be looking at five different criteria for evaluating arguments using generalizations.

1. The Premises Are True. True premises are based on credible evidence. A premise can be false because of flaws in a research design—as happened in the 1936 *Literary Digest* survey on the presidential election. A premise can also be false because it is based on popular misconceptions or stereotypes rather than on actual evidence—as in the following example:

> Nothing can live forever. Nicole's claim that there are some marine animals that are immortal is clearly false.

In this example, the premise "Nothing can live forever" is false. There are some animals, including certain jellyfish, corals, and hydra, that can rejuvenate their bodies indefinitely by cloning or regenerating new parts. As we noted in Chapter 1, good critical thinkers make sure that their information is accurate and their sources are credible before they come to a conclusion.

2. The Sample Is Large Enough. As a general rule, the larger the sample, the more reliable the conclusion.

When our sample is too small, we run the risk of committing the *fallacy of hasty generalization.* For example, a high school senior knows three students who just were accepted by a first-rate 4-year college. In each case, both of their parents were professionals with graduate degrees. From this small sample, the student may hastily conclude that she shouldn't bother applying for admission to this college, since her parents never attended college. In reality, only about 20 percent of the parents of college freshmen have a graduate degree, whereas an even larger number of parents—28 percent—have only a high school education or less.[11]

3. The Sample Is Representative. A sample should be representative of the population being studied. If the sample is not, then the argument is weak (see "Analyzing Images: The Blind Men and the Elephant"). A sample can

ANALYZING IMAGES

The Blind Men and The Elephant According to a Buddhist fable, a group of blind men came upon an elephant. One of the men grabbed the trunk and said, "Elephants are like snakes." "No," replied the second blind man, putting his arms around the elephant's leg, "they're shaped like tree trunks." "Nonsense," chimed in the third blind man as he ran his hands along the elephant's tail. "They're more like ropes."

DISCUSSION QUESTIONS

1. *Why did each of the blind men come to a different conclusion regarding the nature of the elephant? Discuss how the blind men might have used some of the critical-thinking strategies to arrive at a better-reasoned conclusion.*

2. *Discuss a time when you got into a dispute because you made a generalization on the basis of limited experience.*

Women serving combat duty in the United States military has been an issue of contention—but are we against (or for) it for the right reasons?

be large but still not be representative. For example, before the 1980s, almost all clinical drug studies were done only on men. Women were not included, not only because of concern that they might be pregnant but also because of the cultural assumption that men were the norm. Because of this erroneous assumption, women sometimes ended up getting treatments and drugs that were inappropriate for them.

There are other reasons a sample may be unrepresentative. We might poll only people we feel comfortable approaching. Telephone pollsters might do their interviews at a certain time of day or day of the week when most people are at work. In addition, young people are more likely to use cell phones exclusively and, hence, not be listed in the phone directory.

4. The Sample Is Current and Up-to-Date.
A sample may be unrepresentative because it is outdated. It was long believed, on the basis of samples taken decades ago of the water in coastal bays in the United States, that the oceans were so vast that the ocean tides were capable of cleaning out any pollution that entered coastal bays.

Because the sampling data on the purity of coastal water weren't updated, the growing problem of pollution in our bays went unnoticed for many years. While samples from the past are useful for establishing trends, we should be wary about using outdated samples for making generalizations about the current population.

5. The Conclusion Is Supported by the Premise(s).
The conclusion should follow logically from the premises. It should not go beyond what is stated in the premises, as happens in the following example:

> Since men in general are physically stronger than women, women should not be allowed to serve in combat duty in the military.

The conclusion does not follow from the premise in this case, since physical strength may not be essential or even important to be effective in combat. Also, even if it is, some women are physically stronger than some men.

If it is used correctly, generalization is a powerful form of inductive logic. When you make a generalization, it is important that you begin with premises that are true. In addition, your sample should be sufficiently large, representative, and up-to-date.

HIGHLIGHTS

EVALUATING ARGUMENTS THAT ARE BASED ON GENERALIZATION

1. Check whether the premises are true.

2. Decide if the sample is large enough.

3. Decide if the sample is representative.

4. Decide if the sample is current and up-to-date.

5. Determine whether the conclusion is supported by the premise(s).

➤ *APPLICATION: Find an example in the text of each type of evaluation.*

STOP AND ASSESS YOURSELF

1. Evaluate the following poll questions. If the questions are biased, rewrite them.

*a. Do you support increasing airport security to prevent future terrorist attacks using airplanes?

 b. Are you an honest person?

 c. Do you think marriages between homosexuals should or should not be recognized by the law as valid, with the same rights as traditional marriages?

*d. Do you think English should be the official language of the United States?

 e. "Does it concern you or not that when people's homes are broken into and they own a gun, the intruder might take the gun away from the owner and shoot him or her?"[12]

 f. "Should state/local governments be able to pass laws banning handguns?"[13]

*g. Would you support any institution of higher learning that restricts your freedom to think as you wish by establishing zones that limit your freedom of speech?

 h. "With all the gang killings and domestic disputes ending with gun fire, do you think there should be legislation passed to hinder gun ownership?"

 i. Do you want homework on the weekends or the school week extended to include Saturday?

*j. Should we allow children of illegal immigrants to attend state colleges at in-state tuition rates, or should we instead refuse them admission to state colleges?

2. Working in small groups, develop a poll for studying one of the following questions. Discuss the method you will use to ensure that the sample you poll is representative and that the questions are unbiased.

 a. Your college administration is considering banning the use of alcohol on campus. However, the administration first wants to find out if the students will support this idea and how they might react to the ban.

 b. You want to find out how most of the students on your campus feel about allowing cohabitation in the dorms.

 c. The student affairs office at your college is interested in learning more about the short-term goals of students.

 d. The faculty council at your college is concerned about students' plagiarizing from the Internet. They want to learn about the extent of this problem on campus as well as students' attitudes toward the practice.

 e. You live in a college town and are considering running as a Republican for the U.S. Senate against the Democratic incumbent and want to know whether or not you can count on the support of college students living in your district.

3. Evaluate the following arguments:

*a. Every time a stranger comes into our yard, our dog starts barking. From this we can safely conclude that Rex will always bark at strangers.

 b. Barack Obama won 60 percent of the voters under age 30 in the 2012 presidential election. From this we can conclude that most of the students in our logic class probably voted for Obama.

 c. Melissa probably feels down because she wishes she'd brought her dog Rex with us. I read in an airline magazine that 67 percent of U.S. pet owners feel guilty about leaving their pets at home when they travel.

*d. I've noticed that the three Asian students in my calculus class all earn high grades. Asians are just better at math.

 e. We don't need to be concerned about college students having health care coverage because they are covered under their parents' health care insurance.[14]

 f. I don't see why I need a college education. The most successful thinkers in the world never went to college. Abraham Lincoln never graduated from college. And neither did Confucius or Jesus or Socrates or Mohammed—four of the greatest and most influential people ever to walk this Earth.

*g. It seems that whenever I drop a piece of toast, it falls buttered side down. I'd better eat in the kitchen because if I eat in the living room and drop my toast, it will most likely leave a grease mark from the butter on the carpet.

h. The issue of pedophile priests is all over the news. I'm going to pull my children out of St. Mary's School. It's likely that the priests who are their teachers are also molesting children.

i. College students want to see drinking allowed on campus. I took a poll of my fraternity brothers, and we all agreed that drinking should be allowed.

*j. "I hate myself. I'm so much fatter and uglier than other women."
"No, you're not. You look great. Why would you think such a thing?"
"All the women in the television show *Real World* are so thin and beautiful."

k. I don't see why you can't find a job like other college graduates. When I graduated in 1962, we had no trouble finding good jobs.

l. We took a poll in our class and 92 percent of the students supported exemptions for college students if we had a military draft. From this it is clear that young people overwhelmingly oppose the Universal National Service Act, which would only give exemptions to students who are attending high school.

*m. Medical errors aren't nearly as big a problem as some people think. In a national poll of more than 2,000 randomly selected physicians, more than 90 percent said that medical errors are not a serious problem in medicine.

n. According to the World Kennel Club, the average dog weighs about 40 pounds. But my Aunt Celia, who lives in a condo in downtown Toronto, says that the majority of dogs she sees while out on her daily walks are under 25 pounds. Therefore, we can safely conclude that dogs living in Canada tend to be smaller than dogs in the United States.

o. The last three times I asked women out on a date, they turned me down. I should just give up trying to meet someone. Probably any other women I ask out will reject me too.

4. Most of us have been approached on the street or on campus by pollsters toting clipboards and asking for our views about a particular topic or product. Discuss the problems with this methodology for getting a representative sample. Develop a polling methodology to remedy these problems.

5. Some people feel that election polling should be banned, since simply knowing which candidate is ahead in an election can sway undecided voters to vote for that candidate. Working in small groups, come up with a list of premises and a conclusion regarding this issue. Discuss your conclusion with the class.

6. Find out if your college participates in the annual Freshman Survey. If it does, obtain a copy of the report from your administration comparing your college's freshmen to the typical American freshman. Write a few paragraphs about the similarities and differences for discussion in class.

*Answers to selected exercises are found in the Solutions Manual at the end of the book.

ANALOGIES

An **analogy** is based on a comparison between two or more things or events. Analogies often contain words or phrases such as *like*, *as*, *similarly*, or *compared to*. For example, in her article at the end of Chapter 9, Judith Jarvis Thomson draws an analogy between a pregnant woman and a Good Samaritan when she argues that the relationship between a fetus and a woman is like that of a Good Samaritan to a person along the roadside in need of assistance. Using this analogy Thomson concludes in that being a Minimally Decent Samaritan requires us to help those in need if the cost to ourselves is minimal (e.g., phone the police), decency requires that a woman who is in her last months of pregnancy carry the pregnancy to term. However, we are not required to go out of our way to help those in need (e.g., carrying an unwanted pregnancy for nine months) if it would be at great cost to ourselves.

Uses of Analogies

Noticing similarities between things or events is one of the primary ways we learn from experience. A child burns his hand on a candle and afterward stays away from a campfire because of the similarity between the two. To use another example, many early buildings were vulnerable to damage by storms because they were too rigid. Then architects noticed that trees were resilient in strong winds because of their flexibility and adopted this approach in building wind-resistant structures. We've also learned more about how the heart works by comparing it to a mechanical pump.

Connections

How might consumers use arguments by analogy in deciding whether to buy a particular product? *See Chapter 10, p. 308.*

Analogies can exist on their own as descriptive devices, such as in "She's like a bull in a china shop" or "Finding my car in the commuter parking lot is like looking for a needle in a haystack." Analogies can also be used as a means of illustrating a point, as in the following passages:

> The death toll from smoking is comparable to that which would result from three jumbo jet crashes a day, occurring every single day of the year.[15]

> Just as a person puts on new garments after discarding the old ones, similarly, the living entity (or soul) obtains a new body after casting away the old bodies.

The first analogy is used to bring home the point that smoking is considerably more deadly than flying. The second analogy, from the Hindu sacred text the Bhagavad Gita (2:22), is used to illustrate the concept of death and transmigration of souls.

Metaphors, a type of descriptive analogy, are frequently found in literature. In this passage from *Macbeth* (act V), Shakespeare compares life to a stage play.

> Life's but a walking shadow, a poor player
>
> That struts and frets his hour upon the stage
>
> And then is heard no more.

Sometimes it is unclear if a passage is being used metaphorically or if it is meant to be taken literally. This is especially problematic in interpreting ancient scriptural texts, where translation and cultural differences in the use of language can leave us uncertain as to the author's intentions.

The argument from design states that God must exist because the world displays purposefulness.

Arguments Based on Analogies

In addition to standing on their own, analogies can be used as premises in arguments. An argument based on an analogy claims that if two things are similar in one or more ways, they are probably alike in other respects as well.

> *Premise:* X (which is familiar) has characteristics a, b, and c.
>
> *Premise:* Y (which is not as familiar) has characteristics a and b.
>
> *Conclusion:* Therefore, Y probably also has characteristic c.

To illustrate, say you (X) meet someone (Y) at a Sierra Club event on your campus. The person seems pleasant enough and also seems to be interested in you. However, before rushing into a relationship, you first collect more information about this person, including what the two of you might have in common. You already know that you are both interested in environmental issues (characteristic a). After chatting for a bit you learn that Y, like you, also enjoys hiking (characteristic b). After this brief encounter, you conclude, on the basis of your shared interest in the environment and hiking, that Y probably also shares your interest in healthy eating (characteristic c). When you get home, you phone Y and ask Y out for dinner at the local health-food restaurant.

Arguments based on analogies are common in many fields including law, religion, politics, and the military. For example, Shawnee leader Tecumseh (1768–1813) used an analogy to try to convince members of his and other tribes that they needed to unite into a Native American alliance if they were to keep their land from being taken over by the whites. An alliance of tribes, he argued, is like braided hair. A single strand of hair is easy to break. But several strands braided together are almost impossible to break.

One of the most famous arguments based on an analogy is the **argument from design**. This centuries-old argument is one of the most popular "proofs" of the existence of God. It has recently resurfaced in the debate about intelligent design versus evolution, which we'll be examining in depth at the end of Chapter 12.

analogy A comparison between two or more similar events or things.

metaphor A descriptive type of analogy, frequently found in literature.

argument from design An argument for the existence of God based on an analogy between man-made objects and natural objects.

The argument from design begins by noting the similarities between the universe and other natural objects (such as the human eye) and human-made objects (such as a watch). Both natural and human-made objects share the characteristics of both (1) organization and (2) purposefulness. The organization and the purposefulness of a watch are the direct result of an intelligent, rational creator—a watchmaker.

Similarly, the argument goes, the even greater organization and purposefulness of nature must be the product of an intelligent and rational creator. The analogy can be summarized as follows:

Premise: A watch has the following characteristics: (1) organization, (2) purposefulness, and (3) having an intelligent, rational creator.

Premise: The universe (or human eye) also demonstrates characteristics (1) organization and (2) purposefulness.

Conclusion: Therefore, by analogy, the universe (or human eye) also has (3) an intelligent, rational creator, and that creator is God.

Arguments using analogies are also found in science. Scientists come up with hypotheses about the effects of drugs on humans on the basis of the similarities between humans and these other animals by doing experiments on rats and other nonhuman animals. Astronomers make predictions about the characteristics of other planets in the galaxy on the basis of the degree of similarity between Earth and other planets.

In the area of law, courts often look at prior court rulings on similar cases before coming to a decision. We will be studying the doctrine of legal precedent in Chapter 13.

In *Alice's Adventures in Wonderland, the March Hare and the Dormouse use arguments by analogy to refute Alice's argument.*

Connections

How do scientists formulate and test hypotheses? *See Chapter 12, p. 367.*

How are analogies used in courts of laws? *See Chapter 13, p. 415.*

Some analogies use emotively loaded images in an attempt to rally the listener to a particular conclusion. In a speech made on June 22, 1941, the day after Germany invaded the Soviet Union, British Prime Minister Winston Churchill used analogies to convince the British people of the danger posed by Hitler and his army. In his speech, Churchill compared Hitler to a "monster of wickedness, insatiable in his lust for blood," and the Nazi army to a "war machine . . . in constant motion grinding up human lives" and German soldiers to a "swarm of crawling locusts."[16]

Analogies as Tools for Refuting Arguments

Analogies can be used to refute arguments containing weak or false analogies. One way to do this is to respond to the faulty analogy with a new one. A refutation using a new analogy can start out with a phrase such as "You might as well say that" or "That is like saying." The new analogy usually has the same form as the one being refuted, as in the following passage from *Alice's Adventures in Wonderland* by Lewis Carroll in which the March Hare and the Dormouse use analogies to refute Alice's argument that saying what she means is the same as meaning what she says:

"I do [say what I mean]," Alice hastily replied; "at least—at least I mean what I say—that's the same thing, you know."

"Not the same thing a bit!" said the Hatter. "Why, you might just as well say that 'I see what I eat' is the same thing as 'I eat what I see'!"

"You might just as well say," added the March Hare, "That 'I like what I get' is the same thing as 'I get what I like'!"

"You might just as well say," added the Dormouse, which seemed to be talking in its sleep, "That 'I breathe when I sleep' is the same thing as 'I sleep when I breathe'!"

The second way of refuting an argument using an analogy is by extending the analogy used in the argument. Philosopher David Hume (1711–1776), in his refutation of the argument by design, extended the analogy between a watchmaker and God.[17] He noted that the maker of a watch can be several people. Also, the watch might be inferior or defective. The watchmaker(s) might have been senile or up to no good at the time he or she created the watch. Extending the analogy even further,

---

The success of an argument using an analogy depends on the type and extent of relevant similarities and dissimilarities between the things being compared.

Hume argued that we cannot even assume if we come upon a watch that the watchmaker is still alive. Therefore, even if we accept the analogy between God and a watchmaker, we cannot use it to prove that a good and perfect God exists or ever existed.

Evaluating Inductive Arguments Based on Analogies

Some analogies are stronger than others. The success of an argument using an analogy depends on the type and extent of relevant similarities and dissimilarities between the things being compared. The following are steps for evaluating arguments based on analogies.

1. Identify What Is Being Compared. Write down a short summary of the comparison. For example, millions of people have seen the TV ad with eggs in a frying pan representing "Your Brain on Drugs." This ad, in which the brain is being compared with a raw egg and drugs are being compared with a hot frying pan, uses an argument based on analog. The ad, which first aired in 1987, has been one of the most influential of our time.

2. List the Similarities. Make a list of the specific ways in which the two things being compared are similar. Are the similarities strong enough to support the conclusion? As a rule, the greater the similarities, the stronger the analogy. For example, in the "Your Brain on Drugs" analogy, the hot frying pan is similar to drugs in that both can seriously alter and damage organic matter. Another similarity is that both the brain and a raw egg are round and squishy.

After making your list of similarities, cross out those that are not relevant. In this case, the shape and texture of the brain and egg are irrelevant to the argument that drugs can damage the brain. In a good analogy, the remaining relevant similarities should be strong enough to support the conclusion.

3. List the Dissimilarities. Once you have made a list of similarities, make a list of the dissimilarities. Are the dissimilarities or differences relevant in ways that affect the argument? The more the dissimilarities, the weaker the analogy usually is. Are drugs really like a hot frying pan? The use of many drugs, especially in small amounts, does not have such an immediate and catastrophic effect as that of a raw egg being broken into a hot frying pan. Indeed, some drugs such as marijuana may even be beneficial under certain circumstances (see "Critical-Thinking Issues: Perspectives on Legalizing Marijuana" at the end of this chapter).

Some dissimilarities may not be relevant to the argument. As we noted earlier, it is through analogical reasoning that we conclude that, like us, other people feel and are conscious. Since computers or androids are dissimilar from us in far more ways than are other humans, we have more difficulty applying this type of reasoning to beings with artificial intelligence (AI). However, claims that beings with AI can never be conscious or have feelings like humans because they are silicon-based, whereas we are carbon-based, or because they are created and programmed by humans, whereas we are born, are based on irrelevant differences. The material a being is made out of is, as far as we know, not related to the ability to be conscious or feel. Nor is being created by humans relevant, since humans are also created by other humans out of two cells and programmed by their DNA and environment. Of course, this doesn't mean that there are not other dissimilarities between humans and beings with AI that may be relevant.

The claim that beings with AI are not conscious and lack feeling because they are not organic is based on an irrelevant dissimilarity.

4. Compare the Lists of Similarities and Differences. Are the similarities strong enough to support the conclusion? Are the dissimilarities relevant in important ways? Hume refuted the argument from design by pointing out the dissimilarities in the analogy. For example, we cannot conclude from this analogy that the watchmaker, and hence God, still exist. Although a natural object such as an eye and a watch are both organized and purposeful, these similarities are not sufficient to support the conclusion that God created the universe, because the differences between God and a watchmaker are so striking.

5. Examine Possible Counteranalogies. Are the counteranalogies stronger? In "A Defense of Abortion" (see excerpt at the end of Chapter 9), Judith Jarvis Thomson uses the analogy of a Good Samaritan (the pregnant woman) who comes across a person in distress lying along the road (the fetus). Thomson concludes that we are not morally required to assist this person if it would be at a great cost to us. One of the criticisms of her analogy is that while the person beside the road is a total stranger, the fetus is related to us. Using the counteranalogy of coming across a child or other relative, we would be expected, from a moral point of view, to stop and assist our relative even at considerable risk to ourselves.[18]

6. Determine If the Analogy Supports the Conclusion. After comparing the relevant similarities and dissimilarities and looking for possible counterarguments, you are now in position to decide if this is a good argument. Remember, an argument based on analogy does not provide certain proof. It merely provides a stronger or weaker argument.

Analogies can be effective tools in an argument by clarifying the key points. On the other hand, analogies can be deceptively persuasive, since they appeal to our sense of imagination. Because of the power analogies have to shape our worldview, it is important that we learn how to recognize and evaluate arguments containing analogies.

HIGHLIGHTS

EVALUATING ARGUMENTS BASED ON AN ANALOGY

1. **Identify** what is being compared.
2. List the **similarities.**
3. List the **dissimilarities.**
4. **Compare** the lists of similarities and differences.
5. Examine possible **counteranalogies.**
6. **Determine** if the analogy supports the conclusion.

➤ *APPLICATION: Identify in the text an example of each of these steps in evaluating an argument based on analogy.*

STOP AND ASSESS YOURSELF

I. For each of the following, create an analogy, by adding a phrase after the term "is like":

*a. College is like . . .

b. Studying for an exam is like . . .

c. Looking for a job is like . . .

d. Marriage is like . . .

e. Parenthood is like . . .

f. Having thousands of dollars of student loans is like . . .

*g. Using the Internet is like . . .

h. Doing a class presentation is like . . .

i. Finding a good roommate is like . . .

*j. Life is like . . .

k. A first date is like . . .

l. Faith is like . . .

Share your analogies with the class. To what extent does the use of an analogy make it easier for you to express what you think or how you feel?

2. Looking back through previous chapters in the textbook, identify analogies that have been used. Discuss the purpose of each analogy.

3. Evaluate the following arguments that are based on analogies:

a. I don't see what's wrong with buying essays for a class from the Internet. After all, the president of the United States pays someone to write his speeches for him, and no one has a problem with that.

b. We put our beloved pets to sleep when they are very sick and in too much pain to enjoy life. Therefore, we should allow humans who are very sick and in too much pain to enjoy life to die mercifully.

c. A government is like a parent. Just as a child should obey their parents, so too should we obey our government.

*d. Marijuana should be legalized. After all, alcohol is also an addictive drug that is used to enhance mood and it is legal.

e. Hate speech on college campuses should be banned. Hate speech is like yelling "fire" in a crowded theater. It is illegal to yell "fire" in a crowded theater because doing so could cause great harm to people. The same is true of hate speech.

f. Liquid water has been found on Europa, one of Jupiter's moons. Life began in water here on Earth. Therefore, there are probably primitive life forms living on Europa.

*g. "You didn't learn to dance on your first try. Quitting smoking takes practice too."[19]

h. We quarantine people with deadly contagious diseases such as tuberculosis. Therefore, we should quarantine people with AIDS, which is also a deadly, contagious disease.

i. "What is taught on this campus should depend on what the students are interested in. After all, consuming knowledge is like consuming anything else in our society. The teacher is the seller, the student is the buyer. Buyers determine what they want to buy, so students should determine what they want to learn."[20]

*j. Some people reject the comparison of AI with human thinking on the grounds that AI is merely a simulation of thinking. Unlike human thinking, the argument based on analogy goes, so-called intelligent machines only appear to be thinking, much like a child pretending to sip tea at a tea party with her dolls. There is no real tea in the toy cup.

k. I don't tell my mechanic how to fix my automobile. Instead, I trust his expertise. In the same manner, I should not tell my physician how to fix my body.

l. George Bush once said that a vice president should support the president's policy, whether or not he likes it, arguing that "You don't tackle your own quarterback."

*m. "Racists violate the principle of equality by giving greater weight to the interests of members of their own race when there is a clash between their interests and the interests of those of another race. Sexists violate the principle of equality by favoring the interests of their own sex. Similarly, speciesists allow the interests of their own species to override the greater interests of members of other species. The pattern is identical in each case."[21]

4. An analogy is sometimes drawn between the legalization of same-sex marriage and the legalization of mixed-race marriage, which states were barred from forbidding only after a 1967 U.S. Supreme Court ruling. Discuss the analogy.

5. Select one of the following analogies. Using the steps listed on pages 219–220, write a two- to three-page essay evaluating the analogy.

a. In his now classic article "Active and Passive Euthanasia,"[22] James Rachels uses the following well-known analogy to refute the claim that active euthanasia is morally worse than passive euthanasia because it is morally worse to kill someone than to let someone die.[†] Rachels considers the following two cases:

In the first, Smith stands to gain a large inheritance if anything should happen to his six-year-old cousin. One evening while the child is taking his bath, Smith sneaks into the bathroom and drowns the child, and then arranges things so that it will look like an accident.

In the second, Jones also stands to gain if anything should happen to his six-year-old cousin. Like Smith, Jones sneaks in planning to drown the child in his bath. However, just as he enters the bathroom Jones sees the child slip and hit his head, and fall face down in the water. Jones is delighted; he stands by, ready to push the child's head back under if it is necessary, but it is not necessary. With only a little thrashing about, the child drowns all by himself, "accidentally," as Jones watches and does nothing.

Now Smith killed the child, whereas Jones merely "let" the child die. That is the only difference between them. Did either man behave better, from a moral point of view? . . . The preceding consideration suggests that there is really no difference between the two [active euthanasia and passive euthanasia]. So, whereas doctors may have to discriminate between active and passive euthanasia to satisfy the law, they should not do more than that.

b. Former president Lyndon B. Johnson was a tireless advocate of civil rights for African Americans. The following are excerpts from his famous "To Fulfill These Rights" commencement address delivered at Howard University on June 4, 1965:

. . . In far too many ways American Negroes have been another nation: deprived of Freedom, crippled by hatred, the doors of opportunity closed to hope.

In our time change has come to this Nation, too. . . . That beginning is freedom; and the barriers to that freedom are tumbling down. Freedom is the right to share, share fully and equally, in American society—to vote, to hold a job, to enter a public place, to go to school. . . .

But freedom is not enough. You do not wipe away the scars of centuries by saying: Now you are free to go where you want, and do as you desire, and choose the leaders you please.

You do not take a person who, for years, has been hobbled by chains and liberate him, bring him up to the starting line of a race and then say, "You are free to compete with all the others," and still justly believe that you have been completely fair.

Thus, it is not enough just to open the gates of opportunity. All our citizens must have the ability to walk through those gates.

c. In his article "Lifeboat Ethics: The Case Against Helping the Poor," ecologist Garrett Hardin uses the analogy of rich nations as lifeboats in debating whether the rich nations of the world have an obligation to help the poor nations:[23]

If we divide the world crudely into rich nations and poor nations, two thirds of them are desperately poor, and only one third comparatively rich, with the United States the wealthiest of all. Metaphorically each rich nation can be seen as a lifeboat full of comparatively rich people. In the ocean outside each lifeboat swim the poor of the world, who would like to get in, or at least to share some of the wealth. What should the lifeboat passengers do?

6. Think of an analogy that has shaped your thinking and view of the world. Use a specific example to show how this analogy has influenced your decisions. Using the criteria on page 219, evaluate the analogy.

*Answers to selected exercises are found in the Solutions Manual at the end of the book.

†*Active euthanasia* is defined as taking direct action, such as a lethal injection, to kill a person who has a terminal or incurable disease or condition. *Passive euthanasia* is defined as allowing a person who has a terminal or incurable disease or condition to die by withholding life support or medical treatment that would prolong life.

CAUSAL ARGUMENTS

A **cause** is an event that brings about a change or effect. In **causal arguments** it is claimed that something is (or is not) the cause of something else, as the following argument illustrates:

Premise 1 (cause): [You're eating too many French fries] and

Premise 2 (cause): [you don't exercise].

Conclusion (effect): [You're going to gain weight if you don't change your ways].

In this argument, the person is making the argument that eating too many French fries and not exercising will cause weight gain. Like other inductive arguments, the conclusion of a causal argument is never 100 percent certain. You may not gain weight if you eat lots of French fries and don't exercise, because you have a metabolic disorder or a tapeworm.

Causal Relationships

The term *cause* in the commonly used premise indicator *because* is a sign of the importance of cause-and-effect relationships in arguments. Many of our everyday decisions rely on this type of inductive reasoning. If we are to have any level of control over our lives, we need to have some understanding of cause-and-effect relations.

Some causal relationships are well established, such as that between temperature and water freezing, and that between malaria and a protozoan parasite transmitted by mosquitoes. In many instances, however, establishing a causal relationship is not as easy as it may first seem. We might confuse cause and effect when the events are ongoing or recurrent and it's not clear which occurred first. Do we have a headache because we're stressed, or are we stressed because we have a headache? Does playing violent video games cause people to commit violent acts, or are people who are more violent already more likely to play these types of games? For example, was Adam Lanza's obsession with playing violent video games a causal factor in the Sandy Hook school shootings in 2012? See Analyzing Images, page 224.

> **cause** An event that brings about a change or effect.
>
> **causal argument** An argument that claims something is (or is not) the cause of something else.

When we confuse the cause with the effect or assume without sufficient evidence that one thing is the cause of another, we commit the *fallacy of questionable cause*. We are susceptible to this fallacy because, as we noted in Chapter 5, humans have a tendency to see causality and patterns in random events where no cause-and-effect relationship actually exists. In addition, we are inclined to believe that we are in control of or the cause of events that actually are outside our control. Because of these inborn cognitive errors, we need to be careful before concluding that there is a causal relationship between two events.

Most causal relationships are not as straightforward as that between temperature and water freezing. Instead, several causal factors might be involved. Some events or conditions are causal only if other conditions are present. Other conditions may contribute to a certain result—for example, getting good grades in high school may help you to get into an Ivy League college—but they don't guarantee it.

Serial killer Ted Bundy's murder defense was an example of questionable cause. Like many other sexual predators, once caught, he blamed pornography for his crimes. However, scientists are still uncertain about whether pornography makes people sexually violent or whether people who already have a tendency toward sexual violence are more likely to use pornography.

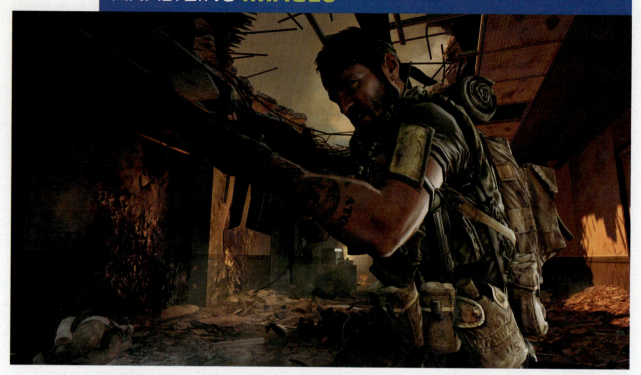

Violent Video Games and the Sandy Hook School Massacre

Do violent video games increase the risk of aggressive behavior? In December 2012, Adam Lanza, aged 20, shot and killed 26 people, including 20 children, at the Sandy Hook Elementary School in Newtown, Connecticut. Earlier that same year, James Holmes opened fire in an Aurora, Colorado, movie theater, killing 12 and injuring 58. And in 1999 two high school students killed 13 and injured 21 at Columbine High School in Colorado before turning their guns on themselves. The four young men involved in these massacres had at least one thing in common: they all played violent video games. The above photo is from Black Ops, the graphically violent fantasy video game that Adam Lanza often played, sometimes for hours a day.

Studies have found a positive correlation between violent video games and aggressive behavior in adolescents.* Wayne LaPierre, CEO of the National Rifle Association (NRA), also blames "vicious video games" for much of the gun violence in this country. See the reading by LaPierre at the end of Chapter 5. However, the question remains: Are people who already have violent tendencies more likely to play violent video games, or do violent video games actually cause or contribute to violent behavior?

DISCUSSION QUESTIONS

1. *Is there a causal connection between violent video games and violent behavior? Research and critically evaluate studies on the subject. Discuss also how you might design a study to determine if there is a causal relationship or simply a correlation between violent video games and violent behavior.* **

2. *If it can be shown that there is a causal connection between playing violent video games and engaging in violent behavior, would this justify banning these games or restricting their sale? Present an argument supporting your position.*

3. *What do you feel when you look at the above image from Black Ops? Discuss how developing your critical thinking skills might help you to override or put into perspective any feelings of aggression that might arise from playing these games.*

* Teena Willoughby, Paul Adachi, and Marie Good, "A Longitudinal Study of the Association Between Violent Video Game Play and Aggression Among Adolescents," *Developmental Psychology*, Vol. 48(4), July 2012, pp. 1044–1057.

** For more on designing and evaluating studies see Chapter 12, pages 367–375.

Correlations

When two events occur together regularly at rates higher than probability, the relationship is called a **correlation**. If the incidence of one event increases when the second one increases, there is a **positive correlation**. There is, for example, a positive correlation between the number of cigarettes smoked and the risk of lung cancer. A **negative correlation** exists when the occurrence of one event increases as the other decreases. There is a negative correlation between smoking and age in adults over the age of 18. The older a person is, the less likely he or she is to smoke.

Although a correlation can indicate a causal relationship, as in the case of smoking and lung cancer, it does not always do so. In the following correlation, it is questionable whether there is a causal relationship as well:

> The greater the distance you sit from the front of the classroom, the lower your final grade is likely to be.

In this argument there is a negative correlation between a student's final grade and his or her distance from the front of the class. However, we cannot assume from the correlation that sitting in the back of the room *causes* a student to get lower grades. The cause and effect could be the opposite. Perhaps poorer students prefer to sit in the back of the room. Or perhaps the teacher

is more likely to notice the contribution of students who sit in front of the classroom and, hence, give them higher grades.

Establishing Causal Relationships

Correlations are often the starting point in determining whether causal relationships exist. To make sure that there aren't other causal factors, or confounding variables, responsible for the correlation, scientists use **controlled experiments**.

In a controlled experiment, the sample under study is randomly divided into an experimental group and a control group. The experimental group receives the treatment whose causal effect is under investigation; the control group does not. For example, in a pharmaceutical experiment, the experimental group may receive a pill containing the drug under study, while the control group receives a harmless placebo, such as a sugar pill, that does not contain the drug. Neither group knows whether the pill they are taking contains the drug.

> **correlation** When two events occur together regularly at rates higher than probability.
>
> **positive correlation** The incidence of one event increases when the second one increases.
>
> **negative correlation** When the occurrence of one event increases as the other decreases.
>
> **controlled experiment** An experiment in which the sample is randomly divided into an experimental and a control group.

The Correlation between Cigarettes Smoked and Lung Cancer

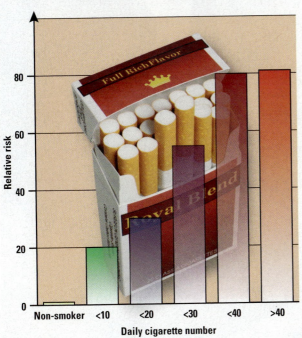

Relative risk / Daily cigarette number

Non-smoker <10 <20 <30 <40 >40

Causal Arguments in Public Policy and Everyday Decision Making

Creating effective public policies and making satisfactory life decisions both depend on being able to correctly infer causal relationships. For example, why are African American students more likely than European American students to drop out of college? Why are college freshmen today more likely than were freshman in 1990 to report that they are frequently bored in class? Why did my last two relationships fail? Until we understand the causes of these events, we can't come up with effective solutions.

When making decisions on the basis of causal arguments, your information should be up-to-date. What was true at one time may no longer be the case. Consider the following argument:

> You should make your children sit at least six feet from the television. Sitting too close can damage their eyes.

Televisions first went on sale in the United States in the 1930s. Before the 1950s, televisions emitted levels

It's Quitting Time: Nicotine 101—College Students and Smoking

About 20 percent of college students smoke. College freshmen are more likely to smoke than are college juniors and seniors. Although tobacco companies have promised not to target their ads toward children, the majority of cigarette ads are still designed to appeal to people under the age of 24, since they are less likely to have the critical-thinking skills to resist taking up smoking. Indeed, 90 percent of adults who smoke began as teenagers. Although college students smoke more than the general public, the smoking rate is almost double among young adults who do not attend college.* These differences in rate of smoking based on age and educational level are due in part to the ability to engage in critical thinking regarding the effects of smoking. People who are inexperienced at critical reasoning are more likely to oversimplify or overlook the complexities of causal relationships. For example, college students who smoke tend to focus on the immediate causal effects—such as smoking helps them to relax, look sophisticated, or fit in with others—and ignore the long-term effects of smoking, such as cancer, heart disease, and a shortened life. In addition to focusing on causal factors associated with immediate gratification, poor critical thinkers are also more likely to think they have more control than they actually do over factors such as developing cancer or other smoking-related health problems.

*See American Legacy Foundation, "Tracking Tobacco Industry Marketing to College Youth," Project 2030 Internship Final Report, 2002.

DISCUSSION QUESTIONS

1. What thoughts or feelings do you have when you look at the students in the photograph? Discuss the extent to which their smoking influences or biases your perception of them.

2. Critically examine some cigarette ads. What causal relationships are the ads trying to establish in the reader's mind? Discuss how effective the ads are in achieving this goal and strategies you might use to make yourself less suseptible to the fallacies and incorrect reasoning used in these and similar ads.

of radiation that in fact could heighten the risk of eye problems in some people after repeated and extended exposure from sitting too close to the screen. However, this causal relationship no longer holds. Modern televisions are built with shielding that controls the emission of radiation.

Most decisions are not clear-cut. In making a decision where there are both beneficial and harmful effects of a particular action or policy, you need to weigh the harms against the benefits. In public policy, this process is known as **cost–benefit analysis**. Arguments about the legalization of marijuana, such as those at the end of this chapter, often revolve around weighing the benefits of legalizing marijuana against the costs or harms of doing so. In your personal life, this type of analysis is useful in situations such as choosing a career path—do you want to spend 8 years in college and incur heavy debts and have to put off having a family, or do you want a less demanding major and career so that you can put more energy into your personal and family life?

Misperception of causes can also lead to misplacing blame or to the perpetuation of harmful behavior and attitudes. Forty-three percent of college women who date report having experienced violent and abusive dating behavior.[24] In the great majority of cases, it involves a man assaulting a woman. What is the cause of dating violence? Most college students believe that it lies in some characteristic of the abuser, such as poor anger control or a history of child abuse. The abuser more often sees the victim's behavior as the major contributing cause of the assault—"She made me angry," "She asked for it," "She was dressed provocatively," or "I did it because she was flirting with another guy."

Those who accept this simplistic assessment of the causes of violence against women are ignoring an important underlying cause of the violence—the cultural power imbalance between men and women. Unfortunately, many of the programs designed to prevent dating violence on campuses steer clear of addressing the inequities in power and instead use sex-neutral materials. These programs have had little effect on the incidence of dating violence. Until power inequalities are addressed as a causal factor in violent heterosexual relationships, these types of prevention programs will remain largely ineffective.

Evaluating Causal Arguments

Knowing how to evaluate causal arguments will help you to make better decisions in your personal life as well as your life as a citizen. The following are four criteria for evaluating a causal argument:

1. The Evidence for a Causal Relationship Should Be Strong.
Do your research before jumping to the conclusion. The more evidence there is for a causal

relationship, the stronger the argument. Be leery of anecdotal evidence. Controlled experiments are one of the best methods for determining if a particular relationship is causal rather than simply a correlation.

> **cost–benefit analysis** A process where the harmful effects of an action are weighed against the benefits.

2. The Argument Should Not Contain Fallacies.
Several types of informal fallacies crop up in causal arguments, the most common of which is the *fallacy of questionable cause,* which occurs when we assume that because one event preceded a second event it was the cause of the second event.

Another common fallacy is the *fallacy of ignorance,* in which we assume that something is the cause simply because no one has proved that it is not or that something is not the cause because no one has proved that it is. A third fallacy that might appear in a causal argument is the *slippery-slope fallacy,* in which we overestimate the influence of a particular cause to bring about a particular effect. For a review of these fallacies, see Chapter 5.

Connections

How are controlled experiments used to test scientific hypotheses? *See Chapter 10, p. 305 and Chapter 12, p. 378.*

> **HIGHLIGHTS**
>
> **EVALUATING CAUSAL ARGUMENTS**
>
> 1. Determine whether the evidence for a causal relationship is strong.
> 2. Make sure that the argument does not contain a fallacy.
> 3. Decide whether the data are current and up-to-date.
> 4. Make sure that the conclusion does not go beyond the premises.
>
> ►APPLICATION: Find examples in the text of each of the steps in evaluating a causal argument.

3. The Data Should Be Current and Up-to-Date.
Before making a decision or accepting an argument that is based on a causal relationship, you should make sure that your information, such as that regarding preferences of college students, is current and up-to-date. A conclusion may be incorrect because a particular causal relationship that was once true may no longer hold.

4. The Conclusion Should Not Go Beyond the Premises. A conclusion goes beyond the premises when we mistake a correlation for a causal relationship or when we attribute more causal power to an event than it actually has over the effect, such as gambler's error. Unless the cause stated in the premise is a sufficient cause, the term *probably* or a similar qualifying term should be used in the conclusion.

Being able to recognize and analyze causal relationships is an important skill in critical thinking. Like other inductive arguments, casual arguments can never be 100 percent certain. Being able to determine the degree to which a particular cause brings about an effect can help us to evaluate causal arguments and make better decisions in our lives.

EXERCISE 7-4

STOP AND ASSESS YOURSELF

1. Discuss whether each of the following relationships is a causal relationship or merely a correlation. Discuss how you would go about verifying which type it is.

*a. There has been an increase in the number of twins being born and a later age of marriage in the past decade.

b. During the past decade there has been a decrease in the size of the Greenland ice cap and an increase in the number of twins being born.

c. People who are members of a religious organization tend to be happier.

*d. Jason drank nine bottles of beer at the party and is having trouble walking straight.

e. In March 2013, after mandatory cuts to the federal budget went into effect, the stock market experienced a string of record closing highs.

f. People living in the southern United States and in southern Europe are significantly more likely to believe in God than people from New England, Canada, and Northern Europe. There seems to be a link between outdoor temperature and faith in God.

*g. Jackie and Jamal ate dinner at a sushi bar this evening, and now they are both feeling nauseated.

h. Almost all of the animals that could flee to higher ground did so shortly before the tsunami struck Indonesia in 2004.

2. Evaluate the following causal arguments:

*a. The majority of people who die are in bed at the time of their death. Clearly, being in bed increases a person's risk of dying. Therefore, if I sleep on the sofa, I have a better chance of living longer.

b. The number of people coming into the hospital emergency room for chest pains increased as the stock market dropped in 2008 and 2009. The drop in the stock market is probably responsible, at least in part, for this increase.

c. There are few women faculty members in the sciences at the Ivy League universities. Women are more likely than men to be discriminated against in hiring. Therefore, discrimination is probably one of the causes of the low number of women faculty members in the sciences at these universities.

*d. "Did you know that young people who use marijuana weekly have double the risk of depression later in life? And that teens aged 12 to 17 who smoke marijuana weekly are three times more likely than non-users to have suicidal thoughts? And if that's not bad enough, marijuana use in some teens has been linked to increased risk for schizophrenia in later years."[25] Therefore, don't let your teens smoke marijuana.

e. Hours after a devastating earthquake struck the coast of South America a tsunami warning was issued for Hawaii.

f. I can't stay home today even though I do have a bad cold because nothing would get done at work and we'll get hopelessly behind in our project. The boss can't get along without me.

*g. I don't have any problem with legalizing marijuana. We all smoked marijuana when I was in college back in the early 1970s and none of us suffered academically because of it.

h. That's ridiculous. It couldn't have been an alien abduction that caused those marks on your body, because no one has proved that aliens even exist.

  i. Fluorine is effective in the prevention of dental decay.

 *j. My brother Mac and his wife Angela are on a three-week Caribbean cruise. I just got a letter from him and he tells me that he and his wife have been enjoying a great sex life ever since he starting putting Matico pepper—something that he bought in Panama—on his food. Whatever is in that stuff must be a powerful aphrodisiac.

  k. Playing sports has a negative effect on intelligence. Studies show that college athletes have a significantly lower graduation rate than non-athletes.

  l. I read my horoscope every morning. You should too. My horoscope said that I would meet an interesting stranger today and, sure enough, I *did*!

 *m. Marijuana is a "gateway" drug. Therefore, you shouldn't smoke marijuana. If you do, you'll no doubt move on to use cocaine. According to studies, children and teens who have used marijuana are 85 times more likely to use cocaine than those who have never used marijuana.

  n. If we allow hikers in the White Mountains to throw their perishable garbage—such as apple cores or orange peels—into the woods, the wildlife will soon become dependent on humans and unable to survive on their own.

4. Advertisers may manipulate people into placing more weight on a contributory cause than it deserves. For example, in before-and-after ads of people who have had cosmetic surgery or who have used a particular cosmetic or exercise product, the people in the before pictures are often glum, wear no makeup, and have unkempt hair, whereas the people in the after pictures are smiling, are wearing makeup, and have neatly groomed hair. Look in magazines and on the Internet for ads that try to manipulate the reader by placing unwarranted emphasis on particular causal factors.

5. Write a letter of application for your ideal job. In the letter include at least one argument using generalization, one argument using an analogy, and one causal argument. Underline and label each of the arguments.

*Answers to selected exercises are found in the Solutions Manual at the end of the book.

THiNK AGAIN

1. How does an inductive argument differ from a deductive argument?
    - Deductive arguments claim that their conclusion necessarily follows from the premises, whereas inductive arguments only claim that their conclusion probably follows from the premises. Deductive arguments can be true or false, whereas inductive arguments are stronger or weaker.

2. How do arguments based on generalizations help us to learn more about a particular population?
    - Arguments based on generalizations can help us learn more about the characteristics of a particular population by studying a representative sample of the population. This can be done through the use of surveys, polls, or scientific experiments.

3. What are some of the uses of arguments by analogy?
    - By drawing a comparison between two or more things or events, arguments by analogy help us to learn more about the world, building on the knowledge that we already have of familiar objects or events. Analogical reasoning is also important in deciding court cases on the basis of rulings in previous similar cases.

4. What role does causal reasoning play in our lives?
    - Knowledge of cause-and-effect relationships is necessary for us to effectively function in the world. Causal arguments help us to determine if the cause and effect are logically related rather than based on questionable assumptions or superstition. Causal reasoning plays a key role in much of scientific observation and experimentation.

Perspectives on Legalizing Marijuana

Marijuana is the most frequently used illegal drug in the United States. Support for legalization of marijuana, at 67 percent, is highest among young people ages 18 to 29 compared to about 50 percent of the general population.[26] According to the Bureau of Justice Statistics, about 30 percent of college students in the United States use marijuana.[27]

Marijuana is prepared from the dried leaves and flowers of *Cannabis sativa* and is usually smoked for its mind-altering effects, which include mild euphoria, relaxation, and increased awareness of sensation. But marijuana use can also cause disruption of memory, paranoia and anxiety, hallucinations, a reduction in motor skills and cognitive performance, irritability, and addiction. Medically, marijuana has been used as an appetite stimulant and pain reliever for AIDS and some types of cancer. As with tobacco, the use of illicit drugs such as marijuana typically begins between the ages of 14 and 17 and is the highest among young people between the ages of 18 and 25.[28]

A U.S. policy on marijuana began with the Marijuana Tax Act of 1937 and has become more restrictive over time. During the late 1960s and 1970s almost all states reduced the penalties for marijuana possession. In 1996, California voters passed Proposition 215, the Compassionate Use Act, which legalized marijuana for medicinal use, with a prescription from a physician, for patients who have glaucoma or pain from cancer, MS, or other serious illnesses. Several other states have since legalized or decriminalized medical marijuana, including Alaska, Arizona, Colorado, Hawaii, Maine, Montana, Nevada, New Mexico, Oregon, Vermont, and Washington. However, in June 2005 the U.S. Supreme Court in *Gonzales v. Raich* ruled that state laws that permit marijuana for medicinal or recreational use are in violation of the federal Controlled Substances Act.

Canada legalized marijuana for medicinal purposes in 2001, and two years later it decriminalized marijuana possession, so that small-time users wouldn't end up going to jail or having a criminal record. This move has created tension between Canada and the United States because in much of the U.S., possession of even a small amount of marijuana is punishable by up to 1 year in jail. There is currently a move underway in the United States to decriminalize marijuana and subject it to regulation and taxation. In March 2013, voters in Washington and Colorado approved referendums that decriminalized marijuana for personal use. Legislation to decriminalize marijuana is pending is several other states.

In the following readings, Karen Tandy argues in favor of the current laws restricting marijuana use, while Joe Messerli argues for the legalization of marijuana.

Keep Marijuana Illegal*

KAREN P. TANDY

Karen Tandy was the head of the U.S. Drug Enforcement Administration from 2003 to 2007. Tandy is a graduate of Texas Tech University and Texas Tech University School of Law. In her article, Tandy argues that marijuana should remain illegal.

The belief that marijuana use is not only an individual's free choice but also is good medicine, a cure-all for a variety of ills, has filtered down to many of our teens, if what I'm hearing during my visits with middle school and high school students across the country is true. . . . Here is what students have told me about marijuana: "It's natural because it grows in the ground, so it must be good for you." "It must be medicine, because it makes me feel better." . . .

The natural extension of this myth is that, if marijuana is medicine, it must also be safe for recreational use. . . .

Myth: Marijuana Is Medicine

Reality: Smoked Marijuana Is Not Medicine

The scientific and medical communities have determined that smoked marijuana is a health danger, not a cure. There is no medical evidence that smoking marijuana helps patients. In fact, the Food and Drug Administration (FDA) has approved no medications that are smoked, primarily because smoking is a poor way to deliver medicine. Morphine, for example has proven to be a medically valuable drug, but the FDA does not endorse smoking opium or heroin. . . .

. . . In truth, the IOM (Institute of Medicine) explicitly found that marijuana is not medicine and expressed concern about patients' smoking it because smoking is a harmful drug-delivery system. The IOM further found that there was no scientific evidence that smoked marijuana had medical value, even for the chronically ill, and concluded that "there is little future in smoked marijuana as a medically approved medication." In fact, the researchers who conducted the study could find no medical value to marijuana for virtually any ailment they examined, including the treatment of wasting syndrome in AIDS patients, movement disorders such as Parkinson's disease and epilepsy, or glaucoma. . . .

Myth: Legalization of Marijuana in Other Countries Has Been a Success

Reality: Liberalization of Drug Laws in Other Countries Has Often Resulted in Higher Use of Dangerous Drugs

Over the past decade, drug policy in some foreign countries, particularly those in Europe, has gone through some dramatic changes toward greater liberalization with failed results. Consider the experience of the Netherlands, where the government reconsidered its legalization measures in light of that country's experience. After marijuana use became legal, consumption nearly tripled among 18- to 20-year-olds. As awareness of the harm of marijuana grew, the number of cannabis coffeehouses in the Netherlands decreased 36 percent in six years. Almost all Dutch towns have a cannabis policy, and 73 percent of them have a no-tolerance policy toward the coffeehouses.

In 1987 Swiss officials permitted drug use and sales in a Zurich park, which was soon dubbed Needle Park, and Switzerland became a magnet for drug users the world over. Within five years, the number of regular drug users at the park had reportedly swelled from a few hundred to 20,000. The area around the park became crime-ridden to the point that the park had to be shut down and the experiment terminated.

Myth: Marijuana Is Harmless

Reality: Marijuana Is Dangerous to the User

Use of marijuana has adverse health, safety, social, academic, economic, and behavioral consequences; and children are the most vulnerable to its damaging effects. Marijuana is the most widely used illicit drug in America and is readily available to kids. Compounding the problem is that the marijuana of today is not the marijuana of the baby boomers 30 years ago. Average THC levels rose from less than 1 percent in the mid-1970s to more than 8 percent in 2004. . . .

Marijuana use can lead to dependence and abuse. Marijuana was the second most common illicit drug responsible for drug treatment admissions in 2002, outdistancing crack cocaine, the next most prevalent cause.

*From "Marijuana: The Myths Are Killing Us," *Police Chief Magazine*, March 2005.

Shocking to many is that more teens are in treatment each year for marijuana dependence than for alcohol and all other illegal drugs combined. . . .

Marijuana is a gateway drug. In drug law enforcement, rarely do we meet heroin or cocaine addicts who did not start their drug use with marijuana. . . . The younger a person is when he or she first uses marijuana, the more likely that person is to use cocaine and heroin and become drug dependent as an adult. One study found that 62 percent of the adults who first tried marijuana before they were 15 were likely to go on to use cocaine. In contrast, only 1 percent or less of adults who never tried marijuana used heroin or cocaine.

Smoking marijuana can cause significant health problems. Marijuana contains more than 400 chemicals, of which 60 are cannabinoids. Smoking a marijuana cigarette deposits about three to five times more tar into the lungs than one filtered tobacco cigarette. Consequently, regular marijuana smokers suffer from many of the same health problems as tobacco smokers, such as chronic coughing and wheezing, chest colds, and chronic bronchitis. In fact, studies show that smoking three to four joints per day causes at least as much harm to the respiratory system as smoking a full pack of cigarettes every day. Marijuana smoke also contains 50 to 70 percent more carcinogenic hydrocarbons than tobacco smoke and produces high levels of an enzyme that converts certain hydrocarbons into malignant cells.

In addition, smoking marijuana can lead to increased anxiety, panic attacks, depression, social withdrawal, and other mental health problems, particularly for teens. Research shows that kids aged 12 to 17 who smoke marijuana weekly are three times more likely than nonusers to have suicidal thoughts. Marijuana use also can cause cognitive impairment, including such short-term effects as distorted perception, memory loss, and trouble with thinking and problem solving. Students with an average grade of D or below were found to be more than four times as likely to have used marijuana in the past year as youths who reported an average grade of A. For young people, whose brains are still developing, these effects are particularly problematic and jeopardize their ability to achieve their full potential.

Myth: Smoking Marijuana Harms Only the Smokers

Reality: Marijuana Use Harms Nonusers

We need to put to rest the thought that there is such a thing as a lone drug user, a person whose habits affect only himself or herself. Drug use, including marijuana use, is not a victimless crime. Some in your communities may resist involvement because they think someone else's drug use is not hurting them. But this kind of not-my-problem thinking is tragically misguided. . . .

Take, for instance, the disastrous effects of marijuana smoking on driving. As the National Highway Traffic Safety Administration (NHTSA) noted, "Epidemiology data from . . . traffic arrests and fatalities indicate that after alcohol, marijuana is the most frequently detected psycho-active substance among driving populations." Marijuana causes drivers to experience decreased car handling performance, decreased reaction times, distorted time and distance estimation, sleepiness, impaired motor skills, and lack of concentration.

The extent of the problem of marijuana-impaired driving is startling. One in six (or 600,000) high school students drive under the influence of marijuana, almost as many as drive under the influence of alcohol, according to estimates released in September 2003 by the Office of National Drug Control Policy (ONDCP). A study of motorists pulled over for reckless driving showed that, among those who were not impaired by alcohol, 45 percent tested positive for marijuana. . . .

Help Spread the Truth about Marijuana

Debunking these myths and arming our young people and their parents with the facts do work. We have proof. . . .

REVIEW QUESTIONS

1. Why do so many students believe that marijuana is safe for recreational use?

2. What evidence does Tandy use to support her conclusion that smoked marijuana is not medicine?

3. According to Tandy, what have been the effects of legalizing marijuana in other countries?

4. What are some of the ways in which marijuana is dangerous to both the users and nonusers?

Should Marijuana Be Legalized under any Circumstances?

Joe Messerli is a writer and creator of the website Balancedpolitics.org. A graduate of the University of Wisconsin, he also works as a technical consultant in web and database management. In the following excerpt, Messerli outlines the arguments in favor of legalizing marijuana.

Yes

1. **The drug generally isn't more harmful than alcohol or tobacco if used in moderation. . . .** [T]he studies of the harmfulness of marijuana are

inconclusive and contradictory. Most doctors would agree that it's not very harmful if used in moderation. It's only when you abuse the drug that problems start to occur. But isn't abuse of almost any bad substance a problem? If you abuse alcohol, caffeine, Ephedra, cigarettes, or even pizza, health problems are sure to follow. Would you want the government limiting how much coffee you can drink or how much cheesecake you take in? Most doctors believe that marijuana is no more addictive that alcohol or tobacco.

2. **Limiting the use of the drug intrudes on personal freedom.** Even if the drug is shown to be harmful, isn't it the right of every person to choose what harms him or her? Marijuana use is generally thought of as a "victimless crime," in that only the user is being harmed. You can't legislate morality when people disagree about what's considered "moral."

3. **Legalization would mean a lower price; thus, related crimes (like theft) would be reduced.** All illegal drugs are higher in price because the production, transportation, and sale of the drugs carry heavy risks. When people develop drug habits or addictions, they must somehow come up with the money to support their cravings. Unless a person is wealthy, he or she must often resort to robbery and other crimes to generate the money needed to buy the drugs. Legalization would reduce the risks and thus reduce the prices. There would therefore be less need for the secondary crimes needed to raise money.

4. **There are medical benefits such as those for cancer patients. . . .** [T]here are a number of medical benefits of marijuana, most notably in the treatment of patients undergoing chemotherapy. Others believe it helps in the treatment of depression. Certain states like California have brought initiatives to legalize the drug for at least medicinal purposes.

5. **Street justice related to drug disputes would be reduced.** Currently, if someone in the drug trade screws you over, there's no police to call or lawyers to litigate. You must settle disputes yourself. This often leads to cycles of retaliatory violence. Legalization would create proper means to settle disputes.

6. **It could be a source of additional tax revenues.** An enormous amount of money is raised through government taxation of alcohol, cigarettes, and other "sins". The legalization of marijuana would create another item that could be taxed. . . .

7. **Police and court resources would be freed up for more serious crimes.** Many consider the War on Drugs an expensive failure. Resources for DEA, FBI, and border security are only the tip of the iceberg. You must add in the cost of police officers, judges, public defenders, prosecutors, juries, court reporters, prison guards, and so on. Legalization of marijuana would free up those people to concentrate on more important things like terrorism, harder drugs, rape, murder, and so on. In addition, an already overloaded civil court docket would be improved; thus, the wait time for other legitimate court cases would be reduced.

8. **Drug dealers (including some terrorists) would lose most or all of their business.** Perhaps the biggest opponents of legalizing drugs are the drug dealers themselves. They make their enormous sums of money because of the absence of competition and the monstrous street prices that come from the increased risk. Legalization would lower prices and open competition; thus, drug cartels (that might include terrorists) would lose all or some of their business.

9. **The FDA or others could regulate the quality and safety of drugs.** Many drug users become sick or die because of poorly-prepared products. After all, there is nothing to regulate what is sold and no way to sue anyone for product liability. By bringing marijuana into the legitimate business world, you can oversee production and regulate sales.

10. **Like sex, alcohol, or cigarettes, marijuana is one of life's little pleasures for some people.** All of us have our guilty pleasures. They are part of what makes life worth living. Several of these little pleasures—coffee, sex, alcohol, cigarettes, etc.—are potentially harmful if abused. Even legal substances like pizza and donuts can be harmful to a person if not consumed in moderation. Would you want to give up all these things for the rest of your life? Would you want someone else telling you what you can and can't have when it is only your body that is affected?

11. **Aside from recreational drug use, *Cannabis* has several industrial and commercial uses, as over 25,000 products can be made from the crop.** The plant used in making marijuana has a ton of alternative uses, including construction and thermal insulation materials, paper, geotextiles, dynamite, composites for autos, and insect repellent. As far back as 1938, *Popular Mechanics* deemed it the "new billion dollar crop", as over 25,000 products can be made from it. Unfortunately, the lack of legality in the U.S. and other countries has squashed the growth and development of these products. We shouldn't limit the use of such a diverse product because *one* use is found objectionable by some.

12. **Drug busts often trap young people in a flawed system that turns them into lifelong criminals.** Imagine an impressionable teenager who is tired of earning minimum wage, who hates living in a poor ghetto area, or who needs to save money for college. He's offered the opportunity to make some decent money simply carrying some drugs across town. Then he's busted. He's thrown in jail as part of a mandatory sentence. There, he spends his time and becomes friends with many other delinquents. He gets meaner in jail since he has to defend himself in a rough crowd. When he gets out of prison, his job and college prospects are slammed because of a felony record and/or disruption of school. This just makes the resumption of a normal crime-free life all

the more difficult. Strapped for cash, he joins some of his new friends in a greater crime like robbery. Suddenly, you have someone who has started down the road of being a lifelong criminal. This story may seem farfetched, but it is all too real for some. The legalization of marijuana would remove another temptation that could lead a young impressionable individual down the wrong road.

Joe Messerli, "Should Marijuana Be Legalized under any Circumstances?" Balancedpolitics.org, August 6, 2011.

Joe Messerli, "Should Marijuana Be Legalized under any Circumstances?" Balancedpolitics.org, August 6, 2011.

REVIEW QUESTIONS

1. On what grounds does Messerli argue that marijuana should be legal even if it can be shown that marijuana might cause harm to the user?

2. According to Messerli, what would be some of the positive results of legalizing marijuana?

3. In Messerli's view, how does keeping marijuana illegal increase the chances of a young person becoming a lifelong criminal?

THiNK AND DISCUSS

PERSPECTIVES ON LEGALIZING MARIJUANA

1. Identify the arguments used in Tandy's and Messerli's articles. Distinguish which arguments are generalizations, analogies, or causal claims. Evaluate each of the arguments. Which of the arguments is most convincing and why?

2. Using the strongest premises from each argument, develop a policy (conclusion) addressing the legal status of marijuana.

3. Should you report to the authorities a student or professor whom you know is using marijuana? Make a list of the factors or premises that are most important in making your decision. Construct an argument supporting your conclusion.

4. Choose a claim from the articles that interests you, such as the potential of marijuana as a medicine, the harms of marijuana to the user, or the effect of decriminalizing marijuana in other countries. Research the claim and compare your findings to those stated in the articles. Share your findings with the class.

5. One of the arguments for legalization of marijuana in the United States is that Prohibition (the prohibition of alcohol from 1919 to 1933) increased crime and forced up the price of liquor. In addition, the illegality of marijuana in the United States puts its growth and distribution under the control of organized crime, whereas if it were sold by licensed businesses it could be regulated and taxed. Evaluate these arguments and discuss how both Tandy and Messerli might each respond to them.

8

DEDUCTIVE
ARGUMENTS

How is the professor using logical argumentation in coming up with mathematical proofs?
How can learning about deductive logic, such as arguments based on mathematics, help us make better-informed decisions?

In Sir Arthur Conan Doyle's mystery story "Silver Blaze," detective Sherlock Holmes uses his extraordinary powers of deductive logic to solve the mystery of the disappearance of racehorse Silver Blaze and the murder of the horse's trainer, John Straker. His head shattered by a savage blow, Straker's body was found a quarter mile from the King's Pyland stables where Silver Blaze was kept. A search is carried out of the surrounding moors and of the neighboring Mapleton stables for the horse.

After interviewing everyone who might have been involved and collecting all the facts, Holmes concludes that Silver Blaze is still alive and hidden in the Mapleton stables, even though the earlier search of the stables had failed to turn up the missing horse.

THiNK FIRST

- What is a deductive argument?
- What are some of the types of deductive arguments?
- What is a syllogism, and how do we know if it is valid?

"It's this way, Watson," [says Holmes]. "Now, supposing that [Silver Blaze] broke away during or after the tragedy, where could he have gone to? The horse is a very gregarious creature. If left to himself his instincts would have been either to return to King's Pyland or go over to Mapleton. Why would he run wild upon the moor? He surely should have been seen by now . . . He must have gone to King's Pyland or to Mapleton. He is not at King's Pyland. Therefore, he is at Mapleton."[1]

As it turns out, Holmes's deduction is right. The missing racehorse is at Mapleton, the silver blaze on its nose covered over to disguise its appearance.

Sherlock Holmes also solves the "murder" of the horse's trainer through deductive logic. He learns from the stable hand that the guard dog did not bark when Silver Blaze was "stolen" from the stables. Therefore, Holmes concludes, the person who took Silver Blaze must have been familiar to the dog. This eliminated suspects who were strangers. Holmes then eliminates, one by one, the other suspects, leaving only the horse. As Holmes stated in another story: "When you have eliminated the impossible, whatever remains, however improbable, must be the truth."[2] He concludes that the horse must have accidentally killed its trainer when Straker, who was something of a scoundrel, used a surgical knife found in his possession to nick the tendons of Silver Blaze's ham so the horse would develop a slight limp and lose the upcoming race. Holmes explains, "Once in the hollow, [Straker] had got behind the horse and had struck a light; but the creature, frightened at the sudden glare, and with the strange instinct of animals feeling that some mischief was intended, had lashed out, and the steel shoe had struck Straker full on the forehead."[3]

To generations of mystery readers, Sherlock Holmes has epitomized the skilled reasoner. In this chapter we'll learn how to evaluate deductive arguments and practice some of the strategies used by Holmes and others who are skilled in deductive argumentation. In Chapter 8 we will:

- Identify the essential attributes of a deductive argument
- Distinguish between validity, invalidity, and soundness in a deductive argument
- Learn how to recognize and evaluate arguments by elimination, mathematical arguments, and argument from definition
- Study the different types of hypothetical syllogisms, including *modus ponens, modus tollens,* and chain arguments
- Learn how to recognize standard-form categorical syllogisms
- Reevaluate categorical syllogisms using Venn diagrams
- Practice putting arguments that are in ordinary language into standard form

Finally, we will analyze different arguments regarding the justification of the death penalty (capital punishment).

WHAT IS A DEDUCTIVE ARGUMENT?

Unlike inductive arguments, in which the premises offer only support rather than proof for the conclusion, in a valid deductive argument the conclusion necessarily follows from the premises. Deductive arguments sometimes contain words or phrases such as *certainly, definitely, absolutely, conclusively, must be,* and *it necessarily follows that.* For example:

> Marilyn is definitely not a member of the swim team, since no freshmen are members of the swim team and Marilyn is a freshman.

Deductive Reasoning and Syllogisms

Deductive arguments are sometimes presented in the form of **syllogisms**, with two supporting premises and a conclusion. For the purpose of analysis, in this chapter the premises and conclusion of a syllogism will usually be presented on separate lines, with the conclusion last.

1. *Premise: All men are mortal.*
2. *Premise: All fathers are men.*
3. *Conclusion: Therefore, all fathers are mortal.*

Deductive arguments may also be diagrammed using the guidelines we learned on pages 181–184. In the case of a syllogism, the two premises are always dependent:

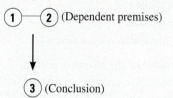

(1)—(2) (Dependent premises)

(3) (Conclusion)

Some deductive arguments are more involved and may have several dependent premises and subconclusions.

Valid and Invalid Arguments

A deductive argument is **valid** if the form of the argument is such that the conclusion *must* be true *if* the premises are true. The **form** of an argument is determined by its layout or pattern of reasoning. In the above case, the form is:

syllogism A deductive argument presented in the form of two supporting premises and a conclusion.

valid A deductive argument where the form is such that the conclusion must be true if the premises are assumed to be true.

form The pattern of reasoning in a deductive argument.

> All X (men) are Y (mortal).
> All Z (fathers) are X (men).
> Therefore, all Z (fathers) are Y (mortal).

This argument is a valid form no matter what terms we use for X, Y, and Z. Because the form is valid, if we substitute different terms for *men*, *mortal*, and *fathers, and* the premises are still true, then the conclusion *must* be true, as in the following example.

> All cats (X) are mammals (Y).
> All tigers (Z) are cats (X).
> Therefore, all tigers (Z) are mammals (Y).

A false conclusion does not necessarily mean that a deductive argument is invalid. In the two arguments we've examined so far, the conclusions were both true because the premises were true *and* the form was valid. The conclusion of a valid argument

Hot or Not?

Are deductive arguments better than inductive arguments?

can be false only if one of the premises is false. In the following example, which uses the same form as our initial argument, we end up with a false conclusion:

> All men are tall people.
>
> Tom Cruise is a man.
>
> Therefore, Tom Cruise is a tall person.

The conclusion in the above argument is false *only* because there is a false premise, not because the form of the argument is invalid. The first premise, "All men are tall people," is false.

If both premises are true and the conclusion is false, then the argument, by definition, is invalid. For example:

> All dogs are mammals.
>
> Some mammals are not poodles.
>
> Therefore, some poodles are not dogs.

It is also possible to have an invalid argument in which the premises are true and the conclusion just happens to be true. Consider this:

> No seniors are freshmen.
>
> All freshmen are college students.
>
> Therefore, some college students are seniors.

In this argument, the premises and conclusion are true. However, the premises do not logically support the conclusion. The invalidity of a form can be demonstrated by substituting different terms for *senior*, *freshman*, and *college students*, and then seeing whether we can come up with an argument using this form in which the premises are true but the conclusion false, as in the following substitutions:

> No fish are dogs.
>
> All dogs are mammals.
>
> Therefore, some mammals are fish.

Sound and Unsound Arguments

An argument is **sound** if (1) it is valid *and* (2) the premises are true. The argument on page 239 about fathers being mortal is a sound argument because it is valid and the premises are true. On the other hand, although the argument about Tom Cruise uses a valid form, it is not a sound argument because the first premise is false. Invalid arguments, because they do not meet the first criterion, are always unsound.

sound A deductive argument that is valid and that has true premises.

Logic is primarily concerned with the validity of arguments. As critical thinkers, we are also interested in the soundness of our arguments and in having our premises supported by credible evidence and good reasoning. We have already discussed in previous chapters guidelines for ensuring that our premises are accurate and credible. In this chapter we'll learn how to identify the different types of deductive arguments and how to use Venn diagrams to evaluate these arguments for validity.

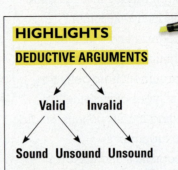

HIGHLIGHTS

DEDUCTIVE ARGUMENTS

Valid   Invalid

Sound Unsound Unsound

Valid argument: The form or layout of the argument is such that if the premises are true, then the conclusion must necessarily be true.

Sound argument: The form of the argument is valid and the premises are true.

➤ **APPLICATION:** Identify in the text an example of an argument that is (a) valid and sound, (b) valid and unsound, and (c) invalid.

"Some mammals are fish" is an example of a false conclusion.

STOP AND ASSESS YOURSELF

1. What do you mean when you say that you can prove something with certainty? Give a specific example of a proof from your everyday experience (keep it as brief as possible). What type of logic does the proof use—inductive or deductive?

2. In the story "Silver Blaze," Sherlock Holmes tells Watson that when it comes to the art of reasoning, many people rely on opinion and unsupported assumptions. The difficulty, he maintains, is to detach the framework of undeniable fact from the embellishments of hearsay and reporters. What do you think he meant by this? Explain using examples from your personal experience.

3. Using substitution, show that the form of each of the following deductive arguments is invalid. Remember: To establish invalidity, your premises must be true when you are substituting new terms for the ones in the original argument.

*a. All fraternity members are men.
No women are fraternity members.
Therefore, no women are men.

b. If it is raining, then it is cloudy.
It is cloudy.
Therefore, it is raining.

c. No mice are humans.
Some mice are rodents.
Therefore, no humans are rodents.

*d. Some married people are college students.
All wives are married people.
Therefore, some wives are college students.

e. All flowers are plants.
All orchids are plants.
Therefore, all orchids are flowers.

f. If my baby sister is a college student, then she is a high school graduate.
My baby sister is not a college student.
Therefore, my baby sister is not a high school graduate.

4. The following arguments are all valid arguments. Determine whether each argument is sound or unsound.

*a. No mammals are birds. Some penguins are mammals. Therefore, some penguins are not birds.

b. Some twins are sisters. All twins are siblings. Therefore, some siblings are sisters.

c. All students are dormitory residents. No dormitory residents are birds. Therefore, no birds are students.

*d. If Mexico is in South America, then Mexico is not a country bordering the United States. Mexico is in South America. Therefore, Mexico is a not country bordering the United States.

e. All people living in England are citizens of the European Union.
All members of the British royal family are people living in England.
Therefore, all members of the British royal family are citizens of the European Union.

f. All millionaires are rich people. Some Americans are not rich people. Therefore, some Americans are not millionaires.

*Answers to selected exercises are found in the Solutions Manual at the end of the book.

TYPES OF DEDUCTIVE ARGUMENTS

There are several types of deductive arguments. In this section, we'll be looking at three types of deductive arguments used in everyday reasoning:

- Arguments by elimination
- Arguments based on mathematics
- Arguments from definition

Arguments by Elimination

An **argument by elimination** rules out different possibilities until only one possibility remains. In the

> **argument by elimination** A deductive argument that rules out different possibilities until only one remains.

introduction to this chapter, we saw Sherlock Holmes using an argument by elimination. He reasoned that Silver Blaze had to be at one of the two stables. Since it wasn't at King's Pyland, it must be at Mapleton. In "Thinking Outside the Box: Bo Dietl" we profile a New York City detective who is skilled in this type of deductive reasoning.

Like detectives, physicians are trained in this type of deductive logic. In diagnosing an illness, a physician starts by doing a physical examination and, often, by ordering tests. If the examination and test results eliminate the most common explanations of the symptoms, then the physician moves on to check out less obvious possibilities until the mystery is solved. Indeed, Dr. Joseph Bell, one of Sir Arthur Conan Doyle's professors at the University of Edinburgh Medical School, was the inspiration for the character Sherlock Holmes.

Arguments by elimination are frequently used in everyday life. For instance, suppose it is the first day of the semester and you arrive on campus with 10 minutes to spare.

THiNKing Outside the Box

BO DIETL, *Top Cop*

Bo Dietl is a modern Sherlock Holmes. Born in Queens, New York, in 1950, Dietl wanted a job where he could make a real difference in people's lives. When he learned about the test to get into the police academy, he decided to give it a try and became a police officer.

One of the most highly decorated detectives in the history of the New York Police Department, Dietl investigated numerous high-profile murders and other felonies, obtaining evidence through research, interviews, and other investigative techniques. He attributes much of his success in solving more than 1,500 felonies to what he calls his "sixth sense—a nontangible feeling good detectives use in solving cases."*

One of the most famous crimes he solved was the 1981 rape and torture of a Catholic nun in an East Harlem convent. Dietl concluded from the evidence that the crime was a burglary gone wrong, rather than a sex crime, thus narrowing his search to people with burglary records. He also knew, from interviewing witnesses, that one of the men was probably tall and that the other had a limp. Days later he received a tip that the two men who committed the crime lived somewhere on 125th Street in Harlem. However, there were hundreds of buildings and thousands of people living on this street. He began the process of elimination by going to the local hangouts and tenements, knocking on doors, giving a brief description of the suspects, and asking questions. He also passed out hundreds of business cards. His efforts paid off, and the two suspects were apprehended and arrested. The 1998 movie *One Tough Cop* is based on Dietl's autobiography of the same name.

1. Discuss how Dietl's method of solving the murder of the nun in the East Harlem convent demonstrates deductive reasoning using an argument by elimination.

2. In Chapter 2 we learned that much of reasoning is unconscious and automatic and that scientists and mathematicians, as well as great detectives, often resolve complex problems without any conscious deliberation. However, to develop this ability, they have spent years consciously resolving problems and mentally rehearsing solutions. Think of a type of problem in your life that you find easy to resolve with little or no conscious deliberation. Discuss what factors, such as your familiarity and experience with the problem, contributed to your ease of resolution.

*Conversation with Bo Dietl on August 8, 2005.

You check your schedule and see that your first class, Introduction to Psychology, is in Winthrop Hall. However, on your schedule the room number is smudged and you can't read it. What do you do? It would take too long to get a new schedule. Instead, you head over to Winthrop Hall and check out the building directory. It lists twelve room numbers. Nine of them are faculty offices, so you eliminate those nine. The remaining three are classrooms A, B, and C. You go into classroom A and ask some students what class it is. They tell you that it's English Literature. You proceed to classroom B and repeat the process; it turns out to be a course in Business Statistics. When you get to classroom C, you just go inside and take a seat. How do you know this is the correct classroom? Through the use of an argument by elimination. Assuming that your premises are true (that your psychology course is being taught somewhere in Winthrop Hall), the third classroom *by necessity* must be your classroom.

> My class is either in room A, B, or C.
>
> My class is not in room A.
>
> My class is not in room B.
>
> Therefore, my class must be in room C.

In the previous example, there were three alternatives. If there are only two alternatives, the argument is referred to as a **disjunctive syllogism**. A disjunctive syllogism takes one of two forms:

> Either A or B.   Either A or B.
>
> Not A.   Not B.
>
> Therefore, B.   Therefore, A.

In determining the whereabouts of Silver Blaze, Sherlock Holmes used a disjunctive syllogism:

> Either Silver Blaze is at King's Pyland or Silver Blaze is at Mapleton.
>
> Silver Blaze is not at King's Pyland.
>
> Therefore, Silver Blaze is at Mapleton.

Here is another example of a disjunctive syllogism:

> Either you finished cleaning your room or you're staying in tonight.
>
> You are not staying in tonight.
>
> Therefore, you finished cleaning your room.

In a disjunctive syllogism, the two alternatives presented in the first premise—clean your room or stay in tonight—must be the only two possibilities. If there are other possible alternatives that have not been stated, then the argument commits the *fallacy of false dilemma*. For example:

> Either we keep Obamacare or we balance the budget.
>
> We are keeping Obamacare.
>
> Therefore, we will not have a balanced budget.

A mouse locates the prize at the end of the maze through the deductive process of elimination.

In this argument, the two alternatives in the first premise do not exhaust all possible alternatives. There are many areas of the federal budget we could cut other than healthcare spending. Because the argument commits the fallacy of false dilemma, it is not a sound argument.

Arguments Based on Mathematics

In an **argument based on mathematics**, the conclusion depends on a mathematical or geometrical calculation. For example:

> My dormitory room is rectangular in shape.
>
> One side measures 11 feet and the side adjacent to it measures 14 feet in length.
>
> Therefore, my room is 154 square feet.

You can also draw conclusions about your new roommate, Chris, even before you meet, using this type of deductive reasoning. You know from e-mail correspondence that Chris plans on trying out for the basketball team and is 6′ 2″ tall. Since you are 5′ 6″ tall, you can conclude (assuming that Chris's information is correct) that Chris is 8 inches taller than you.

These are relatively simple examples. Arguments based on mathematics may be quite complex and require

> **disjunctive syllogism** A type of deductive argument by elimination in which the premises present only two alternatives.
>
> **argument based on mathematics** A deductive argument in which the conclusion depends on a mathematical calculation.

mathematical expertise. For example, scientists at NASA needed to calculate the best time to launch the two *Mars Explorer Rovers*—robotic geologists—so that they would arrive at the Red Planet when Mars would be closest to Earth. Mars takes 687 days to complete a revolution of the Sun, compared to 365 days for Earth. Also, because their orbits differ and because Mars has a slightly eccentric orbit, the distance between Mars and Earth varies widely, ranging from about 401 million miles to less than 55 million miles.[4] The two rovers, *Spirit* and *Opportunity,* were launched from Cape Canaveral, Florida, in the summer of 2003 and landed on Mars in January 2004. The landing was remarkably smooth, thanks to the deductive reasoning skills of the NASA scientists. As of 2013 NASA has lost contact with the rover *Spirit*, which has become stuck in a sand trap. *Opportunity* is still transmitting scientific data back to Earth.

Knowing how to make arguments based on mathematics can help you make better-informed decisions, such as calculating the cost of a vacation to Cancun or determining what type of payment method for your educational expenses is most cost-effective. For example, by taking out a student loan instead of using a credit card to pay for your college expenses, you can save thousands of dollars (see "Critical Thinking in Action: Put It on My Tab: Paying College Tuition by Credit Card—a Wise Move?").

Not all arguments using mathematics are deductive. As we learned in Chapter 7, statistical arguments that depend on probability, such as generalizations, are inductive because we can conclude from these only that something is *likely*—not certain—to be true (see pages 207–209).

How can an understanding of arguments based on mathematics help you evaluate science news? *See Chapter 11, pp. 345–346.*

Connections

argument from definition A deductive argument in which the conclusion is true because it is based on the definition of a key term.

Arguments from Definition

In an **argument from definition**, the conclusion is true because it is based on a key term or essential attribute in a definition. For example:

Paulo is a father.

All fathers are men.

Therefore, Paulo is a man.

This conclusion is necessarily true because a father is, by definition, "a male parent." Being male is an essential attribute of the definition of *father*.

As we discussed in Chapter 3, language is dynamic and definitions may change over time. Consider this example:

Marilyn and Jessica cannot be married, since a marriage is a union between a man and a woman.

This conclusion of this argument was necessarily true at one time, before some states legalized same-sex marriage. Today, because the legal definition of marriage is undergoing change, this argument may no longer be sound.

Arguments by elimination, arguments based on mathematics, and arguments from definition are only three types of deductive arguments. In logic, deductive arguments are often written in syllogistic form, such as the disjunctive syllogism. In the following sections, we'll learn about two other types of syllogisms—hypothetical and categorical—and how to evaluate arguments using these forms.

Put It on My Tab: Paying College Tuition by Credit Card—A Wise Move?

Have you ever wondered why credit-card companies are so keen on signing up college students? According to CreditKarma.com, an online credit tracking site, people between the ages of 18 and 29 have the poorest credit ratings of all age groups. In fact, credit-card companies make most of their money from people who don't pay off their balance each month, which is the case with 80 percent of college students. Many parents and students regard credit cards as a convenient way to pay for tuition. However, if you think carrying a balance on a credit card or charging college expenses such as tuition to a credit card is a smart move, consider the following argument, based on mathematics:

> Your credit card bill is $1,900. This includes $1,350 for tuition and fees at your community college and $550 for books for two semesters. Being frugal, you decide not to use your credit card again, since you don't want to get too far into debt. The minimum monthly payment due on your balance is 4 percent, which comes to $75 the first month. You pay the minimum due faithfully each month.
>
> At this rate, how long will it take you to pay off your first-year college expenses? If the annual percentage rate on your card is 17.999 percent, it will take you 7 years to pay off that balance on your credit card!* In addition to the principal (the amount you charged to the card), you'll have paid a total of $924.29 in interest. This means that the amount of money you actually paid for your first year of college expenses was $2,824!**

What if you had taken out a student loan instead? The annual interest rate on a federal student loan is about 8 percent. If you put $75 a month toward paying off your student loan, it would take you 2 years and 4 months to pay off the loan. Furthermore, you don't have to start paying off your student loan until you graduate. By taking out a student loan to cover your college expenses instead of charging them to a credit card, you wouldn't have to pay anything for the 2 years while you are in college. Even then you would pay off the loan almost 3 years before you would pay off your credit card—and the total interest would come to only $188. In other words, you paid $736 for the "convenience" of charging your tuition, fees, and books for your first year at community college. Multiply this times 2 or even 4 years, and you could be paying out several thousand dollars just in interest simply because you didn't apply your logic and your critical-thinking skills when deciding how to pay for your college expenses.

1. Several colleges, including Tufts University, Boston College, Sarah Lawrence College, and Arizona State University, have discontinued credit-card payments for tuition. In part this is because the credit-card companies charge the college a 1 percent to 2 percent fee on each charge, which ultimately gets added on to the cost of tuition. What is the policy at your college or university? Do you agree with the policy? Construct an argument supporting your answer.

2. Examine your own credit-card use. Discuss ways in which you can use deductive logic to be more economical in your spending habits.

*To calculate what you'll pay on a credit-card balance, go to http://cgi.money.cnn.com/tools/debtplanner/debtplanner.jsp; for what you'll pay on a student loan, go to http://cgi.money.cnn.com/tools/studentloan/studentloan.html.

**For information on applying for federal and private college loans, see http://www.collegeboard.com/student/pay/loan-center/414.html.

STOP AND ASSESS YOURSELF

1. Identify what type of argument each of the following is. If it is a deductive argument, state which type of deductive argument. If the argument is not a deductive argument, explain why. (See Chapter 7 if you need to review inductive arguments.)

*a. Clem either walked to the bookstore or took the shuttle bus. He couldn't have taken the shuttle bus, since it is out of service today. Therefore, he walked to the bookstore.

b. Hisoka is a psychiatrist. Therefore, Hisoka is a physician.

c. A 64-ounce carton of mint chocolate chip ice cream costs $5.99. A 16-ounce carton costs $1.49. Therefore, I'll actually save money by buying four 16-ounce cartons instead of one 64-ounce carton.

*d. Let's see; it's the triplets' third birthday. We have six presents for Matthew, five for Andrew, and one for Derek. If we want to be fair and give each of the triplets the same number of presents, we'll have to take two of the presents we now have set aside for Matthew and one of the presents we have set aside for Andrew and give them to Derek instead.

e. Tokyo, New York City, and Mexico City have the highest populations of any cities in the world. Tokyo has a higher population than New York City. Mexico City has a lower population than New York City. Therefore, Tokyo has the highest population of any city in the world.

f. I was told that Mary is probably in class right now and that if she were not there, to check the library where she spends most of her afternoons. However, Mary isn't in class. So she is most likely at the library.

*g. Jessica is the daughter of Joshua's uncle. Therefore, Jessica and Joshua are cousins.

h. Either Roy Jones Jr. or John Ruiz won the 2003 world heavyweight championship boxing match in Las Vegas. John Ruiz did not win the fight. Therefore, Roy Jones Jr. was the 2003 world heavyweight champion.

i. $A = 5$. $B = 8$. $C = -11$. Therefore, $A + B + C = 2$.

*j. Forrest Gump said that his mother always told him that "life was like a box of chocolates. You never know what you're gonna get." Therefore, there's no point in trying to plan for the future, since you can never know what it holds for you.

k. I know that Singapore uses either the dollar or the British pound as their currency. I checked out the countries that use the British pound and Singapore was not listed. Therefore, Singapore uses the dollar as its currency.

l. Professor Cervera told us that he was born in one of the four largest cities in Cuba, but I can't remember which one. I remember him mentioning that it was in the southeastern part of Cuba and that he could see the ocean from his bedroom window. I checked my almanac, and the four largest cities in Cuba are Havana, Santiago de Cuba, Camagüey, and Holguin. He couldn't have been born in Havana, since it is on the northwestern coast of Cuba. Camagüey and Holguin are both located inland. So Professor Cervera must have been born in Santiago de Cuba.

*m. We should ask Latitia if she is interested in working part time in our marketing department. I read that about 80 percent of freshmen said there was at least some chance they'd have to get a job to pay for college expenses. In addition, women are far more likely to have to seek employment during college than are men. Therefore, Latitia will probably be looking for a part-time job to help with her college expenses.

n. I agree that the storm we had last week was pretty bad, but it was not a hurricane since the winds never got above 70 miles per hour.

o. Either the tide is coming in or the tide is going out. The tide is not coming in. Therefore, the tide is going out.

*p. A Harvard University survey of more than 10,000 teenagers found that 8 percent of girls and 12 percent of boys have used dietary supplements, growth hormones, or anabolic steroids. Therefore, teenage boys are 50 percent more likely than are teenage girls to use products such as steroids to build muscle mass.

2. Select three of the arguments from exercise 1 and diagram them (see Chapter 6).

3. You're having lunch with some friends and mention that you're studying deductive logic. One of your friends rolls his eyes and says, "You can prove anything you want to with logic. Why, you can even prove that cats have thirteen tails. Here's how it works: One cat has one more tail than no cat. And no cat has twelve tails. Therefore, one cat has thirteen tails." Evaluate your friend's argument.

4. At a picnic, Mike went for soft drinks for Amy, Brian, Lisa, and Bill, as well as for himself. He brought back iced tea, grape juice, Diet Coke, Pepsi, and 7-Up. Using the following information (premises), determine which drink Mike brought for each person:

> Mike doesn't like carbonated drinks.
> Amy would drink either 7-Up or Pepsi.
> Brian likes only sodas.
> Lisa prefers the drink she could put lemon and sugar into.
> Bill likes only clear drinks.[5]

5. How do you pay for your tuition and other college expenses? Go to http://www.money.cnn.com/tools and calculate how much it will cost you to pay off your entire debt on the basis of the average you pay each month, or estimate what you will pay monthly after graduation. Given your financial situation, decide what would be the most economical way for you to pay for your college and personal expenses.

*Answers to selected exercises are found in the Solutions Manual at the end of the book.

HYPOTHETICAL SYLLOGISMS

Hypothetical thinking involves "If . . . then . . ." reasoning. According to some psychologists, the mental model for hypothetical thinking is built into our brain and enables us to understand rules and predict the consequences of our actions.[6] We'll be looking at the use of hypothetical reasoning in ethics in greater depth in Chapter 9. Hypothetical arguments are also a basic building block of computer programs.

According to some psychologists, the mental model for hypothetical thinking is built into our brain and enables us to understand rules and predict the consequences of our actions.

A **hypothetical syllogism** is a form of deductive argument that contains two premises, at least one of which is a hypothetical or conditional "if . . . then" statement.

Hypothetical syllogisms fall into three basic patterns: *modus ponens* (affirming the antecedent), *modus tollens* (denying the consequent), and chain arguments.

Modus Ponens

In a *modus ponens* argument, there is one conditional premise, a second premise that states that the antecedent, or *if* part, of the first premise is true, and a conclusion that

asserts the truth of the consequent, or the *then* part, of the first premise. For example:

> *Premise 1*: *If* I get this raise at work, *then* I can pay off my credit-card bill.
>
> *Premise 2*: I got the raise at work.
>
> *Conclusion*: Therefore, I can pay off my credit-card bill.

A valid *modus ponens* argument, like the one above, takes the following form:

> If A (antecedent), then B (consequent).
>
> A.
>
> Therefore, B.

Sometimes the term *then* is omitted from the consequent, or second, part of the conditional premise:

> If the hurricane hits the Florida Keys, we should evacuate.
>
> The hurricane is hitting the Florida Keys.
>
> Therefore, we should evacuate.

Modus ponens is a valid form of deductive reasoning no matter what terms we substitute for A and B. In other words, if the premises are true, then the conclusion must be true. Thus:

> If Barack Obama is president, then he was born in the United States.
>
> Barack Obama is president.
>
> Therefore, he was born in the United States.

In this case, the first premise is true because the U.S. Constitution requires that the president be "a natural born citizen." Therefore, the argument is a sound argument.

> **hypothetical syllogism** A deductive argument that contains two premises, at least one of which is a conditional statement.
>
> **modus ponens** A hypothetical syllogism in which the antecedent premise is affirmed by the consequent premise.

Deductive Reasoning and Computer Programming

In computer programming, special computer languages are used to create strings of code which are comprised almost entirely of deductive logic. Some popular computer languages include C++, Java, JavaScript, Visual Basic, and HTML. Many others exist that specialize in specific tasks. In the following program using C++, a game has been created using hypothetical statements:

```
int main()
{int number = 5}
        int guess;
        cout << "I am thinking of a number between 1 and 10" << endl;
        cout << "Enter your guess, please";
        cin >> guess;
        if (guess == number)
                    {cout << "Incredible, you are correct" << endl;}
            else if (guess < number)
                    {cout << "Higher, try again" << endl;}
            else // guess must be too high
                    {cout << "Lower, try again" <<endl;}
        return 0:}
```

In the game, the computer asks the user to guess a number between 1 and 10. If the user guesses a 5 (the correct answer), the computer will congratulate the user with the message, "Incredible, you are correct." Otherwise, the computer tells the user whether his/her answer was too high or too low.

---

modus tollens A hypothetical syllogism in which the antecedent premise is denied by the consequent premise.

chain arguments A type of imperfect hypothetical argument with three or more conditional propositions linked together.

It is important not to deviate from this form in a *modus ponens* argument. If the second premise affirms the consequent (B) rather than the antecedent (A), the argument is invalid and the conclusion may be false, even though the premises are true.

> If Oprah Winfrey is president, then she was born in the United States.
>
> Oprah Winfrey was born in the United States.
>
> Therefore, Oprah Winfrey is president.

But of course, as we all know, Oprah Winfrey is not president of the United States. This deviation from the correct form of *modus ponens* is known as the *fallacy of affirming the consequent*.

Modus Tollens

In a ***modus tollens*** argument, the second premise denies the consequent, and the conclusion denies the truth of the antecedent:

> If A (antecedent), then B (consequent).

> Not B.
>
> Therefore, not A.

Here is an example of a *modus tollens* argument:

> If Morgan is a physician, then she has graduated from college.
>
> Morgan did not graduate from college.
>
> Therefore, Morgan is not a physician.

Like *modus ponens*, *modus tollens* is a valid form of deductive reasoning. No matter what terms we substitute for the antecedent (A) and consequent (B), if the premises are true, then the conclusion must be true. If we change the form by changing the first premise to read "If not A, then B," we commit the *fallacy of denying the antecedent*.

Chain Arguments

Chain arguments are made up of three conditional propositions—two premises and one conclusion—linked together. A chain argument is a type of imperfect hypothetical syllogism since it may contain more than three propositions.

> If A, then B.
>
> If B, then C.
>
> Therefore, if A, then C.

Empty Promises: If This, Then That—Making Promises and Threats

Promises are often framed as hypothetical statements: "If you do . . . , then I'll . . ." Because hypothetical syllogisms are deductive arguments, the conclusion necessarily follows from the premises. Therefore, we should think twice about the consequences (conclusion) of having to keep such a promise. For example, President Obama vowed before at an international meeting in Prague in 2009 to punish Iran for pursuing a nuclear weapons program, stating that "Rules must be binding. Violations must be punished . . . The world must stand together to prevent the spread of these weapons." When it came to light that Iran may already have a nuclear weapons program, Obama reiterated his position in his May 2009 State of the Union address: "As Iran's leaders continue to ignore their obligations, there should be no doubt: They, too, will face growing consequences. That is a promise." Four years later, despite tighter sanctions against Iran and Obama's continued assurance that he is determined to prevent Iran from getting a nuclear weapon, Iran remains undeterred in its nuclear program and may be only months away from having a nuclear weapon. In failing to follow through effectively on his promise, Obama has damaged his credibility regarding this issue.

People may also use hypothetical statements as threats to try to get their children to behave or to get their boyfriend, girlfriend, partner, or spouse to change their ways. For instance, an exasperated parent may say to a boisterous child: "If you keep misbehaving and making so much noise, Mommy is never going to get better." The child, being a typical child, misbehaves again. A few weeks later, the mother dies of cancer. In such a case, the child will likely draw the logical conclusion that she is to blame for her mother's death (never getting better).

DISCUSSION QUESTIONS

1. Imagine you had been in Obama's position. Using a hypothetical syllogism, discuss how you might word your response to Iran's nuclear program so it does not become an empty promise but one that can be acted on in a responsible manner.

2. Think of a time when you were given an ultimatum in the form of a hypothetical statement in a relationship. What conclusion logically followed from the ultimatum? Did the ultimatum hurt or enhance your relationship? Explain why or why not.

The following is an example of a chain argument:

> If it rains tomorrow, then the beach party is canceled.
>
> If the beach party is canceled, we're having a party at Rachel's house.
>
> Therefore, if it rains tomorrow, we're having a party at Rachel's house.

Just as some arguments by elimination are syllogisms and others are not, we can have a longer chain argument that is still a deductive argument but not a syllogism because it has more than two premises. For example:

> If A, then B.
>
> If B, then C.
>
> If C, then D.
>
> Therefore, if A, then D.

Here is an example of a chain argument with three premises:

> If you don't go to class, you won't pass the final exam.
>
> If you don't pass the final exam, then you won't pass the course.
>
> If you don't pass the course, then you won't graduate this year.
>
> Therefore, if you don't go to class, you won't graduate this year.

A chain argument is valid if it follows the form of using the consequent of the previous premise as the antecedent in the next premise, and so on, with the conclusion using the antecedent from the first premise (A) and the consequent in the last premise (D).

Evaluating Hypothetical Syllogisms for Validity

Not all hypothetical syllogisms are laid out in standard syllogistic form. If an argument isn't already in standard form, put it in standard form with the conditional premise first and the conclusion last. In the case of a chain argument, begin by listing the premise containing the antecedent from the conclusion. In 1758, Ben Franklin included a version of this proverb in his famous *Poor Richard's Almanac*:

> For the want of a nail, the shoe was lost;
>
> For the want of the shoe, the horse was lost;
>
> For the want of the horse, the rider was lost.

Let's test the validity of Franklin's argument by writing it out as a hypothetical syllogism, in this case a chain argument:

> If a nail is missing (A), then the horseshoe will be lost (B).
>
> If the horseshoe is lost (B), then the rider is lost (C).
>
> If the nail is missing (A), then the rider is lost (C).

By rewriting this as a hypothetical syllogism, we can see that it is a valid argument. In some cases, it may be too awkward to restate each use of the antecedents and consequents using the exact same language as in the proverb. In these cases, it is acceptable to use everyday language as long as the meaning remains the same each time it is used. Otherwise, the argument commits the fallacy of equivocation.

A hypothetical syllogism is valid if it follows one of the forms discussed in this chapter—*modus ponens*, *modus tollens*, or chain argument. If you are uncertain whether a hypothetical syllogism is valid, you can also try substituting different terms for those used in the argument under evaluation.

Not all valid arguments are sound. As we noted earlier, a deductive argument can be valid by virtue of its form but still be unsound because one of the premises is false. Rewording arguments in ordinary language in the form of a hypothetical syllogism can help you expose the faulty

> Rewording arguments in ordinary language in the form of a hypothetical syllogism can help you expose the faulty premises.

premises. Suppose you are looking for a new cell phone and find two models that seem to suit your needs—a Samsung and a Motorola. Both have similar features, but the Samsung costs more than the Motorola. So you think: *The Samsung cell phone costs more, so it should be the better phone. I think I'll buy the Samsung.* Putting your argument in the form of a hypothetical syllogism, we have this:

> If a product is expensive, then it must be good.
>
> This brand of cell phone is expensive.
>
> Therefore, it must be good.

However, the first premise is false. Not all expensive products are good, nor are all inexpensive products of poor quality. Therefore, this is an unsound argument. Unfortunately, many people fall for this line of reasoning. Indeed, some clever marketers have found that when they increase the price of certain items, such as jewelry or clothing, it actually sells better!

Putting an argument in the form of a hypothetical syllogism can be helpful in clarifying what's at stake. Consider this argument from the abortion debate:

> If a being is a person (A), then it is morally wrong to kill that being except in self-defense (B).
>
> The fetus is a person (A).
>
> Therefore, it is morally wrong to kill the fetus except in self-defense (B).

Judith Jarvis Thomson, in her essay "A Defense of Abortion" recognizes the strength of this type of deductive reasoning and acknowledges that she must accept the conclusion if she accepts the premises as true. She also realizes that the only way to reject this argument—since it is a valid argument—is to show that one of the premises is false and therefore the argument is unsound. Otherwise, she *must* accept the conclusion. Since she can't prove that the fetus is not a person, she tentatively accepts the second premise as true. Instead, she questions the first premise, arguing that there may be circumstances when we can kill another person for reasons other than self-defense.

Hypothetical arguments are common in everyday reasoning. In addition to being used in promises and ultimatums (see "Critical Thinking in Action: Empty Promises: If This, Then That—Making Promises and Threats" on page 249), they can be used to spell out the outcomes of certain choices you make

in your life: for example, the necessary antecedents you'll need to graduate from college or go on graduate school.

EXERCISE 8-3

STOP AND ASSESS YOURSELF

1. Sometimes the conclusion and/or one of the premises is unstated in a deductive argument, leaving you to complete the argument. Complete the following arguments, using valid forms of hypothetical syllogisms and stating which form you are using:

   *a. If Sam enlists in the army, then he'll have to go to boot camp. But Sam does not have to go to boot camp.

   b. "If you look at another woman one more time, I'm going to leave you." Mike looks at another woman.

   c. If it didn't rain today, I'd have to water the garden. I won't have to water the garden.

   *d. If I call Lisa, then she'll know I'm interested in her. If she knows I'm interested in her, then she might notice me more around campus.

   e. If we as a nation don't do something about our unprecedented deficit problem, then we will not be able to pay off our national debt for decades. If we are not able to pay it off, then our children are going to be burdened with an intolerable debt. If our children are burdened with an intolerable debt, then they will have a lower standard of living than that enjoyed by their parents.

   f. If the exchange rate is good I'm traveling to Italy and Greece over winter break. The exchange rate is favorable.

   *g. If I buy a new car, then I'll have to get a job. I bought a new car.

   h. If I take statistics this semester, I'll have enough credits to complete a major in accounting. Then I'll be able to apply to do an MBA in accounting.

   i. If you don't stop harassing me I'm going to call the police. I'm calling the police right now.

   *j. If Seattle replaced its conventional buses with hybrid-powered buses, they would save several thousands of gallons of fuel annually. In Seattle, the local transit authority has begun taking delivery of 235 hybrid-powered buses.[7]

2. Identify and evaluate each of the following hypothetical syllogisms for validity and soundness.

   *a. Zachary did not get the promotion. If Zachary had gotten the promotion, he would be earning an extra $200 a month. But he is not earning an extra $200 a month.

   b. If the temperature of freshwater at sea level is below 32° Fahrenheit, then it is frozen. The water in our neighbor's freshwater pond is below 32° Fahrenheit. Therefore, the water in the pond must be frozen.

   c. If a newborn baby is diagnosed with AIDS, then he or she will die during the first year of life. Baby Meg was diagnosed with AIDS when she was born. Therefore, she has less than a year to live.

*d. If you love John, you'll listen to what he says. If you listen to what he says, you'll know that John is trying to lose weight. If you know he is trying to lose weight, you'll avoid offering him sweets. If you love John, you'll avoid offering him sweets.

e. If Jamiel is a freshman at State College, then he is a student.
However, Jamiel is not a freshman at State College. Therefore, Jamiel is not a student.

f. If my short story gets accepted by my college literary journal, I'm going to celebrate by going to Seven Moons Restaurant. I just found out that it didn't get accepted. I guess I'm not going to be celebrating at Seven Moons Restaurant.

*g. You told me that if I helped you pay off this month's rent so you didn't get evicted, then you'd do anything for me that I wanted. Well, I paid your rent. So here's what I want you to do for me: I know you work part time in the registrar's office. So I want you to break into the registrar's office computer system and change my grades to all A's.

h. If you smoke marijuana, then you're breaking the law. You're not smoking marijuana; therefore, you're not breaking the law.

i. If a person is a politician, then he always lies. Joe is a politician. Therefore, Joe denies being a politician.

j. If a person commits a murder in Rhode Island, he or she cannot be given the death penalty. Craig Price murdered three women in Rhode Island. Craig Price cannot be given the death penalty.

k. If Chad has a fever, then Chad will stay home today. Chad doesn't have a fever. Therefore, Chad will not stay home today.

*l. If John is a Leo, then John is brave. John is a Leo. Therefore, John is brave.

*m. If I become a member of the band Alien Autopsy, then I'll probably have an opportunity to play my steel drums in front of a live audience. If I have an opportunity to play my steel drums in front of a live audience, then I'm more likely to be noticed by a talent scout. Therefore, if I become a member of the band Alien Autopsy, I'm more likely to be noticed by a talent scout.

3. Think of an issue or goal that is important in your life. Write a hypothetical syllogism related to the issue or goal. Evaluate the syllogism for validity and soundness.

*Answers to selected exercises are found in the Solutions Manual at the end of the book.

CATEGORICAL SYLLOGISMS

categorical syllogism A deductive argument with two premises and three terms, each of which occurs exactly twice in two of the three propositions.

subject (S) term In a categorical syllogism, the term that appears first in the conclusion.

predicate (P) term In a categorical syllogism, the term that appears second in the conclusion.

Categorical syllogisms are a type of deductive argument that categorizes or sorts things into specific classes, such as mammals, students, or countries. A categorical syllogism is composed of a conclusion, two premises, and three terms, each of which occurs exactly twice in two of the three propositions. In the following categorical syllogism, each of the three classes or terms—in this case "mammals," "cats," and "tigers"—appears in two propositions.

> All tigers are cats.
>
> Some mammals are not cats.
>
> Therefore, some mammals are not tigers.

Did You Know

Categorical syllogisms can be written in any of 256 standard forms or combinations. Although 256 may seem to be an unwieldy number, putting syllogisms in standard form greatly simplifies the process of evaluations.

Standard-Form Categorical Syllogisms

When a categorical syllogism is put into standard form, the terms in the conclusion are given the label *S* for the **subject** of the conclusion and *P* for the **predicate** of the conclusion. The term that occurs only in the two premises is labeled *M*, for **middle term**. The premise containing the *P* term from the conclusion is listed first, and the premise with the *S* term is listed second. Because it is found in the first premise, the *P* term is referred to as the **major term**, and the premise in which it appears is the **major premise**. The *S* term is also known as the **minor term**, and the premise in which it appears is called the **minor premise**. In addition, the verb in a standard-form categorical syllogism is always a form of the verb *to be*, such as *is* or *are*. Using these guidelines, the above argument written in standard form would look like this:

> All tigers (*P*) are cats (*M*).
>
> Some mammals (*S*) are not cats (*M*).
>
> Therefore, some mammals (*S*) are not tigers (*P*).

In other words:

> All *P* are *M*.
>
> Some *S* are not *M*.
>
> Some *S* are not *P*.

As with hypothetical syllogisms, if the form of a categorical syllogism is valid, as it is in this case, the argument will be valid no matter what terms we substitute for *S*, *P*, and *M*. If the form is valid and the premises are true, the conclusion is necessarily true.

Quantity and Quality

Each proposition in a standard-form categorical syllogism is written in one of four forms, determined on the basis of its **quantity** (universal or particular) and **qualifier** (affirmative or negative). If a proposition refers to *every* member of a class, then the quantity is universal. "All *S* are *P*" and "No *S* are *P*" are universal propositions. If a proposition refers only to *some* members of the class, then it is particular. "Some *S* are *P*" and "Some *S* are not *P*" are particular propositions. The **quality** of a proposition is either affirmative or negative. "No *S* are *P*" and "Some *S* are not *P*" are negative propositions.

The quantity and quality of the proposition is determined by its form, not by which terms (*S*, *P*, and *M*) appear as subject and predicate. For example, "All *P* are *M*" and "No *M* are *S*" are both universal propositions.

Quality and Quantity of Standard-Form Propositions

Universal affirmative:	All *S* are *P* (e.g., All oak trees are plants).
Universal negative:	No *S* are *P* (e.g., No squirrels are fish).
Particular affirmative:	Some *S* are *P* (e.g., Some Americans are Muslim).
Particular negative:	Some *S* are not *P* (e.g., Some nurses are not women).

Diagramming Propositions with Venn Diagrams

Each of the four types of propositions can be represented using a **Venn diagram**, in which each term appears as a circle. The class of *S*, for example, can be represented as follows:

If there are no members of the class *S* (*S* = 0), the circle is shaded in. The following diagram states that there are no members of the class "unicorns," which is represented here by the term *S*.

If there is at least one member of the class (*S* ≠ 0), you put an *X* in the circle. For example, to diagram the class "dogs," we would use an *X*, since there exists at least one dog in the world.

You can follow the same procedure for diagramming any other class represented in a syllogism. Using this method, you can represent each of the four types of propositions in a categorical syllogism using two overlapping circles, since each proposition has two terms. The intersection of the two classes *S* and *P* is the class *SP*, which contains all things that are members of both classes *S* and *P*.

The universal propositions are represented using shading. For example, "All *S* are *P*" says essentially the same thing as "There is no such thing as an *S* that is not a *P*." To represent this, you shade

middle (M) term In a categorical syllogism, the term that appears once in each of the premises.

major term The predicate (P) term in a categorical syllogism.

major premise The premise in a categorical syllogism that contains the predicate term.

minor term The subject (S) term in categorical syllogism.

minor premise The premise in a categorical syllogism that contains the subject term.

quantity Whether a categorical proposition is universal or particular.

qualifier A term such as *all*, *no*, or *not*, which indicates whether a proposition is affirmative or negative.

quality Whether a categorical proposition is positive or negative.

Venn diagram A visual representation of a categorical syllogism used to determine the validity of the syllogism.

in the part of the *S* circle that does not overlap with the *P* circle.

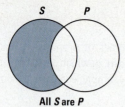

All *S* are *P*

The proposition "No *S* are *P*" states that the class *SP* is empty, or $SP = 0$. To represent this proposition, you shade in the area where the two circles overlap.

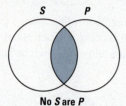

No *S* are *P*

The particular propositions are represented by using an *X*. The proposition "Some *S* are *P*" states that there is at least one member of the class *S* that is also a member of the class *P*. To diagram this, you put an *X* in the area where the two circles overlap.

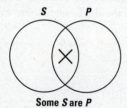

Some *S* are *P*

The proposition "Some *S* are not *P*" tells us that there is at least one *S* that is not a member of the class *P*. To diagram this proposition, you put an *X* in the *S* circle where it does not overlap the *P* circle.

If the proposition stated "Some *P* are not *S*," you would instead put the *X* in the *P* circle where it does not overlap the *S* circle.

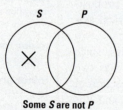

Some *S* are not *P*

Only the Venn diagrams for particular propositions state that there exist members in a class. Venn diagrams for universal propositions, in contrast, only show what doesn't exist. For instance, when we say something like "All tyrannosauruses are dinosaurs," we're not implying that tyrannosauruses actually still exist, just that there is (and was) no such thing as a tyrannosaurus that is *not* a dinosaur.

Venn diagrams engage our spatial reasoning and help us to visualize relationships between classes of things.

Using Venn Diagrams to Evaluate Categorical Syllogisms

Venn diagrams can be used for evaluating the validity of a categorical syllogism. As we noted earlier, Venn diagrams use overlapping circles to represent the terms in a proposition. Since there are three terms (*S*, *P*, and *M*) in a syllogism, you'll need to use three overlapping circles, one for each term. To do this, first draw the two intersecting circles representing the *S* and *P* terms. Then draw the circle representing the *M* term below so that it intersects both the *S* and *P* circles. The area where the *S* and *P* circles overlap makes up the class *SP*, the area where the *S* and *M* circles overlap makes up the class *SM*, and the area where the *P* and *M* circles overlap makes up the class *PM*. The area where all three circles overlap is the class *SPM*.

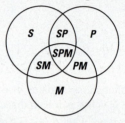

Before diagramming a syllogism, you will need to identify the terms in each proposition. Remember, always start with the conclusion. The first term in the conclusion is *S* and the second term is *P*.

<p style="margin-left:2em;">   *P*   *M*</p>

No (dogs) are (cats).

<p style="margin-left:2em;">   *S*   *M*</p>

Some (mammals) are (cats).

<p>   *S*   *P*</p>

Therefore, some (mammals) are not (dogs).

The next step is to diagram the two premises. If one of the premises is a universal proposition, start by diagramming that premise. In this case, the first premise, "No *P* are *M*," is a universal proposition. To diagram it, you are going to use only the *P* and *M* circles in the Venn diagram. The proposition "No *P* are *M*" tells you that the class *PM*—the area where the *P* (dogs) and the *M* (cats) circles intersect— is empty. In other words, there are no members of the class *PM* or, in this case, there is no such being as a dog that is a cat. To diagram this, shade in the area where the *P* and *M* circles intersect.

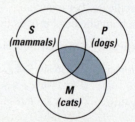

Now diagram the remaining premise "Some *S* are *M*." This proposition tells you that there exists at least one member of the class *S*. In other words, there exists at least one *S* (mammal)

that is also an *M* (cat). To diagram this premise, you put an *X* in the area *SM* where the *S* and *M* circles intersect. Ignore the shaded area where *SM* overlaps *P*, since we know from the first premise that there are no members in *SPM*.

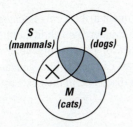

The final step is to determine if the circles contain the diagram for the conclusion, which, in this case, is "Some *S* are not *P*." The conclusion states that there is at least one *S* (mammal) that is not a member of the class *P* (dogs). Diagrammed, this means that there is an *X* in the *S* circle where it does not intersect *P*. Checking this against the diagram of the premises above, we find that there is in fact an *X* in this area. Therefore, this and all other syllogisms of this form are valid.

The following syllogism has already been broken down into its three terms for you:

M   *P*

Some (college students) are (smokers of marijuana).

S   *M*

All (freshmen) are (college students).

S   *P*

Therefore, some (freshmen) are (smokers of marijuana).

In this syllogism the first premise is a particular proposition and the second premise a universal proposition. Therefore, you start by diagramming the second premise. The premise "All *S* are *M*" states that there is no *S* that is not a member of the class *M*. Using only the *S* and *M* circles, shade in the area where the *S* circle does not intersect the *M* circle to show that there are no freshmen who are not also college students.

Next, working only with the *M* and *P* circles, diagram the other premise, "Some *M* are *P*." Place an *X* in the area *MP* where the *M* and *P* circles intersect. Since the *S* circle makes a line through the intersection, draw the *X* on the line to indicate that an *M* (college student) who is a member of the class *P* (smoker of marijuana) may be on either side of this line.

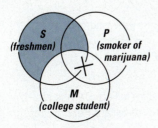

The conclusion states that "some freshmen are smokers of marijuana." In other words, there is an *X* in the class *SP* where the *S* circle and the *P* circle overlap. Looking at the

diagram of the premises, you can see that the conclusion is not contained in the premises, since all that the premises tell us is that there is a member of the class *MP* who may or may not also be a member of the class *SP*. Because the *X* in the premises falls on the line, it is possible that there is a freshman who smokes marijuana, but we can't be sure, since the *X* in the premises may be either in the *SP* circle or only in the *P* circle. Therefore, this argument and all syllogisms that follow this form are invalid.

In using Venn diagrams to determine the validity of a syllogism with two universal or two particular premises, you can start by diagramming either premise. The following is an argument with two universal premises. Begin by labeling the terms in the argument:

P   *M*

All (Americans) are (humans).

S   *M*

No (space aliens) are (humans).

S   *P*

Therefore, no (space aliens) are (Americans).

The first premise states that there are no members of the class *P* (Americans) that are not members of the class *M* (humans). To diagram this, you shade in the area of *P* that does not overlap the *M* circle. The second premise states that there are no *S* (space aliens) that are *M* (humans). Therefore, the area *SM* (human space aliens) is an empty class. To diagram this, you shade in the space where the *S* and the *M* circles overlap, like this:

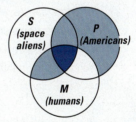

The conclusion states that there are no members of the class *SP* (American space aliens). For this syllogism to be valid, the diagram of the premises must show that *SP* is an empty class. In fact, the area *SP* is shaded in. Therefore, this argument and all syllogisms that follow this form are valid.

Let's look at one last syllogism with two particular premises.

M   *P*

Some (ranchers) are not (horse lovers).

S   *M*

Some (Texans) are (ranchers).

S   *P*

Therefore, some (Texans) are not (horse lovers).

The first premise states that there is at least one rancher who is not a horse lover. To diagram this, place an *X* in the *M* circle where it does not intersect the *P* circle. Remember to put the *X* on that part of the *S* circle where it intersects the *M* circle, since you can't tell from this premise whether this rancher is a Texan. The second premise states that there is at least one Texan (*S*) who is a rancher (*M*). But since this premise does not tell you whether this Texan is a horse lover, put the X on the line in the S circle where the P circle intersects the M circle, since we're not sure which side of the line the Texan belongs on.

Do the premises support the conclusion? To diagram the conclusion, put an X on the line where S intersects M but not P. The conclusion is invalid because the X's from the two premises may be only in the P and M circles. Therefore, this argument is invalid—as are all arguments of this form.

Putting an argument in the form of a categorical syllogism makes it easier to evaluate its validity, either by checking it for formal fallacies or by drawing Venn diagrams. Many everyday arguments can be put into standard-form categorical syllogisms, as discussed in the next section.

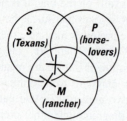

STOP AND ASSESS YOURSELF

EXERCISE 8-4

1. For each of the following propositions, indicate the form of the proposition (universal affirmative, universal negative, particular affirmative, or particular negative), and then draw a Venn diagram for each proposition.

   *a. All beagles are dogs.

   b. Some Democrats are socialists.

   c. Some members of the Tea Party movement are not Republicans.

   *d. No android is a natural object.

   e. Some college students are retired people.

   f. Some scientists are not atheists.

   *g. No atheist is a person who believes in God.

   h. All suns are stars.

   i. Some people who smoke cigarettes are people who get lung cancer.

   *j. Some drugs are not illegal substances.

   k. All professional basketball players are people who are more than 5 feet tall.

   l. No city or town in Australia is a city or town in the Northern Hemisphere.

2. Using Venn diagrams, determine which of the following syllogisms are valid and which are invalid.

   *a. All published authors are writers.
   Some writers are professors.
   Therefore, some professors are published authors.

   b. Some scholars are not geniuses.
   Some scholars are football players.
   Therefore, some football players are not geniuses.

   c. Some Latinos are Republicans.
   All Republicans are American citizens.
   Therefore, some American citizens are not Latinos.

   *d. All members of fraternities are male.
   Some college students are not male.
   Therefore, some college students are not members of fraternities.

   e. Some terrorists are citizens.
   No cats are citizens.
   Therefore, no cats are terrorists.

   f. All members of Congress who voted for the health-care bill are Democrats.
   No members of Congress who voted for the health-care bill are Republicans.
   Therefore, no Republicans are Democrats.

   *g. Some UFO sightings are hallucinations.
   Some UFO sightings are sightings of airplanes.
   Therefore, some sightings of airplanes are hallucinations.

h. No nations that allow capital punishment are members of the European Union.
No European nations are nations that allow capital punishment.
Therefore, all European nations are members of the European Union.

i. All people living in the Netherlands are people living in the European Union.
All people living in Amsterdam are people living in the Netherlands.
Therefore, all people living in Amsterdam are people living in the European Union.

*j. Some Olympic athletes are professional athletes.
No high school cheerleaders are professional athletes.
Therefore, no high school cheerleaders are Olympic athletes.

k. Some actors are comedians.
All comedians are funny people.
Therefore, some funny people are actors.

l. Some scientists are believers in UFOs.
No irrational people are scientists.
Therefore, some irrational people are not believers in UFOs.

*m. Some women are mothers.
No women are men.
Therefore, no men are mothers.

n. All pacifists are opponents of capital punishment.
All pacifists are opponents of war.
Therefore, all opponents of war are opponents of capital punishment.

*Answers to selected exercises are found in the Solutions Manual at the end of the book.

TRANSLATING ORDINARY ARGUMENTS INTO STANDARD FORM

Most of the deductive arguments that we hear or read in our everyday lives are not expressed as standard-form syllogisms. For example, you and your roommate are discussing whether to buy hamburgers or veggie burgers for a picnic you're throwing. She wants to buy veggie burgers, arguing that "it's wrong to eat meat from animals that are capable of reason, such as cows." Is this a valid argument? To answer this question, you first need to rewrite her argument as a standard-form categorical syllogism with three propositions.

Rewriting Everyday Propositions in Standard Form

Start by identifying the conclusion and rewriting it in standard form. Your roommate is trying to prove that it's wrong to eat meat from animals that are capable of reason. To translate this into a standard-form proposition, ask yourself: "What is the quantity (universal or particular) and the quality (positive or negative) of this statement?" Since her conclusion is referring to only some instances of meat eating, the quantity is particular. The quality of her conclusion is positive—she is saying that it *is* wrong to eat meat, as opposed to *is not*. Her conclusion, therefore, is something like this: "Some meat-eating is wrong."

However, this proposition still isn't in standard form. Standard-form propositions have a subject term and a predicate term that are both either nouns or noun clauses and that are connected by a form of the verb *to be*. In this case, the predicate term *wrong* is an adjective. You can rewrite the adjective as a noun phrase by rewording it as *a wrongful act*. The conclusion is now written as a standard-form proposition:

$$S \qquad\qquad P$$

Some (meat-eating) is (a wrongful act).

Determining the quality and quantity of a proposition is not always as straightforward as in the above example. In some instances, you will need to examine the context of the proposition to determine the quality. Consider the following two statements:

Teenagers have more automobile crashes.

Kangaroos are marsupials.

In the first example, does the speaker mean *all* teenagers or only *some* teenagers? In all likelihood, the speaker is referring to only some teenagers. Translating the statement into a standard-form proposition, you have this:

Some (teenagers) are (people who have more automobile crashes than the average driver).

When people intend or interpret statements such as this to be universal, or about *all* young people, they commit the *fallacy of hasty generalization*. We cannot go from a statement about the reckless driving habits of some to a generalization about all teenagers, since many teenagers are safe drivers and some older drivers are a danger on the road.

In the second example, the speaker is making a statement about all kangaroos, since, by definition, a kangaroo is a marsupial. Consequently, this proposition can be translated as a universal positive (*A*) proposition:

All kangaroos are marsupials.

Phrases in ordinary language that indicate that a proposition is universal include the following:

Every *S* is a *P*.   Each *S* is a *P*.
Only *P* are *S*.   *S* are all *P*.
No *P* are *S*.   Whatever is an *S* is a *P*.
Any *S* is a *P*.   If anything is an *S*, then it is a *P*.

Phrases that indicate that a proposition is particular include these:

Some *S* are *P*.   A few *S* are *P*.
Many *S* are *P*.   Most *S* are not *P*.
Not all *S* are *P*.   With few exceptions, *S* are *P*.

Quantity (positive or negative) is usually easier to determine than quality. When the quantity of a proposition is negative, one of the following terms almost always appears somewhere in the original proposition: *no*, *nothing*, *not*, *none*. However, this isn't a hard-and-fast rule. The term *no* may also appear in a universal positive statement, as in this example:

No valid syllogisms are syllogisms with two negative premises.

Translated into standard form, this statement becomes a universal positive proposition:

All syllogisms with two negative premises are invalid syllogisms.

Therefore it is important, when translating a statement into a standard-form proposition, to go back and check to make sure it says the same thing as the original statement.

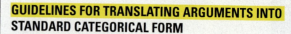

Identifying the Three Terms in the Argument

The next step is to identify the three terms. If you have already translated the conclusion into a standard-form proposition, you have identified two of the terms.

In the opening argument about whether to buy veggie burgers or hamburgers, we recast the conclusion as a standard-form proposition: "Some (meat-eating) is (a wrongful act)." You will notice that there is a term from the original argument that does not appear in the conclusion: "Animals that are capable of reason, such as cows." This term is the middle term (*M*) in the argument. In some ordinary arguments, not all the propositions are explicitly stated. In this case, there is a missing premise that might be worded something like this: "It is wrong to eat animals that are capable of reason." That proposition

is universal and affirmative. Putting it in standard form, you have:

All (killing of animals that are capable of reason, such as cows,) is (a wrongful act).

The second premise can be written as a particular affirmative proposition, since your roommate is saying that only particular types of meat-eating, rather than all meat-eating, are wrong.

Some (meat-eating) is (killing of animals that are capable of reason, such as cows).

Although the verb *involves* would be better English usage here, remember that the verb in a syllogism must be a form of the verb *to be*. Although the wording of this premise is a little awkward, it will do for the purpose of evaluation.

Sometimes there are more than three terms in an ordinary argument. In these cases you will need to reduce the terms to three. If there are two terms that are synonyms, use the same term for both. If there are two terms that are antonyms, or mean the opposite of each other, reduce them to one term by using *not* in front of the antonym. When there are terms that are not essential to the argument, you can simply eliminate them. Consider the following argument:

Not all birds migrate. The spot-breasted oriole, for example, lives on the east coast of Florida year-round.

There are four terms in this argument: *birds, beings that migrate, spot-breasted oriole*, and *beings that live on the east coast of Florida year-round*. In this argument you can combine the second and fourth terms into one by rewriting *beings that live on the east coast of Florida year-round* as *not beings that migrate*. The fact that they live in Florida is not essential to the argument and can be eliminated. The argument now has three terms:

No (spot-breasted orioles) are (beings that migrate).

All (spot-breasted orioles) are (birds).

Therefore, some (birds) are not (beings that migrate).

Putting the Argument into Standard Form

After you have identified the three terms and translated all of the propositions into standard form, you can rewrite the argument as a standard-form categorical syllogism. Going back to our original argument, we have:

All (killing of animals that are capable of reason, such as cows,) is a (wrongful act).

Some (meat eating) is (killing of animals that are capable of reason, such as cows).

Therefore, some (meat-eating) is a (wrongful act).

Once you've set up the argument as a standard-form syllogism, you can easily determine whether it is valid. In this case, it is a valid syllogistic form. In other words, if you agree with the premises, you *must* accept the conclusion. However, you may disagree with the conclusion, even though the argument is valid—but only if you believe that one of the premises is false and the argument therefore unsound. For example, you may argue that the second premise is untrue because only humans are capable of reason and therefore no animals we eat for meat are beings capable of reason. But you'll need evidence to support your position.

Recognizing and evaluating deductive arguments are important skills for everyday decision-making. Using mathematical arguments, arguments by elimination, arguments based on definition, hypothetical syllogisms, and chain arguments, you can use *known* information to discover—with absolute certainty—*unknown* information. Additionally, ordinary arguments used by other people can be translated into standard form to be analyzed for soundness and validity. In Chapter 9, we will discuss the use of critical thinking in moral decision making and in the discussion of ethical issues.

EXERCISE 8-5

STOP AND ASSESS YOURSELF

1. Translate the following arguments into standard-form categorical syllogisms. Identify the form of each syllogism. Determine the validity of each syllogism using Venn diagrams.

*a. "Since man is made in the image of God, then the taking of a man's life is the destruction of the most precious and the most holy thing in the world."[8]

b. If something is a bird then it has feathers. That means my hat must be a bird because it has feathers!

c. The majority of college students are civic-minded, since most college students do some sort of volunteer work and since people who volunteer tend to be civic-minded.

*d. Not everyone who smokes marijuana goes on to use hard drugs. All of my college roommates smoked marijuana, and none of them went on to use hard drugs.

e. Although it's true that most Hispanics are Democrats, this isn't always the case. Cubans, for example, are more likely to vote Republican.

f. Not all parents are heterosexual. I know at least half a dozen gay and lesbian parents.

*g. Teams that wear red uniforms are more likely to win than those who don't. Our team, the Blue Jays, is certain to lose the tournament tonight because we wear blue uniforms, while the opposing team, the Cardinals, will be wearing red uniforms.

h. Not all people who take more than five years to complete a degree are lazy. Some college students take more than five years to complete their degree and no college students are lazy.

i. Many of the abnormal weather patterns we've been experiencing in the past decade are a result of global warming. We've experienced an unprecedented number of droughts and heat spells during the past decade. Many of them are no doubt due to global warming.

*j. Despite what you may have heard, not all college professors are liberals. Some of the professors I know actually voted in favor of free-speech zones on campus, which is something no liberals would do.

2. Find an argument on the Internet or in a newspaper, magazine, or book. Translate the argument into a standard-form categorical syllogism.

*Answers to selected exercises are found in the Solutions Manual at the end of the book.

1. What is a deductive argument?
    - A deductive argument is one in which its conclusion necessarily follows from the premises if the argument is sound. A sound argument is one in which the premises are true and the form of the argument is valid.

2. What are some of the types of deductive arguments?
    - There are many types of deductive arguments, including arguments by elimination, mathematical arguments, arguments from definition, hypothetical syllogisms, and categorical syllogisms.

3. What is a syllogism, and how do we know if it is valid?
    - A syllogism is a deductive argument with exactly two premises and one conclusion. To be valid, the different types of syllogisms have to conform to particular forms. Venn diagrams can be used to determine if the form of a categorical syllogism is valid.

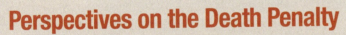

Perspectives on the Death Penalty

In 2011, 93 percent of all known executions worldwide took place in five countries: China, Iran, Iraq, Saudi Arabia, and the United States.[9] The United States is the only Western democracy that still uses the death penalty. More than two-thirds of countries have abolished the death penalty in law or practice, including[10] most Latin American and African countries. Both the European Union and the United Nations support worldwide abolition of the death penalty.

The death penalty was abolished in the United States in 1972 by the U.S. Supreme Court, which ruled that, given the arbitrary and often racially biased patterns in which it was applied, it was "cruel and unusual" punishment.[11] However, the death penalty was reinstated by the U.S. Supreme Court in *Gregg v. Georgia* (1976), which ruled that the death penalty does not violate the U.S. Constitution and for certain extreme crimes is the "only adequate response." Since that time, more than a thousand convicts have been executed. Although as of 2013 capital punishment is legal in thirty-two states, only eleven states and the federal government actually carry out capital punishment, with Texas leading in the number of executions. As of October 2012, there were 3,146 prisoners on death row in the United States.

Even though opposition to the death penalty remains strong among other Western nations, currently the death penalty has widespread support among Americans. A 2013 Gallup Poll found that 63 percent of Americans support the death penalty, up from 47 percent in 1965. Opposition to the death penalty is highest among women and minorities.

In the United States, most executions today are carried out through lethal injection. Because of the lengthy appeal process and the time prisoners spend on death row, the average cost associated with a death penalty case can amount to several million dollars. According to the ACLU, it can cost as much as three times more to keep a prisoner on death row before execution than to maintain a prisoner with a life sentence.

In the following readings, Ernest van den Haag presents arguments for the death penalty, while the American Civil Liberties Union (ACLU) argues against its use.

The Ultimate Punishment: A Defense of Capital Punishment

ERNEST VAN DEN HAAG

Ernest van den Haag is a retired professor of jurisprudence and public policy at Fordham University. An advocate of the death penalty, van den Haag argues that the primary purpose of the death penalty is to satisfy the demands of retributive justice. In his article, he also responds to abolitionists' arguments that capital punishment discriminates against minorities.[12]

The death penalty is our harshest punishment. It is irrevocable: it ends the existence of those punished, instead of temporarily imprisoning them. Further, although not intended to cause physical pain, execution is the only corporal punishment still applied to adults. These singular characteristics contribute to the perennial, impassioned controversy about capital punishment.

I. Distribution Consideration of the justice, morality, or usefulness of capital punishment is often conflated with objections to its alleged discriminatory or capricious distribution among the guilty. Wrongly so. If capital punishment is immoral *in se*, no distribution among the guilty could make it moral. If capital punishment is moral, no distribution would make it immoral. Improper distribution cannot affect the quality of what is distributed, be it punishments or rewards. Discriminatory or capricious distribution thus could not justify abolition of the death penalty. Further, maldistribution inheres no more in capital punishment than in any other punishment.

. . .

Maldistribution of any punishment among those who deserve it is irrelevant to its justice or morality. Even if poor or black convicts guilty of capital offenses suffer capital punishment, and other convicts equally guilty of the same crimes do not, a more equal distribution, however desirable, would merely be more equal. It would not be more just to the convicts under sentence of death.

Punishments are imposed on persons, not on racial or economic groups. Guilt is personal. The only relevant question is: does the person to be executed deserve the punishment? Whether or not others who deserve the same punishment, whatever their economic or racial group, have avoided execution is irrelevant. . . .

Equality, in short, seems morally less important than justice. And justice is independent of distributional inequalities. The ideal of equal justice demands that justice be equally distributed, not that it be replaced by equality. Justice requires that as many of the guilty as possible be punished, regardless of whether others have avoided punishment. . . .

II. Miscarriages of Justice In a recent survey Professors Hugo Adam Bedau and Michael Radelet found that 1,000 persons were executed in the United States between 1900 and 1985 and that 25 were innocent of capital crimes.

. . . Despite precautions, nearly all human activities, such as trucking, lighting, or construction, cost the lives of some innocent bystanders. We do not give up these activities, because the advantages, moral or material, outweigh the unintended losses. Analogously, for those who think the death penalty just, miscarriages of justice are offset by the moral benefits and the usefulness of doing justice. For those who think the death penalty unjust even when it does not miscarry, miscarriages can hardly be decisive.

III. Deterrence Despite much recent work, there has been no conclusive statistical demonstration that the death penalty is a better deterrent than are alternative punishments. However, deterrence is less than decisive for either side. Most abolitionists acknowledge that they would continue to favor abolition even if the death penalty were shown to deter more murders than alternatives could deter.

. . . Deterrence is not altogether decisive for me either. I would favor retention of the death penalty as retribution even if it were shown that the threat of execution could not deter prospective murderers not already deterred by the threat of imprisonment. Still, I believe the death penalty, because of its finality, is more feared than imprisonment, and deters some prospective murderers not deterred by the threat of imprisonment. Sparing the lives of even a few prospective victims by deterring their murderers is more important than preserving the lives of convicted murderers because of the possibility, or even the probability, that executing them would not deter others.

IV. Incidental Issues: Cost, Relative Suffering, Brutalization . . . Some believe that the monetary cost of appealing a capital sentence is excessive. Yet most comparisons of the cost of life imprisonment with the cost of execution, apart from their dubious relevance, are flawed at least by the implied assumption that life prisoners will generate no judicial costs during their imprisonment. At any rate, the actual monetary costs are trumped by the importance of doing justice.

Others insist that a person sentenced to death suffers more than his victim suffered, and that this (excess) suffering is undue according to the *lex talionis* (rule of retaliation). We cannot know whether the murderer on death row suffers more than his victim suffered; however, unlike the murderer, the victim deserved none of the suffering inflicted. Further, the limitations of the *lex talionis* were meant to restrain private vengeance, not the social retribution that has taken its place. Punishment—regardless of the motivation—is not intended to revenge, offset, or compensate for the victim's suffering, or to be measured by it. Punishment is to vindicate the law and the social order undermined by the crime. . . .

Another argument heard . . . is that by killing a murderer, we encourage, endorse, or legitimize unlawful killing. Yet, although all punishments are meant to be unpleasant, it is seldom argued that they legitimize the unlawful imposition of identical unpleasantness. Imprisonment is not thought to legitimize kidnapping; neither are fines thought to legitimize robbery. . . .

V. Justice, Excess, Degradation We threaten punishments in order to deter crime. We impose them not only to make the threats credible but also as retribution (justice) for the crimes that were not deterred. . . . By committing the crime, the criminal volunteered to assume the risk of receiving a legal punishment that he could have avoided by not committing the crime. The punishment he suffers is the punishment he voluntarily risked suffering and, therefore, it is no more unjust to him than any other event for which one knowingly volunteers to assume the risk. Thus, the death penalty cannot be unjust to the guilty criminal.

There remain, however, two moral objections. The penalty may be regarded as always excessive as retribution and always morally degrading.
. . .

Justice Brennan has insisted that the death penalty is "uncivilized," "inhuman," inconsistent with "human dignity" and with "the sanctity of life," that it "treats members of the human race as non-humans, as objects to be toyed with and discarded," that it is "uniquely degrading to human dignity" and "by its very nature, [involves] a denial of the executed person's humanity."

. . . Yet philosophers, such as Immanuel Kant and G. F. W. Hegel, have insisted that, when deserved, execution, far from degrading the executed convict, affirms his humanity by affirming his rationality and his responsibility for his actions. They thought that execution, when deserved, is required for the sake of the convict's dignity. (Does not life imprisonment violate human dignity more than execution, by keeping alive a prisoner deprived of all autonomy?)

. . . This degradation is self-inflicted. By murdering, the murderer has so dehumanized himself that he cannot remain among the living. The social recognition of his self-degradation is the punitive essence of execution. To believe, as Justice Brennan appears to, that the degradation is inflicted by the execution reverses the direction of causality.

Execution of those who have committed heinous murders may deter only one murder per year. If it does, it seems quite warranted. It is also the only fitting retribution for murder I can think of.

REVIEW QUESTIONS

1. How does van den Haag respond to the argument that capital punishment is wrong because it is applied in a discriminatory manner?

2. How does van den Haag respond to the argument that capital punishment is wrong because an innocent person may be executed?

3. How does van den Haag respond to the argument that capital punishment may not be an effective deterrent to crime?

4. According to van den Haag, why do justice and the principle of retribution require capital punishment for some crimes?

The Case Against the Death Penalty

AMERICAN CIVIL LIBERTIES UNION (ACLU)

The American Civil Liberties Union believes the death penalty inherently violates the constitutional ban against cruel and unusual punishment and the guarantees of due process of law and of equal protection under the law. In the following statement, issued on December 11, 2012, the ACLU presents six arguments against the death penalty.

Capital punishment is an intolerable denial of civil liberties and is inconsistent with the fundamental values of our democratic system. The death penalty is uncivilized in theory and unfair and inequitable in practice. Through litigation, legislation, and advocacy against this barbaric and brutal institution, we strive to prevent executions and seek the abolition of capital punishment.

The ACLU's opposition to capital punishment incorporates the following fundamental concerns:

. . .

Capital punishment is cruel and unusual. It is cruel because it is a relic of the earliest days of penology, when slavery, branding, and other corporal punishments were commonplace. Like those barbaric practices, executions have no place in a civilized society. It is unusual because only the United States of all the western industrialized nations engages in this punishment. It is also unusual because only a random sampling of convicted murderers in the United States receive a sentence of death.

Capital punishment denies due process of law. Its imposition is often arbitrary, and always irrevocable—forever depriving an individual of the opportunity to benefit from new evidence or new laws that might warrant the reversal of a conviction, or the setting aside of a death sentence.

The death penalty violates the constitutional guarantee of equal protection. It is applied randomly—and discriminatorily. It is imposed disproportionately upon those whose victims are white, offenders who are people of color, and on those who are poor and uneducated and concentrated in certain geographic regions of the country.

The death penalty is not a viable form of crime control. When police chiefs were asked to rank the factors that, in their judgment, reduce the rate of violent crime, they mentioned curbing drug use and putting more officers on the street, longer sentences and gun control. They ranked the death penalty as least effective. Politicians who preach the desirability of executions as a method of crime control deceive the public and mask their own failure to identify and confront the true causes of crime.

Capital punishment wastes limited resources. It squanders the time and energy of courts, prosecuting attorneys, defense counsel, juries, and courtroom and law enforcement personnel. It unduly burdens the criminal justice system, and it is thus counterproductive as an instrument for society's control of violent crime. Limited funds that could be used to prevent and solve crime (and provide education and jobs) are spent on capital punishment.

Opposing the death penalty does not indicate a lack of sympathy for murder victims. On the contrary, murder demonstrates a lack of respect for human life. Because life is precious and death irrevocable, murder is abhorrent, and a policy of state-authorized killings is immoral. It epitomizes the tragic inefficacy and brutality of violence, rather than reason, as the solution to difficult social problems. Many murder victims do not support state-sponsored violence to avenge the death of their loved one. Sadly, these victims have often been marginalized by politicians and prosecutors, who would rather publicize the opinions of pro-death penalty family members.

. . .

A society that respects life does not deliberately kill human beings. An execution is a violent public spectacle of official homicide, and one that endorses killing to solve social problems—the worst possible example to set for the citizenry, and especially children. Governments worldwide have often attempted to justify their lethal fury by extolling the purported benefits that such killing would bring to the rest of society. The benefits of capital punishment are illusory, but the bloodshed and the resulting destruction of community decency are real.

REVIEW QUESTIONS

1. According to the ACLU, how does capital punishment deny due process of law and violate the Constitution?

2. What does the ACLU mean when it claims that capital punishment is ineffective in controlling crime?

3. How does capital punishment waste limited resources?

4. In what ways does the death penalty violate respect for human life?

THiNK AND DISCUSS

PERSPECTIVES ON THE DEATH PENALTY

1. Working in small groups, summarize the arguments from the readings. Which side presents the strongest argument? Evaluate the arguments.

2. Find a hypothetical argument and a categorical syllogism in one of the readings. Rewrite the argument as a standard-form deductive argument. Evaluate the argument for both validity and soundness.

3. Van den Haag maintains that justice in the form of retribution demands capital punishment for murderers. Do you agree? Discuss how van den Haag would most likely respond to the call from the ACLU to abolish capital punishment.

4. One of the criticisms of the death penalty in the United States is that it is racist. Is this a strong enough concern for abolishing the death penalty? Critically evaluate van den Haag's counter-argument to this concern.

5. Clarence Darrow, a famous American criminal defense attorney (1857–1938), believed that human behavior is determined by circumstances out of our control. In his "Address to the Prisoners in the Cook County (Chicago) Jail," Darrow told the inmates:

   > In one sense, everybody is equally good and equally bad. . . . There were circumstances that drove you to do exactly the thing which you did. You could not help it any more than we outside can help taking the position we take. . . .
   >   I will guarantee to take from this jail, or any jail in the world, five hundred men who have been the worst criminals and law-breakers who ever got into jail. And I will go down to our lowest streets and take five hundred of the most abandoned prostitutes, and go out somewhere where there is plenty of good land, and will give them a chance to make a living, and they will be as good people as the average in the community.

   Identify the premises and conclusion in Darrow's argument. Evaluate the soundness of his argument. Discuss how van den Haag might respond to Darrow's claim that criminals are simply products of their environments and do not deserve to be punished.

6. Should a criminal's level of cognitive development be considered in sentencing? Discuss whether murderers who lack effective critical-thinking skills or who are cognitively immature should receive the death penalty.

9

ETHICS & MORAL
DECISION MAKING

The use of performance-enhancing drugs, substances that are taken to perform better athletically, is prevalent among professional and Olympic athletes. In recent years there also has been a trend toward their use among college athletes, and a study claims that around 5 percent of middle and high school students have used a type of drug called anabolic steroids to bulk up muscle.[1, 2]

Anabolic steroids are synthetic versions of the hormone testosterone and are used to stimulate muscle growth and increase strength, and help athletes recover between workouts or races. However, use of these steroids also increases the risk of heart attacks and strokes and may contribute to the development of liver disease.[3] In addition, some scientists believe that steroid use may contribute to depression, paranoia, and aggressive behavior. In 2007, professional wrestler Chris Benoit strangled his wife and suffocated his 7-year-old son before hanging

What do you think motivated Sean "Diddy" Combs to volunteer his time helping others? How can improving our moral reasoning skills help us to make effective moral decisions that motivate us to take action to improve our lives and those of others?

THiNK FIRST

- How does conscience help us to make moral decisions?
- What is the stage theory regarding the development of moral reasoning?
- In what ways can the different moral theories help us in formulating moral arguments?

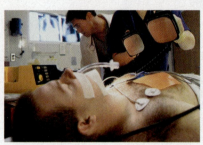

>> himself from a pulley in his basement weight room. His autopsy revealed a high concentration of steroids in his body.[4]

The possession or sale of anabolic steroids without a valid prescription is illegal, and their use is banned by most professional sports leagues as well as the International Olympic Committee (IOC) and National Collegiate Athletic Association (NCAA).

Suppose you are the captain and star player on your college basketball team, and you've made it into the finals. A wealthy entrepreneur, who is an avid basketball fan and alumnus of your college, has promised to make a $60 million donation to your school *if* your team wins the finals. Your college desperately needs the money. It is currently in serious financial trouble and has been forced to cut back on academic programs.

A few weeks before the game, the same entrepreneur offers you a banned performance-enhancing substance known as tetrahydrogestrinone, or THG, one of the new "designer" steroids. When you express concern about getting caught, he assures you that you won't get caught, since THG has been cloaked to avoid detection by drug tests. He also tells you that he will make a $6 million donation, one-tenth of the original amount, even if your team loses, but only on the condition that you take the drug for the next 2 weeks and give the game your best effort. The team you are playing has won the finals the past 3 years in a row.

What should you do? Your school desperately needs the money, and you could do a lot of good for your school by taking the drug. On the other hand, what about possible physical harms of the steroids to yourself? Also, would it be fair to the other team or to sports fans if you had an advantage because of taking this banned drug?

This situation is an example of a moral conflict that requires you to engage in moral reasoning. We are confronted with moral decisions every day of our lives. Fortunately, most of these decisions are fairly straightforward. For the most part we keep promises, don't steal someone else's laptop when their backs are turned, wait our turn in line, and offer a helping hand to those in need. Although we may be unaware of having consciously made these decisions, we have nonetheless engaged in moral reasoning.

Perhaps in no other area are people so prone to engage in rhetoric and resistance as in debates over controversial moral issues such as capital punishment or abortion. Skill in critical thinking can help us to evaluate moral issues from multiple perspectives as well as break through patterns of resistance. In this chapter, we'll be learning how to make moral decisions in our everyday lives as well as how to think about and discuss controversial moral issues. In Chapter 9 we will:

- Examine the relationship between morality and happiness
- Distinguish between moral values and non-moral values
- Learn about the role of conscience and moral sentiments in moral decision making
- Study the stages in the development of moral reasoning
- Examine moral reasoning in college students
- Evaluate the different moral theories
- Learn how to recognize and construct moral arguments
- Apply strategies for resolving moral dilemmas

Finally, we will read and evaluate arguments regarding the morality of abortion and work toward seeking possible resolutions of the issue.

WHAT IS MORAL REASONING?

We engage in **moral reasoning** when we make a decision about what we ought or ought not to do, or about what is the most reasonable or just position or policy regarding a particular issue. Effective moral decision making depends on good critical-thinking skills, familiarity with basic moral values, and the motivating force of moral sentiments.

Aristotle, shown on left, taught that morality is the most fundamental expression of our rational nature and that we are happiest when we put moral values above nonmoral values.

Moral Values and Happiness

Aristotle believed that morality is the most fundamental expression of our rational human nature. It is through being moral, he argued, that we are happiest. The association of morality with happiness and a sense of well-being is found in moral philosophies throughout the world.

Studies support the claim that people who put moral values above nonmoral concerns are happier and more self-fulfilled.[5] **Moral values** are those that benefit yourself and others and are worthwhile for their own sake. They include altruism, compassion, tolerance, forgiveness, and justice. **Nonmoral (instrumental) values** are goal-oriented. They are a means (an instrument) to an end we wish to achieve. Nonmoral values include independence, prestige, fame, popularity, and wealth, which we desire for the most part because we believe they will bring us greater happiness.

moral reasoning Used when a decision is made about what we ought or ought not to do.

moral values Values that benefit oneself and others and are worthwhile for their own sake.

nonmoral (instrumental) values Values that are goal oriented—a means to an end to be achieved.

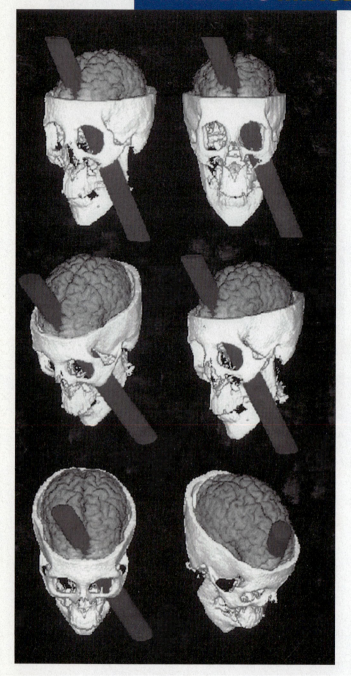

The Brain and Moral Reasoning: The Case of Phineas P. Gage

The frontal lobe cortex in the brain plays a key role in moral decision making. One of the most fascinating studies on the relation between the brain and morality was carried out by a team of scientists on the skull of a nineteenth-century railroad worker, Phineas P. Gage. In 1848, Gage was working on a railway track in Vermont when one of the explosives accidentally went off. The impact sent a long metal rod through his skull just behind his left eye. The rod passed through the frontal lobes of his brain and landed several yards away. This photo shows computer-generated images of the most likely path the rod took as it passed through Gage's skull.

After Gage recovered from the accident, his intellectual and motor skills were found to be unaffected. However, he was no longer able to engage in moral reasoning. Before the accident Gage had been well liked, responsible, and a good worker, whereas afterward he was untrustworthy and obscene and seemed incapable of making even the simplest moral decisions.

DISCUSSION QUESTIONS

1. *Neurologist Jonathan Pincus conducted a study of 14 death row inmates who committed their first murder before the age of 18, and 119 teenagers living in a reform school for delinquents. He found that violent crime is strongly correlated with neurological abnormalities in the brain. If our ability to engage in moral reasoning is dependent on our brain structure, should people such as Gage and criminals whose frontal lobes are abnormal be held morally responsible or punished for their harmful actions? Discuss how we should respond to people who seem to lack a moral sense and hurt others without compunction.*

2. *We expect people to behave morally. When they don't, we're generally taken aback. Think of a situation where you've been surprised because someone seemed to lack a sense of morality. What was your reaction to this person? Discuss why you reacted as you did.*

---

moral tragedy This occurs when we make a moral decision that is later regretted.

conscience A source of knowledge that provides us with knowledge about what is right and wrong.

affective The emotional aspect of conscience that motivates us to act.

moral sentiments Emotions that alert us to moral situations and motivate us to do what is right.

helper's high The feeling that occurs when we help other people.

When buying a car, a person who places nonmoral values above moral values might base his or her decision on stylishness, cost, and a desire to impress other people. A person who places moral values above nonmoral values, in contrast, might place more emphasis on fuel efficiency and environmental friendliness. Although many Americans regard nonmoral values such as career success, financial prosperity, and flashy materialism as the means to happiness, there is in fact little correlation between prosperity or level of income and happiness, except at the lowest levels of income.

On the other hand, there is a positive correlation between level of moral reasoning and critical-thinking ability.[6] This is not surprising, given that critical thinking requires not only that we be aware of our own values but also that we be open-minded and willing to respect the concerns of others.

When we fail to take appropriate moral action or make a moral decision that we later regret, we commit what is called a **moral tragedy**. In the Milgram study on obedience

The Montgomery Bus Boycott began as a protest against the unjust segregation on buses and ended with the U.S. Supreme Court outlawing segregation on buses.

and shaped by our family, religion, and culture.

Conscience has an **affective** (emotional) element that motivates us to act on this knowledge of right and wrong. In Chapter 2, we learned that healthy emotional development can predispose us to make better decisions. Effective moral reasoning involves listening to the affective side of our conscience as well as to the cognitive or reasoning side. Indeed, research shows that psychopaths intellectually recognize right from wrong when presented with a moral dilemma. However, they act violently anyway because they lack the emotional components of sympathy and guilt.[7]

Moral sentiments are emotions that alert us to moral situations and motivate us to do what is right. They include, among others, "helper's high," empathy and sympathy, compassion, moral outrage, resentment, and guilt.

When you help other people, you feel happy and good about yourself. This is known as **helper's high**. The feeling of helper's high is accompanied by the release of or increase in endorphins—morphinelike chemicals that occur naturally in your body. This is followed by a period of increased relaxation and improved self-esteem, which, as we learned in Chapter 1, enhances critical thinking.[8]

Empathy, or *sympathy*, is the capacity for imagining and the inclination to imagine the feelings of others. This moral sentiment expresses itself as joy at another's happiness and sadness at their despair. **Compassion** is sympathy in action and involves taking steps to relieve others' unhappiness. Although most of us are able to feel empathy or sympathy for those who are similar to us, we have a tendency (as we learned in Chapter 4) to divide the world into "us" and "them."

Not all moral sentiments are warm and fuzzy. **Moral outrage**, also known as moral indignation, occurs when we witness an injustice or violation of moral decency. Moral outrage motivates us to correct an unjust situation by demanding that *justice* be done. **Resentment** is a type of moral outrage that occurs when we ourselves are treated unjustly. For example, Rosa Parks's resentment, as well as her courage, motivated her to refuse to give up her seat on the bus to a white man. Her actions sparked the 1955–1956 bus boycott

(see Chapter 1), most of the study subjects who continued to deliver "shocks" to the "learner" knew that what they were doing was morally wrong. However, they lacked the necessary critical-thinking skills to come up with counterarguments to the researcher's argument that "the experiment requires that you must continue."

compassion Sympathy in action.

moral outrage Indignation in the presence of an injustice or violation of moral decency.

resentment A type of moral outrage that occurs when we ourselves are treated unjustly.

Conscience and Moral Sentiments

For most people, a well-developed conscience is the essence of the moral life. The word *conscience* comes from the Latin words *com* ("with") and *scire* ("to know"). A well-developed **conscience** provides us with knowledge about what is right and wrong. Like language, whose basic structure is innate, conscience is nurtured (or neglected)

Connections

What are some of the moral issues involved in a decision to engage in civil disobedience? *See Chapter 13, pp. 410–413.*

SELF-EVALUATION QUESTIONNAIRE: MORAL REASONING*

Case I: Man with an Assault Rifle

Carlos is walking to class one afternoon when he notices a man heading toward a large lecture hall brandishing an assault rifle and swearing under his breath. Carlos, who is interested in pursuing a career in law enforcement, has just come from the shooting range where he enjoys target practice. However, he still has his bag containing his handgun with him, despite the fact that no firearms of any kind are allowed on his campus. No one else has noticed the man with the rifle. If the man starts shooting, should Carlos use his gun on the assailant?

Looking at the following list, determine which considerations are most important to you in deciding what to do. Also determine whether each (1) appeals to personal interests, (2) maintains norms, or (3) appeals to moral ideals or principles. Finally, discuss what other considerations and arguments are important to you in making your decision.

a. Whether stopping the potential assailant or observing the campus's gun code would be better for Carlos's future career in law enforcement

b. Whether the campus's gun code is unjust and getting in the way of protecting unsuspecting students' right to life

c. Whether Carlos's using his gun will anger the public and give his college a bad name

d. Whether Carlos is more responsible to those who created the university's gun code or instead to the students whose lives are in danger

e. Whether Carlos is willing to risk being expelled or going to jail

f. What the basic values are that dictate how people treat one another

g. Whether the man brandishing the rifle deserves to be shot for posing a threat to students

Case II: Buying an Essay from the Internet

Jennifer, a college junior, is taking five courses and doing an internship while trying to maintain her 4.0 grade-point average so that she can get into a good law school and become a civil-rights lawyer. After staying up all night to complete a fifteen-page term paper, Jennifer realizes that she forgot to write a four-page response paper due for an English literature class she's taking. Strapped for time and not wanting to damage her grade in the course, she remembers another student in her class telling her about a Web site that sells essays. She goes to the Web site and finds an essay that fits the assignment. Should Jennifer buy the paper and turn it in as her own?

Looking at the following list, determine which considerations are most important to you in deciding what to do. Also determine whether each (1) appeals to personal interests, (2) maintains norms, or (3) appeals to moral ideals or principles. Finally, discuss what other considerations and arguments are important to you in making your decision.

a. Whether the campus rules against plagiarism should be respected

b. How big the risk is that Jennifer will get caught

c. Whether it is fair to the other students applying to law school if Jennifer isn't caught and gets accepted instead of them because she turned in a plagiarized essay

d. Other students in the class are plagiarizing

e. Whether turning in the paper from the Internet will be best for her future career

f. Whether she is violating the rights of the professor and other students in the class by turning in the essay

g. Whether the professor brought this on himself by placing too many demands on his students

* See page 432 to learn which stage of moral reasoning each answer represents.

in Montgomery, Alabama—one of the turning points in the modern American struggle for civil rights.

While moral outrage calls our attention to an injustice, without effective moral reasoning and critical-thinking skills we may fail to act or may respond ineffectively. Moral outrage or resentment that is not guided by reason may degenerate into feelings of bitterness, blame, or helplessness.

Guilt both alerts us to and motivates us to correct a wrong we have committed. Guilt is a lot like pain. When you cut yourself, you feel pain at the site where the injury occurred. The pain motivates you to repair the injury before it becomes infected and festers. Guilt also motivates us to avoid harming ourselves and others. We refrain from cheating on an exam or from stealing someone's laptop—even when no one is around to see us take it—because the very thought of doing so makes us feel guilty.

Guilt is frequently regarded as a barrier to personal freedom and happiness. Some of us respond to guilt with resistance, either trying to ignore it entirely or getting angry at the person who "made" us feel guilty. But at the same time, we generally regard a person who feels no guilt—such as a sociopath—as inhuman and a monster. This uncertainty about the nature of guilt stems in part from a confusion of guilt with shame.

Guilt is often broadly defined to include shame. However, the two are different. **Guilt** results when we commit a moral wrong or violate a moral principle. **Shame**, on the other hand, occurs as a result of the violation of a social norm, or not living up to someone else's expectations for us. Teenagers who are lesbian, gay, or bisexual may feel shame for not living up to the expectations of their family, church, or society—but they generally do not feel moral guilt. Rather than motivating us to do better, shame leaves us feeling inadequate, embarrassed, and humiliated. As good critical thinkers, it is important that we distinguish between guilt and shame.

Conscience, which has both a cognitive and an affective aspect, can aid in moral decision making. The affective side of conscience includes moral sentiments that motivate us to take action. In the next section, we'll be studying the cognitive or reasoning side of our conscience.

Hot or Not?

Is guilt good or is it a barrier to our happiness?

> **guilt** A moral sentiment that alerts us to and motivates us to correct a wrong.
>
> **shame** A feeling resulting from the violation of a social norm.

Connections

How do marketers manipulate our sense of guilt to get us to buy products we might not otherwise purchase? *See Chapter 10, p. 313.*

EXERCISE 9-1

STOP AND ASSESS YOURSELF

1. Working in small groups, come up with a list of moral values and a list of nonmoral values. Discuss which values are most important to you and why. Discuss also how these values influence your life plan and everyday decisions.

2. Discuss this quotation from Irish poet W. B. Yeats: "Hate is a kind of 'passive suffering,' but indignation is a kind of joy."

3. People who are depressed can become self-preoccupied to the point of becoming indifferent to the consequences of their actions for themselves and others. According to psychiatrist Peter Kramer, author of *Listening to Prozac*, treatment with an antidepressant drug such as Prozac can in some cases "turn a morally unattractive person into an admirable one."[9] In cases where people are depressed to the point of making poor moral decisions, discuss whether it is morally acceptable, or even obligatory, for them to use Prozac or similar drugs to improve their reasoning capacity.

4. Reformers such as Mahatma Gandhi and Martin Luther King, Jr., argued that violence can never be justified by moral outrage. Instead, they insisted, we need to use our moral reasoning to develop nonviolent strategies for responding to violence. Do you agree? Come up with an argument (inductive or deductive) supporting your position.

5. Think of a specific time when you felt guilty and a time when you felt shame. How did you respond in each case? Was your response appropriate, from the point of view of effective critical thinking? If not, discuss how you might develop more appropriate responses to these feelings as well as learn how to better differentiate between them.

6. Looking back at the list of values from your life plan, identify which of these values are moral values and which are nonmoral values. If appropriate, reevaluate and reorganize your values and goals.

THE DEVELOPMENT OF MORAL REASONING

Many psychologists believe that we progress through different stages of moral development during our lives. In this section we'll be looking at theories on moral development and research on moral development in college students.

Lawrence Kohlberg's Stage Theory of Moral Development

According to Harvard psychologist Lawrence Kohlberg (1927–1987), people advance though distinct stages in the development of their moral reasoning capabilities. These stages are transcultural—that is, they are found in every culture of the world.[10] Each new stage represents increased proficiency in critical-thinking skills and greater satisfaction with one's moral decisions.

Kohlberg identified three levels of moral development, each with two distinct stages (see Highlights on page 275). In the first two stages, what Kohlberg called the **preconventional stages**, morality is defined egotistically in terms of oneself. People at this level expect others to treat them morally but generally do not treat other people with moral respect unless doing so benefits them. Most people outgrow the preconventional stages by high school.

People at the **conventional stages** look to others for moral guidance. Earning the approval of others and conforming to peer-group norms are especially important to people at stage 3, the first stage of conventional reasoning. For example, Lynndie England, one of the American guards in the Abu Ghraib prison scandal in Iraq, at her court-martial stated in her defense that she "chose to do what my friends wanted me to."[11] The judge rejected that plea. England completed her three-year prison sentence. She continues to blame the media and others for the scandal.

Most high school seniors and college freshmen are at stage 3 (good boy/nice girl) in their moral development. This stage is associated with the first stage of cognitive development in which students believe that there are right and wrong answers and that those in authority know the right answers.

The next stage of conventional moral reasoning involves substituting the norms and laws of the wider culture for peer-group norms. This type of moral reasoning is also known as *cultural relativism*. The majority of American adults are at this stage. Rather than thinking through decisions about moral issues, they adopt the prevailing view. The mere fact that "everyone" agrees with them confirms, for them, that they must be right.

At the **postconventional stages** of moral reasoning, people recognize that social conventions need to be justified. The fact that something is the law does not make it moral or just. Instead, moral decisions should be based on universal moral principles and on concerns such as justice, compassion, and mutual respect.

A person's stage of moral development is correlated with his or her behavior. Researchers found that only 9 percent of people at stage 2 (egoist) and 38 percent of people at stage 4 (society-maintaining) would offer help to someone who appeared to be suffering from drug side effects; yet all the subjects at stage 6 offered their assistance.[12] Less than 10 percent of American adults ever reach the postconventional level of moral reasoning.[13]

Connections

How does democracy contribute to "tyranny of the majority" and the belief that the majority must know what is right? *See Chapter 13, p. 400.*

preconventional stages Stage of moral development in which morality is defined egotistically.

conventional stages Stage of moral development in which people look to others for moral guidelines.

postconventional stages Stage in which people make moral decisions on the basis of universal moral principals.

STAGES IN THE DEVELOPMENT OF MORAL REASONING

Level—Kohlberg's Description*: Gilligan's Description**

Preconventional

Stage 1—Avoid punishment*: Fear of punishment**

Self-centered *: View your own needs as all that matters**

Stage 2—Egoist *: Put self first; satisfy your own needs; consider needs of others only if it benefits you: "You scratch my back, I'll scratch yours."**

Me   Others

Conventional

Stage 3—Good boy/nice girl *: Put others first; please and help others; maintain good relationships and earn others' approval; conform to peer norms**

Self-sacrificing *: View others' needs as more important than your own**

Stage 4—Society maintaining*: Respect authority and society rules; maintain the existing social order**

Me   Others

Postconventional

Stage 5—Social contract or legalistic*: Obey useful, albeit arbitrary, social rules; appeal to social consensus and majority rule as long as minimal basic rights are safeguarded**

Mature care ethics*: able to balance your own needs and the needs of others**

Stage 6—Conscience and universal moral principles*: Autonomously recognize universal rules, such as justice and equality, that are rational and logically consistent and reflect a respect for equal human rights and the dignity of each individual**

Me   Others

►**APPLICATION: Identify in the text examples of reasoning at the preconventional, conventional, and postconventional stages.**

*Description of Kohlberg's stages adapted from Barbara Panzl and Timothy McMahon, "Ethical Decision-Making Developmental Theory and Practice," speech delivered at a meeting of the National Association of Student Personnel Administrators, Denver, March 1989.

**Description of Gilligan's stages adapted from Carol Gilligan's *In a Different Voice: Psychological Theory and Women's Development* (Cambridge, MA: Harvard University Press, 1982).

People at the lower levels of moral reasoning tend to come up with simplistic solutions. When these solutions don't work or backfire, they become baffled.

People outgrow their old way of thinking when it becomes inadequate for resolving the more complex problems and issues that they encounter in life. Movement to a higher stage is usually triggered by new ideas or experiences that conflict with their worldview.

Carol Gilligan on Moral Reasoning in Women

Kohlberg carried out his research only on men. Psychologist Carol Gilligan argued that women's moral development tends to follow a different path. Men, she said, tend to be duty- and principle-oriented, an approach

she called the **justice perspective**. Women, in contrast, view the world in terms of relationships and caring. She called this the **care perspective**.

Gilligan outlined three stages or levels in the development of moral reasoning in women. Like boys, girls at the preconventional stage are self-centered, putting their own needs first. Women at the conventional stage of moral reasoning, in contrast, tend to be self-sacrificing, putting the needs and welfare of others before their own. The desire to please others can backfire as we saw in the case of Lynndie England (see page 274). Finally, women at the postconventional stage are able to balance their needs and those of others—what Gilligan calls **mature care ethics**.

Although some studies support Gilligan, others have found sex differences to be insignificant.[14] Some women have a strong justice perspective, while some men prefer the care perspective. In addition, most people make use of *both* perspectives in their moral reasoning. Just as the cognitive and the affective sides of our conscience work together, the two types of moral reasoning work and complement each other, helping us to make better decisions.

justice perspective The emphasis on duty and principles in moral reasoning.

care perspective The emphasis in moral development and reasoning on context and relationships.

mature care ethics The stage of moral development in which people are able to balance their needs and those of others.

THiNKing

Outside the Box

GLORIA STEINEM, *Feminist and Writer*

Feminist and writer Gloria Steinem (b. 1934) is a good example of a creative problem solver who was willing to step up to a challenge. Steinem, who was 29 at the time and a struggling journalist, wanted to find a way to make the public aware of how Playboy Clubs exploited women. However, instead of just writing another article, she agreed to participate in a creative solution by going undercover as a Playboy Bunny. Steinem's persistence and willingness to take a risk led to an exposé of the poor working conditions at the Playboy Clubs.

Now in her late 70s, Steinem continues to work for social justice. She also writes and lectures about the importance of strong self-esteem in women's personal development.

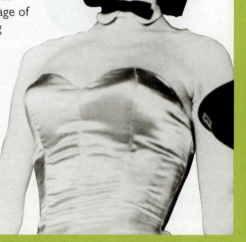

DISCUSSION QUESTIONS

1. Discuss how Steinem's actions in going undercover as a Playboy Bunny relate to the post-conventional stage of moral development as explicated by both Kohlberg and Gilligan.

2. Think of an injustice on your campus or in the world that is of concern to you. Come up with a creative action you might take to make others more aware of this injustice or to change public policy. Share and evaluate your plan of action with others in the class. Discuss how, if at all, working with others helped you come up with a better plan. If appropriate, modify your plan in light of the feedback you receive.

MOHANDAS GANDHI, *Nonviolent Activist*

Mohandas Gandhi (1869–1948), popularly known as Mahatma, or "Great Soul," was born in India, which at the time was ruled by England. As a young lawyer, Gandhi was prohibited by British segregationist practices from sitting where he wanted to on the train and from walking beside his "noncolored" friends. Even worse, he saw people of lower classes or castes being treated with utter contempt by both the Europeans and higher-caste Indians. But rather than acquiesce to cultural norms or internalize his resentment, he responded with moral outrage guided by reason.

His response sparked one of the most effective nonviolent moral reform movements in the history of the world. Following the Massacre at Amritsar in 1919, in which hundreds of unarmed Indian civilians were gunned down by soldiers in the British army, Gandhi launched a policy of nonviolent noncooperation against the British who were occupying India. As a result of his efforts, India gained its independence in 1947.

Gandhi also strove to get rid of the oppressive caste system in India. His respect for the equal dignity of all people and his use of nonviolent resistance as a strategy for political and social reform has had a lasting influence on later civil rights movements, including the 1960s civil rights movement in the United States.

DISCUSSION QUESTIONS

1. Discuss how Gandhi's resolutions to moral issues he confronted in his life reflect thinking at both Kohlberg's and Gilligan's postconventional stages.

2. Think back on a time when you were tempted to respond or responded to violence (verbal or physical) against you with violence. Discuss how a person at the postconventional stage of moral reasoning would most likely have responded and how their reasoning uses the critical thinking skills.

The Development of Moral Reasoning in College Students

A college education is positively correlated with moral development. Many young people in college go through a time of crisis—sometimes called "cognitive disequilibrium"—when they leave home and enter college. They may initially respond to the disruption of their world-views by conforming to their peer culture. The propensity of some freshmen, at the urging of their peers, to engage in self-destructive behavior—smoking, binge-drinking, reckless driving—reflects this conformity.

As we've already seen, freshmen tend to be more black-and-white in their thinking. In a study of moral reasoning in college students, students were presented with the fictional case of "Joe."[15] One day a neighbor discovers that Joe, who has been living the life of a model citizen for several years, is actually an escaped prisoner. Students were then asked, "Should the neighbor turn him in to the authorities?" Freshmen were more likely to say yes because it's what the law dictates. By the time college students reach their senior year, they are still concerned about what the law states; however, they also question whether it would be *fair* for the law to be applied in this case. Those who had reached the postconventional level wanted to know more about Joe and if he had been truly rehabilitated. They also asked which action—reporting or not reporting Joe to the authorities—would most benefit society.

Peer relations at college are important in the development of moral reasoning. Students who have diverse friendships with people different from themselves tend to make greater gains.[16] Discussions of moral issues in classrooms, in which students' ideas are challenged and they are required to support their conclusions, also have the potential to enhance moral reasoning.[17]

Despite these positive influences, most college students do not make the transition to postconventional moral reasoning. Instead, college tends to push students up into a higher stage of conventional reasoning, where they shift to conforming to wider societal norms rather than to those of their peer culture.

Moral reasoning plays an important role in our everyday decisions. Level of moral reasoning is positively correlated with self-esteem, mental health, satisfaction with career goals, honesty, and altruistic behavior.[18] In the next section we will study moral theories that guide our thinking.

Connections

Why is moral reasoning important for college students in deciding how to use social networking on the Internet? *See Chapter 11, p. 348.*

Hot or Not?

Does our current education system inhibit moral development?

EXERCISE 9-2

STOP AND ASSESS YOURSELF

1. Which scheme of moral development—Gilligan's or Kohlberg's—best describes your style and stage of moral reasoning? Discuss situations you've encountered where this stage was adequate for resolving a particular problem or conflict, as well as some situations in which it was inadequate.

2. College tends to move students up to a higher stage of conventional moral reasoning. Working in small groups, discuss why you think this is the case. Make a list of specific suggestions for changes in the curriculum and campus life in general that might promote postconventional moral reasoning.

3. How did you respond to the question on this page about whether you should report "Joe," the escaped prisoner, to the authorities? Are you satisfied with your answer? Explain, referring to the different stages of moral development.

4. Are you less susceptible to peer pressure in making moral decisions than you were in high school or when you first started college? Discuss what factors might have contributed to your ability to think more independently in making moral decisions during your transition from high school to college.

5. Since entering college, have you encountered a situation or problem in which your style of moral reasoning was inadequate? How did you respond? Would you respond differently now? Relate your answers to the stages of moral reasoning.

MORAL THEORIES: MORALITY IS RELATIVE

Moral theories provide frameworks for understanding and explaining what makes a certain action right or wrong. They also help us clarify, critically analyze, and rank the moral concerns raised by moral issues in our lives. There are two basic types of moral theories: (1) those that claim that morality is relative and (2) those that claim that morality is universal. Moral relativists claim that people *create* morality and that there are no universal or shared moral principles. Universalists, in contrast, maintain that there are universal moral principles that hold for all people.

There are two basic types of moral theories: (1) those that claim that morality is relative and (2) those that claim that morality is universal.

The inability of many people to make universal moral judgments on issues such as abortion and capital punishment contributes to the widespread feeling that our positions on moral issues are simply matters of personal opinion and that there is little room for discussion when differences of opinion exist. Critical evaluation of the different theories, however, soon makes it clear that some moral theories are better than others for explaining morality and providing solutions to moral problems.

Ethical Subjectivism

According to **ethical subjectivists**, morality is nothing more than personal opinion or feelings. What *feels* right for you *is* right for you at any particular moment. Consider J. L. Hunter ("Red") Roundtree, who died in 2004 in a Missouri prison at the age of 92. A retired business tycoon, Roundtree pulled his first bank robbery at age 86. "Hold-ups," he said, "made me feel good, awful good."[19] Did the fact that robbing banks made Roundtree "feel good" morally justify what he did? The ethical subjectivist would have to say yes. If Roundtree felt "awful good" about robbing banks, then his actions were morally correct, just as are the actions of a serial killer who feels good about torturing and killing his victims.

Do not confuse ethical subjectivism with the observation that people *believe* in different moral values. Ethical subjectivism goes beyond this by claiming that sincerely believing or feeling something is right *makes* it right for that person. While robbing banks or torturing and killing

people may not be right for you, these actions—according to ethical subjectivism—*are* morally right for Roundtree and serial killers. Since personal feelings are the only standard for what is right or wrong for each individual, a person can never be wrong.

Also, do not confuse ethical subjectivism with tolerance. Ethical subjectivism, rather than encouraging tolerance, allows a person to exploit and terrorize the weak and vulnerable, as long as the perpetrator believes that doing so is right.

Ethical subjectivism is one of the weakest moral theories. Having a right to our own opinion is not the same as saying that all opinions are equally reasonable. Indeed, most people who support ethical subjectivism usually feel quite differently when they are unfavorably affected by someone else's harmful actions.

> **ethical subjectivist** One who believes that morality is nothing more than personal opinion or feelings.
>
> **cultural relativism** People look to societal norms for what is morally right and wrong.

In the previous chapter on deductive reasoning, we learned that hypothetical reasoning can be used to analyze a moral theory by providing us with a means of examining its implications. Consider the following argument:

Premise 1: If ethical subjectivism is true, *then* I am always behaving morally when I act on my personal feelings and opinions, including torturing and raping young children.

Premise 2: Ethical subjectivism is true.

Conclusion: Therefore, I am always behaving morally when I act on my personal feelings and opinions, including torturing and raping young children.

In the above valid hypothetical syllogism, if we are not willing to accept the conclusion as true, then we *must* reject as false the premise: "Ethical subjectivism is true." Ethical subjectivism, if taken seriously, is a dangerous theory. It not only isolates the individual but permits people to exploit and hurt others without ever having to justify their actions or stand in judgment.

Connections

Do we as a society have a moral obligation to restrict certain types of advertising and television shows that may exploit young children? *See Chapter 10, pp. 315–316.*

Cultural Relativism

Cultural relativism, the second form of moral relativism, looks to public opinion and customs rather than to private opinion for moral standards. According to cultural relativists, there are no universal moral principles. Instead, morality is nothing more than socially approved customs. Something that is regarded as morally wrong in one culture—such as polygamy, slavery, spousal abuse, or homosexuality—may be morally neutral or even praiseworthy in another culture.

If you are a cultural relativist, you need only ask what the customs and laws of your culture or society are at this point in time to know what is right and wrong. One hundred and fifty years ago, slavery was considered morally acceptable in the southern part of the United States; today, Americans everywhere condemn slavery as highly immoral. Cultural relativists are not just saying that Americans once *believed* that slavery was morally acceptable. They are claiming that slavery actually *was* moral prior to 1863 when it was outlawed by the Emancipation Proclamation. Indeed—according to the cultural relativists—it was not the slave owners who were immoral but the abolitionists, who opposed the cultural standards of their time.

Cultural relativism can be used to legitimate the oppression of certain groups, as well as perpetuate ethnocentrism (see "Analyzing Images: A Ku Klux Klan Lynching, Indiana, 1930"). The belief that people from other cultures do not have the same basic moral standards that we have can lead to distrust. If two cultures disagree about what is morally right, there are no rational grounds for discussion, since there are no shared universal moral values. If a culture feels offended or threatened by another, the only solutions are isolationism or war.

Cultural relativism corresponds to the conventional stages of moral reasoning. Like ethical subjectivism, cultural relativism is not a correct description of how we make moral judgments. We often pass judgment on our own culture, whether it be about a particular war, abortion, same-sex marriage, or capital punishment.

Connections

Is the "social contract" the source of morality in a culture? *See Chapter 13, p. 397.*

How should we respond when there is a conflict between moral principles and the laws of our society? *See Chapter 13, p. 410.*

Slaves being auctioned. Slavery was once justified as moral by cultural relativists, despite its glaring violation of human rights.

A Ku Klux Klan Lynching, Indiana, 1930 Members of the Ku Klux Klan (KKK) identify morality with the white-supremacist values of their subculture. These values are expressed in hate crimes against African Americans, Hispanic immigrants, Jews, Muslims, illegal aliens, and homosexuals, all of whom the KKK sees as a threat to the American way of life.

The Ku Klux Klan was founded in the South in 1866 and officially disbanded in 1869. It was reorganized in 1915. By the mid-1920s the KKK had 5 million members and had expanded its reign of terror to the northern states as well. In the 1920s, many prominent politicians, including governors, senators, and congressmen, were members of the KKK. It experienced another surge of popularity in the 1950s and the 1960s in opposition to the civil-rights movement. It declined again in the 1980s, only to experience a resurgence following the election of President Obama.

DISCUSSION QUESTIONS

1. *Cultural relativists equate morality with the values of their culture or subculture. However, what happens when the values of one's culture and one's subculture come into conflict with each other? Is the fact that the white-supremacist values of the KKK are currently considered immoral by the government and the majority of American people morally relevant? Would the Klan's values and activities be morally admirable if the majority of Americans believed in them? Support your answers.*

2. *You probably experienced a strong emotional reaction when you first saw this image. What moral sentiments did you experience? Discuss to what extent your response was shaped by cultural values and to what extent it was informed by values that are not culture-bound. Relate your answer to the theory of cultural relativism.*

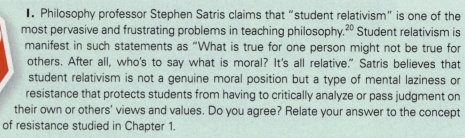

STOP AND ASSESS YOURSELF

1. Philosophy professor Stephen Satris claims that "student relativism" is one of the most pervasive and frustrating problems in teaching philosophy.[20] Student relativism is manifest in such statements as "What is true for one person might not be true for others. After all, who's to say what is moral? It's all relative." Satris believes that student relativism is not a genuine moral position but a type of mental laziness or resistance that protects students from having to critically analyze or pass judgment on their own or others' views and values. Do you agree? Relate your answer to the concept of resistance studied in Chapter 1.

2. What is the source of your moral values? Do you identify with the values of a particular group, such as your peers or religious organization? Are you satisfied with these values when it comes to making moral decisions in your life? Explain using specific examples.

3. Think of a time when you took a moral stand that conflicted with the norms of your peer group. Discuss how you justified your position. Discuss how your peers responded to you. How did you address their concerns?

4. Think of a moral decision you made this past week. Write a short essay discussing which of the values involved in making the decision were moral values and which were nonmoral values. Describe also which moral sentiments played a role in motivating you to carry out this decision. Were you satisfied with your decision? Explain why or why not. If not, how might you use your critical thinking skills to come to a better decision.

*5. In August 1995, 33-year-old Deletha Word jumped to her death from the Belle Isle bridge in Detroit to escape a 19-year-old man who savagely beat her after a fender bender. Dozens of spectators stood by, some even cheering on the attacker. Discuss how an ethical subjectivist would most likely respond to this event.

6. Looking back at the steroids-in-sports question with which we began this chapter, discuss how both an ethical subjectivist and a cultural relativist would have each most likely responded to the hypothetical entrepreneur's proposal.

7. Amina Lawal, age 30, became pregnant after having an affair with her neighbor, who had agreed to marry her. However, he went back on his promise to marry her. Eight days after Lawal gave birth, the police arrested her for adultery, a capital crime in her home state of Katsina in northern Nigeria. She was tried and sentenced to be buried in the ground up to her chest and stoned to death. In her culture, in cases of adultery, typically it is only the woman who is sentenced to death by stoning. There was an outcry in some parts of the world against this practice, and the sentence, at least in Lawal's case, was dropped because of outside pressure. However, on what grounds can we, as Americans, claim that the practice is immoral? Discuss whether our claims that such practices are immoral can be reconciled with cultural relativism.

*8. Working in small groups, write a hypothetical syllogism regarding the implications of cultural relativism (*If* cultural relativism is true, *then . . .*). Share your syllogism with the class for evluation.

9. The U.S. military is grappling with the problem of post-combat guilt among soldiers in Iraq and Afghanistan who have killed in combat. These soldiers believe that the war is right and just. One officer dealing with guilt says, "I know what I did was right. But I'll never lose the sound of that grief-stricken family."[21] Discuss how both an ethical subjectivist and a cultural relativist might explain the phenomenon of guilt in these cases.

*Answers to selected exercises are found in the Solutions Manual at the end of the book.

MORAL THEORIES: MORALITY IS UNIVERSAL

Most moral philosophers believe that morality is universal—that moral principles are binding on all people regardless of their personal desires, culture, or religion. In this section, we'll look at four types of universal moral theories: utilitarianism (consequence-based ethics), deontology (duty-based ethics), natural-rights ethics (rights-based ethics), and virtue ethics (character-based ethics). Rather than being mutually exclusive, as the relativist theories are, these theories enrich and complement each other.

Utilitarianism (Consequence-Based Ethics)

In **utilitarianism**, actions are evaluated on the basis of their consequences. According to utilitarians, the desire for happiness is universal. The most moral action is that which brings about the greatest happiness or pleasure and the least amount of pain for the greatest number. This is known as the **principle of utility**, or the **greatest happiness principle**:

> Actions are right in proportion as they tend to promote happiness, wrong as they tend to produce the reverse of happiness.[22]

In making a moral decision, we need to weigh the benefits and harms (costs) to those affected by an action. English philosopher and social reformer Jeremy Bentham (1748–1832) developed the utilitarian calculus as a means of determining which action or policy is morally preferable. Using **utilitarian calculus**, each potential action is assigned a numerical value—for instance, from 1 to 10, or whatever scale you choose to use—on the basis of the intensity, duration, certainty, propinquity, fecundity, purity, and extent of the pleasure or pain. (Each of these categories is defined in "Highlights: Utilitarian Calculus: Seven Factors to Take into Consideration in Determining the Most Moral Action or Decision," on page 284). The greater the pleasure, the higher the positive numerical value it is assigned; the greater the pain, the lower the value.

Using utilitarian calculus, if a proposed policy or action has a higher total positive value than its alternatives, then it is the better policy. For example, in the case at the beginning of this chapter on using steroids, while the purity of the pleasure may be diluted by any pain to the other team if it loses the game or to you from any short-term physical effects of the drugs, this pain is outweighed by the intensity, duration, and extent of the pleasure or happiness it will bring to your college.

Utilitarian cost–benefit analysis is especially useful in developing policies for the allocation of limited resources. In 1962, there were not enough kidney dialysis machines for everyone who needed them. The Seattle Artificial Kidney Center (now known as the Northwest Kidney Centers) appointed a committee of seven—the so-called God Committee—which decided who should get kidney dialysis on the basis of each patient's capacity to benefit the community. The selection process included criteria such as age, employment history, education level, history of achievements, number of dependents, and involvement in the community. This case points out one of the weaknesses of the utilitarian calculus. While one person may regard the contributions of a poet or artist as having great value to society, another may judge a person's value solely in terms of how much money or material goods they generate.

Utilitarian Jeremy Bentham donated his estate to University College London on the condition that his preserved body (shown with a wax head in the glass cabinet) be presented at board meetings.

In deciding on the best policy, a utilitarian doesn't simply go along with what the majority wants, since people are not always well informed. Nor is happiness the same as going along with personal preferences or feelings. For example, although spending an evening partying may bring you and your friends short-term happiness, your

utilitarianism A moral philosophy in which actions are evaluated based on their consequences.

principle of utility (greatest happiness principle) The most moral action is that which brings about the greatest happiness or pleasure and the least amount of pain for the greatest number.

utilitarian calculus Used to determine the best course of action or policy by calculating the total amount of pleasure and pain caused by that action.

Connections

What are some of the utilitarian arguments for restricting—or not restricting— advertising? *See Chapter 10, p. 309.*

long-term happiness may be better served by studying for an exam you have the next day, so that you can do well in college, graduate, and get a good, well-paying job.

One of the strengths of utilitarian theory is that it requires us to be well informed about the possible consequences of our actions (or inactions) before we make moral decisions. The excuses "I didn't intend any harm" and "Don't blame me—I was just a bystander" don't pass muster with a utilitarian.

deontology The ethics of duty.

categorical imperative Kant's fundamental moral principle that helps to determine what our duty is.

On the other hand, utilitarianism fails to give sufficient attention to individual integrity and personal rights. Restoring peace by arresting and executing an innocent person may bring about the greatest happiness to the greatest number. However, this solution is wrong despite its overall benefit to society because it is wrong to use a person as a means only.

Utilitarian theory is not so much wrong as incomplete. Its primary weakness is not its claim that consequences are important but instead the claim that *only* consequences matter in making moral decisions.

Immanuel Kant is regarded as one of the greatest moral philosophers.

HIGHLIGHTS

UTILITARIAN CALCULUS: SEVEN FACTORS TO TAKE INTO CONSIDERATION IN DETERMINING THE MOST MORAL ACTION OR DECISION

1. *Intensity:* Strength of the pleasure and pain. The greater the pleasure, the higher the positive value; the greater the pain, the more negative the value.

2. *Duration:* Length of time the pain and pleasure will last.

3. *Certainty:* Level of probability that the pleasure or pain will occur.

4. *Propinquity:* How soon in time the pleasure or pain will occur.

5. *Fecundity:* Extent to which the pleasure will produce more pleasure.

6. *Purity:* The pleasure does not cause pain at the same time.

7. *Extent:* The number of sentient beings affected by the action.

▶ APPLICATION: Give an example of each of the seven factors.

Deontology (Duty-Based Ethics)

Deontology claims that duty is the foundation of morality. Some acts are morally obligatory regardless of their consequences. We should do our duty purely out of a sense of goodwill, not because of reward or punishment or any other consequences.

According to German philosopher Immanuel Kant (1724–1804), the most fundamental moral principle is the **categorical imperative**, which (in Kant's famous words) states:

> Act only on that maxim by which you can at the same time will that it should become a universal law.[23]

The categorical imperative, said Kant, must guide our moral decision making. It is inconsistent, for example, to argue that it is wrong for others to lie but that it is okay for us. For example, it was wrong of the journalists to lie to the nurse about their relationship to Kate Middleton, Duchess of Cambridge, who had been hospitalized for morning sickness, even though the journalists may have intended it as a joke and did not expect any harm to come of their "prank" (see page 82). If it is wrong to lie, it is wrong for *everyone* to lie. Moral principles or duties apply to everyone regardless of a person's feelings or culture.

Kant believed that all rational beings will recognize the categorical imperative as universally binding. It is our ability to reason that gives us moral worth. Since humans and other rational beings have intrinsic moral worth or dignity, they should never be treated as expendable, in the way that they can be under utilitarian theory. Because each of us has intrinsic moral worth, according to Kant, our foremost duty is self-respect or proper self-esteem: If we don't respect and treat ourselves well, we're not going to treat others well. This ideal is summed up in Kant's second formulation of the categorical imperative:

> So act as to treat humanity, whether in thine own person or in that of any other, in every case as an end in itself, never as a means only.[24]

This moral obligation is found in moral philosophies and religious ethics throughout the world (see "Critical Thinking in Action: The Golden Rule—Reciprocity as the Basis of Morality in World Religions"). While religious ethics is sometimes considered different from philosophical ethics, the general moral principles recognized by the two are the same.

Kant believed that universalizing moral duties, such as a duty not to lie, requires that these duties be absolutely binding in all circumstances. Most deontologists, while agreeing that moral duties are universal, disagree with Kant, noting that there are situations where moral duties may come into conflict.

Scottish philosopher W. D. Ross (1877–1971) came up with a list of seven duties derived from the categorical imperative (see "Highlights: Seven Prima Facie Duties"). These duties include the future-looking (consequential) duties of the utilitarians, as well as duties based on past obligations and ongoing duties. Ross argued that these duties are **prima facie** (translated "at first view")—that is, they are morally binding unless overridden by a more compelling moral duty.

Let's look at an example. You have promised to pay back, by a certain date, money that you borrowed from a friend. Under ordinary circumstances, you would have a duty of fidelity to pay back the money. Your friend arrives at your door on the due date and is furious because his chemistry professor gave him a failing grade. He is carrying parts for a bomb and demands the money so he can buy the rest of the explosives he needs to blow up the science building. Should you give him the money? In situations such as these, you need to determine which moral duties are the most compelling. In this case, the duty of nonmaleficence—preventing serious harms to other people—overrides your duty to pay back the money.

> **prima facie duty** Moral duty that is binding unless overridden by a more compelling moral duty.

Deontology is a powerful moral theory, especially when it incorporates the insights of the utilitarians. While deontology is strong on moral principle and duty, one of its limitations is the failure to adequately take into account the role of sentiment and care ethics in moral decision making. On the other hand, deontology provides a solid foundation and justification for rights-based ethics—to which we now turn.

Connections

What steps does our judicial process take to ensure that everyone is treated fairly? *See Chapter 13, pp. 414–415.* Do we as citizens have a moral obligation to vote? *See Chapter 13, pp. 401–402.*

HIGHLIGHTS

SEVEN PRIMA FACIE DUTIES

FUTURE-LOOKING DUTIES

- *Beneficence:* The duty to do good acts and to promote happiness.

- *Nonmaleficence:* The duty to do no harm and to prevent harm.

DUTIES BASED ON PAST OBLIGATIONS

- *Fidelity/loyalty:* Duties arising from past commitments and promises.

- *Reparation:* Duties that stem from past harms to others.

- *Gratitude:* Duties based on past favors and unearned services.

ONGOING DUTIES

- *Self-improvement:* The duty to improve our knowledge (wisdom) and virtue.

- *Justice:* The duty to treat all people with dignity and to give each person equal consideration.

➤ *APPLICATION: Provide an example of each of the seven prima facie duties.*

Rights-Based Ethics

In rights-based ethics, moral rights are *not* identical to legal rights, as they are in cultural relativism. Because we have moral rights, others have a duty to honor these rights.

Critical THiNKing in Action

The Golden Rule—Reciprocity as the Basis of Morality in World Religions

Buddhism: "Hurt not others in ways that you yourself would find hurtful." *Udana Varga 5:18*

Christianity: "Always treat others as you would like them to treat you." *Matthew 7:12*

Confucianism: "Do not do to others what you do not want them to do to you." *Analects 15:23*

Hinduism: "This is the sum of the Dharma [duty]: do naught unto others which would cause pain if done to you." *Mahabharata 5:1517*

Islam: "None of you [truly] believes until he wishes for his brother what he wishes for himself." *Number 13 of Iman "Al-Nawawi's Forty Hadiths"*

Judaism: ". . . thou shall love thy neighbor as thyself." *Leviticus 19:18*

Native American spirituality: "Respect for all life is the foundation." *The Great Law of Peace*

DISCUSSION QUESTIONS

1. Discuss the deontologist's claim that the categorical imperative (law of reciprocity) is a universal and fundamental principle of ethics. If you are a member of a religion, discuss ways in which this fundamental principle of ethics is (or is not) expressed in your religion.

2. Most of us have been taught some form of the duty of reciprocity as young children. Using a specific example, discuss the extent to which this duty influences your everyday moral reasoning and behavior.

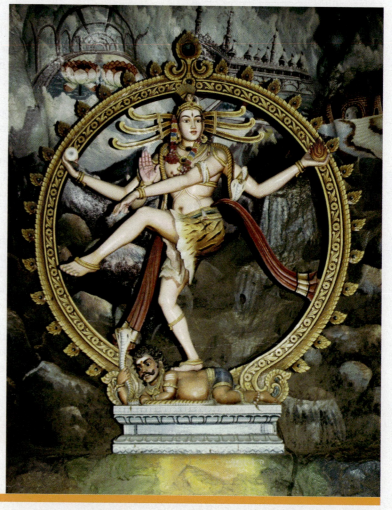

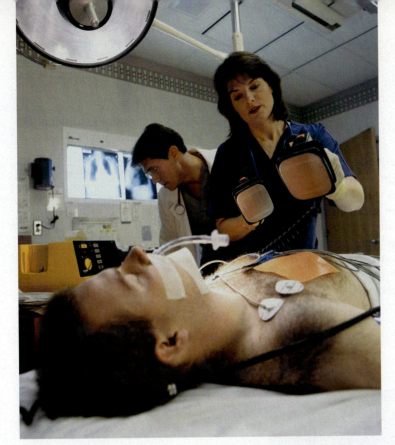

Welfare rights include the right to emergency medical care, regardless of ability to pay.

Connections

To what extent should media speech be protected by freedom of speech? *See Chapter 11, p. 336.* What are some of the moral conflicts raised by potential misuses of the Internet? *See Chapter 11, pp. 350–351.* Does the USA Patriot Act violate people's liberty rights, or does the government's duty to protect citizens override these rights? *See Chapter 13.*

The right to pursue our interests is limited to our **legitimate interests**—that is, those interests that do not harm other people by violating their similar and equal interests.

Moral rights are generally divided into welfare and liberty rights. **Welfare rights** entail rights to receive certain social goods, such as education, and police and fire protection, which are essential for our welfare, or well-being. At the heart of the Affordable Care Act, commonly called Obamacare, is a belief that health care is a welfare right. Welfare rights are important because without them, we cannot effectively pursue our legitimate interests.

Liberty rights entail the right to be left alone to pursue our legitimate interests. A misogynist (a man who hates women) may have an *interest* in keeping women out of the workplace, but this does not give him the *right* to do so, since it violates women's right to equal opportunity—a liberty right—and therefore his is not a *legitimate interest*. Freedom of speech, freedom of religion, freedom to choose our major and career path, the right to privacy, and the right to own property are all examples of liberty rights.

Rights ethics is an important component of a comprehensive moral theory because rights protect our equality and dignity as persons. Like duties, rights may come into conflict with each other or with other duties. When this happens, we need to use our critical-thinking skills to decide which are the more compelling moral rights and/ or duties.

HIGHLIGHTS

UNIVERSAL MORAL THEORIES

- *Utilitarianism:* Morality is based on consequences.
- *Deontology:* Duty is the foundation of morality. We have a duty to act only on principles that we would want to be universal laws.
- *Rights-based ethics:* Rights are the primary moral concern.
- *Virtue ethics:* Character is more important than right actions.

➤ APPLICATION: Find in the text an example of the application of each theory.

---

legitimate interests Interests that do not violate others' similar and equal interests.

welfare rights The right to receive certain social goods that are essential to our well-being.

liberty rights The right to be left alone to pursue our legitimate interests.

Virtue Ethics

Virtue ethics emphasize character over right actions. The sort of person we are constitutes the heart of our moral life. Virtue ethics are not an alternative to moral theories that stress right conduct, such as utilitarian and deontological theories. Rather, virtue ethics and theories of right action complement each other.

virtue ethics Moral theories that emphasize character over right actions.

moral sensitivity The awareness of how our actions affect others.

A *virtue* is an admirable character trait or disposition to habitually act in a manner that benefits ourselves and others. The actions of virtuous people stem from a respect and concern for the well-being of themselves and others. Compassion, courage, generosity,

loyalty, and honesty are all examples of virtues. Because virtuous people are more likely to act morally, virtue ethics goes hand in hand with the other universal moral theories.

Being a virtuous person entails cultivating moral sensitivity. **Moral sensitivity** is the awareness of how our actions affect others. Morally sensitive people are more in tune with their conscience and more likely to feel guilty when they harm another person or to feel moral indignation when they witness an injustice.

Moral theories do not exist in abstraction. They inform and motivate our real-life decisions and actions. By using the universal theories together and drawing from the strengths of each, we can become more proficient at analyzing and constructing moral arguments as well as resolving moral conflicts.

ANALYZING **IMAGES**

DISCUSSION QUESTIONS

1. *According to American social theorist James Q. Wilson, the author of* The Moral Sense *(1993), some people from birth seem to have a great capacity for empathy and justice—what Aristotle called "natural virtue." People at the higher levels of moral development, like the people in the above photo, are more likely to rescue others in distress, even at a risk to their own lives. Does the duty of beneficence require that we help others in distress and, if so, what are the limits, if any, on this duty? Support your answer.*

2. *Discuss ways in which our education system might enhance our moral sensitivity as well as our capacity to help others in need.*

STOP AND ASSESS YOURSELF

*1. Imagine that the government has decided to reinstate the military draft. Using utilitarian calculus, come up with a plan for determining who should be drafted and who, if anyone, should be exempt from the draft.

2. Examine Ross's list of prima facie duties in light of the categorical imperative and ethics of reciprocity. Are the duties consistent with this fundamental moral principle? Working in small groups, come up with examples of each of the above moral duties in your personal lives.

3. Referring back to the case at the beginning of this chapter, use Kant's categorical imperative and Ross's prima facie duties to decide whether you ought to take the steroids.

4. What is your greatest virtue? Discuss how this virtue contributes to your ability to be a better critical thinker.

5. The majority of parents in the United States believe that it is morally acceptable, even praiseworthy, to tell their young children that Santa Claus is a real, physical person. Is it morally right to tell children this, even though it is a lie? Support your answer using the categorical imperative and duty of reciprocity.

6. After the September 11, 2001, terrorist attacks, hundreds of Arab American men were detained for questioning as a means of combating terrorism. Many were arrested and imprisoned, without being told why they were being detained. Discuss whether restricting the rights of certain groups in times of crisis is morally justified and, if so, on what grounds.

7. Utilitarian theory is often used to formulate social policies around issues such as HIV testing, free-speech zones, and the distribution of social goods such as scholarships and medical benefits. Find some examples of utilitarian reasoning in our current government policies or policies at your college. Write a short essay explaining why these policies illustrate utilitarian reasoning. Critically evaluate each policy.

*Answers to selected exercises are found in the Solutions Manual at the end of the book.

MORAL ARGUMENTS

Moral theories provide the foundation for moral arguments and their application to real-life situations.

Recognizing Moral Arguments

A moral argument, like any argument, has premises and a conclusion. However, unlike nonmoral arguments, at least one of the premises is a *prescriptive premise*—that is, it makes a statement regarding what is morally right and wrong or what *ought* to be the case. Moral arguments also contain *descriptive premises* about the world and human nature. In the following argument, the first premise is a prescriptive premise and the second premise is a descriptive (factual) premise.

> *Prescriptive premise*: It is wrong to inflict unnecessary suffering on people.
>
> *Descriptive premise*: Imprisonment causes unnecessary suffering by restricting inmates' freedom of movement.
>
> *Conclusion*: Therefore, it is wrong to imprison people.

Moral arguments may also contain premises that define key or ambiguous terms. In the above example, the argument would be stronger if it provided a definition of the ambiguous term *unnecessary suffering*. *Unnecessary suffering* may be defined as "suffering that is not essential for achieving a particular desired goal." In this case, if our goal is to prevent further harm to the community, is prison the only means of keeping this person from further harming the community, or does imprisonment constitute "unnecessary suffering"?

In making a moral argument, we should first get our facts straight. Incorrect facts or assumptions can lead to a faulty conclusion. Until recently most physicians lied to patients who were dying because they believed that telling patients the truth would upset them and hasten their deaths. It wasn't until the 1960s that a study on the effects of truth-telling showed that people with terminal cancer actually did better and lived longer if they knew the truth about their condition.[25] Good intentions, in other words, are not enough in making moral decisions. If we make unfounded assumptions without first checking our facts, we may end up actually doing more harm than good.

Constructing Moral Arguments

Constructing a moral argument is like constructing any argument, except at least one of the premises must be prescriptive. As with other arguments, begin by clearly identifying the issue. Let's use a simple example. You ride to class with one of your friends. While pulling her car into a parking spot, your friend scrapes the fender of another car. Suppose she starts to pull out and leave the scene of the accident? What should you do? You could say nothing, but by doing so you become complicit in your friend's decision to avoid taking responsibility for the accident.

After deciding that you should say something, your next step is to make a list of descriptive and prescriptive premises. In this case one of the descriptive premises could simply be a factual statement of what happened: Your friend damaged the fender of the car next to her when she pulled her car into the parking spot. In some cases the facts may be more complex and you'll need more premises, but in this case let's assume that the next car was legally parked and not moving, and no one was around to witness the accident except you and your friend.

To come up with prescriptive premises, ask yourself, "What are the moral duties, rights, and values that are relevant to this case?" The principle of reparation is relevant; if we cause harm, whether intentionally or unintentionally through carelessness, we have a moral duty to make up for that harm. The corresponding right in this case is the right of the other person to be compensated for that harm. In fact, one of the reasons we are required to carry automobile insurance is so we can honor the rights of others if we have an accident for which we are responsible.

If you are talking to someone at the postconventional level of moral reasoning, these premises may be sufficient for your friend to come to the conclusion that she ought to take steps to pay for the damage to the other car. However, what if she says, "I don't care" or "If I do, my parents will find out what happened and get angry with me"? If this happens, you need to persist in making your moral argument in a way that is respectful of your friend. You have both a duty of beneficence to be caring as well as a duty of fidelity (loyalty) to your friend. This may require gathering more information. For example, why is she worried about her parents' reaction?

You might also want to add a prescriptive premise containing an application of the principle of reciprocity by asking her, "How would you feel if someone hit your parked car and just drove off? I bet you'd be pretty upset, and rightly so." Remember not to use an accusatory tone in stating your premises—that would mean committing the abusive or ad hominem fallacy. Resorting to this fallacy tends to alienate others and moves you further from a satisfactory moral conclusion or resolution.

The issue and premises can be summarized as follows:

Issue: Your friend scraped the fender of a car in the parking lot. What should she do, and what should you do?

Descriptive premises:

- Your friend damaged the fender of the car next to her when she pulled her car into the parking spot.
- Your friend was driving her parents' car.
- Your friend is concerned that her parents will get angry when they learn about the accident.

Many of the prisoners at Guantanamo Bay were denied access to legal counsel and other protections as required by the United Nations' Geneva Conventions.

may be left out because it is obvious or uncontroversial. Take this example:

> I'm so angry! I have a good grade point average but was refused a college scholarship solely on the grounds that I was a mother of a young child—and, as they said, my place is in the home. That's just not right![26]

The unstated premise in this argument involves the *duty of justice*: The college has a duty to give each student equal consideration. In this case, the only relevant criteria for consideration should have been based on grade point average, not the parental status of the student.

In some moral arguments, a prescriptive premise may be left out because it is controversial or questionable. Consider this argument:

> *Descriptive premise*: The Second Amendment to the United States Constitution protects people's right "to keep and bear arms."
> *Conclusion*: I have a moral right to own a handgun.

The unstated prescriptive premise in this argument is that "an action or policy is morally right if it is constitutional." In other words, this argument assumes cultural relativism is true. However, this is a questionable premise. Owning slaves was a *legal* right, at least prior to the 1865 ratification of the Thirteenth Amendment, which outlawed slavery. But most of us do not consider it to be a *moral* right—either now or before 1865. Similarly, in the argument about handguns, although you may agree with the conclusion, the premises do not support it.

The premises should also be true. If just one premise is false, the argument is unsound. For example, some people support the practice of cohabitation (living together) on the grounds that people who live together before marriage have a better chance of a successful marriage. However, research does not support this claim: The divorce rate is in fact significantly higher among married couples who lived together before their marriage or engagement.[27]

Moral arguments should also be free of informal fallacies. Consider:

> Cloning humans is wrong because it is unnatural. Therefore, human cloning ought to be illegal.

In this argument, the person is making the assumption that if something is unnatural, then it is morally wrong, thereby committing the *naturalistic fallacy*. If immorality were synonymous with what is unnatural, then the use of antibiotics, eyeglasses, or even clothing (at least in warm climates!) would be immoral.

Another fallacy that often appears in moral arguments is the *fallacy of popular appeal*. This fallacy is most likely to be used by a cultural relativist or by a person at the conventional stages of moral reasoning. The *fallacy of hasty*

Connections

What are some of the ethical concerns in designing scientific experiments? *See Chapter 12, pp. 383–384.*

Prescriptive premises:

- We have a moral duty to make up for past harms we cause others (duty of reparation).
- The person whose car your friend struck has a right to be compensated for the damage (welfare right).
- I have a duty to be kind and caring to my friend (duty of beneficence).
- I have a duty of loyalty to my friend (duty of fidelity).
- We should treat others as we would want to be treated (law of reciprocity).

In making a moral argument, the point is not to prove that you are morally superior to others but to come to a conclusion that leads to an action or a policy that is reasonable and most consistent with moral values. Do not come to a conclusion until you've developed a list of relevant premises that you can both agree on. Remain open-minded and flexible. Help your friend seek strategies that encourage her to do the right thing while minimizing possible harm to her from angry parents. Taking the premises into consideration, you may come to the following solution or conclusion:

> *Conclusion*: Your friend should leave a note on the other car with her name and phone number explaining what happened, and you should go with your friend when she tells her parents about the accident.

This is a relatively straightforward moral argument that leads to a solution, taking into account all the relevant moral principles. In a later section, we'll be studying strategies for resolving moral dilemmas, cases in which there is a conflict between moral principles and concerns.

Evaluating Moral Arguments

In evaluating moral arguments, the first step is to make sure that the argument is complete and that no important premises are omitted. In some moral arguments, the prescriptive premise(s) is unstated. A prescriptive premise *generalization* may also be used by a cultural relativist to justify cultural stereotypes and the denial of equal treatment to certain groups of people.

Finally, the *slippery-slope fallacy* is committed in a moral argument when we argue, without sufficient evidence, against a practice on the grounds that if we allow it, then we'll have to permit other similar actions. This fallacy is most common in arguments about new technologies or practices—such as genetic engineering, same-sex marriage, and physician-assisted suicide—where we're not sure of the future consequences on society.

These are only a few of the fallacies that may appear in moral arguments. For a more in-depth review of the different informal fallacies, see Chapter 5.

Resolving Moral Dilemmas

A situation in which we have a conflict between moral values is known as a **moral dilemma**. No matter what solution you choose, it will involve doing something wrong in order to do what is right. We do *not* have a moral dilemma when the conflict is between moral values and nonmoral values, such as popularity or economic success. Solutions to moral dilemmas are not right or wrong, only better or worse.

In resolving a moral dilemma, resist the temptation to start with a "solution" and then rationalize it by selecting only the facts and principles that support it. Instead, a

moral dilemma should be resolved in a systematic manner (see "Highlights: Steps for Resolving a Moral Dilemma").

Consider this classic example of a moral dilemma:

On May 19, 1894, the yacht *Mignonette* sailed from England for Sydney, Australia, where it was to be delivered to its new owner. There were four people aboard: Dudley, the captain; Stephens, the mate; Brooks, a seaman; and Parker, a 17-year-old cabin boy and apprentice seaman. The yacht capsized in the South Atlantic during a storm, but the crew managed to put out in a 13-foot lifeboat. They drifted for 20 days in the open boat. During this time, they had no fresh water except rainwater and, for the last 12 days, no food. They were weak and facing starvation. The captain called them together to make a decision about their fate. What should they do?

The first step in resolving a moral dilemma is to *clearly describe the facts*, including finding answers to any missing information. In the case of the *Mignonette* crew, you may want to know whether it was possible to catch fish (the answer is no); how much longer the crew might live (one was already dying), or whether they were near a shipping lane (no). You may also have questions about the status of the different men: Do they have families back home, how old are they, and so forth.

Next, *list the relevant moral principles and concerns.* We have a *duty to respect life*, as well as a *duty of nonmaleficence*—not to cause harm or to minimize harm. The *duty of justice* and equal treatment of all of the crew members is also relevant in this case. It's not fair to single out one crew member to kill and eat. The

Sailing before the wind : How the dinghy was managed during the last nine days.

crew members also have a *liberty right* to be left alone and not be killed unless they are interfering with someone's equal right to life. On the other hand, the captain has a *duty of fidelity* to his crew, which might put the onus on him to sacrifice his life to save his crew.

Once you have collected all your facts and made a list of the relevant moral principles, *list the possible courses of action*. Now is the time to brainstorm and get feedback from other people. List any possible actions that come to mind. In this dilemma, possible courses of action might include the following:

- The crew can wait and hope for a rescue.
- Everyone can starve to death together.
- Everyone can commit suicide together.
- The crew can eat the first person who dies.
- The crew can kill and eat the weakest person.
- The crew can kill and eat the person with the least social utility.
- Someone can volunteer to be killed and eaten.
- The crew can draw lots to see who gets eaten.

HIGHLIGHTS

STEPS FOR RESOLVING A MORAL DILEMMA

1. Describe the facts.
2. List the relevant moral principles and concerns.
3. List and evaluate possible courses of action.
4. Devise a plan of action.
5. Carry out the plan of action.

▶ APPLICATION: Identify an example of each of the steps in the text.

The next step is to *devise a plan of action*. The crew has already tried the first course of action, but there seems to be no hope of rescue, and they are near death. They now face choosing from the remaining courses of action. To evaluate these, examine each in light of your list of moral principles. Ideally, the best resolution to a moral dilemma is the one that honors as many moral values as possible.

The principle of nonmaleficence requires that you try to minimize harm—in this case, the death of the crew members. Because the second and third courses of action involve the death of everyone, they're not good choices. On the other hand, killing someone without that

> **Ideally, the best resolution to a moral dilemma is the one that honors as many moral values as possible.**

person's permission is a violation of the person's liberty right and is unjust because it discriminates against the person. Eating the person who dies first, although gross, is not immoral—except to cultural relativists, since cannibalism is taboo in our society. Under the circumstances, it may be the best solution, since it honors the most moral principles. However, what if no one has died yet, and instead everyone is on the verge of starvation? The last two solutions both avoid the problem of injustice and may have to be the last resort.

The final step is to *carry out the plan of action*. It's also a good idea to have a backup plan in case the first plan of action doesn't work. In some moral dilemmas, people may agree on the premises but still come to different conclusions because they prioritize the relevant moral duties and concerns differently. For example, the captain may favor utilitarian theory and value the strongest members of his crew, reasoning that keeping them alive and killing the weakest member may increase the chances of at least *one* person surviving. However, the cabin boy, who lacks experience and has become extremely seasick, may value the fidelity of the captain and believe that it is the captain's tacit duty to sacrifice himself for his crew, since he was the one who was responsible for getting them into this precarious position in the first place. On the other hand, a person at the postconventional stages of moral reasoning who favors the justice perspective would probably prefer the last course of action—draw lots to see who gets eaten—since it is the most fair and just solution.

In fact, what happened is that the captain and two crew members killed Parker, the cabin boy, and ate him. The three remaining survivors were eventually rescued by a Swedish ship and returned to England, where they were tried for murder. The court ruled that the killing of Parker was not justified, since it was not in self-defense, and the men were found guilty of murder. This ruling continues to serve as a legal precedent in maritime law.

In this section, we have seen that a moral argument is much like other arguments, except that it must include at least one prescriptive premise. When trying to decide what is the best moral position or course of action, you should begin by listing the premises. Just as you would for other arguments, you must check the descriptive premises for their accuracy. If used correctly, moral reasoning can be a powerful tool for clarifying and resolving issues and dilemmas in your everyday life.

Connections

What is legal precedence, and what type of inductive reasoning is it based on? *See Chapter 13, p. 415.*

STOP AND ASSESS YOURSELF

1. Determine whether each of the following premises is a descriptive premise, prescriptive premise, or a premise containing a definition:

*a. You ought to keep your promise to Chad.

b. Mary is opposed to capital punishment.

c. Torturing prisoners of war is a violation of the Geneva convention.

*d. Steroids are a type of performance-enhancing drug.

e. We are all entitled to freedom of speech.

f. School bullying is a violation of the categorical imperative and the principle of reciprocity.

*g. Doing community service work makes me feel good about myself.

h. Binge drinking is harmful because it can cause acute intoxication and even death.

i. Passive euthanasia is the withholding or withdrawing of medical treatment, resulting in a patient's death.

*j. Americans should give more money to poorer nations.

2. Discuss possible courses of action (conclusions) that your friend who scraped the fender of the car in the parking lot might take in the scenario described on page 290. Support your answer by taking into account the relevant moral duties and rights.

3. Evaluate each of the following moral arguments. If an argument is missing one or more premises, indicate what they are.

*a. You should not drink alcohol in your dorm room. After all, it's against the rules, since we're a dry campus. Also, it's against the law for anyone younger than 21 to drink alcohol, and you're only 18.

b. Euthanasia is wrong because it interferes with the natural dying process. We should wait until it is our time to die.

c. You should think of doing the optional community-service learning project for class. Studies show that doing a community-service project can actually enhance a student's level of moral development.

*d. Professor Dugan is Chris's teacher. Therefore, it would be wrong for Professor Dugan to try to initiate an intimate relationship with Chris.

e. The Affordable Care Act is a step in the right direction, but it doesn't go far enough. We ought to extend Medicare to all American citizens. That way everyone will be assured of the same basic medical coverage.

f. You're only 28. You should wait until you're in your thirties to get married. The duty of fidelity requires that we should do our best to honor our marriage vow "until death do us part," and the older you are when you get married, the less likely you are to divorce.

*g. Animals can feel pain. It is wrong to cause sentient beings pain when it can be avoided. Therefore, it is wrong to eat meat.

h. Cyberbullying is getting out of hand. Social network sites, such as Facebook, should be closely monitored and anyone caught posting intimidating remarks should lose their right to use the site and be reported to the police.

i. Those teenagers who vandalized the Van Zandt property should at least have to repay the owners for the damage and maybe even serve some time in a juvenile detention facility. It's not fair these rich students get off with just a slap on the hand while others, especially black teenagers, are sent to jail for doing the same thing.

*j. Medical research using human embryonic stem cells is morally acceptable. Recent polls show that the majority of Americans think that stem-cell research should be legal.

k. The dining hall should provide kosher meals. Several of the students in our dormitory are Orthodox Jews.

4. Working in small groups and using the five-step method discussed on page 293, resolve the following moral dilemmas:

a. Imagine that your class is on a yacht (you have a very rich professor) 3 miles offshore for an end-of-semester celebration. A storm strikes. There are only enough lifeboats to save half the people on the yacht. What should you do?

b. You are answering a hotline for the local women's resource center as part of a community-service project for school. A college student calls and tells you she is feeling suicidal. She also tells you that she has run away, because she is afraid of her boyfriend with whom she is sharing an apartment. You recognize her from her story, although she doesn't recognize your voice. You make arrangements for her to stay at the shelter belonging to the resource center. However, a few days later, you see her on campus with her boyfriend. Her face and upper arms are bruised. What should you do?

c. You are a member of the National Guard and have been told to evacuate people from an area that is predicted to be hit by a potentially devastating hurricane. You approach a family with three young children that is living in a high-risk area. The parents refuse to evacuate, saying that they rode out the last hurricane and survived and plan to do the same this time. One of the children is frightened and wants to go with you. The parents say no—the family belongs together. What should you do?

d. You are a family physician. One of your patients, a 37-year-old married man, has just found out that he has gonorrhea. He pleads with you not to tell his wife about his condition, since he is worried that she'll leave him if she finds out that he's been unfaithful. His wife is also one of your patients and has scheduled a visit for her annual checkup. The husband asks you to tell his wife, should she ask you, that he is taking antibiotics for a urinary tract infection. What should you do?

e. Tyrone, a 19-year-old college student, lost the use of both his arms and legs after an automobile accident in which his neck was broken. He has been in the hospital for 4 months when he calls in his physician and tells the physician that he no longer wants to go on living. He asks the physician to give him a lethal injection. Assisted suicide is illegal in the state. What should the physician do?

f. Megan is a college student who has been picked up for possession of a small amount of marijuana. In return for not bringing criminal charges against her, since she has no previous record, the police ask if she'll serve as an undercover agent to catch drug dealers on her campus. Should she accept the assignment?

g. Rose and Joe have been living together in a monogamous relationship for the past 2 years—since the beginning of their sophomore year at college. They both agreed, at the time they moved in together, that either could leave the relationship at any time. However, Rose unexpectedly became pregnant. Because she is opposed to abortion, she has resigned herself to having the baby. When Rose is 6 months pregnant, Joe decides to leave. He leaves a short note saying, "It was fun while it lasted, but it's time for me to move on." What should Rose do?

5. Think of a moral conflict in your life. Using the five-step method on page 293, come up with a resolution to the conflict. If you are willing, share your proposed resolution to your conflict with the class. If appropriate, make modifications to your plan on the basis of class feedback.

*Answers to selected exercises are found in the Solutions Manual at the end of the book.

THiNK
AGAIN

1. How does conscience help us to make moral decisions?
    - Conscience has both a cognitive and an affective (emotional) aspect. The cognitive aspect provides us with knowledge and judgment of what is right and wrong, while moral sentiments or feelings, such as empathy, moral indignation, and guilt, motivate us to take action.

2. What is the stage theory regarding the development of moral reasoning?
    - Kohlberg and Gilligan proposed three levels or stages: (1) preconventional, in which people put their needs and concerns before those of others; (2) conventional, in which people conform to peer or societal norms; and (3) postconventional, in which people are able to use universal moral principles and to balance their needs and the needs of others. Most American adults and college students are at the conventional stage of development.

3. In what ways can the different moral theories help us in formulating moral arguments?
    - Moral theories provide the foundation for moral arguments and their application to real-life situations by making us aware of the different moral principles, rights, and concerns and how to prioritize them in making effective moral decisions.

Perspectives on Abortion

Prior to the 1960s, there was little support for reform of the restrictive abortion laws that had been on the books since the turn of the 19th century. Even Margaret Sanger, the founder of Planned Parenthood, opposed abortion in all but a few circumstances as "taking the life of a baby after it begins" (1963 Planned Parenthood brochure). Instead she promoted birth control (contraception) as an alternative to abortion.

In 1962, Sherri Finkbine, the star of a popular children's show, discovered that she had taken thalidomide (a sedative) during the first month of her pregnancy. Thalidomide had just been found to cause serious defects in infants if taken during the early months of pregnancy. The Finkbines decided that the best course of action was to seek an abortion, which was then illegal. Eventually, she got an abortion in Sweden. The baby was terribly deformed. Finkbine's case galvanized the movement to reform abortion laws in the United States.

Abortion was legalized throughout the United States in January 1973 by the U.S. Supreme Court's ruling in *Roe v. Wade*. The Court ruled that the right of personal privacy in the U.S. Constitution includes the abortion decision. Therefore, abortion should remain unregulated by the state, at least in the first trimester prior to viability. Rather than settling the abortion issue once and for all, however, the court ruling continues to deeply divide Americans.

A 2013 Gallup Poll found that 24 percent of Americans thought that abortion should be legal throughout pregnancy for any reason. Fifty-seven percent thought that it should be legal only under certain circumstances, while 14 percent thought that it should always be illegal.[28] Although feminism is associated in most people's minds with the "pro-choice" position, feminists are divided on the issue.

Since 1973 there have been several challenges to *Roe v. Wade*. Most states have passed laws restricting abortion, including parental notification for minors, and requiring waiting periods between the first visit to an abortion clinic and the actual abortion.

In the following readings we examine the abortion issue from both the legal and moral perspectives. In the excerpt from the majority opinion in Roe v. Wade, Justice Blackman maintains that abortion should be legal based on a woman's right to privacy. Fr. Clifford Stevens disagrees. He argues that abortion is unconstitutional and a violation of the rights of the unborn.

A Defense of Abortion

ROE V. WADE (1973)

In the following readings, the U.S. Supreme court, in its landmark Roe v. Wade *decision, extends the right to privacy to include a woman's right to have an abortion. Father Clifford Stevens disagrees. He argues for the moral and constitutional rights of the unborn.*

It is . . . apparent that at common law, at the time of the adoption of our Constitution, and throughout the major portion of the nineteenth century, abortion was viewed with less disfavor than under most American statutes currently in effect. . . .

Three reasons have been advanced to explain historically the enactment of criminal abortion laws in the nineteenth century and to justify their continued existence.

[First] It has been argued occasionally that these laws were the product of a Victorian special concern to discourage illicit sexual conduct. Texas, however, does not advance this justification in the present case, and it appears that no court of commentator has taken the argument seriously. . . .

A second reason is concerned with abortion as a medical procedure. When most criminal abortion laws were first enacted, the procedure was a hazardous one for the woman. . . . Modern medical techniques have altered this situation. . . . Consequently, any interest of the state in protecting the woman from an inherently hazardous procedure, except when I would be equally dangerous for her to forego it, has largely disappeared. . . .

The third reason in the state's interest—some phrase it in the terms of duty—in protecting prenatal life . . . Only when the life of the pregnant mother herself is at stake, balanced against the life she carries within her, should the interest of the embryo or fetus not prevail . . . a legitimate state interest in this area need not stand or fall on acceptance of the belief that life begins at conception or at some other point prior to live birth. In assessing the state's interest, recognition may be given to the less rigid claim that as long as at least potential life is involved the state may assert interests beyond the protection of the pregnant woman alone.

Parties challenging state abortion laws have sharply disputed in some courts the contention a a purpose of these laws, when enacted, was to protect prenatal life. Pointing to the absence of legislative history to support the contention, they claim that most state laws were designed solely to protect the woman. . . . The few state courts called upon to interpret their laws in the late 19th and early 20th centuries did focus on the State's interest in protecting the woman's health rather than in preserving the embryo and fetus. . . .

The Constitution does not explicitly mention any right of privacy. . . . [Earlier Supreme Court] decisions make it clear that only personal rights that can be deemed "fundamental" or "implicit in the concept of ordered liberty" . . . are included in this guarantee of personal privacy. They also make it clear that the right has some extension to activities relating to marriage . . . [and] procreation. . . .

The right of privacy, whether it be founded in the Fourteenth Amendment's concept of personal liberty and restrictions upon stat action, as we feel it is, . . . is broad enough to encompass a woman's decision whether or not to terminate her pregnancy. The detriment that the state would impose upo n the pregnant woman by denying this choice altogether in apparent. . . .

We therefore conclude that the right of personal privacy includes the abortion decision, but that this right is not unqualified and must be considered against important state interests in regulation.

. . . no case could be cited that holds that a fetus is a person within the meaning of the Fourteenth Amendment . . . . All this, together with our observation, supra, that throughout the majority portion of the nineteenth century prevailing legal abortion practices were far freer than they are today, persuades us that the word "person," as uses in the Fourteenth Amendment, does not include the unborn. . . .

There has always been strong support for the view that life does not begin until live birth . . . . Physicians and their scientific colleagues have ... tended to focus either upon conception or upon live birth or upon the interim point at which the fetus becomes "viable," that is, potentially able to live outside the mother's womb, albeit with artificial aid. Viability is usually places at about seven months (28 weeks) but may occur earlier. . . .

With respect to the state's important and legitimate interest in the health of the mother, the compelling point, in the light of present medical knowledge, is at approximately the end of the first trimester. This is so because of the now established medical fact . . . that until the end of the first trimester mortality in abortion is less than mortality in normal childbirth. It follows that, from and after this point, a state may regulate the abortion procedure to the extent the regulation reasonably relates to the preservation and protection of material health. Examples . . . are requirements as to the qualifications of the person who is to perform the abortion . . . .

State regulations protective of fetal life after viability have both logical and biological justifications. If the state is interested in protecting fetal life after viability, it may go so far as to proscribe abortion during that period except when it is necessary to preserve the life of health of the mother. . . .

To summarize and conclude: . . . This holding, we feel, is consistent with the relative weights of the respective interest involved with the lessons and example of medical and legal history, with the lenity of the common law, and with the demands of the profound problems of the present day. The decision leaves the State free to place increasing restrictions on abortion as the period of pregnancy lengthens, so long as those restrictions are tailored to the recognized state interests.

REVIEW QUESTIONS

1. What are the three reasons why criminal abortion laws were in effect through most of the 19th century?

2. On what grounds does the court conclude that most of these reasons for criminalizing abortion are no longer applicable?

3. What is the right to privacy in the U.S. Constitution and how does the court apply this right to the abortion question?

4. According to the court when does life begin and how does this affect their final ruling?

The Rights of the Unborn

FATHER CLIFFORD STEVENS

Clifford Stevens is a priest in Omaha, Nebraska and author of several books on religion, religious history, and morality. In the following reading, Stevens argues that *Roe v. Wade* is a flawed ruling that failed to take into account the basic moral and constitutional rights of the unborn.

A legal victory over abortion will not be achieved by one or two cases, but only by the persistent recourse to the courts, as abortion practices are challenged with new data which demonstrate the violation of constitutional rights. What will gradually emerge as these cases are adjudicated are the facts and the principles of a new juridic development, embryonic law.

That development was opened by the Roe v. Wade decision, as the issue of civil rights was opened by Plessy v. Ferguson, workers' rights by Lochner v. New York, and children's rights by Hammer v. Dagenhart. . . .

Any opposition to abortion in the courts and in the public arena must be a *constitutional* opposition, based on principles enshrined in the Constitution of the United States, on precedents in constitutional law and on rights which the Constitution was fashioned to secure and protect.

At this point in adjudicating the dispute, only one side of the issue has really been heard, the views of those who support abortion. The only history of the question that has been examined, or even aired, is the history of the abortion laws, with an erroneous conclusion drawn from those laws.

The constitutional issue in the abortion question, the *termination of unborn life,* was not faced by the Court, in fact, the Court refused to consider that issue, much as the *Dred Scott Decision* refused to face the question of the manner in which Black Africans were brought to the United States or the inhuman manner of their servitude. This was because *Roe v. Wade* was presented, on the basis of the briefs, as a case of law *facilitating* a basic constitutional right, rather than *constituting* one. Those arguing the case made sure that the question of unborn life and the manner of its destruction would never be faced by the Court.

In *Roe v. Wade,* there was scarcely any appeal to precedent and the precedent chosen, *Griswold v. Connecticut,* had nothing to do with the unborn. Its only link with the abortion issue was that both cases had some relationship to sexual relations and reproductive matters. The hard work of linking the abortion question with its constitutional precedents was simply not done.

In *Roe v. Wade,* abortion was accepted as standard medical practice, just as low wages, appalling working conditions and the grinding poverty of workers were accepted as standard contractual practices in *Lochner v. New York.* In both cases, the judiciary gave those exercising power over others the legal judgment over their own acts. In the case of abortion, the judiciary refused to examine the "medical" result of the surgical operation called abortion, or the claim of medical science that the procedure was merely a medical matter. The will of the patient and the willingness of the doctor were the only factors that entered into that judgment. Just as surely as the failure to recognize that Black slavery involved the oppression, exploitation and violence done to kidnapped Africans was the root of the constitutional contradiction in *Dred Scott,* so the failure to recognize that abortion involves the violent extermination of unborn life is the root constitutional contradiction in *Roe v. Wade.*

The root procedural error in adjudicating *Roe v. Wade* was to look upon the decision as *facilitative* of a basic right, rather than *constitutive* of a right, and that was because of the dependence of the Justices on the written briefs of the NARAL, which had defended the view that abortion laws were fashioned solely to protect a woman from unsafe surgery. In consequence, the abortion issue was not seen in the progression of laws securing constitutional rights, and the issue of the unborn was considered peripheral to the case. As in the case of slavery, segregation, the exploitation of workers and child labor, the constitutional issue was given a legal cover that became the focus of the dispute and the deciding factor in the majority opinion. Only by future litigation can the real constitutional issue emerge. . . .

Just as Liberty of Contract was used as a legal cover for gross injustices to workers, hiding the violation of their constitutional rights, so the Right to Privacy is used in the abortion issue as a legal cover for the violent death of the unborn. Similarly, just as the Court finally recognized that freedom of contract is not unlimited and could be used for the exploitation of others, so the Court has to be persuaded that a right to privacy has its limitations and cannot be used a legal cover for violent actions. . . .

The link that was made in the *Roe v. Wade* decision is with *abortion laws,* the formation of those laws, the purpose of those laws, the obsolescence of those laws. And a judgment was made, based on invalid historical assumptions and erroneous medical information, that those laws were purely medical matters, due to the primitive and unsafe surgical methods of the time, and that therefore the judgment in the matter is a *medical* one, and that it is for the physician to decide whether an abortion is called for in any particular case.

[T]here are no precedents relating directly to abortion. The issue of abortion has to be shown as part of a larger canvas, just as slavery and segregation had to be shown as part of the securing of the human rights laid down in the Constitution for every class of human being. . . .

UNDOUBTEDLY, ABORTION IS THE MOST VEXING constitutional question that has been brought to the Supreme Court, but it is by no means the most difficult or the most unprecedented. Slavery was a far more explosive issue, far more entrenched in legal precedents and supported by positive laws of long standing. Segregation had been given the cover of constitutional precedent and embodied in countless Supreme Court decisions, defended by statesmen and constitutional lawyers and deeply ingrained in the habits of public and private life for vast numbers of people. Child labor was part of a widely accepted economic practice, upon which families and employers depended for their livelihood, and even attempts by the federal government to eliminate the practice were overruled by the Court. There is no long-standing precedent with regard to abortion, certainly none as long-standing as liberty of contract which held as a precedent in workers' rights for almost fifty years, or separate, but equal, which supported segregation laws for fifty-eight years.

REVIEW QUESTIONS

1. On what grounds does Stevens claim that abortion is a violation of Constitutional rights?

2. What are the legal and moral similarities, according to Stevens, between the Supreme Court rulings on slavery and on abortion?

3. Why does Stevens disagree with *Roe v. Wade's* use of the right of privacy to legalize abortion?

4. Why does Stevens maintain that the *Roe v. Wade* decision was made on "invalid historical assumptions and erroneous medical information"?

THiNK
AND DISCUSS

PERSPECTIVES ON ABORTION

1. Identify the main premises in both the *Roe v. Wade* majority opinion and in the reading by Stevens. Break down and diagram both arguments. Identify the different types of arguments (inductive and deductive) in both readings. For the inductive arguments, note which are generalizations, analogies, and causal arguments.

2. Referring back to Question 1, note which premises are descriptive and which are prescriptive. Identify the moral principles and rights in the prescriptive premises. Discuss the relevance of these moral principles and rights to the issue of abortion. Were any moral concerns left out of either's argument? Explain.

3. Stevens argues that the justices in *Roe v. Wade* failed to address the moral issue of the destruction of unborn life and instead focused on the will of the patients and willingness of physicians as well as the fact that abortion was accepted as standard medical practice. Critically evaluate this criticism of *Roe v. Wade*. Discuss also how the justices in *Roe v. Wade* might respond to Stevens.

4. Critically evaluate Steven's analogy between legalized slavery and legalized abortion. Did he successfully make the case that all humans, including the unborn and slaves, ought to have legal and moral rights? Support your answer.

5. Working in small groups, and referring back to the premises you identified in question 1, make a list of the premises that you found most compelling. Using these premises, come up with a policy (conclusion) for addressing the issue of abortion. Share your conclusion with your group. Modify it, if appropriate, in light of the feedback from the group.

10

MARKETING
& ADVERTISING

"Fifteen minutes could save you 15 percent or more on car insurance." Many of us are familiar with the humorous GEICO auto insurance ads featuring the gecko with a British accent. Known for its offbeat ads, GEICO spent $994 million on advertising in 2012 alone. Much of the success of GEICO is the result of its numerous television, billboard, Internet, and radio advertisements that contain memorable and quirky characters. Since the introduction of the caveman ads in 1998, GEICO's share of the auto insurance market has increased from sixth to third place among the major insurance companies.[1]

Why has GEICO been so successful in its marketing and advertising? In this chapter we'll learn about business marketing research and strategies, including those used by GEICO. We will also apply our critical-thinking skills to recognizing and

What statement do you think the man holding the flag is making? In what ways do companies exert influence over our life using marketing and advertising?

THiNK FIRST

- What strategies are used in marketing research and marketing?
- How do marketing and advertising impact the consumer?
- How can we as consumers be more aware of fallacies and rhetorical devices used in advertising?

 evaluating marketing strategies and advertisements that we encounter in our everyday lives. Specifically, we will:

- Learn about the importance of marketing in business
- Study marketing research and strategies
- Relate the SWOT model to marketing strategies
- Consider the impact of marketing and advertising on the consumer
- Look at the relationship between big business, advertising, and mass media
- Examine the use of fallacious reasoning and rhetorical devices in advertising

MARKETING IN A CONSUMER CULTURE

Marketing a product or service is an essential component of doing business in a consumer culture, such as we have in the United States. A **business** is an organization that seeks to make a profit by providing goods and services desired by its customers. (**Profit** is the money left over after all expenses are paid.) A business's success depends on its ability to determine what customers want and then provide it at a reasonable cost. To be competitive, businesses need to plan and implement effective strategies for marketing and advertising these products and services.

business An organization that makes a profit by providing goods and services to customers.

profit The money left over after all expenses are paid.

marketing research Identifying a target market and finding out if it matches customer desires.

Marketing Research

The process of identifying a target market for a product or service and finding out if it matches what the customer wants is called **marketing research**—or, as marketing professionals say, discovering customers' "hot buttons."

Marc Ecko was successful in marketing his new line of urban clothing in part because he first carefully researched his target audience's "hot buttons."

Hot or Not?

What do you see as today's consumer "hot buttons"?

At the age of 20, fashion designer and former graffiti artist Marc Ecko successfully introduced a new line of urban clothing by targeting young males who were into skate-boarding and hip-hop music. The Ecko Unlimited brand, with its airbrushed T-shirts and baggy jeans, quickly amassed a loyal following. Ecko succeeded because he knew his target population's hot buttons. In this case, they wanted a line of clothing that set them apart and that said something about their lifestyle.

There are several approaches to marketing research, including surveys, observation, and experimentation, each of which involves proficiency in critical thinking and inductive logic. Survey research is used to collect information and opinions about a product and can be done at a mall or by mail, e-mail, Internet, or phone. Informal surveys or group brainstorming sessions may be conducted

as well. Southwest Airlines, for instance, holds focus groups with consumers to come up with ways of maintaining or improving the airline's position in the market.[2]

Observation involves directly monitoring customers' buying patterns. A market researcher may watch customers and record their actions, or use sales data such as bar-code inventories to collect information. Nielsen Media Research also uses observation to track the television viewing habits of a representative sample of Americans via a small device attached to their televisions. We'll be looking more at the relationship between advertising and the mass media later in this chapter.

Experimentation—another type of marketing research—measures cause–effect relationships between the purchase of a product or service and selected variables such as packaging, advertising logo, or price. These are changed to determine the effect of the changes on consumers' responses. Since these three approaches all use inductive logic, they only provide information on what products

Connections

How can scientific methodology be used in marketing research? *See Chapter 7, pp. 212–213.*

will most likely be successful in the market—but they do not, in themselves, ensure success.

Avoiding Confirmation Bias and Other Errors in Thinking

Like individuals, a business may fail to do its research or to consider certain evidence because it assumes that its beliefs are correct when in fact they may not be. Information can be distorted by cognitive and social errors such as confirmation bias, probability error, and the "one of us/one of them" error. A business starting out with questionable assumptions can make incorrect predictions, take inappropriate actions, and wind up with disappointing outcomes—a process sometimes referred to as the "doom loop."[3]

escalation of commitment The overcommitment of marketing to a particular answer.

> A business starting out with questionable assumptions can make incorrect predictions, take inappropriate actions, and wind up with disappointing outcomes—a process sometimes referred to as the "doom loop."

In the 1960s, Japanese automobile manufacturers got caught up in the "doom loop" when they marketed cars in the United States with 1,000-cc engines, which were a lot smaller than the 1,500- to 1,600-cc engines in American-built small cars. Given the poor condition of Japanese roads at the time, 1,000 cc was sufficient for the speeds possible in Japan but not for speeds on U.S. highways. Yutaka Katayama, who came to the United States in 1960 as marketing manager for Datsun (now Nissan), challenged the company's assumptions and suggested that 1,000-cc engines were insufficient for the American market. However, managers in Japan were insulted and rejected his advice. It took Katayama almost a decade to convince Datsun to change its preconceptions. By that time, Honda's Civic, which changed its strategy and came out in

Apple promotes its iPod by portraying it as a simple, sleek, and sexy electronic device.

1972 with a 1,169-cc engine and increased its engine size over the next few years, had made significant inroads into the American small-car market.

Confirmation bias, as the Datsun example shows, is an ongoing problem in business. Marketers may misinterpret or distort available information, limit their research to sources that support their view, or dismiss contradictory evidence as an anomaly. Datsun/Nissan was not the only car manufacturer that failed to take into account key evidence in its marketing research.

Confirmation bias may also lead marketing researchers to overcommit to a particular answer rather than exploring other options—what

For many years the swimsuit industry failed to examine its assumption that women liked to wear sexy bathing suits. In 1987 market research conducted by the Swimsuit Manufacturers Association found, as one supplier put it, "that most women would rather have a root canal without Novocain than buy a swimsuit." In their rush to make sexy bathing suits for women with fashion model figures, the industry did not take into account the concern of the majority of women that these bathing suits were embarrassing. It also took swimsuit companies several years to come up with the two-piece tankini in which the top covers up the midriff while the bottom allows ease of use in bathrooms.

is known in the business world as **escalation of commitment** or *loss aversion.* This occurs when a business continues to pursue an erroneous course of action in marketing a product, instead of changing course and cutting its losses. When videotaping went mainstream in the 1970s, two competing and incompatible types of recording systems—Betamax, produced by Sony, and VHS, produced by JVC—were released into the market. Even after it was clear that consumers preferred the cheaper VHS system, Sony continued to manufacture Betamax machines. It wasn't until 1988 that Sony finally decided to cut its financial losses and produce VHS systems instead. And seller's loss aversion contributed to the housing and mortgage crisis that started in 2008 when home sellers refused to

lower the price of homes in the face of a slipping house market. At Lego, escalation of commitment to theme parks nearly drove the company out of business until a new CEO made drastic changes that saved the company (see "Thinking Outside the Box: Jørgen Vig Knudstorp").

Poor communication and listening skills can also lead to poor marketing decisions. A business that assumes that customers share its expectations and preferences about a product may go so far as to distort what customers say to fit its worldview. The firm may describe customers' preferences as "irrational" or talk in terms of what customers *should* want. For example, a fashion company was losing sales. However, when a consumer focus group said that the reason was the unattractiveness of its styles, a representative from the company responded by "explaining" why the items were not unattractive. The focus group politely deferred to him rather than challenge his "authority."[4] In this case, the company representative demonstrated poor listening skills by ignoring what the customers were telling him and changing the "facts" to fit his worldview. As a result, the company continued to lose sales.

Because of the problems of confirmation bias and people's tendency to conform to group pressures, many companies use independent marketing research companies or rely on research carried out by government agencies. These companies and agencies also have expertise in designing surveys and selecting a representative sample from among customers or potential customers. For example, GEICO enlisted the help of the Martin Agency, whose clients also include Walmart and UPS.

Accurate, complete, and unbiased marketing research is particularly important when introducing a product to the international market. What may sell well in one country may not sell in others. Factors such as presentation, packaging, and the name of a product must be researched, as must customers' interest in the product itself. When Proctor & Gamble first marketed its jars of Gerber baby food in one African nation, hardly anyone bought them.[5] On further investigation, Proctor & Gamble realized its mistake. Because many of the people in the country were illiterate, food product labels generally carried pictures of what was inside. Using inductive argument by analogy, the potential customers drew the logical but unsavory conclusion that the jars of baby food contained ground-up babies!

The management of Nissan in Tokyo also failed to do its research when it came up with the name *My Fair Lady* for their first sports car for the American market—hardly a name that connotes the engine power and excitement that most American consumers seek in a sports car. Fortunately, Yutaka Katayama had the foresight to remove the nameplates with *My Fair Lady* and replace them with ones that read *240Z*, the internal designation for the car.[6] The popular sports car came to be known as the Z-car.

In addition to understanding the current market, marketing research must anticipate future trends to take advantage of opportunities. To do this, marketing researchers must put aside their personal biases and be open-minded, attentive, and intellectually curious. What first appears to be a market anomaly may actually be the beginning of a trend. The Western Union telegraph company, which dominated the nation's communications network in the mid-nineteenth century, failed to anticipate the profound effect of the telephone on people's lives. In 1876 it turned down the opportunity to purchase Alexander Graham Bell's patents on the telephone. "This 'telephone,'" concluded Western Union, "has too many shortcomings to be seriously considered as a means of communication."

Connections

How can familiarity with arguments by analogy make companies less likely to commit erros in marketing? *See Chapter 7, p. 216.*

EXERCISE 10-1

STOP AND ASSESS YOURSELF

1. Working in small groups, develop a plan for marketing a new health club, energy drink, credit card, or cell phone to college students. Create a short poll or survey as part of your marketing research. Share your strategy with the rest of the class.

2. Part of marketing research is anticipating future trends. What do you see as possible future markets for artificial intelligence systems? Create a marketing research plan for monitoring this trend.

3. Many businesses provide funding for universities to conduct research for developing and marketing new products. Find examples of this happening at your university. Does this practice give businesses too much control over the educational process? Discuss the pros and cons of this practice.

4. Do marketers have an ethical obligation to consider the wider social and environmental implications of their product and marketing strategy? Discuss using specific examples.

MARKETING STRATEGIES

Only after we have examined our assumptions and gathered the relevant information are we ready to engage in strategic planning. A **strategic plan** is a method by which an organization deploys its resources to realize a goal or objective. In business, strategic planning generally involves the use of a strategic model, which is "... a systematic list of policies that will guide the future specification of inputs, outputs, processes, and values of the complete operations of the business of the corporation."[7]

strategic plan A method by which an organization deploys its resources to realize a goal.

SWOT model Used to analyze a company's strengths, weaknesses, external opportunities, and threats.

The SWOT Model

SWOT is an acronym for "strengths, weaknesses, opportunities, and threats." The **SWOT model** is used to analyze a company's strengths and weaknesses, as well as external opportunities and threats in the business environment. This strategic model can be used for developing a marketing strategy and for deciding (among other things) whether to launch a new business or expand an existing business. The SWOT model is also used by individuals for making major life decisions, such as what career or college major to choose or where to live.

The first two components of SWOT (strengths and weaknesses) require an internal assessment. Opportunities and threats, in contrast, are external to a company. Analyzing a company's resources and competitive capacity is similar to drawing up a balance sheet on which strengths are weighed against weaknesses or deficiencies.

In carrying out a SWOT analysis, we begin by making a list of a company's greatest strengths. *Strengths* are defined as a company's assets and core competencies—in other words, what it does best. A company's strengths contribute to its ability to achieve its goals and do certain things better than its competitors. Toyota, one of the largest car makers, has brand name recognition throughout the world. Other strengths include new investments in factories

Strengths	Weaknesses	Opportunities	Threats
• Location of facilities • Unique selling points • Large customer base • Commitment/ productivity of employees • Ability to meet demand • Quality of product or service • Company reputation • Customer service program • Strong management • Brand recognition • Marketing distribution	• Outdated facility/ equipment • Insufficient information • Debts or limited financial resources • Weak consumer demand • Strong competitors • Poor management • Poor marketing • Inability to meet deadline pressures • Lack of expertise	• New markets • Competitor's vulnerabilities • Industry or lifestyle trends • Technology developments/ innovations • Global influences • Chance to buy out a rival company • Fashion influences • Increase in consumer spending • New partners	• Competitors • Restrictive legal regulations • Global warming • Natural disasters • New technologies • Shift in consumer demands • Consumer dissatisfaction • Slow economy • Negative media coverage • Rising cost of wages/ benefits • Outsourcing

Examples of Components of the SWOT Model

in China and the United States as well as a diverse range of products ranging from large trucks to small hybrid cars.

Since Google was formed in 1998, it has grown to have more than 30,000 employees. An innovative and future-looking company, Google carried out a SWOT analysis to identify its strengths and weakness.[8] In addition to brand loyalty and innovative products, part of its strength is its attention to employees' comforts and needs. It has a "mothers' room," a café, and a game room, among other amenities.

Walmart, which employs over 2 million people, is the world's largest corporation. Its main strength is its efficiency and innovation in getting the lowest price for its customers, which it does primarily by importing 80 percent of its manufactured goods from low-wage China. Walmart has an aggressive and effective marketing strategy and brags of its "always low prices." Another facet of its marketing strategy is its "good works" programs and community philanthropy, in which Walmart aggressively promotes itself as a "good neighbor" in the small communities where it sets up its megastores.

Weaknesses, in contrast, are things that a company lacks or does poorly. They include internal liabilities or inadequacies, such as a lack of expertise, insufficient information, limited financial resources for meeting consumer demand, or poor location. In coming up with a marketing strategy, it is important that a business do an internal survey of its weaknesses. Even the strongest company can be brought down because of an unacknowledged internal weakness or an unanticipated external threat. The use of resistance, such as denial, can blind a business to internal weaknesses. While Japanese automobile makers were developing efficient, automated production facilities, American automobile companies remained more labor intensive, employing four times as many workers to produce a car,[9] contributing to the 2009 bankruptcy of General Motors and Chrysler, who were rescued by an $85 billion federal bailout.

Johnson & Johnson is currently facing numerous lawsuits over a defective hip joint implant because of poor management decisions regarding recalls of the implant. The company knew years

The "How May I Help You?" and the "Always Low Prices" slogans have helped to cement Walmart as a leader among world corporations.

Arturo Moreno (on right) increased the profitability of the Los Angeles Angels by using a marketing strategy that appealed to families and the Hispanic market.

before the implant was recalled in 2010 that it was flawed and could cause physical harm to the patient. However, rather than recalling it, management concealed the information and continued to market the implant even though many physicians had ceased to use it because of problems associated with it. The lawsuits could cost Johnson & Johnson billions of dollars.

One of GEICO's weaknesses was its size, compared with the insurance giants such as State Farm Insurance and Allstate; it also had a hard-to-remember name. One way GEICO overcame this weakness was by coming up with a chatty gecko as its mascot, a marketing strategy to help customers remember its name and to associate the name with fun. GEICO also saturated the airwaves with its ads, spending hundreds of millions of dollars on ads a year.

The last two parts of a SWOT analysis (opportunities and threats) address factors that are external to a company and mostly beyond its control. Developing an effective marketing strategy involves being alert for opportunities—circumstances or pieces of good fortune that a business may be able to take advantage of.

Opportunities include new technology, increases in consumer spending, and untapped markets. For example, there is a lot of oil money in the Middle East looking for a bank. However, Qur'anic laws (the Islamic Sharia) forbid both lending money for profit and investing in activities such as gambling or smoking. (The Sharia is the code of law based on the *Qur'an*.) Citicorp and other banks have taken advantage of this growing market by opening Islamic subsidiary banks in conjunction with Islamic banks and companies from the Middle East, such as the Islamic Bank of Britain. Since most Western banks lack expertise in Qur'anic law, they have compensated for this weakness by hiring top-caliber Sharia scholars to sit on their boards. These banks are now using Islamic laws to break new ground with Islamic credit cards, Islamic mortgages, and Islamic bonds that comply with Islamic law.[10]

As electronic books (e-books) began to gain popularity, Barnes & Noble saw the opportunity and created its own e-book reader, the Nook, and marketed it both in stores and online. In contrast, Borders bookstore chain failed to see the rise in popularity of e-books and continued to focus its attention on selling hardcopy books in its stores—a strategy that had been successful in the past, but eventually contributed to its bankruptcy in 2011.

Open-minded and creative critical thinkers are the most likely to capitalize on an opportunity. When Mexican American billionaire Arturo Moreno purchased the Los Angeles Angels baseball team from Disney in 2003, he saw an opportunity to increase its long-term profitability

Not just a cup of coffee: Starbucks provides coffee drinkers with a relaxing social atmosphere.

Because threats come from outside, a business must be vigilant and have a thorough knowledge of the latest developments in the industry. Nestlé (Nescafé) in Switzerland and General Foods (Maxwell House) in the United States both failed to pay attention to the threat of the gourmet coffee craze until it was too late, allowing upstart competitors such as Starbucks to become firmly entrenched in the North American market. Thus, they lost a large chunk of their coffee market to new competitors.

Instead of ignoring a threat, a company may respond to it by expanding its marketing strategy to appeal to a wider consumer base and by seeking out a new niche for its market. When Starbucks, with its appeal to coffee connoisseurs, began expanding out of its home in Seattle, Washington, Dunkin' Donuts responded by expanding its product line and revamping its marketing strategy—captured in the catchy slogan "America runs on Dunkin'." The new marketing strategy, which was meant to appeal to the busy lifestyle of most Americans, emphasized Dunkin' Donuts' speed and efficiency in contrast to the slower, laid-back atmosphere of Starbucks.

Threats from a competitor can sometimes be dealt with by providing a new service or new line of products. Lego sales began dropping in 2002 due to the rising popularity of video games. It wasn't until 2004, when a new CEO took over and changed the direction of the company, that Lego sales began to rise again (see "Thinking Outside the Box, Jørgen Vig Knudstorp," on page 312).[13]

The consumer electronics corporation Best Buy responded to the threat from Walmart by providing a service Walmart was unable to offer its customers—excellent customer service by in-store teams of experts, cleverly called the Geek Squad. Likewise, Pepsi responded to its competitor, Coca-Cola, by diversifying aggressively into a new line of products, including such nonsoda drinks as Gatorade, Tropicana, and Propel. This marketing strategy has served Pepsi well. When soda sales recently began to drop, Coca-Cola's stock suffered, even though it produced more soda than Pepsi did.

SWOT is only one example of a strategic model used in business. The key in using a strategic model such as SWOT is to develop a successful business and marketing strategy that concentrates on a company's strengths and potential opportunities to overcome internal weaknesses and external threats.

by increasing his marketing strategy to include the area's booming Hispanic population. To appeal to this market, Moreno began by doing the unthinkable for a team owner—he drastically lowered the cost of family-ticket packages and upper-deck seating while increasing the payroll of the players (making it the fourth-highest in the sport) in order to field a more competitive team. Since Moreno has bought the Angels, the number of Hispanic fans has doubled and advertising revenues from such sponsors as Anheuser-Busch, General Motors, and Verizon have tripled.[11]

Threats are negative and unavoidable realities that are contrary to the well-being of a business and may seriously debilitate or even destroy it. Threats include natural disasters, a slow economy, government regulations, a shift in consumer buying patterns, outsourcing, and new competitors. A company may ignore or downplay financial problems brought on by external threats until it is too late. The American automobile industry was successful for so long, until the 1970s, that it started taking its success for granted. Because it failed to take seriously the threat from Japanese automobile makers, it began a slow decline. By 2007, the General Motors manufacturing facilities in Flint, Michigan, had lost 70,000 jobs.[12] This downturn was further aggravated by the world financial crisis that began in 2008. By the end of that year almost half of the remaining jobs had been terminated and GM turned to the government for bailout to save it from bankruptcy.

Consumer Awareness of Marketing Strategies

In marketing a product or service, businesses generally use a blend of strategies.

One of the most popular strategies is brand recognition. A well-known brand name or symbol, such as Levi's 501 jeans, Apple's iPod, or McDonald's golden arches, is one of a company's most important assets. Marketers may spend millions of dollars coming up with a brand name

Thinking Outside the Box

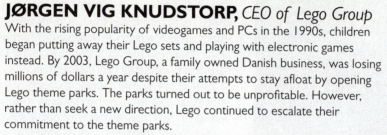

JØRGEN VIG KNUDSTORP, *CEO of Lego Group*

With the rising popularity of videogames and PCs in the 1990s, children began putting away their Lego sets and playing with electronic games instead. By 2003, Lego Group, a family owned Danish business, was losing millions of dollars a year despite their attempts to stay afloat by opening Lego theme parks. The parks turned out to be unprofitable. However, rather than seek a new direction, Lego continued to escalate their commitment to the theme parks.

In 2004, 35-year-old Jørgen Vig Knudstorp was appointed CEO of Lego. Knudstorp, who had joined the company in 2001, was the first head of the company to come from outside the Christiansen family. One of Knudstorp's first steps was to shift the emphasis from "nurturing the child" to making money for the company as the top priority. He sold off the theme parks, which had proven to be a weakness, assessed the threats to the company (the rising popularity of videogames), and sought feedback in redesigning Lego products to meet the demands of the market. To achieve this end, he enlisted the help of thousands of Lego "superusers" and rewarded them for their feedback. Unlike most companies that test children's toys using children, Knudstorp chose to primarily use adult Lego fans. Why adults instead of children? "These superusers," Knudstorp told *Harvard Business Review,* "can articulate the product strengths and weaknesses that young children may sense but can't express."*

As a result of Knudstorp's leadership, Lego Group has rebounded, with profits totaling $336 million in 2012.

DISCUSSION QUESTIONS

1. Relate Knudstorp's strategies to the SWOT model discussed earlier in the chapter.

2. Go online or visit a store, such as Walmart, which carries Lego products. Make a note of how the different Lego products appeal to today's young people. Discuss your findings with the class.

* Andrew O'Connell, "Lego CEO Jørgen Vig Knudstorp on Leading Through Survival and Growth," *Harvard Business Review,* January 2009.

---

that triggers a positive emotional response in the consumer. Pharmaceutical companies, for example, employ branding consultants to come up with a name, such as Viagra, that is positive and memorable and that will appeal to consumers and physicians alike. The entire process of coming up with a brand name for a new pharmaceutical product costs hundreds of thousands of dollars.[14]

In addition to promoting brand recognition, marketing research has found that 70 percent of purchasing decisions are made on the spot in retail stores.[15] This is known as impulse buying. As critical thinkers, we need to be aware of marketing strategies that encourage such impulsiveness. For example, marketers have come up with strategies to get customers to stay in a store long enough to buy something they hadn't planned to buy. Most drugstores, for instance, make customers wait 15 minutes while a prescription is being filled, not because it takes that long to put some pills in a plastic bottle but to give customers time to make additional purchases. A second strategy is to put impulse items, such as candy, in areas where they are most visible, such as end-of-aisle displays, on the middle shelves, or at the checkout counters.

Salespeople and staff members who deal directly with consumers are also part of a marketing strategy. In some stores, a salesperson or another representative greets customers. Marketing research has found that when a customer makes a connection with a salesperson, failing to buy something causes a guilt response in the customer. When this happens, the customer is more likely to make future purchases from that salesperson or store as a kind of reparation. However, this is clearly irrational guilt.[16] Being a smart shopper involves being aware of our reactions so that we don't fall for these marketing ploys.

Marketing, if done properly with an attitude of mutual respect, can result in a win-win situation in which both parties are better off. The consumer gets something he or she wants, and the manufacturer and seller gain economically. However, not all marketing strategies are based on rational appeals. Although much of advertising is informative, advertising in particular has been criticized for manipulating consumers. We'll be looking at advertising in more depth in the next section of this chapter.

The new Cadillac won North American Car of the Year at the 2013 International Car Show in Detroit, Michigan. Hyundai's strengths, its ability to overcome threats, and its pursuit of new opportunities contribute to its being one of the most successful car makers in the world.

STOP AND ASSESS YOURSELF

EXERCISE 10-2

1. Discuss different marketing strategies that you have encountered as a consumer during the past week. Evaluate the strategies. Discuss which ones you found most effective, and which were the least effective.

2. Politicians have adopted many modern marketing strategies with advertising, polling, telemarketing, and demographic targeting. Identify specific examples of marketing strategies being used in political campaigns. Looking back at the section on "Critical Thinking and Democracy" in Chapter 1, discuss ways in which marketing in politics might violate the democratic process.

3. Choose one of your favorite products. Analyze the company's marketing strategy. To what extent did their strategy contribute to your purchasing the product? Discuss ways in which you might improve the strategy without resorting to fallacies or misleading advertising.

4. Think back on the last time you went shopping in a large store such as a Walmart, Best Buy, a supermarket, or even your campus bookstore. Write down a list of the items you purchased that you went there to buy. Next, make a list of items you bought on impulse. Why did you buy the impulse items? Come up with at least three strategies you can use to make yourself less susceptible to impulse buying. Relate these strategies to critical-thinking skills.

5. The SWOT model has been used in business schools to help college students make career and life choices. Select one of the long-term goals from your life plan (see Chapter 1). Carry out a SWOT analysis regarding that goal and the strategies you are using to achieve your goal. Based on your analysis, discuss modifications you might make in your strategies to make achieving your goal more likely.

ADVERTISING AND THE MEDIA

Advertising has three purposes: (1) to create product awareness, (2) to inform consumers about a product or service, and (3) to motivate customer demand for the product, thereby creating brand loyalty. Advertisements appear on television, in magazines, on the Internet, on billboards, store displays, buses, taxis, school bulletin boards, and even people's clothing.

There is no doubt that advertising can provide us with valuable information and options for making our lives easier. On the other hand, the ultimate purpose of advertising is to make money for the advertiser, not to advance truth. Advertising by its very nature is one-sided, persuasive communication. In some instances advertising carries little or no information about the product, instead relying on psychological ploys to create a demand for the product.

We are exposed to advertising in the mass media as well as through store displays, taxis, and on billboards as in this scene of Times Square in New York City.

The Role of Advertising in the Media

Advertising is the keystone of the mass media. We come into contact more with advertising than with any other specific form of media programming. According to the journal *Media Matters,* the average American is exposed to 600 to 625 ads per day, about 270 of which are from traditional mass media sources such as television, radio, magazines, and newspapers.[17] Even inside movie theaters, which used to be ad-free, we now find ourselves subjected to several minutes of advertisements after the lights dim, followed in some cases by an hour and a half of brand-name products strategically placed throughout the movie itself.

Marketers spend a lot of money identifying audiences for their products and creating ads to appeal to the target audience. Readership in print media is measured by circulation figures, as well as by surveys to find out who is reading what. Media research companies also track radio audiences through the use of diaries that record an individual's listening habits. One of the largest media research companies is Nielsen Media Research, which monitors national television viewing habits using a representative sample of more than 5,000 households and 13,000 people. Through monitoring boxes installed on televisions in these households, Nielsen knows exactly when the televisions are turned on and what program is playing. Nielsen also collects demographic information on each member of participating households. Businesses then use this information to determine which programs have the best audiences for their products.

Through this process, media researchers found that *The Big Bang Theory* is one of the most popular shows among young people. Research also shows not only that young people are more likely than the rest of the population to own cell phones but also that people who watch reality television, such as *The Real World* and *American Idol*, are more likely than the general population to switch cellular phone service within the year.[18] Because of this, many of the ads on these types of shows are for cell-phone services.

Internet advertising is also becoming increasingly popular among advertisers. It has the advantage of permitting a more precise targeting of audiences, based on which Web sites people visit. Unlike conventional media advertising, Internet advertising allows two-way communication between the audience and businesses, thus serving as a means of transacting sales and distributing goods, including the downloading of music and video games. The Army National Guard, when it was faced with recruitment shortfalls, turned to advertising on the Internet to appeal to 18- to 25-year-olds. Internet surfers who were willing to scroll through the guard's recruitment message were offered free music through iTunes and video game downloads.

60 percent after the product had a role in the 1982 film *E.T.: The Extra-Terrestrial*. The 2012 James Bond movie *Skyfall* featured both Coca-Cola and Smirnoff vodka martinis. Doritos were featured on the film *Hotel Transylvania*. Product placement in movies is becoming increasingly popular, since viewers cannot turn off a movie the way they can a television. Apple computers is one of the biggest users of product placement with its products appearing in almost half of the top films in the past few years including *Mission Impossible: Ghost Protocol*, *The Possession*, and *The Twilight Saga: Breaking Dawn*, parts I and II. Apple has repeatedly stated that it doesn't pay for product placement. The obvious answer is that Apple gives its products away for use in certain productions. *Transformers 3* (2012) set a record by having more than 100 product placements in the movie.

Some viewers and media corporations prefer product placement rather than commercials because it doesn't take time away from the programming. Sponsors are also looking more to product placement because many more homes now have DVRs (digital video recorders) that allow viewers to record television shows and movies and skip the ads.

The organization Commercial Alert opposes product placement, arguing that product placement is basically deceptive. Unlike regular commercial advertising, it points out, there is no disclosure that these are paid advertisements.[20] In addition, product placements give parents less control over which advertisements their children see, since the placements are not separated from the regular programming, as are traditional commercials.

The advent of the Internet has provided marketers with new opportunities for reaching out to consumers.

Product Placement

Ads may also be embedded in a television program. Product placement is an advertising strategy in which "a real commercial product is used in fictional media, and the presence of the product is a result of an economic exchange"[19] between the media company and the business that produces the product. Most product placements go unnoticed unless we make a conscious effort to notice them. Coca-Cola, which appears on *American Idol*, is one of the brands that has been placed most frequently (see "Analyzing Images: Product Placement in the Media"). Companies may also pay to have their logos used in a show. The logo for a sports apparel company such as *Nike* or Wilson Sporting Goods may appear on sports uniforms and equipment in sports broadcasts. Automobile companies frequently use product placement.

Product placement has also caught on in movies. In the movie *Transformers,* every car was made by General Motors. The sales of the candy Reese's Pieces increased

Television Advertising and Children

Television viewing is the primary after-school activity for school children.[21] According to the 2012 Nielsen Report, the average child watches almost 4 hours of television a day, including having the television on during mealtimes and viewing television on their mobile phones. Seven out of ten children also have a television in their bedroom. This translates to 5 hours of television commercials a week, or about 40,000 commercials a

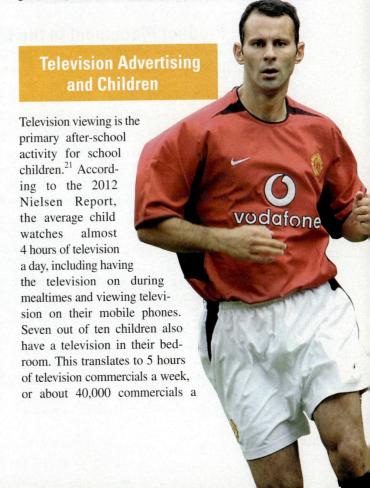

Product Placement in the Media
Product placement on Fox television show *American Idol*: Judges Mariah Carey, Keith Urban, Nicki Minaj, and Randy Jackson shown with their "favorite" beverage.

DISCUSSION QUESTIONS

1. *Discuss the effectiveness of product placement in the photo. Discuss also the extent to which product placements rely on fallacious thinking.*

2. *Imagine that you're an advertising consultant for a show such as* American Idol, *whose target audience is primarily young people. You've been asked to come up with an advertising strategy for an iPod. Discuss which strategies, including product placement or separate commercials, would be most effective in getting the attention of the target audience and why.*

year.[22] Children as young as 18 months of age can identify brand logos such as McDonald's golden arches and the Nike swoosh.[23] According to many psychologists, advertising has a significant impact on child development and health.[24] Children under the age of 8 years lack the cognitive maturity to recognize either the intent of advertising or the fallacious reasoning and rhetorical devices that are frequently used in ads. In addition, the use of characters from children's shows in advertisements blurs the line between advertising and the show itself. Because of children's inability to critically analyze advertisements, the American Psychological Association calls for legislation to restrict advertising targeted at children 8 years of age and younger. See this chapter's Critical Thinking Issues, "Perspectives on Advertising and Children," for a discussion of what restrictions, if any, should be placed on advertisements for children.

Young children are particularly vulnerable to advertising images on television because of their undeveloped critical-thinking skills.

STOP AND ASSESS YOURSELF

1. Make a list of all the advertisements you remember seeing yesterday. Next, select a day and on that day keep a list of all the advertisements you see from the time you get up to the time you go to bed at night. To what extent were you unaware of all the advertisements you saw before doing this assignment? Come up with at least two critical thinking strategies you might use to make yourself more aware of the effects of advertisements in your life. Discuss how being more aware of their presence in your life might make you less susceptible to the allure of advertising.

2. During your next shopping trip to a drugstore or grocery store, check the prices of the brand-name products and of the equivalent generic products. What is the price difference? Which do you normally buy (name-brand or generic) and why? Relate your answer to the strategies used by marketers to get you to buy their brand products. Using the research skills for evaluating evidence in Chapter 2, discuss how you might go about determining which product—the generic or the brand—is the best.

3. Some people feel that product placement borders on deception. The next time you watch television or go to a movie, pay attention to name-brand products that appear in the show or movie. Should product placement be regulated? Discuss the moral issues involved in product placement in both adult and children's programming.

4. In the futurist movie *Minority Report*, starring Tom Cruise, each person has a chip embedded that is scanned by billboard advertisements so that the ads are catered to the particular person. While this movie scenario is still fictional, new cell phone technology, such as Foursquare and 1020 Placecast, allows marketers to track your location and gear the advertisements on your cell phone to your location. For example, if you are near a Starbucks, they might place a Starbucks advertisement on your cell phone. Discuss ethical issues raised by this practice.

5. What is your favorite ad? Why do you like it? What is the target audience for the ad? What values are being communicated by this ad? Critically analyze how, if at all, the ad has influenced you or people you know to purchase the product being advertised.

EVALUATING ADVERTISEMENTS

Much of advertising in the media serves an important role by informing us about different products and services that can improve our lives. However, advertisements can manipulate us into buying a product that we neither need nor would have wanted before being exposed to the advertisement. Rather than using reason, these ads appeal to our emotions through fallacies, rhetoric, and emotionally laden language and images. In addition, some ads omit information or premises that are necessary for us to come to a reasoned conclusion about a particular product or service. Ads that convey false or deliberately misleading information to the consumer are forbidden by law. The use of psychological persuasion and rhetorical devices, on the other hand, are generally permissible in advertising. However, studies have found that the mere thought of the immediate reward of having money or something we want can cause our brain to release dopamine, the "pleasure chemical," and stimulate images in our head, such as a sports car or scantily clothed supermodels.[25] Marketers prey on this human tendency. As critical thinkers, we need to be attentive and learn to sort out the fallacies and rhetorical devices and distinguish the genuine message.

This ad for Diesel clothing uses snob appeal as well as the fallacy of questionable cause by implying that wearing Diesel clothing will make one irresistible to the opposite sex.

Common Fallacies in Advertisements

Connections

How do advertisers use clichés to distract from critically analyzing a product? *See Chapter 1, p. 23.*

How can the use of emotional appeals cloud our thinking when it comes to advertisements and media messages? *See Chapter 2, p. 47.*

How do advertisers use language and images to convince us to buy their products or services? *See Chapter 3, p. 89.*

Many ads rely on fallacies and psychological persuasion rather than credible information and rational argumentation. *Scare tactics*, for example, are used to create anxiety or play on our fears, insecurities, or sense of shame. We are told that we are not good-looking or thin enough; that we have bad breath, body odor, or dandruff; that we have an unattractive personality or the wrong clothes; or that we are poor parents. The ad then promises a solution to the problem—which in some cases we didn't realize we had in the first place. Although some ads that use scare tactics promote products that may actually deliver on their promises, others go on to commit the *fallacy of questionable cause* by creating a false expectation that something wonderful, such as becoming more beautiful, thinner, more popular, or happier, will result if we use the product.

Another common fallacy in ads is the *fallacy of popular appeal* that creates the impression that "everyone" is using this product and therefore you should use it too. As we noted in Chapter 4, people have a strong drive to conform and be part of a group. This type of advertising is particularly effective with teenagers, who tend to define themselves in terms of what their peer group has or is doing. If "everyone" has an Apple iPod or wears Nike athletic shoes, then we need them too. Cravings to have what "everyone" else has can cause some individuals to steal or commit violent crimes. People have been killed for the Nikes they are wearing.

An ad may also use *snob appeal*, a type of popular appeal, by setting up an association between a product and people who are sexy, athletic, popular, or living a desirable lifestyle. Ads for alcohol frequently associate drinking with enjoyable activities and being a fun-to-be-with person. Advertisers, such as the Jeep Liberty, may also associate their product with patriotism by including patriotic language or images of American flags next to their products.

The *fallacy of appeal to inappropriate authority* occurs when advertisers use a celebrity, such as an athlete or movie star, to promote a product that is outside the celebrity's field of expertise. For example, sales of Salton's countertop grill jumped when the company signed former heavyweight champion George Foreman to promote it—a fallacious ad, since Foreman is not an authority on grills or cooking.

Advertising may also reinforce stereotypes by using the fallacy of *hasty generalization*. Women are often portrayed as pencil-thin sex objects and young men as mindless pleasure seekers; blacks get stereotyped as athletes or musicians and Asians as very studious.

Another commonly used fallacy is *amphiboly*. The Holland America Line, a provider of cruises, makes the claim "Lowest fare advertised on Holland America guaranteed." However, this claim commits the fallacy of *amphiboly*, since the grammar leaves us uncertain as to how to interpret it. Is the company referring only to the fares advertised in the line's brochure? Does it mean lowest in comparison to fares on other cruise lines? It's hard to tell.

Other ads may employ the naturalistic fallacy (equating what is natural with what is good for you), false dilemma, or equivocation on a key term such as *free*. Advertisements for Natural American Spirit cigarettes not only commit the fallacy of popular appeal but also suggest, incorrectly, that because their tobacco is "all natural" it is not harmful like other cigarettes. (What tobacco is not "all natural," and why should "all natural" tobacco be safer? The ad doesn't say.) In this case, the Federal Trade Commission (FTC) determined that the ads involved deception and ordered the company to change them.

Rhetorical Devices and Misleading Language

Although the FTC forbids outright deception in advertising, it does permit the use of rhetorical devices. *Euphemisms*, in particular, abound in advertising. In real estate ads, a small house or apartment is "cozy," "quaint," or "compact," while old houses are "charming" or "full of character." A software product is a "solution" and a low-cost item is "economical" or "a great value."

The rhetorical device of *hyperbole*, or exaggeration of claims regarding a particular product, is considered acceptable in the advertising industry as well. NBC's claim that it was "Must See TV" and General Food's assertion that Wheaties is "the Breakfast of Champions" are examples of hyperbole.

In addition, ads frequently contain emotive words and phrases, such as *joystick*, *fresh*, *miracle*, *light*, or *alive with pleasure*, to evoke positive feelings that will become associated with the product. For example, George Foreman's grill was originally known

as the "Lean Mean Fat Reducing Grilling Machine," creating the impression that you can lose weight if you use this grill.

Images and slogans are also used to create a feel-good situation without telling us much about the product. Slogans such as Sprite's "Obey your thirst" convey no actual information about these brands. The use of emotive words and phrases sometimes borders on deception. In 2003, Philip Morris was found guilty of consumer fraud for the use of the term *light* in its ads, which gave the false impression that "light" cigarettes were less harmful or safer than other cigarettes.

Another advertising tactic is the use of vague, ambiguous, or obscure language. Words such as *help*, *can be*, and *up to* are sometimes so vague that they are meaningless. A claim that we can save "up to 50 percent" does not exclude the possibility that we may save nothing or may even pay more than we would for a similar product from a different brand. The use of obscure or technical terms can also be confusing to the consumer. For example, what is a "fixed rate" when it comes to a loan or mortgage, especially when the ad states in tiny letters at the bottom that the rates are subject to daily change?

Connections

What is the fallacy of snob appeal and how is it used by advertisers? *See Chapter 5, p. 146.* **How can hasty generalizations lead to false stereotypes?** *See Chapter 5, p. 149*

Faulty and Weak Arguments

Ads may try to persuade us to buy their product by presenting an inductive argument using an analogy in which they compare their product to something positive or powerful. In some cases, this analogy is weak or false. Take the slogan "Chevy: Like a Rock." In what ways is a Chevy like a rock? We certainly can't drive a rock. Also, rocks are free and last for millennia without needing maintenance on our part. In fact, there are few relevant similarities between a vehicle and a rock.

Some ads may appear to be logical arguments when in fact, key information is missing or statistics are misrepresented. For example, the pharmaceutical company Glaxo-SmithKline ran a magazine ad that appears to be using an inductive argument to oppose Congress's legalizing the importation of drugs from other countries. However, some of the premises are missing.

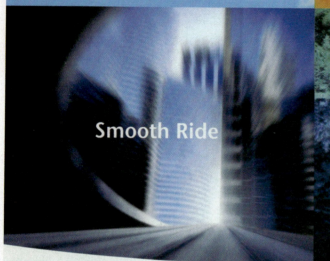

Fresher Air

Fuel Efficiency

Smooth Ride

Quietness

What will your reason be?

Hybrid Synergy Drive, delivers in more ways than one. Fresher air is the result of the lowest CO_2 emissions in its class*. Its fuel efficiency is demonstrated by its ability to travel 650 miles on a single tank of petrol, and its electric motor can take you from 0 to 62 mph in just 10.9 seconds. And just when you thought it could not get any better, the Torque on Demand Control uses the high-output electric motors to deliver a responsive, smooth and quiet acceleration. Will you choose it for yourself, for the earth, or both? Hybrid Synergy Drive. What will your reason be?

HYBRID SYNERGY DRIVE

www.HybridSynergyDrive.com

TODAY TOMORROW TOYOTA

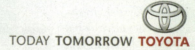

All figures quoted refer to Toyota Prius with Hybrid Synergy Drive. Official Fuel Consumption Figures for the Prius 1.5 Hybrid in mpg (l/100 km): Urban – 56.5 (5.0), Extra-Urban – 67.3 (4.2), Combined – 65.7 (4.3), CO_2 – 104 g/km. * Lowest CO_2 emissions than all other vehicles in the upper medium segment, according to SMMT annual CO_2 report 2006 market overview.

Ad for a Toyota Hybrid

DISCUSSION QUESTIONS

1. *What was your reaction when you first saw this ad? Explain.*

2. *Is the ad effective? Discuss ways in which the advertisement uses emotive words and images to evoke a positive feeling toward the automobile being advertised.*

3. *The advertisement asks: "Will you choose it for yourself, for the earth, or both?" Discuss what fallacy is being used in posing this question and what the advertiser is hoping to accomplish by using this fallacy.*

The ad states: "Experts say 10 percent of the world's drug supply is counterfeit. Can we be sure we import the 90 percent that isn't?" The ad ends by inviting the reader to "do your homework. Do the math. And see if drug importation adds up for you." However, the ad doesn't provide all the information we need to do the math. The statistics in the two premises, while accurate, are misleading to the uncritical reader because they convey the impression that imported drugs are more likely to be counterfeits. Before we can draw any conclusion about the relative safety of the domestic drug supply, we need a third premise providing information on the percentage of counterfeit drugs produced in this country, as well as those coming from countries such as Canada.[26] Indeed, while the World Health Organization estimates that 10 percent of the world's drug supply is counterfeit, the organization also points out that *most* of the counterfeit drugs are from developing nations. This ad also uses scare tactics as well as the *one of us / one of them*

cognitive error by counting on the reader to assume that counterfeit drugs are only a problem in *other* countries, not in *our* country (although this claim is never actually made in the ad).

In some ads, generalizations are made on the basis of statistics without having a control or comparison group or without providing information about how a sample was selected. An ad for Tempur-Pedic mattresses states: "Our sleep technology is recognized by NASA, raved about by the media, recommended worldwide by no less than 25,000 medical professionals." To start with, we have an ambiguous term—*medical professional*. Does it include only physicians and registered nurses? How about chiropractors and massage therapists? Or nurses' aides and hospital orderlies? How large was their sample, and how was it chosen? There are 600,000 physicians in the United States and 2.3 million registered nurses. If we include only these two groups in the category of medical professionals and 25,000 of them recommend Tempur-Pedic, does this mean that 99 percent of medical professionals do *not* recommend Tempur-Pedic mattresses?

Connections

How can using a representative sample strengthen an advertisement's impact?

See Chapter 7, p. 211.

HIGHLIGHTS

QUESTIONS TO CONSIDER IN EVALUATING ADVERTISEMENTS

- Does the ad use scare tactics to persuade us that we need the product?

- Does the ad provide credible evidence and/or statistics to support any causal claims?

- Does the ad play on our tendency to give in to group pressure?

- Does the ad set up a desirable image or lifestyle that may not be related to the product?

- Does the ad use any other informal fallacies?

- Does the ad use emotive language, images, or euphemisms?

- Is the grammar confusing or the wording misleading?

- Is the language vague, ambiguous, or obscure?

- Are the claims exaggerated?

- Does the ad leave out information that is necessary for us to make a decision?

- If the ad uses an analogy, is the analogy relevant?

➤APPLICATION: Answer the questions referring to a specific ad or product in the text to illustrate each question.

A Critique of Advertising

Critics claim that advertising is damaging to society. The fallacies and rhetorical devices used in advertising, they argue, distort consumer thinking and create markets for nonessential goods and services, thereby contributing to a shallow, materialistic mind-set. As ads become increasingly sophisticated and persuasive, more and more of us are going into debt to pay for lifestyles we can't afford. Advertisements can also make people feel they are to blame if they fall short of the ideals portrayed in advertisements.

Another questionable advertising practice is that of targeting minorities and poorer people here and in other countries. Magazines such as *Ebony* and *Latina* have twice as many ads for junk food, cigarettes, and alcohol and one-fourth as many ads for health-promoting products, compared to magazines read primarily by white women such as *Good Housekeeping*.[27] In addition, with more people giving up smoking in developed countries, tobacco companies are stepping up marketing efforts in developing countries, particularly those in Southeast Asia.

Advertising for products such as tobacco and alcohol also encourages addictive behavior. Virginia Slims ads have been credited with contributing to the increase in young female smokers. Studies have also found a direct

Ad for Sabai Wine Spritzer This sultry ad appeared in a magazine geared for the general public.

DISCUSSION QUESTIONS

1. What audience do you think this ad is geared toward? Explain.

2. What did you feel and what thoughts came to your mind when you first saw this ad? What rhetorical devices, fallacies, and/or images are being used by the advertisement to evoke these thoughts and feelings in the viewer?

3. Discuss the relevance of the ad to the actual product being promoted. Is the ad effective? Did it make you feel more likely to buy the product? Explain why or why not.

correlation between exposure to advertisements for alcohol and how much a young person drinks.[28]

Finally, critics point out that advertising is expensive and increases the prices of consumer goods and services, for some products by as much as 30 to 40 percent.[29] Furthermore, the ability of big corporations to spend large sums of money on advertising gives them a huge advantage over smaller companies. Thus, advertising contributes to the decline of small, local businesses and the rise of big business and monopolies.

Defenders of advertising respond that rather than *creating* cultural values, such as materialism, ads merely *reflect* those values. In response to the charge that ads are misleading, they point out that the government protects consumers from deceptive advertising practices. Some people may be taken in by persuasive ads, but most reasonable people are able to use their judgment in interpreting these ads.

In addition, if advertising is sometimes misleading or persuades people to buy things they don't really want, this is offset by the information that advertising does provide consumers so that they can make better-informed decisions. Consumers also have other sources of information, particularly through the Internet, media, and such publications as *Consumer Reports*, about products and the market. Placing restrictions on advertising entails placing restrictions on people's freedom of speech. The harms of restricting freedom of speech in the form of advertising in order to protect gullible consumers outweigh any benefits of censoring advertising, say the defenders of unrestricted advertising.[30]

In response to the argument that advertising puts small businesses at a disadvantage, defenders of advertising argue that restricting large corporations' freedom of speech to protect local businesses will lead to a decline in the quality of products and services. In a free-market society, they say, the best businesses will

---

Advertising is expensive and increases the prices of consumer goods and services, for some products by as much as 30 to 40 percent.

---

rise to the top. They respond to complaints about the high cost of advertising by saying that without advertising, production costs in many cases would be higher, since marketers could not address a mass market. Finally, it is argued that advertising gives media the financial funding it needs, thus allowing it to be free of government interference.

Many ads for products such as alcohol, cigarettes, and junk food target minorities and poorer people.

Whatever position we take regarding advertising, there is no doubt that it has more influence on our buying habits and beliefs than most of us are willing to admit. Because of this, we need to be continually vigilant in using our critical-thinking skills to evaluate advertising messages. The presence of misleading language, fallacies, and rhetorical devices in an ad is not always obvious.

One of the main barriers that keeps us from critically analyzing advertisements is self-serving bias and the assumption that we're more rational and smarter than most people. Recognizing our own shortcomings and learning about strategies used by advertisers so we are able to recognize them will make us less likely to fall for manipulative advertising.

EXERCISE 10-4

STOP AND ASSESS YOURSELF

I. Critically evaluate the following ads. Indicate what fallacies or rhetorical devices, if any, are being used.

*a. "Just as you can depend on the sun to rise, you can count on Metropolitan." (Life Insurance Company)

b. "You're in the Pepsi generation." (Pepsi)

c. "World's greatest newspaper." (Chicago Tribune)

*d. "An army of one." (U.S. Army)

e. "Sometimes you feel like a nut, sometimes you don't." (Almond Joy/Mounds)

f. "Because you're worth it." (L'Oréal cosmetics)

*g. "It will take you as far as your mind wants to go." (Toyota ad for the Avalon)

*h. "Can you hear me now?" (Verizon)

i. "God's gift to women." (Three Musketeers brand miniatures).

*j. "Live richly." (Citi Simplicity credit card)

k. Jessica Alba in ads promoting the Nokia Lumia 920 Window phone

l. "Too good to eat just one." (Lay's potato chips)

*m. "We're back on our feet again but the Gulf Coast community isn't. Purchase an Oreck vacuum and we will donate one in your name to people who are rebuilding their lives." (Oreck)

n. "I'm lovin' it." (McDonald's)

o. "Just one pill lasts up to 12 hours." (Mucinex)

*p. "Over 92 percent of people who own exercise equipment and 88 percent of people who own health club memberships do not exercise." (FastExercise equipment)

2. What are some of the values encouraged by advertising? Use specific examples of advertisements to support your answer. Discuss whether ads create cultural values or merely reflect them.

3. Evaluate the arguments for and against advertising. Should the government place more restrictions on advertising in the media, and if so, what type of restrictions? Construct an argument to support your answer.

4. Pharmaceutical companies now spend many times more on advertising and self-promotion than they do on basic research.[31] Before 1997, pharmaceutical companies were not permitted to advertise prescription drugs directly to the public. Should pharmaceutical companies be allowed to advertise to the public in the mass media, or should they be restricted to advertising to physicians and other medical professionals? Do mass media ads encourage people to overmedicate themselves or rely on medicine instead of lifestyle changes to solve their health problems? Support your answers.

5. Discuss how ads use fallacies and rhetoric to get a consumer to buy a product. Bring in three different ads to illustrate your answer.

6. Discuss in small groups some of the strategies, fallacies, and rhetorical devices used by advertisers and what you might do to make yourself less susceptible to them.

*Answers to selected exercises are found in the Solutions Manual at the end of the book.

THiNK AGAIN

1. What strategies are used in marketing research and marketing?

    ■ Marketing research strategies include discovering consumers' "hot buttons" and the use of surveys, focus groups, and observation. Marketing strategies include targeting advertisements to specific audiences, placement of goods on certain shelves in stores, and application of the SWOT model to determine a company's marketing strengths and weaknesses as well as opportunities and threats.

2. How does marketing and advertising affect the consumer?

    ■ Advertising informs consumers of products and services that can improve our lives. But advertising can promote materialism by creating markets for nonessential goods and services. The media is also affected by the market, since the media needs advertisers for financial support.

3. How can we as consumers be more aware of fallacies and rhetorical devices used in advertising?

    ■ Many ads rely on fallacies and rhetoric rather than credible information and rational argumentation. By being aware of fallacies such as scare tactics, popular appeal, snob appeal, and inappropriate appeal to authority, we will be less likely to accept fallacious arguments about a product. Awareness of rhetorical devices such as hyperbole and the use of euphemisms will also help us to not be fooled by these persuasive tools.

Perspectives on Advertising and Children

Children are one of the fastest-growing consumer groups in the United States. The average American child is exposed to 25,000 to 40,000 advertisements a year.* Almost half of television advertising for children ages 6 through 11 is for food such as sugary cereals, candy, and fast foods, or what is commonly known as "junk food."** Research suggests that by promoting nutritionally deficient and high-calorie foods, these ads may be contributing to the increase in childhood obesity.[†] This, in turn, has led to calls for limits on junk food advertising to children.

Should food advertising aimed at children be regulated? A Yale University poll found that 73 percent of Americans favor restrictions on children's food advertising.[††] Several countries, including Sweden, Norway, Canada, and Greece, have adopted strict measures limiting advertising to children. In the United States, the Federal Communications Commission (FCC) Children's Television Act of 1990 (revised in 1996) states that broadcasters are a "public fiduciary" who are obligated to serve the educational needs of children and to limit the amount of advertising during children's programs.

However, the content of advertising is generally regarded as protected by a business's First Amendment right to freedom of speech. According to this view, any regulation of content should be voluntary.[§] This perspective is defended by Robert Liodice in the second

---

*Anup Shah, "Children as Consumers," http://www.globalissues.org/article/237/children-as-consumers.
**"TV Ads Market Junk Food to Kids, New Study Finds," http://www.news.uiuc.edu/news/05/0824junkfood.html.
[†]The National Academies news release, "Food Marketing Aimed at Kids Influences Nutritional Choices," December 6, 2005.
[††]Institute of Medicine, "Preventing Childhood Obesity: Health in the Balance," 2005, http://www.iom.edu.
[§]For more on First Amendment issues and advertising, see Martin H. Redish, "Tobacco Advertising and the First Amendment," *Iowa Law Review,* Vol. 81, March 1996, p. 589.

essay in this section as well as by the Children's Advertising Review Unit (CARU), a division of the Council of Better Business Bureaus. CARU's guidelines call for self-regulation by children's advertisers rather than legal regulations.[§§]

Not everyone agrees with this voluntary approach. An Institute of Medicine (IOM) study on food marketing calls for a law to limit advertising of unhealthy food to children on both broadcast and cable television if the industry does not take voluntary action to do so. The Center for Science in the Public Interest (CSPI) also supports legal regulation of children's advertising. Whether voluntary self-regulation is sufficient remains to be seen.

In the following two readings by the Center for Science and Public Interest (CSPI) and by Liodice we'll examine arguments both for and against the legal regulation of "junk" food advertising to children.

Limiting Food Marketing to Children

CSPI (CENTER FOR SCIENCE IN THE PUBLIC INTEREST)

The Center for Science in the Public Interest (CSPI) is a consumer advocacy organization that advocates for better health and nutrition and provides consumers with information about health and well-being. In the following reading, the CSPI calls for more restrictions on the advertising of junk food aimed at young children.

The Federal Government

Almost 30 years have passed since the last public debate on food marketing aimed at children. In 1977, two non-profit organizations, Action for Children's Television and the Center for Science in the Public Interest, petitioned the Federal Trade Commission (FTC) to halt television commercials for candy and sugary snack foods directed at young children. That triggered an in-depth and controversial FTC examination of the issue.

In 1978 the FTC issued a staff report that concluded that "television advertising for any product directed to children who are too young to appreciate the selling purpose of, or otherwise comprehend or evaluate, the advertising is inherently unfair and deceptive." . . . The FTC commenced a public hearing on the issue and invited comments on its staff's proposal to ban all (not just junk food) television advertising aimed at young children, ban commercials for sugary snack foods aimed at older children, and other measures. The FTC also asked the public to comment on other approaches, such as requiring health information within ads, restrictions on the techniques used to advertise to young children, and restricting the number of commercials directed at young children.

Broadcasters, ad agencies, and food and toy companies vehemently opposed the FTC's proceedings. They worked to stop the FTC from holding hearings, lobbied Congress to prevent the FTC from using its funding to address children's television, and filed a lawsuit against the Commission. Advertisers also began a voluntary effort to improve food advertising. Although the FTC did hold hearings, before it could act Congress passed the cynically named Federal Trade Commission Improvements Act of 1980 that barred the FTC from issuing industry-wide

regulations to stop unfair advertising practices. As a result, the FTC now regulates advertising aimed at children only on a case-by-case basis.

In 1981, the FTC acknowledged that "child-oriented television advertising is a legitimate cause for public concern" because young children do not understand the persuasive intent of advertising and indiscriminately trust ads. But the FTC concluded that "the only effective remedy would be a ban on all advertisements oriented toward young children, and such a ban, as a practical matter, cannot be implemented," because then there would be no way to fund children's television programs. With that, the FTC's bold initiative to regulate children's television advertising sputtered to an end.

Self-Regulation: Foxes Guarding the Hen House

Today, with broad federal regulation off the table, the only protection of children from inappropriate food marketing is occasional FTC enforcement actions and voluntary industry self-regulation regarding unfair or deceptive advertising. The Children's Advertising Review Unit (CARU), a program of the Council of Better Business Bureaus, runs industry's main self-regulation program. CARU is funded by such food producers as Burger King, Frito-Lay, Hershey, Kellogg, and McDonald's, along with toy manufacturers, National Geographic Kids (which is filled with food advertising), and food and toy trade associations.

CARU's "Self-Regulatory Guidelines for Children's Advertising" gives the appearance of protecting children from deceptive advertising, but those guidelines are not enforceable and depend on voluntary action by a company. Typically, companies withdraw objectionable ads, but replace them with new ads that are little different. The major flaw is that the guidelines focus on narrow advertising techniques and not on the nature of the products being advertised. For instance, advertisers are not supposed to

[§§]For CARU's guidelines, go to http://www.caru.org/guidelines/guidelines.pdf.

actively prod kids to pester their parents to buy a brand of candy, but are permitted without restriction to advertise candy or other junk food.

On the corporate front, Kraft voluntarily does not advertise to children under 6 and in 2005 started limiting to healthier foods its television, radio, and print advertising directed to children 6–11. Also, the soft drink industry continues to refrain from advertising its products on television to young children.

Food Marketing Directed to Children . . .

. . . There is still a lot of advertising, notwithstanding a 1990 law that limits commercials to 10½ minutes per hour on weekends and 12 minutes per hour on weekdays during children's programming. (That law did not reduce the amount of TV advertising, but simply codified what was already the industry norm.) Many of the ads are still for sugary cereals, salty snacks, candy, fast foods, and the like; programs like SpongeBob SquarePants are essentially program-length commercials for foods whose labels feature the licensed characters; and many of the advertisers, such as Kellogg and McDonald's, are the same. The major differences are that cable companies, like Nickelodeon and the Cartoon Network, provide many more hours of children's programming than did Saturday morning broadcast networks in the 1970s, and food manufacturers and restaurants have new marketing venues like Channel One in schools and the Internet.

Recently, industry executives have expressed concern about the childhood obesity epidemic and have mounted modest programs aimed at addressing the problem, but, if history is any indication, as soon as public outcries quiet down, the industry programs will die out and efforts to reduce junk food marketing voluntarily will fade.

REVIEW QUESTIONS

1. Why did some groups oppose the proposal for the FTC to hold hearings on advertising on children's television?

2. On what grounds did the FTC maintain that "child-oriented television advertising is a legitimate cause for public concern"?

3. What is CARU and why does the CSPI reject their approach for regulating children's advertising?

Advertising and Freedom of Speech: Beware of the Food Nanny

ROBERT LIODICE

Robert Liodice is the president and CEO of the Association of National Advertisers. In this blog, he argues that the guidelines suggested by CSPI are a violation of the right to freedom of speech and the free exchange of information.* Liodice also contends that the guidelines are based on misinformation about food advertising and children's television viewing.

Free speech is the most important and fundamental right we have as Americans. It is the foundation for the free exchange of ideas and ideals that drives the lifestyles and livelihoods in this most free of countries. . . .

. . . When those freedoms are jeopardized, we all lose. When you begin to chip away, even marginally, at those freedoms, we all run the risk of sliding down that slippery slope of diminishing rights and privileges.

I am rather stunned that The Center for Science in the Public Interest (CSPI)—or any organization for that matter—would suggest restricting or modifying the free speech of perfectly legal enterprises as an approach to solve a problem. We all recognize that there are a host of societal issues—childhood and adult obesity stands out as one of the most "curable" of them all. But seeking a cure should not follow the path of trampling on our core rights and privileges of Americans. Without question or argument, there are a range of reasonable alternatives and approaches that can be considered and aggressively pursued—and they should [be pursued] with full vigor. But trampling on the First Amendment, whether through government controls or unsupported self-regulatory edicts, should not even be on anyone's radar screen—as a way to solve problems. . . .

Last week the Center for Science in the Public Interest (CSPI) did something that was neither based on science nor beneficial to the public interest. They released a set of ill-conceived, heavy-handed food marketing guidelines. [On the basis of] flawed data and backed by the threat of lawsuits, they intend to coerce the food and marketing industries to conform to their misguided views of what constitutes good nutrition and what represents appropriate commercial communication with consumers.

In issuing these guidelines, CSPI misstates the facts about food advertising and childhood TV viewing; they overlook the broad array of factors—beyond marketing—that influence childhood food consumption; they disregard the significant efforts of food companies to enhance the nutritional content of their products; and they ignore the fact that food and other advertising are already among the most stringently regulated areas in the United States.

*Robert Liodice, "Advertising and Freedom of Speech: Beware of the Food Nanny," January 24, 2005, http://anablogs.com/liodice/2005/01/america-free_sp.html.

Styling themselves as the nation's food nanny, CSPI has proposed a set of extraordinarily overreaching regulations, which specify acceptable nutritional content, portion size, packaging design and logo use. . . .

The guideline specifics are ridiculously restrictive. For example, children are defined as "anyone under 18"; low-nutrition beverages are defined as "drinks with less than 50 percent real juice;" and banned TV shows are those "for which more than a quarter of the audience is children." They are an affront to—and broadside attack on—the marketing freedoms of food and restaurant businesses, broadcasters, entertainment companies, and the entire marketing industry.

So let me specifically address the major flaws inherent in CSPI's guidelines.

First, CSPI speciously claims that the amount of marketing aimed at kids has doubled in the last ten years. In examining measured media, however, a detailed study by Nielsen Media Research covering the period of 1993 to 2003 concludes otherwise. Adjusting for inflation in order to hold the value of dollars constant, real expenditures on food and restaurant advertising on television (including cable) fell over this ten-year period. Furthermore, the actual number of food ads seen by children under 12 declined by 13 percent from the first four years of this period to the last four years. . . .

Second, CSPI's report states that "parents bear the primary responsibility for feeding their children." However, the guidelines then ignore this point and the fact that adults make the vast majority of food purchases for their families, particularly for younger kids. They also disregard what the majority of food experts inherently know: that the best way to encourage good childhood nutrition is to promote healthy, well-balanced diets, rather than attempting to characterize some products as "good foods" and others as "bad foods." When other countries have attempted to ban or severely restrict children's advertising, those efforts have consistently failed to lower obesity rates in comparison to countries where there are no such restrictions.

Finally, let's take a look at the significant, positive steps the food and marketing industries are taking—and have historically taken—to address the special concerns of children. Thirty years ago, the marketing industry established the Children's Advertising Review Unit (CARU) specifically to recognize that material which might be truthful and non-deceptive for adults could still mislead young people. CARU created a detailed code, available at www.caru.org/guidelines, which proactively works to [ensure] that children are not taken advantage of in the advertising marketplace. . . . The record of industry compliance with CARU's guidelines demonstrates an extremely high level of effectiveness.

Equally important are the many, significant steps that food and restaurant companies are taking to bring healthy new offerings to market. For example, they are reformulating products to be lower in cholesterol, fat, and calories. They are removing trans fats, reducing sodium and sugar content, introducing whole grains, and offering more milk products and salad menu items.

There is no question that childhood nutrition and obesity are serious societal issues. However, as the Surgeon General concluded in his groundbreaking 2001 report, "There is no simple or quick answer to this multifaceted challenge." Unlike CSPI's guidelines which mislead the public by narrowly focusing on food advertising, the Surgeon General's report contains thoughtful, specific recommendations on how to address the challenge in a balanced, comprehensive way. It further calls on all of us—companies, individuals, families, schools, governments and the media—to work together in ways that will bring better health to everyone in this country. We accept this challenge and stand ready to collaborate with all other interested, responsible parties to identify solutions that will truly work.

REVIEW QUESTIONS

1. According to Liodice, what is the most important and fundamental right we have as Americans? In what ways do the CSPI guidelines trample on our "core rights and privileges"?

2. On what grounds does Liodice claim that the CSPI guidelines are "ridiculously restrictive" and mistake the facts about food advertising and childhood television viewing?

3. What does Liodice mean when he says that the CSPI guidelines ignore the fact that parents bear the primary responsibility for buying and feeding their children healthy foods?

4. What steps does Liodice suggest that the food and marketing industries take to address the issue of advertising to children and obesity in children?

THiNK AND DISCUSS

PERSPECTIVES ON ADVERTISING AND CHILDREN

1. Critically evaluate the CSPI's and Liodice's arguments regarding government regulation of children's food advertising. Which makes the best argument and why?

2. Discuss whether freedom of speech as a liberty right should apply to advertising of nutritionally poor food to children. Present an argument to support your answer.

3. Discuss who should be primarily responsible—business, the media, government, or parents—for regulating or monitoring food advertising to young children. Discuss how this responsibility should be reflected in public policy regarding food advertising to children.

4. Develop an argument addressing the issue of whether or not corporations, such as Viacom and Kellogg, should be held responsible for damages to children's health that are allegedly related to advertising.

5. Should misleading advertising be legal? Discuss where the line should be drawn between ads that use fallacies and rhetoric and those that are blatantly deceptive, particularly when it comes to children. Use specific ads to illustrate your answer. Construct an argument to support your conclusion.

6. Write a letter to a food company or media corporation that advertises to young children. In the letter, construct an argument presenting a policy that is reasonable and in the best interests of both business and consumers for advertising food to children.

7. Many schools and colleges sell foods of poor nutritional quality in their vending machines, cafeterias, and school stores. Working in small groups, develop a policy regarding this practice at your college (or your former high school or elementary school). Construct an argument supporting your policy.

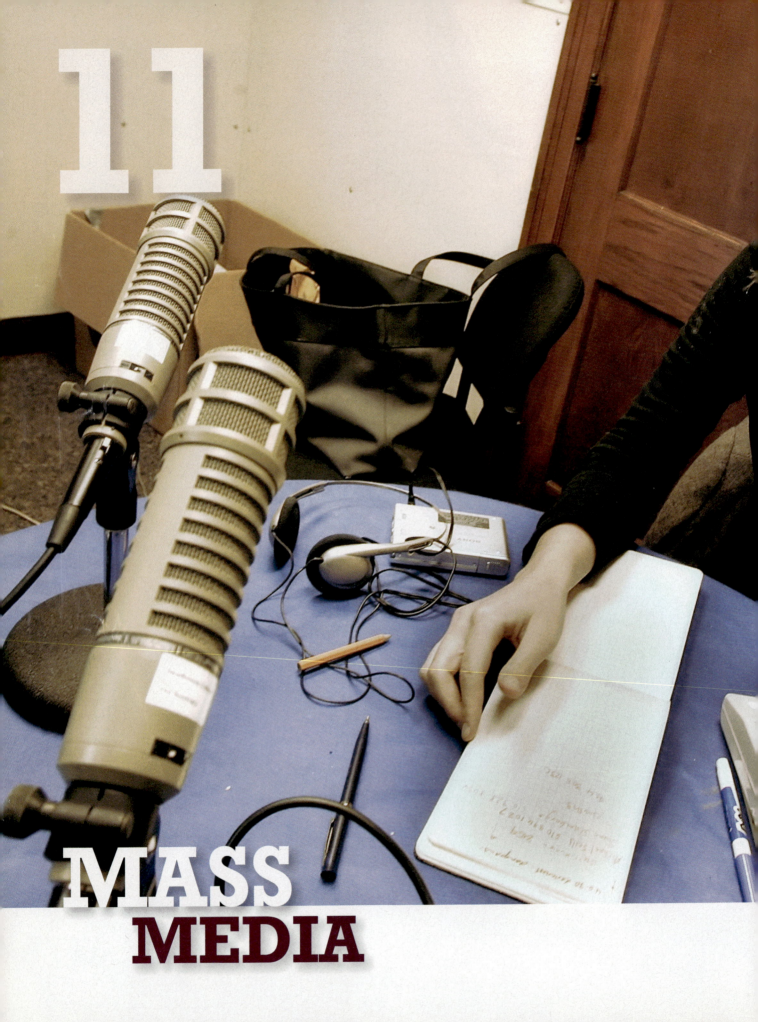

11

MASS MEDIA

A group of students at Swarthmore College who were dissatisfied with the narrow scope of the media coverage of the conflicts in Iraq and Afghanistan decided in 2005 to start their own radio station called War News Radio. "We hear the military talk about Iraq all the time and we even hear stories of U.S. soldiers, but the Iraqis didn't have a voice. We wanted to cover their side of the story," says junior Eva Barboni, who was an associate producer for War News Radio.[1] "We felt that there was really no history or no context to a lot of the stories we see in the mainstream media."

To provide their audience with a better idea of what the war is like, student volunteers at War News Radio have interviewed Iraqi and Afghanistan citizens who experienced the war firsthand. To do this, the student journalists use special Internet software that allows them to make free international phone calls. Although they are limited to interviewing Iraqis who can speak English or who can

How can you, as a college student, use the media to express your views and influence local, national, and international issues?

THiNK FIRST

- What is the relationship between mass media and big business in the United States?
- What are some of the limitations of the news media?
- In what ways has the Internet changed our lives?

 find a translator, the interviews—such as one with a father whose daughter was shot at an American checkpoint and one with an Iraqi artist whose work includes images of war violence—have touched the hearts of the station's many listeners. More recently, the show has broadened its scope to cover Iran, North Korea, and Syria, in addition to topics such as the use of military drones by the U.S. (For more on the issue of drones, see "Critical Thinking Issue: Perspectives on the Use of Drones in War," p. 420.)

The Swarthmore radio show continues to be a huge success and has been picked up by some college and public radio stations in the United States, as well as by radio stations all over the world. It is available for listening at www.warnewsradio.org.

The success of War News Radio has inspired other colleges to consider undertaking similar media productions. It also illustrates one of the limitations of traditional mass media. Unlike most college media, the mass media cannot rely on subsidies and volunteers. Mass media survive by attracting large audiences and finding businesses to sponsor their programming through advertising. Because mass media rely on advertising and circulation, they need to please their sponsors and audience.

Swarthmore College students and an advisor preparing stories for their War News Radio show.

Good critical-thinking skills require that we be able to critically analyze media messages. In Chapter 11 we will:

- Look at the history of mass media in the United States
- Learn about the dependency of mass media on advertising revenues
- Develop skills for critically evaluating news coverage in the media
- Find out how to evaluate reports of scientific findings
- Examine the influence of government on reporting in the media
- Examine the impact of the Internet on our lives
- Cultivate strategies for analyzing media images

MASS MEDIA IN THE UNITED STATES

We live in an information age in which we are bombarded daily with an overwhelming amount of data. The average American spends about 9 hours a day watching television, surfing the Internet, talking on a telephone, reading the newspaper and magazines, or using some other form of media.[2] Although most of us claim that we have a healthy skepticism about what we hear or see, we are more taken in by what the media tells us than we may think. Because of this, it is important that we learn how to think critically when it comes to evaluating what we see, hear, or read in the media.

The Rise of Mass Media

Before the arrival of television in the late 1940s, radio and magazines were the main forms of **mass media**—that is, forms of communication designed to reach and influence very large audiences. **Niche media**, in contrast, are geared to a narrowly defined audience with special interests, such as raising cattle, gardening, or automobile racing, or to an audience with specific demographic or geographic characteristics, such as women, African Americans, or people living in Alaska.

By 1930 half of all American homes had a radio. In the 1930s and 1940s, a few large national radio networks broadcast news and entertainment to the entire country. Large-circulation magazines such as *Life*, *Look*, and the *Saturday Evening Post* also kept the public informed. For visual news, people relied on the weekly newsreels shown in movie theaters. Even after television made its appearance,

soon after World War II, for many years there were only three national commercial stations (ABC, CBS, and NBC), plus in some areas a few independent local TV stations.

The increasing presence of mass media in our culture has changed our lives. Since the 1950s, more and more of our experiences have been shaped by the corporations that control the media rather than by family and educational institutions, on which past generations relied. On the other hand, without these mass-media corporations we would not have the free or relatively inexpensive access to entertainment and information—including news, consumer reviews, and online databases—that we now enjoy.

> **mass media** Forms of communication that are designed to reach and influence very large audiences.
>
> **niche media** Forms of communication geared to a narrowly defined audience.

The Media Today

Today, digital cable television, mobile media, and the Internet offer us a dizzying array of media choices. As a result, audiences have become increasingly fragmented. On television, Nickelodeon is aimed at children and teens,

A newsstand in Hong Kong: About 200,000 different magazines, most of which are geared toward niche markets, are published worldwide.

Where Do We Get Our News?

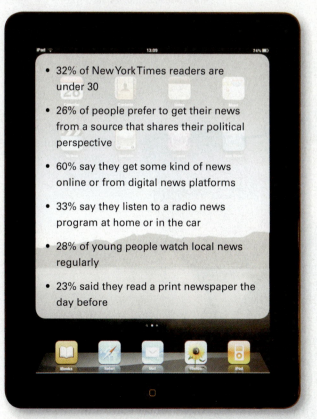

- 32% of New York Times readers are under 30
- 26% of people prefer to get their news from a source that shares their political perspective
- 60% say they get some kind of news online or from digital news platforms
- 33% say they listen to a radio news program at home or in the car
- 28% of young people watch local news regularly
- 23% said they read a print newspaper the day before

http://www.poynter.org/latest-news.mediawire/189819/pew-tv-viewing-habit-grays-as-digital-news-consumption-tops-print-radio. September 2012.

and MTV targets young adults. TV Land, with its reruns, appeals to baby boomers, while Fox Television aims at a young urban audience. There are even 24-hour channels for shoppers, weather-watchers, and those who want instant news at any time of the day or night. Magazines such as *Ski, Wired, Saveur, Islands,* and *Internet World,* as well as many radio stations, are niche media geared toward particular lifestyles or ethnic groups.

In addition, more Americans today are choosing what to listen to or watch on the basis of their political views. Conservative critics accuse the news media of having a liberal bias, a bias that has been confirmed by studies.[3] The majority of the news media outlets, for instance, have in the past supported Democratic presidential candidates, abortion rights, stricter environmental regulations, and cuts in military spending.

At the same time that news media options are proliferating, a select few large corporations are controlling the news media. In 1983, 50 corporations controlled the majority of the news media in the United States. By 2012 the media was controlled by a handful of corporations which included, among others, General Electric, News Corporation, Walt Disney, Viacom, Time Warner, COX, and CBS.[4] The content of a television show, magazine, or newspaper, consequently, is dictated to a large extent by the interests and values of its corporate owner.

In addition to influencing the public through their productions, news media corporations also try to influence public policy directly, by donating millions of dollars

Hot or Not?

Does the fact that only a select number of corporations control the media affect the quality and objectivity of the media?

annually to congressional campaigns and tens of millions more to lobbying efforts.[5] For example, television, radio, and wireless Internet all rely on airway radio frequencies to send and receive messages. Media lobbyists are trying to persuade Congress to privatize these airways, which are currently regulated by the government through the FCC. This pressure on the FCC has contributed to a trend toward government deregulation over the past few decades. In April 2010 a U.S. appeals court ruled against *net neutrality,* which gives all Web sites equal access to Internet broadband, and in favor of Comcast, stating that the FCC has no power to regulate net neutrality. In making this ruling the court gave large powerful Web sites, which can pay to have their Web sites load faster, an advantage over small Web sites.

In addition, as the media corporations control the airways, other businesses influence the public through advertising. Mass media corporations could not survive without the financial backing of other large corporations. Because advertisers pay media corporations, the public can watch broadcast television and listen to the radio for "free." In return for "free" programs, viewers are subjected to ads. If a show does not hold our attention or a magazine does not sell enough copies, sponsors will withdraw their ads, media corporations will lose money, and sooner or later the show or magazine will be dropped. Thus, the need to keep advertisers is the primary concern of media corporations.

The purchase of the Wall Street Journal along with several small New England newspapers by Australian-born global news mogul Rupert Murdoch, who also owns the Fox News Channel and is CEO of News Corporation, has led to concerns of a move toward a partisan conservative position in news coverage.

EXERCISE 11-1

STOP AND ASSESS YOURSELF

I. In *Citizens United v. Federal Election Commission* (2010), the U.S. Supreme Court ruled that there should be no ceiling on political spending by corporations. Critically analyze the consequences of this ruling on our ability to get unbiased news on elections and legislation.

2. Make a list of the different types of media that you experience in the course of one day. Research what corporations control the forms of media that you are exposed to most. Working in small groups, discuss the implications of your findings.

THE NEWS MEDIA

According to the Pew Research Center's "The State of the News Media 2013" report, the influence of newspapers, magazines, and news television has declined 30 percent since its peak in 2000. The paucity of news coverage is due in part to financial problems facing the news industry and the need to cut staff. Television stations have cut news reporting, which is labor intensive, by up to 50 percent, while coverage of sports, weather, and traffic now accounts for 40 percent of content. These problems are exacerbated by dwindling audiences. Almost one-third of people have abandoned a particular news outlet because it no longer provides the news coverage and information they were accustomed to getting. Newspapers and news magazines are also suffering from cutbacks with the growth of digital media and social networking, which are increasingly popular sources of news, especially for young people.[6]

Another change in the past few decades has been a trend away from reporting government and foreign affairs and toward reporting entertainment, lifestyle, and celebrity-scandal news. With cuts in budgets, news broadcast stations are also relying more on citizen or amateur reporters as well as self-interested information providers such as corporations, think tanks, partisan activists, and government press releases. Thus, while Americans have an increasing number of news sources, they are no more informed than they were two decades ago.[7]

At the same time, the news media have played and continue to play a key role in exposing corporate and government scandal. The exposé of John D. Rockefeller and his oil monopoly by editor and journalist Ida Tarbell (1857–1944) resulted in a federal investigation and the Supreme Court's eventual breakup in 1911 of Standard Oil. In the early 1970s, Bob Woodward and Carl Bernstein of the *Washington Post* were instrumental in exposing the 1972 Watergate scandal, which led to President Nixon's resignation in 1974.

Errors can also be perpetuated by the news media. In the rush to be the first to cover breaking news, the news media have sometimes reported news before they have confirmed the information in their reports. Following the Sandy Hook Elementary School massacre in Newton, Connecticut in 2012, news sources incorrectly reported that the shooter was Ryan Lanza, Adam Lanza's older brother, and that their mother Nancy

Connections

How does bias in the media interfere with critical thinking in a democracy? *See Chapter 1, p. 19.*

What types of narrow-mindedness are reinforced by some types of news reporting? *See Chapter 1, pp. 24–26.*

What types of emotional appeals and rhetorical devices, including hyperbole, do the media use to hold our attention? *See Chapter 2, p. 48* and *Chapter 3, p. 70.*

What critical-thinkng tools can we use to evaluate the credibility and reliability of evidence presented by the media? *See Chapter 4, p. 116.*

Percentage of Adults Who Follow the News All or Most of the Time

AGE	PERCENTAGE
18–29	31%
30–49	52%
50–64	65%
65+	73%

After the devastating earthquake in Haiti in early 2010, news features remained focused on Haiti for weeks following the disaster because so many people remained in dire need of assistance.

How does confirmation bias influence our choice of new sources?
See Chapter 4, p. 110.

Connections

was one of the teachers shot and killed inside the school that day. In fact, the shooter turned out to Adam Lanza. The media also speculated based on incorrect information that a possible motive for the shooting was that Adam Lanza had felt neglected because his mother was working at the school. In fact, his mother had never been a teacher at Sandy Hook Elementary School.

Sensationalism and the News as Entertainment

Like other types of mass media, the goal of the news media is not simply to inform and educate the public about critical issues. The news media also selects stories that will appeal to a large number of people and presents the news in a way that keeps us tuned in so that we will view the commercials.

News stories are often selected because of their entertainment value rather than their newsworthiness. Most people prefer heartwarming, true-crime, or disaster stories over critical analysis of national and international issues. Therefore, excessive amounts of time and space, including the front pages and headlines of newspapers, may be devoted to stories about daring rescues, celebrity scandals, kidnapped children, airplane crashes, natural disasters, and gruesome murders. Following the Boston Marathon bombings in April 2013, the news media covered the bombings and the capture of the two suspects almost nonstop for days.

Newscasters and journalists play on our human tendency to engage in the memorable events cognitive error, in which our mind exaggerates the importance of sensational—and usually gruesome—events to hold the audience's attention. After the 1999 Columbine High School shootings in Colorado, in which fourteen people were killed, high-profile stories on school shootings left many people with the false impression that there was an epidemic of such shootings in the United States. This impression was reinforced by the "massacre" in 2007 at Virginia Tech (Virginia Polytechnic Institute and State University), which took the lives of thirty-three college students and professors, and, in 2012, by the Newton, Connecticut, school shootings.

Because we tend to remember sensational events, we come to see them as far more frequent that they really are. In contrast, ongoing problems such as global warming, discrimination, and poverty generally get relatively little coverage in the mainstream news media. This is mainly because in-depth investigation of these issues would be far more time consuming and costly than flying a crew to the site of a disaster.

News as sensationalist entertainment is carried to an extreme in broadcasts by so-called shock jocks. Popular radio talk show host and conservative Rush Limbaugh infuriated many listeners when he referred to Georgetown University Law Center student Sandra Fluke as a "slut" and "prostitute" after she had made a speech the week before in front of the House Democrats supporting mandatory insurance coverage at her college for contraceptives. Limbaugh has been condemned by some as being a "sexist" and a "racist." Although the FCC does have the power to regulate and censor sexually explicit material in the media, some offensive racist and sexist talk has been considered off limits to government regulators.

Depth of News Analysis

As we noted, most people prefer sensationalist news stories, such as one about a heinous crime or a celebrity scandal, rather than in-depth analyses of ongoing issues. While some news shows, such as those on National Public Radio (NPR) and BBC World Service—both government-funded networks that are not dependent on (but NPR does accept some) advertising revenue—go into depth, there is usually little critical analysis of news issues in the news media. In addition, many people have a short attention span and are easily distracted by competing interests, such as the telephone, the Internet, and video games. Consequently, even important news stories are usually presented in small segments with little analysis of the implications of the issue. The lack of in-depth analysis of the Health Care and Education Reconciliation Act of 2010, which will not be fully implemented until 2022, left many Americans confused and even opposed to the bill simply because they didn't know what is in it or how it would affect them.

Did You Know

The amount of time a typical half-hour local newscast devotes to U.S. foreign policy is less than one minute. The amount of time that it spends on sports and weather, in contrast, takes up 40 percent of the newscast.[8]

Not only are viewers or readers usually given little insight into issues, but also visual images and speakers' comments may be taken out of context or important information may be omitted for the sake of "brevity." Captions used with photos can also be misleading and inadvertently promote racism and other negative stereotypes, as you can

Many people are not interested in in-depth analysis of the news and are easily distracted from the news by cell phones and video games.

see in "Analyzing Images: Stereotypes and Racism in the News Media." In these cases, we are often left not knowing the original context of an image or the intent of a speaker.

During the 2000 presidential elections, the team of Republican nominee George W. Bush came up with a political commercial mocking what it said was Vice President Al Gore's claim of having invented the Internet. Although the Republican Party never aired the commercial because it was inaccurate, the story that Gore claimed to have invented the Internet was snatched up by the news media—which never bothered to check the original source of Gore's statement or the context in which it was uttered. In fact, Gore never claimed that he invented the Internet. Instead, he had said in a 1999 interview that "during my service in the United States Congress, I took the initiative in creating the Internet."[9] The context of the comment was regarding his work, not as a scientist or inventor, but as a senator and vice president in actively promoting the development of the Internet and in helping the inventors of the Internet get it to the point where it is today.

In addition, because of time limitations, editors and newscasters must decide which stories to use and which to disregard or shorten. News stories also have to hold the attention of the audience, who may be more interested in sports and weather than in international or national news. This is particularly true with television newscasts.

Because of budget restrictions and the need to air a breaking story before other stations do in order to maintain ratings, the news media often relies on information from government or corporate press conferences and press

releases rather than do its own investigative reporting (which can be very expensive and time-consuming). However, information from press releases may be presented in an oversimplified and biased manner to bolster the image of those giving the press conference. On the basis of information in a government press release in 2002 and 2003, during the buildup to the invasion of Iraq, the American media reported, without ever fully investigating the story, that the United States had found mobile laboratories for creating biological weapons in Iraq. As it turned out, that information may have been incorrect and is believed by some to have been a case of disinformation deliberately disseminated by people in the U.S. administration to build public support for the invasion of Iraq.

In addition to issuing press releases, government officials may call on selected journalists during press conferences and ignore others who might ask unwanted questions. Follow-up questions by other journalists may not be allowed. To be one of the favored journalists, a reporter must be careful not to offend government sources or

Connections

How are words used to reinforce stereotypes in the media? *See Chapter 3, p. 88.*

In what ways does the government appeal to our sense of ethnocentrism and nationalism in their press releases on foreign policy? *See Chapter 1, p. 26.*

In the news coverage following Hurricane Katrina, the caption for an Associated Press (AP) photo (top left) showing a black man wading through the flood waters carrying goods from a store read, "A young man walks through chest-deep flood water after looting a grocery store in New Orleans, Louisiana," whereas the caption for an AP photo (bottom left) of two white people wading through the flood waters carrying goods said, "Two residents wade through chest-deep water after finding bread and soda from a local grocery store after Hurricane Katrina came through their area in New Orleans, Louisiana." In other words, white people "find," whereas black people "loot."

Stereotypes and Racism in The News Media

In addition to using images and quotes out of context (the fallacy of accident), the news media can inadvertently manipulate viewers' perceptions through the use of descriptive language. In the news coverage after Hurricane Katrina in 2005, several readers complained that the captions for the two pictures shown here of people wading through the floodwaters carrying goods from a store showed racial bias.

DISCUSSION QUESTIONS

1. Discuss how, if at all, the two photo captions show racial bias.

2. Bring in examples of photos with captions from magazines and newspapers. Discuss whether the captions are written in a biased fashion. If they are, explain why they are biased and rewrite them using neutral language.

corporate backers. Thus journalists need to think twice about critiquing their sources or printing or airing a story that might offend the hand that feeds them.

Journalists have also accepted money from political sources to promote particular political agendas—a practice known as "pay to sway." United Press International syndicated columnist Maggie Gallagher was paid more than $40,000 in federal funding from the Department of Health and Human Services under the Bush administration to promote in her columns the Marriage Protection Amendment, which would limit marriage to a man and a woman. Her columns ran in newspapers such as the

New York Times, the *Wall Street Journal*, and the *Washington Post*.[10]

Politically motivated government sources may also leak sensitive news to the press. In 2003, former U.S. ambassador Joseph C. Wilson IV told the press that the Bush administration had distorted intelligence on Iraq's suspected weapons of mass destruction program to justify the war. The White House may also use the media to forward a particular political agenda, such as Obama's public clash with President Hamid Karzai of Afghanistan whom Obama regards as corrupt. Then Press Secretary Robert Gibbs told the press that President Karzai had threatened to join the

White House press secretary Jay Carney briefing the press.

Taliban. The Karzai administration responded by denying that Karzai had ever made such a comment and questioned the credibility of the White House media accounts, saying they were "shocked to see such kind of [unsupported] comments in the media."

Bias in the News

Almost invariably, the news media claim to present objective as well as truthful coverage of local, national, and international events and developments. Despite this, 77 percent of Americans believe that the media "tend to favor one side," an increase from 53 percent in 1985. An analysis of bias in the media found that left-leaning and right-leaning reporting tends to balance out across the news media outlets. For example, Fox News tends to be a right-leaning network and MSNBC tends to be a left-leaning news outlet, while on the Internet, the Free Republic is right leaning, while the Huffington Post leans left.[11] News is often reported in a biased way to keep us tuned in. Reporters may exaggerate certain details and omit or down-play others to make a story more interesting and entertaining to the audience. The repeated airing in 2008 on CNN News of *Saturday Night Live* comedian Tina Fey's impersonation of Republican vice-presidential candidate

Some people thought that comedian Tina Fey's biased impersonation of then-Republican vice presidential candidate Sarah Palin was actually Palin.

EDWARD R. MURROW, *Broadcast Journalist*

Edward R. Murrow was a pioneer and legend in news broadcasting. Born in Greensboro, North Carolina, in 1908 to Quaker parents, he majored in speech at Washington State University. In 1935 Murrow went to work for CBS Radio. At the time, CBS did not have a news broadcaster. During World War II, Murrow went to London to cover the war for CBS. Rather than rely on assumptions, hearsay evidence, or government press releases, Murrow hired and trained a corps of war correspondents to assist him. Murrow's accurate and in-depth war coverage of the events from wartime London set high standards for journalistic excellence.

In 1951, Murrow switched to television. His ability to critically analyze issues and events rather than get caught up in cognitive errors or groupthink continued to distinguish his career. During the 1950s, he displayed great integrity and courage in standing up to Senator Joseph McCarthy and McCarthy's Red Scare tactics. Murrow kept the public informed about what was going on despite the fact that doing so brought him into frequent conflict with CBS executives and the show's sponsors. Murrow's coverage helped bring about the downfall of McCarthyism. Murrow also used his news show to promote democratic ideals such as freedom of speech, citizen participation, and the pursuit of truth.

Murrow left CBS in 1961 to become director of the United States Information Agency under President John F. Kennedy. A heavy smoker, he died in 1965 of lung cancer. However, his legend and example as an exemplary critical thinker live on. The movie *Good Night, and Good Luck* (2005) chronicles Murrow's career during the McCarthy era.

DISCUSSION QUESTIONS

1. Think of a current event of national or international importance such as Iraq's nuclear program and missile testing by North Korea. Compare the coverage given to these events by contemporary news broadcasters and journalists with that given to McCarthyism by Murrow.

2. Referring to the event that you selected for the previous question, discuss how you would cover the event if you were a news broadcaster or journalist, keeping in mind that if you lose your sponsors, you may no longer have a medium for voicing your views.

Sarah Palin both entertained viewers as well as left some with the impression—after all, this was a news broadcast—that they were actually watching Palin or that Palin had made all these comments verbatim. News organizations also need to keep their sponsors happy to keep their financial backing. Therefore, they generally avoid airing or printing stories that might alienate or offend their audiences and sponsors. Because of this, the news that reaches us is often one-sided.[12]

Another source of bias in news reporting is gender bias. Although an increasing number of news anchors are women, news is still generally reported from a male perspective. With the sole exception of "lifestyle" stories, men are used as sources of news more than twice as often as women are. In a study of forty-five different news outlets by the Project for Excellence in Journalism, newspapers were found to be the media source most likely to cite at least one female source in a story, while cable news stations were the least likely.[13]

The news media may also play on other cultural biases, such as age bias and people's fears of getting older, to get people's attention. For example, a headline in *Newsweek* read "New Secrets for Youthful Skin."[14] In fact, this article contained no new "secrets" but simply rehashed common-sense advice, such as wear sunblock and use moisturizers, as well as information on surgical procedures for younger-looking skin.

The increased number of news sources and the need to attract and hold an audience have led the various news media to target particular audiences by tailoring their reporting. Simply by choosing which sources of information to use or which experts to interview, the news media can compromise objectivity and bias the reporting. During the 2008 presidential campaign Fox News moved even further to the right, while MSNBC clearly gave its support to Obama. This division between the networks was further deepened when, following the election, officials in the Obama administration stated that Fox News was not really a news organization, but rather was pushing a point of view. The bias, although still present, was more subtle in the 2012 presidential election.

The Pew Research Center has found that the news audience is becoming more and more polarized and "politicized." This tendency to choose our news sources on the basis of our political leanings contributes to confirmation bias. Rather than providing us with new information and challenging our preconceptions, the news show simply confirms our previously held views and biases, thus impeding our growth as critical thinkers.

As critical thinkers, we cannot assume that the news media is presenting an unbiased and balanced coverage of an issue or event. Instead, we need to ask about the reliability and credibility of the sources of the information before accepting a news story as accurate. We should also keep in mind that the news being reported is to a large extent determined by the need to attract and keep advertisers and to hold the interest of the audience.

EXERCISE 11-2

STOP AND ASSESS YOURSELF

1. Where do you get most of your news? Why do you use this source for your news? Working in small groups, critically evaluate each of the news sources for accuracy and comprehensiveness, as well as for bias.

2. The news media prefers to report on memorable events, such as disasters, kidnappings, and killings, rather than covering ongoing issues. Discuss the effect of this type of reporting on how you and others live your daily lives.

3. Working in small groups, choose two or three important current events. Where did you hear about them, and what did you learn? Analyze how the coverage could have been improved. Is there any disagreement in the group about what happened or the interpretation of what happened? If so, discuss why the discrepancy exists.

4. Make a list of recent and upcoming events on your campus, as well as other events and issues that might be of interest to students on your campus. Working in small groups, put together a layout for a two-page campus newspaper. Discuss the criteria you used in deciding how much space should be given to each story and which stories should go on which page and where on that page. Discuss also why you chose these criteria.

5. Where should we draw the line between the media serving a public good and the media simply engaging in sensationalism? Construct an argument to support your conclusion, remembering to clearly define your key terms.

6. Select a current event. Compare how this story was covered on a broadcast network, a cable network, one newspaper, and a Web site such as a blog.

SCIENCE REPORTING

While most of us are skeptical of what we see on television news shows or read in the newspaper, a Yale University study found the opposite to be true when it comes to stories about scientific findings. We tend to trust that such information is true simply because what we are reading is called "science." However, this trust is sometimes misplaced.

Misrepresentation of Scientific Findings

Most reporters are not trained in science and sometimes make mistakes in reporting the results of scientific studies. Reporters may also intentionally distort scientific findings to attract a greater audience. In 1986, *Newsweek* featured a cover story entitled "Too Late for Prince Charming?" which was based on a scientific study on marriage patterns in the United States carried out by Yale and Harvard sociologists. According to the study, a single 35-year-old white, college-educated woman had only a 5 percent chance of getting married, whereas a 40-year-old woman had a 2.6 percent chance. The *Newsweek* article reported that "forty-year-olds are more likely to be killed by a terrorist; they have a minuscule 2.6 percent probability of tying the knot."

The part on the terrorist was not in the original study but was a bit of hyperbole added by the reporter for sensationalism and shock value. Furthermore, the reporter never checked the findings of the study against other surveys and studies. In fact, according to the U.S. Census Bureau, in 1986 the chance that a forty-year-old woman—even a white, college-educated woman—would eventually marry was much higher, at 23 percent for the general population. Nevertheless the *Newsweek* article had a profound impact on Americans and created a sense of anxiety and loss of confidence among educated, older women who had hoped someday to get married, illustrating the control that the news media has over our thoughts and feelings.

Scientific findings may also be sensationalized or misrepresented in the media when they present hypotheses as factual findings rather than as hunches or assumptions. In 2003 astronomers discovered a large asteroid—asteroid 2003 QQ47. Scientists estimated that there was just under a 1-in-a-million chance that this asteroid would hit the Earth in 2014. The media immediately picked up the story, with some hyping it with headlines

How can we recognize and avoid being taken in by the use of hyperbole in the reporting of scientific findings? *See Chapter 3, p. 91.*

Connections

The media may distort scientific findings for the sake of sensationalism, as happened in a 1986 story about a 40-year-old woman's chance of getting married.

such as "Armageddon Set for March 21, 2014" and "Earth Is Doomed."

The media can also convey false information to the public because they fail to take into account that scientific reports are sometimes based on probability or limited information. In 2013, a 10,000 ton meteorite exploded over the Russian city of Chelyabinsk. The meteorite was not only closer to Earth, but 1,000 times larger than originally reported by the media.

Another source of media bias is the interpretation of scientific findings in light of cultural norms and the reporters' own biases, including racial and sex biases. In reports on human evolution, Cro-Magnon man, our direct ancestor, used to be generally depicted as fair-skinned, blond, and inventive, whereas Neanderthal man is depicted as a

Science reporters may unintentionally perpetuate racial and sexual stereotypes.

dark-skinned, black-haired, brutish caveman. In fact, we don't know the skin and hair coloring of either group of early humans.

Sex bias is also evident in some science shows. In a Discovery Channel report, *The Rise of Man*,[15] bias was evident in more than just the title of the show. Men were consistently portrayed as being in the forefront of human evolution, the discovery of fire, the creation of tools, agriculture, and art, with women playing only a very marginal role. In actual fact, scientists don't know whether men or women made these discoveries and advances. Rather, it was the media that perpetuated this bias.

Reporters may simplify a scientific report or report findings in a way to maximize their impact and attract audience interest. For instance, a study conducted by Harvard researchers on the effects of intercessory prayer (prayer offered on behalf of another person) on healing in cardiac-bypass patients[16] was reported in the *Los Angeles Times* under the headline "Largest Study of Prayer to Date Finds It Has No Power to Heal."[17] However, this headline is misleading because the study was only about a very specific type of prayer—intercessory prayer by a group of strangers. It did not study the effect of prayer by the patients themselves or of prayer by friends and relatives on behalf of the patients. (For a summary of the prayer study and an evaluation of the experiment design, see Chapter 12, page 381.)

In addition, the media may report scientific research in a manner that emphasizes its controversial aspects. For example, when reporting on stem-cell research, the media generally focus on the use of embryonic stem cells, ignoring research findings using stem cells that don't come from embryos. Thus, the public is left with the impression that all stem-cell research relies on aborted embryos when in fact much research involves adult stem cells or amniotic stem cells, which do not involve human embryos.

"U.S. Officials Say Dangers of Dioxin Were Exaggerated."[18] The article stated that exposure to dioxin "is now considered by some experts to be no more risky than spending a week sunbathing." Some of the facts presented in the article were false; dioxin is far more toxic than sunbathing, but the reporter did not do enough research to unearth this fact.

In cases where scientific research is government funded, pressure may be brought to bear on scientists to report findings to the public in a way that is consistent with a political agenda. The Bush White House intervened to weaken and even delete sections in reports by Environmental Protection Agency scientists regarding the extent of global warming and the role of industry in creating or accelerating global climate change. Because the media relies primarily on press releases, rather than doing its own investigative reporting, the extent of global warming was underreported in the media for many years. The Obama administration, in contrast, takes global warming seriously and has passed legislation to reduce carbon emissions that contribute to global warming.

Evaluating Scientific Reports

Unlike most news reports, for which we generally do not have access to the primary sources, with science reporting we can often assess a story's credibility by looking up the original source of the scientific study. In evaluating a scientific report in the mass media, the first step is to determine who is making the claim. Is it the reporter, or is the reporter citing a scientist or other expert in the field? In addition, is the reporter using direct quotes, or is the reporter paraphrasing or embellishing on what the scientists found, as in the 1986 *Newsweek* report on single women and marriage?

Government Influence and Bias

Since many reporters rely on press releases, science reporting may be biased in favor of government policy and the interests of big corporations. In the 1980s there was a growing concern among the public about the damaging effects of dioxin. Dioxin is a highly lethal chemical that was used in herbicides such as Agent Orange, a defoliant dumped on jungles during the Vietnam War to destroy vegetation and deprive enemy fighters of hiding places. It is also the byproduct of some industrial chemical processes. In 1991 the *New York Times* featured a story that was based on government reports and was headlined

Dr. Sanjay Gupta, a popular television personality, is a neurosurgeon and assistant professor of neurosurgery at Emory University School of Medicine. These credentials make him well qualified to be chief medical correspondent with CNN.

How can an understanding of deductive arguments help you to evaluate scientific reports in the media? *See Chapter 8, p. 239.*

How can we evaluate the credentials of a source cited by the media? *See Chapter 4, p. 110.*

Connections

What are the credentials of the source(s) cited by the media? Is he or she associated with a respected university, research lab, or other credible organization? Or is the source someone with little or no background in the field of science under discussion—a religious leader, an actress, a novelist, a politician, or an astrologer? In addition, we should ask about the credentials of the reporter. The source may be credible; however, the reporter may lack the necessary scientific background to accurately summarize the findings or make interpretations of the findings. Glenn Beck, for example, has no background in science or even a college degree for that matter, nor did he refer to any reputable scientific studies in his commentary on global warming.

A comprehensive scientific report should name the scientific journal in which the study or article first appeared.

Is it a respectable scientific journal? That is, does it require peer reviews—confirmation of the research results by other qualified scientists—before it publishes an important finding? If you have any questions about the report, many of these journals are now available in the library or in library online databases. Also, to gain a more balanced perspective, look at how other people who are experts in this field are reacting to the scientific findings. For example, are scientists more concerned about global warming than media reports suggest?

HIGHLIGHTS

EVALUATING SCIENTIFIC REPORTS IN THE MEDIA

- Who is making the claim?
- What are the credentials and funding of the source?
- What is the background of the reporter?
- Where was the scientific study or findings first published?
- How are other authorities in the field responding to the report?
- Is the report biased?

➤ *APPLICATION: Find in the text an example of an answer to each of the questions.*

Finally, ask yourself if the media report itself is biased. Does the reporter or the media that he or she represents have a particular political agenda that would cause the reporter to exaggerate certain aspects of the scientific report and downplay or ignore others? Remember, the reporter not only needs to attract the largest audience possible but also needs to avoid offending his or her employer and other powerful interests.

In summary, scientific findings are sometimes misreported or distorted by the media. Reporters may lack the necessary training to accurately summarize a scientific study. In addition, some media outlets have a tendency to sensationalize findings by overemphasizing certain aspects of scientific research and ignoring others, or by masquerading speculation or opinions as facts. Outside interests such as the government and businesses can also influence how scientific findings are reported. As critical thinkers we need to be mindful of these problems when interpreting science reports in the mass media. We'll be looking more at evaluating scientific hypotheses and research in Chapter 12.

Former Fox News personality Glenn Beck made several on-air commentary reports on global warming on his talk show that were accepted by many as fact, although Beck has no scientific degree or background and didn't reference any specific scientific findings.

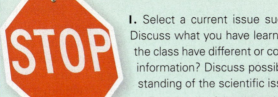

STOP AND ASSESS YOURSELF

1. Select a current issue such as global warming, stem-cell research, or terrorism. Discuss what you have learned from the media regarding these issues. Do people in the class have different or conflicting information? What was the media source of their information? Discuss possible explanations for the discrepancies in students' understanding of the scientific issue.

2. Examine the following science headlines. Discuss what tactics are being used to get your attention. From just looking at the headline, state what you think the story is about.

*a. "'Conclusive Evidence' for Martian Life" (BBC News Online, 2001)

b. "U.S. Bird Flu Study Predicts Millions of Deaths, Billions in Cost" (*San Francisco Chronicle*, May 4, 2006)

c. "Study: Cutting, Self-Abuse Common Among College Students" (FoxNews.com, June 5, 2006)

*d. "Happiness Is Controlled by Your Genes" (*The Guardian* [UK], July 9, 2004)

e. "Harvard Scientists Join Human Cloning Race" (MSNBC, June 6, 2006)

f. "The Gay Terrorist" (*The New York Observer*, March 16, 2010)

*g. "Warning: Medical Websites Damage Your Health" (*The Independent*, [UK], October 4, 2001)

h. "Greece's Debt Crisis: Blaming Nazi Germany" (*Time*, February 26, 2010)

3. Working in small groups, write two paragraphs for your local newspaper summarizing the findings of a study in a scientific journal provided by your instructor. Share your paragraphs with others in the class. Discuss how you might evaluate the accuracy of each other's reports. If there was bias or misrepresentation, discuss possible sources of this bias.

4. Look for an article in the mass media, or a news video clip, that reports the results of a scientific study. Find a copy of the original scientific article written by the scientist(s) who did the study. How accurately did the mass media report the study? If the media report was not accurate, discuss why the media might have misrepresented the story.

*Answers to selected exercises are found in the Solutions Manual at the end of the book.

THE INTERNET

The 1990s were dubbed the "decade of the Internet," with an explosive growth of the Web, e-mail, and electronic commerce. Internet use has more than tripled in the United States since 2000. As of 2012, more than 2.27 billion people worldwide were Internet users, including 78.6 percent of North Americans, 67 percent of Europeans, and 44.8 percent of Asians, with the most rapid growth in Internet use occurring in Africa and the Middle East where Internet use tripled between 2007 and 2012.[19] The pervasive impact of the Internet on global communication and our everyday lives can hardly be overestimated.

Worldwide, Internet use grew by more than 600 percent between the years 2000 and 2012.

Impact of the Internet on Daily Life

According to the 2012 American Freshman Survey, college freshmen report that in their senior year of high school they spent more time on social media sites than studying.[20] People can shop, do their banking, purchase concert or movie tickets, carry out research, play games, gamble, download music, and even earn a college degree online without leaving the comfort of their homes.

In addition to creating new career possibilities such as software engineer,[21] the Internet allows students and other job seekers to find out what job opportunities are available and to post their résumés online. We now can get all our news, watch movies, and read books over the Internet, which may make other forms of the mass media—including television, radio, and printed books—obsolete.

Because of the pervasive and growing influence of the Internet on our lives and decisions, it is important that we learn to think critically about what we see, hear, and post on the Internet. In Chapter 4, we examined different criteria for evaluating Internet resources when doing research on the Internet. In the following pages, we will look at the impact of the Internet on our social and political lives.

Social Networking

The Internet is affecting daily life by reshaping social dynamics among young people. During the 2008 and 2012 elections, Obama supporters used social networks to encourage young people to get out and vote for their candidate. Social networking sites such as Facebook and Twitter continue to grow at a phenomenal rate. These sites rely heavily on messages, photos, stories, personal journals, and music, which users post and other users view. Facebook, the most popular of these Web sites, has more than a billion members worldwide.[22] Ninety-four percent of college freshmen spent time each week on social networking sites, with 25 percent spending more than 6 hours a week on the sites.[23] A study found that there is a full grade point difference between college students who are social network users and those who do not use social networks. The study also found that social network users did not believe there was a connection between their use and their grades.[24]

Communicating with others is certainly worthwhile. However, good communication skills require discernment and thinking beforehand about what message we are sending: What information is being conveyed by the messages we post? What attitudes and feelings are being communicated, both by our verbal and nonverbal or graphic postings?

For example, some of the profiles on social networking sites contain lewd photographs of students or photographs

of students engaging in such illegal activities as smoking marijuana, as well as derogatory remarks about professors and other people. This raises serious questions about the judgment and critical-thinking skills of some of the young people who put their profiles on the sites.

While such postings may have been intended to send a message to our peers that we are a lot of fun or can stand up to authority, these messages may be misinterpreted by a college administrator or potential employer as suggesting that we are irresponsible and mean-spirited.

When posting a message, we need to consider who are the potential recipients, both intended and unintended, of our message. Although Facebook was designed primarily for college students, the Internet is a form of mass media. As such, it is available to the public and most of its users are now off-campus.

Many students assume that their profiles are private. Several college students have been expelled for posting disparaging remarks about professors, racist comments, or threats to kill someone. More and more employers are looking at the profiles of job applicants on these sites as part of a background check, sometimes to the detriment of the college-graduate job-seekers. By not thinking critically before posting a message, these students may place obstacles in the way of achieving their life goals. The police are also looking to personal content in social networking sites as a law enforcement tool. A photo on his Facebook page of Bryant College junior Joshua Lipton dressed as a prison inmate and mockingly sticking out his tongue, just days after he had slammed into two cars seriously injuring one of the drivers, was used as evidence of his lack of remorse in his trial and sentencing. Lipton's blood alcohol was more than twice the legal limit at the time of the accident.[25]

As critical thinkers, you need to do your research about social networking sites and how to use them. You also need to think twice before making a posting. What may seem like a joke or just having fun can end up getting a person expelled from college or denied a coveted job interview.

Hot or Not?

What do you think is a healthy or reasonable amount of time to spend on the Internet each day?

Did You Know

President Obama's Facebook page has more than 35 million followers.

Points to Consider When Posting a Message on a Social Network Site

- What is my goal or intention in posting this message?
- Who is the recipient of the message? Include both intentional and unintentional recipients in your answer.
- What information is being conveyed in the message?
- What feelings and attitudes are being communicated in both the verbal and nonverbal messages?
- Does the message being posted enhance or move me closer to my life goals?

The Internet as "The Great Equalizer"

Since it is so accessible, the Internet has been hailed as "the great equalizer," as "the most participatory form of mass speech yet developed," and as "the best advancement in democracy since universal suffrage."[26] During the 2008 and 2012 presidential elections, blogs such as blog.4president.org/2008 and blog.4president.us/2012 played an important role in dissemination and discussion of information about the candidates and their positions. A free and open flow of information is important in a healthy democracy. Unlike traditional mass media, which is controlled by a handful of large corporations, there is no centralized control of the Internet. In addition, unlike television, which is one-way communication, the Internet is open and accessible to all people. Anyone who has access to the Internet can exchange ideas and post information that is available to people around the world. In his book *The Assault on Reason*, former Vice President Al Gore writes that

> The Internet is perhaps the greatest source of hope for reestablishing an open communicative environment in which the conversation of democracy can flourish. . . . The Internet is not just another platform for disseminating the truth. It's a platform of pursuing the truth, and the decentralized creation and distribution of ideas . . .[27]

The social networking site Twitter was used en mass by Iranians protesting the reelection of President Mahmoud Ahmadinejad in 2009. Because Twitter is free,

quick, and uses both the Internet and SMA, the network used by cell phones for text messaging, it was ideal for the average citizen to communicate their concerns while at the same time difficult for the Iranian government to control or suppress. On the other hand, the information about what was going on in Iran is difficult to verify since it is impossible to authenticate the source of the information.

With increased opportunity comes increased responsibility for us as critical thinkers and participants in a democratic society. Unlike most real-time discussions, exchanging ideas on the Internet allows us time to critically analyze and research the credibility of the premises used in other people's arguments, as well as to develop a response or counterargument that is both logical and backed up by credible sources.

The Internet also has the potential to reverse the growing economic gap between those who enroll in college and those who do not. One of the recent cost-saving developments in higher education is the use of online courses, along with interactive online group study and discussion. In addition tuition at an online university can be less than half that of the average private college.[28] The Internet has the potential to make a higher education accessible not only to more low-income families but also to a greater range of people, including long-distance learners and those who are unable to attend classes on campus because of health issues or work or family obligations.

The Internet has greatly leveled the playing field when it comes to learning, sharing, and discussing ideas—but on the downside, the Internet has also created new opportunities for invasions of privacy, harassment, fraud, and terrorism. As critical thinkers we need to do our research and be knowledgeable regarding the risks involved in Internet use. Unscrupulous people can steal our personal information,

Connections

How can you use your critical-thinking skills to use the Internet more effectively in analyzing political issues? *See Chapter 12, pp. 379–380.*

> The Internet has the potential to make a higher education accessible not only to more low-income families but also to a greater range of people, including long-distance learners and those who are unable to attend classes on campus because of health issues or work or family obligations.

Critical THiNKing in Action

Over Your Shoulder : Monitoring Employees' Internet Use

About 64 percent of employees use the Internet at work every day for personal use, including viewing pornography, shopping, gambling, downloading files, and e-mailing.* According to a Neilsen Company Survey, 28 percent of these employees use their work computer to visit pornography sites. This not only results in loss of productivity but also increases the risk of security breaches and of inadvertently downloading viruses, worms, and spyware. In addition, coworkers may be exposed to offensive pornography.

Although there are laws that prevent employers from spying on their employees, there are exceptions to these laws when employees are using company-owned equipment, such as computers. According to an American Management Association report, about two-thirds of companies monitor their employees' Internet usage, and more than half track and review employees' e-mails.** Most, though not all, of these companies notify employees of their monitoring policy. By notifying employees that personal Internet use is unacceptable, employers make themselves less vulnerable to sexual harassment suits resulting from employees seeing pornography on other employee's Internet sites. Opponents of Internet monitoring argue that it is an invasion of employees' privacy rights and is an ineffective means of improving worker productivity.

DISCUSSION QUESTIONS

1. Discuss the arguments for and against monitoring employee Internet use.

2. Employers, Internet service providers, and spyware that we may inadvertently download can all track the Web sites that we visit. In addition, the USA Patriot Act requires that if requested, college libraries turn over records of student Internet use. In what ways does knowing that you might be monitored affect how you use the Internet? Relate your answer to the levels of moral reasoning discussed in Chapter 9.

*Cheryl Connor, "Employees Really Do Waste Time at Work," Forbes, July 17, 2012.

**Laura Petrecca, "More Employers Use Tech to Track Workers," USA Today, March 2010. http://usatoday30.usatoday.com/money/workplace/2010-03-17-workplaceprivacy15_CV_N.htm

such as our credit card or Social Security numbers, from Internet databases. Hackers, or even worse—cyber-terrorists—can sabotage or alter business, educational, and government records. In addition, Internet technology can be used to distribute damaging computer viruses or to send harassing or fraudulent e-mails to millions of people at one time. Finally, as we noted in Chapter 4, the Internet is replete with sites that are disreputable or biased. Anyone who wants to can set up a Web site. Chat rooms and personal Web sites in particular often have a biased agenda. Because of this, as critical thinkers we need to be especially cautious when using information from the Internet unless it is from a credible source.

Misuse of the Internet: Pornography and Plagiarism

The proliferation of Internet technology over the past decade has raised the question of whether rules regarding freedom of speech in the media should apply to Internet speech, including obscenity and pornography. Sex is currently the most searched topic on the Internet. As of 2012, porn sites accounted for about 30 percent of Internet traffic.[29] One hundred thousand of these Web sites offer illegal child pornography. Pornography is a multibillion-dollar enterprise and one of the fastest-growing businesses on the Internet. Unfortunately, many people do not consider the possible repercussions, both on their family life and their career, of visiting these Web sites. For example, 20 percent of men admit to viewing pornography online at work.[30] In some cases, they have lost their jobs because of this. See "Critical Thinking in Action: Over Your Shoulder: Monitoring Employees' Internet Use."

As parents or potential parents, we should research and consider the potential impact of the Internet on our children. The easy availability of the Internet means that children can access it at home. An estimated 90 percent of children between the ages of 8 and 16 have viewed pornography online. The largest consumers of Internet pornography are teenagers. Ninety percent of boys aged 12 to 17 view online pornography while doing their homework.[31] Parents can regulate the time children watch a television show or keep pornographic literature out of the house, but Internet pornography is available to children 24 hours a day at the click of a button. To address these potential problems, we need to engage in creative critical thinking to come up with effective solutions.

Plagiarism has also raised concerns about misuse of the Internet. Studies suggest that 61 percent of college students have plagiarized material or bought papers online.[32] Although some people mistakenly assume that the presence of something on the Internet makes it public property and available for anyone to use, others copy from the Internet because they think they can get away with it. Educators are increasingly using plagiarism-detection software and Web sites such as TurnItIn.com to catch student plagiarists. While many educators believe that easy access to information provided by the Internet is partly to blame,[33] the ultimate responsibility lies with the plagiarist. Plagiarism involves not only deception but also an inability or unwillingness on the part of the plagiarist to think for him- or herself and to develop his or her critical-thinking skills.

Computers and the Internet have transformed media technology and greatly increased our access to information. Like any new technology, however, the Internet needs to be used with discernment—capitalizing on its strengths and opportunities while avoiding its pitfalls.

Hot or Not?

Does the Internet encourage student plagiarism?

EXERCISE 11-4

STOP AND ASSESS YOURSELF

1. Discuss ways in which the Internet has enhanced our ability to engage in critical thinking.

2. Why do you think social networking on the Internet is so popular among college students? Does social networking improve your critical thinking and communication skills or have the potential to do so? Or, as some people claim, is the current fascination with social networking merely a symptom of young people's narcissism and love of watching themselves endlessly on their monitors? Present an argument to support your conclusion.

3. Discuss Al Gore's argument, in *The Assault on Reason* (quoted earlier), regarding the potential importance of the Internet in a democracy. Use specific examples of ways in which you use the Internet, or could use the Internet, in your answer.

4. Forty percent of college students gamble at least once a month, with Internet poker being the most popular form of gambling. Studies show that 10 percent of students who gamble at least once a month are in debt as a result and that others have anxiety and other psychological problems.[34] Suppose that gambling has become a problem on your campus. Discuss what restrictions or policies, if any, should be put in place regulating Internet gambling on your campus. Construct an argument supporting your position and then critically evaluate your argument.

5. In a highly publicized case at the University of Michigan, a student distributed over the Internet a violent sexual fantasy about a fellow student, whom he explicitly named, in which she was raped, tortured, and finally killed. The judge ruled that although the story was deeply offensive, it was not a crime. Do you agree with the judge's ruling? Critically evaluate whether incidents such as these should be regulated, banned, or criminalized.

6. Google wants to scan books so that they are available to everyone online rather than just to people who can afford to buy them. Discuss arguments for and against downloading copyrighted books, music, and software from the Internet. Relate your answer to the concept of the Internet as the "great equalizer."

7. Go to one of the popular social networking sites such as Facebook or Twitter. If you have your own page at either site, critically evaluate your profile from the viewpoint of a college administrator or employer who is reading it. Evaluate what messages—both visual and written—the profile is communicating.

8. Research the effects of pornography depicting violence against women on society. Develop an argument addressing the issue of whether Internet pornography should be regulated or censored.

9. How should colleges respond to Internet plagiarism by students? Construct arguments to address this question. Develop a policy for your college that is based on your conclusion.

MEDIA LITERACY: A CRITICAL-THINKING APPROACH

Media literacy is the ability to understand and critically analyze the influence of the mass media on our lives, as well as the ability to use effectively different forms of media, including entertainment and news outlets. Media literacy is important in a democracy, where we are expected to participate in discussions of issues and make informed decisions in elections. If we are unaware of the impact media has on our lives and decisions, or if we engage in self-serving bias by fooling ourselves into thinking that the media affects others but not ourselves, we run the risk of being controlled by the media rather than being in control of our own lives.

media literacy The ability to understand and critically analyze the influence of the mass media.

Experiencing the Media

The three-tier model of thinking—experience, interpretation, and analysis—can be used in fostering media literacy skills. (For a review of the three-tier model, see Chapter 1, pages 21–22.) In applying this model, the first step is to develop an awareness of the *experience* of the media in your life.

Most people have no idea how much time they actually spend tuned into the media. A study in which researchers observed and recorded media use by adults found that actual media use was double that reported by standard questionnaires or phone survey methods.[35] Try keeping a tally of the television and radio shows you tune into, the newspapers and magazines you read, and Internet sites you visit in a typical day. You'll probably be surprised at the amount of time you spend on the media.

Experience also involves understanding the process involved in creating media messages. Who created each message, and what was the creator's goal? For example, is the article you are reading or the show you are watching intended to be factual—or is it primarily intended as entertainment? Sometimes the two are mixed, as in talk shows, such as the *Tonight Show,* or news satires such as *The Daily Show with Jon Stewart* on Comedy Central. Even reputable news sources, as we noted earlier, can present news in

Some television shows, such as **The Daily Show with Jon Stewart,** *combine news and entertainment.*

a misleading manner because of the need to hold and entertain an audience.

Also ask yourself what issues are being addressed. Write a summary of the message(s) using nonemotive language. There might be several messages or bites of news, information, or entertainment. Note the images used, including the set and appearance of the commentators, performers, or guests on the show—their sex, race, ethnicity, and so forth. Note the use of music and graphics: Are they upbeat, soothing, inspiring, edgy, gloomy, or ominous? Note as well the amount of time or space devoted to advertisements. What products are being advertised, and how do these products reinforce the message?

Interpreting Media Messages

Once you have collected all your facts, the next step is *interpretation*, or trying to make sense of the experiences. What values and points of view are being expressed in the program's message? Describe your reaction or interpretation of the message or particular show or article. Examine your reaction. Why did it make you feel this way? What effect did the language, music, and visuals have on you? Are there certain media individuals you identified with or felt positive toward and others who evoke a negative reaction? What prompted your reactions?

You might have enjoyed *The Daily Show* because of the way Jon Stewart pokes fun at conservatives, or *Nashville*

HIGHLIGHTS

ANALYZING MEDIA MESSAGES

- Who **created** the message?
- What is the **purpose** of the message?
- What **techniques** are used to attract and hold your attention?
- What **values and points of view** are represented in the message?
- What was your **reaction** to the message?
- Is your **interpretation** of the message reasonable and well informed?
- How might different people **interpret the** message?
- Is the message **biased?**
- Is the message backed by **good reasoning and facts?**
- What are the possible **effects of the message** on individuals and society?

➤ APPLICATION: *Find an example of an answer to each of these questions in the text.*

---

on ABC because of the country music and the beautiful young musicians, or *Hawaii Five-0* on CBS because of all the exciting action scenes. What do these reactions say about you and how you interpret the world around you, as well as your particular biases and types of resistance? Do you watch only those shows that confirm your political and social worldview and avoid those that don't?

Only watching programs that confirm your worldview contributes to confirmation bias and narrow-mindedness. To overcome this bias, watch or read coverage of the same issue or news event on a different channel or in a different magazine or newspaper. Once again, apply the three-tier model of thinking, noting your interpretation of the experience and then critically analyzing your interpretation. Expanding your range of media experiences can help you overcome narrow-mindedness.

In interpreting media from the perspective of a critical thinker, it is important to take into account diverse points of view, without assuming that yours is the correct or only interpretation. Don't assume that everyone agrees with your interpretation or with the messages being promoted by your favorite shows. In addition, other people may interpret a media message entirely differently. Ask other people what they thought about a particular show or article. For example, Jon Stewart's show may be interpreted by someone else as disrespectful and anti-American. Another viewer may see the beautiful young women on *Hawaii Five-0* as degrading to women or setting up impossible standards of beauty for women. And the exciting action scenes in the same show may be interpreted by another person as a reflection of rampant crime in our culture. Remember, at this point you are just making a list of interpretations, not evaluating them. Some of our interpretations may be well founded; others may be based merely on our opinions or personal feelings and prejudices, as you will discover when you carry out an analysis.

Analyzing Media Messages

The third step entails carrying out a critical *analysis* of your interpretations. Analysis often begins by asking a question. You may use your reaction to a particular media message as a starting point in your analysis by asking, "Why did this show or article make me feel this way?" Emotional reactions such as sympathy or moral outrage may be quite appropriate if they are balanced by reason and analysis of the issue. On the other hand, emotional reactions such as anger or contempt may be indicative of underlying prejudices or distorted worldviews.

Keep in mind that analysis is most productive when it is done collectively, since we each bring different experiences and interpretations to a message. As you begin the process of analysis, note any resistance on your part if your interpretations are challenged. For example, do you roll your eyes or get annoyed if someone suggests that certain shows or magazines are degrading to women?

In analyzing a media message, identify the purpose or conclusion of the message. How does the message contribute to making us better informed about events, issues, and scientific findings? Is the message backed by good reasoning and facts, or is it based on rhetorical devices and fallacious arguments? To what extent is the portrayal of events or developments biased or sensationalized? Does the media presentation contribute to stereotypes and materialism in our culture, or to poor self-esteem and fear of crime? How about our concepts of what is morally right and wrong? Analysis may require research on your part. Does pornography in the media harm women? Are people who view violence in the media more likely to act violently? What is the effect of the media on children?

The mass media plays an essential role in a democracy because it keeps us informed about issues and events. Indeed, the news media is sometimes called the fourth branch of government because it acts as a check on the executive, judicial, and legislative branches. On the other hand, because the mass media depends on business advertising for financial support, it may be more concerned with holding the audience's attention than with providing information on important issues and developments. As critical thinkers, we need to develop media literacy so that we can understand the influence of the media on our lives and have the skills to critically analyze its messages.

EXERCISE 11-5

STOP AND ASSESS YOURSELF

1. Working in small groups, select a television or radio show that everyone, or almost everyone, has seen or heard. Using the three-tier model of thinking, write down what type of show it is (for example, news, comedy, documentary, reality show, drama, or sitcom) and a summary of the show. Next, make a list of the different interpretations students in your group have of the show. Finally, carry out a critical analysis of the interpretations, noting which ones are most reasonable.

2. Discuss ways in which your media experiences reinforce your existing worldviews and values as well as ways in which they challenge or expand your views. Be specific.

3. Referring back to Exercise 7 on page 352, critically analyze the social networking site using your media literacy skills.

4. Select a television show, newspaper, or magazine that you would not ordinarily watch or read because it doesn't fit with your personal beliefs. As you experience it, note the types of resistance you may feel and what messages prompt the resistance. Evaluate how being aware of your use of resistance can help you to overcome it and be more open to rationally analyzing the messages rather than simply dismissing them.

THiNK AGAIN

1. What is the relationship between mass media and big business in the United States?

    ■ Much of mass media today is controlled by a few large corporations. In addition, big business influences what appears in the media, since to receive advertising revenue, the media generally needs to promote, or at least not contradict, the values of their sponsor.

2. What are some of the limitations of the news media?

    ■ With an increasing selection of news sources, including the Internet, people are tending to select news outlets that are consistent with their own worldviews. To attract and keep an audience, news stories are often selected because of their entertainment value and sensationalism rather than their newsworthiness or in-depth analysis of important national and international issues.

3. In what ways has the Internet changed our lives?

    ■ The Internet is becoming the primary source of news and information for many North Americans. It is also used in job searches, for posting information, and for communication

Internet Plagiarism Among College Students

Today almost everyone is familiar with the advantages of the Internet as a source of information. However, one of the downsides is that the Internet has made it easier for students to commit plagiarism. *Plagiarism* is fraudulent copying that involves deception and the intent to mislead the reader, in this case the professor.*

In a 2012 survey, 75 percent of college students admitted to cheating, with 90 percent of students saying they thought they would not get caught and 85 percent claiming that "cheating was necessary to get ahead."** In 2012, in one of the largest cases of academic dishonesty, nearly half of the 279 students in a Harvard class on "Introduction to Congress" allegedly plagiarized their answers or inappropriately collaborated on a take-home exam.***

Internet plagiarism has also become more common in high schools and on college applications where students are vying with each other for scholarships and admission to prestigious colleges.[†] The rising cost of a college education and a highly competitive job market has exacerbated this trend.

Many people blame students for the increase in Internet plagiarism. Others feel faculty bear part of the blame. Also under fire are Web sites known as "paper mills" that sell essays and dissertations to students and have proliferated since the 1990s. The development of

---

*For a more extensive discussion of the definition of plagiarism, see Richard A. Posner, *The Little Book of Plagiarism* (New York: Pantheon Books, 2007).

**Rebecca Castagna and Andy Landolfi, "Cheating, Plagiarism Still Exist in College Classrooms," *The Quinnipiac Chronicle*, October 10, 2012.

***Rebecca D. Robbins, "Harvard Investigates 'Unprecedented' Academic Dishonesty Case," *The Crimson*, August 8, 2012.

[†]See David Callahan, *The Cheating Culture: Why More Americans Are Doing Wrong to Get Ahead* (Orlando, FL: Harcourt Books, 2004), Chapter 7.

antiplagiarism software such as TurnItIn.com has made it easier for teachers to find out if a student paper has been plagiarized.

While some states have passed laws trying to restrict computer-aided plagiarism, they've made little headway in stemming the use of these sites. Defenders of paper mills argue that legal attempts to restrict the exchange of scholarly material would be a violation of the First Amendment freedom of speech.

The victims of Internet plagiarism extend beyond the intended reader(s). Other students also suffer, as well as the plagiarist, who receives no direct educational benefit from the assignment. Finally, society is harmed because students learn that cheating pays and carry this attitude over into their careers.

In the following readings, the authors discuss the reasons for and consequences of Internet plagiarism and what steps academic communities might take to curtail it. Brook Sadler argues that plagiarism is wrong and should be severely penalized. Russell Hunt, in contrast, regards Internet plagiarism as an opportunity for the academic community to rethink the traditional model of knowledge that, he argues, encourages plagiarism.

The Wrongs of Internet Plagiarism: Ten Quick Arguments   BROOK J. SADLER

Brook J. Sadler is an associate professor of philosophy at the University of South Florida. In the following reading, she presents several arguments for why plagiarism is wrong. She also examines reasons why students plagiarize and the negative effects of this practice on the offending student, the academic community, and society in general.

What is wrong with plagiarism?

. . . First, plagiarism, regardless of the copyright issue, can be viewed as a type of theft: the taking of someone else's property and using it as one's own. . . .

Second, plagiarism involves the intent to deceive. . . . The professor's activity in grading is one that is predicated on academic honesty; when students knowingly deceive professors about their work, they enlist professors in an activity to which professors would not consent were they fully informed.

Third, plagiarism violates the trust upon which higher education is established. Students trust that professors will do their best to give them an honest education—not unduly biased, not misrepresenting the facts, not deliberately omitting relevant evidence, not distorting the findings of research in the field, not grading students' work on the basis of prejudice, personal feeling, or arbitrary criteria. . . . Professors give time and energy to educating students on the presumption that students are open *to being educated*. When a student commits any form of academic dishonesty, he or she is shutting down the possibility of being educated; the student does not learn from the effort required to produce the work on her own, nor from the constructive feedback the professor gives in grading the assignment. . . . The trust that underwrites education, especially university education, is disrupted, even annihilated, by academic dishonesty.

Fourth, plagiarism is unfair to other students in the class. Especially when the source of the plagiarism is a professional research paper, the plagiarized paper may be much better than the work produced by the other students in the class. If a professor does not detect the plagiarism, the fact that the plagiarized paper is of higher quality than others throws off a professor's sense of her students' capabilities regarding the material covered by the assignment.

It makes the work of honest students appear comparatively weak. This has two detrimental effects. One is that it may alter a professor's grade scale, disadvantaging honest students. . . . The second detrimental effect is that plagiarism makes it difficult for a professor to assess the effectiveness of her instruction. . . . Thus, plagiarism undermines the professor's effort to mold her instruction to students' actual abilities and does an injustice to other students who stand to benefit from that instruction.

Fifth, a student who plagiarizes does not benefit from the process of struggling with the material on her own. She does not truly learn the material or engage the assignment. The quality of her education is thereby diminished. She does not acquire the skills that the assignment requires her to exercise or to develop. With respect to writing papers, a large part of the value of the assignment consists not in the finished product, but in the process of working on it.

Sixth, the plagiarizing student indulges in vices distinct from the deception mentioned above. The vice will depend upon the student. Perhaps it is laziness or a kind of cowardice borne of low self-esteem: . . . Plagiarizing students thus habituate themselves to indolence, dishonesty, cowardice, or low self-esteem and incapacitate themselves to do the kind of work assigned.

Seventh, students who get away with academic dishonesty may come to believe, quite generally, that the best way to "get ahead" in life is to cheat, deceive, violate trust, or take the easy route. Such a belief may undercut the student's ability to partake of the internal goods of a wide variety of practices, limiting his or her rewards to the external goods of money or status and instilling a corollary belief that the primary attainments in life are gained through competition with others, not through cooperation or by challenging oneself to meet the standards of excellence established by practices. . . .When this attitude is tolerated, overlooked, or even promoted in the university, it would not be surprising were students to carry it with them to other public contexts. . . .

Eighth, unpunished academic dishonesty diminishes the value of a university degree. Employers expect students who graduate from a university to have certain demonstrable skills acquired in their education. . . . Students who plagiarize their way through the degree do not possess these skills. They have not truly earned the degree. . . . When university-educated students do not possess the skills or knowledge to participate intelligently in public discourse or business, it is no wonder if the public harbors a suspicion about the value of higher education.

. . . Ninth, plagiarism and academic dishonesty preclude opportunities for the student both to take pride in creative self-expression and to come to terms with one's epistemic and intellectual limitations. It is sometimes supposed that the problem with plagiarism is that it violates a value characterized as intellectual or scholarly integrity; however, the average (undergraduate) student does not see her- or himself as involved in a long-term intellectual project whose integrity is at stake. The student is simply writing a paper as outlined by the professor's assignment. . . . Nonetheless, it is awareness of the circumscribed nature of students' papers that can afford students the opportunity to recognize their own epistemic and intellectual limitations in a way that inspires appreciation for the achievements of researchers and scholars. In confronting the difficulty of producing their own work, students stand to gain a valuable form of humility that may inspire further education and stoke curiosity at the same time that it inspires students to take pride in their own intellectual development and to value their own creative expression.

Tenth, one of the ideas behind higher education is that students can learn something from their courses, from their assignments, from their professors that they cannot learn (at all, as easily, or as well) outside of the university. . . . One of the distinctive values of university education consists in the interpersonal engagement that happens between students and between professors and students. The university does not exist merely to serve as a conduit for the transference of information: from (anonymous) professor to (anonymous) student, as if the process consisted simply in the handing-off of pre-packaged goods. . . . Although grades *do* represent assessments of quality, the act of grading papers and engaging with students' work involves more than this: it involves an engagement with a particular student's struggle to express herself, to navigate concepts, to enlarge her world-view, to come to know and to understand. This engagement is not possible when a student plagiarizes, and if I am right that one of the fundamental and distinguishing features of higher education is the interpersonal engagement it affords, then plagiarism thwarts or defeats that purpose.

. . . Plagiarism is wrong because it is detrimental to students, to professors, to the university, to the project of higher education, and even to the public perception of the value of higher education. . . .

REVIEW QUESTIONS

1. In what ways does plagiarism violate trust between students and professors?

2. Why is plagiarism unfair to the other students in a class?

3. In what ways does plagiarism harm the plagiarist?

4. How does plagiarism undermine the value of a university education and the enterprise of higher education?

Four Reasons to Be Happy about Internet Plagiarism   RUSSELL HUNT

Russell Hunt is a professor of English at St. Thomas University in Fredericton, New Brunswick, Canada. Hunt views the issue of Internet plagiarism as an opportunity for educators to reexamine the old model of knowledge that encourages Internet plagiarism and to develop a model of knowledge that is more active, cooperative, context-bound, and problem- and project-based.

The "information technology revolution" is almost always presented as having cataclysmic consequences for education—sometimes for the better, but often, of course, for the worse. In postsecondary circles, perhaps the most commonly apprehended cataclysm is "Internet Plagiarism." . . .

It's almost never suggested that all this might be something other than a disaster for higher education. But that's exactly what I want to argue here. I believe the challenge of easier and more convenient plagiarism is to be welcomed. This rising tide threatens to change things—for, I predict and hope, the better. Here are some specific practices which are threatened by the increasing ease with which plagiarism can be committed.

1. **The institutional rhetorical writing environment (the "research paper," the "literary essay," the "term paper") is challenged by this, and that's a good thing**. Our reliance on these forms as ways of assessing student skills and knowledge has been increasingly questioned by people who are concerned with how learning and assessment take place, and can be fostered, and particularly with how the ability to manipulate written language ("literacy") is developed. The assumption that a student's learning is accurately and readily tested by her ability to produce, in a completely arhetorical situation, an artificial form that she'll never have to write again

once she's survived formal education (the essay examination, the formal research paper), is questionable on the face of it, and is increasingly untenable. If the apprehension that it's almost impossible to escape the mass-produced and purchased term paper leads teachers to create more imaginative, and rhetorically sound, writing situations in their classes, the advent of the easily-purchased paper from SchoolSucks.com is a salutary challenge to practices which ought to be challenged. . . . Many other equivalent arguments that assignment can be refigured to make plagiarism more difficult—and offer more authentic rhetorical contexts for student writing—have been offered in recent years.

I'm unconvinced that we can address the problem by assuring students that "they are real writers with meaningful and important things to say," or invite them to revise their work where we can see the revisions, as long as we continue giving them more decontextualized, audienceless and purposeless writing exercises. . . .

2. **The institutional structures around grades and certification are challenged by this, and that's a good thing**. Perhaps more important is the way plagiarism challenges the overwhelming pressure for grades which our institutions have created and foster, and which has as its consequence the pressure on many good students to cut a corner here and there (there's lots of evidence that it's *not* mainly the marginal students in danger of failing who cheat; it's as often those excellent students who believe, possibly with some reason, that their lives depend on keeping their GPA up to some arbitrary scratch). An even more central consideration is the way the existence of plagiarism itself challenges the way the university structures its system of incentives and rewards, as a zero-sum game, with a limited number of winners.

University itself, as our profession has structured it, is the most effective possible situation for encouraging plagiarism and cheating. If I wanted to learn how to play the guitar, or improve my golf swing, or write HTML, "cheating" would be the last thing that would ever occur to me. It would be utterly irrelevant to the situation. On the other hand, if I wanted a *certificate* saying that I could pick a jig, play a round in under 80, or produce a slick Web page (and never expected actually to perform the activity in question), I might well consider cheating (and consider it primarily a moral problem). This is the situation we've built for our students: a system in which the only incentives or motives anyone cares about are marks, credits, and certificates. . . .

3. **The model of knowledge held by almost all students, and by many faculty—the tacit assumption that knowledge is stored information and that skills are isolated, asocial faculties—is challenged by this, and that's a good thing**. When we judge essays by what they contain and how

logically it's organized (and how grammatically it's presented) we miss the most important fact about written texts, which is that they are rhetorical moves in scholarly and social enterprises. In recent years there have been periodic assaults on what Paolo Freire called "the banking model" of education. . . . A model of the educational enterprise which presumes that knowledge comes in packages . . . invites learners to think of what they're doing as importing prepackaged nuggets of information into their texts and their minds.

Similarly, a model which assumes that a skill like "writing the academic essay" is an ability which can be demonstrated on demand, quite apart from any authentic rhetorical situation, actual question, or expectation of effect (or definition of what the "academic essay" actually *is*), virtually prohibits students from recognizing that all writing is shaped by rhetorical context and situation, and thus renders them tone-deaf to the shifts in register and diction which make so much plagiarized undergraduate text instantly recognizable. . . .

4. But there's a reason to welcome this challenge that's far more important than any of these— . . . It's this: **by facing this challenge we will be forced to help our students learn what I believe to be the most important thing they can learn at university: just how the intellectual enterprise of scholarship and research really works**. Traditionally, when we explain to students why plagiarism is bad and what their motives should be for properly citing and crediting their sources, we present them in terms of a model of how texts work in the process of sharing ideas and information which is profoundly different from how they actually work outside of classroom-based writing, and profoundly destructive to their understanding of the assumptions and methods of scholarship. . . .

Scholars—writers generally—use citations for many things: they establish their own *bona fides* and currency, they advertise their alliances, they bring work to the attention of their reader, they assert ties of collegiality, they exemplify contending positions or define nuances of difference among competing theories or ideas. They do not use them to defend themselves against potential allegations of plagiarism.

The clearest difference between the way undergraduate students, writing essays, cite and quote and the way scholars do it in public is this: typically, the scholars are achieving something positive; the students are avoiding something negative.

The conclusion we're driven to, then, is this: offering lessons and courses and workshops on "avoiding plagiarism"—indeed, posing plagiarism as a problem at all—begins at the wrong end of the stick. It might usefully be analogized to looking for a good way to teach the infield fly rule to people who have no clear idea what baseball is.

1. How do most people in postsecondary education view the information technology revolution?

2. In what ways does the issue of Internet plagiarism present a challenge to academia's current system of rewards?

3. What is the old model of knowledge, and why does Internet plagiarism challenge this model?

4. Why is Hunt happy about Internet plagiarism?

THiNK AND DISCUSS

PERSPECTIVES ON INTERNET PLAGIARISM AMONG COLLEGE STUDENTS

1. Critically analyze the responses of both Sadler and Hunt to the issue of Internet plagiarism. Which person presents the best argument and why?

2. In *The Little Book of Plagiarism*, Richard Posner maintains that students who plagiarize are also victims since they derive no direct educational benefit from the assignment. On the other hand, these students receive indirect benefits in terms of better grades and improved career opportunities. Imagine a student who is considering purchasing an essay from the Internet because she has a heavy academic workload and does not have the time to research and write an essay. She also needs a good grade in the course to get into graduate school. Referring to Chapter 9, pages 283–284, discuss also how a utilitarian might advise the student.

3. MasterPapers.com provides a "custom essay, term paper and dissertation writing service." The site states:

   > Experience your academic career to the fullest—exactly the way you want it! . . . Our company is perfectly aware that a number of tutors do not appreciate when their students resort to essay writing services for help. We strongly believe that professional and legitimate research paper writing services do not hamper students [sic] progress in any way, while the contemporary academic environment often leaves them absolutely no choice but to take advantage of our help.

   Critically analyze the argument by MasterPapers.com that using a writing service is justified because (1) it does not interfere with students' progress, and (2) the current academic atmosphere sometimes leaves students no other choice. Discuss how Sadler and Hunt might each respond to the argument.

4. In the United States, Canada, and most Western nations, published information is regarded as belonging to a particular person. But in some cultures, such as much of India, people regard information on the Internet as communal property that's free for the taking. Given this difference in cultural values, discuss how professors should respond if they find that a student from another cultural background has plagiarized an essay.

5. Some colleges reject plagiarism software and Web sites, such as TurnItIn.com, and instead prefer to use an honor code or lecture their students about the evils of plagiarism. Are these approaches naïve as some claim?* Discuss your answer in light of your answer to question 2.

---

*Richard A. Posner, *The Little Book of Plagiarism* (New York: Pantheon Books, 2007), pp. 82–83.

12

SCIENCE

Sea levels have risen nearly 7 inches in the last hundred years because of global warming, according to the Environmental Protection Agency (EPA), and they are expected to rise another foot by 2100.[1] In the past few decades, global warming has accelerated. The hottest 9 years on record since we began recording the temperature in 1850 have occurred since 2000. Temperatures are expected to increase another 2 to 11 degrees by 2100.[2] With its widespread droughts, deadly heat waves, and massive storms, 2012 was the hottest year on record in the continental United States.

The melting of the polar ice sheets in response to the increased warming of Earth is in part responsible for rising sea levels. In 2002, a piece of the Antarctic ice shelf the size of Rhode Island broke off and fell into the ocean. If the West Antarctic ice sheet

What do you think the scientist is thinking as she evaluates the glass flask? How can learning about scientific methodology make us better at evaluating scientific claims?

THiNK
FIRST

- What is the scientific method?
- How does science differ from pseudoscience?
- What are some of the different types of scientific experiments and research methods?

>> were to completely melt—a process that has begun and is occurring at a much faster rate than previously predicted by scientists—the sea level could rise by as much as 30 inches by 2050.[3] In other words, if these trends continue, by the time today's typical college freshman retires, most of the world's coastal cities and communities will be under water.[4]

Rising sea levels will also contribute to land erosion, as well as to the salinization of freshwater and agricultural land in low-lying areas, thus disrupting our food and water supply. In addition, major storms are predicted to increase in number and intensity, while the warmer climate will ensure that infectious diseases, especially such tropical diseases as malaria, will flourish in places like the southern United States.

Some scientific research on global warming and other natural processes is more rigorous and better at explaining and predicting phenomena than other research. As critical thinkers, we need to be able to interpret and evaluate science stories in the news media, as well as research reports in scientific journals. We need to decide not only whether they are worth considering but also how scientific findings can be applied to our lives and to public policy. Even more basic to this process is the capacity to think critically about science itself as a method for discovering truth. In this chapter we'll:

- Learn about the history of science
- Identify and critically analyze the assumptions underlying science
- Study the scientific method
- Learn how to evaluate scientific explanations
- Distinguish between science and pseudoscience
- Learn about the different types of scientific experiments and how to evaluate them
- Look at ethical concerns in scientific experimentation
- Examine Thomas Kuhn's theory of normal science and paradigm shifts

WHAT IS SCIENCE?

Science rests on reasoning that moves from observable, measurable facts to testable explanations for those facts. The task of scientists is to discover, observe, and collect facts in a systematic manner and to explain relationships among them.

Modern science has a profound impact on our lives. Because it is so pervasive in our culture, we tend to assume that science is the natural method for obtaining and testing knowledge about the world. In this section, we'll examine the development of modern science, as well as some of the assumptions underlying science.

The Scientific Revolution

Prior to the seventeenth century, the teachings of Christianity, and in particular those of the Catholic Church, were regarded as the final source of truth in Western Europe. Nicolaus Copernicus (1473–1543), a Polish astronomer, launched the scientific revolution with his assertion that the sun, not the Earth, is the center of the

Copernicus launched the scientific revolution with his observation that the Earth revolves around the sun, and not vice versa.

solar system. Many historians, however, recognize English philosopher and statesman Sir Francis Bacon (1561–1626), who systematized the scientific method, as the father of modern science. In his *Novum Organum* (1620), Bacon put forth a method based on direct observation for discovering truths about the world. Bacon's scientific method, which begins with carrying out systematic observations about the world and using testing and experimentation to draw inferences that are based on these observations, has been tremendously successful in advancing our knowledge about the world and our ability to manipulate nature.

> **science** The use of reason to move from observable, measurable facts to hypotheses to testable explanations for those facts.
>
> **empiricism** The belief that our physical senses are the primary source of knowledge.
>
> **objectivity** The assumption that we can observe and study the physical world without any observer bias.

Assumptions Underlying Science

Science is the primary way in Western culture of interpreting reality. However, it is important to keep in mind that science is a system created by humans and, as such, is based on a particular worldview or set of assumptions.

Empiricism. **Empiricism**, the belief that our physical senses are the primary source of knowledge, is one of the most basic assumptions of science. Scientists consider the empirical method the only reliable method for obtaining knowledge. Consequently, the more data and observations that scientists accumulate over the generations, the greater is science's ability to correctly explain the workings of nature.

Objectivity. A related assumption underlying modern science is **objectivity**, the belief that we can observe and study the physical world "out there" as an object outside of us without bias on the part of the scientist/observer. Because the world is objective and independent of the individual observer, the presumption is that systematic observation will lead to agreement among scientists. This assumption has been called into question by quantum physics, which has found that the mere act of observing a quantum event changes it.

Connections

How can the methods of doubt and belief be used in science? *See Chapter 1, p. 10.*

What is the relationship between religious beliefs and reason? *See Chapter 2, pp. 53–54.*

What are some of the critical thinking strategies used in the reasoning process? *See Chapter 2, p. 39.*

Although early empiricists (including Bacon) thought that objectivity was achievable, most scientists now also acknowledge that past social experiences, as well as inborn cognitive and perceptual errors, can influence how even the best-trained scientists perceive the world. For example, as we noted in Chapter 4, we have a tendency to see order in random phenomena. One of the most famous examples of this type of error was the Martian canals. See Analyzing Images "The 'Canals' of Mars."

Despite the fact that complete objectivity is unattainable, scientists strive as much as possible to be aware of their biases, to be objective in their observations, and to be precise in their use of language.

Materialism. With the doctrine known as **materialism**, empiricism goes one step further. Scientific materialists argue that *everything* in the universe is physical matter. (*Materialism* in this sense has nothing to do with being obsessed with acquiring money, consumer goods, and other "material things.") According to scientific materialism, perceptions, thoughts, and emotions can all be reduced to descriptions of physical systems, such as brain waves or stimulus and response. There is no need to bring into scientific descriptions and explanations extraneous, nonmaterial concepts such as a conscious mental life. Because of its materialistic roots, science has made little, if any, progress in explaining how matter is or can become conscious.

Predictability. Scientists have traditionally assumed that the physical world is *orderly and predictable*. The universe consists of interconnected causal relationships that can be discovered through systematic observation and inductive reasoning. Quantum mechanics in particular challenges the idea of an ultimately predictable, determinist, material reality, suggesting that there are forces at play in the universe other than strictly physical causal laws. For example, the Heisenberg uncertainty principle states that it is impossible to predict both the position and momentum of a particle simultaneously, even under ideal conditions of measurement.

Unity. Associated with the belief in predictability is the assumption that there is an *underlying unity of*

the universe, or a unified dynamic structure that is present in all phenomena. These unified structures can be translated into scientific laws that are universally applicable. Indeed, Albert Einstein devoted considerable effort during his lifetime in search of a grand unified theory, a search that to date has been unfruitful.

Limitations of Science

Despite its obvious strengths in enabling us to build a body of knowledge about the natural world, science has some limitations. One of these, at least from a philosophical viewpoint, is that it uses the existence of a physical world as its starting point. But as the seventeenth-century French philosopher René Descartes noted, we only have an idea in our mind of a world outside of us—not direct evidence that the world "out there" actually exists.[5] In other words, the very starting point of science—the existence of a physical world—cannot be empirically proven!

Empiricism and the use of sensory experience as the foundation of science also limits science to observable, shared phenomena. However, there are aspects of the physical world—such as dark energy and dark matter, certain electromagnetic waves, and subatomic particles—that are imperceptible to human senses and to the scientific instruments that are designed to function as extensions of our senses. In addition, according to string theorists, physicists who use mathematical reasoning, there are at least nine dimensions, not just three, that our brain is able to perceive and process.

Hot or Not?

Is science the best tool for learning about the world?

Connections

How do perception errors and personal and social bias interfer with scientific objectivity?
See Chapter 4,
pp. 113–116, 126 and 130.

materialism The belief that everything in the universe is composed of physical matter.

HIGHLIGHTS

ASSUMPTIONS OF SCIENCE:

- **Empiricism:** Sensory experience is the source of truth.
- **Objectivity:** We can study the physical world without bias.
- **Materialism:** Everything in the universe is made up of physical matter.
- **Predictability:** The universe is made up of interconnected causal relationships.
- **Unity:** The universe has an underlying unified dynamic structure.

➤ APPLICATION: Identify an example in the text of each of the assumptions.

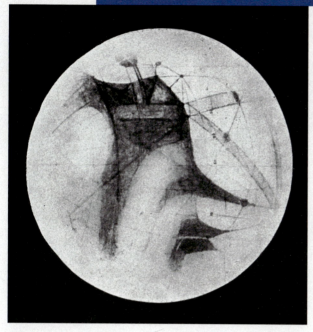

Drawing of Mars in 1895.

Photo of Mars in 2012.

The "Canals" of Mars

Many astronomers continued to believe in the Martian canals until 1965, when the space probe *Mariner 4* flew close to Mars and took photos of the planet's surface. No canals showed up in the photos. It turned out that the "canals" were a combination of an optical illusion and our brain's tendency to impose order on random data, as well as the expectation on the part of scientists that canals existed on Mars.

DISCUSSION QUESTIONS

1. *Discuss how language shapes your expectations and observations of natural phenomena, as occurred with the "canals" of Mars. Use specific examples to illustrate your answer.*

2. *Think of a time when you drew an incorrect conclusion on the basis of observation alone. How did you discover that your observation was misleading? Discuss the role scientific knowledge played in correcting your misperception?*

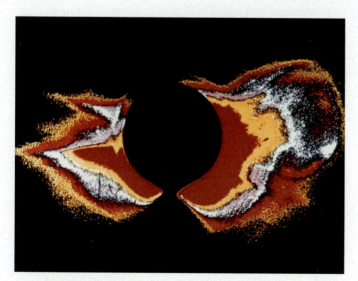

Magnetic energy is imperceptible to human senses.

Some philosophers argue that observation alone, no matter how many times we observe one event to follow another, cannot logically establish a necessary causal connectedness between the two events. Immanuel Kant in particular maintained that causality is a property of our mind, not of the outside world.* In other words, how we experience reality is dependent on the structure of our brain, which organizes and gives meaning to input from our senses.

Science and Religion

There are four basic positions regarding the relationship between science and religion: (1) science always trumps religion when there is a conflict; (2) religion always trumps

*For a review of Kant's theory of the mind and critique of empiricism, see Chapter 4, pages 103–104.

Michelangelo's rendition of the Genesis story of "The Creation of Man." The religious belief that humans are qualitatively different than other animals is one of the underlying assumptions of modern science.

science when there is a conflict; (3) science and religion operate in two separate and mutually exclusive realities; and (4) science and religion are concerned with the same reality and are compatible and complementary.

Most scientists and Western philosophers adopt the position that science always trumps religion when there is a conflict between them. This attitude has created antagonism between science and religion, especially fundamentalist religions. Many conservative Christians believe that the Bible is the literal and infallible word of God not only in the religious sphere but also in science.

People who adopt the third position, such as Judge John E. Jones (see "Critical Thinking Issue: Evolution versus Intelligent Design"), deny that there is a conflict. They argue instead that science and religion each deal with separate and mutually exclusive realms. Science deals with the objective, empirical reality; religion is concerned with values and a subjective, spiritual reality. Science asks how and what; religion asks why. Therefore, we can accept evolution without relinquishing our religious convictions regarding the special creation of human beings in the image of God. One of the problems with this approach is that in some cases science and religion make claims about the same phenomenon, whether it is the origin of human life, the effect of prayer on healing, or the occurrence of the Biblical Great Flood. When these claims are in conflict, logically they cannot both be true.

According to the fourth view, science and religion are dealing with the same reality and, as such, are compatible. This view

How does anthropocentrism act as a barrier to critical thinking? *See Chapter 1, p. 26.*
Are faith and reason compatible? *See Chapter 2, pp. 53–55.*

Connections

> . . . how we experience reality is dependent on the structure of our brain, which organizes and gives meaning to input from our senses.

is found in Judaism, Hinduism, Islam,[6] and some mainstream Protestant denominations. If scripture conflicts with the claims of science, then scripture should be reinterpreted. For example, the creation story in Genesis should be seen as a metaphor rather than taken literally. British chemist and theologian Arthur Peacocke supports this approach. Religion and science, he argues, are both dealing with different aspects of the same reality. As such, they must always "be ultimately converging. . . . The scientific and theological enterprises [are] interacting and mutually illuminating approaches to reality."[7] With the election of Pope Francis I, who accepts the theory of evolution, the Catholic Church is expected to move closer to this view of science and religion as compatible.

Though scientists often reject religious explanations for natural phenomena, there are strands of religious belief in science. The Judeo-Christian view that God gave humans dominion over the world legitimates the use of science to control and alter nature for our benefit. In addition, *anthropocentrism*—the assumption that humans are the central reality in the universe and are qualitatively different from other animals—allows scientists to confine and use other animals in research and experiments as a means to better the lives of humans. Some scientists take anthropocentricism even further and argue that the universe exists so that conscious human life would have a place to arise—a doctrine known as the *anthropic principle*.[8]

As noted previously, science is grounded in a set of unproven assumptions. However, this does not mean that science is invalid or even that these assumptions are false. Instead, we need to keep in mind that science has limitations in addition to its strengths. As we already noted, science has been extremely successful in uncovering many of the mysteries of the universe. Science has also been responsible for producing new technology for improving our lives.

THE SCIENTIFIC METHOD

The **scientific method** involves the identification of a problem and the rigorous, systematic application of observation and experimentation in testing an explanation for the problem.

As such, it is similar to the three levels of thinking—experience, interpretation, and analysis—that we studied in Chapter 1. Alone, experience or sensory data tell us nothing. They have to be interpreted in light of existing scientific knowledge and theories. Like the three levels of thinking, the scientific method is dynamic and recursive rather than linear, with analysis returning to observation to check for consistency, and interpretation being revised in light of further analysis and observation.

Experimentation/Testing (Analysis)

↑ ↓

Hypothesis (Interpretation)

↑ ↓

Observation (Experience)

The scientific method includes specific steps to guide a scientist through this process of systematically analyzing his or her observations. Although there is some variation in the steps between the different scientific disciplines, the steps basically are as follows: (1) identifying the problem, (2) developing a hypothesis, (3) gathering additional information and refining the hypothesis, (4) testing the hypothesis, and (5) evaluating the results of the tests or experiments. We'll examine each of these steps in turn in this section.

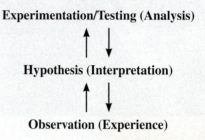

Connections

How can improving our research and inquiry skills make us better scientists? *See Chapter 1, pp. 9–10.*

How does the scientific method use the three levels of thinking? *See Chapter 1, p. 21.*

What are some of the research resources scientists might use in gathering evidence? *See Chapter 4, p. 110.*

1. Identify the Problem

The scientific method begins with the identification of a problem for investigation. This requires good observation skills, an inquisitive mind, and the ability to ask the right questions. Biologist Russell Hill, in his study of athletes on British soccer teams, observed that the teams that wore red uniforms seemed to win more often. He asked the question: Might there be a causal relationship at work?[9]

A problem may also arise as the result of previous work in the field. The Human Genome Project developed out of previous genetic research, including Watson and Crick's 1953

> **scientific method** A process involving the rigorous, systematic application of observation and experimentation.

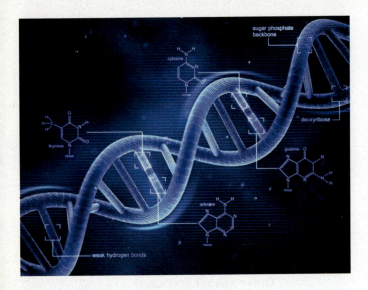

a term is generally a theoretical or operational definition. Operational definitions provide precise measures that can be used in data collection, interpretation, and testing.* For example, meteorologists studying weather and climate changes define El Niño as an oceanic condition where the temperature continues at +0.5°C or higher, averaged over 3 or more consecutive months.[10] If a hypothesis introduces a new term, a stipulative definition must be provided.

A scientific hypothesis should provide a testable explanation for the problem being investigated. To facilitate this, hypotheses are often formulated as hypothetical ("If . . . then . . .") propositions. Writing Hill's soccer hypothesis as a hypothetical proposition, we have: If a team is wearing red (Antecedent), then the team is more likely to win the game than is a team wearing blue (Consequent).

> If A, then C.
> A.
> Therefore, C.

In this case we have a *modus ponens* argument.** Does the consequent or conclusion—"the team is more likely to win the game than is a team wearing blue"—regularly follow the antecedent—"a team is wearing red"? If it does follow, then the first premise (the hypothesis) is worth further testing. If it does not follow, then the first premise (the hypothesis) is false and the hypothesis should be discarded. We'll look at additional criteria for evaluating scientific explanations later in this chapter.

hypothesis A proposed explanation for a particular set of phenomena.

scientific theory An explanation for some aspect of the natural world based on well-substantiated facts, laws, inferences, and tested hypotheses.

discovery of the structure of DNA. Or a problem may be brought to the attention of a scientist by a politician, by a government agency, or by concerned citizens. For example, beginning in the fall of 2006, beekeepers in both North America and Europe began noticing that their honeybees were disappearing, with some reporting losses of as much as 90 percent of their hives.

2. Develop an Initial Hypothesis

Once a problem has been identified, the next step in the scientific method is to develop a working hypothesis. A **hypothesis** is basically an educated guess—a proposed explanation for a particular set of phenomena, which can serve as a starting point for further investigation. Several hypotheses were put forth regarding the cause of the collapse of the honeybee colonies, a phenomenon now called colony collapse disorder (CCD). Some researchers hypothesized that the use of insecticides known as neonicotinoids was responsible. Others thought a pathogen or fungus may be killing the bees. Still others suggested that radiation from cell phones may be interfering with honeybee navigation.

Hypotheses are put forth tentatively and may be changed on the basis of further observation. A scientific theory, on the other hand, is usually more complex and supported by previous work in the field. The U.S. National Academy of Sciences defines a **scientific theory** as "a well-substantiated explanation of some aspect of the natural world that can incorporate facts, laws, inferences, and tested hypotheses." Because the scientific method is inductive, scientists can never prove with absolute certainty that a theory or a hypothesis is true.

A well-formulated hypothesis uses precise language with key terms clearly defined. The scientific definition of

3. Gather Additional Information and Refine the Hypothesis

Since we cannot possibly take in all the sensory data coming at us, hypotheses are used to guide and focus the collection of additional information. Without a hypothesis to guide our observations, we don't know what is relevant and what to ignore.

*For a review of the different types of definitions, see Chapter 3, pages 74–77.

**For a review of hypothetical reasoning, see Chapter 8, pages 247–248.

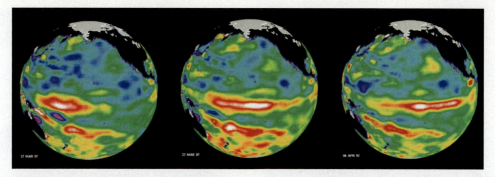

Since the 1970s, El Niño has become both more frequent and more intense. In these images, showing 3 months of sea surface temperature, the yellow and red areas indicate where waters are relatively warmer than average. El Niño contributed to massive snow blizzards in California in the winter of 2009–2010 and to the megastorms that struck the Midwest in 2012.

Scientific observation may be direct or indirect. To aid their senses and to minimize observer bias and cognitive and perceptual errors, scientists use instruments such as microscopes, telescopes, tape recorders, and stethoscopes.

The initial hypothesis may be modified on the basis of further observation. Since we can never be certain that our hypothesis is correct, collecting information is an ongoing process in science. It is vital that scientists strive to be as objective as possible and systematically record their observations without bias.

It may be only after an examination of their observations that scientists notice an unexpected pattern. When Charles Darwin as a young man of 22 traveled aboard a British naval vessel, the HMS *Beagle*, as the ship's naturalist, he collected specimens and took abundant notes on the flora and fauna of the Galapagos Islands. However, it wasn't until after he returned to England that he noticed patterns and from these, years later, developed his theory of evolution.

In collecting information, scientists avoid anecdotal and hearsay evidence. They are skeptical and do not accept at face value what people tell them, unless they have compelling firsthand evidence that what is being said is true. For example, as we learned in Chapter 7, people have a tendency to tell an interviewer what makes them look good or what they think the interviewer wants to hear.

As a graduate student in anthropology, Margaret Mead (1901–1978) was interested in finding out whether the troubles that plague adolescence in our culture are also found in so-called primitive or simpler cultures. Her hypothesis was that in these cultures, adolescence would present a different, less troubled, picture. To gather data, Mead lived with, observed, and interviewed sixty-eight young women, ages 9 to 20, in a small village in Samoa, an island in the South Pacific.

On the basis of her interviews, she concluded that Samoan girls experienced a carefree adolescence and engaged in casual sex from an early age, a finding that shocked many Westerners.[11] Many years later, the now-elderly Samoan women who had been interviewed by Mead confessed that they had lied to her, mainly as a joke. In this case, Mead's attachment to her hypothesis and her reliance on anecdotal evidence biased the way she gathered her information.

Scientists cannot rely on observations alone to determine whether a particular hypothesis is the best explanation of a phenomenon. Observations may be incomplete

Connections

What are the two types of precising definitions? *See Chapter 3, p. 75.*

What factors can bias scientists' efforts to gather evidence? *See Chapter 4, p. 116.*

How are inductive arguments using generalization used in the scientific method? *See Chapter 7, p. 206.*

Margaret Mead lived with Samoan villagers to conduct an observational study to test her hypothesis that adolescence in simpler cultures was more carefree for girls than in Western society. She is shown here, many years later, being interviewed about claims that some of the information she received was false.

1. Geospiza magnirostris.
2. Geospiza fortis.
3. Geospiza parvula.
4. Certhidea olivacea.

FINCHES FROM GALAPAGOS ARCHIPELAGO.

Darwin's Drawings of Galapagos Island Finch Beaks

DISCUSSION QUESTIONS

1. *Look at the drawings and create a list of possible explanations for the differences in the beaks of the finches.*

2. *Review the list of critical-thinking skills for reading scientific papers on page 384. Discuss the role that these skills played in Darwin's formulation of his theory of evolution.*

or biased because of poor collection methods, social expectations, or cognitive and perceptual errors. Instruments themselves may also be biased, since it is human inventors who determine what the instruments measure. For example, in the search for new life forms, both on Earth and beyond the Earth, scientists use instruments that measure the presence of DNA in soil, water, rock, and atmospheric samples. However, it is possible that non-DNA life forms exist (or once existed), such as those based on RNA.[12]

4. Test the Hypothesis

After completing the observations and data collection and refining the hypothesis, the next step in the scientific method is to test the hypothesis. Russell Hill and his fellow scientist Robert Barton tested the hypothesis about the relationship between a team's uniform color and winning by carrying out a study of team events at the 2004 Olympics.

Testing may also be done in a laboratory using a controlled experiment. To determine the effectiveness of a vaccine made from anthrax germs, Louis Pasteur designed an experiment in which he inoculated twenty-five animals with the vaccine. He also had a control group of twenty-five animals that did not receive the vaccine. Through scientific experimentation, he found that the vaccine was effective against anthrax. We'll be studying experimental design in more detail later in this chapter.

Testing a new hypothesis may take time if it depends on direct testing of empirical evidence that doesn't occur very often. For example, Einstein's theory of relativity predicted that the sun's gravitational pull would bend starlight. However, to test this prediction, scientists had to wait several years, until (in 1919) a total eclipse of the sun occurred. It may also take several years to thoroughly test a hypothesis. The Minnesota Twin Family Study is a longitudinal study begun in 1989 conducted to identify the genetic and environmental influences on psychological development. Researchers are following the development of more than 8,000 pairs of twins and their families. By carefully comparing traits in identical twins with those in fraternal twins, the researchers have been able to determine, for example, that about 40 percent of the variation in religious behavior, such as praying and attending religious services, is due to genetic rather than environmental factors.[13] The study is ongoing.

Testing and experimentation is a critical step in the scientific method, since some hypotheses that we assume to be true are, in fact, poorly supported and fall apart when tested. The more testing confirms one's hypothesis, the more confidence we can feel that the hypothesis is *probably* true. However, as we noted earlier, we will never be able to be absolutely certain that it is true.

5. Evaluate the Hypothesis on the Basis of Testing or Experimental Results

The last step in the scientific method is to evaluate the hypothesis using testing and experimentation. If the results or findings do not support the hypothesis, then scientists reject it and go back to step 2, come up with a new hypothesis, and repeat the process. We'll be learning how to interpret experimental results in the section "Evaluating an Experimental Design."

HIGHLIGHTS

THE SCIENTIFIC METHOD

1. Identify the problem
2. Develop an initial hypothesis
3. Gather additional information and refine the hypothesis
4. Test the hypothesis
5. Evaluate the hypothesis on the basis of results of testing or experimentation

➤ *APPLICATION: Identify an example in the text of each of the five steps.*

The scientific method is ongoing. Old hypotheses and theories may be revised or discarded in light of new evidence or be replaced by hypotheses with greater explanatory power. After four years of research into the cause of honeybee colony collapse, a 2010 study at Penn State College of Agriculture found unprecedented levels of a particular pesticide chemical in honeybees' pollen and hives.[14] However, this hypothesis, while one of the most promising, has yet to be substantiated. Because of uncertainty, it is important than scientists remain open-minded and do not overcommit to one hypothesis. Scientists are still exploring other explanations for CCD.[15]

Any theory, including those as well accepted as Darwin's theory of evolution or Einstein's theory of relativity, is always subject to replacement if new data contradicts it. In the next section we'll be examining some of the criteria used for evaluating scientific explanations.

STOP AND ASSESS YOURSELF

1. Working in small groups, come up with hypotheses to explain each of the following observations. Refine your hypotheses on the basis of feedback from the class.

*a. The moon looks larger when it is on the horizon than when it is high in the sky.

b. During the past few years the number of American students attending Canadian colleges increased by 50 percent over the 2001 figure.[16]

c. Since the 1950s, tens of thousands of people claim to have seen UFOs.

*d. Women are significantly underrepresented in senior faculty positions in science and math departments at Ivy League colleges.

e. More than one out of eight babies in the United States is born at least 3 weeks before the due date. This represents a 36 percent increase since 1980.[17]

f. Rates of the diagnosis of autism have risen dramatically in the past 30 years.

*g. Left-handed people die an average of 9 years earlier than the general population.[18]

h. Eating fish regularly decreases the chance of stroke.

i. The average person will lose five pounds a month by drinking two cups of green tea a day.

*j. Married people live about 3 years longer, on the average, than unmarried people.[19]

2. Select three of your hypotheses from the previous exercise and discuss what preliminary observations you might carry out to gather more information about them. Modify or refine your initial hypotheses on the basis of your observations and new information.

3. Select one of your hypotheses from question 2. Word the hypothesis in the form of a hypothetical argument. Discuss how you might test your hypothesis.

4. "The real purpose of [the] scientific method," writes Robert Pirsig, author of *Zen and the Art of Motorcycle Maintenance*, "is to make sure Nature hasn't misled you into thinking you know something you actually don't know." What do you think he meant by this? Relate your answer to the study of informal fallacies in Chapter 5 and the study of cognitive, perceptual, and social errors in Chapter 4.

5. Think of a problem or question in your life, such as why your car isn't getting better gas mileage, the most efficient way to study for an exam, or whether you should drink less coffee. Write an essay explaining how you would apply the scientific method to coming up with an answer to the problem.

6. Austrian zoologist Konrad Lorenz once gave the following advice: "It is a good morning exercise for a research scientist to discard a pet hypothesis every day before breakfast. It keeps him young."[†] What are some of your pet hypotheses about your life and the way the world works? Applying the characteristics of a critical thinker found in Chapter 1, decide whether you should discard some or all of these hypotheses.

*Answers to selected exercises are found in the Solutions Manual at the end of the book.
[†]Quoted in Singh Simon, "How a Big Idea Is Born," *New Scientist*, Vol. 184, Issue 2476, December 4, 2004, p. 23.

EVALUATING SCIENTIFIC HYPOTHESES

Different scientists observing the same phenomenon might come up with different hypotheses or explanations. We've already mentioned a few criteria for a good scientific hypothesis: It should be relevant to the problem under study, use precise language, and provide a testable explanation. Other criteria for evaluating a scientific explanation include consistency, simplicity, falsifiability, and predictive power.

Relevance to the Problem Under Study

First of all, a good hypothesis or explanation should be relevant to the problem under study. In other words, it should be related to the phenomenon it is intended to explain. Obviously, we cannot include all observations and facts in a hypothesis. Instead, we need to decide which are relevant to the problem under investigation. Polish chemist Marie Curie (1867–1934), for example, focused specifically on the atomic properties of radium and polonium in coming up with her initial hypothesis about the nature of radioactivity; Hill focused on the color of a sport team's uniform in his hypothesis.

Consistency with Well-Established Theories

Science is a system of logically consistent hypotheses or theories. Scientific explanations are preferred if they are consistent with well-established theories in the field—what American historian of science Thomas Kuhn refers to as "normal science." (We'll be studying Kuhn's concepts of normal science and paradigms later in this chapter.) This system forms a *paradigm*, or particular way of looking at and explaining the world. For example, the new hypothesis that "internal processes in the ocean such as the release of oceanic methane hydrate deposits that exist on the sea floor on continental margins are the primary cause of global warming" is considered a good hypothesis by environmental scientists since it is consistent with the established paradigm that global warming is the result of a combination of man-made and natural physical and chemical changes in the earth.

The intelligent design theory, on the other hand, does not meet this criterion because

it is inconsistent with the well-established theory of evolution (see "Critical Thinking Issue: Evolution versus Intelligent Design").

However, scientists do not automatically discard explanations that contradict well-established theories, especially if they meet the other criteria for a good explanation. Einstein's theory of relativity, which stated that time and space are relative, was not compatible with Newtonian physics, in which time and space are fixed and absolute. As it turned out, the theory of relativity—bizarre as it first sounded—turned out to be a better explanation of some phenomena. While Newton's theory remains a valid predictor at the level of phenomena that we can detect with our "normal" powers of observation, it fails at extreme conditions, such as those involving the speed of light (186,000 miles per second). Einstein's theory of relativity led to a radical rethinking of physics on the cosmic level.

Simplicity

If rival hypotheses or explanations both satisfy the basic criteria, scientists generally accept the one that is simpler, a logical principle known as Ockham's razor (named for the medieval philosopher William of Ockham). The great majority of scientists reject intelligent design theory because, among other reasons, the theory of evolution is simpler than that of intelligent design. The process of evolution alone, scientists argue, can explain the gradual development of complex organs such as the human eye, beginning with the light-sensitive cells that primitive organisms possess. There is no need to add the idea of an intelligent designer to the process.

Did You Know

Karl Popper believed that "Darwinism is not a testable scientific theory, but a metaphysical research program."[20]

On the other hand, there is nothing about the physical world itself that points to a preference for simplicity. Simplicity is a preference on the part of scientists. When there are competing hypotheses, the more complex hypothesis may turn out to be correct. For example, Einstein's theory of relativity failed the test of simplicity. However, it explained certain phenomena better and had more predictive power than the competing and simpler Newtonian theory of absolute space and time.

ALBERT EINSTEIN, *Inventor*

One of Albert Einstein's high school teachers told his father: "It doesn't matter what he does—he will never amount to anything." However, young Einstein (1879–1955) was not one to let others' opinions determine the course of his life. A mediocre student in school, he preferred learning on his own and taught himself mathematics and science. Having a curious, creative, and analytical mind, he soon realized the inadequacies of Newtonian physics and by the age of sixteen had already developed the basics of his theory of relativity.

Einstein graduated from the Swiss Federal Polytechnic School at Zurich in 1900 with a degree in physics. Unable to find a teaching position, he accepted a job in the Swiss patent office. In his spare time he continued to work on physics and completed a doctorate in physics in 1905. In the same year he published the papers that introduced his theory of relativity and would later revolutionize physics. His papers were initially met with skepticism and ridicule. However, his theory eventually won support and in 1914 he was offered a professorship at the University of Berlin. In 1921 he won the Nobel Prize for physics.

By the 1930s Einstein, who was a Jew, was high on Hitler's enemy list. He moved to the United States in 1933 and accepted a position at the Institute for Advanced Research at Princeton, New Jersey. Einstein was a humanist and pacifist who saw science in its wider social context. Fearful that Germany was building an atomic bomb, he wrote a letter to President Franklin D. Roosevelt in 1939, urging him to develop the bomb first. He also stressed in his letters to the president that the bomb should never be used on people. He was appalled when the U.S. dropped the atomic bombs on Hiroshima, Japan.

After Hiroshima, Einstein became an anti-nuclear and anti-war activist, and a leading figure in the World Government Movement. He was invited to become president of Israel, an offer he declined. During his later years Einstein worked on the construction of a unified field theory in physics, which would reconcile his theory of relativity with the quantum theory, but never succeeded. He died in his sleep in 1955.

DISCUSSION QUESTIONS

1. Referring to the moral principles and concerns discussed in Chapter 9, construct an argument about whether or not scientists have a moral obligation to refuse to engage in research that might be used to produce destructive technology.

2. In what ways might young Einstein's rebelliousness against authority have aided him in remaining open-minded and questioning established scientific paradigms? Relate your answer to your own attitudes toward accepted science.

Testability and Falsifiability

A hypothesis or explanation should be presented in a form that is testable and can be replicated by other scientists. In addition to being testable, an explanation must be able to be falsified.[21] Philosopher Karl Popper (1902–1994) pointed out that logically no number of positive experimental outcomes or observations can confirm a scientific theory; however, a single counter example is logically decisive since it proves that the theory is false. Therefore, one of the main tasks of a scientist in testing a hypothesis is the search for the negative, falsifying instances. For example, the hypothesis that "all swans are white" was based on observations of hundreds of thousands of swans, every one of which was white. However, the hypothesis was falsifiable, since it would take only one non-white swan to prove it false, which happened when black swans were discovered in Australia. Resistance to falsification is a constant struggle in science because of confirmation bias. A good scientist seeks evidence and carries out experiments that might falsify his or her theory.

On the other hand, theories that are able to accommodate all challenges have a critical weakness, because they cannot be tested for falsity. For example, Sigmund Freud's theories about the Oedipus complex fail the falsifiability criterion since, if a man claims that he does not have this complex, Freudians argue that he has repressed it into his unconscious.* However, unconscious thoughts, by their very nature, are untestable. Therefore, there is no way of falsifying Freud's theory.

Predictive Power

Finally, a good hypothesis or explanation has predictive power and can be used to accurately predict and explain the occurrence of similar events. The greater the predictive power, the more fruitful the hypothesis is. A hypothesis is fruitful if it suggests new ideas for future research.

The big bang theory, for example, was able to predict not only that the universe was expanding but also the amount of helium in the universe and the distribution of the galaxies. It alone was also able to explain the existence of microwave background radiation throughout the universe, which was first detected in 1965. Likewise, one of the reasons Einstein's theory of general relativity became so widely accepted was

*The Oedipus complex is the theory that young boys have sexual feelings toward their mothers that often involve rivalry with the father for the mother's affection. Freud considered this part of normal development.

because of its predictive power. His theory of relativity predicted with greater accuracy certain eclipses than did Newton's theory.

Good scientific explanations meet all or most of the criteria that we have described so far. In the subsection that follows, we'll be looking at the differences between scientific explanations or hypotheses and those of pseudoscience.

Distinguishing between Scientific and Pseudoscientific Hypotheses

Pseudoscience is a body of explanations or hypotheses that, in an attempt to gain legitimacy, masquerades as science. However, unlike science in which explanations are grounded in the scientific method, including systematic observation, reason, and testing, pseudoscience is based on emotional appeals, superstition, and rhetoric. Astrology, psychic healing, numerology (the study of numbers, such as one's date of birth or 9/11/2001, to determine their supernatural meaning), tarot card readings, and mind reading are all examples of pseudoscience.

While scientific explanations and hypotheses use precise wording, those of pseudoscience are usually framed in such ambiguous language that it is impossible to determine what would count as verification of the hypothesis. Astrological descriptions, for example, are usually so vague that they apply to anyone. Because of this, pseudoscientific claims are unfalsifiable.

Did You Know

Twenty-six percent of Americans believe in the accuracy of astrology.[22]

For the most part, no tests or experiments are carried out to check out the validity of pseudoscientific explanations. The few studies that are carried out, such as those on extrasensory perception or ghosts, are generally poorly designed and rarely replicable. Pseudoscience may also explain the failure of its explanations to stand up

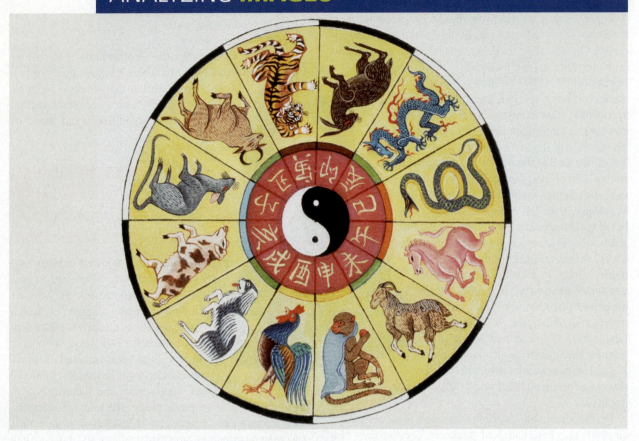

Science Versus Pseudoscience

DISCUSSION QUESTIONS

1. *According to Gall polls, about ¼ of Americans believe in astrology. Referring back to Chapter 5 on informal fallacies, critically examine the claims that are used to support this conclusion.*

2. *Using the criteria discussed in this section, evaluate the hypothesis that astrology is a good scientific hypothesis.*

to scientific scrutiny by blaming the subject. For example, it might be said that a person was not healed by a faith healer because he or she did not have enough faith.

Pseudoscientific explanations also fail to meet the criteria of predictability. Most are so broadly worded that just about anything would bear out their predictions. Not surprisingly, most pseudoscientific predictions are done after the fact. Nostradamus, a sixteenth-century writer of prophecies, is today credited with foreseeing events such as the French Revolution, the rise of Nazism in Germany, and the September 11, 2001, attacks on the World Trade Center. Like the first two prophecies, the one that "predicted" 9/11 was brought to people's attention only *after* the attacks had already occurred.[23] Because the language used in prophecies tends to be so vague and

Nostradamus's prophecies tended to be so vague that they could only be "proven" after they had happened.

obscure, it can be manipulated to fit many similar events, as in the following example from Nostradamus that "predicted" 9/11.

> Ennosigee, fire of the center of the earth,
> Shall make an earthquake of the New City,
> Two great rocks shall long time war against each other,
> After that, Arethusa shall color red the fresh water.[24]

Despite its lack of scientific legitimacy, belief in pseudoscience is widespread.

Pseudoscience literally means "fake science." To avoid falling for the empty promises of pseudoscience, we need to know how to critically evaluate the claims of pseudoscience, using the criteria listed on page 384. We should also be aware of how cognitive and social errors can distort our thinking and make us vulnerable to the lure of pseudoscience.

HIGHLIGHTS

CRITERIA FOR EVALUATING A SCIENTIFIC HYPOTHESIS

- Is it **relevant** to the problem under investigation?
- Is it **consistent** with well-established theories?
- Is it the **simplest** explanation for the problem?
- Does it provide a **testable** and **falsifiable** explanation of the problem?
- Can it be used to **predict** the outcome of similar events?

▶ **APPLICATION:** *Find an example in the text of an answer to each of the above questions.*

EXERCISE 12-3

STOP AND ASSESS YOURSELF

I. Evaluate the following hypotheses using the five criteria for a good scientific explanation (see pages 372–375). If the hypothesis is inadequate, formulate a new hypothesis and discuss why it is better.

  *a. People who consume diet soda are more likely to gain weight than those who do not.

  b. Kwanda was having trouble with her computer. It would often freeze up when she was using her word processing program. She concluded that the problem must be a computer glitch.

  c. Pastor Luke Robinson believes that God inflicted his wrath on New York City in the form of Superstorm Sandy in response to Mayor Bloomberg's support of same-sex marriage.

  *d. Marijuana use leads to heroin addiction.

  e. Regular use of Facebook harms academic performance.

  f. Humans and dolphins are the only animals that engage in sex for fun.

  *g. Everything we do and everything that happens is determined by the original state of the universe.

  h. Having a pet cat or a dog increases a person's life expectancy.

  i. The avian flu is transmitted to humans through eating the flesh of an affected bird.

  *j. Whatever happens, happens for the best.

  k. The increase in carbon dioxide in the atmosphere is contributing to an increase in pollen-related allergies in people.

  l. In the new century a fire will erupt into the sky, bringing destruction on the land.

2. Polls find that young adults are more likely than older adults to believe in astrology. Why do you think this is the case? Relate your answer to the development of critical-thinking skills and the stages of cognitive development in Chapter 1.

3. Working in small groups, design and carry out an experiment to test for the existence of telepathy. Evaluate your findings.

4. Read your horoscope for the day in the newspaper or on the Internet. How accurate, in your opinion, is the prediction? Is the prediction falsifiable? Write down events that would definitively falsify the horoscope.

*Answers to selected exercises are found in the Solutions Manual at the end of the book.

RESEARCH METHODOLOGY AND SCIENTIFIC EXPERIMENTS

Scientists use research and experimentation to test their hypotheses. In this section, we'll look at the basics of research methodology and will examine three research methods that use experimentation: field experiments, controlled experiments, and single-group (pretest–posttest) experiments.

Research Methodology and Design

Research methodology is a systematic approach to gathering and analyzing information based on established scientific

research methodology A systematic approach in science to gathering and analyzing information.

scientific experiment Research carried out under controlled or semicontrolled conditions.

independent variable The factor in a controlled experiment that is being manipulated.

dependent variable A factor in a controlled experiment that changes in response to the manipulation.

controlled experiment An experiment in which all variables are kept constant except for the independent variable(s).

procedures and techniques. Experimentation is only one type of research method. **Scientific experiments** are carried out under controlled or semicontrolled conditions and involve systematic measurement and statistical analysis of data. Other research methods include observation, surveys, and interviews (see Chapter 7). For example, rather than carrying out an experiment in a laboratory under simulated sunlight or starlight,

which are controlled conditions that scientists may use, ethnologist Jane Goodall used observation of chimpanzees in their natural habitat in Tanzania. Astronomer Arthur Eddington, in his research on the effect of gravity on light, used observation during a solar eclipse as a research method.

In coming up with a research design, scientists need to consider which methodology is best suited to the hypothesis under investigation. For example, in astronomy and meteorology, although some experiments are carried out in laboratories using simulations, it is generally not feasible to use simulation experiments, since humans have little or no control over the variables that affect the action of celestial bodies or the weather.

In designing an experiment, scientists begin by writing up a plan in which they clearly define the purpose or objective of the experiment in terms of the hypothesis that is being tested, the variables that are going to be measured, and the type of measurement that will be used. The **independent variable** is the factor that the experimenter is manipulating, while the **dependent variable** is the one that changes in response to the manipulation. Sometimes the variables under study naturally fall into place in a relatively controlled setting without having to set up an experiment. Biologist Russell Hill, for example, was able to test his hypothesis by observing four combat events, such as boxing, at the 2004 Olympics. In these events, red and blue uniforms (the independent variable) were randomly assigned to each team. Hill found that the athletes who wore red uniforms beat the blue teams 60 percent of the time, a rate higher than probability.[25]

In a **controlled experiment**, all variables are kept constant except for the independent variable(s). Variables that are not accounted for or controlled by the experimental

Ethnologist Jane Goodall used observation as a research method to test her hypothesis that chimpanzees use tools.

design are known as **confounding variables**. This is particularly a problem in field experiments and observational research.

Experimental material is the group or class of objects or subjects that is being studied, such as pea plants, light rays, or college freshmen. If a sample is going to be used, it should be precisely defined in terms of how large it will be and how it will be selected.[26] It is also important that the sample be representative of the population under study.

In addition, ethical considerations may place restrictions on what type of experimental design is suitable. For example, it would be unethical to use a controlled experiment to research the effects of smoking on children by randomly assigning half the children to a group where they are made to smoke. Instead mice or other lab animals are used as subjects, a practice that raises ethical concerns with some people, such as animal rights activists, as well as those who note that experiments done on animal models cannot always be generalized to humans.

Field Experiments

In some cases, studying a phenomenon in its natural setting may be the best method of testing a hypothesis. Field experiments use contrived situations designed to appear to the study subjects as natural occurrences. Two or more similar groups of study subjects are nonrandomly assigned to different treatments or experimental interventions. The groups are then compared to determine the effect of the treatment variable.

For example, to test their hypothesis that "bystanders are more likely to aid victims of their own race than those of a different race," psychologists Daniel Wegner and William Crano used a field experiment. An experimenter would "accidentally" drop a deck of cards he or she was carrying in a campus building when he or she was one step away from a preselected study subject. The study subjects were unaware of the design of the experiment.[27]

If the study subject immediately helped the experimenter, the actions were recorded as an instance of helping. The data were then analyzed, comparing the difference in performance between groups on the basis of their race.

Hot or Not?

Are field experiments real scientific experiments?

The disadvantage of field experiments is that natural conditions cannot be controlled and manipulated as easily as conditions in a laboratory setting. For example, the study subjects in the Wegner and Crano field experiment might have been stressed because of final exams and therefore not as willing to stop and help as they might have otherwise been. Also, the assumption that the groups were similar in all respects except for race is questionable.

Controlled Experiments

Some people regard field experiments as quasi-experiments and maintain that controlled experiments are the only true type of scientific experiment. Controlled experiments are used to determine whether there is a causal relationship between the independent and dependent variable. To rule out other confounding causal variables that may be responsible for a change, in a controlled experiment there is generally only one independent variable. To ensure that both groups are virtually identical, study subjects are randomly assigned to an experimental or control group. The experimental group receives the treatment (independent variable), while the control group does not receive it. With human study subjects, participants do not know whether they are in the experimental or control group. The results obtained from each group are then compared and statistically analyzed to determine the effect of the treatment or independent variable.

Although there are several variations on the research design in a controlled experiment, the basic design is this:

> **confounding variable** A factor that is not accounted for or controlled by the experimental design.
>
> **experimental material** The group or class of objects or subjects that is being studied in an experiment.

Connections

What types of bias and errors in thinking are reduced by the use of an appropriate research design? *See Chapter 4, p. 108.*

What types of sampling errors might occur in scientific research? *See Chapter 5, p. 148, and Chapter 7, pp. 207–208.*

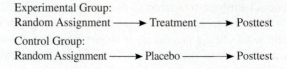

Experimental Group:
Random Assignment ⟶ Treatment ⟶ Posttest

Control Group:
Random Assignment ⟶ Placebo ⟶ Posttest

PLATE IV.—MENDELIAN INHERITANCE OF THE COLOUR OF THE FLOWER IN THE CULINARY PEA

Two flowers of a plant
of a pink-flowered race.

Two flowers of a plant produced by
crossing the pink with the white.

Two flowers of a plant
of a white-flowered race.

Connections

How do controlled experiments involve the use of inductive causal arguments? *See Chapter 7, p. 225.*

placebo A substance used in experiments that has no therapeutic effect.

In Augustinian monk Gregor Mendel's (1822–1884) famous experiments on heredity in successive generations of pea plant hybrids, he controlled for the influence of environment on traits by carrying out his experiments in a laboratory setting where variables such as light, heat, and water were kept constant, leaving only genes as the independent variable. His methodology, which established the foundations of the modern science of genetics, was radical at the time and provided a model for future research in science.

The advantage of doing a controlled experiment is that scientists have more control over the different variables that might affect the outcome of the study. One of the potential disadvantages is that human study subjects know they are part of an experiment and adjust their expectations accordingly. This is particularly problematic in medical and psychology research.

To ensure that receiving the treatment does not confound the outcome, the control group may be given a placebo. A **placebo** is a substance, such as a sugar pill or a bogus treatment, which has no therapeutic effect.

Placebos are used because the influence of expectation and self-fulfilling prophecies is so powerful that if study subjects believe that they may be receiving a particular beneficial treatment, their condition often actually improves even though they are getting only a placebo.

Single-Group (Pretest–Posttest) Experiments

Instead of using a control group and an experimental group, a *single-group experiment* uses only one group of study subjects. The variable under investigation is measured by a pretest before the intervention and again with a posttest after the intervention. Generally the same test is used in both the pre- and posttest.

Single Group:
Pretest ⟶ Treatment ⟶ Posttest

For example, in studying the effect of community service on moral reasoning, the Defining Issues Test (DIT)—a test of moral reasoning—is administered to a group of college students before their community service and then again at the end of the semester after they complete the service. It was found that the students score significantly higher on the DIT at the end of the semester.[28] Can we conclude from this that community service (the independent variable) was responsible for the improvement in the scores (the dependent variable)? No, we can't, not with the same degree of certainty that we could if there was a control group.

One of the weaknesses of the single-group study is that without a control group, it doesn't control for other

Critical THiNKing in Action

Science and Prayer

A controlled experiment conducted by Harvard scientists found that therapeutic inter-cessory prayer provided no health benefits to patients recovering from cardiac bypass surgery.* Eighteen hundred patients were randomly assigned to experimental and control groups. The experimental group was divided into those who knew they were being prayed for and those who did not know but in fact were being prayed for. The control group did not know whether they were being prayed for and, as the control, were not being prayed for. The first names of those in the two groups receiving prayers were given to members of two Catholic monasteries and one Protestant group. They each offered up the same prayer for 30 days for the names on their lists asking for "a successful surgery and a quick, healthy recovery and no complications." There was no statistical difference in the recovery of the three groups.

Does this study prove that prayer does not work? "I am always a little leery about intercessory prayer," says Rev. Dean Marek. "What we have in mind for someone else may not be what they have in mind for themselves. . . . It is clearly manipulative of divine action and personal choice." Another critic of the study states that "science is powerful and wonderful in determining the orbit of the Earth, . . . the power of a new drug. But now we've asked science to study something that occurs outside of space and time. This shows you shouldn't try to prove the power of the supernatural."**

1. Evaluate the experimental design in this study. Does this study prove that prayer does not work? Are the criticisms of the study valid? If so, explain how you might go about improving the design of the study.

2. Do you personally believe that prayer works? In answering this, provide an operational definition of *prayer*. In other words, what do you mean in terms of observable, measurable effects when you say that prayer does or does not work? Discuss what evidence supports your belief regarding the effectiveness of prayer.

*H. Benson et al., "Study of the Therapeutic Effects of Intercessory Prayer (STEP) in Cardiac Bypass Patients: A Multicenter Randomized Trial of Uncertainty and Certainty of Receiving Intercessory Prayer," *American Heart Journal*, Vol. 151, Issue 4, April 15, 2006, pp. 762–764.

**Quotes from Denise Gellene and Thomas H. Maugh II, "Largest Study of Prayer to Date Finds It Has No Power to Heal," *Los Angeles Times*, March 31, 2006, p. A-8.

variables that might be affecting the outcome, such as maturation and familiarity with the test from the pretest. For this reason, single-group studies, because they are easier to set up and administer than studies with control groups, are often used as exploratory experiments, which, if the results are promising, are followed up with a controlled experiment.

In some research, however, single-group experiments may be preferable to controlled experiments, especially when it is clear that the variable under study is having a significant positive effect on the experimental group. For example, a new cancer drug is being tested on children with leukemia using a controlled experiment. After 3 months it is found that the children taking the new drug are doing significantly better than those taking the placebo. At this point the experimenters have an ethical obligation to stop the controlled experiment and switch to a single-group experimental design in which all the children are receiving the drug.

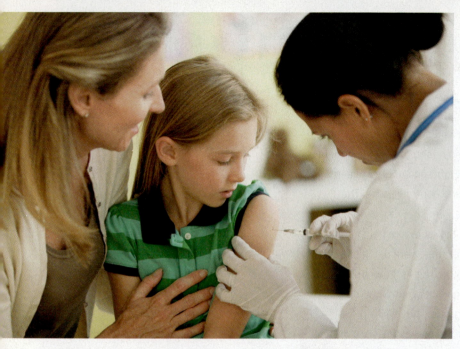

Sometimes single-group experiments are necessary, such as when a drug is found right away to be very effective.

Evaluating an Experimental Design

As we noted, there are several types of experimental design. However, good designs all have certain characteristics in common. One of the foremost is being able to *discriminate between different hypotheses*. If the same experimental results can be used to support two competing hypotheses, then the experiment was poorly designed. For example, you decide to conduct an experiment to test your hypothesis that hanging garlic on your front door will keep vampires away. You hang up the garlic and use a hidden camera to record the number of vampire visits during the next month. No vampires come to your house during the month. Does this prove your hypothesis that garlic keeps vampires away? Not necessarily, because the results of your experiment also support the competing hypothesis that vampires don't exist.

A well-designed experiment is *unbiased*. It uses checks and controls to minimize experimental error, which can result from small sample size, an unrepresentative sample, or subject or experimenter bias. A 1998 study published in the *Lancet*, a British medical journal, suggesting a link between autism and childhood vaccinations was based on testing of only twelve children with autism; there was no control group for comparison. Unfortunately, the media publicized these findings and many parents took them seriously, despite scientists' criticisms of

Why is being aware of confirmation bias and the fallacy of questionable cause important in evaluating scientific evidence?
See Chapter 1, p. 8 and Chapter 5, p. 155.

Connections

Hot or Not?

Should pregnant women, or women who might become pregnant, be allowed to participate in drug tests?

the experimental design and the lack of corroborating evidence.

This explanation of autism has since been called into question. Scientists in Denmark have carried out a 20-year unbiased study of nearly 700,000 births and have discovered that certain factors in the pregnant mother, such as rheumatoid arthritis, celiac disease, and other autoimmune disorders, significantly elevate their child's probability of having autism. These scientists have also found that women living in areas where they are exposed to parasites and microbes have stronger immune systems and are less likely to have autoimmune disorders and children with autism. While they acknowledge that what they have are correlations, scientists plan to carry out further studies to look for causal connections.[29]

A third criterion of a good design is that the *measurements of the outcome of the variable under investigation are reliable as well as accurate and precise*. Measurement tools are reliable if they provide consistency of results over time and when used by different people. An IQ test is reliable if it gives the same results when used by two different experimenters on study subjects and if the results remain consistent when the test is used on the same study subject over a period of time.

An accurate measurement is one that is consistent with other standards used for measuring a phenomenon. Measurement should also be precise. Precision depends on the problem under investigation. Days or even years may be a precise enough measurement of time in a study of the effect of global warming on the retreat of glaciers in Alaska. However, we need a more precise definition of time for calculating the timing of chain reactions in nuclear fission, which are measured in milliseconds.

Accurate and precise measurements allow the experiment to be *replicated or reproduced* by other scientists. One of the purposes of writing up experiments in a scientific journal is to provide enough details on the experimental design so that other scientists can replicate it—that is, run the same experiment and obtain the same results. Replicability is necessary because the results of one study might have occurred by chance, might have used a faulty sample, or might even have been fabricated (see pages 384–385).

The final criterion is *generalizability*. A well-designed experiment produces results that can be generalized from the sample used in the experiment. A problem with generalizability occurs when the sample in a study is not representative of the overall population that it is supposed to represent. Prior to the 1980s, most medical and psychological studies used only white males as study subjects. However, when scientists generalized the results to all people, they sometimes ran into problems. For example, we have since learned that women wake up earlier from anesthesia than do men—a fact that could have easily led to horrific surgical experiences for female patients. In 1985, the U.S. Food and Drug Administration began requiring clinical trials sponsored by drug manufacturers to include data about sex as well as age and race.

Interpreting Experimental Results

Once an experiment is complete and the data have been analyzed, the results are usually published in a scientific journal. Most scientific journals, though not all, require that articles published in them follow the organization outlined in "Critical Thinking in Action: How to Read a Scientific Paper." Some prestigious scientific journals, such as *Science* and *Nature*, which appeal to a wider audience, have space limitations, and thus some sections in articles may be condensed or combined.

The results section in a scientific paper provides information on how the data were analyzed and which findings were statistically significant. Experimental results are generally expressed in terms of averages or correlations between variables. Experimental results that falsify (that is, disprove) a hypothesis are just as important to scientific knowledge as those that support a hypothesis.

Each time an experiment is replicated with a new sample and significant results are obtained, the confidence level becomes higher, since the total sample size tested becomes larger. If the results are not replicated in subsequent experiments, the hypothesis should be reexamined.

Hot or Not?

Is it desirable, or even possible, for science to be value-neutral?

Ethical Concerns in Scientific Experimentation

A scientific experiment may be well designed and produce significant results but still be inappropriate because it violates moral principles and guidelines. Ethical considerations of informed consent, rights, and nonmaleficence (no harm) are particularly important when working with human study subjects.

Some of the most unethical scientific experiments were those performed on Jews, prisoners of war, and other captives in Nazi concentration camps. Members of marginalized groups have also been used, without their consent, in scientific experiments in other countries. Between 1930 and 1953 the U.S. Department of Health Services conducted a study of the effects of syphilis, known as the Tuskegee study, using poor black men living in Macon County, Alabama. None of the men were told that they had syphilis, and no attempt was made to treat them. The study continued even after penicillin was discovered as a cure, resulting in the death of many of the men purely for the sake of advancing scientific knowledge.

Since the 1970s there has been growing concern for the rights of human subjects in scientific experiments. Studies like the 1963 Milgram experiment and the 1971 Stanford Prison experiment (both discussed in Chapter 1), which put people at risk for psychological or physical harm, are today considered unethical.

The concept of the neutrality of science and ethical concerns over the use of scientific results for unethical purposes was poignantly raised by the creation of the atomic bomb. Albert Einstein, who was involved in launching the American effort to build a nuclear weapon during World War II, came to regret his

---

HIGHLIGHTS

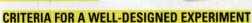

CRITERIA FOR A WELL-DESIGNED EXPERIMENT

- **Unbiased:** The experiment has checks or uses controls to eliminate the possibility of subject and experimenter bias

- **Measurement:** The measurements used are appropriate and reliable as well as accurate and precise

- **Replicable:** The experiment can be reproduced by other scientists

- **Generality:** The experimental results can be generalized to the population under study

➤ *APPLICATION: Find an example in the text of the application of each of these criteria.*

Connections

How can an understanding of moral reasoning and moral principles help us recognize and avoid ethical problems in scientific experiments?
See Chapter 9, p. 274.

Critical THiNKing in Action

How to Read a Scientific Paper

A paper in a scientific journal is usually organized as follows:

- **Abstract:** A brief summary of the major findings of the study
- **Introduction:** The hypothesis under investigation and background information on similar studies
- **Methods:** Detailed description of the experimental design, including the specific procedures and methods used, and the experimental material used, such as the sample, and how it was selected
- **Results:** Review of the rationale for the experiment and an explanation of how the data were analyzed and summary of which findings were statistically significant; may include graphs and tables summarizing results
- **Discussion:** An analysis and interpretation of the data, an explanation of how the findings logically follow from the data, and a discussion of the significance of the findings and how they contribute to the field as well as the limitations of the study and suggestions for future research
- **References:** List of articles, books, and other works cited from which information was drawn

DISCUSSION QUESTIONS

1. Select an article from a scientific journal that interests you. After reading its abstract and introduction, read the methods sections and evaluate the experimental design in terms of whether it meets the criteria of a well-designed experiment. Describe any limitations in the design and ways in which it might be improved.

2. Read the results and discussion section of the paper. Discuss whether the conclusions of the paper are supported by the experimental findings. Discuss some of the implications of this study for future research.

> It is up to the community of scientists to employ their critical-thinking skills to analyze the work of other scientists in their field and to expose frauds.

role in its creation, calling his part in it the "one great mistake" in his life. More recently, ethical concerns are being raised about genetic engineering research and the possibility of human cloning.

Ethical considerations in scientific experimentation and reporting of research findings also include integrity and honesty on the part of scientists. In cases in which research is government-funded, pressure may be brought to bear on scientists to report findings to the public in a way that is consistent with the current political agenda. For example, officials in the Bush administration had intervened to weaken and even delete sections in reports by Environmental Protection Agency scientists regarding the extent of

Scientists' role in the creation of the atomic bomb raised ethical concerns among some scientists.

global warming and the role of industry in global warming. In addition, because the promotion process is often dependent on publications—the enormous pressure to "publish or perish"—scientists may exaggerate results or be selective in what they choose to report.[30]

Research carried out on behalf of pharmaceutical companies may be unreliable because of pressure to get findings published and to get a new drug on the market. New drugs may be compared against inferior, ineffective drugs that are already on the market. In addition, observations are often carried out on a small number of cases without proper controls, and data for outcomes may be based on biased reports or self-reported symptoms ("my chest felt better") rather than survival rates. Indeed, one study estimated that "as much as 90 percent of published medical information" that doctors rely on is based on flawed research.[31]

It is up to the community of scientists to employ their critical-thinking skills to analyze the work of other scientists in their field and to expose frauds. Although peer review is an effective process for safeguarding against ethical wrongdoing, procedural errors, and fraud, reviewers tend to reject for publication scientific hypotheses and studies that fall outside the established norms in science. In the next section, we'll be looking at paradigms in normal science.

EXERCISE 12-4

STOP AND ASSESS YOURSELF

1. Discuss which type of experimental design would be best for testing each of the following hypotheses and why:

*a. Fred noticed that his hens as well as those on the neighboring farm laid more eggs when the children were away at summer camp in June and July. He hypothesized that the children's absence caused the hens to lay more eggs.

b. Students who drink a cup of coffee before a test perform better than those who do not.

c. Men are more likely to look at women who have blond hair than women who have brown or black hair.

*d. Taking antibiotics doubles a woman's risk of getting breast cancer.

e. Nonhuman mammals are able to anticipate an earthquake or tsunami hours before it strikes.

f. Good-looking couples are more likely to have daughters.

*g. Computers are conscious.

2. Read the article by Russell Hill and Robert Barton in the May 19, 2005, issue of *Nature*.[32] Evaluate the experimental design used by Hill and Barton in their study of the effect of the color red on winning, as well as the significance of their results. Working in small groups, design an experiment to test their experimental results regarding the relationship between color of team uniform and winning.

3. Millions of men take drugs such as Viagra for erectile dysfunction, but are these drugs safe? According to a 2005 report, forty-three men who had taken Viagra had developed a form of blindness. The question now facing researchers is: "Was Viagra a causal factor?" The Food and Drug Administration has hired you to come up with a controlled experiment to test this question. Working in small groups, develop an experimental design to test the hypothesis.

4. Discuss the use of placebos in controlled experiments. Is their use immoral because it involves deception? Present a logical argument to support your conclusion.

5. Psychology professors sometimes use their students as subjects in experiments or studies and may even require that students participate as part of their grade in the course. Discuss the ethical issues involved in this practice.

6. Nazi experiments on hypothermia involved submerging prisoners for long periods of time in icy water. Although the experiments resulted in the death of many of the study subjects, they were well-designed experiments that yielded valuable results, which could save the lives of people who have hypothermia. Analyze whether it is morally acceptable to use the data from these and other Nazi death camp experiments to save the lives of people.

7. Bring in an example of a graph or table from a science journal, textbook, or a Web site. Discuss how the use of visuals makes it easier to understand the significance of the results.

8. Look for an article in the mass media, or a news clip, that reports the results of a scientific study. Find a copy of the original scientific article written by the scientists who did the study. How accurately did the mass media report the study? Looking back at the discussion of mass media in Chapter 11, discuss why the media sometimes distort, either intentionally or unintentionally, scientific findings.

*Answers to selected exercises are found in the Solutions Manual at the end of the book.

THOMAS KUHN AND SCIENTIFIC PARADIGMS

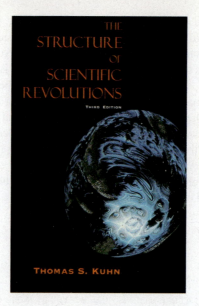

THE STRUCTURE OF SCIENTIFIC REVOLUTIONS

THIRD EDITION

THOMAS S. KUHN

In his landmark book, *The Structure of Scientific Revolutions* (1962), American physicist and historian of science Thomas Kuhn (1922–1996) challenged the idea that the scientific method is objective and that science is progressive. He argued that science, like other human enterprises, is a social construct—a product of its society. As such, it is biased by social expectations and professional norms that determine what is an acceptable hypothesis.

Normal Science and Paradigms

Kuhn put forward three key concepts: normal science, paradigms, and scientific revolutions. **Normal science** refers to "research firmly based upon one or more past scientific achievements, achievements that some particular scientific community acknowledges for a time as supplying the foundation of its further practice."[33] Normal science is conveyed in science journals and textbooks.

normal science Scientific research that is based on past achievements and is recognized by most scientists.

paradigm The accepted view of what the world is like and how we should go about studying it.

scientific revolution A paradigm shift in which a new scientific theory replaces a problematic paradigm.

The achievements of normal science provide paradigms or models for research in the field. A **paradigm** is the accepted view of what the world is like and how we should go about studying it. A paradigm becomes part of normal science if it is both successful in solving problems that scientists are working on and also able to attract a large group of adherents.

Paradigms, according to Kuhn, can influence not only what is considered to be a problem worth studying but also our actual perceptions of a phenomenon. For example, it is a current paradigm in science that consciousness is organically based and therefore will never be emulated by computers or artificial intelligence (AI). Consequently, the majority of scientists perceive the actions or operations of computers, even intelligent ones, in purely mechanical terms.

Although normal science is tremendously successful in generating results and new technology, Kuhn argued that it does not seek novelty. This in turn contributes to confirmation bias. When an anomaly is found, it is often dismissed out of hand, or scientists may try to reconcile it to the existing paradigm. For example, the orbit of Mars was an anomaly that could not be explained by the old geocentric (Earth-centered) paradigm of the universe and hence was ignored for many years by Western scholars until Copernicus.

Scientific Revolutions and Paradigm Shifts

Scientific progress, according to Kuhn, is not strictly linear—that is, it does not proceed in a straight line. A crisis, Kuhn argues, is necessary for the emergence of a new paradigm. If anomalies persist or cannot be explained by the current paradigm, a "crisis" may occur that leads to a rejection of the old paradigm.

A **scientific revolution**, or paradigm shift, occurs when a new scientific theory is made available to replace a problematic paradigm. Copernicus's theory that the Earth goes around the sun, Einstein's theory of relativity, German earth scientist Alfred Wegener's tectonic-plate or continental-drift theory, and Darwin's theory of human evolution all represented paradigm shifts in their respective fields.

A paradigm shift requires a new way of looking at the world and may take several decades to complete. It is

When the author was in elementary school, one of her classmates pointed to the world map on the wall and excitedly pointed out that Africa and Europe fit into North and South America like a puzzle, asking if they used to be part of one great continent. She thought that the student made a great point and was quite excited by her "discovery." However, the idea was ridiculed at length by the teacher as preposterous and unscientific (pseudoscience). It wasn't until years later that continental-drift theory, which had been proposed as early as 1912 by Alfred Wegener, became accepted by the scientific community. This experience, and the importance of keeping an open mind, has always stuck with her.

especially difficult for scientists who have been brought up and worked under the old paradigm to make the shift. Since they have invested years of their lives as well as their professional reputations in proving a particular theory, most will defend it vigorously when challenged, even in the face of contradictory evidence.

Those who fail to conform to the standards of normal science are often ridiculed as frauds, and their research findings get rejected by mainstream scientific journals. When Wegener first proposed the theory of continental drift in 1912, he too was attacked by his fellow scientists. The idea that something as large as a continent could move was considered ludicrous. However, by the early 1960s the evidence for the tectonic-plate and continental-drift theory eventually became so overwhelming that it could no longer be ignored.

New paradigms generally win adherents from young scientists and people who are new to or outside of the field and are not heavily invested in the old paradigm. For example, Einstein was only 26 when in 1905 he first published his hypothesis regarding relativity.

Kuhn's critique of normal science has been tremendously valuable in making scientists and others more aware of the role that social expectations and confirmation bias play in science. As critical thinkers, we need to be aware of the assumptions and paradigms of normal science and to remain open-minded to hypotheses that might not conform to these norms. In evaluating a new hypothesis, we should apply the criteria discussed in this chapter rather than dismissing the hypothesis because it does not conform to the paradigms of normal science.

EXERCISE 12-5

STOP AND ASSESS YOURSELF

1. Looking back at the list of assumptions at the beginning of this chapter on pages 363–364, discuss how they have shaped the current paradigms in science. Use specific examples.

2. In Chapter 2 we studied artificial intelligence (AI). Identify at least one hypothesis in this relatively new field that challenges some of the accepted paradigms of normal science. Discuss what scientific findings regarding AI would be most likely to precipitate a scientific revolution and why.

3. Discuss, hypothetically, what evidence in the field of human evolution would result in a paradigm shift and giving up the savannah theory (that humans originated on the grassy plains of Africa) for a new paradigm.

THiNK AGAIN

1. What is the scientific method?
   - The scientific method, which was first systematized by Francis Bacon, involves the identification of a problem and the rigorous, systematic application of observation and experimentation in testing an explanation for the problem.

2. How does science differ from pseudoscience?
   - Pseudoscience is a body of explanations or hypotheses that are based on emotional appeals, superstition, and rhetoric rather than scientific observation, reasoning, and testing. Furthermore, unlike scientific hypotheses, those of pseudoscience are often worded so vaguely as to be untestable.

3. What are some of the different types of scientific experiments and research methods?
   - Scientific experiments are carried out under controlled or semicontrolled conditions and involve systematic measurement and statistical analysis of data. Other research methods include observation, surveys, and interviews.

Evolution versus Intelligent Design

The legal conflict between religion and science in the classrooms dates back to 1925 when the judge in the Scopes Monkey Trial ruled that it was illegal for public schools to teach anything that contradicted the Biblical story of creation. In 1987, this ruling was reversed in *Edwards v. Aguillard* when the U.S. Supreme Court ruled that creationism was a religious theory and that teaching it in schools violated the Constitutional separation of church and state.

The conflict has recently resurfaced under the banner of intelligent design (ID) versus evolution. The theory of ID was developed in the 1980s by a group of scientists who argued that some biological structures are so complex that they can't be the result of natural selection but can be explained only by the existence of an intelligent designer.

ID is presented by its proponents as an evidence-based scientific theory. Evolutionists argue that ID is not a scientific theory at all but a religious viewpoint, since it requires a supernatural explanation of the beginning of life. In addition, evolution by natural selection does a better job of explaining the available fossil and DNA evidence and is supported by 150 years of research.

The majority of scientists (87 percent) believe that living things have evolved due to natural processes, a belief that is shared by only about one-third (32 percent) of the public.* A 2012 poll showed that 46 percent believe the ID view that God created humans in their present form within the last 10,000 years.**

*Pew Research Center for People & the Press, "Public Praises Science; Scientists Fault Public, Media," July 9, 2009. http://www.people-press.org/2009/07/09/public-praises-science-scientists-fault-public-media.
**Gallup Poll, Evolution, Creationism, Intelligent Design. http://www.gallup.com/poll/21814/evolution-creationism-intelligent-design.aspx.

In a highly publicized trial, the American Civil Liberties Union brought suit against the School Board of Dover, Pennsylvania, for requiring high school biology teachers to teach ID theory alongside the theory of evolution. In 2005, Judge John E. Jones ruled against the school board, stating that there was "overwhelming evidence" that intelligence design was not a scientific theory and that "ID cannot uncouple itself from its creationist, and thus religious antecedents."[†] As such, it violates the First Amendment clause regarding separation of church and state.

Both Michael Behe and Kenneth Miller, whose views are included here, participated as expert witnesses in the Dover School Board trial. In the first reading, Michael Behe argues that ID theory and the concept of irreducible complexity is the best scientific explanation for life. Kenneth Miller's article offers a response to Behe's argument. In it, Miller contends that scientific evidence does not support ID theory but rather is consistent with the theory of evolution.

[†]Kitzmiller v. Dover Area School District, United States District Court for the Middle District of Pennsylvania, December 20, 2005, Case No. 04cv2688. http:www.pamd.uscourts.gov/kitzmiller/kitzmiller_342.pdf.

Irreducible Complexity: Obstacle to Darwinian Evolution*

MICHAEL BEHE

Biochemist Michael Behe is a professor of biological sciences at Lehigh University. He maintains that Darwin's theory of evolution is unable to explain the origin of life and that only an intelligent designer could have created the irreducible complexities of cellular organisms.

In his seminal work *On the Origin of Species*, Darwin hoped to explain what no one had been able to explain before—how the variety and complexity of the living world might have been produced by simple natural laws. His idea for doing so was, of course, the theory of evolution by natural selection. . . .

It was an elegant idea, and many scientists of the time quickly saw that it could explain many things about biology. However, there remained an important reason for reserving judgment about whether it could actually account for all of biology: the basis of life was as yet unknown. . . .

In light of the enormous progress made by science since Darwin first proposed his theory, it is reasonable to ask if the theory still seems to be a good explanation for life. In *Darwin's Black Box: The Biochemical Challenge to Evolution* (Behe 1996), I argued that it is not. The main difficulty for Darwinian mechanisms is that many systems in the cell are what I termed "irreducibly complex." I defined an irreducibly complex system as: a single system that is necessarily composed of several well-matched, interacting parts that contribute to the basic function, and where the removal of any one of the parts causes the system to effectively cease functioning (Behe 2001). As an example from everyday life of an irreducibly complex system, I pointed to a mechanical mousetrap such as one finds in a hardware store. Typically, such traps have a

number of parts: a spring, a wooden platform, a hammer, and other pieces. If one removes a piece from the trap, it can't catch mice. . . .

Irreducibly complex systems seem very difficult to fit into a Darwinian framework, for a reason insisted upon by Darwin himself. In the *Origin*, Darwin wrote that "[i]f it could be demonstrated that any complex organ existed which could not possibly have been formed by numerous, successive, slight modifications, my theory would absolutely break down. But I can find out no such case" (Darwin 1859, 158). Here Darwin was emphasizing that his was a gradual theory. Natural selection had to improve systems by tiny steps, over a long period of time. . . . However, it is hard to see how something like a mousetrap could arise gradually by something akin to a Darwinian process. For example, a spring by itself, or a platform by itself, would not catch mice, and adding a piece to the first nonfunctioning piece wouldn't make a trap either. So it appears that irreducibly complex biological systems would present a considerable obstacle to Darwinian evolution.

The question then becomes, are there any irreducibly complex systems in the cell? Are there any irreducibly complex molecular machines? Yes, there are many. In *Darwin's Black Box*, I discussed several biochemical systems as examples of irreducible complexity: the eukaryotic cilium, the intracellular transport system, and more. Here I will just briefly describe the bacterial flagellum. . . . The flagellum can be thought of as an outboard motor that bacteria use to swim. It was the first truly rotary structure discovered in nature. It consists of a long filamentous tail that acts as a propeller; when it is spun, it

*Michael Behe, "Irreducible Complexity: Obstacle to Darwinian Evolution." In W. A. Dembski and M. Ruse, *From Darwin to DNA* (Cambridge, MA: Cambridge University Press, 2004), pp. 352–370.

pushes against the liquid medium and can propel the bacterium forward. The propeller is attached to the drive shaft indirectly through something called the hook region, which acts as a universal joint. The drive shaft is attached to the motor, which uses a flow of acid or sodium ions from the outside to the inside of the cell to power rotation. Just as an outboard motor has to be kept stationary on a motorboat while the propeller turns, there are proteins that act as a stator structure to keep the flagellum in place. . . .

As with the mousetrap, it is quite difficult to see how Darwin's gradualistic process of natural selection sifting random mutations could produce the bacterial flagellum, since many pieces are required before its function appears. . . .

Second, a more subtle problem is how the parts assemble themselves into a whole. The analogy to an outboard motor fails in one respect: an outboard motor is generally assembled under the direction of a human—an intelligent agent who can specify which parts are attached to which other parts. The information for assembling a bacterial flagellum, however (or, indeed, for assembling any biomolecular machine), resides in the component proteins of the structure itself. . . . Thus, even if we had a hypothetical cell in which proteins homologous to all of the parts of the flagellum were present (perhaps performing jobs other than propulsion) but were missing the information on how to assemble themselves into a flagellum, we would still not get the structure. The problem of irreducibility would remain.

Because of such considerations, I have concluded that Darwinian processes are not promising explanations for many biochemical systems in the cell. Instead, I have noted that, if one looks at the interactions of the components of the flagellum, or cilium, or other irreducibly complex cellular system, they look like they were designed—purposely designed by an intelligent agent. . . .

Rather than showing how their theory could handle the obstacle, some Darwinists are hoping to get around irreducible complexity by verbal tap dancing. . . . Kenneth Miller actually claimed . . . that a mousetrap isn't irreducibly complex because subsets of a mousetrap, and even each individual part, could still "function" on their own. The holding bar of a mousetrap, Miller observed, could be used as *a toothpick*, so it still has a "function" outside the mousetrap. Any of the parts of the trap could be used as a paperweight, he continued, so they all have "functions." And since any object that has mass can be a paperweight, then any part of anything has a function of its own. *Presto*, there is no such thing as irreducible complexity!

. . . Of course, the facile explanation rests on a transparent fallacy, a brazen equivocation. Miller uses the word "function" in two different senses. Recall that the definition of irreducible complexity notes that removal of a part "causes the *system* to effectively cease functioning." Without saying so, in his exposition Miller

shifts the focus from the separate function of the intact *system* itself to the question of whether we can find a different use (or "function") for some of the *parts*. However, if one removes a part from the mousetrap I have pictured, it can no longer catch mice. The *system* has indeed effectively ceased functioning, so the *system* is irreducibly complex. . .

With the problem of the mousetrap behind him, Miller then moved on to the bacterial flagellum—and again resorted to the same fallacy. . . . Without blinking, Miller asserted that the flagellum is not irreducibly complex because some proteins of the flagellum could be missing and the remainder could still transport proteins, perhaps independently. . . . Again, he was equivocating, switching the focus from the function of the system, acting as a rotary propulsion machine, to the ability of a subset of the system to transport proteins across a membrane. . . .

Future Prospects of the Intelligent Design Hypothesis

The misconceived arguments by Darwinists that I have recounted here offer strong encouragement to me that the hypothesis of Intelligent Design is on the right track. . . .

The important point here for a theory of Intelligent Design is that molecular machines are not confined to the few examples that I discussed in *Darwin's Black Box*. Rather, most proteins are found as components of complicated molecular machines. Thus design might extend to a large fraction of the features of the cell, and perhaps beyond that into higher levels of biology.

Progress in twentieth-century science has led us to the design hypothesis. I expect progress in the twenty-first century to confirm and extend it.

References

Behe, M. J. 1996. *Darwin's Black Box: The Biochemical Challenge to Evolution*. New York: The Free Press.

———. 2001. Reply to my critics: A response to reviews of *Darwin's Black Box: The Biochemical Challenge to Evolution. Biology and Philosophy* 16: 685–709.

Darwin, C. 1859. *The Origin of Species*. New York: Bantam Books.

REVIEW QUESTIONS

1. What does Behe mean by an "irreducibly complex system"?

2. According to Behe, why is it difficult to fit this concept into a Darwinian framework of evolution through natural selection?

3. According to Behe, how do both the mousetrap and the bacterial flagellum illustrate the concept of irreducibly complex systems?

4. Why does Behe believe there must be an intelligent designer of life?

5. How does Behe respond to Kenneth Miller's criticism of ID theory?

Answering the Biochemical Argument from Design*

KENNETH R. MILLER

Kenneth Miller is a professor of biology at Brown University. Miller critically examines Behe's concept of irreducible complexity in biological structures, concluding that such complexity is not irreducible and can be explained through the evolutionary mechanism of natural selection. Therefore, there is no need to evoke the existence of an intelligent designer.

One of the things that makes science such an exhilarating activity is its revolutionary character. As science advances, there is always the possibility that some investigator, working in the field or at a laboratory bench, will produce a discovery or experimental result that will completely transform our understanding of nature. . . .

In 1996, Michael Behe took a bold step in this scientific tradition by challenging one of the most useful, productive, and fundamental concepts in all of biology—Charles Darwin's theory of evolution. Behe's provocative claim, carefully laid out in his book, *Darwin's Black Box*, was that whatever else Darwinian evolution can explain successfully, it cannot account for the biochemical complexity of the living cell. . . .

Behe's argument is crafted around the existence of complex molecular machines found in all living cells. Such machines, he argues, could not have been produced by evolution, and therefore must be the products of intelligent design. . . . What I propose to do in this brief review is to put this line of reasoning to the test. I will . . . pose the most fundamental question one can ask of any scientific hypothesis—does it fit the facts?

An Exceptional Claim

For nearly more than a century and a half, one of the classic ways to argue against evolution has been to point to an exceptionally complex and intricate structure and then to challenge an evolutionist to "evolve this!" Examples of such challenges have included everything from the optical marvels of the human eye to the chemical defenses of the bombardier beetle. At first glance, Behe's examples seem to fit this tradition. . . .

Given that the business of science is to provide and test explanations, the fact that there are a few things that have, as yet, no published evolutionary explanations is not much of an argument against Darwin. Rather, it means that the field is still active, vital, and filled with scientific challenges. Behe realizes this, and therefore his principal claim for design is quite different. He observes, quite correctly, that science has not explained the evolution of the bacterial flagellum, but then he goes one step further. No such explanation is even *possible*, according to Behe. Why? Because the flagellum has a characteristic that Behe calls "irreducible complexity."

. . . To make his point perfectly clear, Behe uses a common mechanical device, the mousetrap, as an example of irreducible complexity. . . .

Since every part of the mousetrap must be in place before it is functional, this means that partial mousetraps,

ones that are missing one or two parts, are useless—you cannot catch mice with them. Extending the analogy to irreducibly complex biochemical machines, they also are without function until all of their parts are assembled. What this means, of course, is that natural selection could not produce such machines gradually, one part at a time. They would be non-functional until all of their parts were assembled, and natural selection, which can only select functioning systems, would have nothing to work with. . . .

In Behe's view, this observation, in and of itself makes the case for design. If the biochemical machinery of the cell cannot be produced by natural selection, then there is only one reasonable alternative—design by an intelligent agent. . . .

If Behe's arguments have a familiar ring to them, they should. They mirror the classic "Argument from Design," articulated so well by William Paley nearly 200 years ago in his book *Natural Theology*. Darwin was well aware of the argument . . ., Darwin's answer, in essence, was that evolution produces complex organs in a series of fully functional intermediate stages. If each of the intermediate stages can be favored by natural selection, then so can the whole pathway. . . .

Getting to the Heart of the Matter

To fully explore the scientific basis of the biochemical argument from design, we should investigate the details of some of the very structures used in Behe's book as examples of irreducibly complex systems. One of these is the eukaryotic cilium, an intricate whip-like structure that produces movement in cells as diverse as green algae and human sperm. . . .

Remember Behe's statement that the removal of any one of the parts of an irreducibly complex system effectively causes the system to stop working? The cilium provides us with a perfect opportunity to test that assertion. If it is correct, then we should be unable to find examples of functional cilia anywhere in nature that lack the cilium's basic parts. Unfortunately for the argument, that is not the case. Nature presents many examples of fully functional cilia that are missing key parts. One of the most compelling is the eel sperm flagellum, which lacks at least three important parts normally found in the cilium. . . .

The key element of Behe's claim was that "any precursor to an irreducibly complex system that is missing a part is by definition nonfunctional." But the individual parts of the cilium, including tubulin, the motor protein dynein, and the contractile protein actin, are fully functional elsewhere in the cell. What this means, of course, is that a selectable function exists for each of the major parts of the cilium, and therefore that the argument is wrong. . . .

*Kenneth R. Miller, "Answering the Biochemical Argument from Design," in Neil Manson, ed., *God and Design* (New York: Routledge Press, 2003) pp. 291–306.

Disproving Design

. . .

As we have seen, these facts demonstrate that the one system most widely cited as the premier example of irreducible complexity contains individual parts that have selectable functions. What this means, in scientific terms, is that the hypothesis of irreducible complexity is falsified. . . .

Caught in the Mousetrap

Why does the biochemical argument from design collapse so quickly upon close inspection? I would suggest that this is because the logic of the argument itself is flawed. Consider, for example, the mechanical mousetrap as an analogy of irreducibly complex systems. Behe has written that a mousetrap does not work if even one of its five parts is removed. However, with a little ingenuity, it turns out to be remarkably easy to construct a working mousetrap *after* removing one of its parts, leaving just four. . . .

. . . It is possible, in fact, to imagine a host of uses for parts of the "irreducibly complex" mousetrap.

The meaning of this should be clear. If portions of a supposedly irreducibly complex mechanical structure are fully functional in different contexts, then the central claim built upon this concept is incorrect. . . . Natural selection could indeed produce elements of a biochemical machine for different purposes. The mousetrap example provides, unintentionally, a perfect analogy for the way in which natural selection builds complex structures. . . .

What Is the "Evidence" for Design?

What follows is the logical chain of reasoning leading from the observation of biochemical complexity to the conclusion of intelligent design.

1. *Observation:* the cell contains biochemical machines in which the loss of a single component may abolish function. *Definition:* such machines are therefore said to be "irreducibly complex."

2. *Assertion:* any irreducibly complex structure that is missing a part is by definition non-functional, leaving natural selection with nothing to select for.

3. *Conclusion:* therefore, irreducibly complex structures could not have been produced by natural selection.

4. *Secondary conclusion:* therefore, such structures must have been produced by another mechanism. Since the only credible alternate mechanism is intelligent design, the very existence of such structures must be evidence of intelligent design.

When the reasoning behind the biochemical argument from design is laid out in this way, it becomes easy to spot the logical flaw in the argument. The first statement is true—the cell does indeed contain any number of complex molecular machines in which the loss of a single part may affect function. However, the second statement, the assertion of non-functionality, is demonstrably false. As we have seen, the individual parts of many such machines do indeed have well-defined functions within the cell. Once this is realized, the logic of the argument collapses. If the assertion in the second statement is shown to be false, the chain of reasoning is broken and both conclusions are falsified.

The cell does not contain biochemical evidence of design.

References

Behe, M. (1996a) *Darwin's Black Box*, New York: The Free Press.

REVIEW QUESTIONS

1. How is the "revolutionary character" of science relevant to Behe's challenge of Darwin?

2. What does Miller mean when he says that Behe's argument mirrors the classic "Argument from Design"?

3. According to Miller, what are the two principle claims of ID?

4. According to Miller, what evidence disproves the argument of irreducible complexity?

5. How does Miller summarize the chain of reasoning from the observation of biochemical complexities to the conclusion that they are evidence of an intelligent designer, and what is his analysis of the reasoning?

THiNK
AND DISCUSS

PERSPECTIVES ON EVOLUTION VERSUS INTELLIGENT DESIGN

1. Using the criteria for evaluating an analogy in an inductive argument listed in Chapter 7, pages 217–218, evaluate the mousetrap analogy used by Behe. Discuss whether the analogy supports his conclusion regarding irreducible complexity in biology and the existence of an intelligent designer.

2. Was Miller successful in disproving ID and irreducible complexity? Evaluate his argument. Discuss how effective Behe's counterarguments were in responding to Miller's criticisms.

3. Evaluate both the theory of evolution and the theory of intelligent design using the criteria for evaluating a hypothesis listed on page 377. Discuss what evidence or experimental findings might falsify the ID theory/hypothesis. Discuss what evidence or experimental findings might falsify the theory of evolution by natural selection.

4. Former President George W. Bush endorsed the teaching of ID alongside evolution, stating, "Both sides ought to be properly taught so people can understand what the debate is all about." Author and physicist Robert Ehrlich disagrees. He writes that "to require intelligent design to be taught alongside evolution makes as little sense as requiring flat-Earth theory to be taught in science courses, so that students 'can make up their own minds' whether the Earth is round or flat." Discuss whether access to all sides of an argument, even ones that may be mistaken, is important in developing students' critical-thinking skills in science.

13

LAW &
POLITICS

What point do you think the demonstrators are trying to make? Why is it important to understand how the legal and political system work in order to be effective citizens in a democracy?

Illegal immigration has become one of the central issues in American politics. An illegal or unauthorized immigrant is a person who has entered the United States without government permission or who has stayed beyond the termination date of their visa. According to the Pew Hispanic Research Center, there are 11 million unauthorized immigrants living in the United States. The majority of these immigrants are from Mexico and Central America.[1] According to the U.S. Border Patrol, about 2,000 people have died trying to cross the hostile dessert that forms the border between the United States and Mexico. How should the U.S., as a democracy and one of the wealthiest countries in the world, respond to the influx of undocumented immigrants into the country, many at the risk of their own lives? What is a country's moral obligation to the people of the world who live in poverty and how should responsibility for this be legislated?

THiNK FIRST

- What are the two main types of democracy?
- What are the three branches of government?
- How can citizens get involved in the government process in the United States?

>> According to an April 2013 Gallup Poll, two-thirds of Americans favor a law that "would allow illegal immigrants living in the United States the chance to become permanent legal residents if they meet certain requirements." Support is particularly high for those brought to this country as children. Studies have found that children of unauthorized immigrants are at risk of lower educational performance, have limited opportunities for economic mobility, and find themselves "perpetual outsiders."[2] Opponents of granting legal status to undocumented immigrants argue that this will only encourage illegal immigration.

The Development, Relief and Education for Alien Minors Act (called the DREAM Act) is a legislative proposal first introduced in 2001 that provides conditional permanent residency to illegal aliens who came to the U.S. as minors and who meet certain qualifications. In 2012, following failed attempts to pass the DREAM Act, President Obama signed a memo called the Deferred Action for Childhood Arrivals (DACA). This program gives legal status, though not a direct path to citizenship, to the 250,000 young people under the age of 31 who were brought to the United States illegally before the age of 16. So far more than 99 percent of the applications for legal status have been approved by the U.S. government.

What is the process by which bills, such as the DREAM Act, get enacted into law? What happens if a law violates a citizen's civil liberties or the rights and welfare of undocumented immigrants? How can we, as citizens living in a democracy, use our critical-thinking skills to evaluate public policy and to positively influence the political process? In this chapter we will address some of these questions. Specifically, we will

- Learn about the social contract theory of government and the concept of sovereignty
- Study the development of U.S. democracy

- Critically evaluate the different types of democracy and their justifications
- Identify and discuss the rights and obligations of citizens in a democracy
- Examine the election process and whether we have a duty to vote
- Learn about the three branches of government—executive, legislative, and judicial
- Learn about the process of making a law and how citizens can participate in the process
- Study the relationship between law and morality
- Examine the use of and logical foundation of rules of evidence and legal precedence in the court system

THE SOCIAL CONTRACT THEORY OF GOVERNMENT

Why should we obey laws? Indeed, why have government and laws in the first place? Shouldn't we be free to make our own decisions? Doesn't government, by imposing constraints and laws on us, compromise our autonomy as critical thinkers and our ability to make rational decisions about our lives?

The State of Nature

Most political theorists would answer no to the last two questions. They argue that people are better off living under a government than without a government—a condition referred to as a **state of nature**.[3] Although a state of nature may sound like the ideal condition for exercising our freedoms, without a government the strongest people would be able to impose their will on others.

In the state of nature we would live a life, to use the words of English political philosopher Thomas Hobbes (1588–1679), where there is "continual fear, and danger of violent death; and the life of man, solitary, poor, nasty, brutish and short . . . a constant war of every man with every man."[4] Under such conditions, our everyday decisions would be based primarily on the fallacy of appeal to force or scare tactics rather on than rational discussion and argumentation.

Social Contract Theory

The ideas of English philosopher John Locke (1632–1704) greatly influenced the development of the American government. According to Locke, the primary purpose of forming a government is to protect us in our exercise of our natural rights.[5] Without government, our right to freedom of speech and the right to openly debate controversial ideas, which is so important to critical thinking, would be at grave risk.

Locke thought that our natural rights would best be protected by a government that recognizes the existence of a **social contract**: a voluntary and generally implicit, unanimous agreement among the people in a society to unite as a political community and to obey the laws enacted by the government they select. Under social contract theory people accept the government's **sovereignty**—its exclusive right to exercise political authority—only so long as the government actually protects the people from harm and does not abuse them. A social contract must be mutually beneficial to both citizens and the government; otherwise, there would be no point in our giving up our life in a state of nature to live in a civil society. The United

Connections

What is a liberty right and how does government protect these rights? *See Chapter 9, p. 287.*

How would a cultural relativist view social contract theory? *See Chapter 9, pp. 279–280.*

state of nature The condition in which people lived prior to the formation of a social contract.

social contract A voluntary agreement among the people to unite as a political community.

sovereignty The exclusive right of government to exercise political power.

Thomas Hobbes (1588–1679). Hobbes believed that in a state of nature without government, life would be nasty, brutish, and short.

John Locke (1632–1704). Locke's political philosophy influenced the development of American government.

States Constitution, which was written under the influence of Locke's ideas, is an example of a written social contract. Its Preamble states:

> We the People of the United States, in Order to form a more perfect Union, establish Justice, insure domestic Tranquility, provide for the common defense, promote the general Welfare, and secure the Blessings of Liberty to ourselves and our Posterity, do ordain and establish this Constitution for the United States of America.

Locke argued that the act of remaining in a country and enjoying its benefits constitutes **tacit consent** to abide by the social contract and laws of the country. However, when he put forward his concept of tacit consent, there were still unclaimed areas of the world (at least from the point of view of the Europeans) such as the Americas, where people could move to if they disagreed with or rejected their government. Without this option, tacit consent today no longer has the voluntary quality that it did when Locke was writing. Many of us lack the resources to pick up and move to another country, or we may not qualify for immigration status in the country of our choice. In this latter case, since people naturally want the best for themselves and their family, they may opt to illegally immigrate to another country, which raises a whole new set of issues regarding the limits of national sovereignty and the rights of individuals.

tacit consent The implicit agreement to abide by the laws of a country by remaining there.

Hot or Not?

Why should we obey the laws of our country?

International Law

Today the world is divided into sovereign nations, each with a defined territory. Individuals who disagree with their government cannot opt to be world citizens, since there is no world government. Although there is a body of law known as international law, which includes the Geneva Conventions and the United Nations Universal Declaration of Human Rights, international law regulates relations between nations rather than between individuals. The use of military drones has raised the question of whether drones, which sometimes unintentionally kill civilians, violate the Geneva Conventions. See Critical Thinking Issue: "Perspectives on the Use of Drones in Warfare" at the end of this chapter.

In addition, international law presents a dilemma because it conflicts with the concept of absolute national sovereignty. The current United Nations is not a world government but a collection of independent, sovereign nations. Therefore, international laws are not strictly laws in the sense of those issued by the legislatures of sovereign nations. Because the United Nations lacks sovereign power over its member nations, it has no legitimate power to enforce international law and treaties.

Although compliance with international law is voluntary in the absence of a world government with sovereign power, there are consequences for ignoring it. The force of international law usually comes not from logical argumentation but from pressure by stronger nations that find it in their interest to enforce the law. If a nation refuses to comply, it can face economic disincentives, threats, sanctions, or even war by the more powerful nations. In other words, as long as nations retain absolute sovereign power, the nations of the world essentially live in a Hobbesian state of nature, with the more powerful being able to impose their will on weaker nations.

EXERCISE 13-1

STOP AND ASSESS YOURSELF

1. Imagine a scenario, such as that on the television show *Lost* or in William Golding's novel *Lord of the Flies,* in which people are living without government and laws. Discuss whether the people in this situation would be better off with or without a government.

2. Analyze the concept of tacit consent. Present an argument addressing the question of whether or not tacit consent provides sufficient justification for why you are bound to obey the laws of this country.

3. Do people who are living in poverty have a moral right to seek a better life for their families by immigrating (if necessary, illegally) to a country where they and their families can enjoy a decent life? Referring to the discussion of moral rights and duties in Chapter 9, create an argument addressing these questions.

4. Globalization and the increasing economic dependency of nations on each other have made the formation of an international government even more of a critical issue. Is it time that individual nations considered relinquishing some of their sovereignty to a world government by expanding the power of the United Nations in exchange for the benefits and protection of such a government? Evaluate arguments both for and against a world government.

5. Discuss ways in which resistance and narrow-mindedness (see Chapter 1, pages 22 to 26), both on an individual and a national level, interfere with global security and world peace. Discuss also possible steps we might take for counteracting this type of thinking.

THE DEVELOPMENT OF DEMOCRACY IN THE UNITED STATES

In a democracy, the **legitimate authority** of the government comes from the people themselves. In return for the benefits and protection that the government provides, we have a duty to obey the laws because we entered into a voluntary contract—that is, we have given our tacit consent—to live under the government. In a democracy based on a social contract, it is particularly important for us as citizens to be well informed about the government and current issues. Most Americans, unfortunately, are not that knowledgeable about their government. In a 2006 survey, only 1 percent of Americans could name the five freedoms protected by the First Amendment (freedom of speech, religion, press, assembly, and petition), while 20 percent knew the names of the cartoon Simpson family members.[6]

In the following sections we'll be learning more about how our democracy works and how we as citizens can use our critical-thinking skills to influence the political process.

James Madison (1751–1836), was the fourth president of the United States. Unlike many of his elitist colleagues, he leaned more toward egalitarianism and listening to the voice of the people.

Representative Democracy: A Safeguard Against the Tyranny of the Majority

In a **direct democracy**, all the people directly make laws and govern themselves. In a **representative democracy**, such as the United States, the people turn over this authority to their elected representatives. The founders of the U.S. Constitution set up a representative democracy in part because the United States, with its 4 million people (including 1 million slaves) in the late 1780s, was too large for direct democracy. Another reason was the founders' belief that the general public is not in a position to make the best decisions when it comes to public policies and legislation. Not only are most people prone to errors in their thinking and fallacious reasoning but also many of us are misinformed or lack the necessary information to make important policy

Connections

How can being at the conventional stage of moral reasoning make us vulnerable to tyranny of the majority? *See Chapter 9, p. 274.*

legitimate authority In a democracy, the right to rule given to the government by the people.

direct democracy A type of democracy in which all of the people directly make laws and govern themselves.

representative democracy A form of democracy in which people turn over their authority to govern to their elected representatives.

decisions. Because of this, the majority could end up imposing on the country poorly-thought-out policies and

tyranny of the majority The majority impose their policies and laws on the political minorities.

populism A belief in the wisdom of the common people and in the equality of all people.

elitism A belief in the rule of "the best people."

liberal democracy A form of democracy emphasizing liberty of individuals.

federalism A system in which power is divided between the federal and state governments.

separation of powers A system in which three separate branches of government act as a check on one another.

laws that are detrimental to political minorities as well as to the greater good—a scenario known as the **tyranny of the majority**. To counter this, representative democracy entrusts day-to-day political judgments to representatives who are elected by the people because—at least ideally—of these representatives' ability to make rational, well-informed public policy decisions.

The fear of direct democracy and majority rule, coupled with the founding fathers' mistrust of the British monarchy and of any government with too much power, has contributed to two distinct and sometimes conflicting assumptions—populism and elitism. **Populism** is the belief in the wisdom and virtue of the common people and the belief in equality of all people. **Elitism**, in contrast, is rule by "the best people" in terms of socioeconomic class, sex, ethnic group, education, and (in the case of a monarchy) royal blood.

The U.S. Constitution was initially more elitist than it currently is. For many decades, the ideals of individual freedom and equality in the Constitution applied only to white males of European descent. American democracy has moved gradually from an elitist model to one of populist democracy with voting rights first being extended to adult males of any race and skin color, including former slaves, in 1870 and to women in 1920. In 1978, the Twenty-Sixth Amendment extended the right to vote to those age 18 and older.

Despite these changes, doublethink—in this case, a simultaneous belief in both elitism and populism—is still evident in modern politics. The belief that political office should be available to all people conflicts with the need for a candidate to have his or her own wealth to finance a run for high office. To use another example, the conscription laws of the Vietnam War era placed a greater burden on people who were poor and uneducated. About 60 percent of eligible men did not serve because they received legal exemptions or deferments because they were in college. Other young men, whose parents had political or other connections, received assignments to noncombat service in the United States, such as in the reserves of the

How can narrow-mindedness limit our ability to effectively participate in a representative democracy? *See Chapter 1, p. 24.*

Connections

various military branches. This led to outcries of unfairness and, eventually, to the end of the draft and the institution of an all-volunteer army in 1973.

Liberal Democracy: Protection of Individual Rights

Thomas Jefferson is credited with having said: "A democracy is nothing more than mob rule, where fifty-one percent of the people may take away the rights of the other forty-nine."[7] Because of fear of the tyranny of the majority, the Bill of Rights, or first ten amendments, was added to the Constitution to place certain rights beyond the reach of majority vote and popular opinion. Because of this, in addition to being a representative democracy, the United States is a **liberal democracy** in which the liberties of individuals, including the right to vote, freedom of religion, and freedom of speech, are protected.

To protect citizens from abuses of power by government, the authors of the Constitution built in checks against unlimited power. One of these checks is **federalism**. This is a system of government in which power is divided between a central authority—the federal government—and constituent state governments. Another check is the division of the federal government into three branches: the executive, the legislative, and the judicial. Each of the three branches of government is separate and has authority to act on its own, a principle known as **separation of powers**. To prevent the abuse of power by one branch of government, a system of checks and balances was put in place, giving each branch some power to block the others' actions. We'll be studying each of the three branches of government in greater depth later in this chapter.

Political Campaigns and Elections

Political campaigns and elections are an important aspect of representative democracy. Through campaigns, we learn about the people who want to represent us, and through elections, we can express our political choices. On the other hand, because elections are held so frequently in the United States, parties and candidates are more likely to focus on policies that bring short-term benefits to the electorate, such as cutting taxes. Long-term policies, such as eliminating poverty, tend to get ignored. As critical thinkers, our responsibility does not end with voting. We must insist that our representatives be held accountable for their decisions, and we need to be able to evaluate government policies critically and respond effectively to challenges such as poverty, global warming, job outsourcing, immigration, and terrorism.

During the 2012 presidential election, Barack Obama and Mitt Romney each spent more than a billion dollars on their respective campaigns, thus far outspending any previous presidential campaign. In presidential elections the effect of campaign spending is usually modest, except in

In 2012 Barack Obama ran on a platform of "Forward," thus taking advantage of people's fears that a Republican president would move America backward.

very close races. Ninety percent of the variation in the outcome of presidential campaigns is determined before the campaign actually begins, with party affiliation being one of the primary determinants of how a citizen votes.[8]

Although democracy allows citizens to participate in the political process through elections, political campaigns do not always guarantee that the best-qualified people will represent us. Political campaigns are very expensive—a factor that favors candidates who have huge personal fortunes or have won the backing of wealthy contributors, corporations, and interest groups. Campaign spending is a greater problem in congressional campaigns, where the level of spending is one of the primary factors in who wins the election.[9] The distribution of campaign funds in these races tends to be unequal. Incumbents—politicians already in office—generally receive a much larger share of contributions.[10] Candidates who challenge an incumbent usually have to rely heavily on their own personal resources, making a Senate seat feasible only for people who are wealthy or well connected.

Another factor that influences the outcome of an election is the media portrayal of a candidate's image, personal qualities, such as experience and integrity, and positions on controversial issues. For example, John F. Kennedy's standing in the 1960 presidential race was greatly bolstered by his charismatic presence in his television debates with Richard Nixon, akin to Obama's captivating speeches on the campaign trail in 2007 and 2008.

Beginning with the Kennedy–Nixon contest in 1960, the mass media have dramatically transformed political campaigning. Because of the need to appeal to a large number of viewers, the media, rather than informing citizens and critically analyzing important issues, tend to rely heavily on rhetorical devices and to reinforce positive or negative views of the candidates that people already have. To further compound the problem of confirmation bias, most people watch only those news shows and read only those newspapers that confirm their preexisting views of the candidates and parties.

The growing role of public opinion polls has also influenced the election process. Although some polls, such as the Gallup Poll, are reputable and unbiased, other polls word their survey questions to produce a desired result rather than accurately measure the views of those being polled. In addition, the availability of polling information makes it easier for candidates to shape their campaigns toward appealing to the majority and to avoid taking unpopular stands. Polling also influences how we vote, since people have a tendency to change their position to conform to that of the majority.

The Internet has the potential to dramatically change democracy by connecting parties, politicians, and citizens in a network of political activity. During the 2012 campaign Obama raised over 600 million dollars online, mostly from fundraising e-mails.

The Supreme Court of Delaware, in *John Doe v. Patrick Cahill* (2005), described the Internet as "a unique democratization medium unlike anything that has come before." The Internet permits people to express their opinions to thousands through blogs and message boards. Other blogs offer analyses of polling results. Statistician Nate Silver's FiveThirtyEight blog in the New York Times (http://fivethirtyeight.blogs.nytimes.com) analyzes polling results and ranks polling sites by their accuracy. Silver also supplies his own projections on the outcome of elections, so far with impressive accuracy. The Internet also opens up the possibility of direct voting on candidates and issues from our home or library. We have yet to see how extensively the Internet will transform elections and politics.[11]

Connections

What types of rhetorical devices are used by politicians? *See Chapter 3, p. 90.* Does the moral duty of fidelity create an obligation for us to vote? *See Chapter 9, p. 285.*

Voting: A Right or a Duty?

One of the primary ways we as citizens participate in a representative democracy is through voting. Despite the crucial role of voting, voter turnout in the United States is

One of the criticisms of election polls is that voters tend to swing toward the candidate who is ahead in the polls.

one of the lowest in the world. Compare the percentages shown here with some of the countries with the top voter turnouts—Vietnam (98.85 percent), Rwanda (98.5 percent), Equitorial Guinea (96.45 percent), Australia (95.17 percent), Italy (92.5 percent), Bahamas (92.13 percent) and Belgium (91.08 percent).

In the United States responsibility for voting is left up to the individual. The high value placed on personal freedom and liberty rights in American democracy rests on the belief that citizens should be allowed to engage voluntarily in economic and political activities, including voting, without interference from government regulations. In contrast, in some democracies such as Australia, Belgium, and Luxemburg, voting in national elections is mandatory, and thus voter turnout is very high.

Some people who favor mandatory voting question whether our system of voluntary voting in the United States skews our elections toward elitism because of the high positive correlation between voter turnout and educational level and socioeconomic class. Those who don't vote are disproportionately younger people, the economically disadvantaged, people with less formal education, and members of certain ethnic and minority groups. In addition, only 28 percent of Hispanic citizens voted. Turnout in the 2008 presidential election was the highest in at least twenty years, in part because of the higher turnout of young, Hispanic, and African-American voters who voted overwhelmingly for Barack Obama. Nevertheless, the youth vote was still lower than that of older voters, with only about 51 percent of eligible people under the age of 30 voting in

the election. Opponents of mandatory voting argue that citizens should not be forced to exercise their rights. Forcing people to vote who are not motivated or informed or who do not have the necessary critical-thinking skills for evaluating the various candidates and issues would not contribute to the election of the best-qualified representatives.

As responsible citizens, we need to remain open-minded when making a decision on how we will vote. The information we gather should be accurate and unbiased. We should be alert to faulty reasoning, including fallacies and rhetorical devices, used in political campaigns. We also need to keep in mind that when it comes to stating positions on controversial issues, candidates have a strong incentive, if they want to get elected, to outwardly adopt a position that will appeal to as many voters as possible or to be vague or ambiguous about their position to avoid offending potential supporters.

In summary, according to social-contract theory, the legitimate authority of a government comes from the people. Over the past two centuries, the United States has moved from being an elitist democracy to one based more on populism, or government by the people. Although the Constitution, our social contract, imposes duties on the government to protect individual rights and the social good, we as citizens have an obligation to obey laws and vote in elections. Even failure to vote or to engage in public discussions on critical issues is a form of participation in that it supports the status quo or the most vocal and powerful group.

Year Voted	Percent of Total Population
2012	57.5*
2010	45.2
2008	58.2
2006	43.6
2004	58.3
2002	42.3
2000	54.7
1998	41.9
1996	54.2
1994	45.0
1992	61.3
1990	45.0
1988	57.4
1986	46.0
1984	59.9
1982	48.5
1980	59.3
1978	45.9
1976	59.2
1974	44.7
1972	63.0
1970	54.6
1968	67.8
1966	55.4
1964	69.3

Sources: U.S. Census Bureau, IDEA International, http://www.idea.int/vt/viewdata.cfm
*http://www.abc15.com/dpp/news/national/election-results-2012-voter-turnout-lower-than-2008-and-2004-report-says.

Reported Voting in the United States: 1964 to 2012

As responsible citizens, we need to remain open-minded when making a decision on how we will vote.

Did You Know

You can go to http://www.usa.gov/Citizen/Topics/Voting/Register.shtml to learn how and where to register to vote.

STOP AND ASSESS YOURSELF

1. In his book *The Wisdom of Crowds*, James Surowiecki notes that when we calculate the average answer of a large group of people—who are each unaware of the answers the others are giving—the average answer is generally very accurate when it comes to solving cognitive problems, such as guessing how much an ox weighs or how many jelly beans are in a jar. Given this, he asks whether the "wisdom of crowds" would prevail in creating solutions for problems of the type we find in the democratic process.[12] In particular, can voters be trusted to elect the candidates who will make the best decisions? Discuss how, if at all, the voting process would have to be changed to take advantage of the "wisdom of crowds."

2. The use of public opinion polls to influence policy decisions, where everyone's judgment is considered equally valid whether or not they are an expert, is an example of one of the pitfalls of democracy. Should we put restrictions on the use of polling, or should we give greater weight to the answers of experts? Present an argument to support your answer.

3. Why is voter turnout lower in the United States than in most democracies? Should voting in federal elections be mandatory? Should voting be held on weekends, as it is in most of Europe? Discuss reforms you could make or legislation you might pass to improve voter turnout, particularly among young people.

4. Because of the tendency to go along with the majority, some people question the wisdom of publishing preelection polls, since they have the effect of swaying the electorate in favor of the leading candidate. Should preelection polls be banned? Develop an argument addressing the issue of whether or not preelection polls should be restricted or banned.

5. To become an American citizen, an immigrant must first pass a test on the history and principles of the U.S. government. Discuss whether passing this test should be a requirement for native-born citizens to be eligible to vote. Relate your answer to the importance of critical-thinking skills for effective participation in democracy.

6. Make a list of ways in which the Internet has made direct democracy possible for the first time in this country's history. Discuss the advantages and disadvantages of moving in the direction of a direct democracy. Present your analysis in the form of an argument.

7. If eligible, did you vote in the last federal, state, and/or local elections? Why or why not? To what extent did polls influence your voting decisions? Relate your answer to your critical-thinking skills.

THE EXECUTIVE BRANCH OF GOVERNMENT

In the United States, the executive branch of the federal government is headed by the president, who is the head of state and the highest government official in the country. In addition to the president and his White House staff, the executive branch of the federal government includes the agencies that carry out much of the work of government.

The Role of the Executive Branch

The executive branch is made up of the president's executive staff, a cabinet, and fifteen executive departments, including the Department of Defense and the Department of Education. The cabinet consists of the vice president and the fifteen department heads. The nominal purpose of the cabinet is to advise the president, although today their primary purpose is running their departments. The executive branch administers government departments and public services, conducts foreign affairs, commands the armed forces, and, with the approval of the Senate, appoints federal judges (including Supreme Court justices), ambassadors, and other high-level government officials. The executive branch is also charged with enforcing or executing the law through the administration of prisons, the police force, and the prosecution of criminals in the name of the state.

Executive Orders and National Security

The executive branch of government traditionally has more power in times of war. For this reason, it is especially important during a national crisis or war that we use our critical-thinking skills in evaluating government policy and directives, rather than simply conforming to what the authorities say. During the Civil War, President Lincoln suspended

President Obama signing an executive order on February 2013 designed to improve the cybersecurity of the country's critical infrastructure.

habeas corpus (a procedure that serves as a protection against being detained or imprisoned illegally). President Woodrow Wilson jailed Socialist and former presidential candidate Eugene V. Debs for protesting the entry into World War I. And, during World War II, Franklin D. Roosevelt had Japanese Americans sent to internment camps (see "Analyzing Images: Japanese American Internment Camps and Executive Order 9066"). These policies, which might or might not have been justified, were all put in place with little protest from citizens. As a check on executive power, Congress passed the Non-Detention Act in 1971, which states that "no citizen shall be imprisoned or otherwise detained by the United States except pursuant to an Act of Congress."

The George W. Bush administration exercised executive privilege to detain enemy combatants indefinitely and to deny them access to lawyers or courts. The former Bush administration also expanded its interrogation techniques to include torture and the wiretapping and reading of e-mails of U.S. citizens without first getting court-approved warrants. Some of these actions are in violation of federal law and in some cases international law, and—say critics—some appear to overstep constitutional guarantees against "unreasonable" search and seizure. Bush justified these actions on the grounds that our nation faces the continuing

threat of terrorism and that these activities are necessary to protect national security and effectively fight the war on terror. Opponents argue that Bush exceeded his executive power. In 2009, President Obama issued an executive order revoking the use of enhanced interrogation techniques and ensuring lawful interrogations for terrorist suspects.

Checks on Executive Power

The danger of executive power is that it can be taken too far, to the point where the violations of individual rights exceed the requirements of national security. The legislature serves as one of the primary checks against excesses of executive power. Congress has to approve any declarations of war (although Congress has not been asked to issue a declaration of war since World War II).* In addition, Congress can withhold funding from particular programs it wishes to check and can pass legislation to limit executive power if it feels

*The Korean War (1950–1953) was a United Nations "police action," and the Vietnam War was fought under the Gulf of Tonkin Resolution. In the case of the recent war in Iraq, Congress authorized the use of force rather than issuing an actual declaration of war.

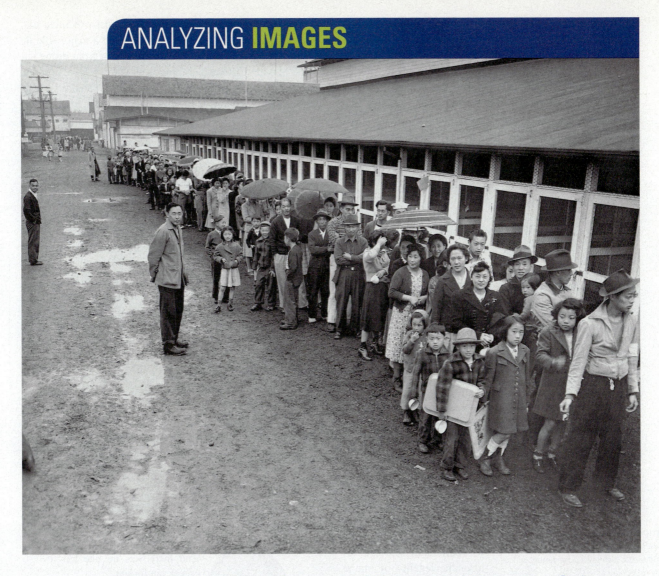

Japanese American Internment Camps and Executive Order

9066 On December 7, 1941, during World War II, the Japanese bombed the U.S. military base at Pearl Harbor in Hawaii. Within days, the United States declared war against Japan, Germany, and Italy. On February 19, 1942, President Franklin D. Roosevelt issued Executive Order 9066, declaring that no one of Japanese ancestry could live on the West Coast of the United States.

As a result of this executive order, about 120,000 Japanese American families were forced to give up their jobs, homes, and most of their belongings and were sent to internment camps such as the one in this photo at the Tanforan Assembly Center in San Bruno, California. Some internees spent several years in the camps, behind barbed-wire fences, surrounded by armed guards, and under minimally adequate living conditions. Protests against the internment policy were unsuccessful. In *Korematsu v. the United States* (1944), which contested the government's authority to intern people on the basis of their ancestry, the U.S. Supreme Court sided with the federal government

In 1988 President Ronald Reagan signed the Civil Liberties Act, which provided a presidential apology and reparation in the form of a payment of $20,000 apiece to internees and other American citizens of Japanese descent who lost their liberty and property as a result of Executive Order 9066.

DISCUSSION QUESTIONS

1. *Using your moral reasoning skills from Chapter 9, discuss whether Executive Order 9066 was morally justified.*

2. *Construct an argument addressing the question of whether there should have been reparations to those affected by the order and, if so, whether the reparation was adequate.*

that the executive branch is overstepping its powers. For example, the Freedom of Information Act (FOIA) was passed by Congress to protect citizens' access to government information. There are several exemptions in the FOIA, however, including unlimited presidential power to withhold information affecting national security. This exemption has been particularly frustrating to members of the press who feel it interferes with their mandate to keep the public well informed. Despite President Obama's call for transparency in government, the Obama administration has invoked these exemptions on more than 70,000 occasions in response to requests to release information to the public.[13]

The final recourse of the legislative branch against abuse of executive power is **impeachment**, the process by

---

> ## "The very core of liberty secured by our Anglo-Saxon system of separated powers has been freedom from indefinite imprisonment at the will of the Executive."

---

which the House of Representatives formally brings charges against a high-level government official and the Senate puts the official on trial and, if it convicts, removes him or her from office.

The judicial branch also has the power to limit or challenge executive power. Several cases came before federal courts challenging former President George W. Bush's detainment of citizens without the benefit of habeas corpus, particularly the right to have the legality of one's detention assessed by a court. Bush argued that these detainees are not ordinary criminals but "enemy combatants," a term adopted for the purpose of detaining terrorist suspects so that they fall outside the protection of the Non-Detention Act. The Supreme Court disagreed, affirming the right of citizen "enemy combatants" to legal counsel and a court hearing in *Hamdi v. Rumsfeld* (2004). In this ruling, Justice Antonin Scalia wrote: "The very core of liberty secured by our Anglo-Saxon system of separated powers has been freedom from indefinite imprisonment at the will of the Executive." In line with this ruling, President Obama favored trying terrorist suspects in federal rather than military courts. He also opposed indefinite imprisonment and was initially working toward closing the prison at Guantanamo Bay Naval Base. However, he has since signed the Defense Authorization Act, which allows terrorist suspects to be held indefinitely. This legislation raises the possibility of the military sending terrorists who are U.S. citizens to Guantanamo Bay. As of April 2013, there are still more than 160 detainees being held at Guantanamo Bay.

impeachment The process by which Congress brings charges against and tries a high-level government official for misconduct.

The media also acts as a check against executive excesses. For example, the media has played a major role in calling attention to civilian deaths resulting from drone attacks. See the Critical Thinking Issue "Perspectives on the Use of Drones in Warfare." For this reason, freedom of the press is one of the most carefully guarded rights in a democracy. Indeed, the press has been called the fourth branch of government because of its critical role as a watchdog against government corruption and abuse of power. Large newspapers such as the *New York Times*, the *Los Angeles Times*, the *Wall Street Journal*, and the *Washington Post*—the latter, for example, exposed the Watergate scandal during the Nixon era (1969–1974)—have been particularly significant in keeping us informed about government doings and misdoings and in presenting carefully researched arguments for or against particular policies and decisions.

Finally, we, the citizens, act as an important check against abuse of power. Martin Niemoeller, one of the Protestant leaders in Germany who defied the nation's Nazi rulers, once said:

First they came for the communists, and I did not speak out—

because I was not a communist;

Then they came for the socialists, and I did not speak out—

because I was not a socialist;

Then they came for the trade unionists, and I did not speak out—

because I was not a trade unionist;

Then they came for the Jews, and I did not speak out—because I was not a Jew;

Then they came for me—

And there was no one left to speak out for me.

The transformation of German democracy into a dictatorship in the 1930s happened in part because people did not speak out loudly enough against abuses by an unscrupulous few, including Adolf Hitler before his rise to power. As critical thinkers, we need to be vigilant and well informed; we also need to be willing to protest to our representatives or write to the media if we have good reasons to support our claim that executive power, or the power of any other government branch, is being misused.

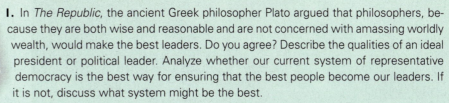

STOP AND ASSESS YOURSELF

1. In *The Republic*, the ancient Greek philosopher Plato argued that philosophers, because they are both wise and reasonable and are not concerned with amassing worldly wealth, would make the best leaders. Do you agree? Describe the qualities of an ideal president or political leader. Analyze whether our current system of representative democracy is the best way for ensuring that the best people become our leaders. If it is not, discuss what system might be the best.

2. Franklin D. Roosevelt was a very popular president who was elected for four terms. In 1951, the Twenty-Second Amendment to the U.S. Constitution limited a president to two elected terms of office. Discuss whether the Twenty-Second Amendment is desirable for our democracy.

3. Benjamin Franklin once said, "Those who would sacrifice liberty for security deserve neither." What do you think Franklin meant by this? Discuss, as if you were an adviser to the president, what criteria you would use in coming up with balance between the need for security and citizens' liberty rights in the current "war on terrorism."

4. Opponents of conscription (the military draft) argue that it is an infringement on individuals' liberty rights. Those who favor conscription, on the other hand, regard military service as a responsibility incurred because of our membership in a democratic political community. Although conscription may restrict our liberties, they argue that this is offset by the necessity in times of crisis to go to war to protect these liberties and our national security. Using a conscripted army to fight an unpopular war, supporters point out, thus acts as a check against an overzealous executive branch. Discuss these particular arguments for and against conscription.

5. In his 1935 novel *It Can't Happen Here*, American writer Sinclair Lewis asked whether an ambitious and unscrupulous politician could use a U.S. presidential election to make himself a dictator as Hitler did in Germany in 1933. Discuss how you would answer Lewis's question.

6. Find examples of the news media acting as a check on presidential power. Share your examples with the class.

7. Citizens are one of the most important checks against abuse of power by the government. Think of an executive policy that you feel strongly about. It could be a presidential policy, a state executive office issue, or a policy developed by one of the fifteen departments of the executive branch. Research the policy and write a one-page letter presenting a logical argument supporting your position. Send or e-mail the letter to the appropriate government official.

THE LEGISLATIVE BRANCH OF GOVERNMENT

In a democracy we have what is known as the **rule of law**, in which government authority must be exercised in accordance with written laws that have been established through proper procedures. The rule of law protects citizens from the **rule of men**, where members of the ruling class can make arbitrary laws and rules for individual cases.

The Role of the Legislative Branch

In the United States, Article I of the Constitution created the federal government's legislative branch, Congress, and gave it the power to make laws. Congress consists of two houses: the Senate and the House of Representatives.

During each two-year session of Congress, thousands of bills are introduced. Of these, fewer than 500 will eventually become laws. It can take several years or only a few days for a bill to become a law. The USA Patriot Act was introduced to the House of Representatives on October 23, 2001, and passed through both houses of Congress in only two days with little dissent. In contrast, it took several years for the civil rights legislation of the 1960s to pass, as well as many years to abolish slavery and to enact legislation giving women the right to vote. Most laws are permanent, unless they are overturned by the Supreme Court or changed by Congress. Others, such as the USA Patriot Act and the Endangered Species Act, are valid only for a specified time, and thus Congress has the options of renewing or modifying them or allowing them to lapse.

> **rule of law** The idea that governmental authority must be exercised in accordance with established written laws.
>
> **rule of men** A system in which members of the ruling class can make arbitrary laws and rules.

Congress, the legislative branch of government, enacts laws and acts as a check on executive power.

interest groups have paid lobbyists to promote their interests. As of 2012 there are about 12,500 registered lobbyists in Washington—that is, more than 20 lobbyists for each legislator in Congress. In addition, it is estimated that there may be up to seven times as many unregistered lobbyists for grass-root initiatives.[14]

Since the civil rights movement of the 1960s, there has been a huge increase in the number of public-interest groups and single-issue advocacy groups. Two of the most influential public-interest groups are Common Cause, which lobbies for a wide range of causes including improved government ethics and government reform, and Public Citizen, a collection of advocacy groups headed by Ralph Nader that lobby for a variety of causes including consumer safety, the environment, and regulatory reform. The Center on Conscience & War, in contrast, is a single-issue advocacy group that focuses its lobbying efforts on expanding legal protection for conscientious objectors and protesting proposed bills such as the Universal National Service Act, which would require that all residents in the United States between ages 18 and 42 carry out national service for a period of two years.

Lobbying is protected under the First Amendment, which states that "Congress shall make no law . . . prohibiting the free exercise thereof; or abridging the freedom . . . to petition the Government for a redress of grievances." The framers of the Constitution believed that lobbying by public and private interest groups encourages full competition among interest groups. Lobbying also benefits the political system by providing information and expertise on particular issues and bills, by explaining difficult subjects in understandable language, and by speaking for various economic, business, and citizen interests.

Critics of lobbying argue that lobbying groups, especially those financed by large corporations and business interests, such as the tobacco, pharmaceutical, and petroleum industries, exert undue influence over government. This becomes particularly a problem when these lobbying groups, rather than relying on rational arguments and credible evidence to make their points, also try to influence legislators by giving gifts, providing entertainment, and making campaign contributions to candidates and parties.

Citzens groups can also have a profound influence on government policy. The Tea Party Movement, a

Citizens and Legislation

Despite barriers to direct participation in the lawmaking process, there are several ways in which we as citizens can participate in the legislative process.

Lobbying is the practice of private advocacy to influence the government by promoting a point of view that benefits an individual or an organization's goals. Most lobbying in the United States is done by interest groups. Major corporations, trade associations, unions, advocacy groups, and political

lobbying The practice of private advocacy to influence the government.

Top Five Spenders on Lobbying 2012*

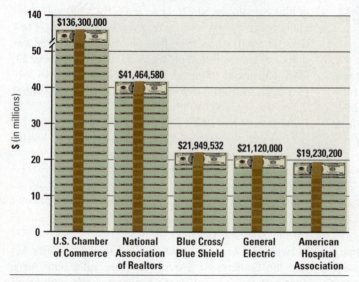

*Statistics from the Senate Office of Public Records; compiled by the Center for Responsive Politics at www.Opensecrets.org

Protesters from the group Grandmothers Against the War protesting in New York City in April 2013 against the government's use of drones.

grassroots conservative citizen movement, emerged shortly after the election of President Barack Obama and quickly took root across the nation. The Tea Party Movement staged rallies across the country against big government, high taxation, government-run health care, the growing cost of entitlements, and bailouts for large corporations.

Anti-war protests, while not as common as they were during the Vietnam War period, have been held to try to get the government to change their policy on war and the use of unmanned drones. According to the Gallup Polls, people over 65 in the United States are significantly more likely to be anti-war than are younger people.

As individual citizens we can influence the legislative process by contacting our legislators regarding a particular bill or an issue. If you are not sure who your members of Congress are, go to http://www.govtrack.us/congress/members and type in your zip code. The page has direct e-mail links to your two senators and your representative and also allows you to monitor their legislative activities. The Web site http://www.congress.org provides information on your legislators, assists you in registering to vote, posts action alerts regarding legislation, and forwards your e-mail to your legislators.

The Legislative Information System Web sites (http://www.senate.gov and http://www.house.gov) contain up-to-date information on all the bills pending in each chamber of Congress. Because there are so many bills under consideration at one time, it is generally most efficient to focus on an area of public policy that is of interest to you. For names of federal and state agencies associated with the issues that interest you, the best place to start is http://www.firstgov.gov.

initiatives Laws or constitutional amendments proposed by citizens.

If there is a particular issue that interests you, you can also join a citizen advocacy or watchdog organization, such as Amnesty International USA, or the National Rifle Association, that tracks legislation regarding particular issues. This approach has the advantage of having a reputable citizens group doing the research on pending bills for you and keeping you up-to-date. Most of these organizations will also let you know, generally through an e-mail list, when it is important for you to contact your legislators regarding a relevant bill.

Putting together an effective argument requires good analytical skills and open-minded skepticism as well as knowledge of the legislative process. Obviously, the sounder and more cogent your argument and the more complete your research, the more likely you are to get a positive response.

About half of the states have initiative and referendum laws that allow citizens to directly vote on issues. **Initiatives** include laws or constitutional amendments

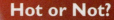

Hot or Not?

Do lobbyists undermine the basic principles and goals of democracy?

referenda Laws or constitutional amendments put on the ballot by state legislators.

libertarian A person who opposes any government restraints on individual freedom.

proposed by citizens. Writing an initiative requires a lot of research and getting feedback from experts and constituents who will be affected by the initiative. This process also requires collecting enough signatures on a petition to have the initiative added to the ballot. **Referenda** are similar to initiatives, but they are put on the ballot by state legislators.

Some people applaud initiatives and referenda because they are forms of direct democracy, but opponents argue that they are subject to the whims of the majority—the fallacy of popular appeal—rather than the reasoned judgment of more informed representatives. For example, some people believe that initiatives such as California's Proposition 98, which requires the state spend 40 percent of its budget on public schools at the expense of other state-run programs such as higher education and the courts, has contributed to the current fiscal crisis faced by the state.

Another criticism is that the availability of only two options—yes or no—on initiatives and referenda dealing with complex issues creates a false dilemma for the voter. Still another objection is that today enormous amounts of money are needed to wage an initiative or referendum campaign allowing major interest groups and large corporations to dominate the process.

If you like hands-on experience and want a chance to hone your critical-thinking skills, there are many opportunities for college students to serve as interns in a government department or to do volunteer work with a political campaign or a lobbying or public-interest group. For example, each semester about 400 students from around the country participate in the Washington Semester Program. This internship involves spending a semester in Washington, D.C., and participating in a full-credit program offered through American University (or more information, go to http://www.american.edu/spexs/washingtonsemester). State and local governments also offer internships in locations such as the governor's

Connections

Why are critical-thinking skills essential in a democracy? *See Chapter 1, pp. 18–21.* How can being aware of narrow-mindedness in ourselves and others make us more effective citizens? *See Chapter 1, pp. 24–25.*

office, state legislature, city government, and the public defender's office.

Unjust Laws and Civil Disobedience

Although there is a difference between "moral laws" and "legal laws," in a democracy we expect that laws should be just and not violate universal moral principles. Some laws—such as which side of the street to drive on or the deadline for filing income tax returns—have little to do with morality.

Behaviors that are immoral because of the harm they cause others are generally considered the province of criminal law. The primary purpose of criminal law is to make offenses against morality—such as murder, rape, stealing, extortion, and blackmail—illegal. However, behaviors that are harmful to ourselves, such as smoking cigarettes, personally using (but not selling) marijuana, and motorcycling without a helmet are in a morally gray area.

Libertarians are those who oppose any government restrains on individual freedom. They argue that we have a liberty right to engage in activities that might harm us as long as doing so doesn't harm others. Critics of libertarianism respond that in society there is no such thing as an individual action that does not affect others. For example, if we ride a motorcycle without a helmet and as a result sustain a permanent brain injury, we are saddling society with the cost of caring for us for the rest of our lives, as well as depriving society of the benefit of our talents and skills.

Hundreds of African-American sanitation workers protesting unfair and inhumane work conditions, Memphis, Tennessee, 1968.

Thinking Outside the Box

ROSA PARKS, *Civil Rights Activist*

On December 1, 1955, Rosa Parks (1913–2005) refused to give up her seat to a white man on a segregated bus. Parks was arrested and jailed for breaking the segregation laws. Her moral indignation at always being asked to "give in" and her resulting act of defiance sparked the Montgomery, Alabama, bus boycott. Hundreds of workers risked their jobs and even their lives by refusing to ride in second-class conditions. Parks's case went all the way to the Supreme Court, which ruled segregation on buses unconstitutional.

Parks went on to travel all over the country speaking out for justice for African Americans. Her perseverance and courage inspired the civil rights movement. She continued to work tirelessly for justice well into her eighties.

DISCUSSION QUESTIONS

1. Discuss ways in which Rosa Parks's action illustrates the importance of emotion in critical thinking.

2. Think of a time when you felt indignant because of your or others' unfair treatment but failed to act on your feeling. Evaluate your reasons for not responding. Taking into account the roles of both reason and emotion in critical thinking, develop a plan for a response that would have been more effective in bringing an end to the unfair treatment.

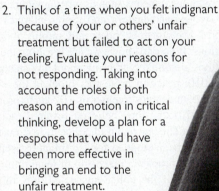

Responsible citizenship requires that we be aware of the basic moral principles and rights, described in Chapter 9, and not simply go along with what our culture says is right. We should be able to develop arguments that balance both prescriptive and descriptive premises in supporting or rejecting particular laws and policies on issues such as capital punishment, same-sex marriage, or the legal status of undocumented immigrants. Some moral offenses, such as engaging in hate speech or being rude to our parents and friends, are not illegal, since the negative consequences of making these actions illegal, in terms of restrictions on our liberty rights and freedom of speech, outweigh the benefits.

Although we may face cultural censure if we break a moral norm, only legal claims carry the weight of official punishment or fines. Unfortunately, not all laws are just. A law that is discriminatory, degrading to humans, or a violation of our basic freedoms may be an unjust or immoral law. For example, the Jim Crow laws that legalized segregation and other forms of discrimination against African Americans in the South were unjust laws. In Chapter 9, we learned that when there is a conflict between a moral and a nonmoral concern, including what the law states, morality takes priority. This may require that we engage in legal protest against the unjust law or, if that is not effective, in civil disobedience.

> **civil disobedience** The active, nonviolent refusal to obey a law that is deemed unjust.

Civil disobedience is the active, nonviolent refusal to obey a law that is deemed to be an unjust law for the purpose of trying to bring about a change in legislation or government policy. During the civil rights movement, Rosa Parks employed civil disobedience by sitting in the part of a Montgomery, Alabama, city bus that was by law designated "White only." Civil disobedience was also used during the

---

In 1846, American writer and great critical thinker Henry David Thoreau went to jail rather than pay a state tax in support of the Mexican-American War, which he opposed as an unjust war intended to expand the slave states.

1930s and 1940s by the nonviolent resistance movement in India against British colonialism, as well as in later struggles against apartheid in South Africa and China.

During the 2011 presidential elections in Egypt, thousands of people flooded into Tahrir Square demanding that Egyptian courts disqualify former Prime Minister Ahmed Shafik as a candidate and demanding an end to the military-controlled government. Similar illegal nonviolent protests were staged in cities throughout Iran in 2009 protesting the election of Mahmoud Ahmadinejad, and at least 36 protestors were killed by government forces during the demonstrations. Nonviolent civil disobedience was also used in Iran against the Shah during the Iranian Revolution in the late 1970s as well as in China in 1989 when thousands turned out in Tianamen Square to protest China's communist government (see page 420). Since the early nineteenth century, Americans have engaged in civil disobedience by helping runaway slaves, resisting unjust wars, protesting segregation, and refusing to comply with military conscription. In 1846, American writer and great critical thinker Henry David Thoreau went to jail rather than pay a state tax in support of the Mexican-American War, which he opposed as an unjust war intended to expand the slave states. Although his protest was short-lived (against his wishes, his friend Ralph Waldo Emerson paid the fine and got him released the next day), this was one of the first significant acts of civil disobedience in American history. In 1849, in his essay "Civil Disobedience," Thoreau outlined four criteria for an action to be considered civil disobedience. First, we should use only moral and nonviolent means to

achieve our goals. These methods include boycotting, illegal picketing, and nonviolent resistance. Second, we should first try to bring about a change in the unjust law through legal means such as writing letters to the editor or lobbying our senators and representatives in Congress. Third, we must be open and public about our illegal actions. If no one knows we are breaking the law, then our actions are unlikely to bring about any changes in the law. In 2010, peaceful protestors blocked the entrance to an immigrant detention center in Arizona to protest a new law (SB 1070) that they believed fostered racial and ethnic profiling. The law required police in Arizona to ask people, who had been stopped for legitimate reasons, to provide proof of citizenship or legal immigration status if the police suspected they might be in the country illegally. Fourth, we should be willing to accept the consequences of our actions. These might include imprisonment, fines, deportation, loss of a job, or social disapproval. For example, dozens of protestors were arrested in Arizona for blocking the detention center.

Before making a decision to use civil disobedience—which could land us in jail or worse—we need to step back and critically analyze the situation and come up with the most effective strategy for protesting a law. This strategy may or may not involve civil disobedience. Rather than resorting to fallacies and rhetorical devices, we need to be prepared to use well-reasoned arguments and assertive communication to back our position. Some people may

After the 2009 presidential election in Iran some peaceful protesters were attacked, beaten, and even killed by policemen.

HIGHLIGHTS

THOREAU'S FOUR CRITERIA FOR CIVIL DISOBEDIENCE

1. Use only moral and nonviolent means to achieve our goals.

2. First make an effort to bring about change through legal means.

3. Be open and public about our actions.

4. Be willing to accept the consequences of our actions.

➤ *APPLICATION: Find an example in the text of the application of each of these criteria.*

protest an unjust law by leaving the country. During the Vietnam War, about 90,000 so-called draft dodgers immigrated to Canada. Many of them still live there. Because they chose not to remain in the United States and make their protest public, as did a much smaller number of draft resistors who stayed here and ended up in jail, they were not engaging in civil disobedience.

In summary, in the United States lawmaking belongs to the legislature. There are several ways in which we as citizens can participate in the lawmaking process. This includes directly contacting legislators, lobbying, volunteering, interning, and getting an initiative on the ballot. When we consider a particular law to be unjust, we can protest the law or engage in civil disobedience.

Connections

How does moral indignation motivate us to engage in civil disobedience? *See* Chapter 2, pp. 45–46.

EXERCISE 13-4

STOP AND ASSESS YOURSELF

1. The House of Representatives was created to represent the interests of ordinary people. However, is the House truly representative? Would the interests of the public be better served by selecting representatives through a lottery-based system, such as we use in calling citizens for jury duty, so that it is a random sample of American people? Present an argument to support your answer.

2. Working in small groups, write an initiative for legislation relating to a current issue on your campus such as free-speech zones or affirmative action. Have the class vote on and critique each of the initiatives.

3. Discuss the justifications for (or against) laws that do the following:

a. Allow children of undocumented immigrants to attend state colleges at in-state tuition rates

b. Outlaw hate speech

c. Legalize same-sex marriage

d. Legalize nude bathing on public beaches

e. Decriminalize prostitution

f. Decriminalize marijuana

g. Make voting mandatory in federal elections

h. Outlaw downloading music from the Internet

i. Have criminal penalties for adultery

4. Billions of dollars are spent every year on lobbying. In 2012, for example, $230 million was spent on health-care lobbying alone. Should the amount of money an organization or business, such as a pharmaceutical company, can spend on lobbying and donations to candidates' campaigns be limited? Or does placing limits on lobbying violate the First Amendment? Support your answers.

5. Howard Zinn (1922–2010), American historian, political theorist, and educator, wrote about our capitalist society: "The role of law does not do away with the unequal distribution of wealth and power, but reinforces that inequality with the authority of law. It allocates wealth and poverty . . . in such complicated and indirect ways as to leave the victims bewildered." Do you agree with Zinn? Support your answer using specific examples.

6. You have just received a notice from the Selective Service System conscripting you to serve in a war that you believe is unjust. However, the SSS has rejected your petition for conscientious objector status. Discuss what you would do. Relate your answer to this chapter's section on civil disobedience.

7. Go to http://thomas.loc.gov/ and click on the "Bills, Resolutions" link. Identify a bill that is of interest to you and answer the following questions: (a) What is the bill (write a one- or two-paragraph summary of the bill)? (b) Who is sponsoring the bill? (c) Where is the bill being sponsored (which house)? (d) When is it being heard in committee or voted on? Write a one- to two-page letter to one of your legislators using sound arguments regarding your position on the bill, as well as changes, if any, you would like to see in the bill (if it still has to go to committee) and how you would like your legislator to vote (if it is going to one of the houses for a vote). Send the letter to your legislator, either by e-mail or regular mail.

8. C-SPAN and C-SPAN2 televise live the proceedings of the House of Representatives and the Senate. Spend an hour watching either channel. Write a few paragraphs describing what you learned about the working of the legislature and how it differed, if at all, from your expectations.

9. Determine which of the following are examples of civil disobedience. If they are not, explain why and discuss, if appropriate, what type of civil disobedience a person might engage in to effectively protest the law.

   a. In 1995 Timothy McVeigh blew up the Oklahoma City Federal Building, killing 168 people, as a protest against the government's killing eighty Branch Davidians near Waco, Texas.

   b. For many years Buddhist monks have been engaging in protest walks against the Burmese government's use of violence against the people of Burma. In 2007 a group of monks took some government officials hostage and torched their cars.

   c. Several young people withdrew their applications from the University of Arizona in 2010 as a protest against the new illegal immigration law.

   d. Irish Anne Bonny, born 1700, thought it was unfair that only men were allowed to be crew on ships. So she disguised herself as a man so she could take up the life of a pirate.

   e. Matt's wife is undergoing chemotherapy and is experiencing nausea and loss of appetite. He reads a scientific study which shows that marijuana can help alleviate these symptoms. However medical marijuana is illegal in his state. After writing a letter to his Senator protesting the law and getting no results, Matt crosses the border into Canada to purchase some marijuana, which he sneaks back into the United States for his wife.

THE JUDICIAL BRANCH OF GOVERNMENT

Article III of the U.S. Constitution created the federal government's judicial branch. The Founding Fathers considered the judicial branch—the court systems—to be the least dangerous branch of government, since the judges are usually appointed and serve for life. Because of this, they are not subject to pressure from the majority in the way elected officials are. The founders also recognized that judges need protection from political pressure by elected officials.

rules of evidence A set of rules that ensure fairness in the administration of law.

The Role of the Judicial Branch

While legislators consider what the law should be, the judicial branch asks when the law should be applied and how it should be interpreted. Courts also have the power to impose sentences in criminal cases and to award damages in civil trials. The judicial branch does not have the power to enforce laws or sentences. Instead, it relies on the executive branch of government to enforce its decisions. For example, following the U.S. Supreme Court's decision in *Brown v. Board of Education* (1954), which overturned laws permitting or requiring school segregation based on race, law enforcement agencies had to be called in several school districts to enforce compliance with desegregation orders.

The U.S. Supreme Court is the highest court in the land. The role of the Supreme Court is to evaluate the law and strike down any law, federal or state, that it determines to be unconstitutional. The Supreme Court also acts as a check on executive and congressional power. For example, in 1989 Congress passed the Flag Protection Act, which criminalized anyone who knowingly defaces an American flag. Protestors argued that the act violated their First Amendment right to freedom of speech. The U.S. Supreme Court agreed and struck down the act as unconstitutional.

Rules of Evidence

One distinctive feature of our judicial system is that we conduct cases by pitting two sides against each other. In civil cases, one party sues another over a dispute; in criminal cases, the government (representing the people) confronts a criminal defendant accused of breaking the law. Because our system is based on an adversarial model, the judicial procedure is governed by strict **rules of evidence**. The purpose of these rules is to ensure "fairness in the administration of law . . . and the promotion of growth and development of the law of evidence to the end that the truth may be ascertained and proceedings justly determined."[15]

The rules of evidence prohibit the use of claims based on

The U.S. Supreme Court Justices.

fallacious and faulty reasoning. Personal attacks (the ad hominem fallacy) are specifically prohibited. Statements about the character of a person or witness that are not related to the truthfulness of and qualification of the person to be a witness are generally inadmissible in federal and state courts. In addition, witnesses may not testify about a matter unless it can be shown that they have personal knowledge of the matter or are credible experts in the field. Hearsay evidence is forbidden, except in some cases where a witness is unavailable to testify (see "Analyzing Images: The Salem Witch Trials").

It is the role of the judge to determine whether the evidence at trial is admissible, to impose reason on a dispute, to instruct the jury regarding the rules of evidence, and to reach a decision that is both fair and enforceable under the law. The effectiveness of lawyers and judges in a court of law depends on their ability to construct and understand arguments. Judges, in particular, need to be proficient in interpreting arguments and judging how sound and convincing an argument is.

Because a member of a jury may be biased or prone to cognitive errors and faulty reasoning, a court cannot rely on the jurors alone to decide a case. If the judge believes that a lawyer in the case has tried to influence the jurors through faulty reasoning, the judge can instruct the jurors to ignore certain testimony in reaching their conclusion. If the judge believes that the jury has made a decision that violates the rules of evidence or cannot be supported under the law, the judge may even overrule the jury's decision.

> . . . in 1989 Congress passed the Flag Protection Act, which criminalized anyone who knowingly defaces an American flag.

Legal Reasoning and the Doctrine of Legal Precedent

Legal reasoning makes use of the same types of deductive and inductive logical arguments that we use in our everyday life. Legal reasoning frequently involves inductive arguments using analogies. These analogies take the form of an appeal to precedents. In the American judicial system, there is an expectation that a judge will respond in a manner that is consistent with how a previous case was decided by a higher court in the same jurisdiction, even though court rulings are not actually laws. Legal precedents form what is known as **common law**. Unlike laws or constitutional amendments, which come from the legislative branch of government, common law is a system of case-based law that is derived from judges' decisions over the centuries.

Legal precedence is important because in a just society laws should be applied in a consistent and fair manner. According to the **doctrine of legal precedent**, if previous legal cases are similar in relevant ways to the current case, then the current case should be decided in the same way. However, because precedents are based on analogies or

common law A system of case-based law that is derived from judges' decisions over the centuries.

doctrine of legal precedent The idea that legal cases should be decided in the same way as previous, similar legal cases.

Connections

Why is it important for judges to not let themselves be persuaded by emotive language? *See Chapter 3, p. 68.*

The Salem Witch Trials
The rules of evidence were established by the judiciary to prevent court proceedings from degenerating into unfounded accusations, where public opinion and hysteria is substituted for credible evidence, as happened in the 1692 witch trials in Salem, Massachusetts. Judge William Stoughton, who was a clergyman with no training in law, presided over the trials. Nineteen people, mostly women, were sentenced to death for witchcraft on the basis of the most flimsy evidence. Only one person was found innocent.

The impropriety of the Salem witch trials had a profound influence on the development of the American judicial system. The public outrage elicited by these trials brought an end to the Puritans' control of the courts in Massachusetts and is reflected in the "innocent until proven guilty" philosophy of today's court system.

DISCUSSION QUESTIONS

1. *Discuss how the application of the rules of evidence might have affected the outcome of the Salem witch trials in colonial America.*

2. *Think of a time when you mistakenly accused someone, or were accused yourself, of a wrongdoing. Discuss how applying the rules of evidence might have helped you, or the person who accused you, to make a better and fairer decision.*

---

case brief Researching the case under consideration and summarizing its relevant details.

Why is knowing how to evaluate evidence and credibility important in courts of law? *See Chapter 4, p. 105.*

Connections

inductive logic, they are never definitive, merely stronger or weaker. Nor are they binding on Congress. In some cases, decisions based on precedents may be overturned in later rulings.

The first step in determining whether there is a legal precedent is to prepare a **case brief**. This involves researching the case under consideration and summarizing its relevant details.

After a list of relevant details is compiled, a search for other similar court decisions addressing the same general principle(s)—for example, privacy rights or eminent domain—is conducted. The final step is to evaluate the analogy. What are the relevant similarities? How strong are these similarities? How can your case be distinguished? Are there relevant dissimilarities that might weaken the analogy? What was the ruling in each of the cases? Does the current case warrant the same decision?

The landmark *Roe v. Wade* (1973) U.S. Supreme Court decision, which ruled that a "woman's decision whether or not to terminate her pregnancy" is protected by "the 14th Amendments' concept of personal liberty," set a legal precedent for similar future court rulings regarding the legality of abortion and restrictions that can placed upon women seeking abortions. For example, in *Planned Parenthood v. Casey (1992),* the U.S. Supreme Court declared unconstitutional, based on the precedent set by *Roe v. Wade,* several Pennsylvania state regulations that placed restrictions on abortion, including the spousal and parental notification rules and the 24-hour hold before a woman could obtain an abortion. (See excerpts from *Roe v. Wade* at the end of Chapter 9, pages 298–299).

Precedents are ordinarily authoritative on later court decisions, unless it can be shown that a previous decision differs in some relevant way or that it was wrongly decided. In *Citizens United v. Federal Election Commission* (2010) the Supreme Court overruled two precedents* that placed restrictions on campaign spending by corporations and unions, arguing that the corporation's First Amendment freedom of speech was being violated by the government placing restrictions on corporate political spending in candidate elections. President Obama denounced the ruling, calling it "a major victory for big oil, Wall Street Banks . . . and the other powerful interests that marshal their power every day in Washington to drown out the voices of everyday Americans."[17] To be valid and binding, precedents must be based on reason and justice. The U.S. Supreme Court's *Dred Scott v. Sanford* decision of 1857 upheld laws that defined slaves as property, arguing that "the right of property in a slave is distinctly and expressly affirmed in the Constitution." However, because this ruling violated the principle of justice, it was not binding in later cases; indeed, in 1865 the Thirteenth Amendment, banning slavery, was added to the U.S. Constitution.

In some cases there are no precedents. This often happens with cases involving the use of new technologies. For example, does downloading, or prohibiting downloading, from the Internet violate the First Amendment right to freedom of speech? Does electronic wiretapping violate the protection "against unreasonable searches and seizures" clause in the Fourth Amendment?

Because the Constitution is more than 200 years old and written before the advent of modern technology, it is difficult to know how to interpret the constitutionality of some of the newly created laws. For example, does the equal-protection clause of the Fourteenth Amendment protect a woman's legal right to have an abortion? Does the Second Amendment, which was written in 1791, guarantee the right of individual citizens to own automatic weapons?* Issues such as these raise the question of whether portions of the Constitution are too outdated and should be amended.

Although the Supreme Court does not use juries to decide cases, as do most lower courts (but not courts of appeals), citizens and citizens groups whose interest may be affected by the outcome of a case may file an amicus curiae, or "friend of the court," brief. An amicus curiae brief presents arguments for a particular position on a case or brings to the court's attention matters or evidence that have not yet been considered.

Connections

How does knowing the fallacies of relevance make it more likely that the rules of evidence will be followed? *See Chapter 5, p. 141.*

Why is an understanding of the principle of justice as well as expertise in knowing how to resolve moral dilemmas important in ensuring a fair trial? *See Chapter 9, p. 285 and pp. 292–294.*

Jury Duty

In the United States, unlike many other countries, jurors play an important role in the judicial system. One of the fundamental rights guaranteed by the Sixth Amendment of the Constitution is the right of citizens to a trial by an impartial jury of their peers. To serve on a jury, a person must be a U.S. citizen and at least 18 years old. The court selects potential jurors by randomly choosing names from voter

---

Austin v. Michigan Chamber of Commerce (1990) and *McConnell v. Federal Election Commission* (2003).

*Amendment II states: "A well regulated Militia, being necessary to the security of a free State, the right of the people to keep and bear Arms, shall not be infringed."

The right of citizens to a trial by a jury of their peers is one of the fundamental Constitutional rights in the United States.

Connections

What types of cognitive and social errors might lead a member of a jury to make a poor decision? *See Chapter 4, p. 127.*

lists or combined voter and driver lists. Because random selection is required for there to be an unbiased sample, people may not volunteer for jury duty. Some people are called for jury duty several times during their lives; others are never called. For more information on jury duty and how the court system works, go to http://www.uscourts.gov/faq.html.

Good critical-thinking skills are crucial for an effective juror. A Canadian study found that people who are most advanced in their ability to engage in legal reasoning are best prepared for jury duty. These people also tend to dominate jury deliberations, thus encouraging the other jurors to engage in critical thinking and providing a positive influence on their views and analysis of the case.[18] Serving on a jury, in other words, has the potential to improve our critical-thinking skills. Jurors also need to be aware of the CSI effect (so-called because of the television show *CSI*), in which jurors expect more scientific and forensic evidence than is available or necessary for a conviction. In addition to being challenged by interesting cases and exposed to the arguments of other jurors who may be better than we are at critical thinking, jurors receive instruction from the court justices, who are trained in critical thinking about the rules of evidence.

The judicial branch of government is concerned with how law should be interpreted. The judicial procedure is governed by rules of evidence and legal precedent, which involves inductive reasoning by analogy. One of the ways citizens participate in the judicial system is through jury service.

EXERCISE 13-5

STOP AND ASSESS YOURSELF

1. Someone in your class has been cheating on exams. A slip of paper with test answers has been found on the floor of the classroom near the desk of a student who has subsequently been accused of cheating. Carry out a mock trial using the rules of evidence. Appoint a defendant, a judge, and lawyers for the defense and prosecution. The rest of the class will serve as the jury.

2. In 1982 the Supreme Court ruled that states must educate undocumented immigrants through the twelfth grade, arguing that children of undocumented immigrants need an education to be able to participate economically in society. However, the court said nothing about education at the college level. Should undocumented immigrants who are residents of a state and have been educated in the public schools be eligible for in-state tuition at the state colleges? Support your argument.

3. Imagine that you have been appointed to a committee to review the Constitution and make suggestions for its revision regarding new technology and issues that are currently facing the Supreme Court. Discuss what revisions you would recommend, and why.

4. The LSAT (Law School Admission Test) is a required exam for entrance to most U.S. law schools. Because of the importance of effective critical-thinking and logic skills in the practice of law, two of the five sections on the LSAT are devoted to testing these skills. Go to http://www.lsat-center.com/sampletest1.html and take the sample LSAT test in reasoning. Check your answers against the correct answers and explanations. Discuss how the questions engaged your critical-thinking skills.

5. Watch a case being tried on Court TV or another station that televises actual court cases. Note how the court procedures conform to the rules of evidence. Evaluate and discuss what steps the judge took to enforce the rules if the lawyers or jury didn't heed them.

6. Referring to the "Critical Thinking Issue: Perspective on Free-Speech Zones on College Campuses" at the end of Chapter 3, imagine that you are a Supreme Court justice and that FIRE (The Foundation for Individual Rights in Education) has brought a case before the court challenging the constitutionality of restricting controversial speech on college campuses to free-speech zones. Research possible precedents for the case. Analyze the analogies between these cases and the FIRE case. Discuss whether these cases provide a solid legal precedent for deciding for or against restricting controversial speech to free-speech zones on campuses and, if so, whether the precedents were just and should apply in this case.

7. President Dwight D. Eisenhower once said, "Politics should be the part-time profession of every American." Looking back through this chapter, examine the different ways you might participate in politics. Write a two-page essay describing at least two specific ways in which you might make politics your part-time profession, whether at the local, state, national, or international level.

1. What are the two main types of democracy?
   ■ In a direct democracy, all of the people directly make laws and govern themselves. In a representative democracy, such as that in the United States, the people turn over this authority to their elected representatives.

2. What are the three branches of government?
   ■ The three branches of government in the United States are the executive, legislative, and judicial.

3. How can citizens get involved in the governmental process in the United States?
   ■ Citizens can get involved through participating in a political campaign, voting in elections, lobbying legislators, joining advocacy groups, serving as interns in government departments, serving on juries, and engaging in civil disobedience to protest unjust laws.

Perspectives on the Use of Drones in Warfare

Unmanned aerial vehicles, also known as drones, were first used by the CIA for targeted killings in 2002 in Afghanistan in an unsuccessful attempt to kill Osama bin Laden. Since 2002, the Pentagon's fleet of drones has grown to over 7,000. More than one-third of the Air Force fleet now consists of unmanned drones. Armed drones have been used by the United States in Afghanistan, Pakistan, Yemen, and Somalia against militant targets.

One advantage of drones is their precision in targeting high-level terrorist suspects without risk to those carrying out the attack. Since 2004, when they were first used in large numbers, drone strikes have killed an estimated 3,000 people in Pakistan alone, including hundreds of civilians and young children.*

Opponents of drones point out that people living in countries targeted by the U.S. are upset by the devastation caused by drone attacks. Since drones are invisible to the people below, drones cause psychological trauma to people who never know when their village might be struck. In addition, because of the death of civilians and destruction of nonmilitary property, drones may increase anti-American sentiment and convert non-radical individuals into terrorists. The *New York Times* reported that "drones have replaced Guantanamo as the recruiting tool of choice for militants."**

Proponents of drones point out that the use of drones result in fewer deaths overall than conventional warfare. In the following readings, David Bell argues that drones are simply an extension of modern warfare and, as such, are justified. David Cole disagrees. He argues that our current policy is indefensible and a violation of the rule of law.

*Lev Grossman, "Drone Home," *Time Magazine*, February 11, 2013, pp. 27–33.
**Jo Becker and Scott Shane, "Secret 'Kill List' Proves a Test of Obama's Principles and Will," *New York Times*, May 29, 2012.

In Defense of Drones: A Historical Argument

BY DAVID BELL

David Bell is a professor of history at Princeton University and a contributing editor to the *New Republic*. Bell argues that the use of drones and remote warfare is morally justified since it makes war safer by allowing us to have fewer soldiers in the battlefield. This article appeared in the January 27, 2012, edition of *New Republic*.

Once upon a time, American military might was symbolized by the heavy boots of the Marine Corps, stomping ashore to reestablish order in unruly parts of the world. Today, increasingly, it is symbolized by unmanned drone aircraft, controlled from thousands of miles away, dropping bombs on accused terrorists. And to judge by the Obama Administration's new defense plan, released earlier this month, this shift will be strongly reinforced in the years to come. The plan aims to cut troops, ships and planes while concentrating our military energies more than ever on drones, spy technology, cyber warfare, jammers, and special operations forces.

With its explicit embrace of advanced technology over traditional methods of combat, the strategy seems designed to provoke the increasingly vocal critics who doubt the morality, effectiveness, and political implications of "remote control warfare." . . . Peter W. Singer of the Brookings Institution called unmanned systems "a technology that removes the last political barriers to war"—and thereby undermines democracy—because it allows politicians to take aggressive military action without having to face the electoral consequences of young Americans coming home in coffins.

. . . Drone technology certainly opens up a new, and in some ways extreme chapter. But it is far from certain that the arc of the story points in the dangerous directions feared by the critics.

It is a commonplace that, from the very beginnings of warfare, combatants have sought technological advantages that allow them to kill their enemies with minimum risk to themselves. And for a very long time, these advances have provoked criticism. We don't know if anyone excoriated the inventor of the bow and arrow as a dishonorable coward who refused to risk death in a hand to hand fight. But we certainly have evidence of the scorn some late medieval critics reserved for the crossbow—a weapon that supposedly allowed poorly skilled archers to kill honorable knights from safe cover. . . . Not surprisingly, then, when the first gunpowder weapons appeared, critics unloosed a torrent of chivalric outrage. . . .

Needless to say, the technological innovations have continued nonetheless—and so have the criticisms, although in modern times they increasingly condemned the innovations as immoral, rather than dishonorable. . . .

. . . Combat now depended on artillery and massed infantry salvos in which relatively few soldiers knew what their bullets had hit, and no amount of rhapsodizing about pikes was going to change this reality.

In the next two centuries, advances in military technology only further increased the distance—both literal and metaphorical—between opposing forces, and added to the anonymity of killing. True, in World War I, much of the British high command held fast to the fantasy that if they could only break through the German trenches, the cavalry could swoop back into action, wielding pistols and swords. Field Marshal Sir John French even insisted on wearing spurs with his uniform at headquarters. But the battlefield belonged to machine guns, poison gas, aerial bombardment and long-distance artillery. . . . All of these developments provoked criticism very similar to that now heard against drone warfare.

. . . If all sectors of society have to share the risks of war, it is said, then a country will be less likely to engage in unnecessary military adventures. The syndicated columnist David Sirota, for instance, has claimed that drone warfare and the end of conscription have combined to "eliminate deterrents to institutional violence, as evidenced by our multiple wars and never-ending occupations."

But again, the story is somewhat more complicated. For one thing, while conscription may raise the stakes of going to war for civilian politicians, it can also lead to much greater carnage on the battlefield itself. As military historians have long observed, generals tend to be much more protective of long-serving, highly-motivated and well-trained professional soldiers than of poorly-motivated, quickly-trained draftees. . . . Today, this purely military logic reinforces the moral and political imperative behind drone warfare. In our all volunteer force, soldiers are a scarce commodity. Things would look different if we brought back the draft.

It is also crucial to note that in the last few decades, the historical move towards the sort of mass warfare characterized by anonymous killing and massive conscript armies has been quite strikingly reversed. Since 1975, the United States, with the exception of the two short campaigns against the army of Saddam Hussein, has largely fought against irregular, insurgent forces and terrorists, and actual combat has mostly taken place at much closer range than it did for the average infantryman of either world war. This development ought to serve as some solace to the critics who worry about the moral and political implications of anonymous, long-distance killing: Those soldiers who do remain on the battlefield—and none more than the special operations forces that the administration plans to rely on so heavily—are more likely to see their enemies up close than their grandfathers did, and to run very great risks indeed.

. . . The critics of drone warfare argue that without Americans running the risk of death, a vital restraint upon murderously aggressive military action will disappear, and countless innocent civilians will die. But in combating insurgents and terrorists, an action's political effects matter just as much, if not more, than their purely military ones, and high civilian death tolls are not just moral outrages, but political disasters.

. . .

... What the history of war makes clear is that the administration's embrace of "remote control warfare" does not signal an abolition of restraints on war's destructive power. Using technology to strike safely at an opponent is as old as war itself. It has been seen in eras of highly-controlled and restrained warfare, and in eras of unrestrained total war— and the present day, thankfully, belongs to the first category. Ultimately, restraints upon war are more a matter of politics than of technology. If you are concerned about American aggression, it is not the drones you should fear, but the politicians who order them into battle.

David Bell is a contributing editor at The New Republic.

REVIEW QUESITONS

1. Why do critics, such as Peter Singer, oppose the use of unmanned drones in warfare?

2. On what grounds does Bell argue that drone warfare is simply a continuation of historic military technical advances?

3. According to Bell, how does the use of drone warfare reduce risks to our soldiers and reduce "carnage on the battlefield"?

What's Wrong With Obama's Drone Policy

DAVID COLE

This article appeared in the March 4, 2013 edition of *The Nation.* David Cole is a Georgetown University Law Center faculty member and the legal affairs correspondent for *The Nation.* He is also author of *The Torture Memos: Rationalizing the Unthinkable.* In the following article Cole argues that our current policy on the use of drones is indefensible and a violation of the rule of law.

Imagine that Russian President Vladimir Putin had used remote-controlled drones armed with missiles to kill thousands of "enemies" (and plenty of civilians) throughout Asia and Eastern Europe. Imagine, further, that Putin refused to acknowledge any of the killings and simply asserted in general terms that he had the right to kill anyone he secretly determined was a leader of the Chechen rebels or "associated forces," even if they posed no immediate threat of attack on Russia. How would the State Department treat such a practice in its annual reports on human rights compliance?

Conveniently, the State Department's country reports leave out the United States. Otherwise, it might have to pass judgment on President Obama's use of drones to kill thousands of our "enemies," and lots of civilians, many of them far from any battlefield. But as citizens in whose name the president is exercising this power, we need to pass judgment. The challenge is that Obama has kept so much of the policy and practice under wraps that it is almost impossible to do this. The leak of a Justice Department white paper defending the legality of killing even US citizens provides the most detailed look yet at this disturbing practice. The more we learn, the more troubling the practice is.

Some critics indiscriminately decry all drone strikes as "extrajudicial assassinations," arguing that killing is never lawful beyond the battlefield and even comparing the practice to former President George W. Bush's authorization of torture. But those criticisms are exaggerated and misguided. Killing and torture are fundamentally different. ... And even in the absence of an existing war, and therefore outside any battlefield, states are permitted to use lethal force to respond to an imminent armed attack.

. . .

So it won't do to dismiss the drone program as illegal assassinations, full stop. A more nuanced critique is necessary. The program is fundamentally flawed in at least four respects:

1. The power to kill with drones should be governed by clear, transparent rules, not by a secret playbook. ... We don't know, for example, what procedures are used to determine whether a person is properly placed on the "kill list," nor even what standard of proof is required. Does anyone, for example, play the role of devil's advocate, defending the absent target and questioning the government's case? Surely if the president claims the power to kill any of us without trial, we have a right to know the standards and procedures he will use.

2. Killing in self-defense should always be a last resort. The white paper concedes, at least as to citizens, that a drone strike off the battlefield is appropriate only if the target poses an imminent threat and capture is not feasible—the traditional requisites for self-defense. But it then says a threat can be imminent even if it is not immediate. It presumptively treats all operational leaders of Al Qaeda or its undefined "associated forces" as "continually" planning attacks and therefore always posing an imminent threat—even if they are sleeping. Anwar al-Awlaki, a US citizen killed by a drone in Yemen in September 2011, was reportedly on the kill list for more than a year before he was killed. How could he have posed an imminent threat for more than a year? The imminence requirement is designed to ensure that lethal force is a last resort; if no attack is on the horizon, there may be time to address the threat by less extreme means, such as capture and trial.

3. At least when it comes to American citizens, it cannot be constitutional for the president to deliberately kill and then refuse to acknowledge doing so. ... How can a government that is supposed to be of, by and for the people have the power to kill its own while keeping secret the fact that it has done so? Accountable and limited government begins with transparency.

4. The power to kill by remote control anywhere in the world should not unilaterally reside in the executive branch. The white paper dismissively claims that courts cannot second-guess the executive's "predictive" judgments about national security. But courts already do this. . . . If we demand that a court authorize even a temporary wiretap, shouldn't we also demand that a court review a decision to end a human life? Some have questioned the utility of a necessarily one-sided and secret warrant process, but warrants have served us well for centuries by interposing an independent decision-maker between the executive and the citizenry. Due process may require advance notice to the target in some instances and/or judicial review after the fact, as the Israeli Supreme Court requires. But we can't leave this awesome power exclusively in executive hands.

Some object that since ordinary uses of armed force in wartime do not require this sort of public accountability, judicial review and due process, those requirements ought not to apply to drone strikes. During World War II, FDR did not have to issue criteria for a kill list, involve courts or publish his officers' specific rules of engagement. But the technology of drones, coupled with the murky scope of this "war," make those features essential now. Because they permit the killing of people without putting boots on the ground or risking American lives, and because they are,

at least in theory, surgically precise, drones reduce the considerable practical disincentives to lethal force.

The ambiguous definitions of the scope of this war and even of the enemy risk establishing a precedent that drones can be used against anyone a government considers even a long-term threat. . . .

Much like transnational wars against nonstate actors, drones challenge traditional legal and ethical categories. The root of the problem is that they make it too easy to kill. We need not and cannot forswear their use. We should not confuse them with assassinations and torture. But we must insist on clear restrictions, transparent practices, independent oversight and accountability—in short, the rule of law. . .

Review Questions

1. Why does Cole say that citizens need to pass judgment on "Obama's use of drones"?
2. On what grounds does Cole dismiss the argument that all drone strikes are extrajudicial or illegal assassinations?
3. What four arguments does Cole use to support his conclusion that the drone program is "fundamentally flawed"?
4. How does drone technology differ from the traditional use of armed force in war?

THiNK AND DISCUSS

PERSPECTIVES ON THE USE OF DRONES IN WARFARE

1. Critically analyze Bell's argument about the use of drones being simply a continuation of advancements in modern warfare. Discuss how Cole might respond to Bell's argument.
2. Bell argues that the use of drones will reduce the need for conscription. However, studies have found that when a country has conscription, people are more reluctant to go to war. Discuss whether the use of drones and the power to kill remotely may make the U.S. more likely to go to war. Discuss also how Cole might respond to this possibility.
3. Critically analyze Cole's argument that drones should only be used in self-defense if there is an "imminent threat and capture is not possible." Discuss also how Bell might respond to Cole's argument.
4. During the war in Afghanistan, dozens and possibly hundreds of civilians were killed by drone strikes. Discuss whether or not the targeting of civilians—by government forces or by individuals such as the Tsarnaev brothers purportedly acting on behalf of a cause—is justified, whether they are intentional or "collateral damages."
5. U.S. law enforcement is expanding its use of drones for aerial surveillance in the United States. Discuss whether the use of drones to monitor the activities of citizens or people residing in this country is justified and, if so, under what circumstances. If not, why not. Relate your answer to the role of government in protecting national security.

Answers to Selected Exercises in the Text

3 Language

EXERCISE 3-1, p. 73

1. a. Informative
  d. Expressive and informative
  g. Informative and expressive
  j. Directive

EXERCISE 3-2, p. 78

4. a. Theoretical (precising)
  d. Lexical
  g. Persuasive
  j. Persuasive

EXERCISE 3-3, p. 80

1. a. Figurative language
  d. Good definition
  g. Circular
  j. Obscure definition when used for policymakers and the public.
  m. Too broad; cats and parakeets are household pets.
  p. Emotive language

3. a. Disagreement in fact
  d. Verbal dispute; the first person is using the term "girl" to mean women, whereas the second person is using the term "girl" to mean female child.
  g. Factual dispute over the law regarding meaning of DWI.

EXERCISE 3-5, p. 93

2. a. Euphemism
  d. Doublethink
  g. Dysphemism
  k. Hyperbole
  n. Dysphemism

5 Informal Fallacies

EXERCISE 5-2, p. 140

1. a. equivocation on "arguments"
  d. division
  g. accent
  j. amphiboly
  m. division
  p. equivocation on "equal"

EXERCISE 5-3, p. 151

1. a. red herring
  d. straw man
  g. hasty generalization
  j. appeal to force
  m. personal attack
  p. red herring
  s. appeal to pity
  v. no fallacy
  y. personal attack

EXERCISE 5-4, p. 160

1. a. loaded question
  d. loaded question—you may have a dime to spare but don't want to give it to a panhandler
  g. appeal to inappropriate authority
  j. naturalistic
  m. false dilemma
  p. questionable cause
  s. loaded question—a person may believe in gender equality and at the same time be opposed to the draft for both men and women
  v. false dilemma

6 Recognizing, Analyzing, and Constructing Arguments

EXERCISE 6-1, p. 173

1. a. For example: Should there be free speech zones on campuses? Should the administration have the power to censor material in student-run newspapers? Do students have the right to boo unpopular guest speakers on campus so they can't be heard? Should colleges censure politically incorrect speech or hate speech?
  d. For example: Copyright theft, individual freedoms, the Internet as public domain.
  g. For example: Does prayer in schools violate the separation of church and state? Should we have separation of church and state? Does prohibiting prayers violate our freedom of speech? What is "prayer" (for example, is a period of silence "prayer")?

2. a. For example: Who should be responsible for paying for higher education—the individual or the state? Does raising tuition constitute discrimination against poorer families? What is the effect of having to work to pay for college on students' academic performance?
  d. For example: Should special interest groups be allowed to promote their views on college campuses? Do we have a moral obligation not to eat animals? What is the best way to reach college students with a message, given their level of cognitive development?
  g. For example: Did China have a right to take over Tibet? Do we have a moral obligation to assist in liberating Tibet? What moral obligations does an occupying country have to the residents of the occupied country? How should people of an occupied country respond to an occupying force?

EXERCISE 6-2, p. 177

3. a. Not a proposition. This is simply an expressive of emotion.
  d. Proposition
  g. This is not a proposition since it is a directive statement.
  j. A proposition, albeit a false one.
  m. A proposition.

4. a. Definitional
   d. Analogy
   g. Analogy
   j. Definitional

6. a. Explanation
   d. Argument
   g. Conditional statement
   j. Conditional statement
   m. Conditional statement

EXERCISE 6-3, p. 185

1. a. ①[Be an optimist.] ②[There is not much use being anything else.]

d. ①[Drinking alcohol is stupid.] ②[Alcohol has no taste at all, it's just a burning sensation.] ③[You don't drink to have a good time,] ④[you drink to forget a bad time.]

g. ①[India should adopt a one-child policy like China.] ②[India's population has tripled in the last thirty years] and ③[it won't be long before food production will not be able to keep up with population growth.]

2. a. ①"[It is impossible to exaggerate the impact that Islam has on Saudi culture] since ②[religion is the dominant thread that permeates every level of society.]"

d. ①[We should not buy a new car for Jack for his graduation.] ②[Jack is irresponsible] because ③[he doesn't care for the things he already owns.] Also, ④[we don't have enough money to buy him a new car.]

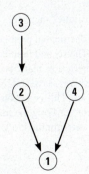

g. ①"[An unbalanced diet can depress serotonin levels—and bingo, you're a grouch!] ②*Too much alcohol unbalances our diet.* ③[Alcohol gives

serotonin a temporary bump but then dramatically lowers it,] ④ so [it pays to go easy on the sauce.]"

j. ①"[There's a need for more part-time or job-sharing work.] ②[Most mothers of young children who choose to leave full-time careers and stay home with their children find enormous delights in being at home with their children], not to mention ③[the enormous relief of no longer worrying about shortchanging their kids.] On the other hand, ④[women who step out of their careers can find the loss of identity even tougher than the loss of income.]"

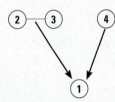

m. ①["In schools, we should give equal time with Darwinism to theories of intelligent design or creationism.] ②[Darwin's theory of evolution is a theory, not a fact.] ③[The origin of life, the diversity of species and even the structure of organs like the eye are so bewilderingly complex that they can only be the handiwork of a higher intelligence."]

p. ①[You shouldn't bother trying out for that internship] because ②[you won't get it.] ③[The company wants only students who are business majors.] ④[*You aren't a business major.*] ⑤ Besides, [the company isn't on a bus line, and you don't own a car.]

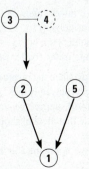

1. a. The argument needs a premise linking illegal immigrants to loss of jobs for Americans.
  d. This argument is weak since the single premise focuses only on one particular aspect of fraternities.
  g. Good argument.
  j. The word *troublemaker* is ambiguous.

2. a. The unstated premise is "Single mothers do not perform well in premed programs." Stating the premise would strengthen the argument, if facts support it. Otherwise, it would weaken the argument.
  d. The unstated premise is "Friskie is a cat."
  g. The unstated premise is "People who are abused as children are more likely to become child abusers themselves when they grow up." The premise is not supported by evidence since the causal relationship is weak.

7 Inductive Arguments

EXERCISE 7-1, p. 205

2. a. Inductive
  d. Deductive
  g. Inductive
  j. Inductive

EXERCISE 7-2, p. 215

1. a. Slanted to elicit a positive response.
  d. Loaded question. It assumes that the U.S. should have only one official language. However, several nations, including Canada, have more than one official language.
  g. Slanted to elicit a "no" response.
  j. False dilemma. There are other alternatives such as charging them out-of-state tuition.

3. a. Conclusion goes beyond the premises. We can only conclude that Rex very likely will bark at strangers.
  d. Hasty generalization based on too small a sample.
  g. False premise based on confirmation bias. We remember the times when toast falls butter-side down because it inconveniences us more. However, studies show that toast only falls butter-side down about half the time.
  j. Hasty generalization based on an unrepresentative sample.
  m. Biased sample because only physicians were polled and also because of the self-serving error.

EXERCISE 7-3, p. 221

1. a. bootcamp for intellectuals
  d. a business partnership
  g. travel without leaving home
  j. a never ending roller coaster ride

3. a. Weak analogy since the president does not pretend he wrote the speeches, only that he provided the ideas.
  d. Premise doesn't support the conclusion. One might also conclude that alcohol should be illegal since marijuana is.
  g. Weak analogy; not being able to dance is not addictive as is smoking.

j. Perhaps a weak analogy. Herbert A. Simon, Nobel Prize winner and "father of artificial intelligence," argues that this is an incorrect analogy. Computers are not merely pretending to think; they do think. They process real input and produce a real solution based on the input. Intelligent computers also perform transformations on the problems and solutions, and come up with creative solutions, just as the human mind does.
  m. Good analogy if one believes that other species have moral value and rights; otherwise, a weak analogy.

EXERCISE 7-4, p. 228

1. a. This is a causal relationship since older couples are more likely to use fertility treatment, which results in more multiple births.
  d. A causal relationship
  g. This could be a causal relationship or it could be a correlation. They might both have the flu and eating at the sushi bar has nothing to do with their nausea.

2. a. Fallacy of questionable cause. There is a positive correlation between being in bed and time of death because of a third factor—very ill people are more likely to be bedridden.
  d. The premises are not strong enough to support the conclusion. It is not clear whether there is a causal relationship or simply a correlation between marijuana use and depression and other mental disorders.
  g. Outdated data. Marijuana today is generally much more potent.
  j. Most likely, simply a positive correlation. The real cause is probably the opportunity to relax and have a good time.
  m. Although there is a high positive correlation between marijuana use and later use of cocaine, the causal relationship is unclear. Later cocaine use could be due to other causal factors such as easy access to drugs or peer pressure to use drugs. The speaker is also committing the slippery slope fallacy by exaggerating the potential effects of trying marijuana.

8 Deductive Arguments

EXERCISE 8-1, p. 241

3. a. Invalid (e.g., substitute "high school dropouts" for "women").
  d. Invalid. Substitute "men" for "college students."

4. a. Unsound—The second premise is false.
  d. Unsound—The second premise is false. Mexico is not in South America, as many people incorrectly assume. Instead Mexico is classified by geographers as part of North America. This is a good example of the importance of verifying the truth of the premises in determining if a valid argument is also sound.

EXERCISE 8-2, p. 246

1. a. Deductive argument by elimination
  d. Deductive argument based on mathematics
  g. Deductive argument based on definition
  j. Inductive argument based on analogy
  m. Inductive argument using generalization

3. It's true that one cat, with the exception of a Manx, has one more tail than no cats. The problem lies in the treatment of "no cat" as an actual being which actually has twelve tails. In fact, if there is no cat, there is no tail (he has committed the fallacy of amphiboly). Once this is straightened out, using an argument based on mathematics, it follows that an actual cat does have one more tail than a nonexistent cat—which, because it is nonexistent, has zero tails.

4. This problem involves the use of argument by elimination. Mike has the grape juice, Amy the Pepsi, Brian the Diet Coke, Lisa the iced tea, and Bill the 7-Up.

EXERCISE 8-3, p. 251

1. a. *Modus tollens* argument. Unstated conclusion: "Sam did not enlist in the Army."

d. Chain argument. Unstated conclusion: "Therefore, if I call Lisa, she might notice me more around campus."

g. *Modus ponens* argument. Unstated conclusion: "I have to get a job."

j. A *modus ponens* argument with an unstated conclusion: "Therefore, Seattle will save several thousands of gallons of fuel annually."

2. a. A valid *modus tollens* argument. The conclusion is stated at the beginning of the argument followed by the conditional premises.

d. A valid chain argument

g. A valid *modus ponens* argument—and an example of the importance of thinking before you speak.

h. Valid *modus ponens* argument

j. Valid *modus ponens* argument

m. Valid chain argument

EXERCISE 8-4, p. 256

1. a. Universal affirmative

d. Universal negative

g. Universal negative

j. Particular negative

2. Using Venn diagrams, determine which of the following syllogisms are valid and which are invalid.

P   M

a. All (published authors) are (writers).

M   S

Some (writers) are (professors).

S   P

Therefore, some (professors) are (published authors).

Invalid Argument

P   M

d. All (members of fraternities) are (male).

S   M

Some (college students) are not (males).

S   P

Therefore, some (college students) are not (members of fraternities).

Valid Argument

M   P

g. Some (UFO sightings) are (hallucinations).

M   S

Some (UFO sightings) are (sightings of airplanes).

S

Therefore, (some sightings of airplanes) are

P

(hallucinations).

Invalid Argument

P   M

j. Some (Olympic athletes) are (professional athletes).

S   M

No (high school cheerleaders) are (professional athletes).

S   P

Therefore, no (high school cheerleaders) are (Olympic athletes).

Invalid Argument

P   M

m. Some (women) are (mothers).

S   M

No (women) are (men).

S   P

Therefore, no (men) are (mothers).

Invalid Argument

EXERCISE 8-5, p. 259

M   P

1. a. No (beings created in the image of God) are (beings whose lives should be destroyed).

S   M

All (men) are (beings created in the image of God).

S   P

Therefore, no (men) are (beings whose lives should be destroyed).

Valid Argument

M   P

d. No (college roommates of mine) are (people who go on to use hard drugs).

M   S

All (college roommates of mine) are (people who smoked marijuana).

S

Therefore, some (people who smoked marijuana) are

P

not (people who go on to use hard drugs).

Invalid Argument

M   P

g. Some (teams wearing blue uniforms) are (teams that will win).

S   M

All (teams named Blue Jays) are (teams wearing blue uniforms).

Therefore, all (teams named Blue Jays) are (teams that will win).

Invalid Argument

j. No (liberals) are (people who favor free speech zones on campus).

Some (people who favor free speech zones on campus) are (college professors).

Therefore, some (college professors) are not (liberals).

Valid Argument

9 Ethics and Moral Reasoning

EXERCISE 9-3, p. 282

5. An ethical subjectivist would have to reply that, if a person watching Word being bludgeoned to death felt like watching and even cheering the attacker, then this was the right thing for him or her to do. And if the attacker felt it was morally acceptable to beat another person to death because she dented his fender, then it *was* morally right, and perhaps morally obligatory, for him to do so.

8. Sample answer: Premise 1: If cultural relativism is true (morality is nothing more than cultural customs), then people who oppose cultural customs or break laws in protest, such as Gandhi, Elizabeth Cady Stanton, and Martin Luther King, Jr., are immoral people. Premise 2: Cultural relativism is true. Conclusion: Therefore, people who oppose and break cultural norms, such as Gandhi, Stanton, and King, are immoral people.

EXERCISE 9-4, p. 289

1. For example: Should college students be drafted? Should women be drafted? How about parents of young children?

EXERCISE 9-5, p. 294

1. a. Prescriptive
   d. Definition
   g. Descriptive

3. a. Missing prescriptive premise: The law is a moral and just law.
   d. Missing premise: The duty of justice entails equality. A relationship where one partner has power over the other is by its nature unequal. If you accept this premise, this is a good argument.
   g. Good deductive argument if you accept the second premise. However, it might be stronger, depending on the audience, if the term "sentient" was defined.
   j. Missing premise and fallacy of popular appeal: The unstated prescriptive premise makes the questionable claim that morality is determined by what the majority of people in a culture think is moral.

10 Marketing and Advertising

EXERCISE 10-2, p. 313

2. Examples might include the use of fallacies rather than rational arguments in marketing a candidate, as well as the unequal access to campaign funds, which would give an advantage to the candidate with the most money.

EXERCISE 10-3, p. 317

1. Relate this to the importance of mindfulness and attentiveness in critical thinking. See Chapter 1.

4. Issues include invasion of privacy and the exposure of other onlookers, such as children, to inappropriate ads.

EXERCISE 10-4, p. 324

1. a. A false analogy. The similarities between the regularity of the sun rising and Metropolitan Life are superficial at best.
   d. Snob appeal. This ad plays into the self-serving bias that we are in control and will maintain our independence even in the military.
   g. False analogy. Can we drive an Avalon to another galaxy?
   j. Euphemism for "use your credit card to buy what makes you happy." The word *richly* is emotively loaded, calling attention to the benefits of credit card use rather than the debts incurred.
   m. Popular appeal. Association of the vacuum cleaner with being a good American. To reinforce this patriotic message, the person shown beside the vacuum cleaner is wearing a tie with the American flag on it.
   p. Incomplete statistics. No source is cited for the statistics or explanation given of how the sample was selected. Nor is *exercise* ever defined in the ad.

2. Ads generally promote the nonmoral values of wealth, status, competition, popularity, beauty, and youth.

11 Mass Media

EXERCISE 11-3, p. 347

2. a. The headline is misleading and based on the fallacy of hasty generalization. The news story is about a tiny crystal of magnetite found in a meteorite that scientists believe originated on Mars. Since magnetite crystals are formed by bacteria here on Earth, the evidence for life on Mars is far from conclusive. It is possible the meteorite was contaminated after it landed on Earth or that the crystals formed under high heat when the meteorite passed through the Earth's atmosphere.
   d. The headline is a distortion of the scientific findings. In fact, the word *happiness* does not even appear in the story that appeared in the journal *Science* about the discovery by scientists of a genetic mechanism which influences serotonin level in the brain and may explain why some people are more susceptible to debilitating psychiatric disorders.
   g. This headline uses hyperbole and distortion, implying that the findings apply to the general population. In fact, the article is about a small group of people known as "cyberchondriacs" who use the Web for

self-diagnosis and to garner information on disorders in order to convince their physicians they have illnesses that they don't really have.

12 Science

EXERCISE 12-1, p. 367

1. For example, the prevailing attitude is that science is not to be questioned. People who question science are often ridiculed and seen as "heretics" engaging in pseudoscience. Also, science is generally seen as the source of truth and as our salvation or the solution to humans' problems.

EXERCISE 12-2, p. 372

1. **a.** Possible hypotheses: "It's an illusion based on a perceptual error," "The moon is closer to the Earth when it is on the horizon," and "The Earth's atmosphere makes the moon look bigger when it's near the horizon."

   d. Possible hypotheses: "Women have less innate ability than men at science and math," "Women have child-minding duties that keep them from working the long hours necessary for promotion," and "Women are being held back because of gender discrimination."

   g. Possible hypotheses: "Left-handed people are more accident-prone because we live in a world made for right-handed people," and "Left-handedness is associated with certain innate health problems that contribute to a shorter life span."

   j. Possible hypotheses: "Married people are more likely to have a higher combined income and thus better health care," "Healthy people are more likely to get married," "Married people are more likely to have children to care for them in their old age," and "Married people are happier than single people and happier people live longer."

EXERCISE 12-3, p. 377

1. **a.** Good hypothesis. Ask students, if this hypothesis turns out to be true based on observation and testing, to come up with a new hypothesis regarding an explanation of this phenomenon.

   d. A good hypothesis. This hypothesis is based on the observation that 90 percent of heroin users used marijuana before becoming addicted to heroin. However, the hypothesis may be false. It's possible that there are environmental and/or genetic variables that play a key causal role in both heroin and marijuana use.

   g. Unfalsifiable hypothesis. The philosophical theory of determinism is unfalsifiable: the person putting forward the hypothesis can always claim that we were unable to predict a particular event because there must be causes that we don't know about.

   j. Poor hypothesis. The word "best" would have to be operationalized in order for it to be tested. What do we mean by "best"? If a person replies, "Whatever happens, happens" he or she is engaging in circular reasoning.

EXERCISE 12-4, p. 385

1. **a.** This could be done by a field experiment in which the two families stagger the dates that their children go to summer camp. The egg-laying rate of the two farms could then be compared. What they would probably find is that the confounding variable is length of daylight, which is correlated to both the timing of the children's summer camp and the number of eggs the hens from each farm are laying.

   d. Students would need to do a controlled experiment with a randomly selected experimental and control group. A field experiment is not sufficient here, since taking antibiotics is sometimes related to having a disease, which would confound the study.

   g. To test this, students first need to come up with an operational definition of consciousness. They then have to develop a test, such as the Turing test, to test for the presence of consciousness in intelligent computers. This may be done by conversing with a chatbot and determining whether or not the computer met the students' definition of consciousness.

2. Hill and Barton found that nineteen of the twenty-nine classes or sporting events observed had more red winners, while only six had more blue winners. The difference was significant at $p \leq 0.015$ (98.5 percent confidence level). However, they used a field experiment so there may have been confounding variables that were not controlled for. In addition, the experimental design limited the generalizability of the results to a particular type of contact sporting event. Finally, the results were only significant for male athletes. In addition to a good experimental design that overcomes some of the shortcomings in Hill's naturalistic experimental design, students need to consider the feasibility of actually conducting the experiment on their campus.

EXERCISE 12-5, p. 387

3. The first requirement would be another hypothesis to take the place of the Old Savannah paradigm. The second requirement would be that the new hypothesis is better at explaining the evidence. This evidence, in the case of Aquatic Ape Hypothesis (the hypothesis that the human species evolved as an aquatic or wading ape in a time when the Earth was warm and the water level much higher than it is today) might include finding human fossil remains in areas that were covered by shallow water or lagoons at the time our ancestors evolved into bipeds. (For more information, refer students to Elaine Morgan, *The Aquatic Ape Hypothesis*, 1997.)

13 Law and Politics

EXERCISE 13-4, p. 414

9. **a.** Not civil disobediance: McVeigh used deadly violence against people.

   b. Civil disobedience. Although the monks took people hostage they did not harm or use violence against them.

   c. Not civil disobedience: The students' actions were not illegal.

   d. Not civil disobedience. Anne Bonny was not open and public about her action in dressing like a man.

   e. Not civil disobedience: Matt was not open and public about bringing the marijuana back from Canada.

Answers to Highlights Applications Questions*

1 Critical Thinking: Why It's Important

"COGNITIVE DEVELOPMENT IN COLLEGE STUDENTS" p. 8

Stage 1: More likely to follow authority figure.

Stage 2: Regard challenges to other's views as "judgmental" and even disrespectful.

Stage 3: Willing to change their position should new evidence come to light.

"CHARACTERISTICS OF A SKILLED CRITICAL THINKER" p. 13

Analytical skills: Provide logical support for their arguments.

Communication skills: Good listeners.

Research skills: Competent at gathering, evaluating, and synthesizing evidence.

Flexible: Can adapt to changes and accommodate new evidence.

Open-minded skepticism: Work toward overcoming personal prejudices and biases.

Creative problem solver: View problems from multiple perspectives.

Attentive, mindful, and intellectually curious: Seek new points of view.

Collaborative learning: Take context and relationships into consideration in making decisions.

"MY LIFE PLAN" p. 15

1. Financial security.
2. Musical talent.
3. Lack of technical expertise.
4. (a) Exercise more; (b) Open a free medical clinic in Mexico City.
5. Study hard in college.
6. Invest money from earnings to save for clinic.

"TYPES OF RESISTANCE AND NARROW-MINDEDNESS" p. 26

Avoidance: Hanging out only with people who agree with us.

Anger: Glaring at a person who has an opposing viewpoint.

Clichés: "To each his own."

Denial: I'm not drunk.

Ignorance: We just don't want to know.

Conformity: Fear of rejection by peers if we disagree.

Struggle: "Analysis paralysis."

Distractions: Television.

Absolutism: There is absolutely correct knowledge.

Fear of challenge: Viewing challenges to our beliefs as personal attacks.

Egocentrism: I am the center of the universe.

Ethnocentrism: Uncritical nationalism.

3 Language & Communication

"TYPES OF DEFINITIONS" p. 77

Stipulative: Bytes.

Lexical: Homely.

Precising: Legal definition of date rape.

Theoretical: Medical definition of alcoholism.

Operational: Obese in terms of body mass index.

Persuasive: Taxation as a form of theft.

"FIVE CRITERIA FOR EVALUATING DEFINITIONS" p. 79

1. Mother as a woman, who had given birth to a child.
2. War as an armed conflict.
3. Teacher as a person who teaches.
4. Love is like a red, red rose.
5. Man as an oppressor of women.

"COMMUNICATION STYLES" p. 83

Assertive: Striving for mutually satisfactory solutions.

Aggressive: Using control tactics to get what we want.

Passive: Avoiding confrontation.

Passive-aggressive: Using devious means of manipulation to get our way.

4 Knowledge, Evidence & Errors in Thinking

"SOCIAL ERRORS AND BIASES" p. 127

"One of us/one of them": The war in Rwanda.

Societal expectations: Salem witchcraft mania.

Group pressure and conformity: Asch experiment.

Diffusion of responsibility: Kitty Genovese case.

5 Informal Fallacies

"FALLACIES OF AMBIGUITY" p. 140

Equivocation: Not clearly defining the word "right" as a moral right or a legal right.

*****Note:** The answers for the Application questions in the Highlight Boxes are merely possible answers. There may be other answers as well.

Amphiboly: Use of "and" in "Wear this fragrance and be happy."

Fallacy of accent: Taking a scriptural verse out of context.

Fallacy of division: Danny DeVito must be tall because men are taller than women.

Fallacy of composition: The rooms in this hotel are small so the hotel is small.

"FALLACIES OF RELEVANCE" p. 150

Personal attack: Insulting other candidates during election campaigns.

Appeal to force: Use of intimidation in a relationship.

Appeal to pity: Trying to get out of a speeding ticket.

Popular appeal: Ads featuring movie stars.

Appeal to ignorance: God does not exist because no one can prove God exists.

Hasty generalization: Racial and sexist stereotypes.

Straw man: Supporters of same-sex marriage want to destroy heterosexual marriage.

Red herring: Support the national health care bill; it is important for all Americans to be healthy.

"FALLACIES INVOLVING UNWARRANTED ASSUMPTIONS" p. 159

Begging the question: "The Bible is the word of God, therefore God must exist."

Inappropriate appeal to authority: Use of celebrities as experts in ads.

Loaded question: "Have you stopped beating your girlfriend?"

False dilemma: "America—love it or leave it!"

Questionable cause: Babe Ruth and jinx on the Red Sox.

Slippery Slope: Army of clones.

Naturalistic: Tobacco is natural.

6 Recognizing, Analyzing & Constructing Arguments

"HOW TO BREAK DOWN AN ARGUMENT" p. 179

Argument in one or several sentences: "I think, therefore, I am" is in one sentence.

Bracket propositions: [I think], therefore, [I am].

Identify the conclusion: "I am" is the conclusion in [I think], therefore, [I am].

Conclusion may be preceded by a conclusion indicator: [I am] is preceded by "therefore."

Identify the premise(s): "I think" is the premise in [I think], therefore, [I am].

"GUIDELINES FOR EVALUATING AN ARGUMENT" p. 189

Clarity: Asking for clarification of the term "ruin" in argument about Hispanic immigrants.

Credibility: Research the claim that Hispanic immigrants are a burden on our public welfare system.

Relevance: Is the claim that most doctors are men relevant to my daughter's wanting to be a doctor?

Completeness: Is there a missing premise that is important to the argument, such as "A woman who gives birth to a child should also raise that child"?

Soundness: Is the premise true that Hispanic immigrants are burdens on our welfare system and, if so, does it support the conclusion?

"STEPS FOR CONSTRUCTING AN ARGUMENT" p. 195

State the issue: Should the United States have stricter gun-control laws?

List premises: The majority of patients actually do better if they know the truth about their illness.

Eliminate weak premises: Senator X, who opposes legalization of marijuana, is a hypocrite because he used it in college.

Establish conclusion: We should build another parking garage [on campus].

Organize your argument: Discuss dependent premises in the same paragraph.

Try out your arguments: Don't resort to fallacies if the other person disagrees with you.

Revise argument as appropriate: My argument for capital punishment is weak so I need to revise my conclusion.

Action: Write to your senator about legalization of marijuana.

7 Inductive Arguments

"QUESTIONS TO ASK IN DETERMINING IF A POLL OR SURVEY IS RELIABLE" p. 211

Who conducted poll or survey? Higher Education Research Institute at UCLA conducted American Freshman Survey.

How was sample selected? All American colleges and universities invited to participate in survey.

Is sample large enough? Twenty percent of American freshmen participate in survey, which is larger than actually needed.

Is sample representative? Freshman survey sample is not representative.

What was method used? To make freshman sample representative the responses of underrepresented populations of freshman are weighed so that they count for more.

What questions were asked? Questions about a freshman's background, demographics, study habits, and position on issues.

Were questions well-written and unbiased? Yes, the Freshman Survey questions were well-written so as not to be biased.

Are there other polls on this issue? Yes, but not ones that are as extensive or done on a regular basis.

Are findings of this poll consistent with other polls? Yes.

"EVALUATING ARGUMENTS THAT ARE BASED ON GENERALIZATION" p. 214

Are premises true? Premise that most pedophiles are homosexual is not true.

Is sample large enough? Sample of three parents is too small to draw conclusion about professional and educational level of most college students.

Is sample representative: Pollsters who poll by land-line phones are not getting a representative sample because many young people use only cell phones.

Is sample current? Samples of pollution in waters from decades ago are outdated.

Is conclusion supported by premises? Premise that men are stronger than women does not support the conclusion that woman should not be allowed to serve in combat duty.

"EVALUATING ARGUMENTS BASED ON A ANALOGY" p. 220

Identify what is being compared: God is being compared to a watchmaker.

List similarities: A watch and natural objects such as the eye are both organized and purposeful.

List dissimilarities: The watchmaker is mortal and may no longer be alive, while God is immortal and eternal.

Examine counteranalogies: In argument for abortion, if we are uncertain whether something, such as the fetus, is human then we should err on side of caution like a hunter not being sure if movement in bushes is a human or a deer.

Determine if analogy supports conclusion: The Argument from Design does not support the conclusion that God exists because there are too many dissimilarities between God and a watchmaker.

"EVALUATING CAUSAL ARGUMENTS" p. 227

Is evidence for causal relationship strong? Controlled experiments are effective means of establishing a causal relationship (see also page 385).

Are there fallacies in the argument? Watch out for fallacy of questionable cause.

Is the data current and up-to date? Need to use current information on freshman preferences.

Does the conclusion go beyond the premise? In gambler's error, the gambler believes his or her actions have a greater causal effect than they actually do.

8 Deductive Arguments

"DEDUCTIVE ARGUMENTS" p. 240

Valid argument: All men are mortal. All fathers are men. Therefore, all fathers are mortal.

Sound argument: The above argument about men, fathers, and mortality is sound as well as valid since the premises are true.

"VALID FORMS OF HYPOTHETICAL SYLLOGISMS" p. 251

Modus Ponens: If Barack Obama is president, then he was born in the United States. Barack Obama is president. Therefore, he was born in the United States.

Modus Tollens: If Morgan is a physician, then she has graduated from college. Morgan did not graduate from college. Therefore, Morgan is not a physician.

Chain Argument: If it rains tomorrow, then the beach party is canceled. If the beach party is canceled, we're having a party at Rachel's house. Therefore, if it rains tomorrow, we're having a party at Rachel's house.

"GUIDELINES FOR TRANSLATING ARGUMENTS INTO STANDARD CATEGORICAL FORM" p. 258

Rewrite each proposition in standard form: "Meat eating is wrong" in standard form becomes "Some meat eating is a wrong act."

Use of context and grammar of original arguments: "Whatever is a dog (S) is a mammal (P)" translated into standard form becomes "All S (dogs) are P (mammals)."

Identify the three terms: The three terms in the argument against meat eating are "meat eating," "a wrongful act," and "killing of animals that are capable of reason."

Rewrite each term as a noun phrase. The term "wrong" in the argument against meat eating is rewritten as a "a wrongful act."

Verb should be form of the verb "to be": In "Not all birds migrate" where the verb is "migrate," the proposition can be rewritten as "Some birds are not beings that migrate."

Put the syllogism in standard form: Returning to the argument on meat eating, it can be written as the following standard-form syllogism: "All (killing of animals that are capable of reason, such as cows), is (a wrongful act). Some (meat eating) is (killing of animals that are capable of reason, as cows). Therefore, some (meat eating) is (a wrongful act)."

9 Ethics and Moral Decision Making

"STAGES IN THE DEVELOPMENT OF MORAL REASONING" p. 275

Preconventional: Stage 1: Some criminals. Stage 2: Most junior high students are egoists.

Conventional: Stage 3: High school and college students who identify morality with conforming to peer norms. Also, women who put others needs before their own (one of our cultural norms). Stage 4: Slave owners who thought slavery was morally acceptable because it was legal.

Preconventional: Stage 5: A person who looks to the U.S. Constitution for moral guidance in interpreting law. Stage 6: Gandhi who fought for justice and equal dignity for all people.

"UTILITARIAN CALCULUS" p. 284

Intensity: Pain from knee injury if you play basketball.

Duration: Long-term benefits of using steroids to your college.

Certainty: We will almost certainly lose if I don't take the steroids.

Propinquity: My college will get the money it needs soon, right after the game.

Fecundity: Many students now and in the future will get a better education here if we win.

Purity: Pleasure of winning.

Extent: Large number of students who will benefit from college getting money.

"SEVEN PRIMA FACIE DUTIES" p. 285

Beneficence: Volunteering with Habitat for Humanity.

Nonmaleficence: Preventing person from blowing up science building.

Fidelity: Paying back money you borrowed.

Reparation: Apologizing to someone we have harmed.

Gratitude: Thanking a person who has done us a favor.

Self-improvement: Getting a college degree.

Justice: Treating people equally regardless of race or gender.

"UNIVERSAL MORAL THEORIES" p. 287

Utilitarianism: The Seattle Artificial Kidney Center committee of seven.

Deontology: Principle of reciprocity.

Rights-based ethics: Right to pursue our legitimate interests.

Virtue-based ethics: Moral sensitivity.

"STEPS FOR RESOLVING A MORAL DILEMMA" p. 293

1. The yacht *Mignonette* capsized in the South Atlantic during a storm and the crew drifted for 20 days with no fresh water except rainwater and no food for the last 12 days.
2. The duty of justice and equal treatment of all the crew members.
3. The crew can starve to death together.
4. Draws lots to see who will be eaten or eat the first person who dies.
5. The crew ate Parker, the cabin boy, who was on the verge of death.

10 Marketing & Advertising

"QUESTIONS TO CONSIDER IN EVALUATING ADVERTISEMENTS" p. 321

Use of scare tactics: We need to buy breath mints so we don't have bad breath.

Credible evidence: Where is the evidence to support the claim that 10 percent of the world's drug supply is counterfeit?

Group pressure: You should buy Nike athletic shoes because everyone is wearing them.

Desirable image or lifestyle: Wearing Diesel clothing will make you irresistible to the opposite sex.

Other informal fallacies: Use of boxer George Forman to advertise Salton's grills is an example of the fallacy of appeal to inappropriate authority.

Emotive language: A cigarette is "alive with pleasure."

Confusing grammar: "Lowest fare advertised on Holland America guaranteed."

Vague, ambiguous, or obscure language: Take out a mortgage at a "fixed rate."

Exaggerated claims: Wheaties is the "Breakfast of Champions."

Information left out: How many pharmaceutical drugs made in the United States are counterfeit compared to the rest of the world?

Relevancy of analogy: In what ways is a Chevy "Like a Rock"?

11 Mass Media

"EVALUATING SCIENTIFIC REPORTS IN THE MEDIA" p. 346

Who is making the claim? Glenn Beck of Fox News Radio made the claims about climate science.

Credentials and funding: Fox News is a news show, not a science show; funding is from commercial sponsors of Fox News.

Background of the reporter: Glenn Beck does not have a background in science.

Findings published: Beck did not refer to reputable scientific publications in making his statements on global warming.

Response of authorities in field: Climate scientists disagreed with Beck's "analysis" as well as the truth of his statements.

Biased: Fox News is biased toward a conservative viewpoint and audience with conservatives being less likely than liberals to believe in global warming.

"POINTS TO CONSIDER WHEN POSTING A MESSAGE ON SOCIAL NETWORKING SITE" p. 349

What is my goal? Joshua Lipton's goal was to amuse his friends and show that he didn't take seriously the possibility of a prison sentence for causing an auto accident.

Who is the recipient of the message? Lipton may have assumed that it was just his friends but, in fact, the Internet is a public venue and others, including the lawyer handling the case against him, saw the message as well.

What information is being conveyed in the message? Lipton was conveying his lack of respect for the justice system and the belief that he was above it.

What feelings and attitudes are being communicated? Lipton's lack of remorse and concern for the people he harmed in the accident as well as contempt for the justice system.

"ANALYZING MEDIA MESSAGES" p. 353

Who created the message? The Bush White House created the press release downplaying global warming.

What is the purpose of message? To promote a particular political pro-industry agenda in the case of Bush press releases on global warming.

What techniques are used? In the speech by Georgetown Law student Sandra Fluke, hyperbole and sensationalism were used to hold our attention.

What point of view is represented? The use of comedian Tina Fey's impersonation of Sarah Palin on CNN news promoted an anti-Republican point of view.

What was our reaction? We tend to react favorably to news coverage that is biased to confirm our previous worldviews. Democrats tended to be entertained by Fey's impersonation of Palin while Republicans tended to find it offensive.

What interpretation is reasonable? The interpretation that prayer has no power to heal based on study of effects of intercessory prayer was unreasonable since the conclusion went beyond the premises that dealt only with intercessory prayer.

Do other people have different interpretations? The one-in-a-million chance an asteroid will strike the Earth in 2014 can be interpreted pessimistically (especially if we are prone to probability error) as in the heading "Earth is doomed"; or, it can be interpreted as there being only a very, very small probability that the asteroid will actually strike the Earth.

Is the message biased? The science report on "The Rise of Man" had both gender and racial bias in it.

Is the message backed by good reasoning and facts? The government report that the chemical dioxin was no more risky to our health than sunbathing was not backed by solid reasoning and facts.

What are possible effects of the message? Effect of the *Newsweek* story "Too Late for Prince Charming" was the creation of a sense of anxiety and loss of confidence among older single women who hoped to get married some day.

12 Science

"ASSUMPTIONS OF SCIENCE" p. 364

Empiricism: Francis Bacon's method based on direct observation for discovering truths.

Objectivity: The canals of Mars.

Materialism: All thoughts and emotions can be reduced to descriptions of physical systems.

Predictability: The universe consists of orderly interconnected causal relationships.

Unity: The grand unification principle.

"THE SCIENTIFIC METHOD" p. 371

Identify problem: The disappearance of large numbers of honey bees since the fall of 2006.

Initial hypothesis: Maybe cell phones are the cause of the honey bees' deaths.

Additional information: Could pesticides, a fungal infection, or pathogens that were found in some of the honey bee colonies be the cause of the colony collapses?

Test hypothesis: Analyze samples of dead bees for pesticides, fungi, and other pathogens.

Evaluate: Penn State did a statistical analysis on the levels of pesticides and other chemicals in the dead bees to determine which were most prevalent.

"CRITERIA FOR EVALUATING A SCIENTIFIC HYPOTHESIS" p. 377

Is it relevant? Hill's focus on uniform color was relevant to a team's chances of winning.

Is it consistent with other theories? Einstein's theory of relativity was not consistent with Newtonian physics.

Is it the simplest explanation? The theory of evolution is simpler than the intelligent design theory.

Is it testable and falsifiable? The hypothesis about the Oedipus complex is not falsifiable.

Can it be used to predict future events? Nostradamus's "predictions" are only useful after the fact.

"CRITERIA FOR A WELL-DESIGNED EXPERIMENT" p. 383

Unbiased: The use of randomly assigned experimental and control groups in Hill's experiment on uniform color and probability of winning.

Measurement: The use of an IQ test in studies that give consistent and reliable results over time.

Replicable: Mendel's controlled experiments on heredity using hybrid pea plants were able to be reproduced by other scientists.

Generality: Many medical experiments prior to the 1980s were done only on males and, therefore, the results could not be reliably generalized to women.

13 Law and Politics

"THOREAU'S FOUR CRITERIA FOR CIVIL DISOBEDIENCE" p. 412

Moral and nonviolent means: Gandhi used only nonviolent means in the resistance movement in India against British colonial rule.

Effort to bring about change through legal means: Grandmothers Against War marched to protest the use of military drones.

Open and public about actions: Rosa Parks sat in the "white only" section of a public bus during rush hour.

Willing to accept the consequences: Some "draft dodgers" in Vietnam War stayed in United States and willingly went to jail rather than move to Canada.

"LEGAL PRECEDENTS" p. 417

1. **Research present case:** Each of the examples in this section required that the judges first research possible similarities or analogies between the present case and any past cases.

2. **Possible precedents:** Two earlier cases were considered as possible precedents in the U.S. Supreme Court case *Citizens United v. Federal Election Commission* (2010).

3. **Shared general principles:** In *Planned Parenthood v. Casey* (1992) the Supreme Court ruled that restrictions on abortion access was unconstitutional based on the similarlity of this case to *Roe v. Wade* (1973), which legalized abortion.

4. **Evaluate the analogy:** In *Citizens United v. Federal Election Commission,* the court rejected the analogy with former cases.

Answers to Think Tank and Self-Evaluation Questions

1 Critical Thinking: Why It's Important

THINK TANK, "SELF-EVALUATION QUESTIONNAIRE" p. 6

1–3. The first three statements illustrate each of the three stages of cognitive development in college students (pp. 7–8).

4. A low rating on the fourth statement illustrates flexibility and open-mindedness in critical thinking (pp. 10–11).

5. The higher the rating on the fifth statement, the better the students' communication skills—assuming they are answering honestly (see p. 9 and Chapter 3).

6. A high rating on the sixth statement relates to the importance of healthy self-esteem for effective critical thinking (p. 16).

7. A high rating on the seventh statement indicates the ability to think independently and not be pressured by authority figures (see pp. 3–5, and Chapter 5, p. 153).

8. A low rating on the eighth statement indicates openness to multiple perspectives (pp. 12–13), whereas a high rating indicates a tendency to use resistance when worldviews are challenged (pp. 22–26).

9. The ninth statement addresses three points: (a) the ability to work collaboratively (p. 10); (b) the problem of egocentrism (p. 26); and (c) the self-serving biases in our thinking (see Chapter 4, pp. 119–122). This is a good basis for class discussion, as students can explore their reasons for a particular rating. For example, while a higher rating might indicate the ability to work collaboratively, egocentric people or those who engage in self-serving biases have a tendency to overrate themselves on this scale.

10. A high rating on the tenth statement indicates lack of openness to personal growth and resistance to change (pp. 14–16 and 22).

11. A high rating on the eleventh statement might be indicative of poor critical-thinking skills (p. 16 & Chapter 4, p. 121).

12. A high rating on the twelfth statement is indicative of being in Gilligan's conventional stage of moral reasoning and fear of offending others, whereas a low score can be indicative of either egoism, or at the other end of the spectrum, a competence in moral reasoning. This is also a good basis for class discussion, as students can explore their reasons for a particular rating (see pp. 10–11 and Chapter 9, pp. 275–276).

13. This statement is true in some circumstances. Gender differences in communication are addressed in Chapter 3 (pp. 73–74).

14. A high score on the fourteenth statement is based on a mistaken belief about the accuracy of eyewitness reports (See Chapter 4, pp. 104–105).

2 Reason and Emotion

THINK TANK, "SELECTED QUESTIONS FROM AN EMOTIONAL IQ TEST" p. 46

The lower the rating on each question, the higher the Emotional IQ.

3 Language & Communication

SELF-EVALUATION QUESTIONNAIRE, "COMMUNICATION STYLE" p. 82

For each question, answer "a" indicates a passive communication style, "b" an aggressive communication style, and "c" an assertive communication style. If a student has mostly "a" answers, they have a passive communication style; mostly "b" answers they have aggressive communication style; and mostly "c" answers they have an assertive communication style. If students use more than one communication style, as most of us do, have students note in which of the scenarios they are most likely to use each communication style. If there is at least one scenario where they use an assertive communication style, ask why (often it is around familiar situations) and how they might expand the use of this style into the other scenarios.

4 Knowledge, Evidence & Errors in Thinking

THINK TANK, "SELF-EVALUATION QUESTIONNAIRE" p. 103

1. The first question asks whether the student is primarily an empiricist (5) or a rationalist (1). In fact, we get knowledge through both our senses and our reason (see pp. 103–104).

2. The second question asks if the student engages in confirmation bias, a cognitive error that distorts our evaluation of evidence (see p. 108). The higher the answer students give, the more likely they are to engage in this error in thinking.

3. A high or "5" answer to this question indicates that the student is unaware of the problems with eyewitness reports and false memories (see pp. 104–105).

4. Any answer to this question is fine. This question is about our brain's tendency to see patterns in random data (see pp. 113–116). While this in itself is not a problem, being unaware of this perceptual error in our thinking, and hence unable to correct for it, can lead us to draw faulty conclusions.

5. "5" is the correct answer to this question. Because we are prone to "probability error" most students will give a low answer to this question (see pp. 118–119).

6. A high answer on this question indicates that the student is committing the self-serving bias of believing they have more control over events in their lives than they actually do (see pp. 119–122).

7. This question is related to the previous question. A high answer on this question indicates that the student is prone to the above self-serving bias and may also be at risk for depression, since it is impossible for us to have perfect control over our lives (see p. 121).

8. This question is based on the self-serving bias in which we tend to overrate ourselves in comparison to others. Most students will answer "3," "4," or "5" on this question. A low answer may be an indication of low self-esteem.

9. A high answer on this question indicates that students may be committing the "one of us/one of them" error in which we tend to think that "we" (our country, culture, social group) are better than "them" (see pp. 124–125). Students who are cultural relativists (see Chapter 9) are the most likely to subscribe to this thinking.

9 Ethics & Moral Decision Making

SELF-EVALUATION QUESTIONNAIRE, "MORAL REASONING" p. 272

Case 1

Preconventional (egoism)

Postconventional (universal moral principles)

Conventional (good boy/nice girl)

Postconvention (social contract)

Preconventional (egoism)

Postconvention (universal moral principles)

Conventional (legalistic)

Case 2

Conventional (legalistic)

Preconventional (egoism)

Postconventional (universal moral principles)

Preconventional (egoism)

Preconventional (egoism)

Postconventional (universal moral principles)

Conventional (good boy/nice girl)

A

accent The meaning of an argument changes depending on which word or phrase in it is emphasized.

ad hominem fallacy Instead of presenting a counterargument, we attack the character of the person who made the argument.

affective The emotional aspect of conscience that motivates us to act.

agnostic A person who believes that the existence of God is ultimately unknowable.

amphiboly An argument that contains a grammatical mistake which allows more than one conclusion to be drawn.

analogical premise A premise containing an analogy or comparison between similar events or things.

analogy A comparison between two or more similar events or things.

anecdotal evidence Evidence based on personal testimonies.

anthropocentrism The belief that humans are the central or most significant entity of the universe.

appeal to force (scare tactics) The use or threat of force in an attempt to get another person to accept a conclusion as correct.

appeal to ignorance The claim that something is true simply because no one has proven it false, or that something is false simply because no one has proven it true.

appeal to pity Pity is evoked in an argument when pity is irrelevant to the conclusion.

argument Reasoning that is made up of two or more propositions, one of which is supported by the others.

argument based on mathematics A deductive argument in which the conclusion depends on a mathematical calculation.

argument by elimination A deductive argument that rules out different possibilities until only one remains.

argument from definition A deductive argument in which the conclusion is true because it is based on the definition of a key term.

argument from design An argument for the existence of God based on an analogy between man-made objects and natural objects.

artificial intelligence The study of the computations that make it possible for machines to perceive, reason, and act.

atheist A person who does not believe in the existence of a personal God.

B

begging the question The conclusion of an argument is simply a rewording of a premise.

business An organization that makes a profit by providing goods and services to customers.

C

care perspective The emphasis in moral development on context and relationships.

case brief Researching the case under consideration and summarizing its relevant details.

categorical imperative Kant's fundamental moral principle that helps to determine what our duty is.

categorical syllogism A deductive argument with two premises and three terms, each of which occurs exactly twice in two of the three propositions.

causal argument An argument that claims something is (or is not) the cause of something else.

cause An event that brings about a change or effect.

ceremonial language Language used in particular prescribed formal circumstances.

chain arguments A type of imperfect hypothetical argument with three or more conditional propositions linked together.

civil disobedience The active, nonviolent refusal to obey a law that is deemed unjust.

cognitive development The process by which one becomes an intelligent person.

cognitive dissonance A sense of disorientation that occurs in situations where new ideas directly conflict with a person's worldview.

common law A system of case-based law that is derived from judges' decisions over the centuries.

compassion Sympathy in action.

conclusion The proposition in an argument that is supported on the basis of other propositions.

conditional statement An "If . . . then . . ." statement.

confirmation bias The tendency to look only for evidence that supports our assumptions.

confounding variable A fact that is not accounted for or controlled by the experimental design.

connotative meaning The meaning of a word or phrase that is based on past personal experiences or associations.

conscience A source of knowledge that provides us with knowledge about what is right and wrong.

controlled experiment An experiment in which all variables are kept constant except for the independent variable(s).

conventional stage Stage of moral development in which people look to others for moral guidelines.

correlation When two events occur together regularly at rates higher than probability.

cost–benefit analysis A process where the harmful effects of an action are weighed against the benefits.

critical rationalism The belief that faith is based on direct revelation of God and that there should be no logical inconsistencies between revelation and reason.

critical thinking A collection of skills we use every day that are necessary for our full intellectual and personal development.

cultural relativism People look to societal norms for what is morally right and wrong.

cyborgs Humans who are partially computerized.

D

deductive argument An argument that claims its conclusion necessarily follows from the premises.

definitional premise A premise containing the definition of a key term.

democracy A form of government in which the highest power in the state is invested in the people and exercised directly by them or, as is generally the case in modern democracies, by their elected officials.

denotative meaning The meaning of a word or phrase that expresses the properties of the object.

deontology The ethics of duty.

dependent premise A premise that supports a conclusion only when it is used together with another premise.

dependent variable The fact in a controlled experiment that changes in response to the manipulation.

descriptive premise A premise that is based on empirical facts.

diffusion of responsibility The tendency, when in a large group, to regard a problem as belonging to someone else.

direct democracy A type of democracy in which all of the people directly make laws and govern themselves.

directive language Language used to direct or influence actions.

disjunctive syllogism A type of deductive argument by elimination in which the premises present only two alternatives.

doctrine of legal precedent The idea that legal cases should be decided in the same way as previous, similar legal cases.

doublethink Involves holding two contradictory views at the same time and believing both to be true.

dysphemism A word or phrase chosen to produce a negative effect.

E

egocentrism The belief that the self or individual is the center of all things.

elitism A belief in the rule of "the best people."

emotion A state of consciousness in which one experiences feelings such as joy, sorrow and fear.

emotional intelligence The ability to perceive accurately, appraise, and express emotion.

emotive language Language that is purposely chosen to elicit a certain emotional impact.

emotive words Words that are used to elicit certain emotions.

empathy The capacity to enter into and understand the emotions of others.

empirical fact A fact based on scientific observation and the evidence of our five senses.

empiricism The belief that our physical senses are the primary source of knowledge.

empiricist One who believes that we discover truth primarily through our physical senses.

equivocation A key term in an argument changes meaning during the course of the argument.

escalation of commitment The overcommitment of marketing to a particular answer.

ethical subjectivist One who believes that morality is nothing more than personal opinion or feelings.

ethnocentrism The belief in the inherent superiority of one's own group and culture is characterized by suspicion and a lack of understanding about other cultures.

euphemism The replacement of a term that has a negative association by a neutral or positive term.

evidence Reasons for believing that a statement or claim is true or probably true.

experimental material The group or class of objects or subjects that is being studied in an experiment.

explanation A statement about why or how something is the case.

expressive language Language that communicates feelings and attitudes.

F

faith Belief, trust, and obedience to a religious deity.

fallacy A faulty argument that at first appears to be correct.

fallacy of ambiguity Arguments that have ambiguous phrases or sloppy grammatical structure.

fallacy of composition An erroneous inference from the characteristics of a member of a group or set about the characteristics of the entire group or set.

fallacy of division An erroneous inference from the characteristics of an entire set or group about a member of that group or set.

fallacy of relevance The premise is logically irrelevant, or unrelated, to the conclusion.

false dilemma Responses to complex issues are reduced to an either/or choice.

false memory syndrome The recalling of events that never happened.

federalism A system in which power is divided between the federal and state governments.

fideism The belief that the divine is revealed through faith and does not require reason.

form The pattern of reasoning in a deductive argument.

formal fallacy A type of mistaken reasoning in which the form of an argument itself is invalid.

G

gambler's error The belief that a previous event affects the probability in a random event.

generalization Drawing a conclusion about a certain characteristic of a population based on a sample from it.

groupthink The tendency to conform to group consensus.

guilt A moral sentiment that alerts us to and motivates us to correct a wrong.

H

hasty generalization A generalization is made from a sample that is too small or biased.

hearsay Evidence that is heard by one person and then repeated to another.

helper's high The feeling that occurs when we help other people.

hyperbole A rhetorical device that uses an exaggeration.

hypothesis A proposed explanation for a particular set of phenomena.

hypothetical syllogism A deductive argument that contains two premises, at least one of which is a conditional statement.

I

impeachment The process by which Congress brings charges against and tries a high-level government official for misconduct.

inappropriate appeal to authority We look to an authority in a field other than that under investigation.

independent premise A premise that can support a conclusion of its own.

independent variable The factor in a controlled experiment that is being manipulated.

inductive argument An argument that only claims that its conclusion probably follows from the premise.

informal fallacy A type of mistaken reasoning that occurs when an argument is psychologically or emotionally persuasive but logically incorrect.

informative language Language that is either true or false.

initiatives Laws or constitutional amendments proposed by citizens.

issue An ill-defined complex of problems involving a controversy or uncertainty.

J

justice perspective The emphasis on duty and principles in moral reasoning.

K

knowledge Information which we believe to be true and for which we have justification or evidence.

L

language A system of communication that involves a set of arbitrary symbols.

legitimate authority In a democracy, the right to rule given to the government by the people.

legitimate interests Interests that do not violate others' similar and equal interests.

lexical definition The commonly used dictionary definition.

liberal democracy A form of democracy emphasizing liberty of individuals.

libertarian A person who opposes any government restraints on individual freedom.

liberty rights The right to be left alone to pursue our legitimate interests.

lie A deliberate attempt to mislead without the prior consent of the target.

loaded question A fallacy that assumes a particular answer to another unasked question.

lobbying The practice of private advocacy to influence the government.

logic The study of the methods and principles used to distinguish correct or good arguments from poor arguments.

M

major premise The premise in a categorical syllogism that contains the predicate term.

major term The predicate (P) term in a categorical syllogism.

marketing research Identifying a target market and finding out if a product or service matches customer desires.

mass media Forms of communication that are designed to reach and influence very large audiences.

materialism The belief that everything in the universe is composed of physical matter.

mature care ethics The stage of moral development in which people are able to balance their needs and those of others.

media literacy The ability to understand and critically analyze the influence of the mass media.

memorable-events error A cognitive error that involves our ability to vividly remember outstanding events.

metaphor A descriptive type of analogy, frequently found in literature.

method of belief A method of critical analysis in which we suspend our doubts and biases and remain genuinely open to what people with opposing views are saying.

method of doubt A method of critical analysis in which we put aside our preconceived ideas and beliefs and begin from a position of skepticism.

middle term In a categorical syllogism, the term that appears once in each of the premises.

minor premise The premise in a categorical syllogism that contains the subject term.

minor term The subject (S) term in a categorical syllogism.

modus ponens A hypothetical syllogism in which the antecedent premise is affirmed by the consequent premise.

modus tollens A hypothetical syllogism in which the antecedent premise is denied by the consequent premise.

moral dilemma A situation in which there is a conflict between moral values.

moral outrage Indignation in the presence of an injustice or violation of moral decency.

moral reasoning Used when a decision is made about what we ought or ought not to do.

moral sensitivity The awareness of how our actions affect others.

moral sentiments Emotions that alert us to moral situations and motivate us to do what is right.

moral tragedy This occurs when we make a moral decision that is later regretted.

moral values Values that benefit oneself and others and are worthwhile for their own sake.

N

naturalistic fallacy A fallacy based on the assumption that what is natural is good.

negative correlation When the occurrence of one event increases as the other decreases.

niche media Forms of communication geared to a narrowly defined audience.

nonmoral (instrumental) values Values that are goal oriented—a means to an end to be achieved.

normal science Scientific research that is based on past achievements and is recognized by most scientists.

O

objectivity The assumption that we can observe and study the physical world without any observer bias.

operational definition A definition with a standardized measure for use in data collection and interpretation.

opinion A belief based solely on personal feelings rather than on reason or facts.

P

paradigm The accepted view of what the world is like and how we should go about studying it.

persuasive definition A definition used as a means to influence others to accept our view.

placebo A substance used in experiments that has no therapeutic effect.

politically correct The avoidance or elimination of language and practices that might affect political sensibilities.

poll A type of survey that involves collecting information from a sample group of people.

popular appeal An appeal to popular opinion to gain support for our conclusion.

populism A belief in the wisdom of the common people and in the equality of all people.

positive correlation The incidence of one event increases when the second one increases.

postconventional stages Stage in which people make moral decisions on the basis of universal moral principals.

precising definition A definition, used to reduce vagueness, that goes beyond the ordinary lexical definition.

preconventional stages Stage of moral development in which morality is defined egotistically.

predicate term In a categorical syllogism, the term that appears second in the conclusion.

premise A proposition in an argument that supports the conclusion.

prescriptive premise A premise in an argument containing a value statement.

prima facie duty Moral duty that is binding unless overridden by a more compelling moral duty.

principle of utility (greatest happiness principle) The most moral action is that which brings about the greatest happiness or pleasure and the least amount of pain for the greatest number.

probability error Misunderstanding the probability or chances of an event by a huge margin.

profit The money left over after all expenses are paid.

proposition A statement that expresses a complete thought and can be either true or false.

pseudoscience A body of explanations or hypotheses that masquerades as science.

push poll A poll that starts by presenting the pollsters' views before asking for a response.

Q

qualifier A term such as *all*, *no*, or *not*, which indicates whether a proposition is affirmative or negative.

quality Whether a categorical proposition is positive or negative.

quantity Whether a categorical proposition is universal or particular.

questionable cause (post hoc) A person assumes, without sufficient evidence, that one thing is the cause of another.

R

random sampling Every member of the population has an equal chance of becoming part of the sample.

rationalism The belief that religion should be consistent with reason and evidence.

rationalist One who claims that most human knowledge comes through reason.

reason The process of supporting a claim or conclusion on the basis of evidence.

red herring fallacy A response is directed toward a conclusion that is different from that proposed by the original argument.

referenda Laws or constitutional amendments put on the ballot by state legislators.

representative democracy A form of democracy in which people turn over their authority to govern to their elected representatives.

representative sample A sample that is similar to the larger population from which it was drawn.

research methodology A systematic approach in science to gathering and analyzing information.

resentment A type of moral outrage that occurs when we ourselves are treated unjustly.

rhetoric The defense of a particular position usually without adequate consideration of opposing evidence in order to win people over to one's position.

rhetorical devices The use of euphemisms, dysphemisms, hyperbole, and sarcasm to manipulate and persuade.

rule of law The idea that governmental authority must be exercised in accordance with established written laws.

rule of men A system in which members of the ruling class can make arbitrary laws and rules.

rules of evidence A set of rules that ensure fairness in the administration of law.

S

sampling Selecting some members of a group and making generalizations about the whole population on the basis of their characteristics.

sarcasm The use of ridicule, insults, taunting, and/or caustic irony.

science The use of reason to move from observable, measurable facts to hypotheses to testable explanations for those facts.

scientific experiment Research carried out under controlled or semicontrolled conditions.

scientific method A process involving the rigorous, systematic application of observation and experimentation.

scientific revolution A paradigm shift in which a new scientific theory replaces a problematic paradigm.

scientific theory An explanation for some aspect of the natural world based on well-substantiated facts, laws, inferences, and tested hypotheses.

self-selected sample A sample where only the people most interested in the poll or survey participate.

separation of powers A system in which three separate branches of government act as a check on one another.

shame A feeling resulting from the violation of a social norm.

slanted question A question that is written to elicit a particular response.

slippery slope The faulty assumption that if certain actions are permitted, then all actions of this type will soon be permissible.

social contract A voluntary agreement among the people to unite as a political community.

social dissonance A sense of disorientation that occurs when the social behavior and norms of others conflict with a person's worldview.

sound A deductive argument that is valid and that has true premises.

sovereignty The exclusive right of government to exercise political power.

state of nature The condition in which people lived prior to the formation of a social contract.

stereotyping Labeling people based on their membership in a group.

stipulative definition A definition given to a new term or a new combination of old terms.

strategic plan A method by which an organization deploys its resources to realize a goal.

straw man fallacy An opponent's argument is distorted or misrepresented in order to make it easier to refute.

subconclusion A proposition that acts as a conclusion for initial premises and as a premise for the final conclusion.

subject term In a categorical syllogism, the term that appears first in the conclusion.

SWOT model Used to analyze a company's strengths, weaknesses, external opportunities, and threats.

syllogism A deductive argument presented in the form of two supporting premises and a conclusion.

T

tacit consent The implicit agreement to abide by the laws of a country by remaining there.

theoretical definition A type of precising definition explaining a term's nature.

Turing test A means of determining if artificial intelligence is conscious, self-directed intelligence.

tyranny of the majority The majority impose their policies and laws on the political minorities.

U

unwarranted assumption A fallacious argument that contains an assumption that is not supported by evidence.

utilitarian calculus Used to determine the best course of action or policy by calculating the total amount of pleasure and pain caused by that action.

utilitarianism A moral philosophy in which actions are evaluated based on their consequences.

V

valid A deductive argument where the form is such that the conclusion must be true if the premises are assumed to be true.

Venn diagram A visual representation of a categorical syllogism used to determine the validity of the syllogism.

virtue ethics Moral theories that emphasize character over right actions.

W

welfare rights The right to receive certain social goods that are essential to our well-being.

Notes

What Do You Believe? (p. 1)

(From top to bottom): Gallup Poll, June 1, 2012. http://www.gallup.com/poll/155003/hold-creationist-view-human-origins.aspx; Gallup Poll, March 30, 2012. http://www.gallup.com/poll/153608/global-warming-views-steady-despite-warm-winter.aspx; CNN/*Essence Magazine*/Opinion Research Corporation Poll, March 26–April 2, 2008; "Cloning Humans," Gallup Poll, May 3–6, 2010. http://www.gallup.com/poll/6028/cloning.aspx; Quinnipiac University Poll, "Immigration," http://www.ppolintionreport.co/immigration.htm; Pew Research Center, "Majority Now Supports Legalizing Marijuana," April 3, 2013. http://www.people-press.org/2013/04/04/majority-now-supports-legalizing-marijuana/; Gallup Poll, "U.S. Death Penalty Support Stable at 63%," Jan. 9, 2012. http://www.gallup.com/poll/159770/death-penalty-support-stable.aspx; Gallup Poll, "Marriage," Nov. 26–29. http://gallup.com/poll/117328/marriage.aspx; Gallup Poll, "U.S. Confidence in Organized Religion at Low Point," July 12, 2012. http://gallup.com/poll/155690/Confidence-Religion-Low-Point.aspx; Alon Harish, "UFOs Exist, Say 36 Percent in National Geographic Survey," June 27, 2012.

Chapter 1

1. Stanley Milgram, *Obedience to Authority* (New York: Harper & Row, 1974).

2. See Zimbardo, P. G. "The Power and Pathology of Imprisonment." *Congressional Record.* (Serial No. 15, October 25, 1975).

3. Milgram, p. 22.

4. For an excellent summary and analysis of the Milgram study, see John Sabini and Maury Silver, "Critical Thinking and Obedience to Authority," *National Forum: The Phi Kappa Phi Journal*, winter 1985, pp. 13–17.

5. Irving Copi, *Symbolic Logic* (New York: Macmillan, 1954), p. 1.

6. Ron Catrell, Fred A. Young, and Bradley C. Martin, "Antibiotic Prescribing in Ambulatory Care Settings for Adults with Colds, Upper Respiratory Tract Infections and Bronchitis," *Clinical Therapeutics*, Vol. 24, Issue 1, January 2002, pp. 170–182.

7. See "Extending the Cure: Policy Responses to the Growing Threat of Antibiotic Resistance," Robert Wood Johnson Foundation, March 2007.

8. "Trends in Reportable Sexually Transmitted Diseases in the United States, 2005," Centers for Disease Control and Prevention, December 2006.

9. William G. Perry, *Forms of Intellectual and Ethical Development in College Years: A Scheme* (New York: Holt, Rinehart and Winston, 1970).

10. http://dictionary.reference.com.

11. See Milgram study on pages 1–2.

12. Chau-Kiu Cheung, Elisabeth Rudowicz, Anna S.F. Kwan, and Xiao Dong Yue, "Assessing University Students' General and Specific Critical Thinking," *College Student Journal*, December 2002, Vol. 36, Issue 4, pp. 504–525.

13. Charles G. Lord, Lee Ross, and Mark R. Lepper, "Biased Assimilation and Attitude Polarization," Journal of Personality and Social Psychology, Vol. 37 (11), Nov. 1979, pp. 2098-2109.

14. Charles E. Murray, "Financial Fraud Targets Youth," *Washington Times*, August 8, 2004; "The Demographics of Identity Fraud," April 2006. A Publication of Javeline Strategy & Research. http://www.javelinstrategy.com.

15. Dwight Boyd, "The Problem of Sophomoritis: An Educational Proposal," *Journal of Moral Education*, Vol. 6, Issue 1, October 1976, pp. 36–42.

16. Stephen A. Satris, "Student Relativism," *Teaching Philosophy*, September 1986, pp. 193–200.

17. American Association of Community Colleges, "Students at Community Colleges," 2012. http://www.aacc.nche.edu/.

18. National Assessment of College Student Learning: 1995, pp. 15–16.

19. René Descartes, "Discourse on the Method of Rightly Conducting One's Reason and Seeking the Truth in the Sciences," in *The Philosophical Writings of Descartes*, eds. John Cottingham, Robert Stoothoff, and Dugald Murdoch (Cambridge, England: Cambridge University Press, 1985), p. 120.

20. Bradley J. Fisher and Diana K. Specht, "Successful Aging and Creativity in Later Life," *Journal of Aging Studies*, Vol. 13, Issue 4, winter 1999, p. 458.

21. Kimberly Palmer, "Creativity on Demand," *U.S. News & World Report*, April 30, 2007, p. EE2.

22. Shunryu Suzuki, *Zen Mind, Beginner's Mind* (New York, Weatherhill, 1989), pp. 13–14 and 21.

23. Sharon Begley, *Train Your Mind, Change Your Brain* (New York: Ballantine Books, 2007.)

24. "Transcendental Meditation in the Workplace," 1999, www:tmscotland.org/popup/businesses.html.

25. Evelyn Fox Keller, *Gender and Science* (New Haven, CT: Yale University Press, 1985).

26. W. Steward Wallace, "Military History," *The Encyclopedia of Canada*, Vol. 3 (Toronto: University Associates of Canada, 1948), pp. 171–172.

27. Michael D. Yapko, PhD, "The Art of Avoiding Depression: Skills and Knowledge You'll Need to Prevent Depression," *Psychology Today*, May 1, 1997; Michael D. Yapki, *Breaking the Patterns of Depression* (New York: Doubleday Publishing, 1988). For further references on the role of faulty reasoning in depression, see "Cognitive Therapy for Depression," http://psychologyinfo.com/depression/cognitive.htm.

28. American College Health Association, *National Health Assessment: Spring 2003* (Baltimore: AMCH, 2003). See also Daniel McGinn and Ron DePasquale, "Taking Depression On," *Newsweek*, August 23, 2004, p. 59.

29. The National Institute of Mental Health, "Major Depressive Disorder among Adults," www/nimh.nih.gov/statistics/1mdd_adult.shmt1.

30. W. Irwin and G. Bassham, "Depression, Informal Fallacies, and Cognitive Therapy: The Critical Thinking Cure," *Inquiry: Critical Thinking Across the Disciplines*, 2002, Vol. 21, pp. 15–21, and Tom Gilbert, "Some Reflections on Critical Thinking and Mental Health," *Teaching Philosophy*, Vol. 26, Issue 4, December 2003, pp. 333–349.

31. John Rawls, *A Theory of Justice* (Cambridge, MA: Harvard University Press, 1971), pp. 408–409.

32. Cooperative Institute Research Program, *The American Freshman National Norms for Fall 2013*, Higher Education Research Institute, University of California, December 2013.

33. For more on the Myers-Briggs test, see Paul D. Tieger and Barbara Barron-Teiger, *Do What You Are: Discover the Perfect Career for You Through the Secrets of Personality Type* (Boston: Little, Brown, 1992) and David Keirsey and Marilyn Bates, *Please Understand Me: Character and Temperament Types* (Del Mar, CA: Prometheus Nemesis Books, 1984).

34. Michael D. Yapko, PhD, "The Art of Avoiding Depression: Skills and Knowledge You'll Need to Prevent Depression," *Psychology Today*, May 1, 1997, and Richard Paul, "Critical Thinking: Basic Question and Answers," *Think* (April 1992).

35. Allen N. Mendler, *Smiling at Yourself: Educating Young Children About Stress and Self-Esteem* (Santa Cruz, CA: Network, 1990), p. xvi.

36. Letter to David Harding (1824).

37. Einstein came in second. See Walter Isaacson, *Einstein: His Life and Universe* (New York: Simon and Schuster, 2007).

38. Daryl G. Smith and Natalie B. Schonfeld, "The Benefits of Diversity: What the Research Tells Us," *About Campus*, November–December 2000, p. 21.

39. ibid, p. 19.

40. University of California Los Angeles, *The American Freshman National Norms,* 2009. http://www.heri.ucla.edu/prdisplay.php?prQry=42.

41. Immanuel Kant, "Proper Self-Esteem," in *Lectures on Ethics* (Indianapolis: Hackett, 1775–1780/1963), p. 127.

42. Raymond V. Raehn, "The Historical Roots of Political Correctness," *Altermedia Scotland*, June 29, 2004. http://scot.altermedia.info/index.php?p=568.

43. Al Gore, *The Assault on Reason* (New York: Penguin Press, 2007), p. 11.

44. "The Real Meaning Behind Horowitz Advertisement," Op-Ed, *Brown Daily Herald* Vol. 139, no. 93, 2001 http://www.browndailyherald.com.

45. Bureau of Justice Statistics, www.ojb.usdoj.gov/bjs.

46. Kate Pickert, "What Choice?" Time, January 14, 2013, p. 45.

47. http://www.cdc.gov/ncipc/factsheets/drving.htm.

48. L. F. Ivanhoe, "Future World Oil Supplies: There is a Finite Limit." http://dieoff.org/page 88.htm.

49. Quoted on Bill Moyers's 1990 PBS broadcast of Pierre Sauvage's 1989 television documentary *Weapons of the Spirit*.

50. Elise J. West, "Perry's Legacy: Models of Epistemological Development," *Journal of Adult Development*, Vol. 11, Issue 2, April 2004, p. 62.

51. Ibid, p. 61.

52. Anne Harrigan and Virginia Vincenti, "Developing Higher-Order Thinking Through an Intercultural Assignment," *College Teaching*, Vol. 52, Issue 3, p. 117.

53. World Governance Indicators, http://worldbank.org/governance.wgi.index.

54. A. H. Martin, "An Experimental Study of the Factors and Types of Voluntary Choice," *Archives of Psychology*, 1922, Vol. 51, pp. 40–41.

55. Peggy Orenstein, *Schoolgirls: Young Women, Self-Esteem, and the Confidence Gap* (New York: Doubleday, American Association of University Women, 1994).

56. Alice Domar and Lynda Wright, "Could You Harbor Unconscious Prejudice?" *Health*, July/August 2004, Vol. 18, Issue 6, p. 139.

57. Tim Driver, "How Men and Women Use Their Time," Salary.com, Inc.

58. Leon Festinger, *A Theory of Cognitive Dissonance* (Stanford, CA: Stanford University Press, 1957), pp. 120–121.

59. John Leach, "Why People 'Freeze' in an Emergency: Temporal and Cognitive Constraints on Survival Responses," *Aviation, Space, and Environmental Medicine*, June 2004, Vol. 75, Issue 6, pp. 539–542.

60. Quoted in Amanda Ripley, "How to Get Out Alive," *Time*, May 2, 2005, p. 62.

61. Zehra R. Peynircioglu, Jennifer L. W. Thompson, and Terri B. Tanielian, "Improvement Strategies in Free-Throw Shooting and Grip-Strength Tasks," *Journal of General Psychology*, April 2000, Vol. 127, Issue 2, pp. 145–156.

62. Analogy used in a speech. Quoted in Douglas Adams, *The Salmon of Doubt: Hitchhiking the Galaxy One Last Time* (London: Macmillan, 2002).

63. Jessica Howell, "Assessing the Impact of Eliminating Affirmative Action in Higher Education," *Journal of Labor Economics,* Vol. 28, Issue 1, January 2010, pp. 113–166.

Chapter 2

1. Fyodor Dostoyevsky, *Crime and Punishment*, trans. by Jessie Coulson (Oxford University Press, 1953). For an online edition of the novel, go to http://www.bartleby.com/318/.

2. This logic problem is based on one from Gregory Bassham et al., *Critical Thinking* (New York, McGraw-Hill, 2005), p. 56.

3. The correct answer is E (to see if the vowel has an even number on its reverse side) and the 7 (to check that there's no vowel on the reverse side).

4. Quoted in S. F. Spontzis, *Morals, Reason, and Animals* (Philadelphia: Temple University Press, 1987), p. 33.

5. Clive D. L. Wynne, *Do Animals Think?* (Princeton, NJ: Princeton University Press, 2004).

6. Temple Grandin, Matthew Peterson, and Gordon L. Shaw, "Spatial-temporal versus language-analytical reasoning: the role of music training," *Arts Education Policy Review*, July–August 1998, vol. 99, no. 6, pp. 11–14.

7. See Jonathan Barnes, *Articles on Aristotle: Ethics and Politics* (Duckworth, 1977).

8. For other examples of this type of thinking, see Jean-Jacques Rousseau's *Emile* (1762), Hegel's *Philosophy of Right* (1872), and Friedrich Nietzsche's *Beyond Good and Evil*, Part VII (1886).

9. See Steven Goldberg, "The Logic of Patriarchy," in *Fads and Fallacies in the Social Sciences* (Amherst, NY: Humanity Books, 2003), pp. 93–108.

10. For more on research on sex differences, see Kingsley Browne, *Biology at Work: Rethinking Sexual Equality* (New Brunswick, NJ: Rutgers University Press, 2002); Anne Fausto-Sterling, *Sexing the Body: Gender Politics and the Construction of Sexuality* (New York: Basic Books, 2000); Melissa Hines, *Brain Gender* (New York: Oxford University Press, 2004); Steven Rhoads, *Taking Sex Differences Seriously* (San Francisco: Encounter Books, 2004); Leonard Sax, *Why Gender Matters: What Parents and Teachers Need to Know About the Emerging Science of Sex Differences* (New York: Doubleday, 2005).

11. "Over 30 and Over the Hill," *The Economist*, Vol. 371, Issue 8381, June 26, 2004, p. 60.

12. See Bruce Bower, "A Thoughtful Angle on Dreaming," *Science News*, June 2, 1990, Vol. 137, Issue 22, p. 348.

13. Quoted in Barbara Kantrowitz and Karen Springen, "What Dreams Are Made Of," *Newsweek*, August 9, 2004, p. 44.

14. J. L. McClelland, "Toward a Pragmatic Connectionism." In P. Baumgartner and S. Payr, eds., *Speaking Minds: Interviews with Twenty Eminent Cognitive Scientists* (Princeton, NJ: Princeton University Press, 1995), p. 141.

15. Deidre Barrett, *The Committee of Sleep: How Artists, Scientists and Athletes Use Their Dreams for Creative Problem Solving* (New York: Crown/Random House, 2001).

16. Mark Nelson, "Sleep On It: Solving Business Problems," *Nation's Business*, December 1987, Vol. 75, Issue 12, pp. 72–73.

17. For more information on the role of sleep and dreams in solving problems and reducing stress, read Eric Maisel's book *Sleep Thinking* (Avon, MA: Adams Media Corp. 2001).

18. Reuven Bar-Levav, *Thinking in the Shadow of Feelings* (New York: Simon & Schuster, 1988), p. 20.

19. This exercise is adapted from Daniel Rigney, "What If You Could Be Instantly Smarter? A Thought Experiment," *The Futurist*, Vol. 38, Issue 2, March-April 2004, pp. 34–36.

20. Barbara J. Thayer-Bacon, "Feminism and Critical Thinking," in Joe L. Kincheloe and Danny Weil, *Critical Thinking and Learning: An Encyclopedia for Parents and Teachers* (Westport, CT: Greenwood Press, 2004), p. 280.

21. *Random House Webster's College Dictionary* (New York, Random House, 2001).

22. Reuver Bar-Levav, *Thinking in the Shadow of Feelings* (New York: Touchstone Book, 1988), p. 116.

23. W. J. Ndaba, "The Challenge to African Philosophy," http://singh.reshma.tripod.com/alternation/alternation6_1/12JNDABA.htm.

24. Edward R. Howe, "Secondary Teachers Conceptions of Critical Thinking in Canada and Japan: A Comparative Study," *Teacher and Teaching*, Vol. 10, Issue 5, November 2004, pp. 505–525.

25. Janette Warwick and Ted Nettelbeck, "Emotional Intelligence Is . . . ?" *Personality and Individual Differences*, Vol. 37, Issue 5, October 2004, pp. 1091–1100.

26. J. D. Mayer and P. Salovey, "What Is Emotional Intelligence," in P. Salovey and D. J. Sluyter, eds., *Emotional Development and Emotional Intelligence: Educational Implications* (Basic Books: New York, 1997), p. 10.

27. Al Gore, *The Assault on Reason* (New York: Penguin Press, 2007), pp. 154–155.

28. For more on the importance of emotional intelligence in everyday life, see David Goleman's *Emotional Intelligence: Why It Can Matter More Than IQ* (1995).

29. Delores Gallo, "Educating for Empathy, Reason, and Imagination," in Kerry S. Walters, ed., *Re-Thinking Reason: New Perspectives in Critical Thinking* (Albany, NY: State University of New York Press, 1994), p. 56.

30. Matthew P. Walker, Conor Liston, J. Allan Hobson, and Robert Stickgold, "Cognitive Flexibility Across the Sleep-Wake Cycle: REM-Sleep Enhancement of Anagram Problem Solving," *Cognitive Brain Research*, Vol. 14, Issue 3, November 2002, pp. 317.

31. Nel Noddings, *Caring: A Feminine Approach to Ethics and Moral Education* (Berkeley: University of California Press, 1984).

32. Kerry S. Walters, "Critical Thinking, Rationality, and the Vulcanization of Students," in Kerry S. Walters, ed., *Re-Thinking Reason: New Perspectives in Critical Thinking* (Albany, NY: State University of New York Press, 1994), pp. 61–63.

33. W. J. Ndaba, "The Challenge to African Philosophy," http://singh.reshma.tripod.com/alternation/alternation6_1/12JNDABA.htm.

34. Patrick Henry Winston, *Artificial Intelligence*, 3rd ed. (Reading, MA: Addison-Wesley Publishing Co., 1993).

35. For more on the Turing test, go to http://www.turing.org.uk.

36. See http://newsvote.bbc.co.uk/2/hi/uk_news/magazine/3503465.stm and Charles W. Bailey, Jr., *Truly Intelligent Computers* (Library & Information Technology Association, 1992), http://www.cni.org/pub/LITA/Think/Bailey.html.

37. http://www.ai.mit.edu/projects/humanoid-robotics-group/kismet/kismet.html. Also see "Robot Pals" on PBS Nova for more on Kismet and Leonardo.

38. Ray Kurzweil, *The Age of Spiritual Machines: When Computers Exceed Human Intelligence* (New York: Viking, 1999), p. 4.

39. Herbert A. Simon, "Machines as Mind," in Kenneth M. Ford, Clark Glymour, and Patrick J. Hayes, eds., *Android Epistemology* (Menlo Park, CA: AAAI Press, 1995), p. 36.

40. See Roger Penrose's *The Emperor's New Mind* (Oxford University Press, 1989) and *Shadows of the Mind* (Oxford University Press, 1994).

41. Steven Pinker, "Using Our Minds to Help Heal Ourselves," *Newsweek*, September 27, 2004.

42. Jennifer L. Collinger et al, "High-performance neuroprosthetic control by an individual with tetraplegia," *The Lancet,* Vol. 381, Issue 9866, February 16, 2012, pp. 557–564.

43. Margaret A. Boden, "Could a Robot Be Creative?" in Kenneth M. Ford, Clark Glymour, and Patrick J. Hayes, eds., *Android Epistemology* (Menlo Park, CA: AAAI Press, 1995), pp. 69–70.

44. For a more in-depth coverage of this topic, refer to Paul Helm, ed., *Faith and Reason* (Oxford, Oxford University Press, 1999).

45. Quoted in Brian Kolodiejchuk, *Mother Teresa: Come Be My Light* (New York: Doubleday, 2007).

46. For more on the work and writings of Billy Graham, go to http://www.billygraham.org/.

47. For an example of fideism, read Danish existentialist Søren Kierkegaard's "Concluding Unscientific Postscript to the *Philosophical Fragments.*"

48. Richard Dawkins, "Viruses of the Mind." In Paul Kurtz and Timothy J. Madigan, *Challenges to Enlightenment: In Defense of Reason and Science* (Buffalo, NY: Prometheus Books, 1994), p. 197.

49. Dean Hamer, *The God Gene: How Faith Is Hardwired into Our Genes* (New York: Doubleday, 2004).

50. Lippman Bodoff, "Was Abraham Ready to Kill His Son?" in Hershel Shanks, ed., *Abraham and Family: New Insights into the Patriarchal Narratives* (Washington, D.C.: Biblical Archaeology Society, 2000).

51. For more on this argument, see colonial American theologian Jonathan Edward's sermon on "Reason No Substitute for Revelation," in Paul Helm, ed., *Faith and Reason* (Oxford, Oxford University Press, 1999), pp. 221–222.

52. Keith A. Roberts, *Religion in Sociological Perspective* (Homewood, IL: Dorsey Press, 1984), p. 62.

53. Cited in "College Students Losing Faith?" *A Chronicle of the Christian Faith*, August 24, 2004. http://www.inthefaith.com/2004/08/24/college-students-losing-faith/.

54. http://www.worldnetdaily.com/news/article.asp?ARTICLE_ID=34540.

55. "Special Report: Muslim World," Gallup World Poll, 2006.

56. Globus: International Affairs Poll, The Associated Press Poll, May 13–26, 2005.

Chapter 3

1. Noam Chomsky, *On Language and Nature* (Cambridge, UK: Cambridge University Press, 2002). See also Mark C. Baker, *The Atoms of Language: The Mind's Hidden Rules of Grammar* (New York: Basic Books, 2001).

2. Geoffrey Sampson, *The 'Language Instinct' Debate* (London: Continuum International, 2005).

3. "Language," *The Columbia Encyclopedia*, 6th ed. (New York: Columbia University Press, 2000), p. 22073.

4. Veanne N. Anderson, Dorothy Simpson-Taylor, and Douglas J. Herrmann, "Gender, Age, and Rape: Supportive Rules," *Sex Roles: A Journal of Research*, Vol. 50, Issue 1, January 2004, pp. 77–90.

5. Lindsley Smith, "Juror Assessment of Veracity, Deception, and Credibility" (for publication), http://www.uark.edu/depts/comminfo/CLR/smith1.html.

6. Estes Thompson, " 'Moral Call' Led Soldier to Expose Prison Abuse," http://aolsvc.news.aol.com/news/article.adp?id=20040803033109990001.

7. Sarah Childress, "A New Controversy in the Fetal-Rights Wars," *Newsweek*, March 29, 2004, p. 7.

8. All passages are from *The New English Bible* (New York: Cambridge University Press, 1972).

9. For more on the development of the English language, see David Wilton, "A (Very) Brief History of the English Language," http://www.wordorigins.org/index.php/site/comments/a_very_brief_history_of_the_english_language3/.

10. This exercise is from Clive Wynne's book *Do Animals Think?* (Princeton, NJ: Princeton University Press, 2004), p. 108.

11. Lois Pineau, "Date Rape: A Feminist Analysis," *Law and Philosophy*, Vol. 8, 1989, pp. 217–243.

12. "General Information about Learning Disabilities," Fact Sheet Number 7 (FS7), 1997. http://www.kidsource.com/NICHCY/learning_disabilities.html.

13. Prior HHS Poverty Guidelines and Federal Register References, U.S. Department of Health & Human Services, http://aspe.hhs.gov/poverty/11computations.shtml.

14. Mary Daly, *Beyond God the Father* (Boston: Beacon Press, 1985).

15. Chapter 48 of the Texas Statutes Human Resources Code, http://tlo2.tlc.state.tx.us/statutes/docs/HR/content/pdf/hr.002.00.000048.00.pdf.

16. http://www.answers.com/topic/community-college.

17. Samuel Johnson, *Dictionary of the English Language*, 1755.

18. Chris Mooney, "Emotional Rescue," *Seed Magazine*, May/June. 2007, pp. 26–28.

19. *Random House Webster's College Dictionary* (New York: Random House, 2001), pp. 1253–1254.

20. Cherrie Moraga, *Loving the War Years* (Boston: South End Press, 1983).

21. http://www.gutenberg.org/files/12242/12242-h/12242-h.htm.

22. Shelly L. Gable, Harry T. Reis, and Geraldine Downey, "He Said, She Said: A Quasi-Signal Detection Analysis of Daily Interactions Between Close Relationship Partners," *Psychological Science*, Vol. 14, Issue 2, March 2003, p. 102.

23. Diana K. Ivy and Phil Backlund, *GenderSpeak: Personal Effectiveness in Gender Communication*, 3rd ed. (Boston: McGraw-Hill, 2004), p. 211.

24. Deborah Tannen, *You Just Don't Understand: Women and Men in Communication* (New York: Morrow, 1990), p. 42.

25. Amy Clements, "Study Confirms Males/Females Use Different Parts of Brain in Language and Visuospatial Tasks," *Brain and Language*, Vol. 98, August 2006, pp. 150–158.

26. For a debate on this issue, go to http://www.pbs.org/thinktank/transcript216.html.

27. "Hillary Clinton's Masculine Communication Style Just Might Win the Prize," *Women's Media Center*, November 13, 2007, http://womensmediacenter.com/article/C/Politics-21.

28. Mark P. Orbe, "Remember, It's Always Their Ball: Descriptions of African American Male Communication," *Communication Quarterly*, Vol. 42, Issue 3, summer 1994, pp. 287–300.

29. Jean Chatzky, "Wheel and Deals," *Time*, October 18, 2004, p. 94.

30. Michelle LeBaron, "Culture-Based Negotiation Styles," Intractable Conflict Knowledge Base Project, University of Colorado, 2003, http://www.beyondintractability.org/m/culture_negotiation.jsp.

31. Phil Williams and Veronica Duncan, "Different Communication Styles May Be at Root of Many Problems Between African American Males and Females," University of Georgia News Bureau, October 8, 1998, http://www.uga.edu/columns/101998/campnews3.html.

32. Li-Jun Ji, Zhiyong Zhang, and Richard E. Nisbett. "Is It Culture or Is It Language? Examination of Language Effects in Cross-Cultural Research on Categorization," *Journal of Personality and Social Psychology*, Vol. 87, Issue 1, July 2004, PsychARTICLES, http:// content.apa.org/journals/psp/87/1/57.html, p. 2.

33. AnneMarie Pajewski and Luis Enriquez, Teaching from a Hispanic Perspective: A Handbook for Non-Hispanic Adult Educators (Phoenix, AZ: Arizona Adult Literacy and Technology Resource Center, 96), http://www.literacynet.org/lp/hperspectives/hispcult.html.

34. Ibid.

35. For more information on fashion as language, see Stuart Hall, *Representation: Cultural Representations and Signifying Practices* (London: Sage Publications, 1997), p. 37.

36. Daniel Okrent, "The War of the Words: A Dispatch from the Front Lines," *New York Times*, March 6, 2005.

37. Neil Gross, "The Indoctrination Myth," March 3, 2012. http://www.nytimes.com/2012/03/04/opinion/sunday/college-doesnt-make-you-liberal.htm.

38. Joseph Massad, "The 'Arab Spring' and other American Seasons," *al-Jazeera*, August 29, 2012.

39. "Tourism: Do Slogans Sell?" *Newsweek*, August 30, 2004, p. 9.

40. George Orwell, *Nineteen Eighty-Four* (New York: New American Library, 1949), pp. 176–177.

41. Gallup poll, 2002, p. 45.

42. "Gay Marriage in Oregon," Letters to the editor, *Newsweek*.

43. March 22, 2004, p. 45.

44. Bernard N. Nathanson and Richard N. Ostling, *Aborting America* (Garden City, NY: Doubleday, 1979), p. 193.

45. Mark G. Frank and Thomas Hugh Feeley, "To Catch a Liar: Challenges for Research in Lie Detection Training," *Journal of Applied Communication Research*, Vol. 31, Issue 1, February 2003, p. 60.

46. Nationally televised speech by President Clinton, CNN, August 17, 1998.

47. Denis Boyles, "A Guide to Everything that Matters." AARP, September/October 2004, p. 108.

48. Mark G. Frank and Thomas Hugh Feeley, "To Catch a Liar: Challenges for Research in Lie Detection Training," *Journal of Applied Communication Research*, Vol. 31, Issue 1, February 2003, p. 59.

49. Carrie Lock, "Deception Detection," *Science News*, Vol. 166, Issue 5, July 13, 2004, p. 72.

50. Frederic Golden, "Face the Music: How New Computers Catch Deceit," *Time Europe*, March 13, 2000, Vol. 155, no. 10, p. 46.

51. Richard H. Escobales, Jr., "The Heated Debate over Stem Cell Research," Letter to the editor, *Newsweek*, Nov. 8, 2004, p. 16.

52. David Ansen, "Not So Great," *Newsweek*, November 29, 2004, p. 60.

53. Sarah Childress and Dirk Johnson, "The Hot Sound of Hate," *Newsweek*, November 29, 2004, p. 30.

54. Marvin Olasky, "Blue-State Philosopher," *World*, November 27, 2004, p. 34.

55. Michael D. Lemonick, "In Search of Sleep," *Newsweek*, September 27, 2004, p. 44.

56. Josh White, "Tillman Killed by 'Friendly Fire'," *Washington Post*, May 30, 2004, p. A01.

57. Jonathan Swift, "A Modest Proposal," 1729.

58. Sarah Palin's Facebook page, August 7, 2009.

59. Headline from the March 22, 2004, *Weekly World News*, pp. 26–27.

60. Brooke Noel Moore and Richard Parker, *Critical Thinking* (New York: McGraw-Hill, 2004), p. 144.

61. James Geary, "Deceitful Minds: The Awful Truth about Lying," *Time Europe*, March 13, 2000, Vol. 155, Issue 10. http://www.time.com/time/europe/magazine/2000/313/deceit.html.

62. Christian Mignot, "Lawsuits, Debate Intensify over University 'Free Speech Zones,'" *Daily Bruin (UCLA)*, October 1, 2002.

63. "Campus Speech Rules Scrutinized by Courts, Students, Advocates: Opponents Say Policies Violate First Amendment Right to Protest and Distribute Material," *College Censorship*, Vol. XXI, Issue 1, Winter 2002–2003, p. 6.

64. Greg Lukianoff, "Feigning Free Speech on Campus," *New York Times*, Oct. 24, 2012.

65. Robert J. Scott, "Reasonable Limits Are Good," *USA Today*, May 27, 2003, p. 14a.

Chapter 4

1. Dan Childs, "Medical Errors, Past and Present," Nov. 27, 2007, www.abcnews.go.com.

2. Yasuharu Tokuda, Noaki Kishida, Ryota Konishi, and Shunzo Koizumi, "Cognitive Error as the Most Frequent Contributory Factor in Cases of Medical Injury," *Journal of Hospital Medicine* 2011, 6 (3), 109–114.

3. Kevin B. O'Reilly, "Diagnostic Errors: Why They Happen," www.amednews.com, Dec. 6, 2012.

4. For more on string theory, see Brian Greene, *The Elegant Universe: Superstrings, Hidden Dimensions, and the Quest for the Ultimate Theory* (New York: W.W. Norton, 2003), or go to: http://superstringtheory.com/basics/.

5. U. Neisser and H. Harsch, "Phantom flashbulbs: False recollection of hearing the news about *Challenger*." In E. Winograd & U. Neisser, eds., *Affect and Accuracy in Recall: Studies of "Flashbulb Memories"* (New York: Cambridge University Press, 1992).

6. Elizabeth F. Loftus and John Palmer, "Reconstruction of Automobile Destruction," *Journal of Verbal Learning and Verbal Behavior*, Vol. 13, 1974, pp. 585–589.

7. Brandon Keim, "Science of Eyewitness Memory Enters Courtroom," July 2012. http://www.wired.com.wiredscience/2012/7/eyewitness-memory/.

8. I.E. Hyman, T.H. Husband, and I.J. Billings (1995). "False Memories of Childhood Experiences," *Applied Cognitive Psychology*, Vol. 9, 1995, pp. 181–197.

9. Elizabeth Loftus, "Creating False Memories," *Scientific American*, Vol. 277, 1997, pp. 70–75.

10. For a summary of studies on the effect of marijuana, see http://www.gdcada.org/statistics/marijuana.htm. For more specifics on the effects of marijuana and alcohol on driving, go to the National Highway Traffic Safety Administration Web site at http://www.nhtsa.dot.gov/people/outreach/safesobr/15qp/web/iddrug.html.

11. Diane Feskanich, Walter C. Willett, Meir J. Stampfer, and Graham A. Colditz, "Milk, Dietary Calcium, and Bone Fractures in Women: A 12-Year Prospective Study," *American Journal of Public Health*, Vol. 87, Issue 6, June 1997, pp. 992–997.

12. Michael Isikoff, Andrew Murr, Eric Pape, and Mike Elkin, "Mysterious Fingerprint," *Newsweek*, May 31, 2004, p. 8.

13. J. Cocker, "Biased Questions in Judgment of Covariation Studies," *Personality and Social Psychology Bulletin*, Vol. 8, June 1982, pp. 214–220.

14. Thomas Gilovich, *How We Know What Isn't So* (New York: Free Press, 1991), p. 54.

15. David Brooks, "Why Men Fail," *New York Times*, Sept. 10, 2012.

16. See abcnews.com.World News Tonight, ABC News, Peter Jennings, March 31, 1998.

17. Matt Ridley, "How Bias Heats up the Global Debate," *The Wall Street Journal*, August. 3, 2012.

18. Michael Sherman, "The Political Brain," *Scientific American*, July 2006, p. 36.

19. "Bin Laden Movie Torture Scenes are Totally Fiction: Ex-CIA Official," Agence France-Presse, Jan. 7, 2103.

20. National Advisory Mental Health Council, "Basic Behavioral Science Research for Mental Health Thought and Communication," *American Psychologist*, March 1996, Vol. 51(3), p. 181.

21. See Theodore Schick, Jr., and Lewis Vaughn, *How to Think About Weird Things*, 4th ed. (New York: McGraw-Hill, 2005), pp. 51–52.

22. Joe Kline, "Listen to What Katrina is Saying," *Newsweek*, September 12, 2005, p. 27.

23. J. Liu and S. A. Siegelbaum, "Change of Pore Helix Conformation State Upon Opening of Cyclic Nucleotide-Gated Channels," *Neuron*, Vol. 28, 2000, pp. 899–909.

24. Curtis White, *The Middle Mind* (San Francisco, CA: HarperCollins, 2003), pp. 105–106.

25. Donn C. Young and Erinn M. Hade, "Holidays, Birthdays, and Postponement of Cancer Death," *Journal of the American Medical Association*, Vol. 292, Issue 24, December 29, 2004, pp. 3012–3016.

26. Robert Ladouceur, "Gambling: The Hidden Addiction," *Canadian Journal of Psychiatry*, Vol. 49, Issue 8, August 2004, pp. 501–503.

27. "Numbers," *Time*, March 21, 2005, p. 20.

28. Edward S. Kubany, "Thinking Errors, Faulty Conclusion, and Cognitive Therapy for Trauma-Related Guilt," *NCP Clinical Quarterly*, Vol. 7, Issue 1, winter 1997. http://www.cbt.ca/trauma-related_guilt.htm.

29. Pew Charitable Trusts, "Social Trends Poll: Americans See Weight Problems Everywhere But in the Mirror," April 11, 2006.

30. Douglas T. Kenrick, Steven L. Neuberg, and Robert B. Cialdini, *Social Psychology: Unraveling the Mystery*, 3rd ed. (Boston: Pearson Education, 2005), p. 84.

31. Amy Joyce, "We All Experience Office Conflict, But It's Never Our Fault," *Providence Sunday Journal*, June 13, 2004, p. H3.

32. Carol Tavris and Elliot Aronson, *Mistakes Were Made (But Not By Me): Why We Justify Foolish Beliefs, Bad Decisions, and Hurtful Acts* (New York: Harcourt, 2007).

33. Douglas T. Kenrick, Steven L. Neuberg, Robert B. Cialdini, *Social Psychology: Unraveling the Mystery*, 3rd ed. (Boston: Pearson Education, 2005), p. 84.

34. Ian I. Mitroff and Harold A. Linstone, *The Unbounded Mind: Breaking the Chains of Traditional Business Thinking* (New York: Oxford University Press, 1993), p. 94.

35. Tiffany A. Ito, Krystal W. Chiao, Patricia G. Devine, Tyler S. Lorig, and John T. Cacioppo, "The Influence of Facial Feedback on Racial Bias," *Psychological Science*, Vol. 17, Issue 3, 2006, pp. 256–261.

36. Sally Lehrman, "The Implicit Prejudice," *Scientific American*, June 2006, pp. 32–34.

37. "Noise Like an Airplane. Fire Island Surfman Heard It in the Air: Sure It Was Not Geese," *Boston Herald*, December 13, 1909, p. 1.

38. "Thousands See Big Airship over Worcester," *Boston Journal*, December 23, 1909, p. 1.

39. Robert E. Bartholomew and Benjamin Radford, *Hoaxes, Myths, and Manias: Why We Need Critical Thinking* (Amherst, NY: Prometheus Books, 2003), p. 210.

40. Joy D. Osofky, "Prevalence of Children's Exposure to Domestic Violence and Child Maltreatment: Implications for Prevention and Intervention," *Clinical Child and Family Psychology Review*, Vol. 6, Issue 3, Sept. 2003, pp. 161–170. See also the work of Dr. Richard Gelles.

41. Solomon Asch, "Effects of Group Pressure upon the Modification and Distortion of Judgments," in Harold Guetzkow, *Groups, Leadership and Men* (New York: Russell and Russell, 1963), pp. 177–190.

42. Ian I. Mitroff and Harold A. Linstone, *The Unbounded Mind: Breaking the Chains of Traditional Business Thinking* (New York: Oxford University Press, 1993), p. 23.

43. "LifeEtc.," *AARP Magazine*, September/October 2004, p. 110.

44. Edward U. Condon, *Scientific Study of Unidentified Flying Objects* (Boulder, CO: Regents of the University of Colorado, 1969).

45. Natalie DiBlaso, "A Thid of Earthlings Believe in UFOs would Befriend Aliens," *USA Today*, June 26, 2012.

46. J. Allen Hynek, *The UFO Experience: A Scientific Inquiry* (New York: Marlowe, 1972), pp. 214–222, 226–227.

47. Royston Paynter, "Physical Evidence and UFOs," 1996, http://www.geocities.com/Area51/Corridor/8148/physical.html.

Chapter 5

1. Lynette Clemetson, "The Alarming Growth of Campus Cults," *Newsweek*, August 1999, p. 35.

2. Bates College Office of the Chaplain, "A Word about Cults," 1997.

3. Laura Withers, "Students Susceptible to Cults' Lures," *The Post* (online edition), Ohio University, February 15, 2002.

4. From "The Battle Over Terri Schiavo," *AOL News*, March 27, 2005.

5. CBS News Poll, Jan. 6–10, 2010.

6. Arthur Jensen, "How Much Can We Boost IQ and Scholastic Achievement?" *Harvard Educational Review* 39, winter 1969, pp. 1–23.

7. See American Freshman Survey, Fall 2009; and *The American Freshman: Thirty-Five Year Trends*, January 2013.

8. Brian Burrell, *Postcards from the Brain Museum: The Improbable Search for Meaning in the Matter of Famous Minds* (New York: Broadway Books, 2005).

9. Philip Terzian, "A Self-Inflicted Wound," *Providence Sunday Journal*, May 9, 2004, p. 19.

10. Quoted in Mike Billips, "Confronting a Scandal's Debris," *Time*, May 24, 2004, p. 50.

11. Harold A. Herzog, "Conflicts of Interest: Kittens and Boa Constrictors, Pets and Research," *American Psychologist*, Vol. 46, Issue 3, 1991, pp. 246–248.

12. Editor's Desk, "The Conversation," *Time*, Feb. 18, 2013, p. 3.

13. Jonathan Alter, "We're Dodging the Draft Issue," *Newsweek*, October 4, 2004, p. 39.

14. Argument paraphrased from Francis Fukuyama, *Our Posthuman Future: Consequences of the Biotechnology Revolution* (New York: Picador, 2002), pp. 169–170.

15. Hazel Erskine, "The Polls: Politics and Law and Order," *Public Opinion Quarterly*, Vol. 38, Issue 4, Winter 1974–1975, pp. 623–634.

16. Quote in "Notebook," *Time*, April 19, 2004, p. 19.

17. See Dan Shaughnessy, *The Curse of the Bambino* (New York: Penguin Putnam, 1990).

18. http://www.heri.ucla.edu/PDFs/pubs/briefs/brief-pr012110-09FreshmanNorms.pdf.

19. For more on this topic, see John A. Robinson, "The Question of Human Cloning," *Hastings Center Report*, Vol. 24, Issue 2, 1994, pp. 6–14, and Leon Kass, "The Wisdom of Repugnance: Why We Should Ban the Cloning of Humans," *The New Republic*, Vol. 216, Issue 22, 1997, pp. 17–26.

20. Carroll Bogert of Human Rights Watch. Quoted in Jonathan Alter, "The Picture the World Sees," *Newsweek*, May 17, 2004, p. 35.

21. Sura 2:191.

22. Daniel Ryan, "Morals and Hazards: Pros and Cons of the Bailout," September 29, 2008. http://www.enterstageright.com/archives/articles/1008/1008bailoutprocon.htm.

23. Diana Ravitch, "The Big Idea—It's Bad Education Policy," March 14, 2010, *Los Angeles Times*. http://articles.latimes.com/2010/mar/14/opinion/la-oe-ravitch14-2010mar14.

24. Gunpolicy.org. See also "List of Countries and Firearm-related Death Rate," *Wikipedia*.

25. Christ Christoff and Ilan Kolet, "American Gun Deaths to Exceed Traffic Fatalities by 2015," *Bloomberg*, December 19, 2012.

26. NBC Poll, Feb. 21–24, 2013.

27. Pew Poll, February 13–18, 2013.

Chapter 6

1. Sohail H. Hashmi, "Interpreting the Islamic Ethics of War and Peace." In Terry Nardin, ed., *The Ethics of War and Peace* (Princeton: Princeton University Press, 1996), pp. 146–166.

2. Abraham Lincoln, Seventh Debate with Stephen A. Douglas, Alton, Illinois, October 15, 1858.

3. Ellis Cose, "A Dream Deferred," *Newsweek*, May 17, 2004, p. 59.

4. This question was asked of my spring 2005 critical-thinking class. The majority gave this answer.

5. Marisa Helms, Minnesota Public Radio, May 20, 2004.

6. "Adopt a College Program Launched," *Vegan Spam*, August 25, 2003. http://www.veganoutreadh.org/enewsletter/20030825.html.

7. "10 Questions for the Dalai Lama," *Time*, October 25, 2004, p. 8.

8. *Webster's College Dictionary* (New York: Random House, 2001), p. 22.

9. Psychiatrist Dr. Edward Volkman, quoted in Paul Nussbaum, "Beheadings Terrorize Like Nothing Else," *Providence Sunday Journal*, June 27, 2004, p. A18.

10. A summary of the British economist David Ricardo's 1817 argument for free trade. In Doug Keklak, "Goodbye to All That," letter to the editor, *Newsweek*, January 31, 2005, p. 14.

11. Joseph Collins, MD, "Should Doctors Tell the Truth?" *Harper's Monthly*, Vol. 155, August 1927, pp. 320–326.

12. Pierre C. Haber, letter to the editor, *Newsweek*, October 31, 1983, p. 6.

13. Winston Churchill.

14. Letter to the editor, *Time*, November 8, 2004, p. 9.

15. "Saudi Arabia: Gateway to the Middle East," special advertisement compiled by London Press, londonpress@london.com.

16. Brad Edmondson, "Who's Grumpy?!!?" *AARP Bulletin*, September 2004, p. 11.

17. Paraphrased from Claudia Wallis, "The Case for Staying Home," *Time*, March 22, 2004, p. 55.

18. Paraphrased from Michael D. Lemonick, "Stealth Attack on Evolution," *Time*, January 31, 2005, pp. 53–54.

19. For a summary of this study, see: "Despite High Levels of Poverty, Latino Immigrants Less Likely to Use Welfare," at http://www.azteca.net/aztec/immigrat/lat_imi2.html.

20. Donald Oken, "What to Tell Cancer Patients: A Study of Medical Attitudes," *JAMA*, Vol. 175, 1961, pp. 1120–1128.

21. James Rachels, "Active and Passive Euthanasia," *New England Journal of Medicine*, January 9, 1975, pp. 78–81.

22. "Gay Marriage: Key Points from Pew Research," Feb. 7. 2013/ www.pewresearch.org/2013/02/07/gay-marriage-key-data-points-from-pew-research.

Chapter 7

1. Pew Research Social and Demographic Trends, "A Gender Reversal on Career Aspirations," April 19, 2012.

2. Cooperative Institutional Research Program, The American Freshman National Norms for Fall 2009, Higher Education Research Institute, University of California, Los Angeles, December 2009, pp. 37–38.

3. Maggie Mahar, "Cesareans and Induced Births," Healthbeatblog.com, Feb. 15, 2011.

4. Stanley Milgram, *Obedience to Authority* (New York: Harper Colophon Books, 1974), p. 35.

5. If you are interested in learning more about polls, read Michael W. Link and Robert W. Oldendick, "'Good' Polls/'Bad' Polls—How Can You Tell? Ten Tips for Consumers of Survey Research," *South Carolina Policy Forum*: a publication of the University of South Carolina Institute for Public Service and Policy Research, fall 1997. You can also read the complete article on the Web at http://www.ipspr. sc.edu/publication/Link.htm.

6. For a list of the major polling organizations go to http://www.ropercenter.uconn.edu/research/other_data_archives.html.

7. For information on sampling and the Gallup Poll, go to http://www.gallup.com/.

8. For more on the sampling techniques used by the Freshman Survey, see Cooperative Institutional Research Program, The American Freshman National Norms for Fall 2004, Higher Education Research Institute, University of California, Los Angeles, December 2004, pp. 156–166.

9. For more on these studies, go to http://www.religioustolerance.org/hom_chil.htm.

10. Other estimates range from 3 to 5 percent.

11. The American Freshman: Thirty-Five Year Trends, p. 4.

12. Lou Harris Poll, 1993.

13. Pew Research Center Poll, March 10–14, 2010.

14. Arelis Hernandez, "College Students are Health Care's Invisible Minority," *Diverse: Issues in Higher Education*, Vol. 26, Issue 18, October 15, 2009, pp. 10–11.

15. Kenneth E. Warner, "The Effects of Publicity and Policy on Smoking and Health," *Business and Health* Vol. 2, Issue 1, November 1984, pp. 7–14.

16. Winston Churchill, "The German Invasion of Russia," reprinted in *Winston S. Churchill: His Complete Speeches 1897–1963*, ed. R. R. James (New York: Chelsea House Publishers, 1974), pp. 6428–6429.

17. See David Hume, *Dialogues Concerning Natural Religion* (London, 1779).

18. John Noonan, "An Almost Absolute Value in History," *The Morality of Abortion: Legal and Historical Perspectives* (Cambridge, MA: Harvard University Press, 1970), pp. 51–59.

19. Ad for Commit Nicotine Lozenges.

20. S. Morris Engel, *With Good Reason: An Introduction to Informal Fallacies* (New York: St. Martin's Press, 1982), p. 130.

21. Peter Singer, *Animal Liberation* (HarperCollins, New York, 1990), p. 9.

22. James Rachel, "Active and Passive Euthanasia," *New England Journal of Medicine*, vol. 292(2), 1975, pp. 78–80.

23. *Psychology Today*, September 1984.

24. Robin H. Gray, "Dating Abuse Statistics," Campus *Safety Magazine*, Dec. 11, 2012.

25. Ad in *Time* magazine from "Parents. The Anti-Drug." (www. theantidrug.com).

26. Quinnipiac University Poll, Dec. 6, 2012. http://www .quinnipiac.edu/institutes-centers/polling-institute/national/ release-detail?ReleaseID=1820.

27. "Drug Use," http://www.ojp.usdoj.gov/bjs/dcf/du.htm.

28. "Drug Use Trends," http://www.whitehousedrugpolicy.gov/ publications/factsht/druguse/index.html.

Chapter 8

1. Sir Arthur Conan Doyle, "Silver Blaze." In *The Best of Sherlock Holmes* (Franklin Center, PA: Franklin Library, 1977), p. 249.

2. Sir Arthur Conan Doyle, *The Sign of Four* (New York: Doubleday), p. 111.

3. Sir Arthur Conan Doyle, "Silver Blaze." In *The Best of Sherlock Holmes* (Franklin Center, PA: Franklin Library, 1977), p. 260.

4. For more information on Mars, go to http://nssdc.gsfc.nasa.gov/ planetary/factsheet/marsfact.html. For more information on the rovers' mission, go to http://marsrovers.jpl.nasa.gov/.

5. From Gregory Bassham, William Irwin, Henry Nardone, and James M. Wallace, *Critical Thinking: A Student's Introduction*, 2nd ed. (Boston, MA: McGraw-Hill, 2005), pp. 56–57.

6. J. St. B. T. Evans and D. E. Over, "Explicit representations in hypothetical thinking," *Behavioral and Brain Sciences*, 1999, Vol. 22, Issue 25, pp. 763–764.

7. 2005 GM ad for hybrid cars, trucks, and buses (reworded slightly).

8. William Barclay, *The Plain Man's Guide to Ethics*. Quoted in *The Watchtower*, February 1, 2005, p. 3.

9. Amnesty International, "Figures on the Death Penalty." Available at http://www.amnesty.org/en/death-penalty/numbers.

10. For updates on death penalty statistics go to: http://www .deathpenaltyinfo.org.

11. According to the Eighth Amendment to the U.S. Constitution, "Excessive bail shall not be required, nor excessive fines imposed, nor cruel and unusual punishments inflicted."

12. Ernest van den Haag, "The Ultimate Punishment: A Defense of Capital Punishment." *Harvard Law Review*, 1986, Vol. 99, pp. 1662–1669. Notes have been omitted.

Chapter 9

1. Fox News, Nov. 19, 2012.

2. For more information on steroids, go to http://www.drugabuse.gov/ ResearchReports/Steroids/anabolicsteroids2.html.

3. "Wrestler Strangled Wife, Suffocated Son, Hanged Self," Foxnews.com, June 27, 2007; http://www.foxnews.com/story/ 0,2933,286737,00.html.

4. "College Athletes and Anabolic Steroid Abuse," http:// athleticscholarships.net/steroids.htm.

5. In the 1980s Dutch sociologist Ruut Veenhoven carried out an extensive study of 245 other studies on happiness from all around the world, including the United States. See Ruut Veenhoven, *Conditions of Happiness* (Dordrecht, Netherlands: D Reidel, 1984).

6. Rosalinda Alfaro-LeFevre, *Critical Thinking in Nursing* (Philadelphia: W. B. Saunders, 1995), p. 20.

7. Marc D. Hauser, *Moral Minds* (New York: HarperPerennial, 2006).

8. Hans Seyle, *The Stress of Life* (New York: McGraw-Hill, 1956).

9. Peter D. Kramer, *Listening to Prozac* (New York: Viking, 1993), p. 294.

10. Lawrence Kohlberg, *Essays in Moral Development*, Vol. II. *The Psychology of Moral Development* (San Francisco: Harper & Row, 1984).

11. "Perspectives," *Newsweek*, January 2, 2006, p. 117.

12. M. Kitwood, *Concern for Others: A New Psychology of Conscience and Morality* (London: Routledge & Kegan Paul, 1990), pp. 146–147.

13. Lawrence Kohlberg, *Essays in Moral Development*, Vol. II. *The Psychology of Moral Development* (San Francisco: Harper & Row, 1984).

14. For a list of some of these studies, see Judith A. Boss, *Ethics for Life*, 3rd ed. (New York: McGraw-Hill, 2004), pp. 216 and N-7.

15. W. Pitt Derryberry and Stephen J. Thoma, "The Friendship Effect: Its Role in the Development of Moral Thinking in Students," *About Campus*, May–June 2000, pp. 13–18.

16. Ibid.

17. Stephen P. McNeel, "College Teaching and Student Moral Development," in James R. Rest and Darcia Narvaez, *Moral Development in the Professions* (Hillsdale, NJ: Lawrence Erlbaum Associates, 1994), p. 36.

18. See James R. Rest and Darcia Narváez, *Moral Development in the Professions: Psychology and Applied Ethics* (Hillsdale, NJ: Lawrence Erlbaum Associates, 1994).

19. "Notebook: Milestones," *Time*, December 6, 2004, p. 27.

20. Stephen A. Satris, "Student Relativism," *Teaching Philosophy*, Vol. 9, Issue 3, September 1986, pp. 193–200.

21. Greg Jaffe, "Military Debates Morality of Killing," *Providence Sunday Journal*, August 21, 2005, p. E1.

22. John Stuart Mill, "Utilitarianism," in Mary Warnock, ed., *Utilitarianism* (New York: Meridian, 1962), p. 257.

23. For a more in-depth discussion of the categorical imperative, see Immanuel Kant, *Principles of the Metaphysic of Ethics*, translated by Thomas Kingsmill Abbott (London: Longman's Green and Col, Ltd., 1873), pp. 44–79.

24. Kant, *Principles of the Metaphysic of Ethics*, 79.

25. Donald Oken, "What to Tell Cancer Patients: A Study of Medical Attitudes," *Journal of the American Medical Association*, Vol. 175, 1961, pp. 1120–1128.

26. This example is based on a real-life case. I—the author—had both my children as a young undergraduate in Australia. In Australia, students who attained a certain grade point average in their first year of college were given a scholarship that paid all their tuition plus a small living allowance. I attained that average, but was denied a scholarship. Fortunately, I was motivated by my moral outrage at being unjustly treated to send a complaint to the federal government. As a result, I got the scholarship, including all the back payments I was due.

27. http://health.discovery.com/centers/loverelationships/articles/ divorce.html.

28. For the latest polling results, go to www.pollingreport.com/ abortion.htm.

29. Judith Jarvis Thomson, "A Defense of Abortion," *Philosophy and Public Affairs*, Vol. 1, Issue 1, 1971, pp. 47–66.

Chapter 10

1. Becky Yerak, "Reporter's Notebook: Geicko Nipping at No. 2 Auto Insurer Allstate's Heels," *Chicago Tribune*, Jan. 4, 2013.

2. Matthew Creamer, "Southwest Rings $20M in Fares with Killer Application," *Advertising Age*, Vol. 76, Issue 28, July 11, 2005, p. 88.

3. Eileen C. Shapiro, *The Seven Deadly Sins of Business* (Oxford, UK; Capstone Publishing Ltd., 1998).

4. Shapiro, *Seven Deadly Sins*, pp. 180–181.

5. See "Geo Gaffes," *BrandWeek*, Vol. 39, Issue 8, February 23, 1996.

6. Shapiro, *Seven Deadly Sins*, p. 2.

7. Frederick Betz, "Strategic Business Models," *Engineering Management Journal*, Vol. 14, Issue 1, May 2002, p. 21.

8. www.strategicmanagementinsight.com/swot-analyses/google-swot-analysis.html.

9. Doron Levin, "Toyota Rise Plus for U.S. Economy," *Bloomberg News*, April 27, 2007.

10. Owen Matthews, "How the West Came to Run Islamic Banks," *Newsweek*, October 31, 2005, p. E30.

11. Sean Gregory, "The Arte of Baseball," *Time*, June 2005, pp. A33–A34.

12. Brian Padden, "Can an American Auto Industry Town Regain Past Prosperity?" *Voice of America*, April 26, 2007, http://www.voanews.com/english/2007-04-26-voa57.cfm.

13. http://www.lego.com/eng/info/default.asp?page=pressdetail&contentid=12504&countrycode-2057.

14. Julie Kirkwood, "What's in a Name?" *The Eagle-Tribune*, September 1, 2003, www.igorinternational.com/press/eagletrib-drug-names.php.

15. Casey Clapper, "Reaching Customers with the Touch of a Button," *Aftermarket Business*, September 2005, p. 10.

16. Darren W. Dahl, Heather Honea, and Rajesh Manchanda, "Three Rs of Interpersonal Consumer Guilt: Relationships, Reciprocity, Reparation," *Journal of Consumer Psychology*, Vol. 15, Issue 4, 2005, pp. 307–315.

17. "Our Rising Ad Dosage: It's Not as Oppressive as Some Think," *Media Matters,* Feb. 15, 2007.

18. "Nielson to Measure the Mobile Media Consumer," June 6, 2007, http://www.nielsen.com/media/2007/pr_07060.html.

19. "Product Placement," BusinessDictionary.com. Available at http://www.businessdictionary.com/definition/product-placement.html.

20. See http://www.commercialalert.org/issues/culture/productplacement.

21. "Watch What Your Kids Watch," *Mediawise*, Vol. 10, 2005.

22. Elizabeth S. Moore, "Children and the Changing World of Advertising," *Journal of Business Ethics*, Vol. 52, Issue 2, 2004, pp. 161–167.

23. Jonathan Freedland, "The Onslaught," *Guardian*, October 25, 2005. See http://www.guardian.co.uk/media/2005/oct/25/advertising/food.

24. Rebecca A. Clay, "Advertising to Children: Is It Ethical?" *Monitor on Psychology*, Vol. 31, Issue 8, September 2000. See http://www.apa.org/monitor/sep00/advertising.html.

25. Todd House and Tim Loughran, "Cash Flow Is King? Cognitive Errors by Investors," *Journal of Psychology & Financial Markets*, Vol. 1, Issue 2/3, 2000, pp. 161–175.

26. For more information on the FDA's proposed initiative for curbing counterfeit prescription drugs, go to http://findarticles.com/p/articles/mi_m1370/is_/ai_109906674.

27. "Doctor's Orders: Bad Health for Sale: Does Advertising Hit Minorities Harder?" *Time*, August 29, 2005, p. 75. Available at http://www.time.com/time/magazine/article/0,9171,1096508,00.html.

28. "Children, Health and Advertising: Issue Briefs" (Studio City, CA: Mediascope Press, 2000).

29. Paul W. Farris and David J. Reibstein, "Consumer Prices and Advertising." In *Blackwell Encyclopedia of Business: Ethics*, 2nd ed. (Oxford, UK: Blackwell Publishers, 2005), p. 107.

30. For more on the issue of freedom of speech and advertising, see Martin H. Redish, "Tobacco Advertising and the First Amendment," *Iowa Law Review*, Vol. 81, March 1996.

31. "Keeping Well, at a Cost," *Newsweek*. Vol. 144, Issue 15, Oct. 11, 2004, pp. 20. Letters, Michael R. Heyman. Roseburg, Ore.

Chapter 11

1. Jim Martyka, "College Station Gives 'Average' Iraqi Voices Global Reach," *Associated Collegiate Press*, February 23, 2006. Available at http://www.studentpress.org/acp/trends/~warnews.html.

2. Leela de Kretser and Lorena Mongelli, "Mesmerized by the Media—We're Obsessive Watchers, Listeners and Readers," *The New York Post*, Dec. 15, 2006, p. 35.

3. "Media Bias Is Real, Finds UCLA Political Scientist," *UCLA News*, December 14, 2005. Available at http://newsroom.ucla.edu/portal/ucla/Media-Bias-Is-Real-Finds-UCLA-6664.aspx.

4. http://www.businessinsider.com/these-6-corporations-control-90-of-the-media-in-america-2012-6.

5. Ben Clark, "Power Surge," *San Francisco Bay Guardian*, September 20, 2000. Available at http://www.sfbg.com.

6. "The State of the Media 2013." http://stateofthemedia.org.

7. http://www.pewresearch.org/2012/03/19/state-of-the-news-media-2012/.

8. "Numbers," Time, February 28, 2005, p. 24.

9. "Inventing the Internet. Did Al Gore Invent the Internet?" http://www.perkel.com/politics/gore/internet.htm.

10. Media Matters for America, "Media Watchdog, Government Ethics and Advocacy Groups Call for Action on 'Pay-Sway' Scandal," January 27, 2005. See http://mediamatters.org/items/200501270003.

11. Pew Research Poll, July 2011. www.archive.mrc.org/biasbasics/.

12. "Local TV News Faces Challenge." www.pewresearch.com (2012).

12. Kristen Purcell et al., "Pew Internet Research: Understanding the Participatory News Consumer, March 1, 2010, p. 9.

13. "The Gender Gap: Women Are Still Missing as Sources for Journalists," Project for Excellence in Journalism, May 23, 2005. Available at http://www.journalism.org/node/141.

14. Jennifer Barrett, "New Secrets for Youthful Skin," *Newsweek*, April 24, 2006, pp. 74–76.

15. Aired June 1, 2006.

16. H. Benson, J. A. Dusek, J. B. Sherwood et al., "Study of the Therapeutic Effects of Intercessory Prayer (STEP) in Cardiac Bypass Patients: A Multicenter Randomized Trial of Uncertainty and Certainty of Receiving Intercessory Prayer," *American Heart Journal*, Vol. 151, Issue 4: pp. 762–764, April 15, 2006.

17. Quotes from Denise Gellene and Thomas H. Maugh II, "Largest Study of Prayer to Date Finds It Has No Power to Heal," *Los Angeles Times*, March 31, 2006.

18. K. Scheider, "U.S. Officials Say Dangers of Dioxin Were Exaggerated," *New York Times*, August 5, 1991, p. 1.

19. http://royal.pingdom.com/2012/04/19/world-internet-population-has-doubled-in-the-last-5-years/

20. "The American Freshman: National Norms for 2012." http://www.gseis.ucla.edu/heri/heri/html.

21. http://money.cnn.com/magazines/moneymag/bestjobs/top50/index.html.

22. http://money.cnn.com/2012/10/04/technology/facebook-billion-users/index.html.

23. "The American Freshmen Norms," Fall 2012.

24. Edward Fitzpatrick, "Fallout from Facebook is Forever," *The Providence Sunday Journal*, October 5, 2008, p. A1.

25. Eric Tucker, "Facebook Used as Character Evidence, Lands some in Jail," *USA Today*, July 19, 2008.

26. Reid Goldsborough, "Free Speech in Cyberspace—Both a Privilege and a Burden," *Community College Week*, Vol. 12, Issue 1, August 23, 1999, p. 27.

27. Al Gore, *The Assault on Reason* (New York: Penguin Press, 2007), p. 260.

28. See www.universityofphoenix.com.

29. Patrick Crane, "30 percent of Web's Total Traffic is for Porn," *Tech Magazine,* April 22, 2012.

30. Marysia Weber, "Internet Pornography: An Occasion of Sin for Our Time," 2010. http://catholiceducation.org/articles/sexuality/se0197.htm.

31. Marysia Weber, "Internet Pornography: An Occasion of Sin for Our Time," 2010. http://catholiceducation.org/articles/sexuality/se0197.htm.

32. Brian Hansen, "Is the Internet Causing More Students to Copy?" *CQ Researcher*, Vol. 13, No. 32, September 19, 2003.

33. "8 Astonishing Stats on Academic Cheating," Dec, 2010, http://oedb.org/library/features/8-astonishing-facts-on-academic-cheating.

34. Wendy Koch, "It's Always Poker Night on Campus," *USA Today*, December 23, 2005. Available at http://www.usatoday.com/news/nation/2005-12-22-gamble-college_x.htm.

35. "People use media twice as much as they think they do," http://www.bsu.edu/icommunication/news/stories/february/2_25_03.html.

36. Brian Stelter, "8 Hours a Day Spent on Screens, Study Finds," *The New York Times*, March 26, 2009.

Chapter 12

1. United Nations Environmental Programme, "Sea Level Rise Due to Global Warming." http://www.grida.no/climate/vital/19.htm.

2. Tom Mosakowski, "2008 Will Be Among the Ten Hottest Years on Record." http://www.naturalnews.com/022658.html.

3. For more statistics, go to the U.S. Environmental Protection Agency Web site on global warming at http://epa.gov/climatechange/index.html.

4. United Nations Environmental Programme, "Sea Level Rise Due to Global Warming." http://www.grida.no/climate/vital/19.html.

5. For a review of Descartes' position of epistemological skepticism see Chapter 1, pages 8–9.

6. For a summary of the Islamic position on science, see Todd Pitock, "Science and Islam," *Discover*, July 2007, pp. 36–45.

7. Arthur Peacocke, *Intimations of Reality: Realism in Science and Religion* (Notre Dame: University of Notre Dame Press, 1984), p. 51.

8. John D. Barrow, Frank J. Tipler, and John A. Wheeler, *The Anthropic Cosmological Principle* (New York: Oxford University Press, 1988).

9. See Russell A. Hill and Robert A. Barton, "Psychology Enhances Human Performance in Contests," *Nature*, Vol. 435, May 19, 2005, p. 293.

10. B. Nyenzi and P. F. Lefale, "El Niño Southern Oscillation (ENSO) and Global Warming," *Advances in Geosciences*, Vol. 6, January 2006, pp. 95–101.

11. See Margaret Mead, *Coming of Age in Samoa* (New York, W. Morrow & Company, 1928).

12. Carl Zimmer, "Aliens Among Us: Do We Share Our Planet with Alternative Forms of Life?" *Discover*, July 2007, pp. 62–65.

13. For their operational definition of *religiousness*, see Laura Koenig et al., "Genetic and Environmental Influences on Religiousness: Findings for Retrospective and Current Religiousness Ratings," *Journal of Personality*, Vol. 73, Issue 2, April 2005, pp. 471–488.

14. Janet Radoff, "Bees Face Unprecedented Pesticide Exposure at Home and Afield," *Science News*, March 21, 2010. http://www.science news.org.

15. U.S. Department of Agriculture, "Honey Bees and Colony Collapse Disorder," May 7, 2012. http://www.ars.usda.gov/News/docs.htm?docid=15577.

16. "More Americans Applying to Canadian Universities," http://scholarships.com.

17. Christine Gorman, "Born Too Soon," *Time*, October 18, 2004, pp. 73–74.

18. Stanley Coren, PhD, *The Left-Handed Syndrome: The Causes and Consequences of Left-Handedness* (New York: Simon & Schuster, 1992).

19. "Healthbeat," *Newsweek*, January 17, 2005, p. 69.

20. For more on the concept of falsifiability, see Karl Popper, *The Logic of Scientific Discovery* (New York: Basic Books, 1959).

21. Karl Popper, *Unended Quest: An Intellectual Autobiography* (La Salle, Indiana: Open Court Press, 1976).

22. Harris Poll, Dec. 15, 2009.

23. For a list of these predictions, go to http://farshores.org/dy09.htm.

24. http://en.wikipedia.org/wiki/Nostradamus.

25. See Megan Mansell Williams, "Should Losers Wear Red?" *Discover*, August 2005, p. 11.

26. For a review of sampling methods, see Chapter 7, pp. 206–209.

27. Daniel M. Wegner and William D. Crano, "Racial Factors in Helping Behavior: An Unobtrusive Field Experiment," *Journal of Personality and Social Psychology*, Vol. 32, No. 5, 1975, pp. 901–905. Available at http://www.wjh.harvard.edu/~wegner/pdfs/Wegner%20&%20Crano%201975.pdf.

28. Judith A. Boss, "The effect of community service work on the moral development of college ethics students." *Journal of Moral Education*, Vol. 23, Issue 2, 1994, pp. 183–198.

29. Andrew J. Wakefield, "MMR Vaccination," *The Lancet*, Vol. 354, Issue 9183, pp. 949–950, 11 Sept. 1999.

30. See John Ioannidis, "Contradicted and Initially Stronger Effects in Highly Cited Clinical Research," *Journal of the American Medical Association*, Vol. 294, 2005, pp. 218–228, and Joao Medeiros, "Dirty Little Secret," *Seed*, May/June 2007, p. 20.

31. Ibid.

32. Russell A. Hill and Robert A. Barton, "Psychology: Red Enhances Human Performance in Contests," *Nature*, Vol. 435, May 19, 2005, p. 293.

33. Thomas Kuhn, *The Structure of Scientific Revolutions* (Chicago: University of Chicago Press, 1962), p. 10.

Chapter 13

1. http://www.pewhispanic.org/2013/01/29/a-nation-of-immigrants/.

2. Julia Preston, "Risks Seen for Children of Illegal Immigrants," *New York Times*, Sept. 21, 2011.

3. The state of nature is purely hypothetical, since all known human societies have at least a rudimentary form of government.

4. Thomas Hobbes, *Leviathan* (1651), Chapter VIII.

5. John Locke, *Two Treatises of Government*, 1699.

6. The survey was conducted by the McCormick Tribune Freedom Museum. See "Poll: Simpsons Better Known Than 1st Amendment," *Providence Sunday Journal*, March 5, 2006, p. D5.

7. UVE EText Jefferson Digital Archive: Thomas Jefferson on Politics and Government, "Majority Rule," http://etext.lib.virginia.edu/jefferson/quotations/jeff0500.htm.

8. Gary C. Jacobson, *Money in Congressional Elections; The Politics of Congressional Elections*, 5th ed. (New York: Longman Publishers, 2001).

9. George R. Will, "An Election Breakwater," *Newsweek*, February 27, 2006, p. 68.

10. Daron R. Shaw, "The Effect of TV Ads and Candidate Appearances on Statewide Presidential Votes, 1988–1996," *American Political Science Review*, Vol. 93, June 1999, pp. 345–362.

11. Anita Fore, "Battle in the Blogosphere: *John Doe v. Patrick Cahill*," *Authors Guild Bulletin*, Winter 2006, p. 10.

12. James Surowiecki, *The Wisdom of Crowds* (New York: Doubleday, 2004), pp. 268–271.

13. John Byrne, "Obama agencies invoking secrecy provision more often than under Bush," March 16, 2010. http://rawstory.com/2010/03/obama-agencies-invoking-secrecy-provision-bush/

14. "Fact Box: How Many Lobbyists are there in Washington?" September 13, 2009. http://www.reuters.com/article/idUSN13488032520090813.

15. The complete *Federal Rules of Evidence* are available at http://uscourts.gov/rules/.

16. James Hutson, "A Wall of Separation," Library of Congress Information Bulletin, June 1998.

17. Adam Liptak, "Justices, Five-Four, Reject Corporate-Spending Limit," New York Times, Jan. 21, 2010.

18. Ken J. Rotenberg and Mike J. Hurlbert, "Legal Reasoning and Jury Deliberations," *Journal of Social Psychology*, August 1992, Vol. 132, Issue 4, pp. 543–544.

PHOTO CREDITS

Prokhorov/E+/Getty Images RF; p. 369 (top): © JPL via San Gabriel Valley Newspapers/AP Images; p. 369 (bottom left): © Comstock/Alamy RF; p. 369 (bottom right): © Arthur Swoger/Archive Photos/Getty Images; p. 370: © Mary Evans Picture Library/The Image Works; p. 371: © Barbara Penoyar/Getty Images RF; p. 373: © Bettmann/Corbis; p. 374: © Library of Congress Prints & Photographs Division [LC-DIG-ggbain-32094]; p. 375: © Simon Wilkinson/Riser/Getty Images; p. 376: © Photo12/The Image Works; p. 378: © Karl Ammann/Corbis; p. 379: © Mario Beauregard/Corbis; p. 380: © World History/Topham/The Image Works; p. 381: © Thinkstock/Punchstock RF; p. 382: © KidStock/Blend Images/Getty Images RF; p. 384 (top): © Image Club RF; p. 384 (bottom): © Bettmann/Corbis; p. 386 (top): © Studio 101/Alamy; p. 386 (bottom): © D'Arco Editori/De Agostini Picture Library/Getty Images; p. 387: © Tim Pannell/Corbis RF; p. 388: © Tom Brakefield/Getty Images RF.

Chapter 13

Opener: © Steve Rhodes/Demotix/Corbis; p. 396: © Sean Adair/Reuters/Corbis; p. 397 (left): © The Print Collector/HIP/The Image Works; p. 397 (right): © Bettmann/Corbis; p. 398: © Digital Archive Japan/Alamy RF; p. 399: © Roger-Viollet/The Image Works; p. 401 (top): © Brendan Smialowski/AFP/Getty Images; p. 401 (bottom): © Linda Davidson/The Washington Post/Getty Images; p. 404: © Zhang Jun/Xinhus Press/Corbis; p. 405: © Seattle Post-Intelligencer Collection; Museum of History and Industry/Corbis; p. 406: © Dmitri Kessel/Time Life Pictures/Getty Images; p. 408: © Kevin LaMarque/Reuters/Corbis; p. 409: © Matt Rourke/AP Images; p. 410: © Rolls Press/Popperfoto/Getty Images; p. 411: © Don Cravens/Time & Life Images/Getty Images; p. 412: © Stringer/Getty Images; p. 414: © Hisham F. Ibrahim/Getty Images RF; p. 415: © Chip Somodevilla/Getty Images; p. 416: © American School/The Bridgeman Art Library/Getty Images; p. 418: © Tim Pannell/Corbis RF; p. 420: © DOD/Handout/Corbis.

TEXT CREDIT LINES

Chapter 1

p. 8, "Cognitive Development in College Students," adapted from Ron Sheese and Helen Radovanovic, W.G. Perry's "Model of Intellectual and Ethical Development: Implications of Recent Research for the Education and Counseling of Young Adults" (paper presented at the Annual Meeting of the Canadian Psychological Association, Ottawa, Ontario, June 1984). Used by permission of Ron Sheese, York University, Toronto.

p. 16, Copyright © 1963 Dr. Martin Luther King, Jr. © Renewed 1991 Coretta Scott King. Reprinted by arrangement with The Heirs to the Estate of Martin Luther King Jr., c/o Writers House as agent for the proprietor New York, NY.

p. 28 (figure), U.S. Census Bureau.

p. 33, Nancy Cantor, excerpt from "Affirmative Action and Higher Education: Before and After the Supreme Court Rulings on the Michigan Cases" from *The Chicago Tribune* (January 28, 2003). Copyright © 2003. Reprinted with the permission of Nancy Cantor.

Chapter 2

p. 44, "Emotion" from *Random House Webster's College Dictionary.* Copyright © 1995, 1992, 1991 by Random House, Inc. Used with permission.

p. 49, Excerpt from 2001: A Space Odyssey, MGM, 1968

p. 49, From *The Age of Spiritual Machines: When Computers Exceed Human Intelligence* (New York: Viking, 1999). Reprinted by permission of Ray Kurzweil & Laksman Frank.

p. 53, *The Hitchhiker's Guide to the Galaxy,* by Douglas Adams, Copyright © 1979, Published by harmony Books, a division of Random House. Used with permission.

Chapter 3

p. 61, From *Summa Theologica* (London: Burns, Oates, and Washbourne, 1920).

p. 62, Excerpts from THE GOD DELUSION by Richard Dawkins. Published by Bantam Press. Copyright © 2006 by Richard Dawkins. Reprinted by permission of Houghton Mifflin Harcourt Publishing Company and The Random House Group, Limited.

p. 82, From Donald A. Cadogan, "How Self-Assertive Are You?" (1990), www.oaktreecounceling.com/assrtquz.htm. Reprinted with the permission of Donald A. Cadogan.

p. 84, From WOOD. *Gendered Lives, 4E.* © 2001 Wadsworth, a part of Cengage Learning, Inc. Reproduced by permission. www.cengage.com/permissions.

p. 97, By Greg Lukinoff (originally published in the *New York Times,* Oct. 24, 2012. Used with permission.

p. 98, Robert J. Scott, "Reasonable Limits Are Good" from *USA Today* (May 27, 2003). Reprinted with permission of Robert J. Scott.

Chapter 4

p. 109, Matt Ridley, "How Bias Heats Up the Warming Debate." Reprinted by permission of Wall Street Journal. Copyright © 2012 Dow Jones & Company, Inc. All Rights reserved worldwide. License number 3220341092145.

p. 111, The CRAAP Test from Meriam Library, California State Universtity, Chico.

pp. 131–132, J. Allen Hynek, excerpts from *The UFO Experience: A Scientific Inquiry.*

pp. 132–133, Royston Paynter, "Physical Evidence and Unidentified Flying Object." Reprinted with the permission of Royston Paynter.

Chapter 5

p. 139, Copyright © 2013; Reprinted courtesy of Bunny Hoest.

pp. 165–166, National Rifle Association Press Release (Dec. 21, 2012).

pp. 166–167, Testimony by Mark Kelly, Senate Judiciary Committee hearing on gun violence on Jan. 30, 2013.

Chapter 6

p. 181, From American Civil Liberties Union.

p. 200, Matthew Spalding, " A Defining Moment for Marriage and Self-Government".

Chapter 7

p. 208, Higher Education Research Institute, "Cooperative Institutional Research Program 2012 Freshman Survey, page 1.

p. 213, Copyright © John Pritchett. Reprinted by permission.

pp. 232–233, Karen P. Tandy, "Marijuana: The Myths Are Killing Us," From *The Police Chief,* Vol. 72, No. 3, March 2005. Copyright held by the International Association of Chiefs of Police, 515 North Washington Street, Alexandria, VA 22314. Reprinted with permission.

pp. 233–234, Joe Messerli, "Should Marijuana be Legalized Under Any Circumstances?" Balancedpolitics.org, August 6, 2011.

Chapter 8

p. 262, Edward van den Haag, "The Ultimate Punishment: A Defense of Capital Punishment" from *The Harvard Law Review 99* (May 1986): 1662–1669. Copyright © 1986 by The Harvard Law Review Association. Reprinted with the permission of The Harvard Law Review via Copyright Clearance Center.

pp. 263–264, *The Case Against the Death Penalty* was first published by the ACLU as a pamphlet in 1973. The original text was written by Hugo Adam Bedau, Ph.d, who also contributed to several subsequent editions of the pamphlet. This version was most recently revised by the ACLU in 2012.

Chapter 9

p. 298, Brannigan and Boss, *Healthcare Ethics in a Diverse Society,* © McGraw-Hill/ Roe v. Wade ???

pp. 299–300, From LIBERTY DEFINED by Ron Paul. Copyright © 2011 by The Foundation for Rational Economics and Education, Inc. (FREE).

Chapter 10

pp. 329–330, Robert Liodice, "America = Free Speech – Whether WE Like It or Not" (January 24, 2005), http://ana.blogs.com/liodice/2005/01/america_free_sp.html. Reprinted by permission.

pp. 328–329, Limiting Food Marketing to Children, Center for Science in the Public Interest.

Chapter 11

pp. 356–357, Brook J. Sadler, "The Wrongs of Plagiarism: Ten Quick Arguments" *Teaching Philosophy,* Volume 30, Issue 3, September 2007, pp. 283–291.

pp. 357–358, Excerpts from "Four Reasons to be Happy About Internet Plagiarism," by Russell Hunt, teacher at St. Thomas University, Canada. Originally published in *Teaching Perspectives 5* (December 2002). Reprinted with permission of Russell Hunt.

Chapter 12

pp. 389–390, Excerpt from "Irreducible: Obstacle to Darwinian Evolution," by Michael Behe, Ph.D in *Debating Design: From Darwin to DNA* edited by W.A. Dembski and M. Ruse. Copyright © 2004, 2006 by Cambridge University Press. Reprinted with the permission of Cambridge University Press.

pp. 391–392, Excerpt from "Answering the Biochemical Argument from Design" by Kenneth R. Miller in Neil Manson, *God and Design: The Teleological Argument and Modern Science* (New York: Routledge, 2003), pp. 291–306. Copyright © 2003. Reprinted with the permission of Taylor & Francis Books UK and Kenneth R. Miller.

Chapter 13

pp. 421–422, "In Defense of Drones: A Historical Argument," By David Bell, *The New Republic,* January 27, 2012.

pp. 422–423, "What's Wrong with Obama's Drone Policy," by David Cole. Reprinted with permission from the March 4, 2013 issue of *The Nation.* For subscription information, call 1-800-333-8536. Portions of each week's Nation magazine can be accessed at http://www.thenation.com.

Resources Available with

THiNK

Online Learning Center:
www.mhhe.com/boss3e

Resources

Instructor's Manual
Test Bank
Computerized Test Bank
PowerPoints

Now with Connect Critical Thinking

Ask your McGraw-Hill sales representative for details.